10 YEARS

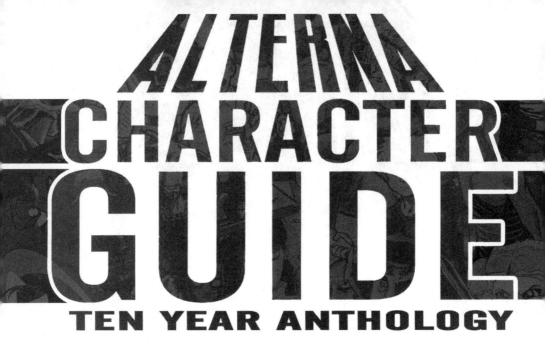

ALTERNA CHARACTER GUIDE
TEN YEAR ANTHOLOGY

ALTERNA COMICS
ALTERNACOMICS.COM

PETER SIMETI
PRESIDENT AND PUBLISHER

FUBAR PRESS
FUBARPRESS.COM

JEFF McCOMSEY
PRESIDENT AND PUBLISHER

JEFF McCLELLAND
STORY EDITOR

ALTERNA ANNIVERSERIES ANTHOLOGY
9781934985526
2016 FIRST PRINTING
Published by Alterna Comics, Inc.

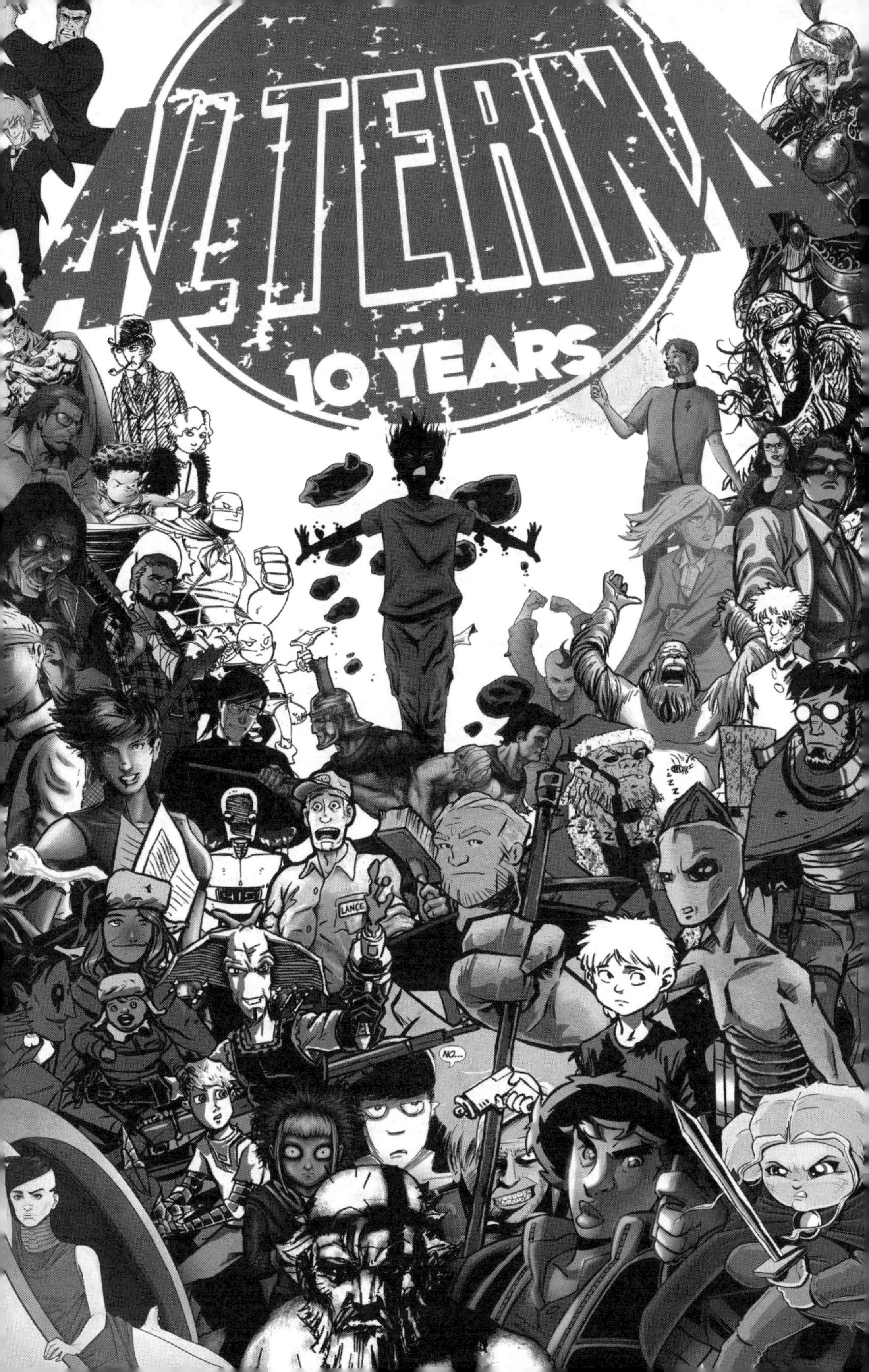

ALTERNA
10 YEARS
LANCE
NO...

"IT WAS A DARK AND STORMY NIGHT ON JANUARY 6TH, 2006. I HAD $600 TO MY NAME... AND NO IDEA WHAT I WAS DOING."

WELL, IT WASN'T THAT DRAMATIC BUT ALL THE FACTS REMAIN THE SAME. WHEN I SIGNED ALL THE PAPERS TO TURN ALTERNA INTO A FUNCTIONING LEGAL BUSINESS, IT WAS DURING A SNOWSTORM AND I DID ONLY HAVE $600 IN THE BANK AT THE TIME (WORKING TWO PART-TIME JOBS WITHOUT MUCH TO SHOW FOR IT) AND BARELY ANY IDEA AS TO WHAT I WAS GOING TO DO BUT I KNEW I HAD TO DO SOMETHING.

HOW DID I END UP IN THAT SITUATION?
LET'S GO BACK TO THE BEGINNING BEFORE THE "BEGINNING"...

I HAD CREATED MY OWN COMIC IN 2005 (ALMOST AROUND THE SAME TIME I GRADUATED COLLEGE) AND USED THE "ALTERNA COMICS" NAME AS AN ALIAS BECAUSE IT SOUNDED BETTER AND LESS SELF-SERVING THAN "SIMETI PUBLISHING" OR WHATEVER ELSE I COULD THINK OF AT THE TIME. THE BOOK SOLD ABOUT TWO HUNDRED COPIES OR SO AT A FEW CONVENTIONS AND A HANDFUL OF STORES (ONLINE SALES WERE ALMOST NON-EXISTENT BACK THEN) BUT WHAT RESULTED WAS SOMETHING I NEVER SAW COMING: PEOPLE WERE SENDING IN SUBMISSIONS TO ME, THINKING THAT ALTERNA WAS A LEGITIMATELY ESTABLISHED PUBLISHING COMPANY.

AT FIRST, I SENT LETTERS AND EMAILS TO PEOPLE WITH APOLOGIES ATTACHED, EXPLAINING THAT ALTERNA WAS MOSTLY JUST A MONIKER I USED FOR MY SELF-PUBLISHING. BUT EVENTUALLY THE STORIES OF REJECTION FROM OTHER CREATORS WORE ME DOWN AND I STARTED TO LEARN EVERYTHING I COULD ABOUT PUBLISHING, EDITING, MARKETING - EVERY FACET OF THE BUSINESS - BECAUSE I JUST WANTED TO HELP HOWEVER I COULD. IT WAS JUST AN AWFUL FEELING, SEEING SO MANY TALENTED PEOPLE THAT WERE TURNED AWAY; TOLD THEIR IDEAS OR SKILLS WERE NO GOOD. A FEW MONTHS LATER, I FILED THE PAPERWORK TO TURN ALTERNA INTO A REAL, OFFICIAL COMPANY.

I KNEW WHAT I WANTED TO DO, BUT I DIDN'T KNOW HOW I WOULD DO IT OR WHAT I NEEDED TO DO TO GET THERE. THERE'S NO TRAINING MANUAL WHEN IT COMES TO RUNNING YOUR OWN BUSINESS (ESPECIALLY IN AN INDUSTRY THAT IS MOSTLY DOMINATED BY TWO VERY WELL-KNOWN AND WELL-LOVED COMPANIES). IT'S A TRIAL BY FIRE FROM START TO FINISH AND YOU HAVE TO DO YOUR BEST NOT TO GET BURNED TOO BADLY (I SAY "TOO BADLY" BECAUSE YOU WILL GET BURNED). STILL, I KNEW THAT THERE WERE A LOT OF TALENTED CREATORS OUT THERE THAT I WANTED TO HELP AND I BELIEVED THAT THERE WAS STRENGTH IN NUMBERS. SO WITH THAT BELIEF, I DID MY BEST TO HELP OTHERS SUCCEED.

THE PUBLISHER

FAST FORWARD TEN YEARS LATER (AND SPARE YOU ALL THE BORING AND NOT-SO-BORING DETAILS) AND ALTERNA HAS GROWN TO A POINT THAT LEAVES ME IN AWE. WE'VE MANAGED TO SURVIVE AGAINST THE ODDS WITH THE HELP OF PEOPLE LIKE YOU (APOLOGIES FOR SOUNDING LIKE THE END OF YOUR FAVORITE PBS PROGRAM). SO MANY PUBLISHERS CAME OUT IN THE MID 2000'S (I KNEW MOST OF THEM IN SOME WAY, SHAPE, OR FORM) AND IT'S SAD TO THINK THAT SO MANY OF THEM ARE NO LONGER IN BUSINESS. "LUCK" WOULD BE THE WRONG WORD BUT IT FEELS APPROPRIATE IN TIMES LIKE THESE. EVERYONE WORKS HARD, SO HARD WORK ISN'T EXACTLY THE END ALL BE ALL. EVERYONE IN THIS BUSINESS IS TALENTED AND CREATIVE TOO SO THAT'S NOT IT EITHER. WHATEVER IT IS, I'M GRATEFUL FOR IT AND THE FACT THAT I'M WRITING A "SO IT'S BEEN TEN YEARS..." PIECE, JUST EMPHASIZES IT EVEN MORE.

IT'S SURREAL, IS WHAT IT IS.

AS WE MOVE FURTHER INTO 2016, I'D LIKE TO STRESS THAT WE WILL CONTINUE WHAT WE'VE BEEN DOING IN THE PAST TEN YEARS AS WELL AS EXPANDING ON IT. WE'LL CONTINUE TO PUBLISH CREATOR-OWNED WORKS (LICENSED COMICS ARE GREAT BUT YOU WON'T FIND THEM AT ALTERNA) AND WE'LL ALSO BE PUBLISHING MORE TITLES IN PRINT & DIGITAL WITH HALF OF 2016'S BOOKS BEING IN FULL COLOR. WE'VE GOT A FEATURE FILM COMING OUT THIS YEAR AS WELL (BASED ON MY GRAPHIC NOVEL THE CHAIR) AND IT'S CURRENTLY AT THE TAIL END OF POST-PRODUCTION. WE'RE ALSO IN THE PROCESS OF FINALIZING A DEAL THAT COULD SEE THE EXPANSION OF ALTERNA COMICS TITLES INTO BOOK STORES AND RETAIL CHAINS ACROSS THE WORLD. EXCITING TIMES! AND ALL OF THIS WOULD NOT BE POSSIBLE WITHOUT YOU AND YOUR BELIEF IN US. THANK YOU FOR THAT.

THANKS AGAIN FOR THE PAST TEN YEARS AND WE HOPE YOU'LL JOIN US FOR THE NEXT TEN (AND MORE),

PETER SIMETI
FOUNDER & PUBLISHER
ALTERNA COMICS

THE ACTUAL ROGER

ADAM WRECK
AND THE KALOSIAN SPACE PIRATES

ALL MY GHOSTS

AMERICAN TERROR
CONFESSION OF A HUMAN SMART BOMB

BEE STING

THE BLACK HAND

BLEEN

BLOOD FOR STONE

CANNONS IN THE CLOUDS

THE CHAIR

CLUSTERF@#K

COMPLEX

CORKTOWN

THE DEADBEAT

DIARY OF THE BLACK WIDOW

THE DOLRIDGE SACRAMENT

EMPIRE OF THE WOLF

FREELANCE BLUES
GWENDOLYN
IF (1)
IF (2)
THE LAST WEST
LILITH DARK
THE MACHINE STOPS
METAPHASE
MOTHER RUSSIA
MYTH
NOVO
RAYGUN
SATANIC HELL
SECRET ADVENTURES OF HOUDINI
SPRING-HEELED JACK
TRESPASSER
UNIT 44
WOLVES OF SUMMER

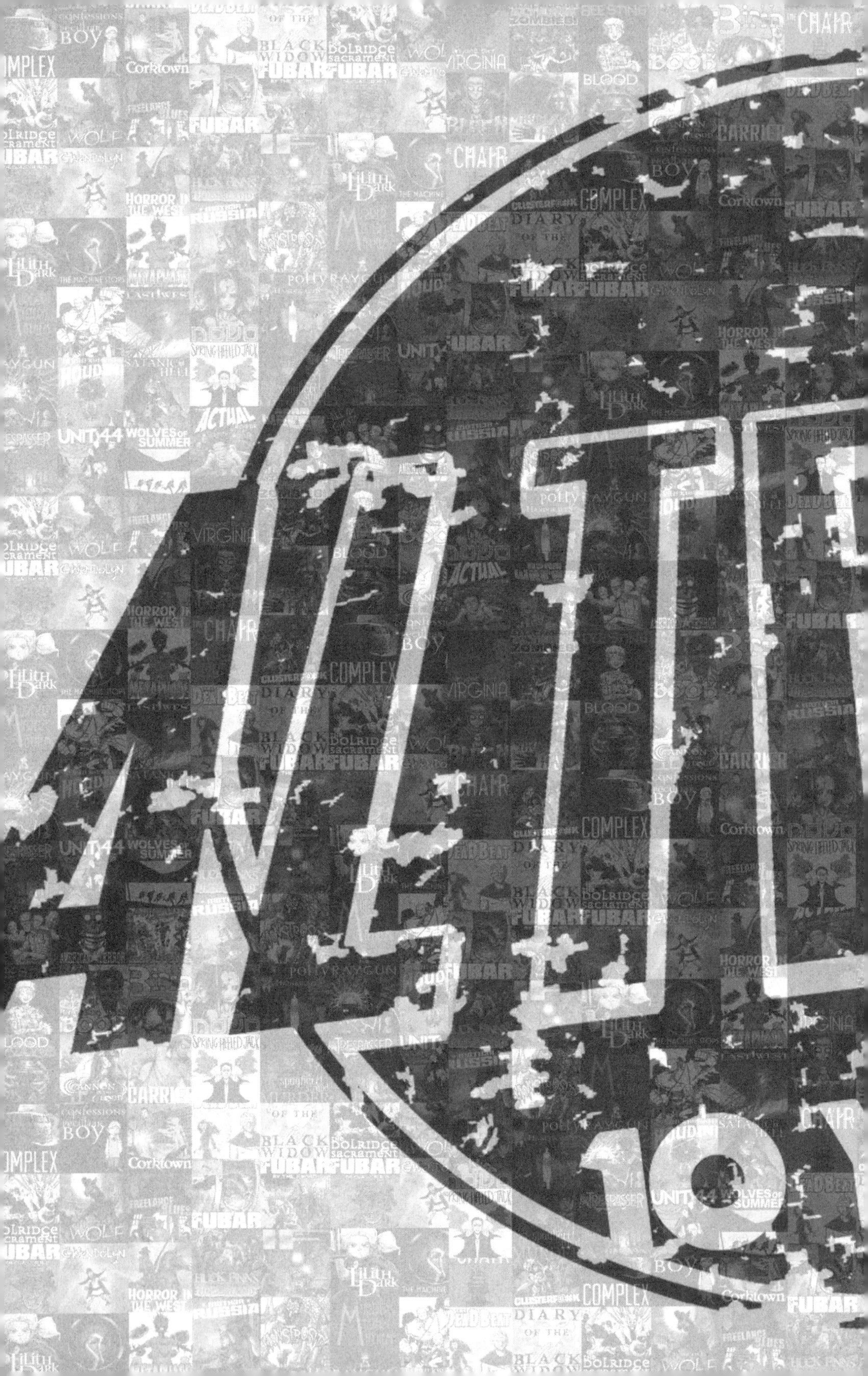
FUBAR
COMPLEX
Corktown
CHAIR
BLOOD
BOY
VIRGINIA
DIARY OF THE BLACK WIDOW
Dolridge sacrament
HORROR IN THE WEST
UNIT 44
WOLVES OF SUMMER
LILITH DARK
SPRING HEELED JACK
CARRIER
POLLY RAYGUN
ACTUAL
CONFESSIONS

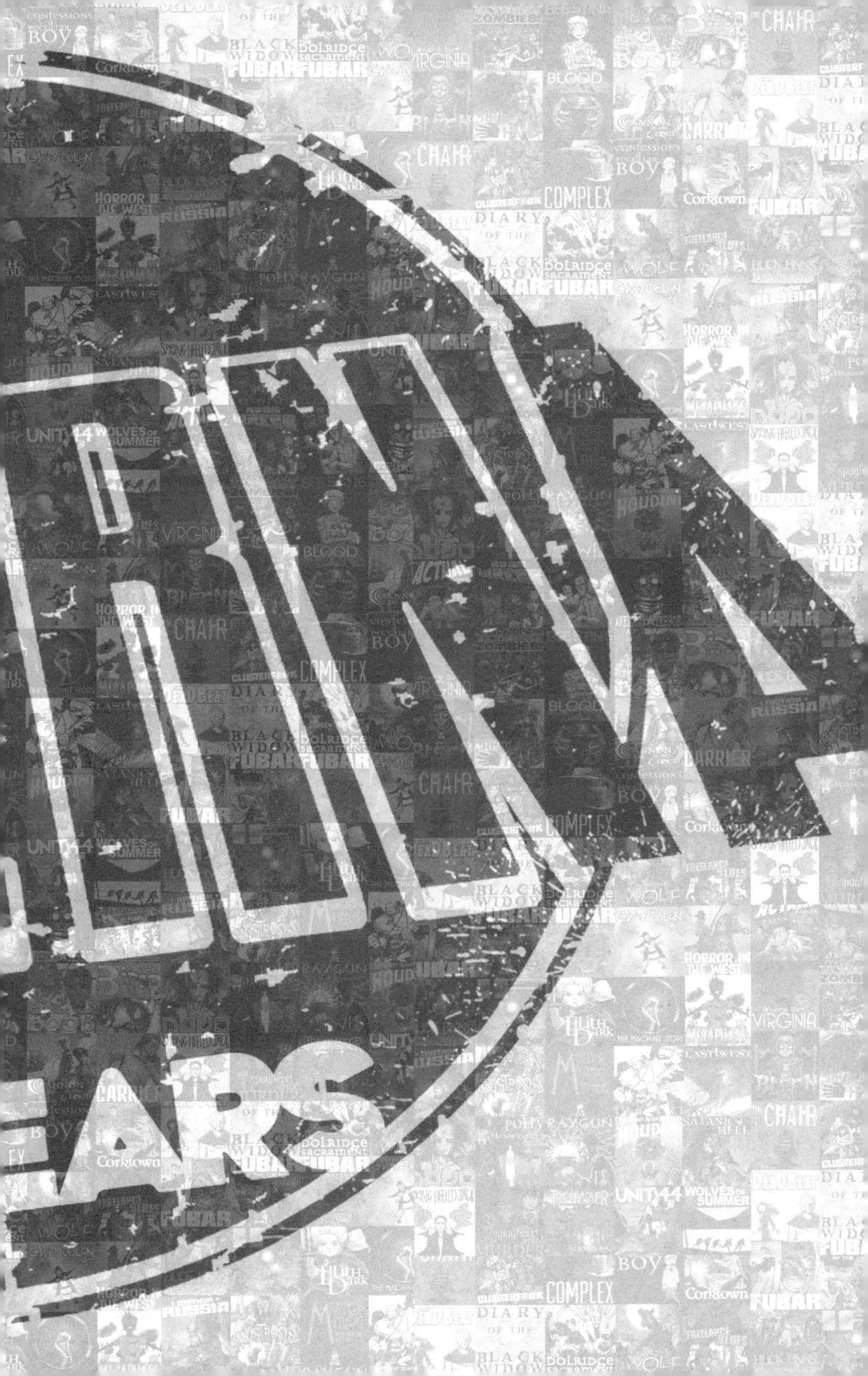

FUBAR
CHAIR
COMPLEX
BLOOD
VIRGINIA
Corktown
CARRIER
HORROR IN THE WEST
RUSSIA
UNIT 44
WOLVES of SUMMER
DIARY OF THE BLACK WIDOW
Dolridge sacrament
polly RAYGUN
CLUSTERFUNK
DEADBEAT

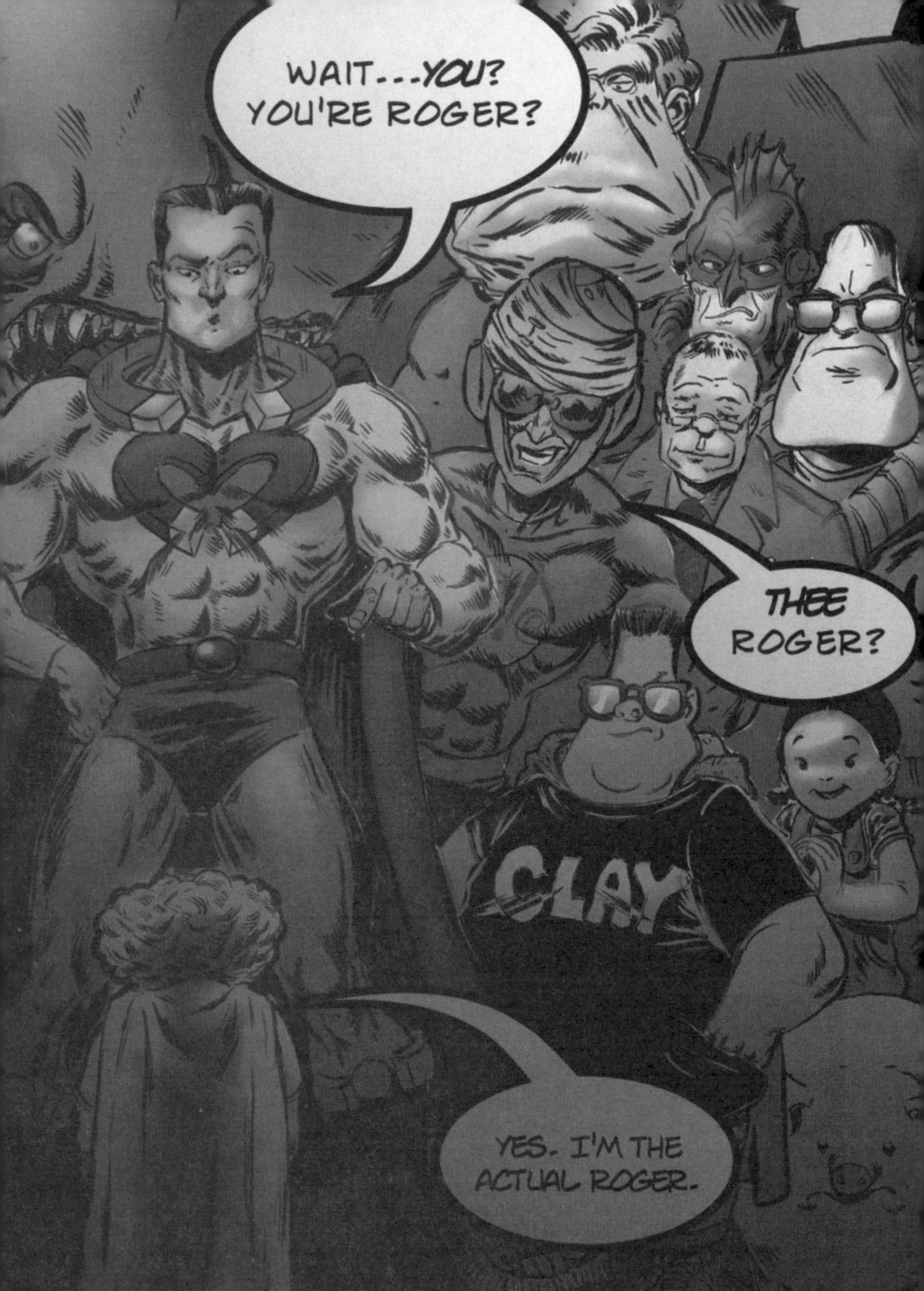
WAIT...YOU? YOU'RE ROGER?
THEE ROGER?
CLAY
YES. I'M THE ACTUAL ROGER.

THE ACTUAL ROGER

THE ACTUAL ROGER

ROGER & MAGNANIMO

"Um, I think I'm being bullied..."

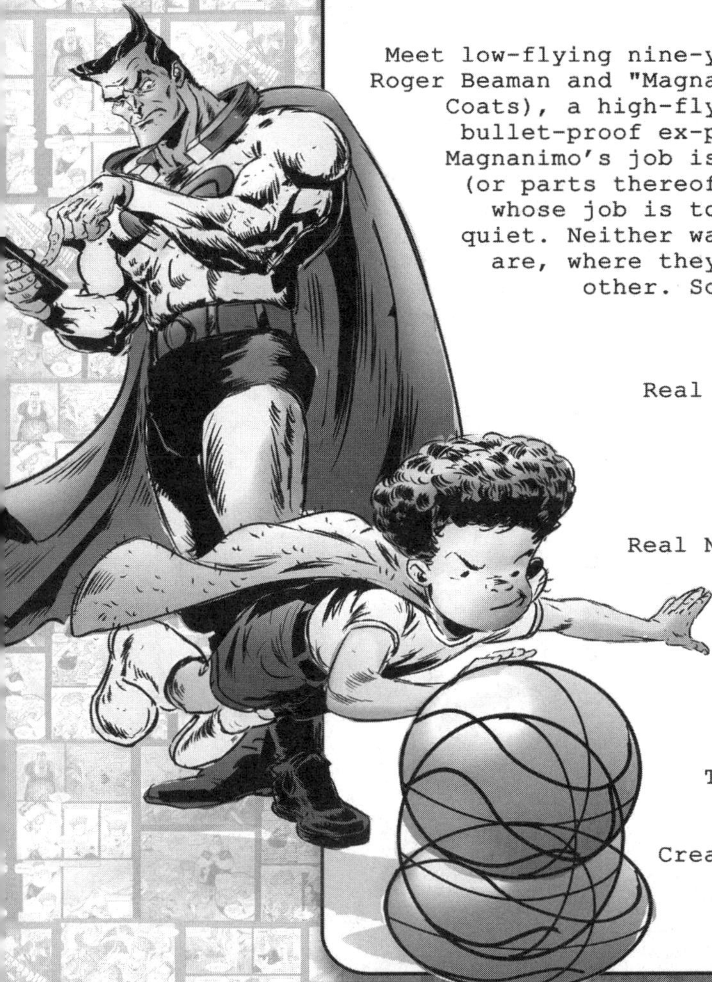

Meet low-flying nine-year-old Lakers fan Roger Beaman and "Magnanimo" (aka: Claude Coats), a high-flying, super-strong, bullet-proof ex-particle physicist. Magnanimo's job is to save the world (or parts thereof) and train Roger, whose job is to be trained and be quiet. Neither want to be what they are, where they are, or with each other. Sounds great, right?

The Actual Roger
Real Name: Roger Beaman
Age: 9
Height: 4' 5"
Weight: 55 lbs.

Magnanimo
Real Name: Claude Coates
Age: 47
Height: 6' 4"
Weight: -235 lbs.

First Appearance
THE ACTUAL ROGER #1
(2013)

Created by Hank Tucker
Illustration by
Hank Tucker

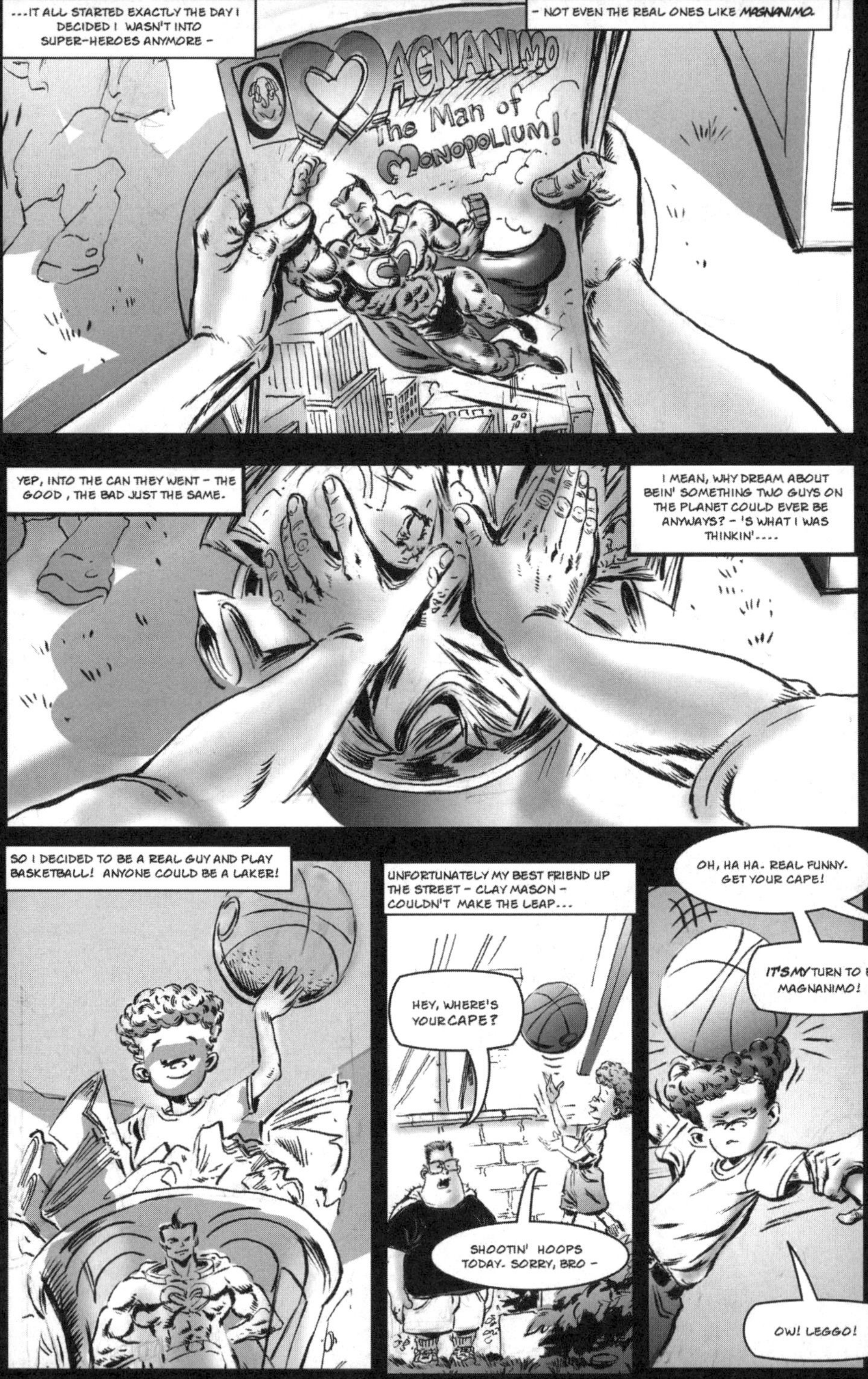
...IT ALL STARTED EXACTLY THE DAY I DECIDED I WASN'T INTO SUPER-HEROES ANYMORE -
- NOT EVEN THE REAL ONES LIKE MAGNANIMO.
MAGNANIMO
The Man of Monopolium!
YEP, INTO THE CAN THEY WENT - THE GOOD , THE BAD JUST THE SAME.
I MEAN, WHY DREAM ABOUT BEIN' SOMETHING TWO GUYS ON THE PLANET COULD EVER BE ANYWAYS? - 'S WHAT I WAS THINKIN'....
SO I DECIDED TO BE A REAL GUY AND PLAY BASKETBALL! ANYONE COULD BE A LAKER!
UNFORTUNATELY MY BEST FRIEND UP THE STREET - CLAY MASON - COULDN'T MAKE THE LEAP...
HEY, WHERE'S YOUR CAPE?
SHOOTIN' HOOPS TODAY. SORRY, BRO -
OH, HA HA. REAL FUNNY. GET YOUR CAPE!
IT'S MY TURN TO BE MAGNANIMO!
OW! LEGGO!

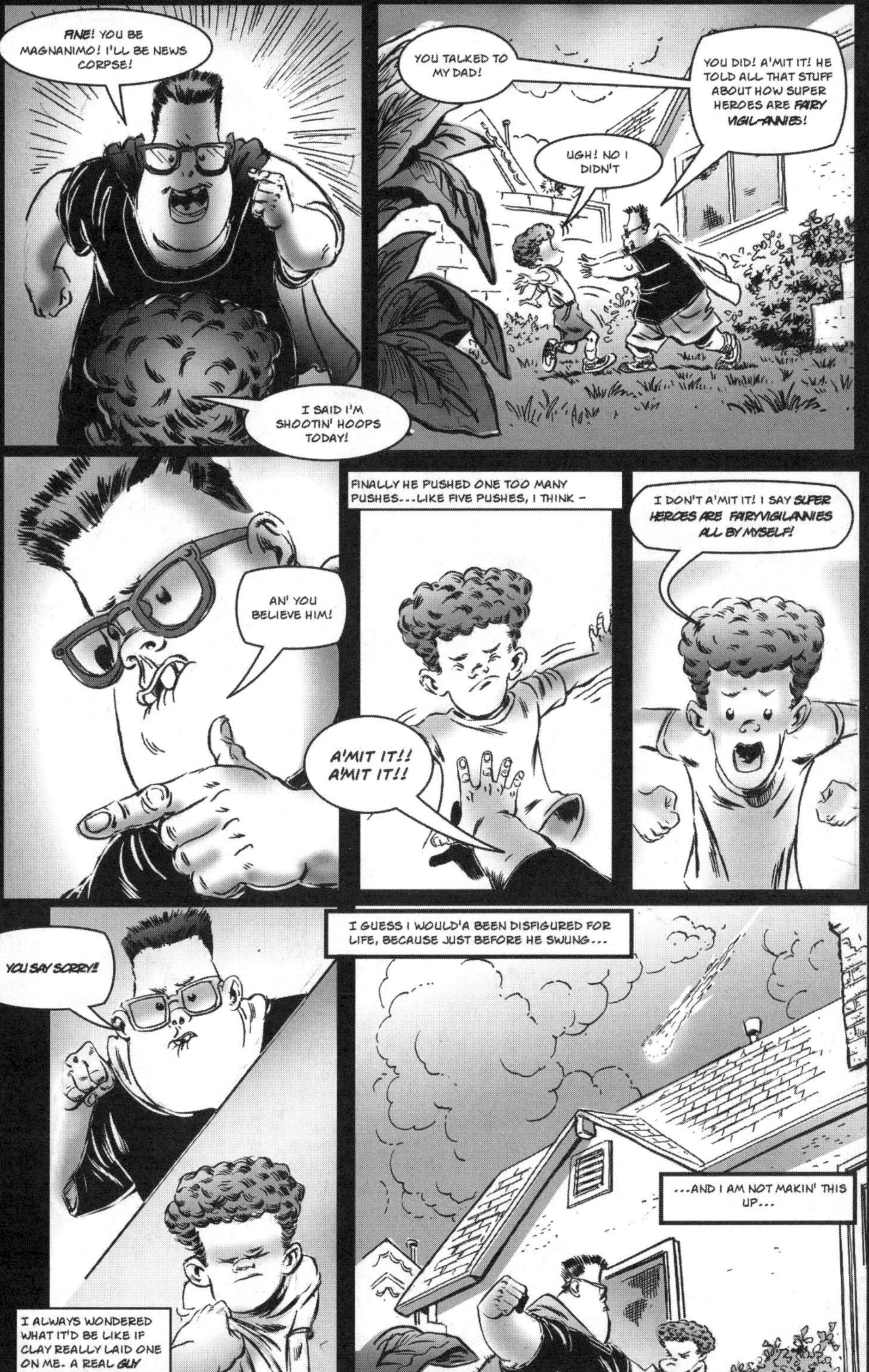
FINE! YOU BE MAGNANIMO! I'LL BE NEWS CORPSE!
I SAID I'M SHOOTIN' HOOPS TODAY!
YOU TALKED TO MY DAD!
YOU DID! A'MIT IT! HE TOLD ALL THAT STUFF ABOUT HOW SUPER HEROES ARE FAIRY VIGIL-ANNIES!
UGH! NO I DIDN'T
AN' YOU BELIEVE HIM!
FINALLY HE PUSHED ONE TOO MANY PUSHES...LIKE FIVE PUSHES, I THINK -
A'MIT IT!! A'MIT IT!!
I DON'T A'MIT IT! I SAY SUPER HEROES ARE FAIRYVIGILANNIES ALL BY MYSELF!
YOU SAY SORRY!!
I ALWAYS WONDERED WHAT IT'D BE LIKE IF CLAY REALLY LAID ONE ON ME. A REAL GUY COULD TAKE A PUNCH!
I GUESS I WOULD'A BEEN DISFIGURED FOR LIFE, BECAUSE JUST BEFORE HE SWUNG...
...AND I AM NOT MAKIN' THIS UP...

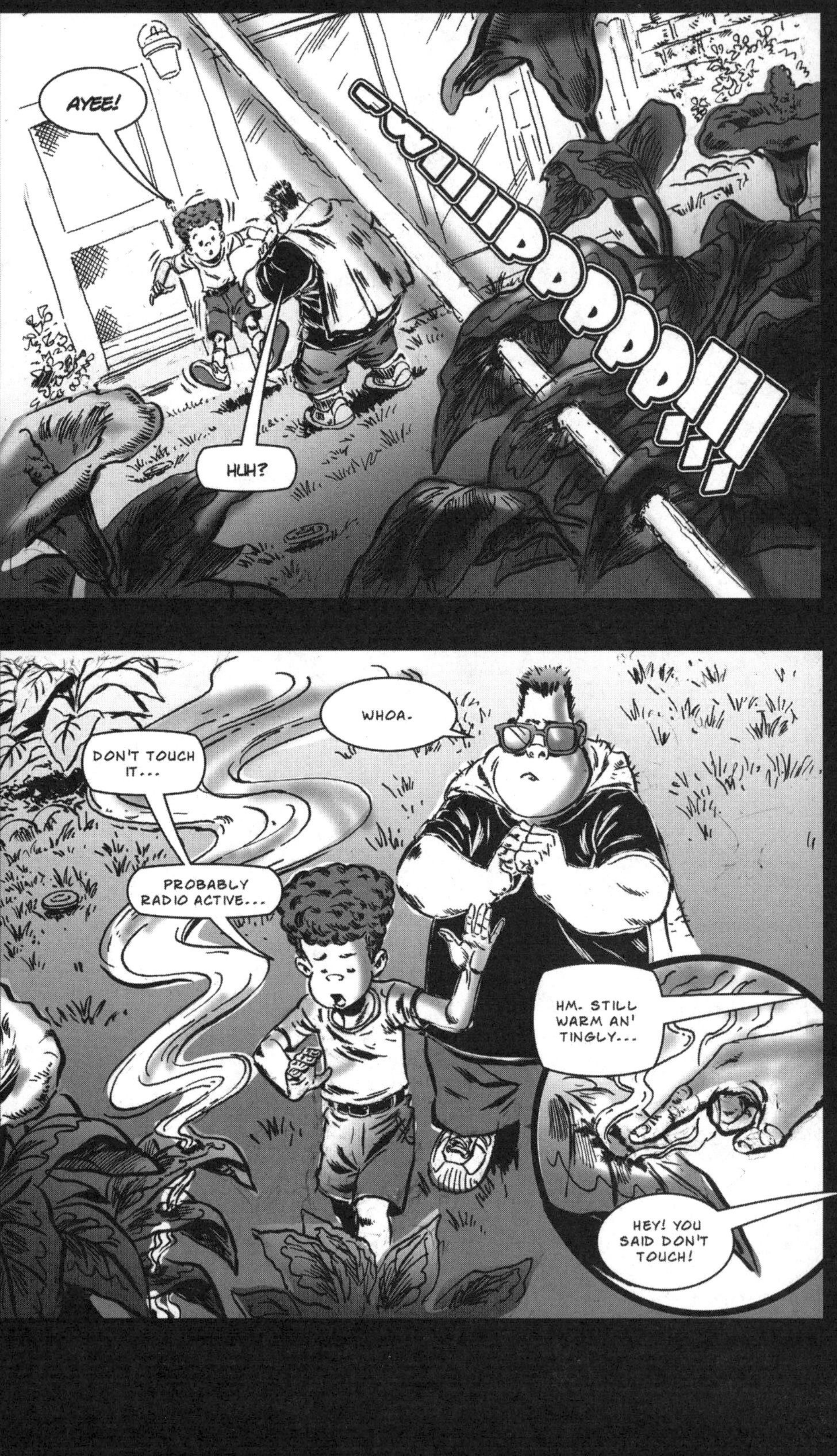
AYEE!
FWIIIPPPP!!!
HUH?
WHOA.
DON'T TOUCH IT...
PROBABLY RADIO ACTIVE...
HM. STILL WARM AN' TINGLY...
HEY! YOU SAID DON'T TOUCH!

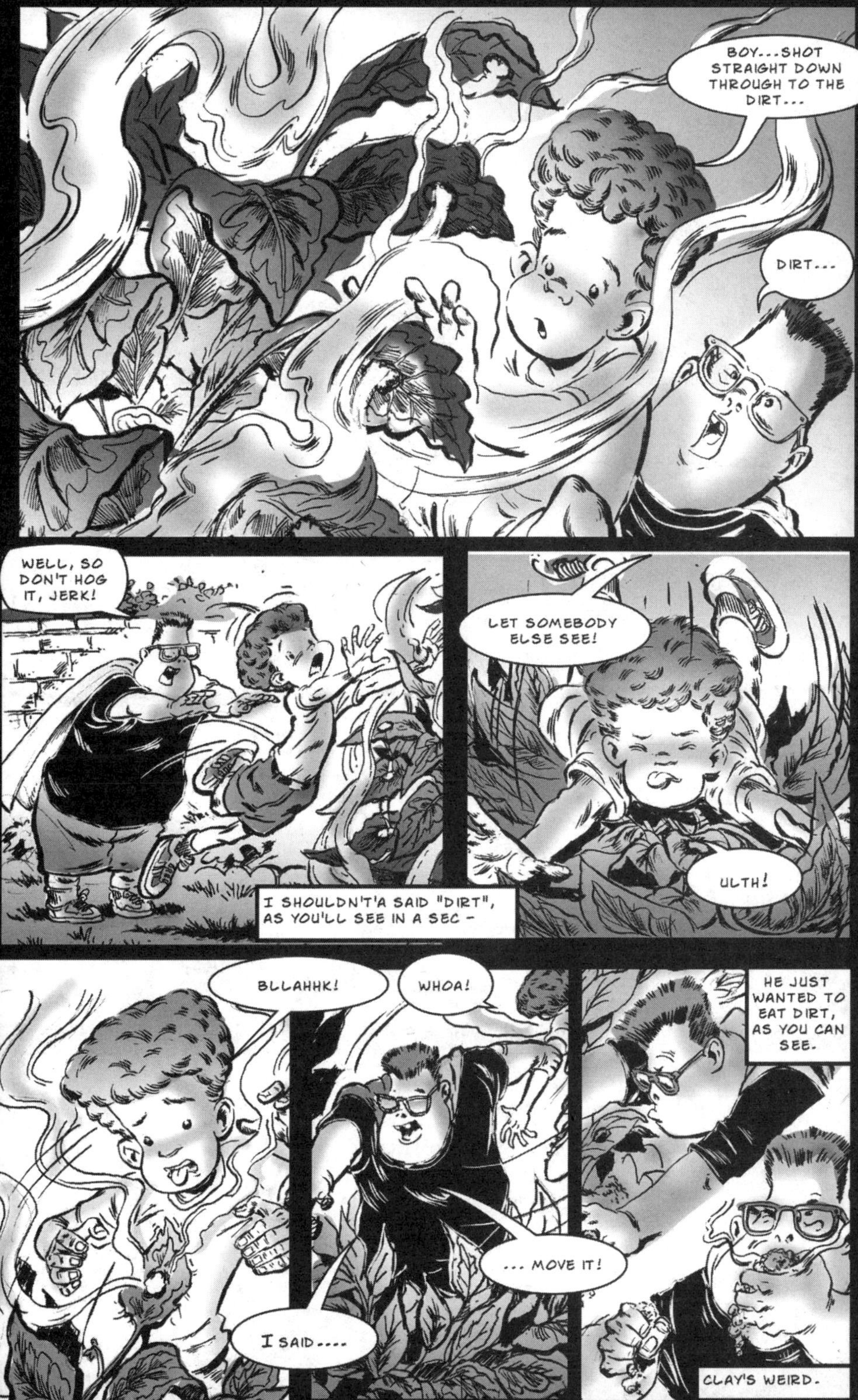
BOY...SHOT STRAIGHT DOWN THROUGH TO THE DIRT...
DIRT...
WELL, SO DON'T HOG IT, JERK!
I SHOULDN'T'A SAID "DIRT", AS YOU'LL SEE IN A SEC -
LET SOMEBODY ELSE SEE!
ULTH!
BLLAHHK!
WHOA!
I SAID....
... MOVE IT!
HE JUST WANTED TO EAT DIRT, AS YOU CAN SEE.
CLAY'S WEIRD.

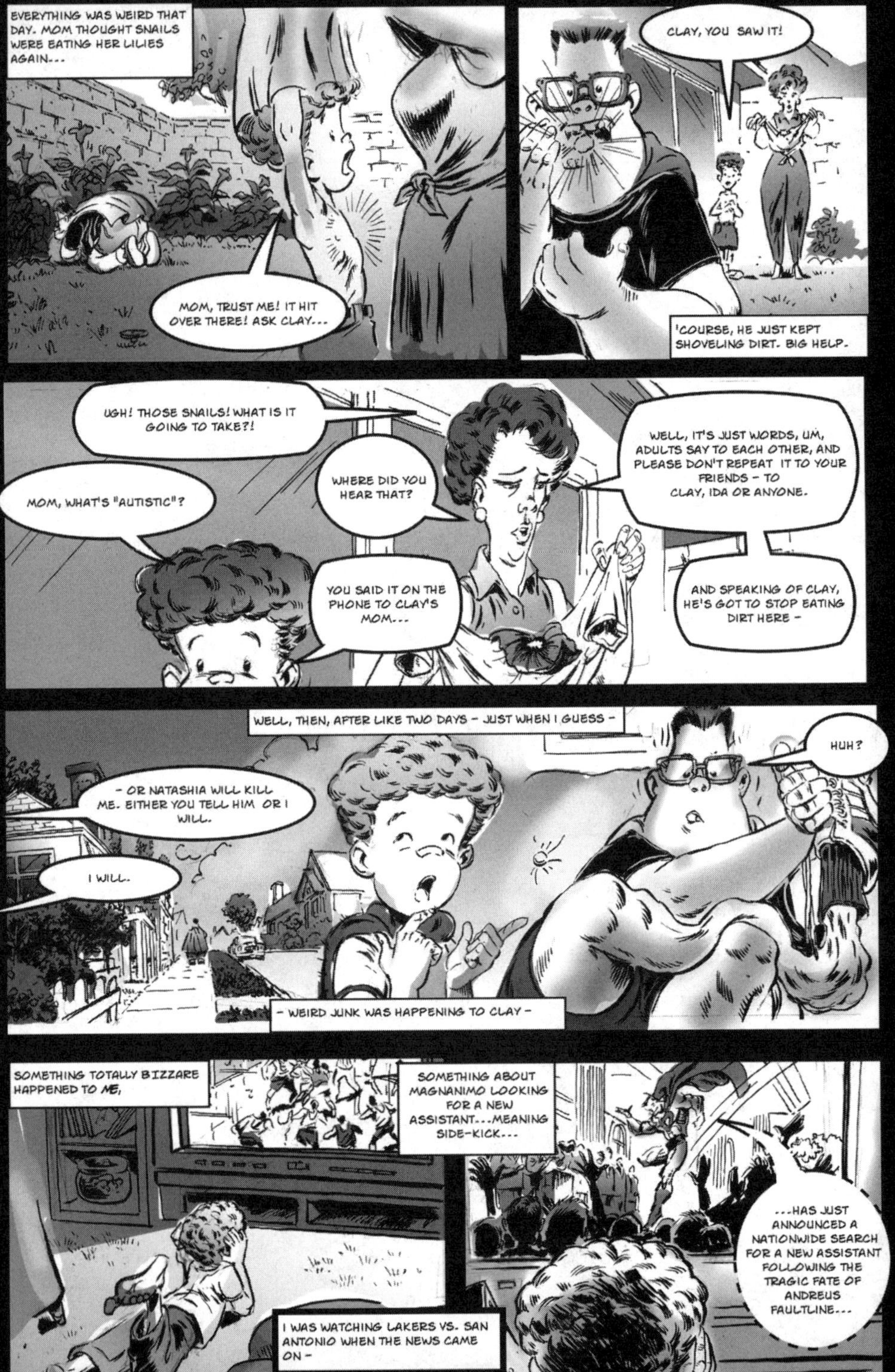
EVERYTHING WAS WEIRD THAT DAY. MOM THOUGHT SNAILS WERE EATING HER LILIES AGAIN...
MOM, TRUST ME! IT HIT OVER THERE! ASK CLAY...
CLAY, YOU SAW IT!
'COURSE, HE JUST KEPT SHOVELING DIRT. BIG HELP.
UGH! THOSE SNAILS! WHAT IS IT GOING TO TAKE?!
MOM, WHAT'S "AUTISTIC"?
WHERE DID YOU HEAR THAT?
YOU SAID IT ON THE PHONE TO CLAY'S MOM...
WELL, IT'S JUST WORDS, UM, ADULTS SAY TO EACH OTHER, AND PLEASE DON'T REPEAT IT TO YOUR FRIENDS - TO CLAY, IDA OR ANYONE.
AND SPEAKING OF CLAY, HE'S GOT TO STOP EATING DIRT HERE -
WELL, THEN, AFTER LIKE TWO DAYS - JUST WHEN I GUESS -
- OR NATASHIA WILL KILL ME. EITHER YOU TELL HIM OR I WILL.
I WILL.
HUH?
- WEIRD JUNK WAS HAPPENING TO CLAY -
SOMETHING TOTALLY BIZZARE HAPPENED TO *ME*,
SOMETHING ABOUT MAGNANIMO LOOKING FOR A NEW ASSISTANT...MEANING SIDE-KICK...
...HAS JUST ANNOUNCED A NATIONWIDE SEARCH FOR A NEW ASSISTANT FOLLOWING THE TRAGIC FATE OF ANDREUS FAULTLINE...
I WAS WATCHING LAKERS VS. SAN ANTONIO WHEN THE NEWS CAME ON -

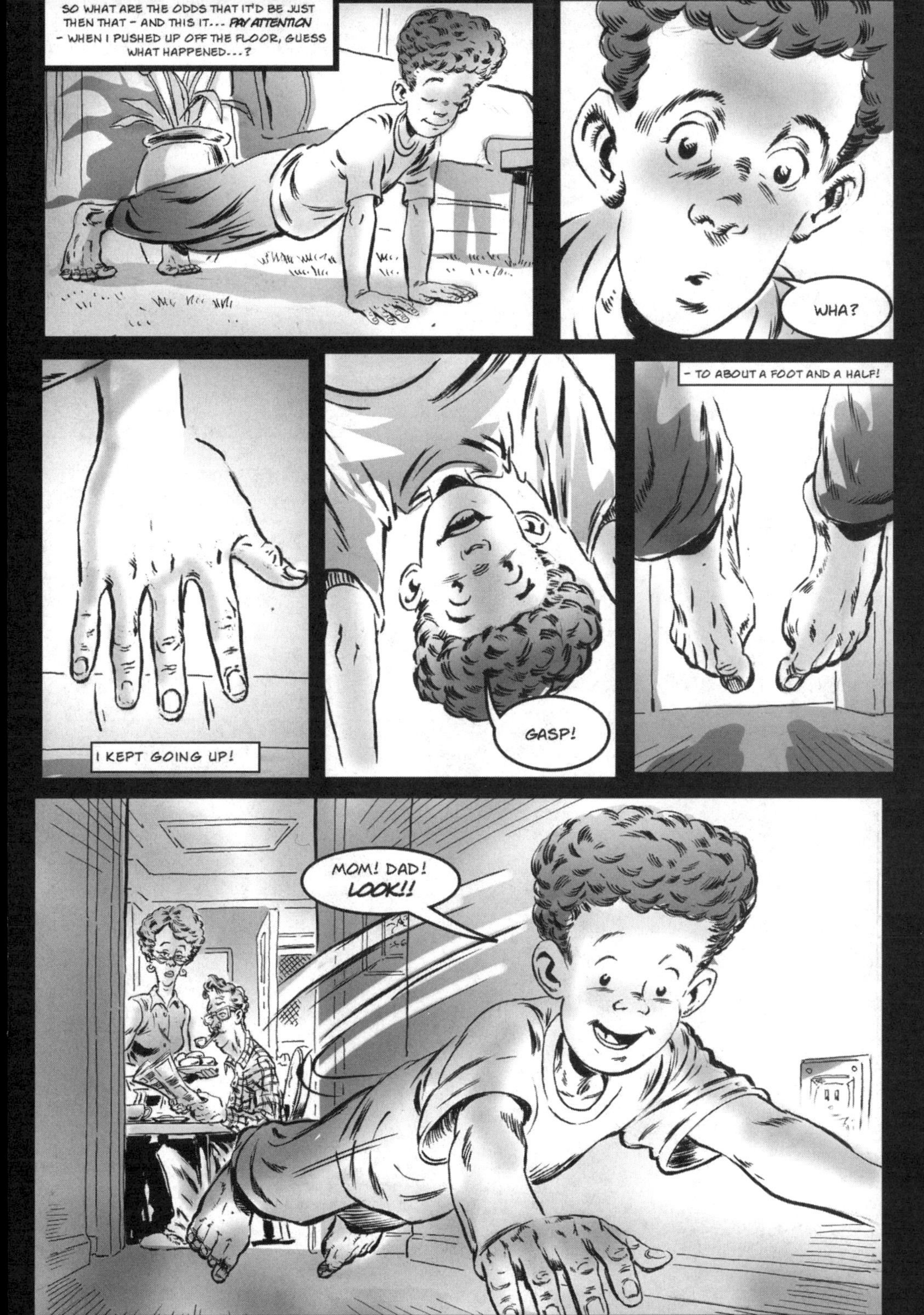
SO WHAT ARE THE ODDS THAT IT'D BE JUST THEN THAT – AND THIS IT... PAY ATTENTION – WHEN I PUSHED UP OFF THE FLOOR, GUESS WHAT HAPPENED...?
WHA?
I KEPT GOING UP!
GASP!
– TO ABOUT A FOOT AND A HALF!
MOM! DAD! LOOK!!

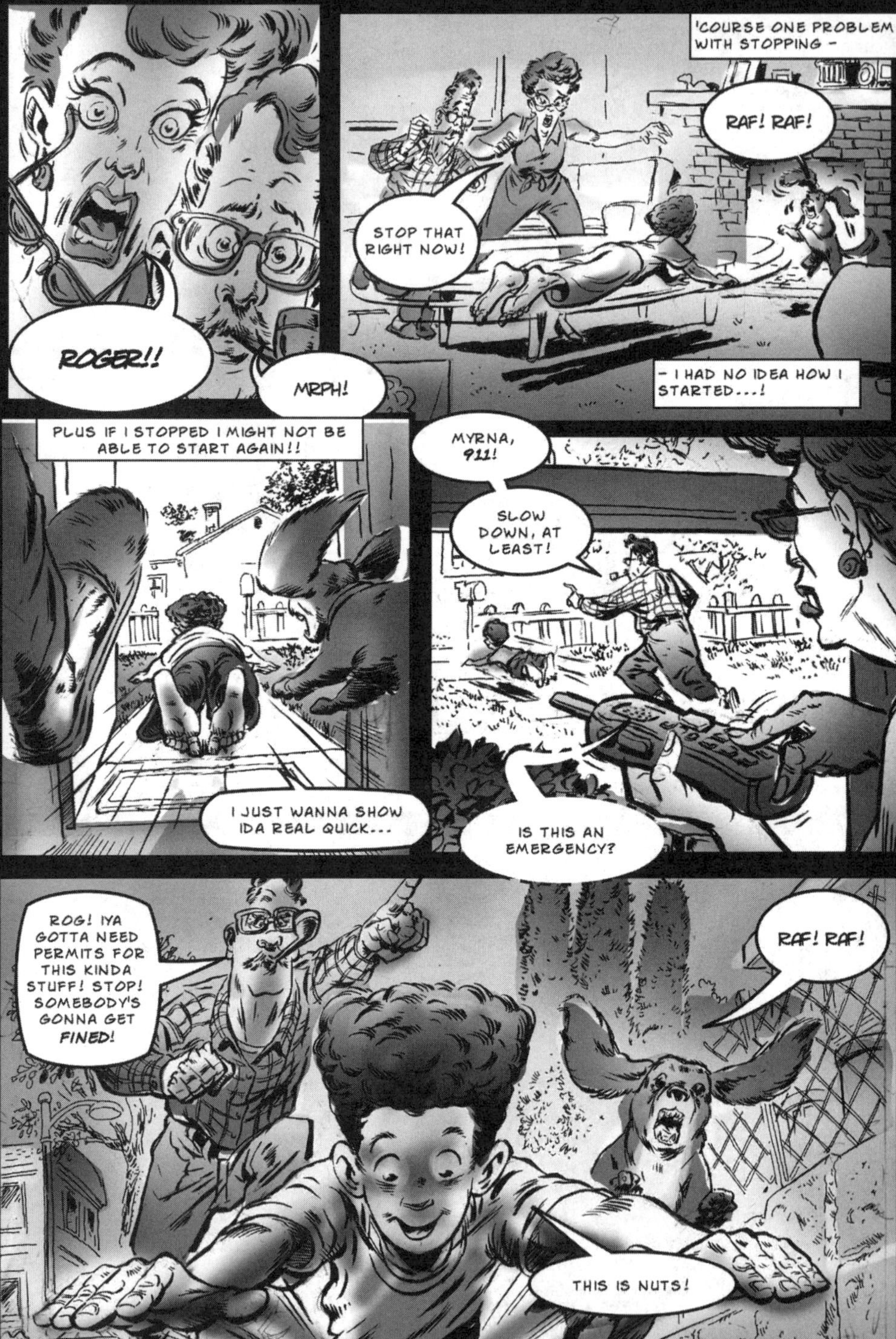
ROGER!!
MRPH!
'COURSE ONE PROBLEM WITH STOPPING -
RAF! RAF!
STOP THAT RIGHT NOW!
- I HAD NO IDEA HOW I STARTED...!
PLUS IF I STOPPED I MIGHT NOT BE ABLE TO START AGAIN!!
I JUST WANNA SHOW IDA REAL QUICK...
MYRNA, 911!
SLOW DOWN, AT LEAST!
IS THIS AN EMERGENCY?
ROG! IYA GOTTA NEED PERMITS FOR THIS KINDA STUFF! STOP! SOMEBODY'S GONNA GET FINED!
RAF! RAF!
THIS IS NUTS!

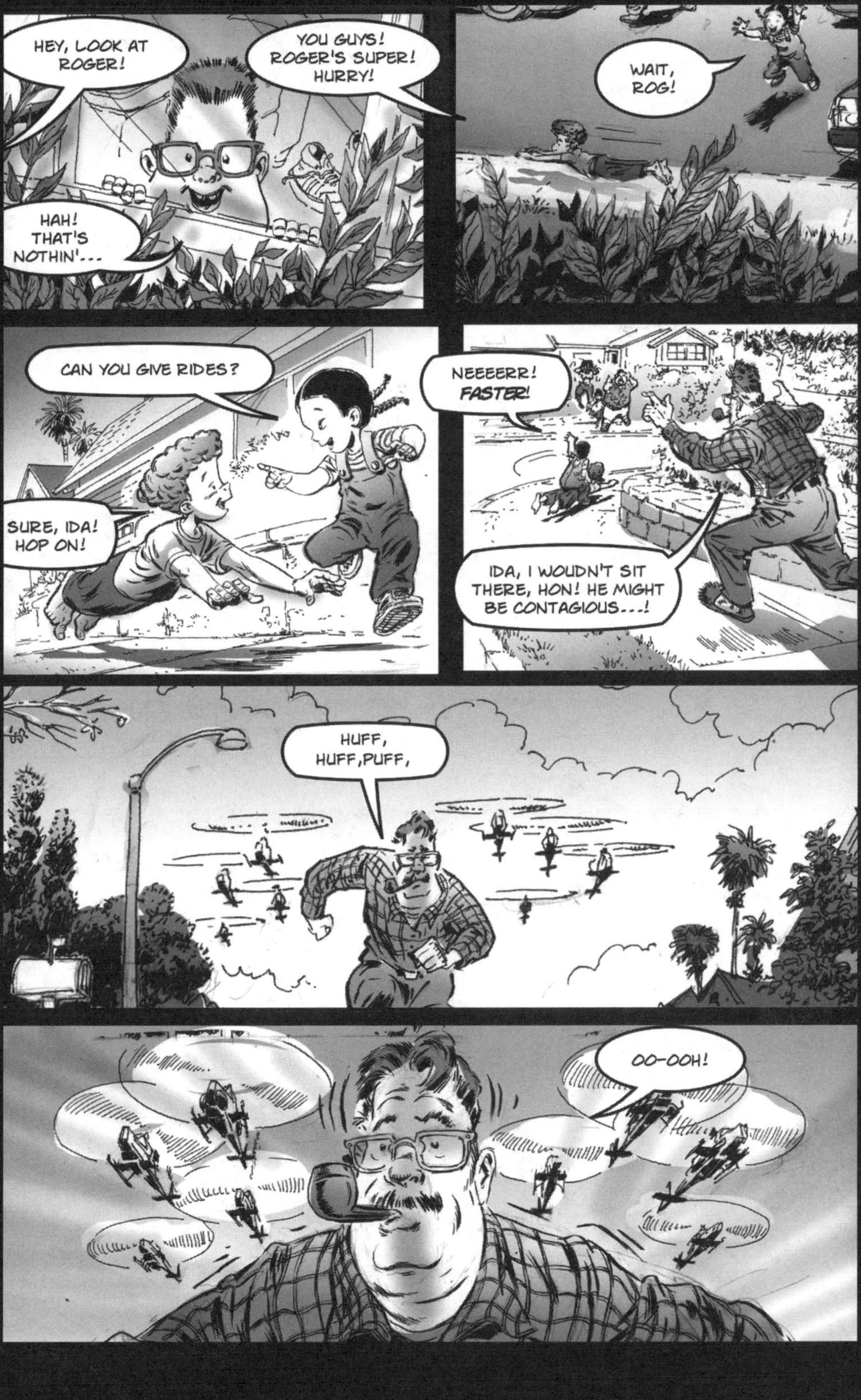
HEY, LOOK AT ROGER!
YOU GUYS! ROGER'S SUPER! HURRY!
HAH! THAT'S NOTHIN'...
WAIT, ROG!
CAN YOU GIVE RIDES?
SURE, IDA! HOP ON!
NEEEERR! FASTER!
IDA, I WOUDN'T SIT THERE, HON! HE MIGHT BE CONTAGIOUS...!
HUFF, HUFF,PUFF,
OO-OOH!

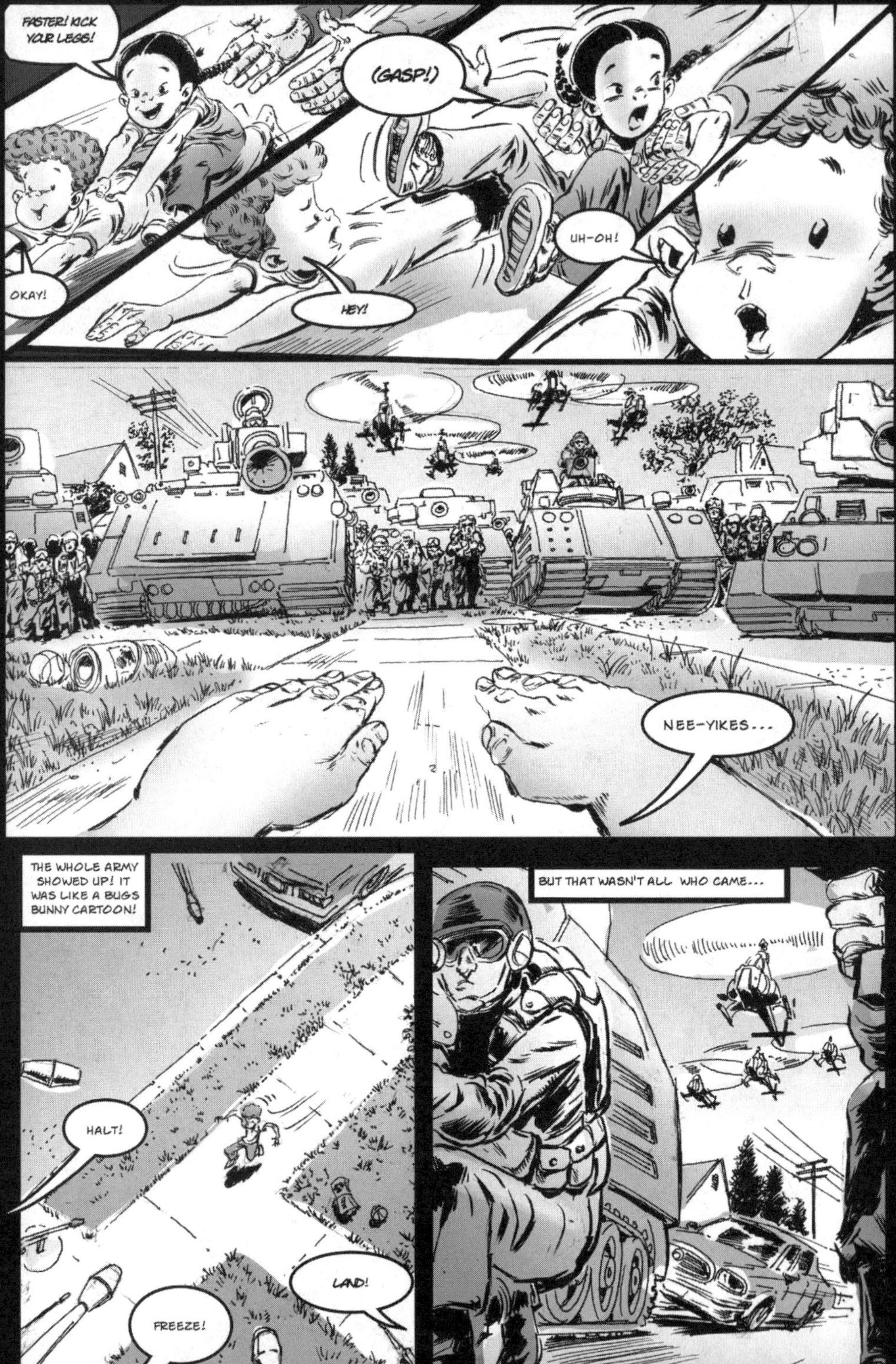
FASTER! KICK YOUR LEGS!
OKAY!
(GASP!)
HEY!
UH-OH!
NEE-YIKES...
THE WHOLE ARMY SHOWED UP! IT WAS LIKE A BUGS BUNNY CARTOON!
HALT!
LAND!
FREEZE!
BUT THAT WASN'T ALL WHO CAME...

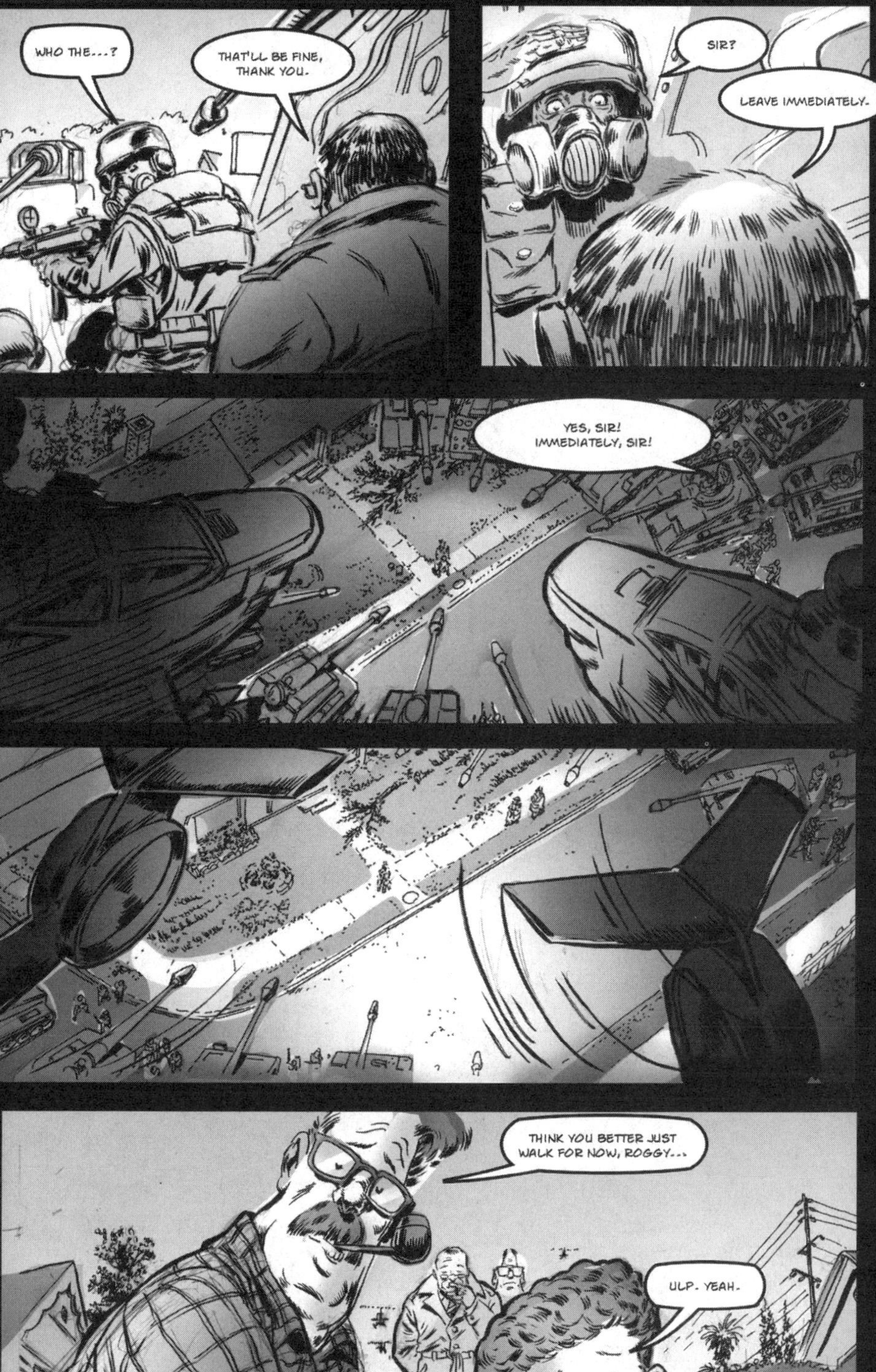
WHO THE...?
THAT'LL BE FINE, THANK YOU.
SIR?
LEAVE IMMEDIATELY.
YES, SIR! IMMEDIATELY, SIR!
THINK YOU BETTER JUST WALK FOR NOW, ROGGY...
ULP. YEAH.

CONTINUED IN THE PAGES OF 'THE ACTUAL ROGER'

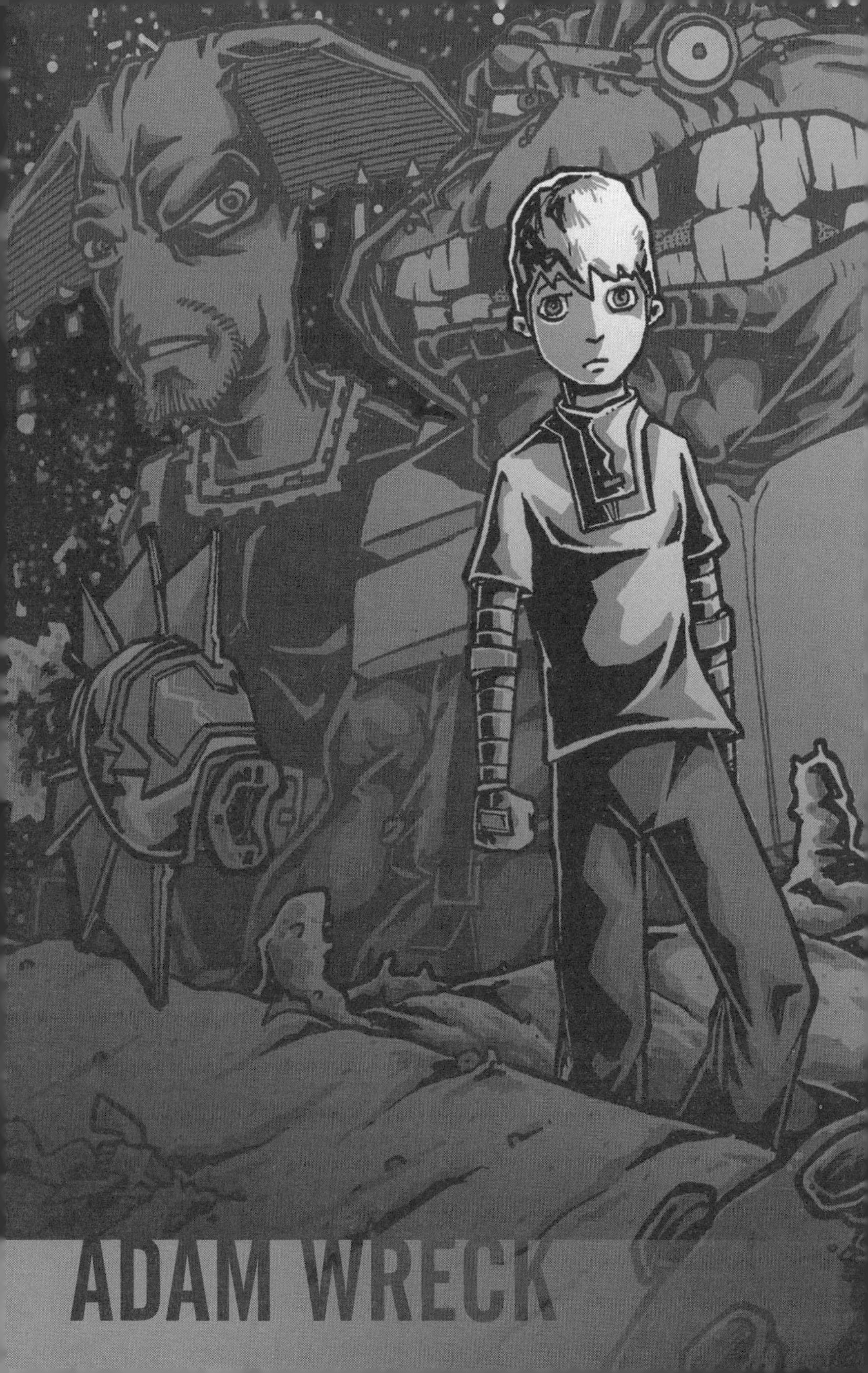

ADAM WRECK

ADAM WRECK

ADAM & VORIC

"Who cares about stars and planets! I want to see some space aliens!"

Adam Wreck is the son of genius space explorer parents, Albert and Betty Wreck. Dragged along on an exploration mission through the far reaches of space, Adam has come to learn one thing… OUTER SPACE CAN BE VERY BORING! At least it *was* "boring" until Adam's parents got captured by dastardly space pirates! Now it's up to Adam and the reluctant treasure-hunting Voric, to save Adam's family from certain doom!

ADAM WRECK
Age: 12
Height: 5'1"
Weight: 105 lbs.

CAPTAIN VORIC
Age: 34 cycles
Height: 6'3"
Weight: 220 lbs.

First Appearance:
ADAM WRECK AND THE KALOSIAN
SPACE PIRATES (2009)

Created by Michael S. Bracco
Illustration by
Michael S. Bracco

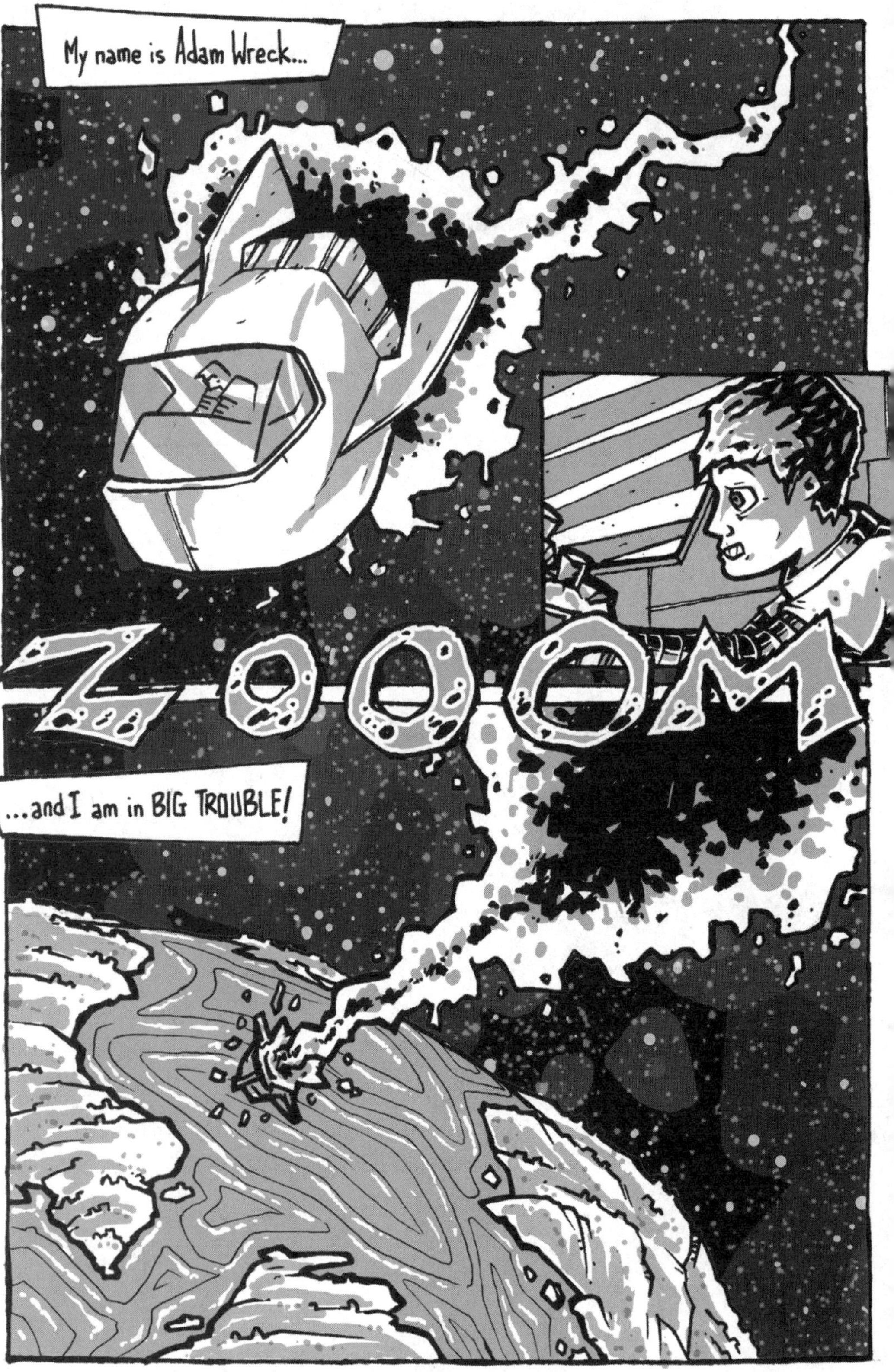
My name is Adam Wreck...
ZOOOOM
...and I am in BIG TROUBLE!

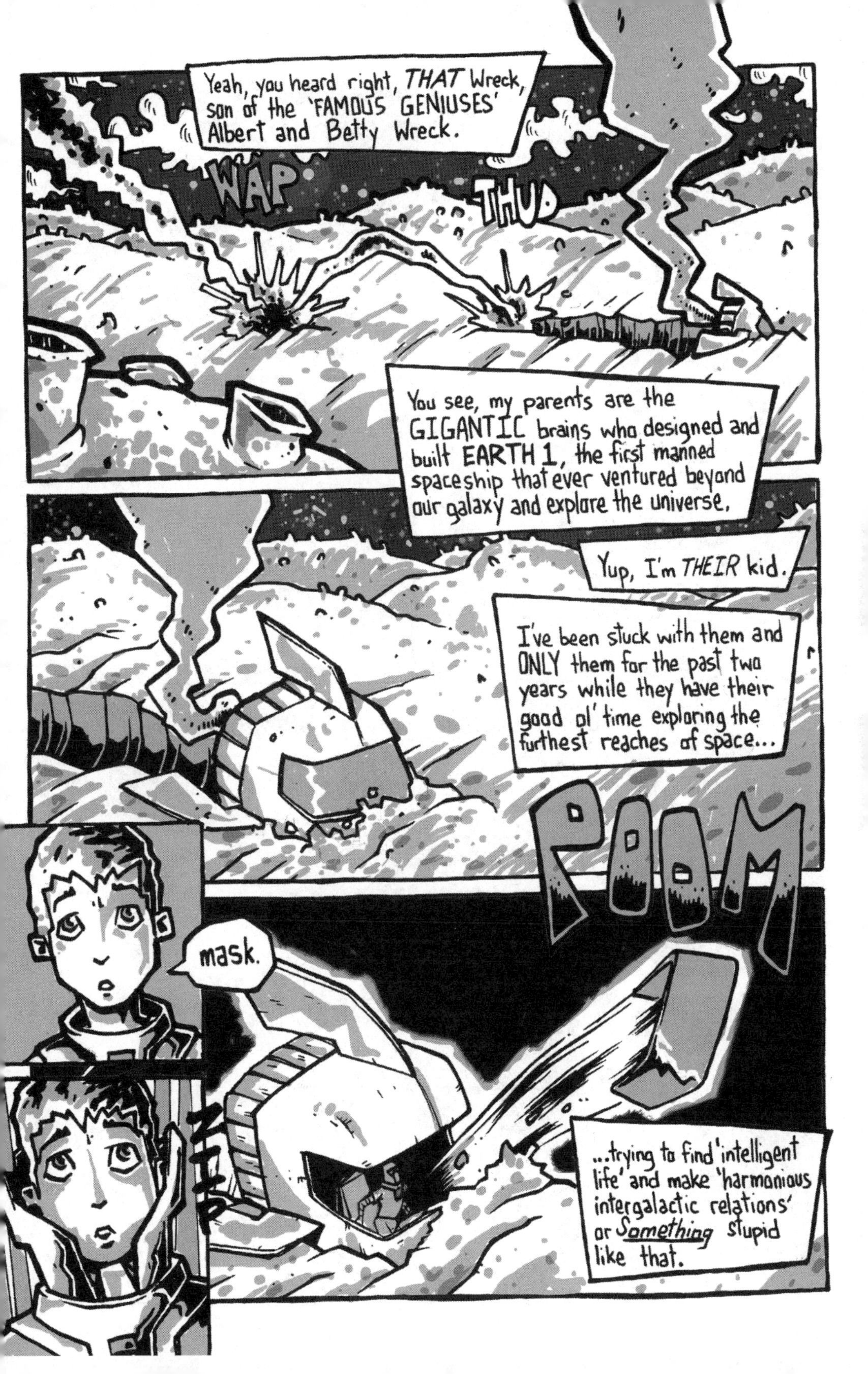
Yeah, you heard right, THAT Wreck, son of the 'FAMOUS GENIUSES' Albert and Betty Wreck.
WAP
THUD
You see, my parents are the GIGANTIC brains who designed and built EARTH 1, the first manned spaceship that ever ventured beyond our galaxy and explore the universe.
Yup, I'm THEIR kid.
I've been stuck with them and ONLY them for the past two years while they have their good ol' time exploring the furthest reaches of space...
POOM
mask.
...trying to find 'intelligent life' and make 'harmonious intergalactic relations' or Something stupid like that.

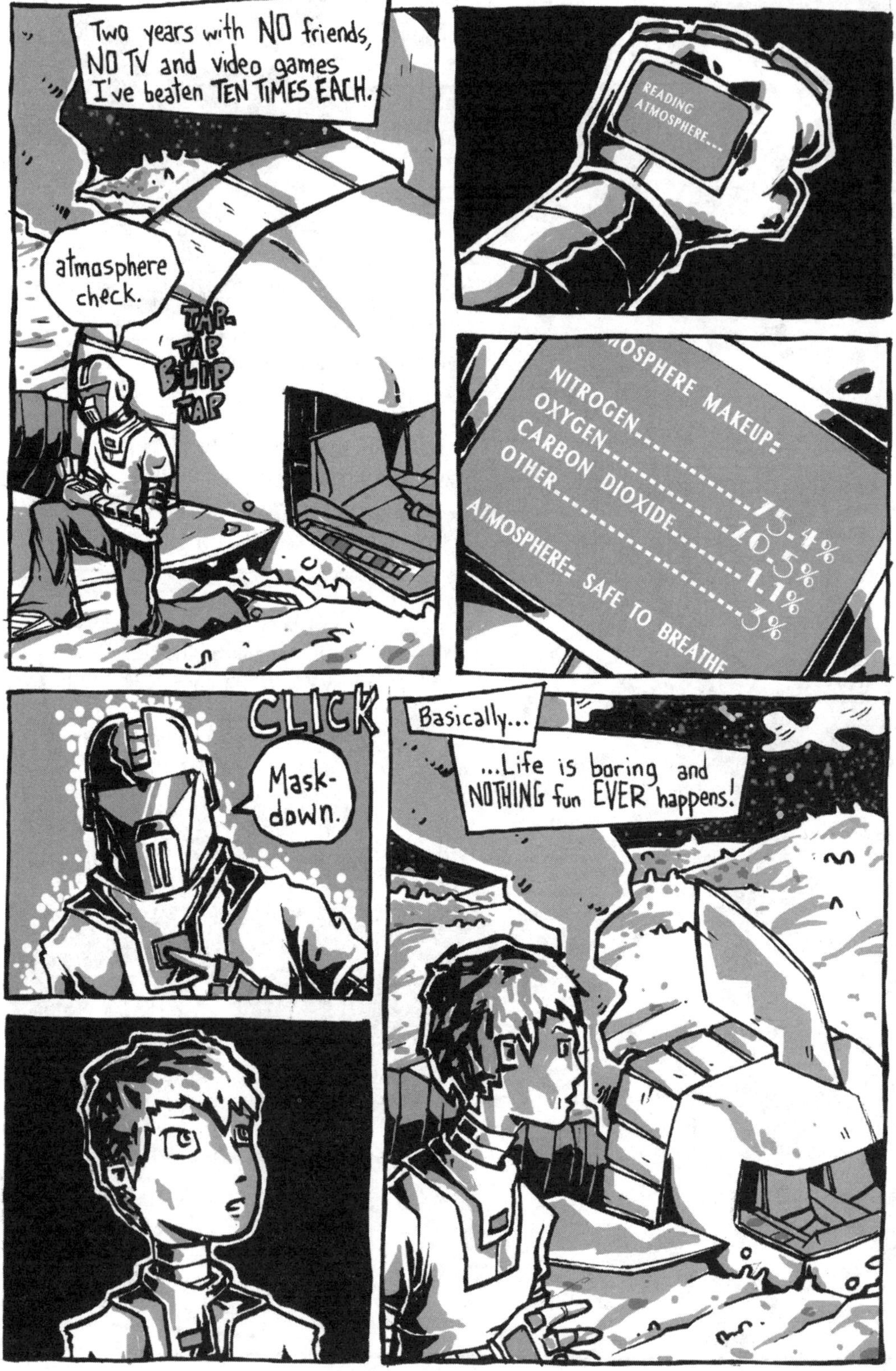
Two years with NO friends, NO TV and video games I've beaten TEN TIMES EACH.
atmasphere check.
TAP-TAP BLIP TAP
READING ATMOSPHERE...
MOSPHERE MAKEUP:
NITROGEN..............75.4%
OXYGEN..............20.5%
CARBON DIOXIDE..........1.1%
OTHER..................3%
ATMOSPHERE: SAFE TO BREATHE
CLICK
Mask-down.
Basically...
...Life is boring and NOTHING fun EVER happens!

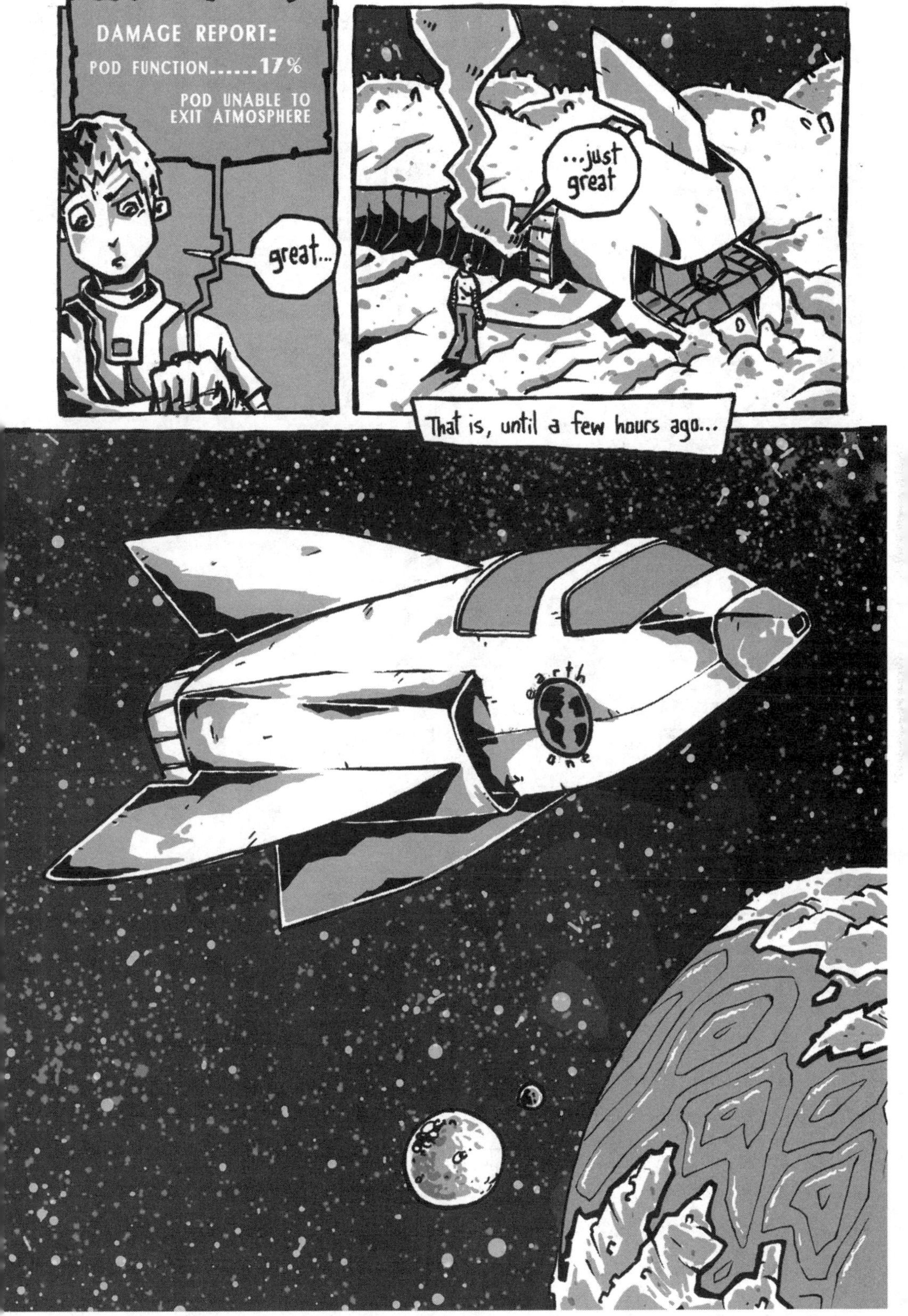
DAMAGE REPORT:
POD FUNCTION.......17%
POD UNABLE TO EXIT ATMOSPHERE
great...
...just great
That is, until a few hours ago...
earth one

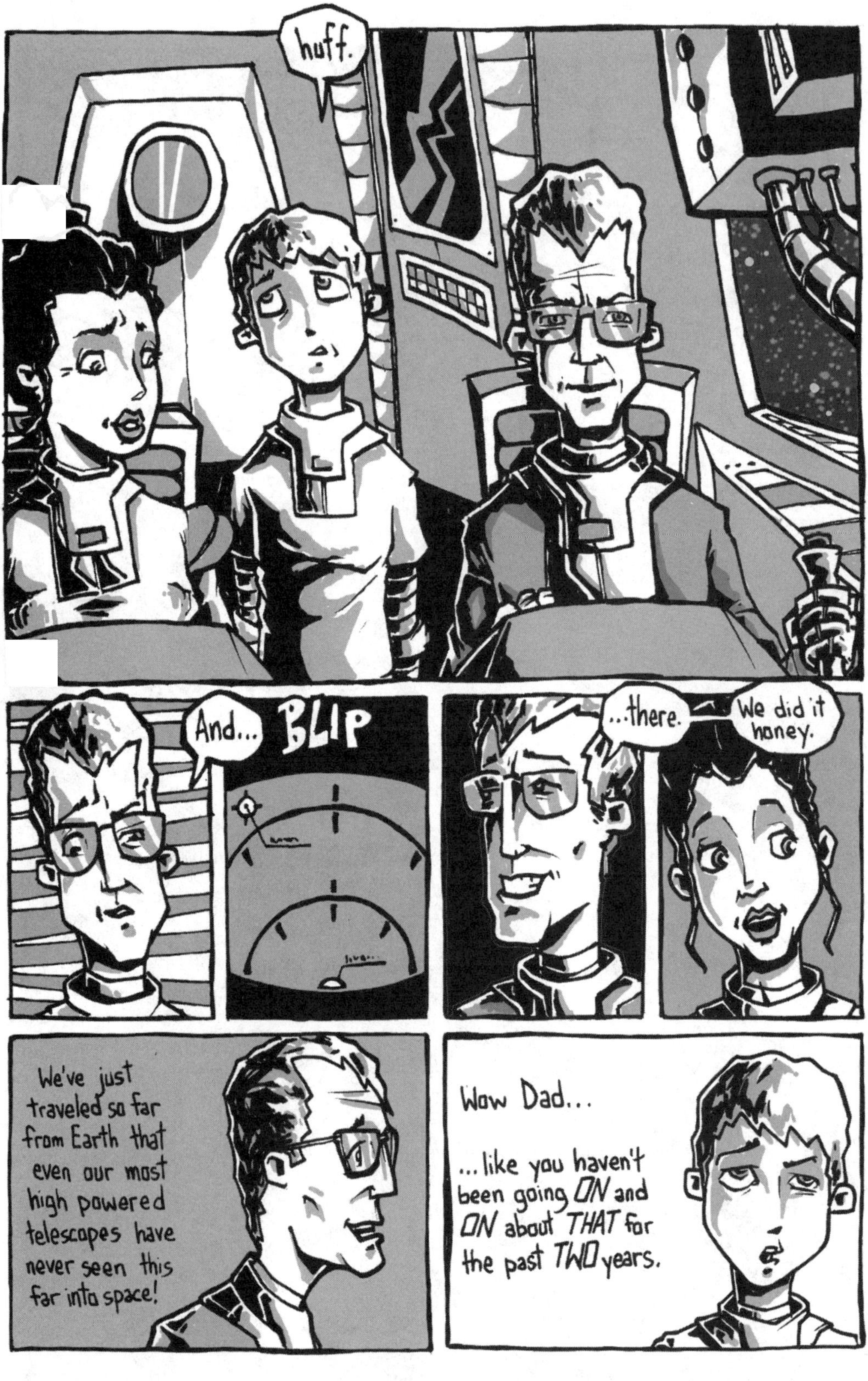
huff.
And...
BLIP
...there.
We did it honey.
We've just traveled so far from Earth that even our most high powered telescopes have never seen this far into space!
Wow Dad...
...like you haven't been going ON and ON about THAT for the past TWO years.

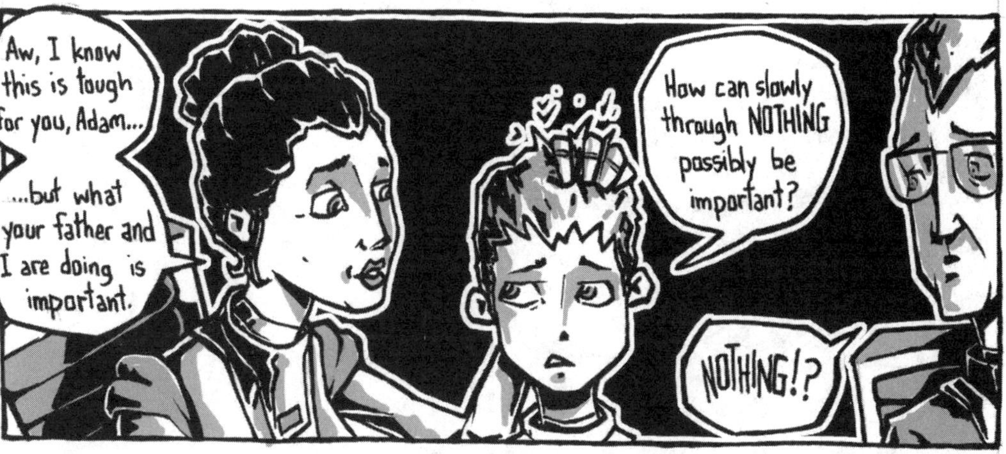
Aw, I know this is tough for you, Adam...
...but what your father and I are doing is important.
How can slowly through NOTHING possibly be important?
NOTHING!?

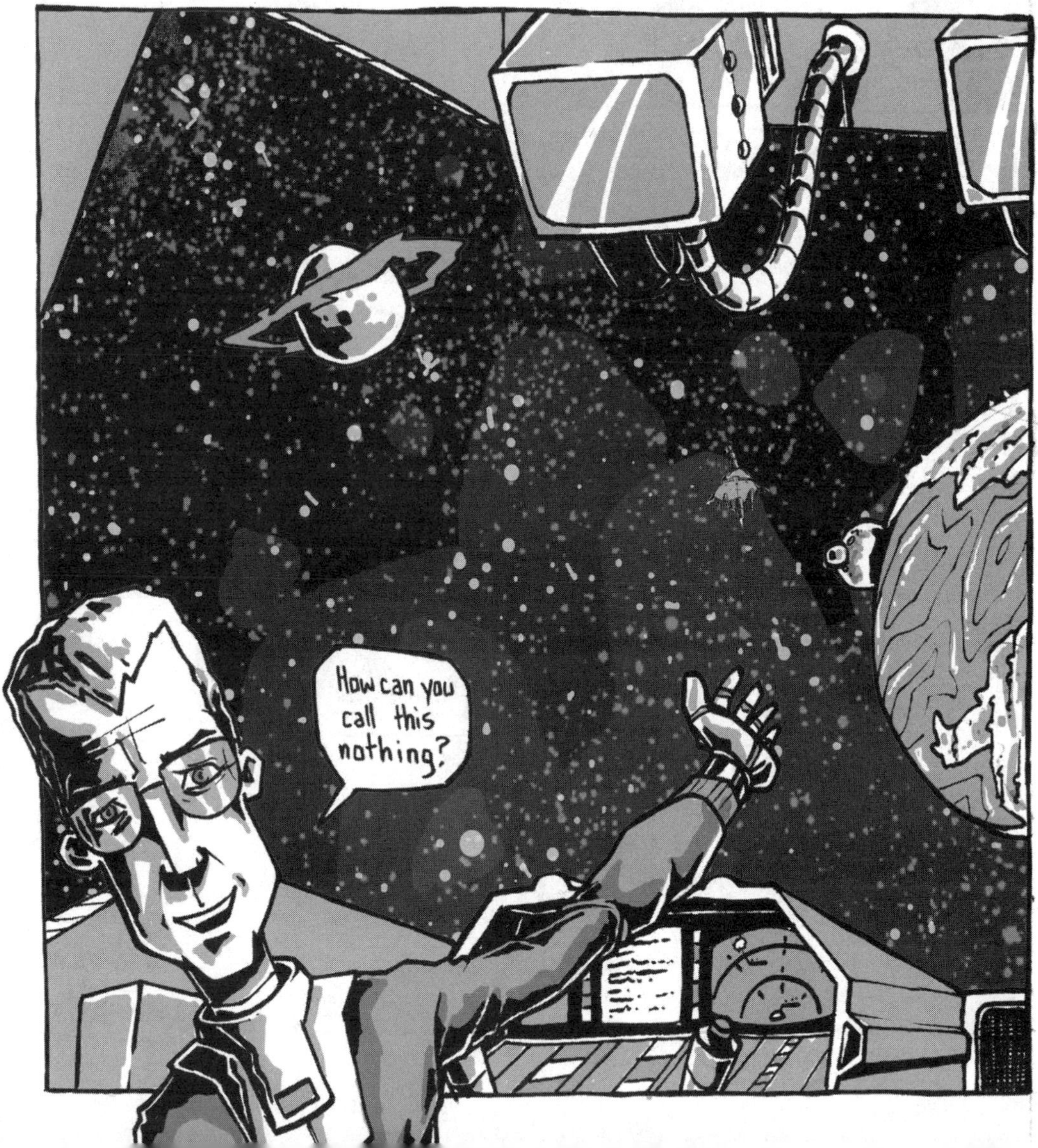
How can you call this nothing?

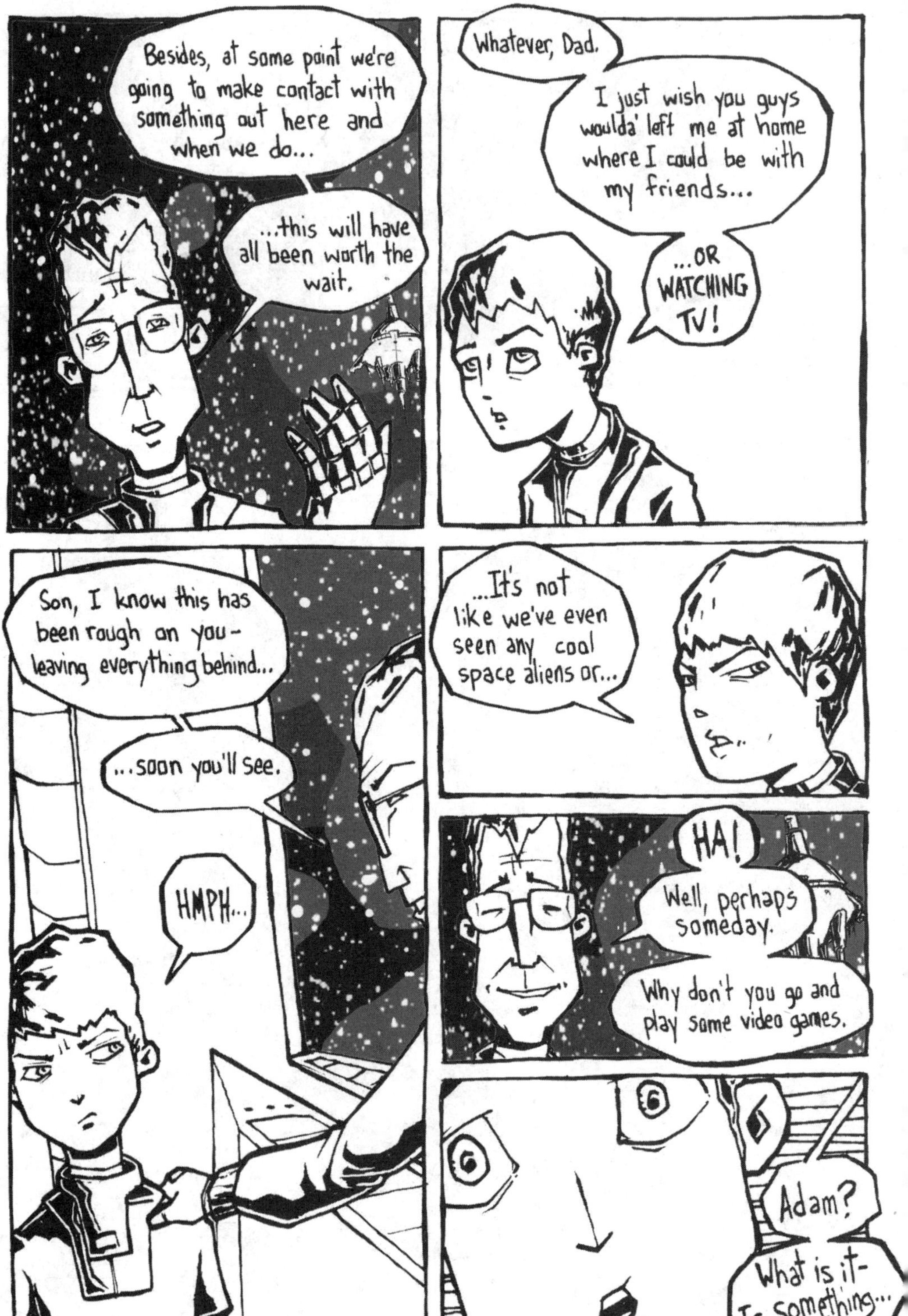
Besides, at some point we're going to make contact with something out here and when we do...
...this will have all been worth the wait.
Whatever, Dad.
I just wish you guys woulda' left me at home where I could be with my friends...
...OR WATCHING TV!
Son, I know this has been rough on you- leaving everything behind...
...soon you'll see.
HMPH...
...It's not like we've even seen any cool space aliens or...
HA!
Well, perhaps someday.
Why don't you go and play some video games.
Adam?
What is it- Is something...

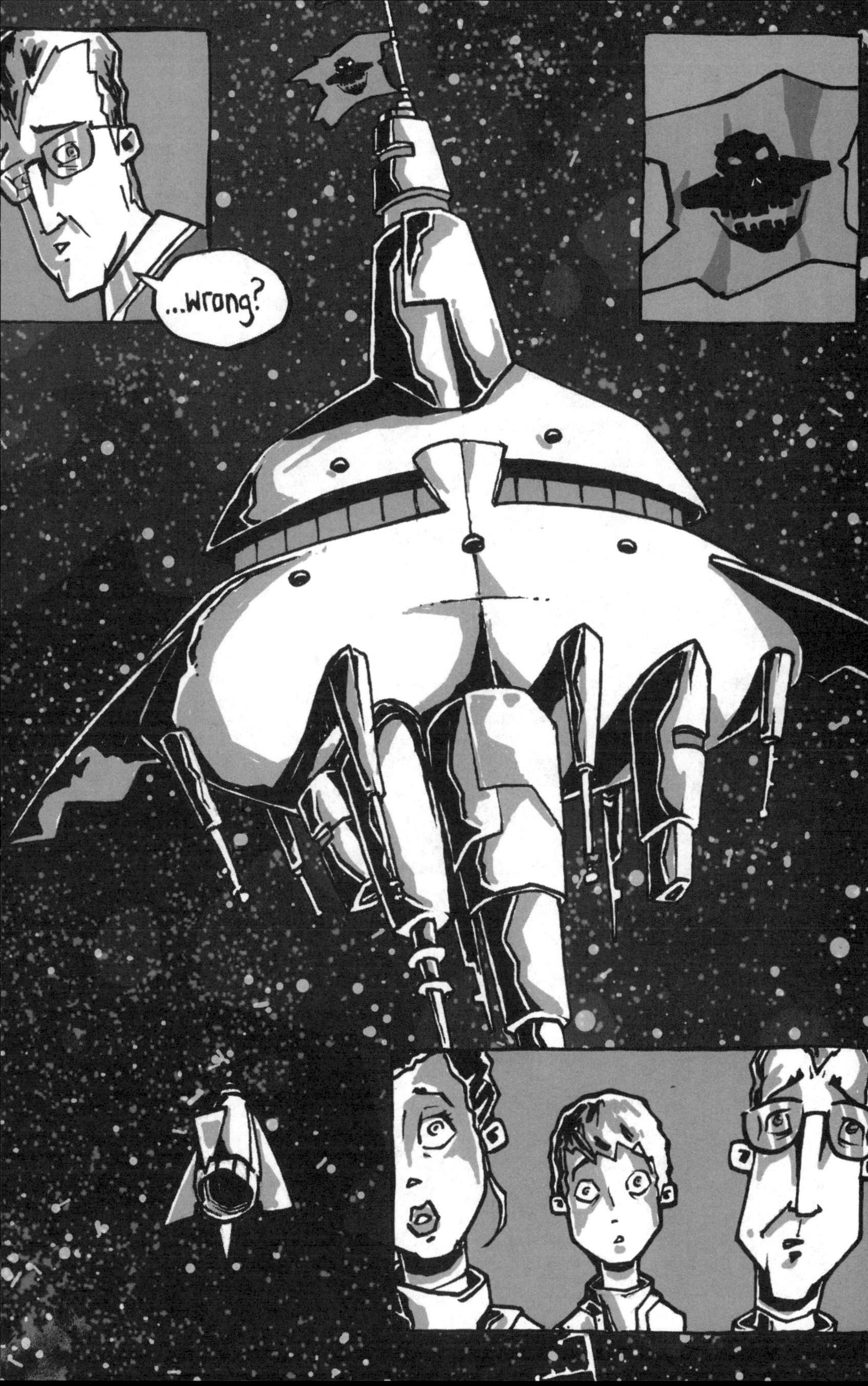
...wrong?

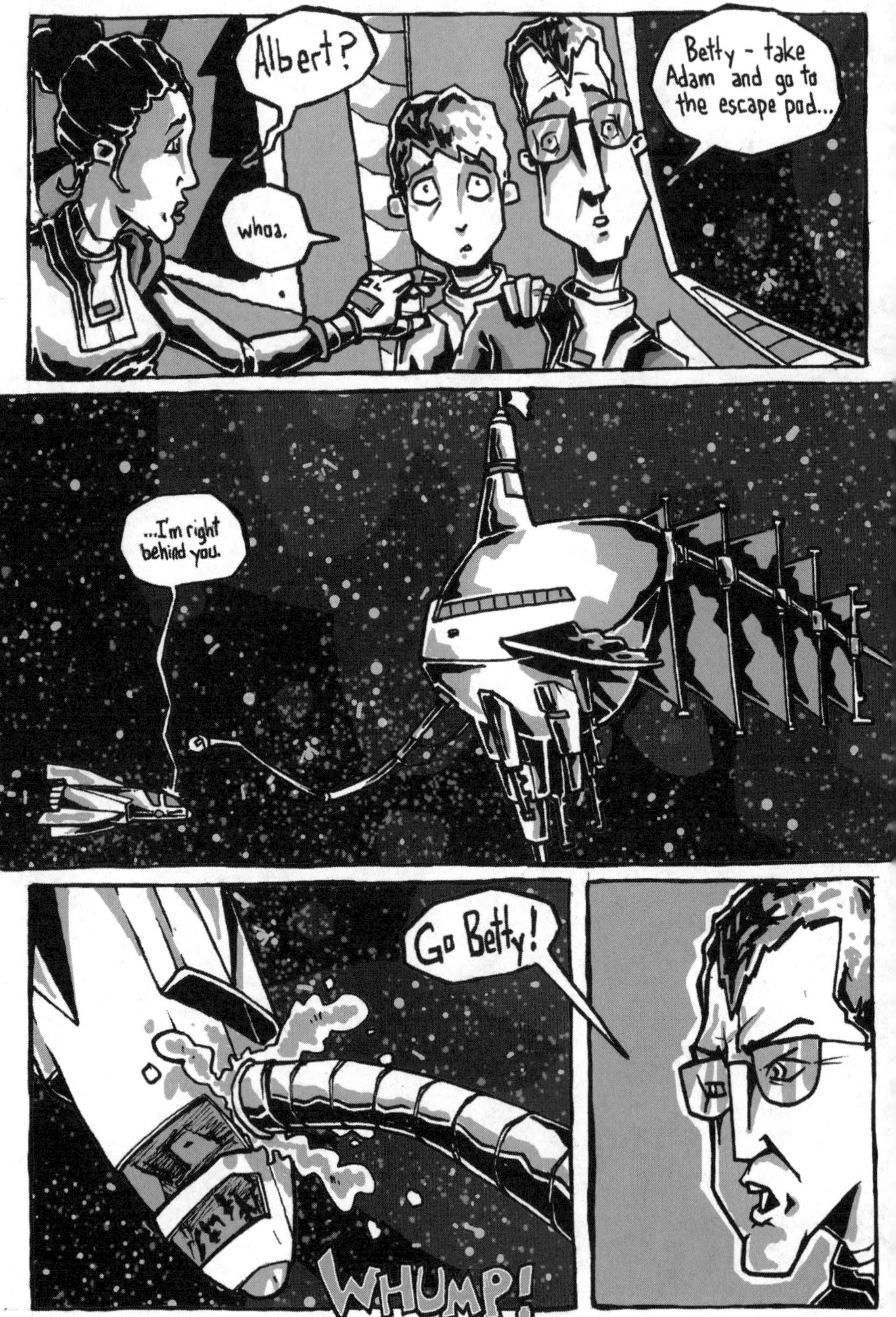
Albert?
Betty - take Adam and go to the escape pod...
whoa.
...I'm right behind you.
Go Betty!
WHUMP!

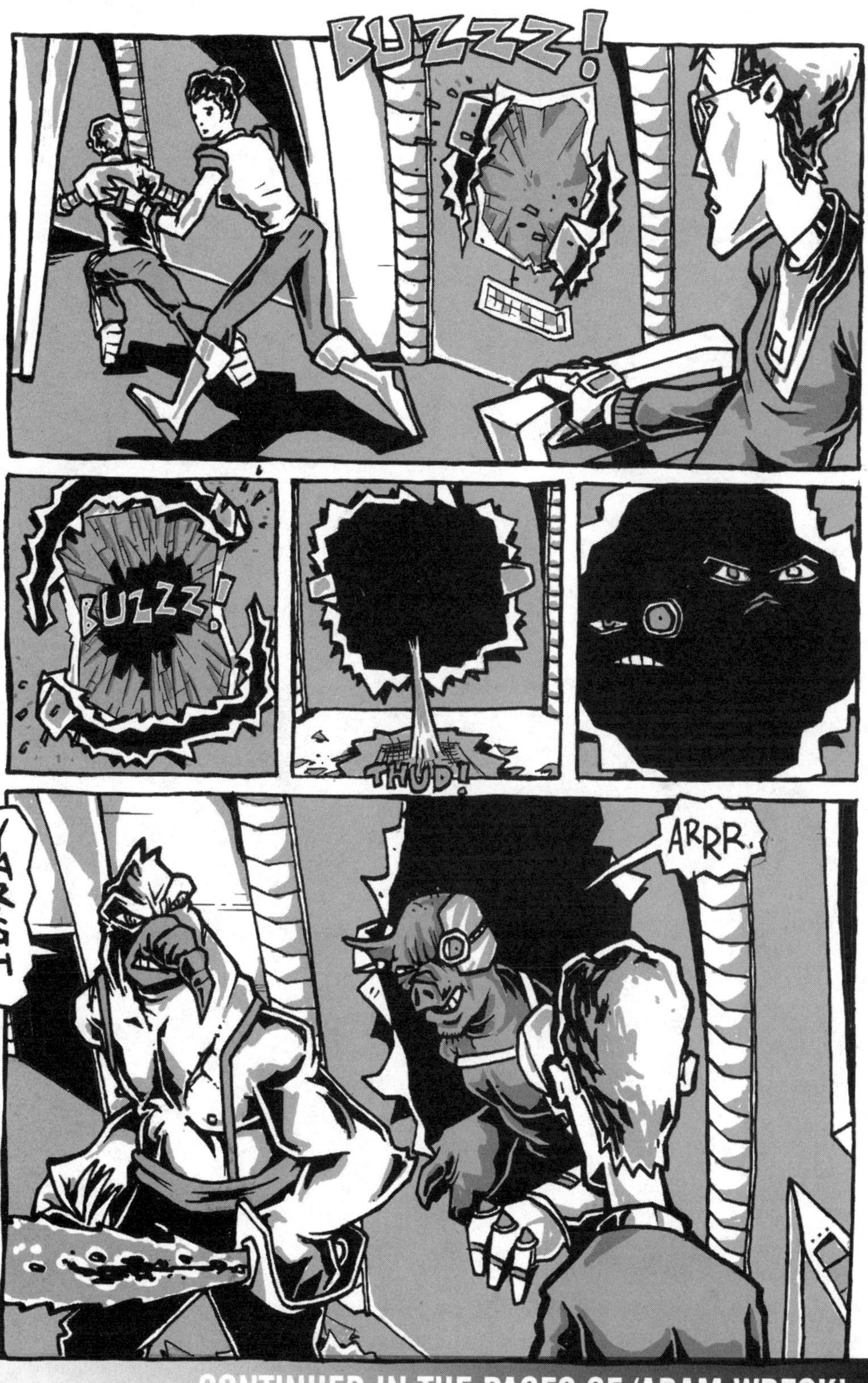
BUZZZ!
BUZZZ!
THUD!
YARGH
ARRR.

CONTINUED IN THE PAGES OF 'ADAM WRECK'

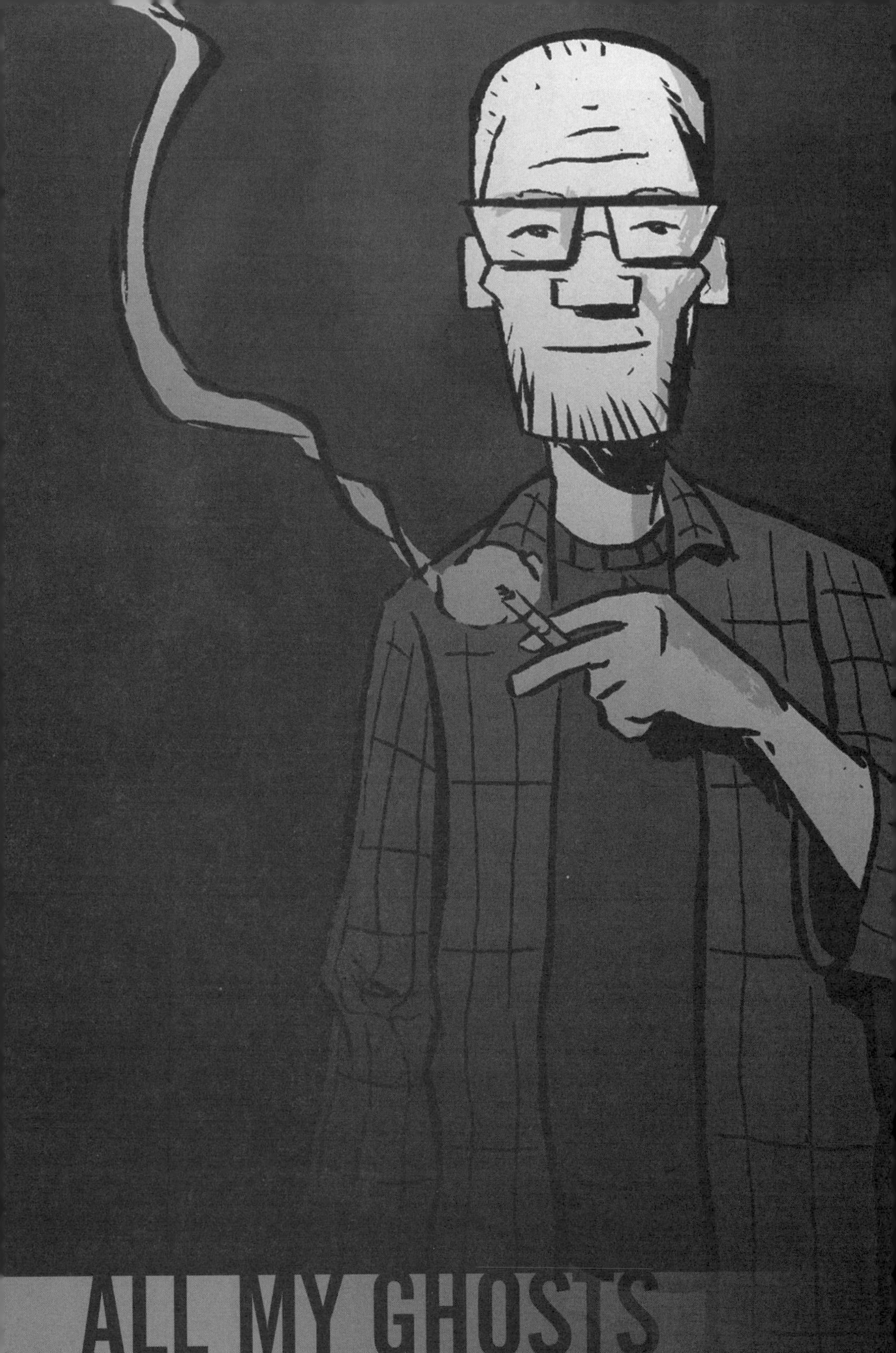

ALL MY GHOSTS

ALL MY GHOSTS

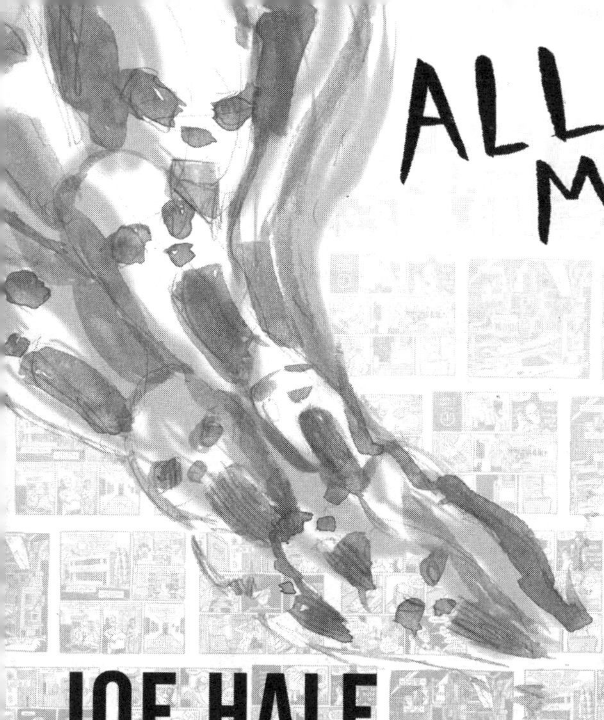

JOE HALE

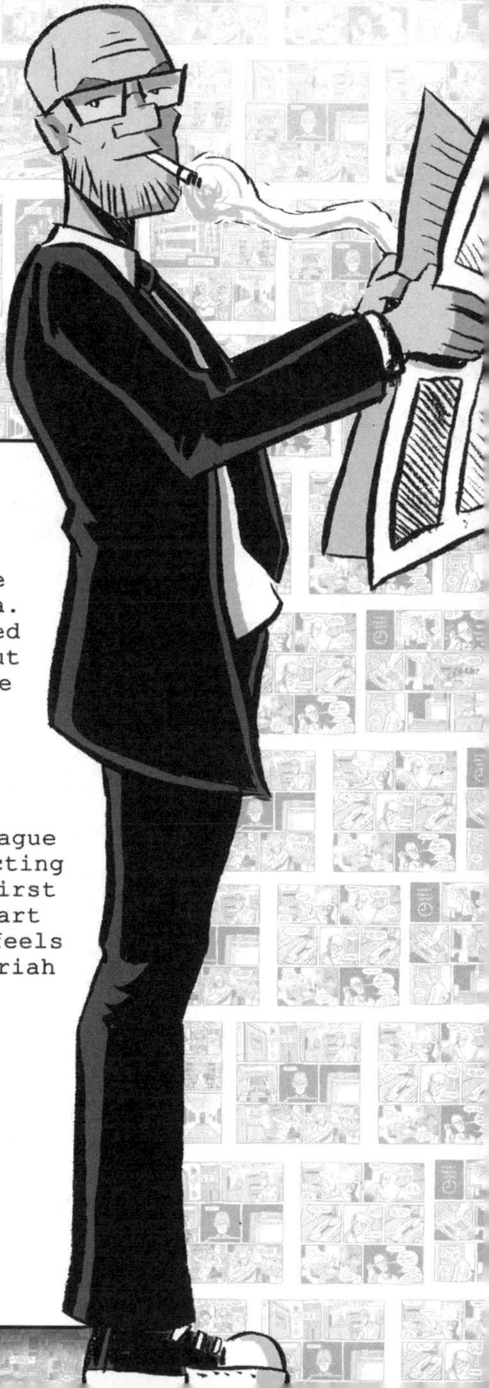

"F@#K IT!!"

Joe lives in a small town in the Appalachian Mountains of Virginia. The local newspaper has been owned by his family for generations, but tough times force Joe to sell the business his family built.

Now strange things are starting to happen.

Ghost sightings and weird events plague the building, and they've got Joe acting odd as well. Feeling free for the first time in his life, he decides to start writing again. Writing whatever he feels and thinks, Joe becomes the town pariah - which actually isn't so bad.

Age: 47
Height: 6'1"
Weight: 180 lbs.

First Appearance:
ALL MY GHOSTS #1 (2013)

Created by Jeremy Massie
Illustration by Jeremy Massie

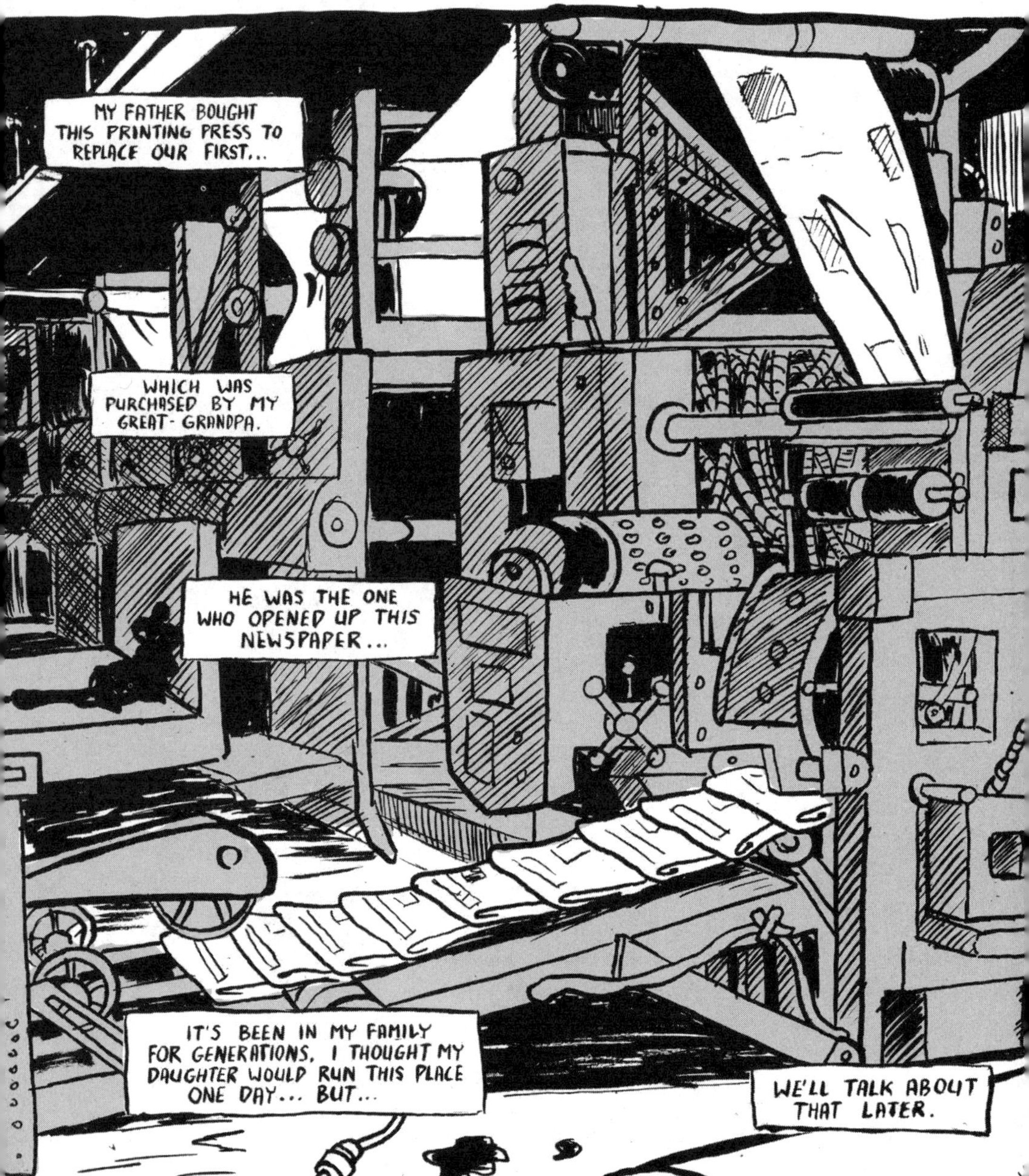
MY FATHER BOUGHT THIS PRINTING PRESS TO REPLACE OUR FIRST...
WHICH WAS PURCHASED BY MY GREAT-GRANDPA.
HE WAS THE ONE WHO OPENED UP THIS NEWSPAPER...
IT'S BEEN IN MY FAMILY FOR GENERATIONS. I THOUGHT MY DAUGHTER WOULD RUN THIS PLACE ONE DAY... BUT...
WE'LL TALK ABOUT THAT LATER.

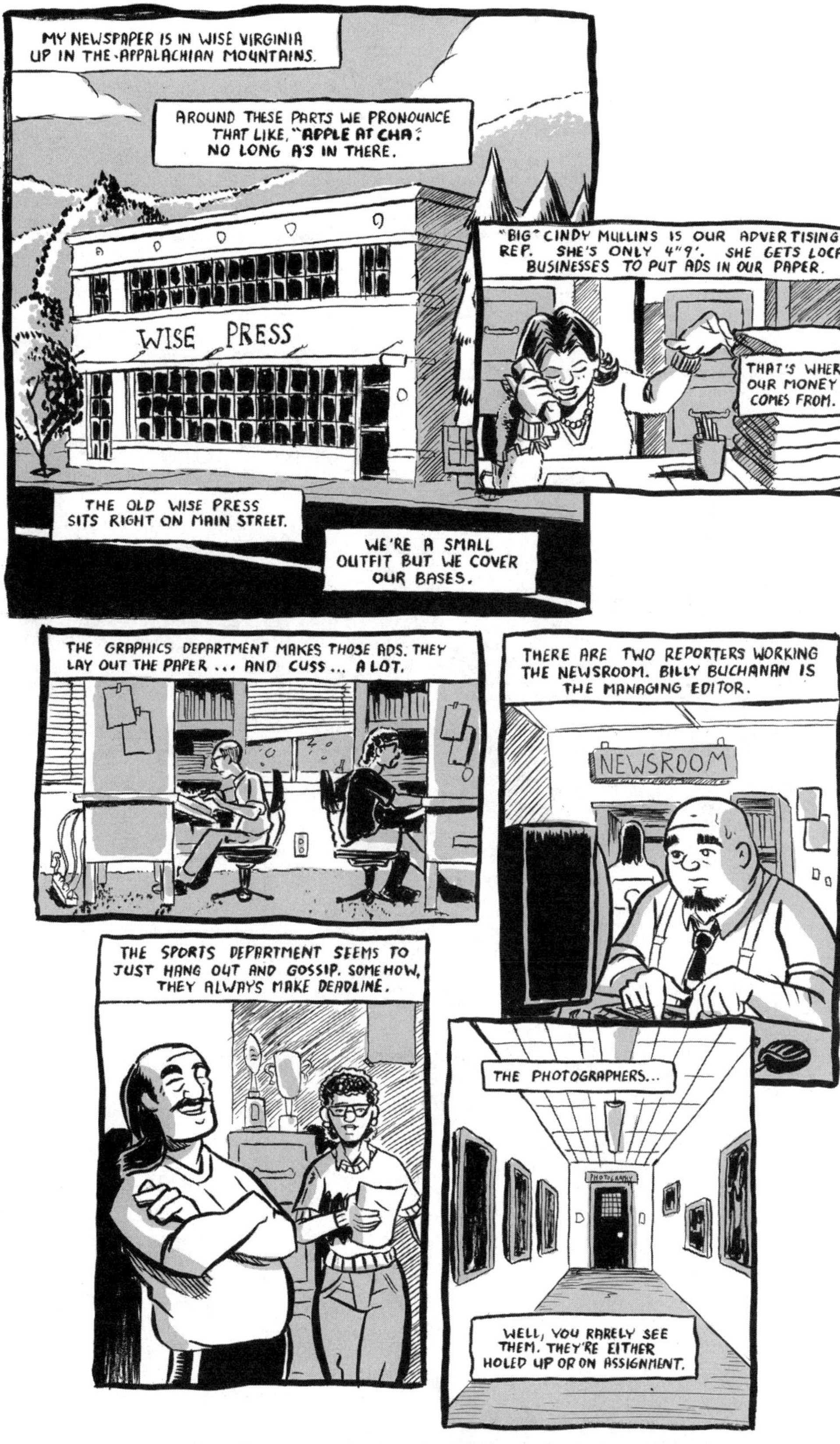
MY NEWSPAPER IS IN WISE VIRGINIA UP IN THE APPALACHIAN MOUNTAINS.
AROUND THESE PARTS WE PRONOUNCE THAT LIKE, "APPLE AT CHA". NO LONG A'S IN THERE.
WISE PRESS
THE OLD WISE PRESS SITS RIGHT ON MAIN STREET.
WE'RE A SMALL OUTFIT BUT WE COVER OUR BASES.
"BIG" CINDY MULLINS IS OUR ADVERTISING REP. SHE'S ONLY 4"9'. SHE GETS LOCAL BUSINESSES TO PUT ADS IN OUR PAPER.
THAT'S WHERE OUR MONEY COMES FROM.
THE GRAPHICS DEPARTMENT MAKES THOSE ADS. THEY LAY OUT THE PAPER ... AND CUSS ... A LOT.
THERE ARE TWO REPORTERS WORKING THE NEWSROOM. BILLY BUCHANAN IS THE MANAGING EDITOR.
NEWSROOM
THE SPORTS DEPARTMENT SEEMS TO JUST HANG OUT AND GOSSIP. SOMEHOW, THEY ALWAYS MAKE DEADLINE.
THE PHOTOGRAPHERS...
PHOTOGRAPHY
WELL, YOU RARELY SEE THEM. THEY'RE EITHER HOLED UP OR ON ASSIGNMENT.

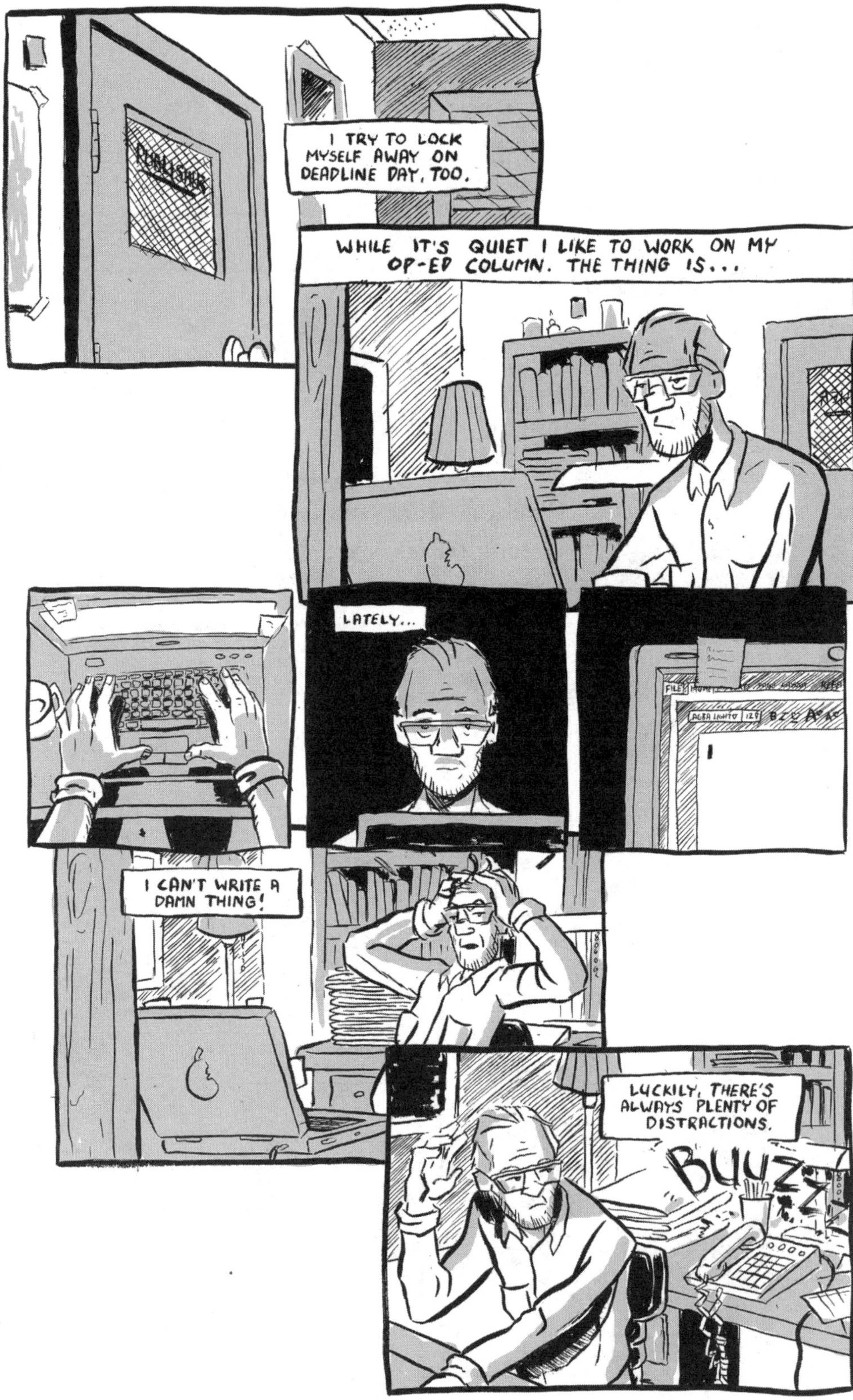
I TRY TO LOCK MYSELF AWAY ON DEADLINE DAY, TOO.
WHILE IT'S QUIET I LIKE TO WORK ON MY OP-ED COLUMN. THE THING IS...
LATELY...
I CAN'T WRITE A DAMN THING!
LUCKILY, THERE'S ALWAYS PLENTY OF DISTRACTIONS.
BUUZZ

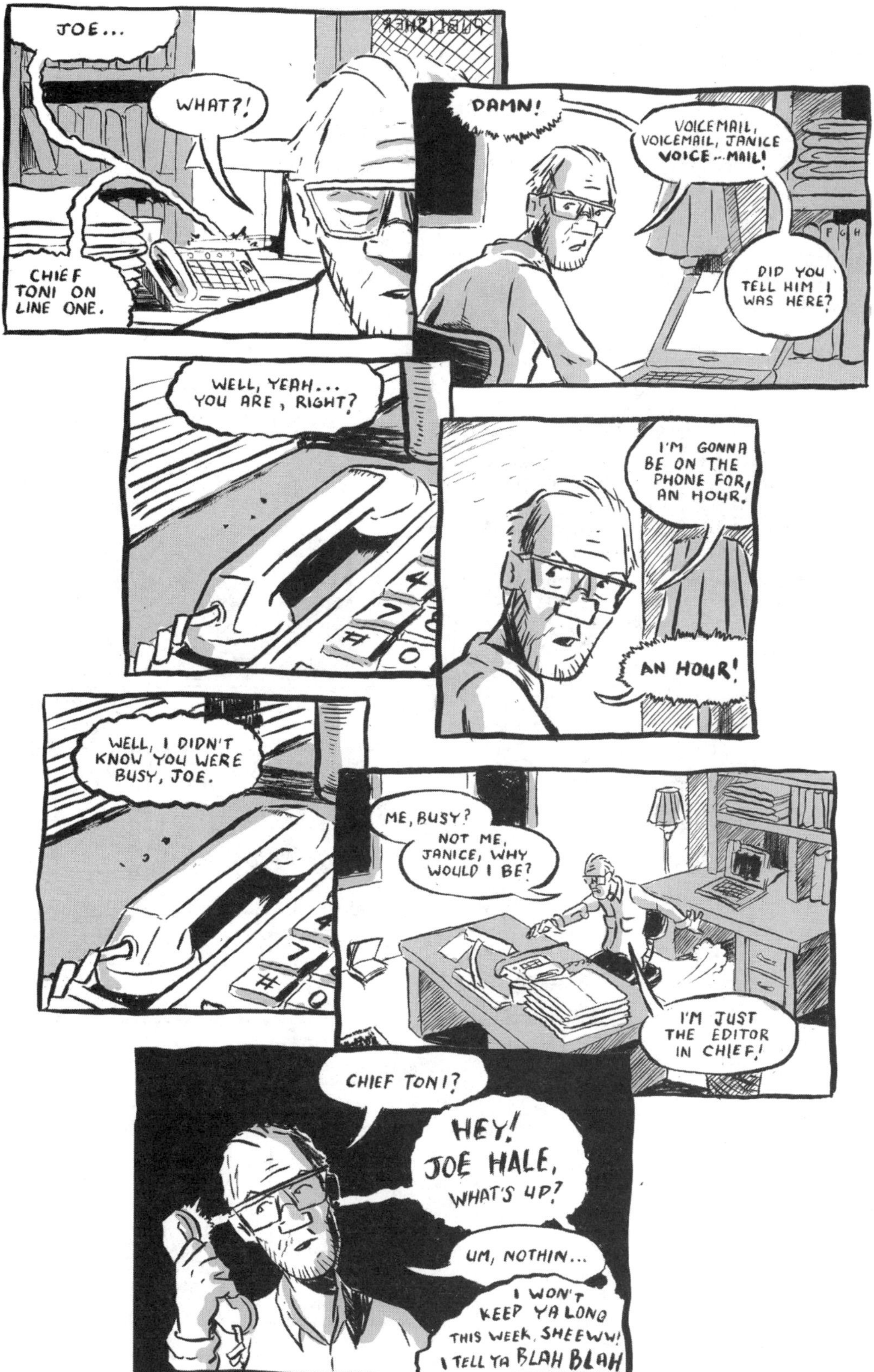

PUBLISHER
JOE...
WHAT?!
CHIEF TONI ON LINE ONE.
DAMN!
VOICEMAIL, VOICEMAIL, JANICE VOICE...MAIL!
DID YOU TELL HIM I WAS HERE?
WELL, YEAH... YOU ARE, RIGHT?
I'M GONNA BE ON THE PHONE FOR AN HOUR!
AN HOUR!
WELL, I DIDN'T KNOW YOU WERE BUSY, JOE.
ME, BUSY?
NOT ME, JANICE, WHY WOULD I BE?
I'M JUST THE EDITOR IN CHIEF!
CHIEF TONI?
HEY! JOE HALE, WHAT'S UP?
UM, NOTHIN...
I WON'T KEEP YA LONG THIS WEEK, SHEEWW! I TELL YA BLAH BLAH

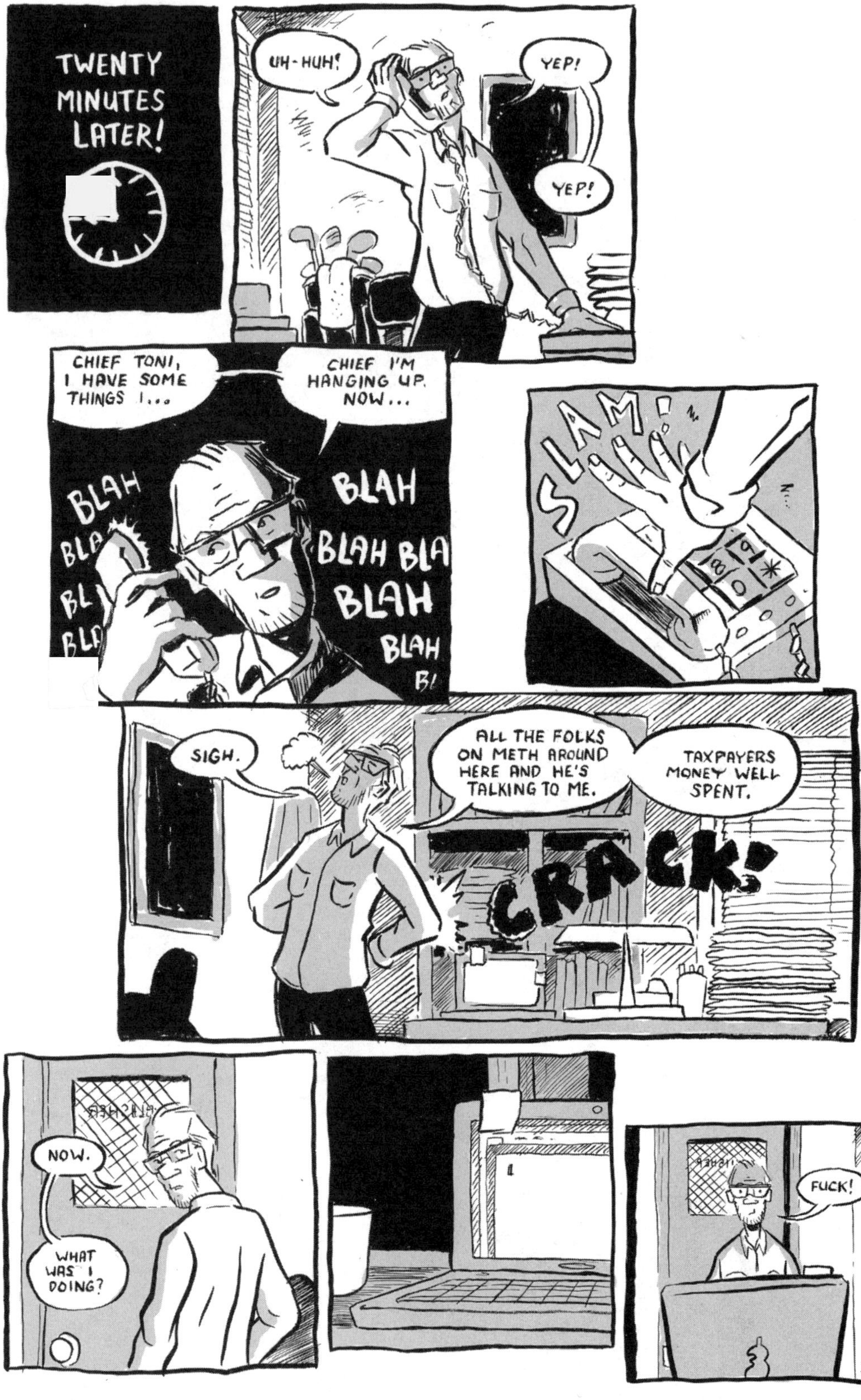
TWENTY MINUTES LATER!
UH-HUH!
YEP!
YEP!
CHIEF TONI, I HAVE SOME THINGS I...
CHIEF I'M HANGING UP. NOW...
BLAH
BLAH
BLAH BLA
BLAH
BLAH
SLAM!
SIGH.
ALL THE FOLKS ON METH AROUND HERE AND HE'S TALKING TO ME.
TAXPAYERS MONEY WELL SPENT.
CRACK!
NOW.
WHAT WAS I DOING?
FUCK!

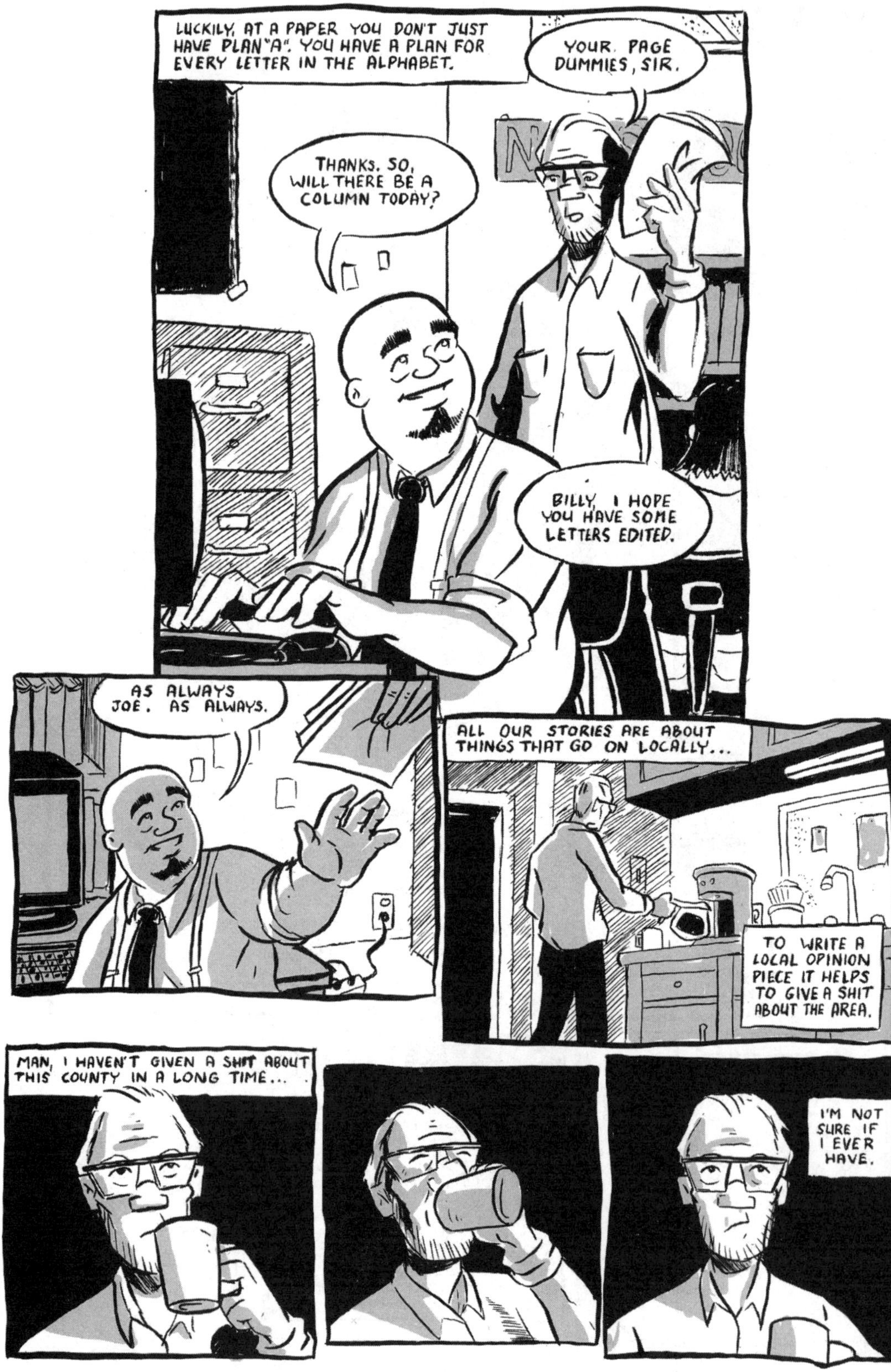
LUCKILY, AT A PAPER YOU DON'T JUST HAVE PLAN "A". YOU HAVE A PLAN FOR EVERY LETTER IN THE ALPHABET.
YOUR PAGE DUMMIES, SIR.
THANKS. SO, WILL THERE BE A COLUMN TODAY?
BILLY, I HOPE YOU HAVE SOME LETTERS EDITED.
AS ALWAYS JOE. AS ALWAYS.
ALL OUR STORIES ARE ABOUT THINGS THAT GO ON LOCALLY...
TO WRITE A LOCAL OPINION PIECE IT HELPS TO GIVE A SHIT ABOUT THE AREA.
MAN, I HAVEN'T GIVEN A SHIT ABOUT THIS COUNTY IN A LONG TIME...
I'M NOT SURE IF I EVER HAVE.

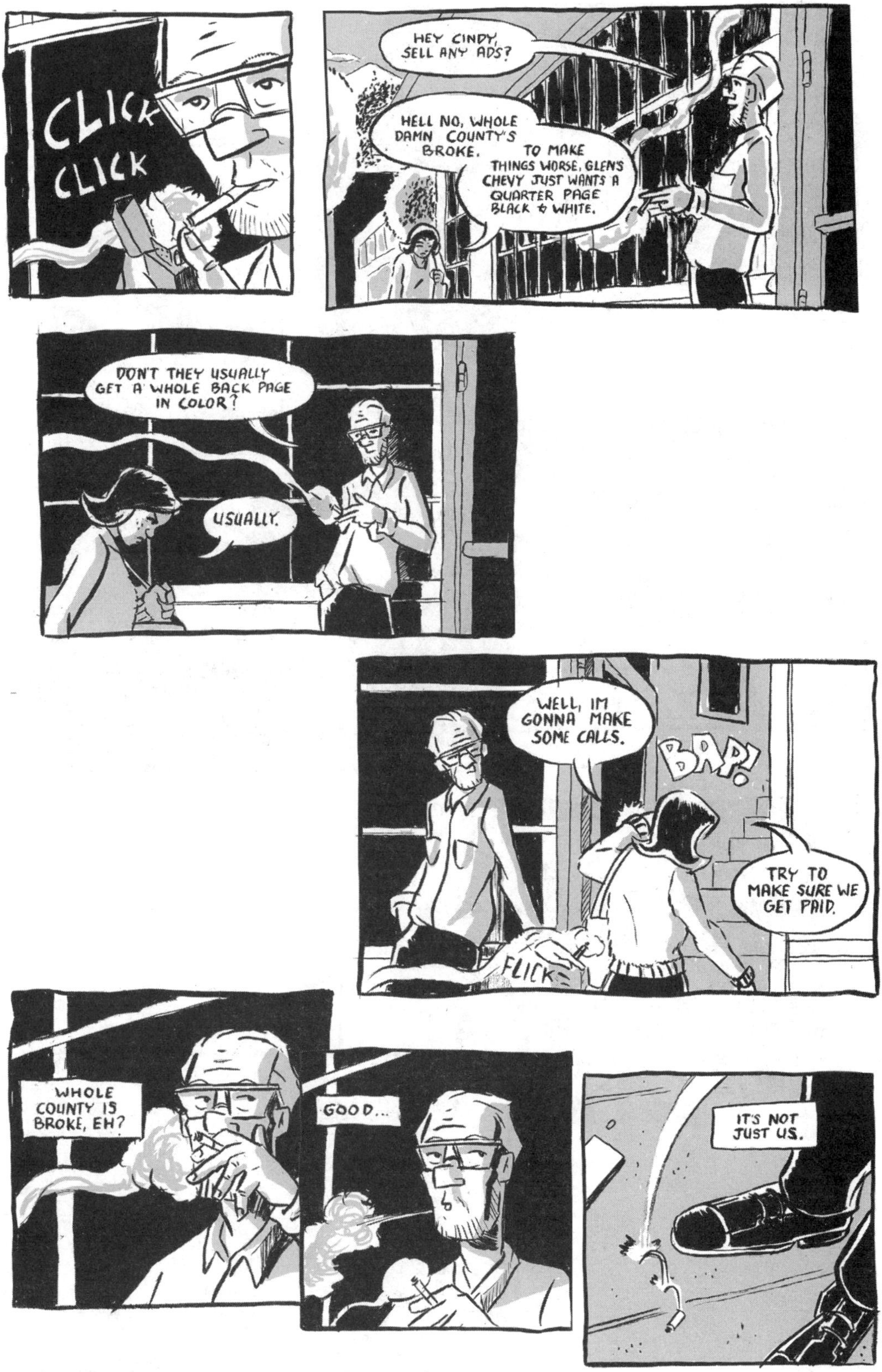
CLICK
CLICK
HEY CINDY, SELL ANY ADS?
HELL NO, WHOLE DAMN COUNTY'S BROKE.
TO MAKE THINGS WORSE, GLEN'S CHEVY JUST WANTS A QUARTER PAGE BLACK & WHITE.
DON'T THEY USUALLY GET A WHOLE BACK PAGE IN COLOR?
USUALLY.
WELL, IM GONNA MAKE SOME CALLS.
BAP!
TRY TO MAKE SURE WE GET PAID.
FLICK
WHOLE COUNTY IS BROKE, EH?
GOOD...
IT'S NOT JUST US.

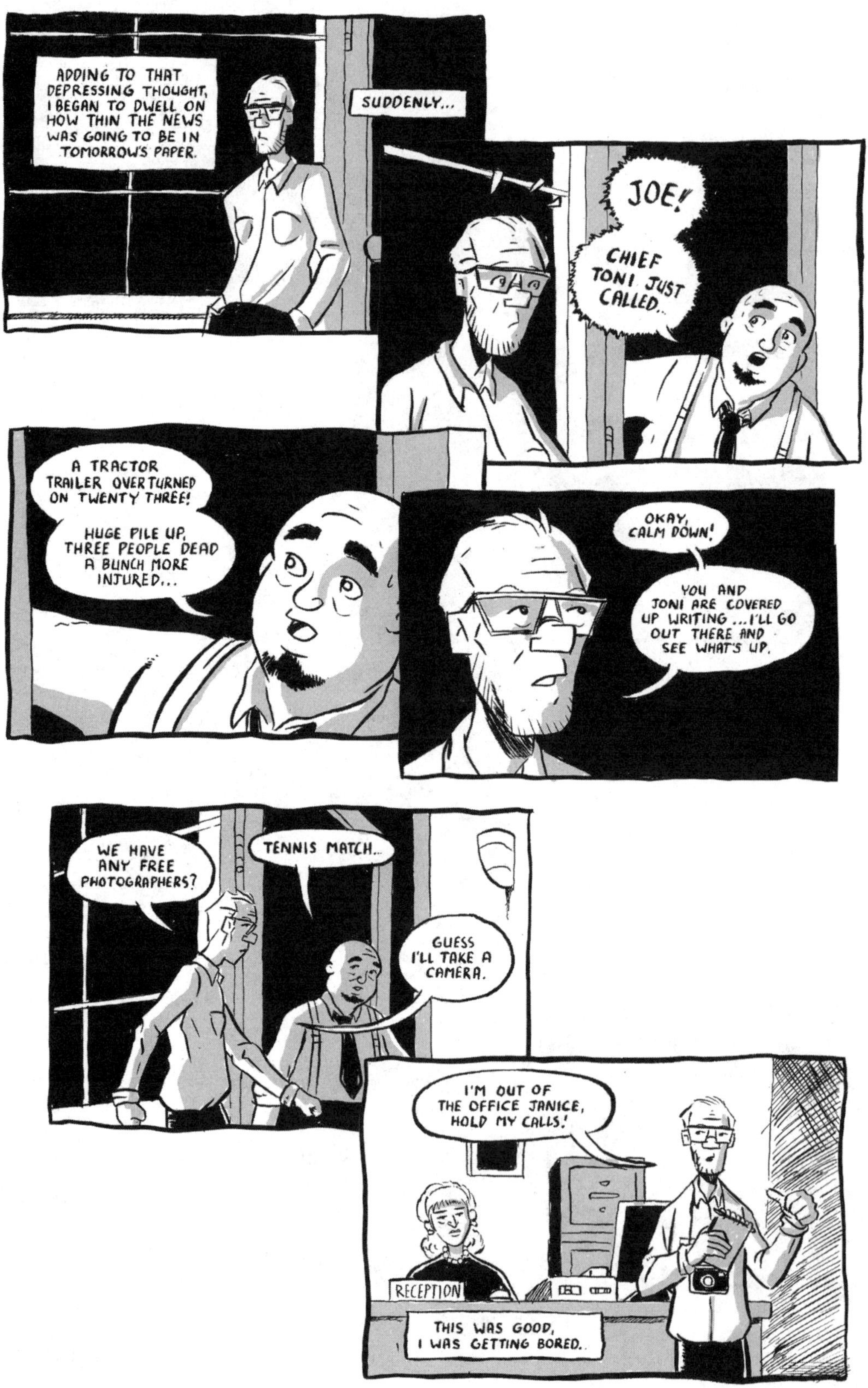
ADDING TO THAT DEPRESSING THOUGHT, I BEGAN TO DWELL ON HOW THIN THE NEWS WAS GOING TO BE IN TOMORROW'S PAPER.
SUDDENLY...
JOE!
CHIEF TONI JUST CALLED...
A TRACTOR TRAILER OVERTURNED ON TWENTY THREE!
HUGE PILE UP, THREE PEOPLE DEAD A BUNCH MORE INJURED...
OKAY, CALM DOWN!
YOU AND JONI ARE COVERED UP WRITING ... I'LL GO OUT THERE AND SEE WHAT'S UP.
WE HAVE ANY FREE PHOTOGRAPHERS?
TENNIS MATCH...
GUESS I'LL TAKE A CAMERA.
I'M OUT OF THE OFFICE JANICE, HOLD MY CALLS!
RECEPTION
THIS WAS GOOD, I WAS GETTING BORED...

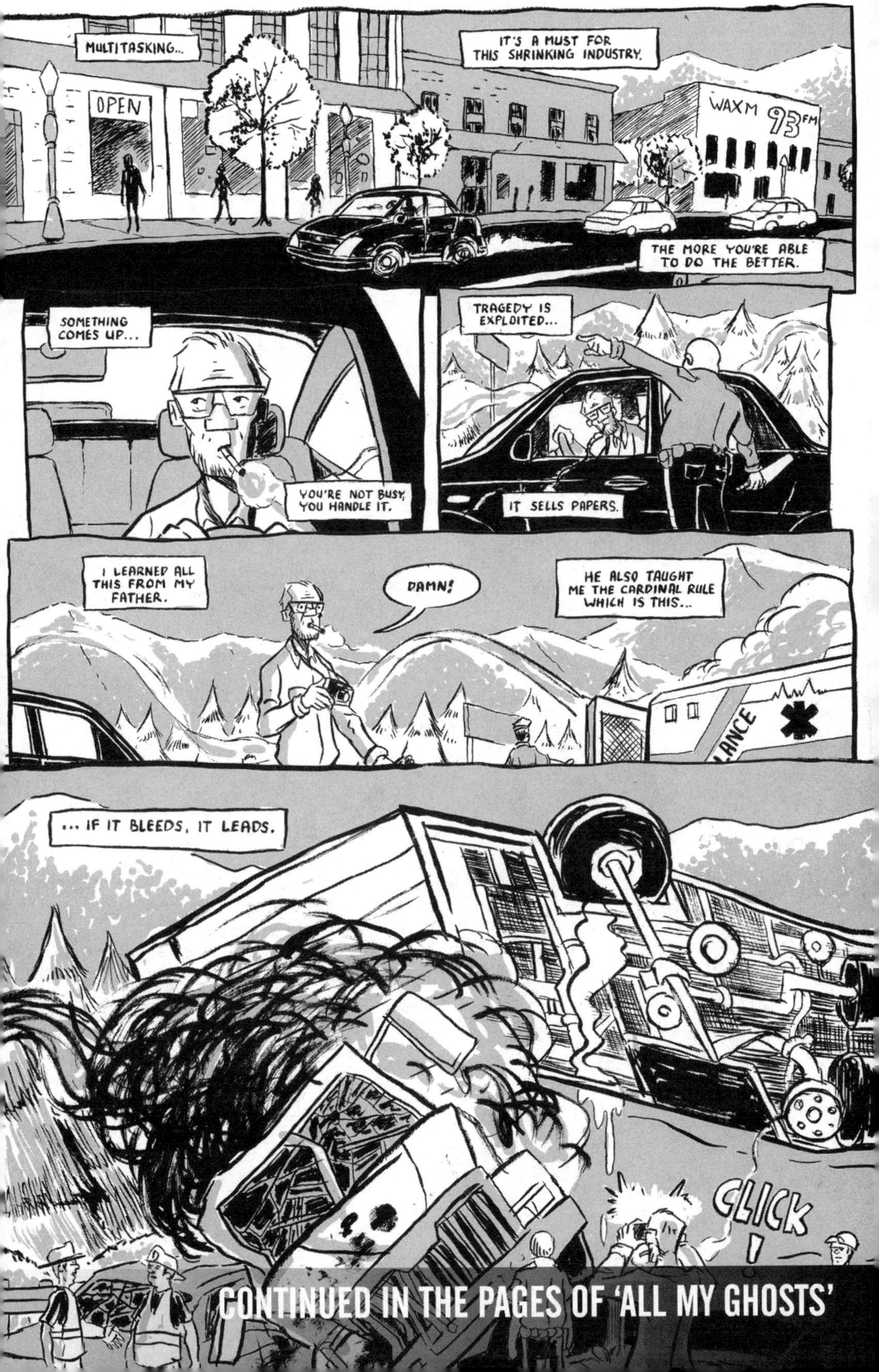
MULTITASKING...
IT'S A MUST FOR THIS SHRINKING INDUSTRY.
OPEN
WAXM 93 FM
THE MORE YOU'RE ABLE TO DO THE BETTER.
SOMETHING COMES UP...
YOU'RE NOT BUSY, YOU HANDLE IT.
TRAGEDY IS EXPLOITED...
IT SELLS PAPERS.
I LEARNED ALL THIS FROM MY FATHER.
DAMN!
HE ALSO TAUGHT ME THE CARDINAL RULE WHICH IS THIS...
...IF IT BLEEDS, IT LEADS.
CLICK!
CONTINUED IN THE PAGES OF 'ALL MY GHOSTS'

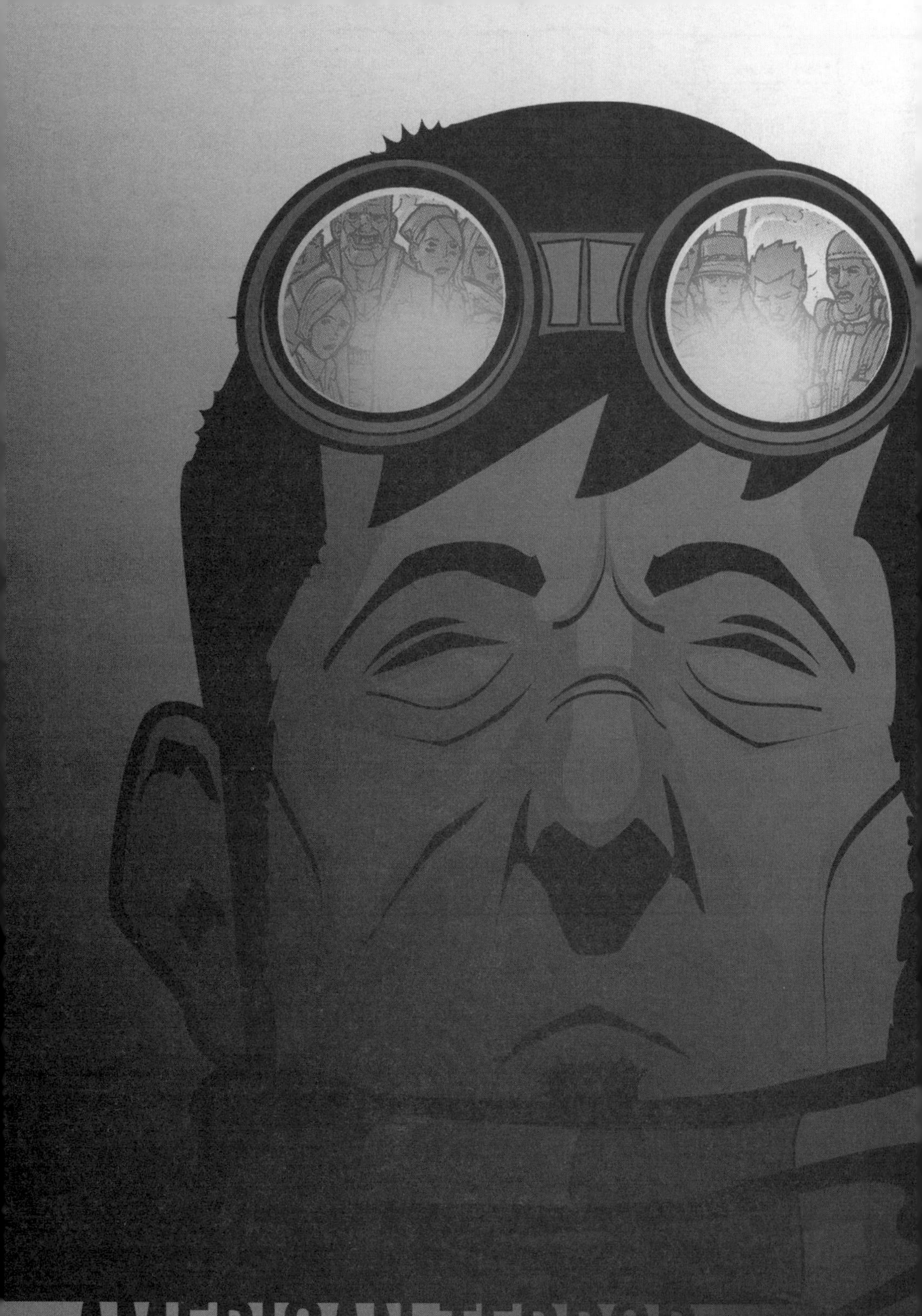

AMERICAN TERROR

AMERICAN★TERROR

CONFESSION OF A HUMAN SMART BOMB

VICTOR SHEPPARD

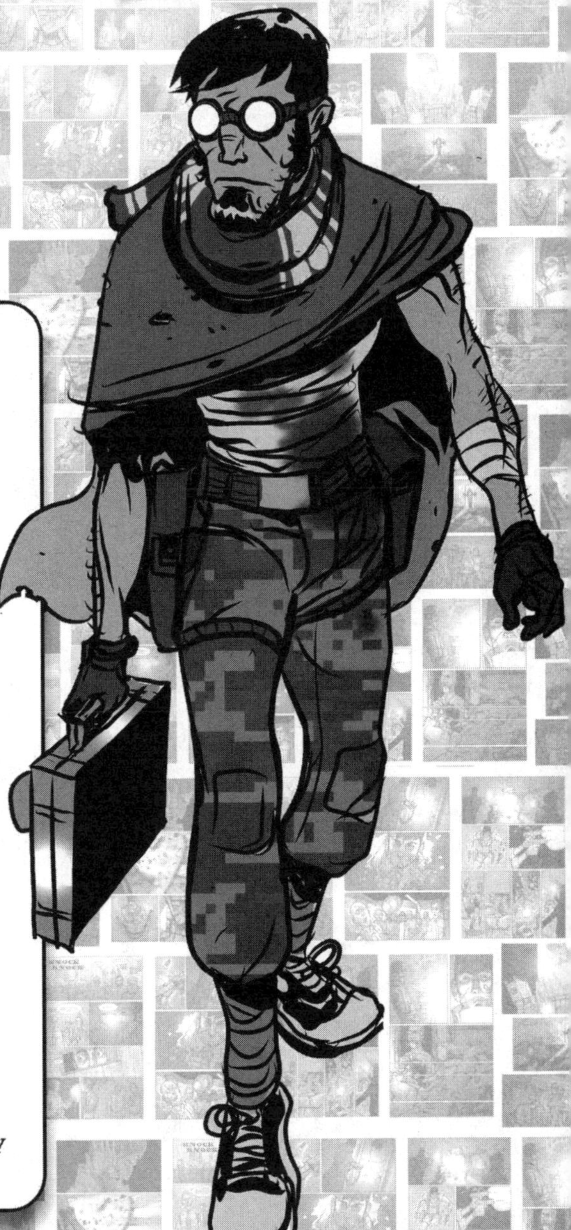

"Sounds like a lost cause. I'm in."

Disgraced soldier Victor Sheppard is out to prove that the only thing more dangerous than an army for sale is a man who is not.

Trained by old school cold warriors, Victor is on a one man mission to liberate the third world from a looming corporate sovereignty movement. He might just pull it off too, if he could stop getting shot at.

Age: 38
Height: 5'11"
Weight: 185 lbs.

First Appearance:
AMERICAN TERROR #1 (2008)

Created by Jeff McComsey
Illustration by Jeff McComsey

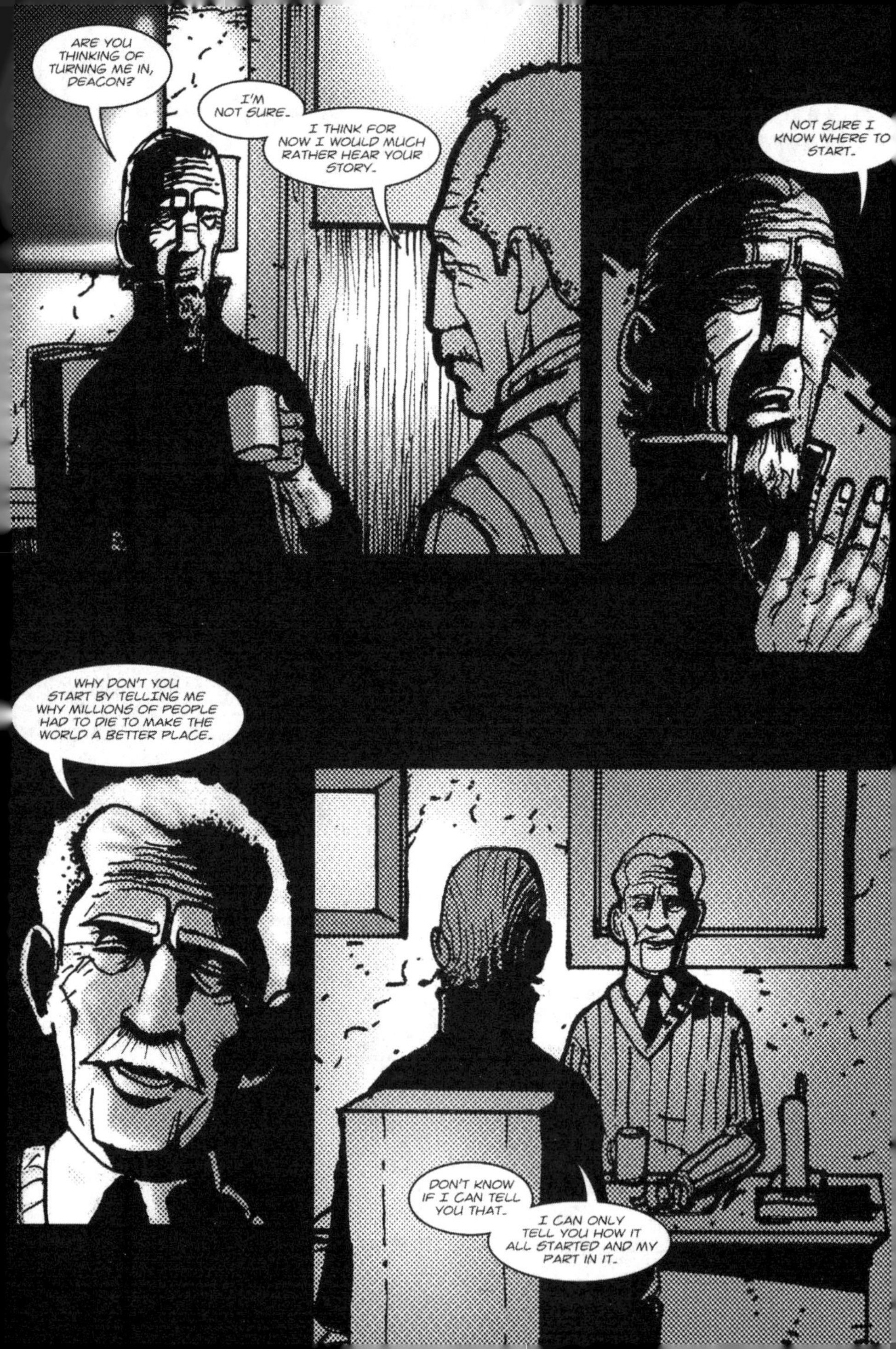
ARE YOU THINKING OF TURNING ME IN, DEACON?
I'M NOT SURE.
I THINK FOR NOW I WOULD MUCH RATHER HEAR YOUR STORY.
NOT SURE I KNOW WHERE TO START.
WHY DON'T YOU START BY TELLING ME WHY MILLIONS OF PEOPLE HAD TO DIE TO MAKE THE WORLD A BETTER PLACE.
DON'T KNOW IF I CAN TELL YOU THAT.
I CAN ONLY TELL YOU HOW IT ALL STARTED AND MY PART IN IT.

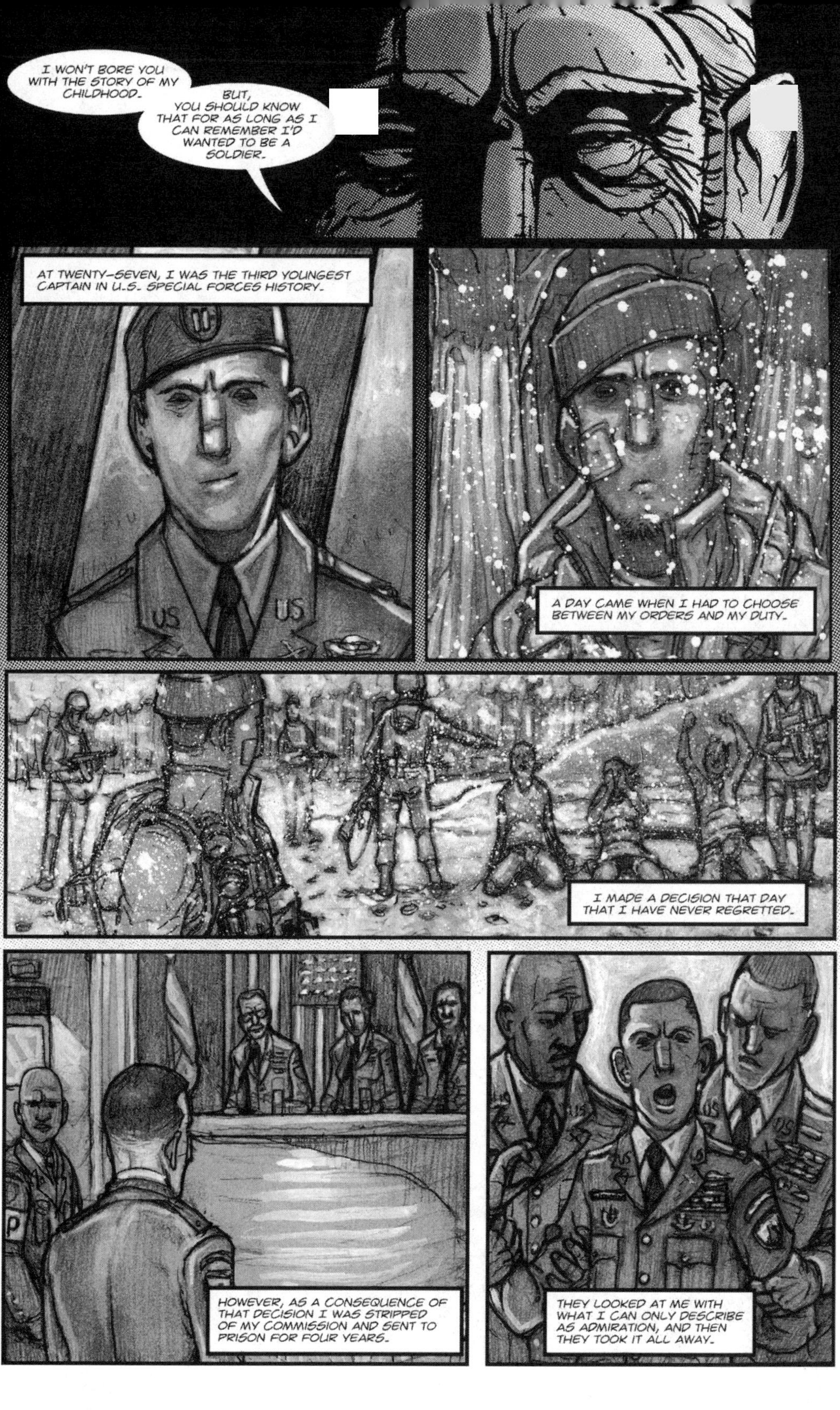

I WON'T BORE YOU WITH THE STORY OF MY CHILDHOOD.
BUT, YOU SHOULD KNOW THAT FOR AS LONG AS I CAN REMEMBER I'D WANTED TO BE A SOLDIER.
AT TWENTY-SEVEN, I WAS THE THIRD YOUNGEST CAPTAIN IN U.S. SPECIAL FORCES HISTORY.
US
US
A DAY CAME WHEN I HAD TO CHOOSE BETWEEN MY ORDERS AND MY DUTY.
I MADE A DECISION THAT DAY THAT I HAVE NEVER REGRETTED.
HOWEVER, AS A CONSEQUENCE OF THAT DECISION I WAS STRIPPED OF MY COMMISSION AND SENT TO PRISON FOR FOUR YEARS.
THEY LOOKED AT ME WITH WHAT I CAN ONLY DESCRIBE AS ADMIRATION, AND THEN THEY TOOK IT ALL AWAY.

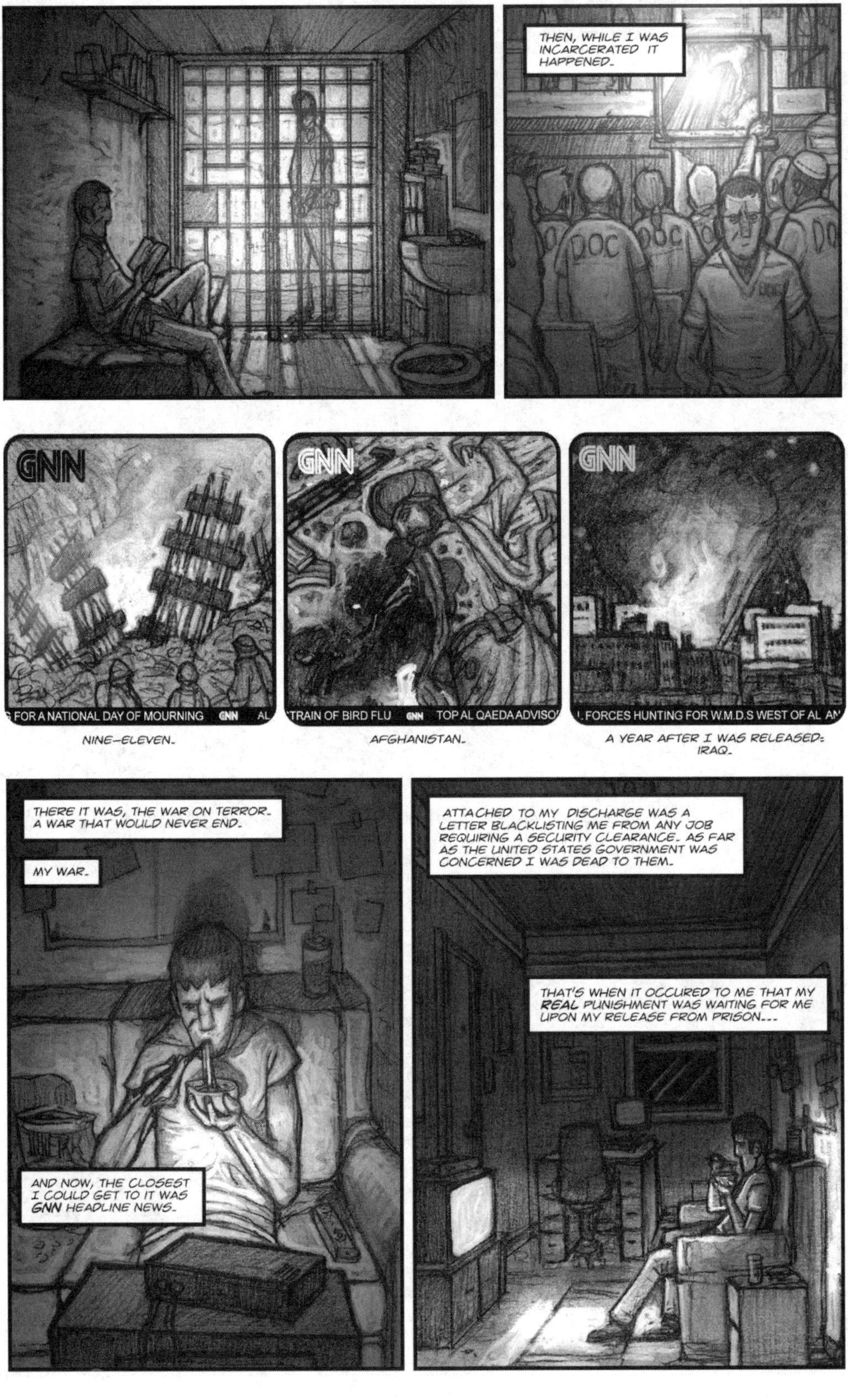
THEN, WHILE I WAS INCARCERATED IT HAPPENED.
D.O.C
DOC
GNN
FOR A NATIONAL DAY OF MOURNING
GNN
TRAIN OF BIRD FLU
TOP AL QAEDA ADVISO
FORCES HUNTING FOR W.M.D.S WEST OF AL
NINE-ELEVEN.
AFGHANISTAN.
A YEAR AFTER I WAS RELEASED: IRAQ.
THERE IT WAS, THE WAR ON TERROR. A WAR THAT WOULD NEVER END.
MY WAR.
AND NOW, THE CLOSEST I COULD GET TO IT WAS GNN HEADLINE NEWS.
ATTACHED TO MY DISCHARGE WAS A LETTER BLACKLISTING ME FROM ANY JOB REQUIRING A SECURITY CLEARANCE. AS FAR AS THE UNITED STATES GOVERNMENT WAS CONCERNED I WAS DEAD TO THEM.
THAT'S WHEN IT OCCURED TO ME THAT MY REAL PUNISHMENT WAS WAITING FOR ME UPON MY RELEASE FROM PRISON...

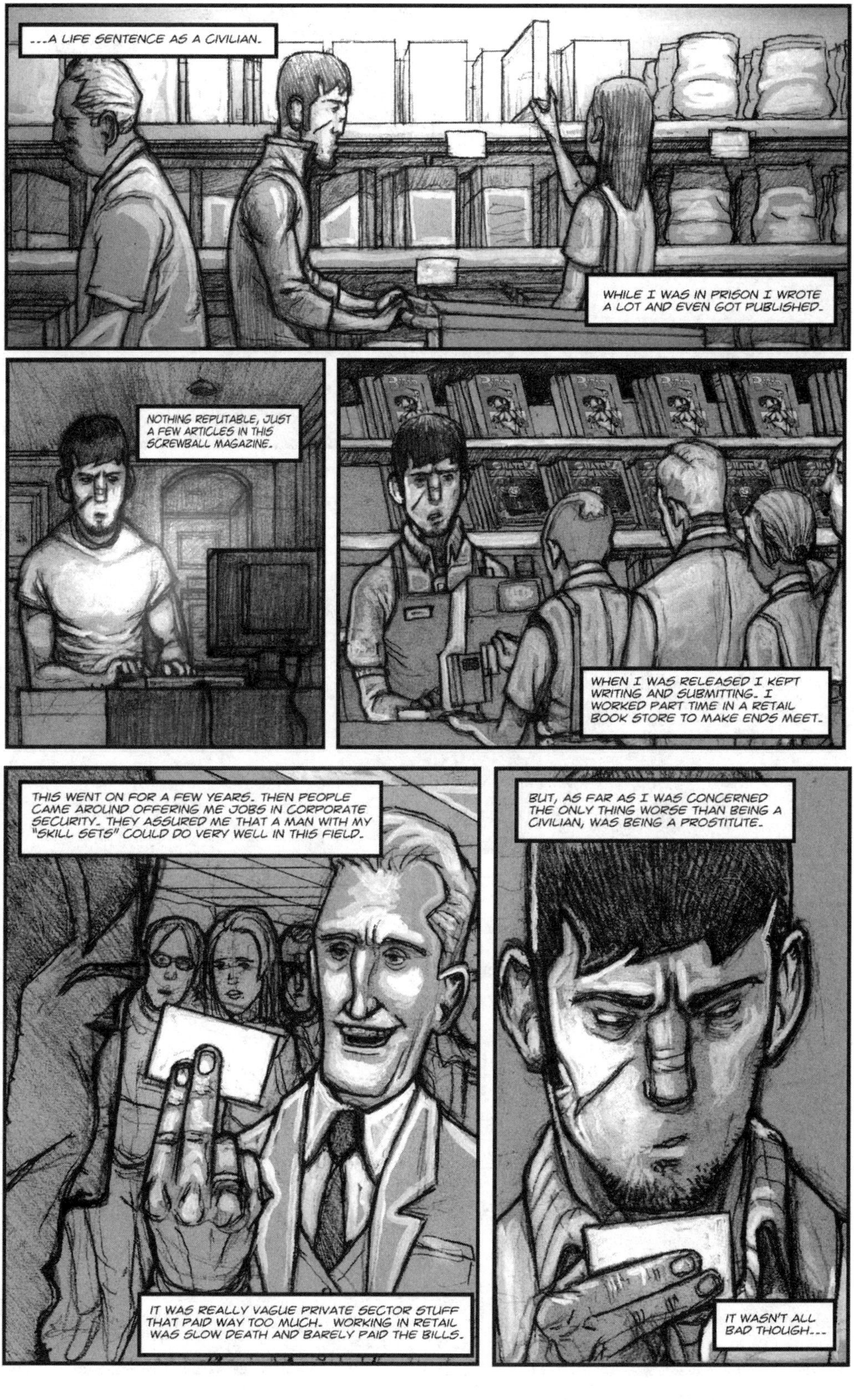
...A LIFE SENTENCE AS A CIVILIAN.
WHILE I WAS IN PRISON I WROTE A LOT AND EVEN GOT PUBLISHED.
NOTHING REPUTABLE, JUST A FEW ARTICLES IN THIS SCREWBALL MAGAZINE.
WHEN I WAS RELEASED I KEPT WRITING AND SUBMITTING. I WORKED PART TIME IN A RETAIL BOOK STORE TO MAKE ENDS MEET.
THIS WENT ON FOR A FEW YEARS. THEN PEOPLE CAME AROUND OFFERING ME JOBS IN CORPORATE SECURITY. THEY ASSURED ME THAT A MAN WITH MY "SKILL SETS" COULD DO VERY WELL IN THIS FIELD.
IT WAS REALLY VAGUE PRIVATE SECTOR STUFF THAT PAID WAY TOO MUCH. WORKING IN RETAIL WAS SLOW DEATH AND BARELY PAID THE BILLS.
BUT, AS FAR AS I WAS CONCERNED THE ONLY THING WORSE THAN BEING A CIVILIAN, WAS BEING A PROSTITUTE.
IT WASN'T ALL BAD THOUGH...

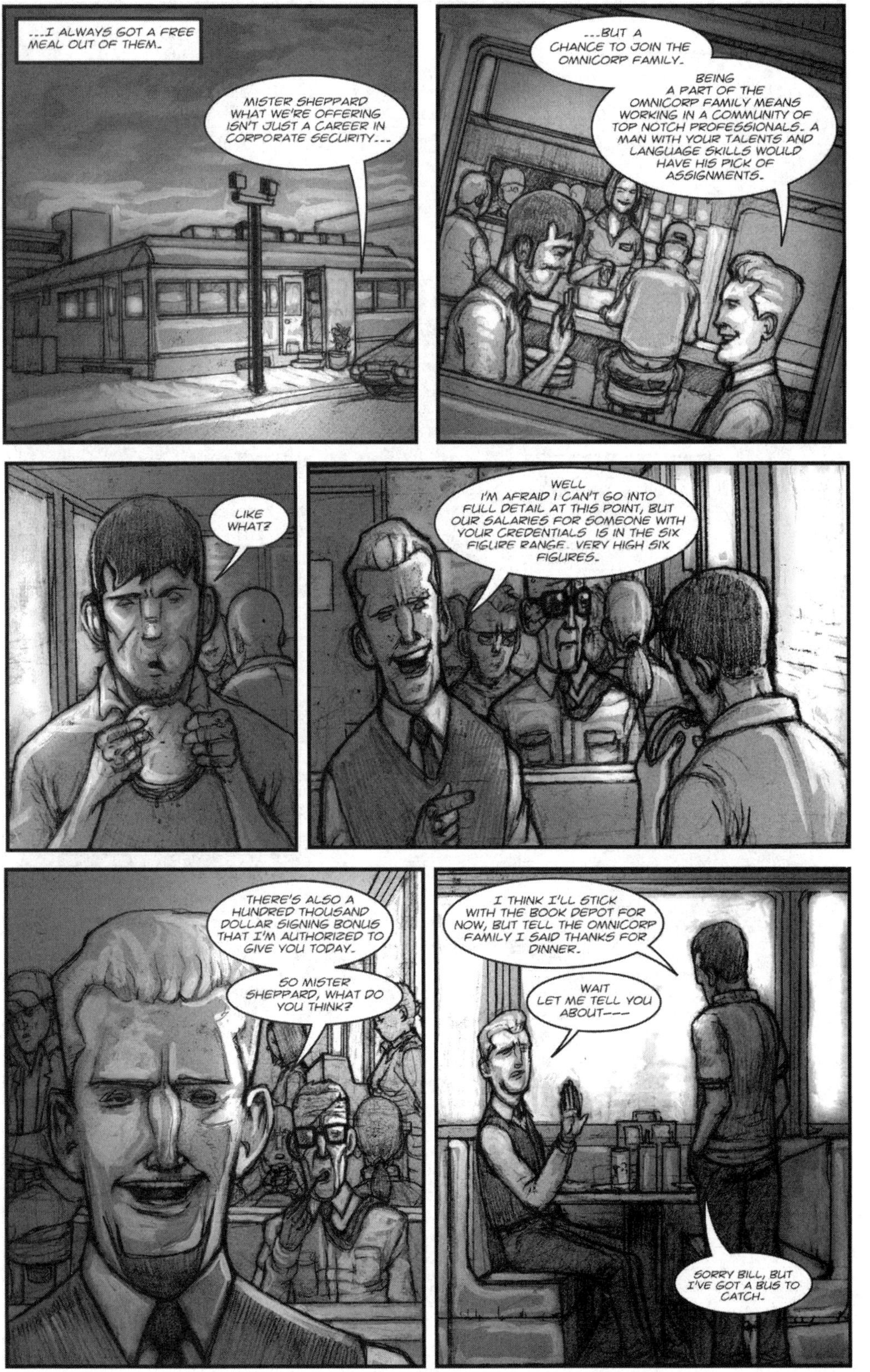
...I ALWAYS GOT A FREE MEAL OUT OF THEM.
MISTER SHEPPARD WHAT WE'RE OFFERING ISN'T JUST A CAREER IN CORPORATE SECURITY...
...BUT A CHANCE TO JOIN THE OMNICORP FAMILY.
BEING A PART OF THE OMNICORP FAMILY MEANS WORKING IN A COMMUNITY OF TOP NOTCH PROFESSIONALS. A MAN WITH YOUR TALENTS AND LANGUAGE SKILLS WOULD HAVE HIS PICK OF ASSIGNMENTS.
LIKE WHAT?
WELL I'M AFRAID I CAN'T GO INTO FULL DETAIL AT THIS POINT, BUT OUR SALARIES FOR SOMEONE WITH YOUR CREDENTIALS IS IN THE SIX FIGURE RANGE. VERY HIGH SIX FIGURES.
THERE'S ALSO A HUNDRED THOUSAND DOLLAR SIGNING BONUS THAT I'M AUTHORIZED TO GIVE YOU TODAY.
SO MISTER SHEPPARD, WHAT DO YOU THINK?
I THINK I'LL STICK WITH THE BOOK DEPOT FOR NOW, BUT TELL THE OMNICORP FAMILY I SAID THANKS FOR DINNER.
WAIT LET ME TELL YOU ABOUT---
SORRY BILL, BUT I'VE GOT A BUS TO CATCH.

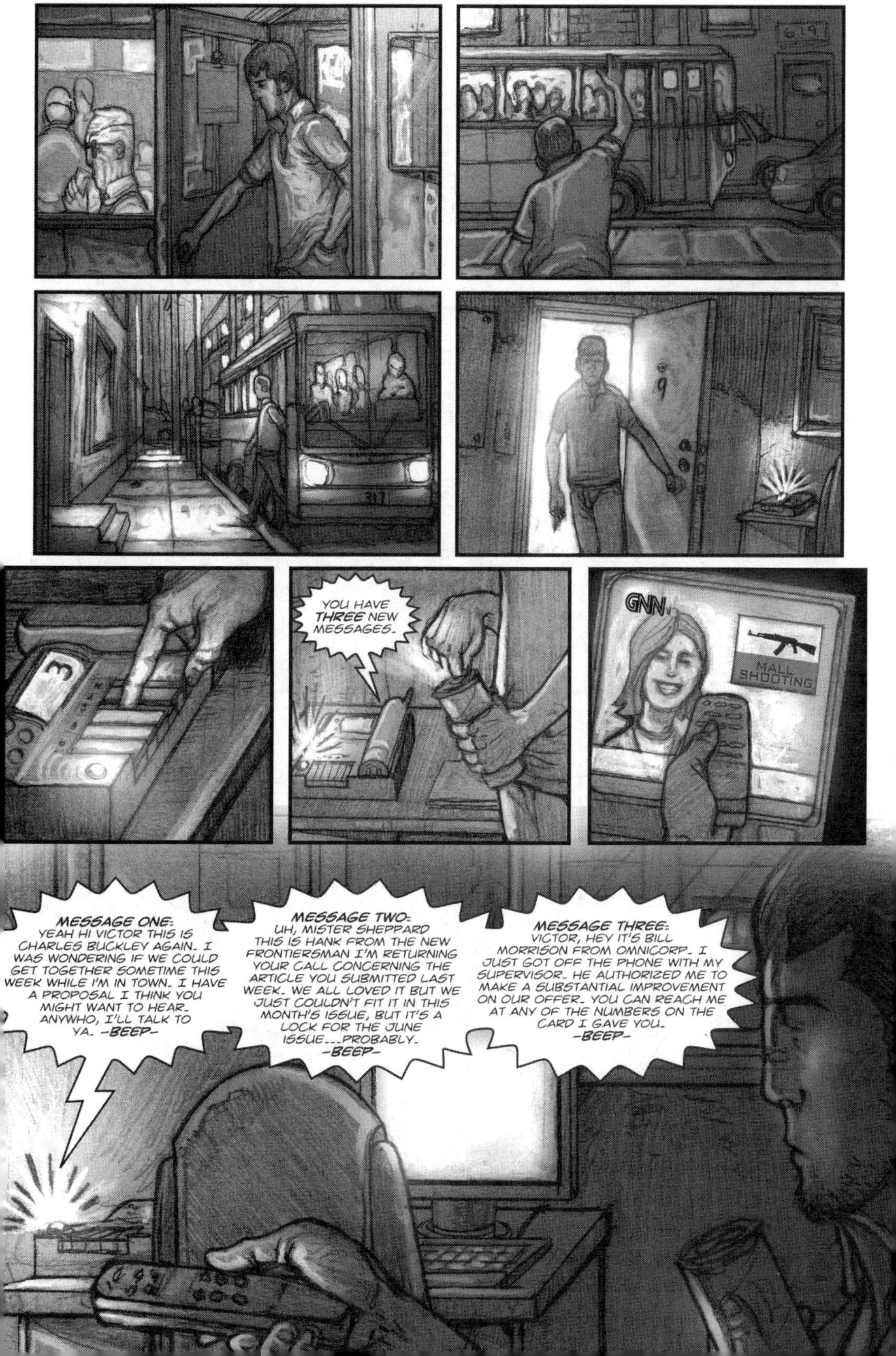
GNN
MALL SHOOTING
YOU HAVE THREE NEW MESSAGES.
MESSAGE ONE: YEAH HI VICTOR THIS IS CHARLES BUCKLEY AGAIN. I WAS WONDERING IF WE COULD GET TOGETHER SOMETIME THIS WEEK WHILE I'M IN TOWN. I HAVE A PROPOSAL I THINK YOU MIGHT WANT TO HEAR. ANYWHO, I'LL TALK TO YA. -BEEP-
MESSAGE TWO: UH, MISTER SHEPPARD THIS IS HANK FROM THE NEW FRONTIERSMAN I'M RETURNING YOUR CALL CONCERNING THE ARTICLE YOU SUBMITTED LAST WEEK. WE ALL LOVED IT BUT WE JUST COULDN'T FIT IT IN THIS MONTH'S ISSUE, BUT IT'S A LOCK FOR THE JUNE ISSUE...PROBABLY. -BEEP-
MESSAGE THREE: VICTOR, HEY IT'S BILL MORRISON FROM OMNICORP. I JUST GOT OFF THE PHONE WITH MY SUPERVISOR. HE AUTHORIZED ME TO MAKE A SUBSTANTIAL IMPROVEMENT ON OUR OFFER. YOU CAN REACH ME AT ANY OF THE NUMBERS ON THE CARD I GAVE YOU. -BEEP-

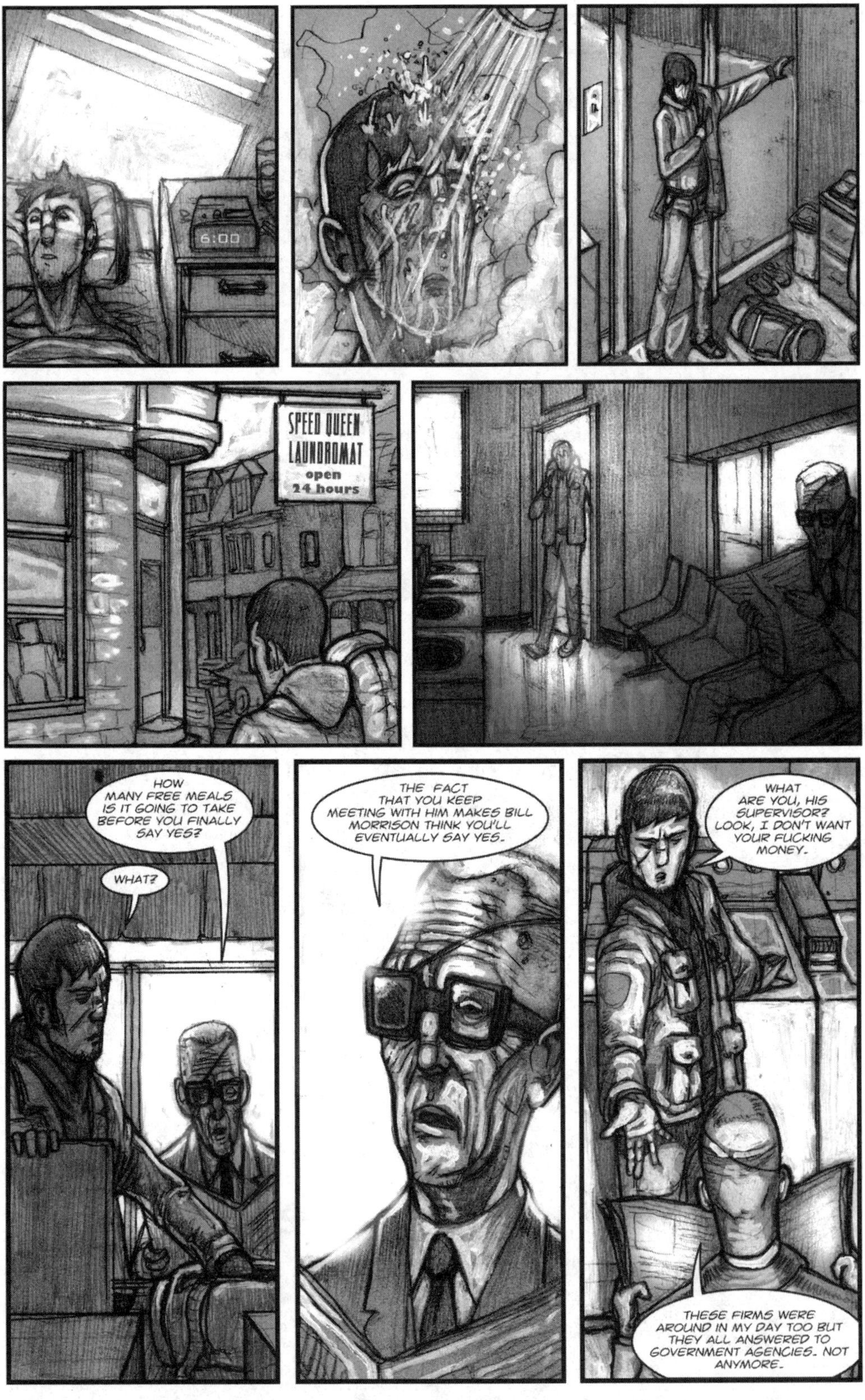
6:00
SPEED QUEEN LAUNDROMAT open 24 hours
HOW MANY FREE MEALS IS IT GOING TO TAKE BEFORE YOU FINALLY SAY YES?
WHAT?
THE FACT THAT YOU KEEP MEETING WITH HIM MAKES BILL MORRISON THINK YOU'LL EVENTUALLY SAY YES.
WHAT ARE YOU, HIS SUPERVISOR? LOOK, I DON'T WANT YOUR FUCKING MONEY.
THESE FIRMS WERE AROUND IN MY DAY TOO BUT THEY ALL ANSWERED TO GOVERNMENT AGENCIES. NOT ANYMORE.

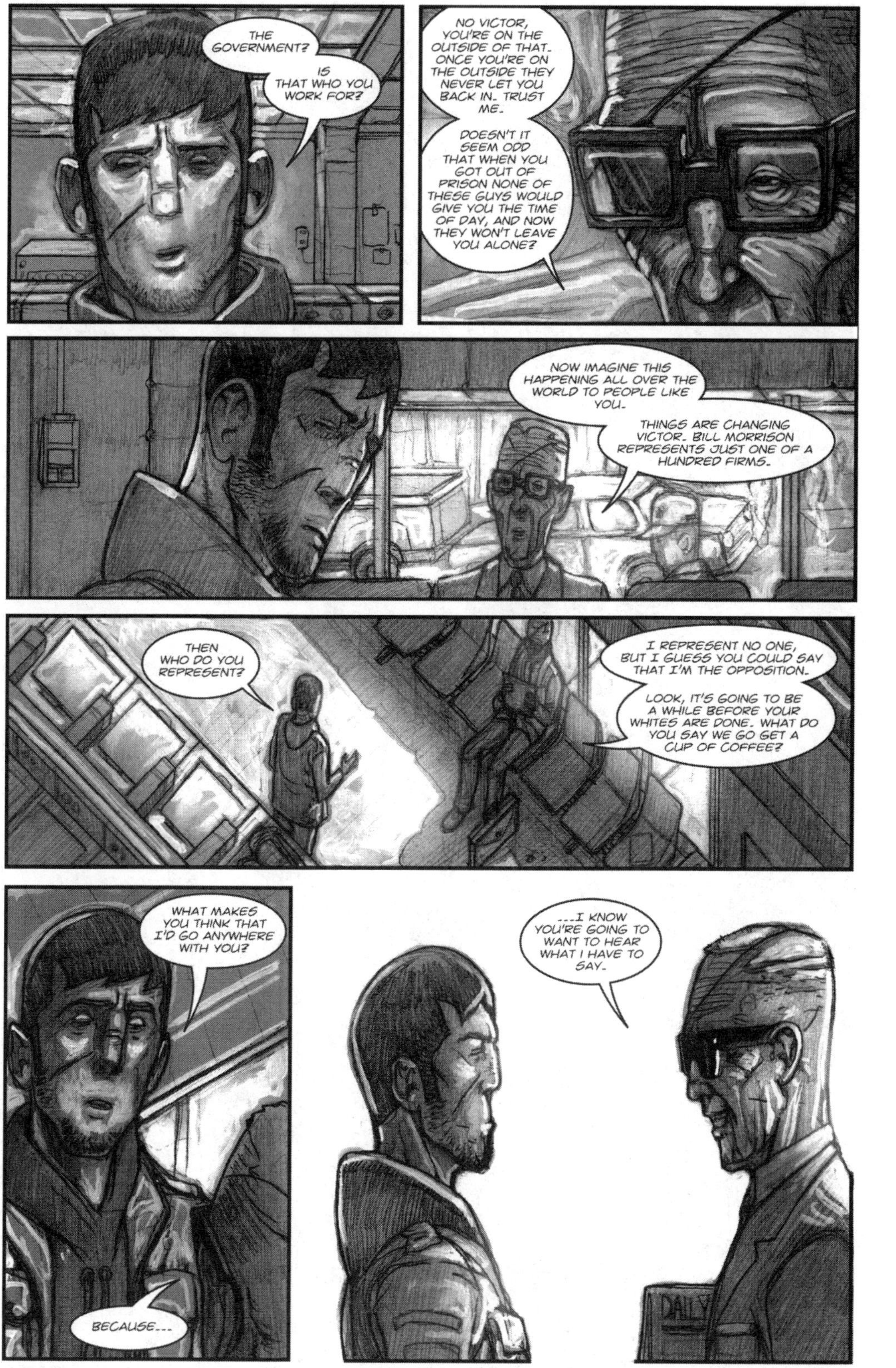
THE GOVERNMENT?
IS THAT WHO YOU WORK FOR?
NO VICTOR, YOU'RE ON THE OUTSIDE OF THAT. ONCE YOU'RE ON THE OUTSIDE THEY NEVER LET YOU BACK IN. TRUST ME.
DOESN'T IT SEEM ODD THAT WHEN YOU GOT OUT OF PRISON NONE OF THESE GUYS WOULD GIVE YOU THE TIME OF DAY, AND NOW THEY WON'T LEAVE YOU ALONE?
NOW IMAGINE THIS HAPPENING ALL OVER THE WORLD TO PEOPLE LIKE YOU.
THINGS ARE CHANGING VICTOR. BILL MORRISON REPRESENTS JUST ONE OF A HUNDRED FIRMS.
THEN WHO DO YOU REPRESENT?
I REPRESENT NO ONE, BUT I GUESS YOU COULD SAY THAT I'M THE OPPOSITION.
LOOK, IT'S GOING TO BE A WHILE BEFORE YOUR WHITES ARE DONE. WHAT DO YOU SAY WE GO GET A CUP OF COFFEE?
WHAT MAKES YOU THINK THAT I'D GO ANYWHERE WITH YOU?
BECAUSE...
...I KNOW YOU'RE GOING TO WANT TO HEAR WHAT I HAVE TO SAY.

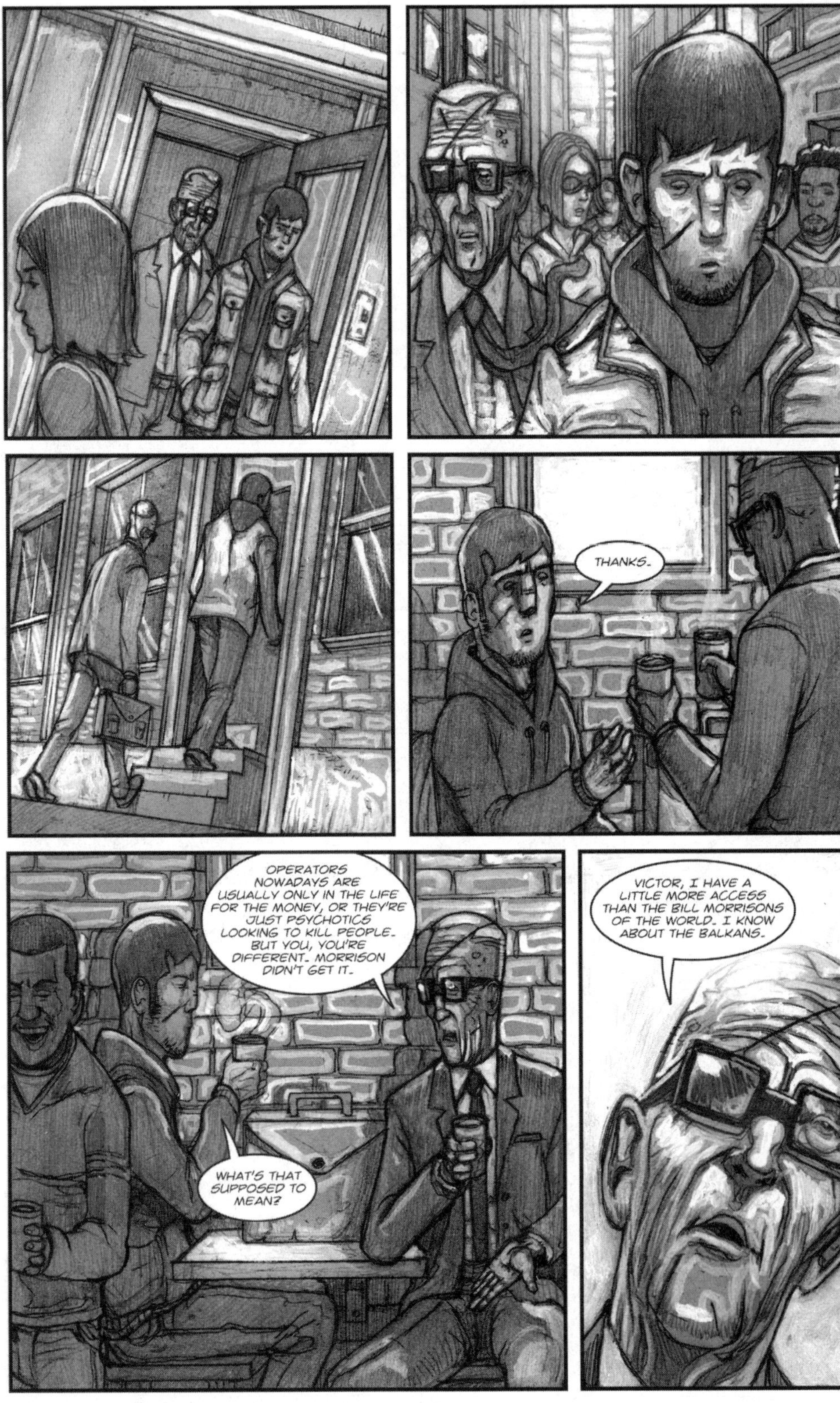
THANKS.
OPERATORS NOWADAYS ARE USUALLY ONLY IN THE LIFE FOR THE MONEY, OR THEY'RE JUST PSYCHOTICS LOOKING TO KILL PEOPLE. BUT YOU, YOU'RE DIFFERENT. MORRISON DIDN'T GET IT.
WHAT'S THAT SUPPOSED TO MEAN?
VICTOR, I HAVE A LITTLE MORE ACCESS THAN THE BILL MORRISONS OF THE WORLD. I KNOW ABOUT THE BALKANS.

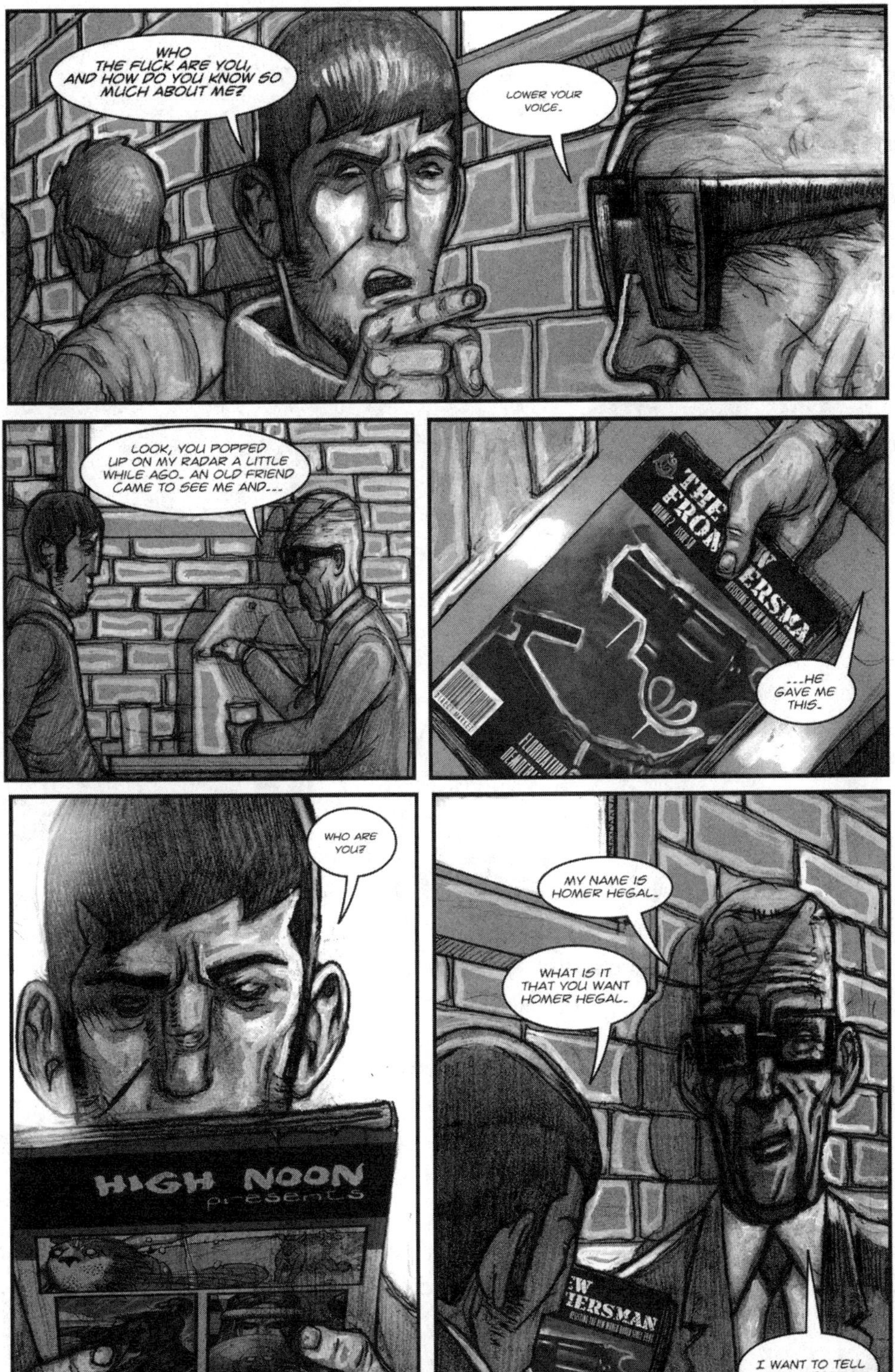
WHO THE FUCK ARE YOU, AND HOW DO YOU KNOW SO MUCH ABOUT ME?
LOWER YOUR VOICE.
LOOK, YOU POPPED UP ON MY RADAR A LITTLE WHILE AGO. AN OLD FRIEND CAME TO SEE ME AND...
...HE GAVE ME THIS.
WHO ARE YOU?
HIGH NOON presents
MY NAME IS HOMER HEGAL.
WHAT IS IT THAT YOU WANT HOMER HEGAL.
I WANT TO TELL YOU A STORY.

CONTINUED IN THE PAGES OF 'AMERICAN TERROR'

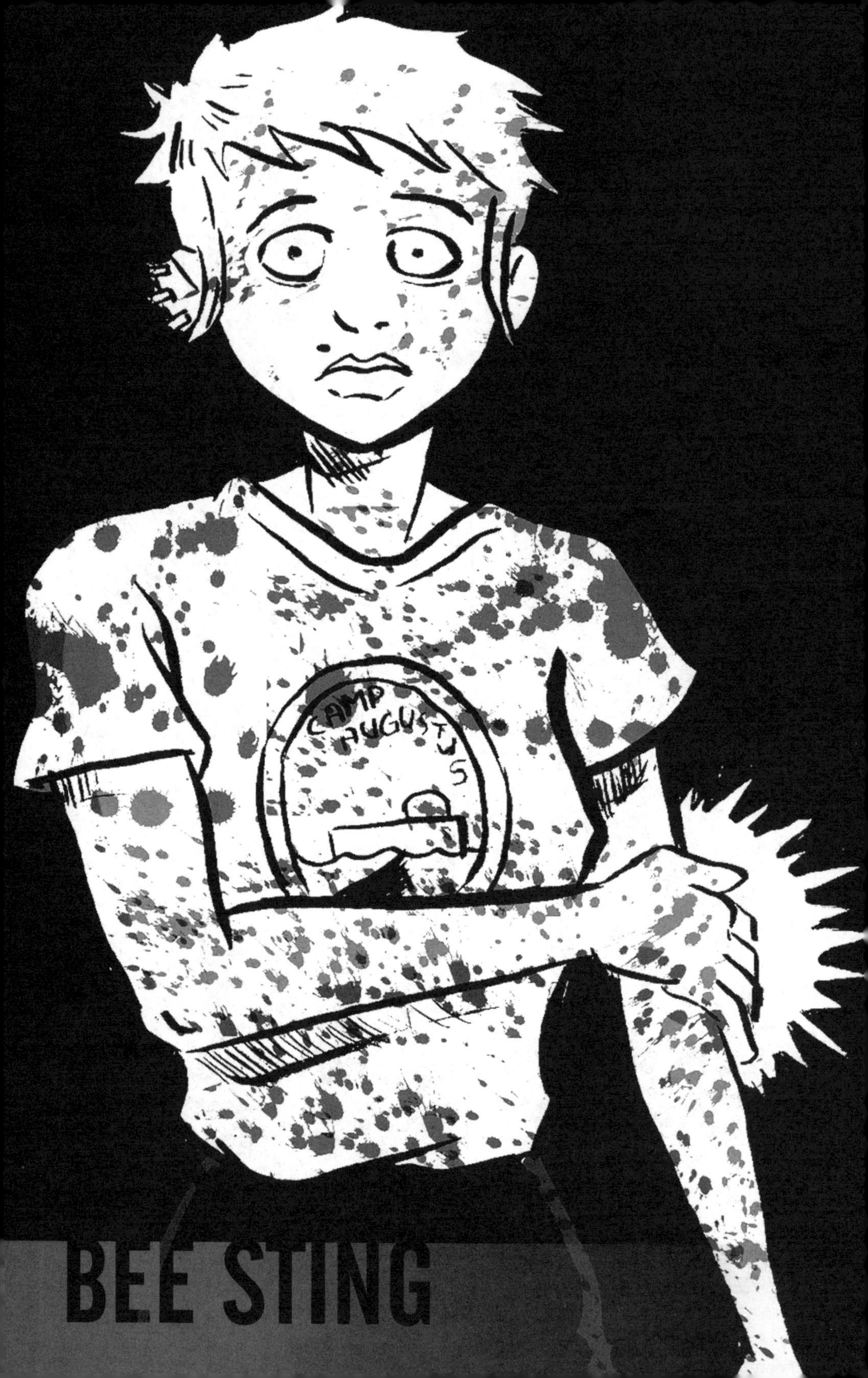
CAMP AUGUSTUS

BEE STING

BEE STING

LOU

"Meat is MURDER!"

Lou is the proprietor of Lou's Butcher Shop,
located near Camp Augustus. He prides himself on his choice
cuts of beef, which he usually serves to his family and friends
at gatherings and parties. However, the counselors at the local
camp do not realize these premium beef cuts are coming from the
other missing campers! Lou is a fine connoisseur of these rare
meats and a firm believer that adrenaline pumping through the
bodies of scared camp counselors increases the tastiness
of the meal!

Age: 45   Height: 6'5"   Weight: 320 lbs.

First Appearance: BEE STING (2013)

Created by Matthew D. Smith
Illustration by Jeremy Massie

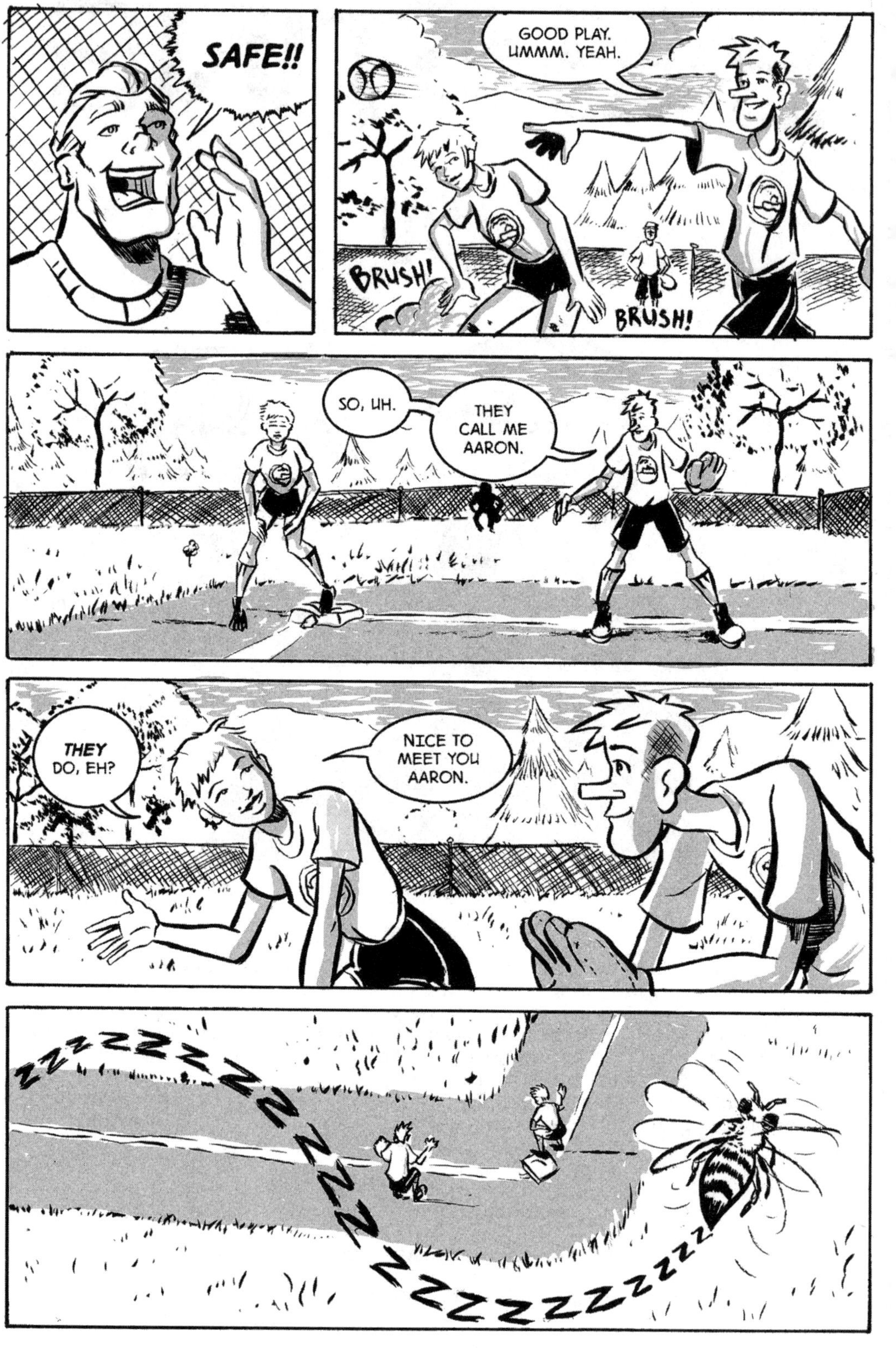
SAFE!!
GOOD PLAY. UMMM. YEAH.
BRUSH!
BRUSH!
SO, UH.
THEY CALL ME AARON.
NICE TO MEET YOU AARON.
THEY DO, EH?

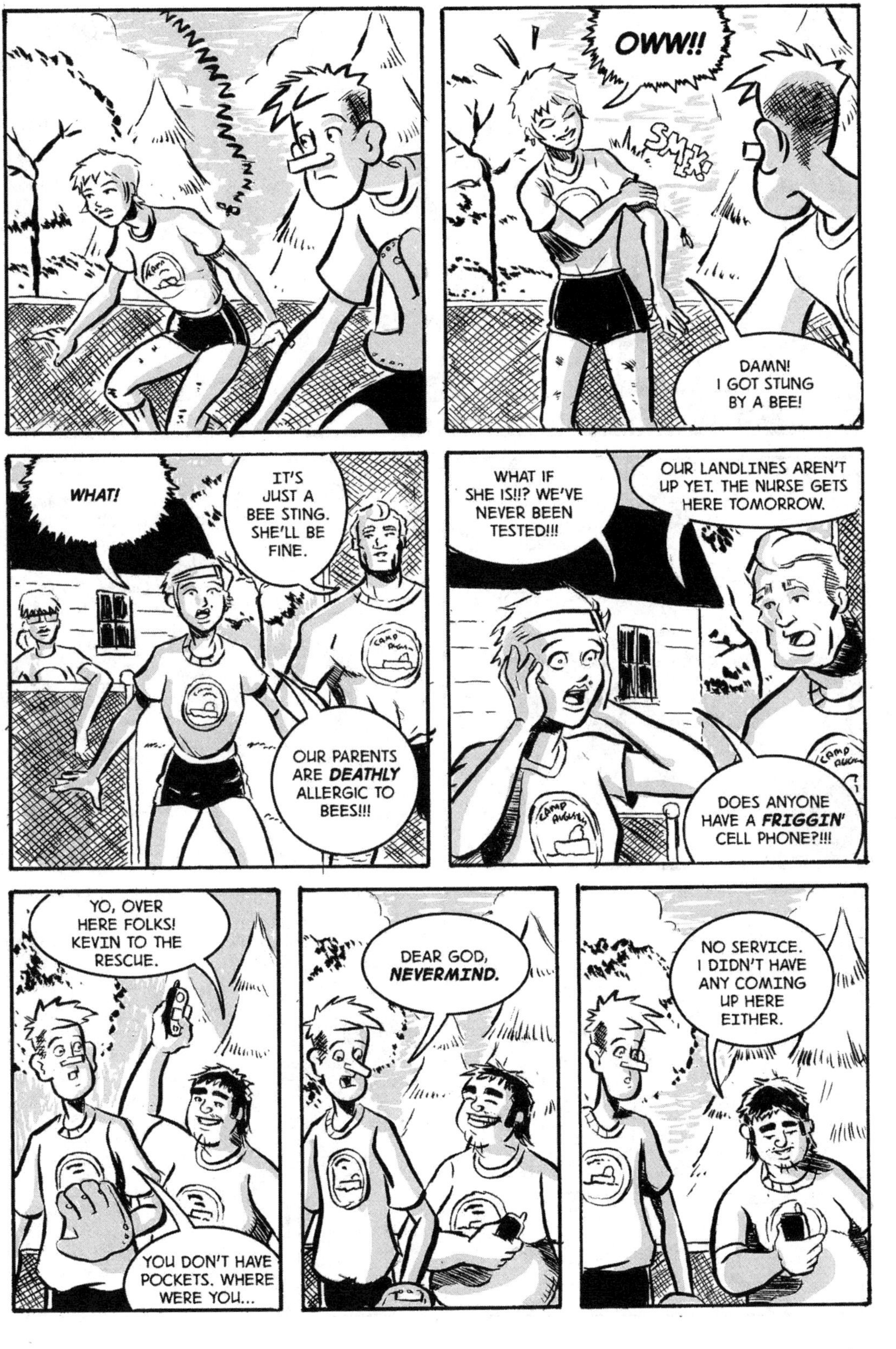
ZZZZZZZZZZZZZZ
OWW!!
SMAK!
DAMN! I GOT STUNG BY A BEE!
WHAT!
IT'S JUST A BEE STING. SHE'LL BE FINE.
OUR PARENTS ARE ***DEATHLY*** ALLERGIC TO BEES!!!
WHAT IF SHE IS!!? WE'VE NEVER BEEN TESTED!!!
OUR LANDLINES AREN'T UP YET. THE NURSE GETS HERE TOMORROW.
DOES ANYONE HAVE A ***FRIGGIN'*** CELL PHONE?!!!
YO, OVER HERE FOLKS! KEVIN TO THE RESCUE.
YOU DON'T HAVE POCKETS. WHERE WERE YOU...
DEAR GOD, ***NEVERMIND.***
NO SERVICE. I DIDN'T HAVE ANY COMING UP HERE EITHER.

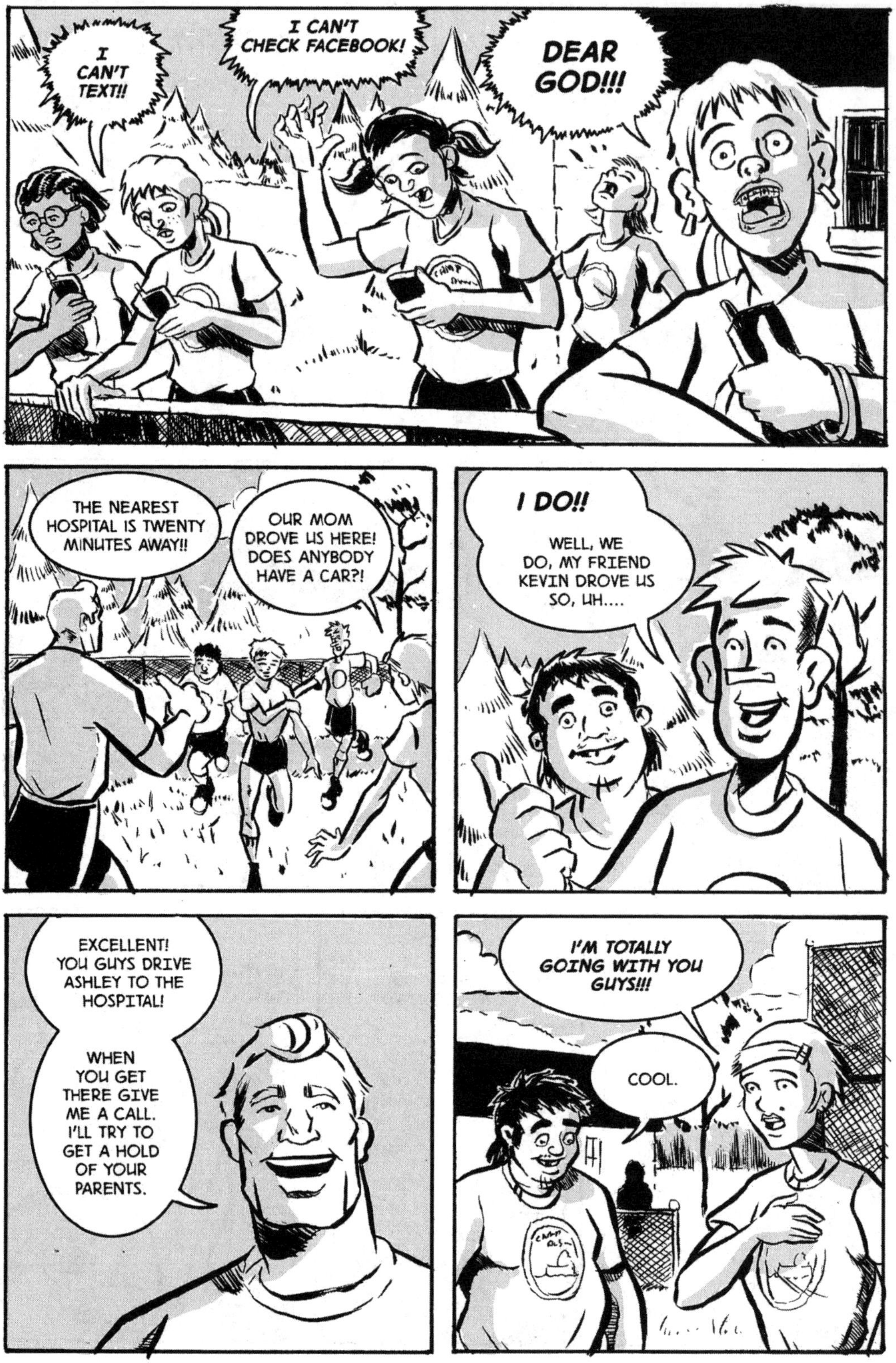
I CAN'T TEXT!!
I CAN'T CHECK FACEBOOK!
DEAR GOD!!!
THE NEAREST HOSPITAL IS TWENTY MINUTES AWAY!!
OUR MOM DROVE US HERE! DOES ANYBODY HAVE A CAR?!
I DO!!
WELL, WE DO, MY FRIEND KEVIN DROVE US SO, UH....
EXCELLENT! YOU GUYS DRIVE ASHLEY TO THE HOSPITAL!
WHEN YOU GET THERE GIVE ME A CALL. I'LL TRY TO GET A HOLD OF YOUR PARENTS.
I'M TOTALLY GOING WITH YOU GUYS!!!
COOL.

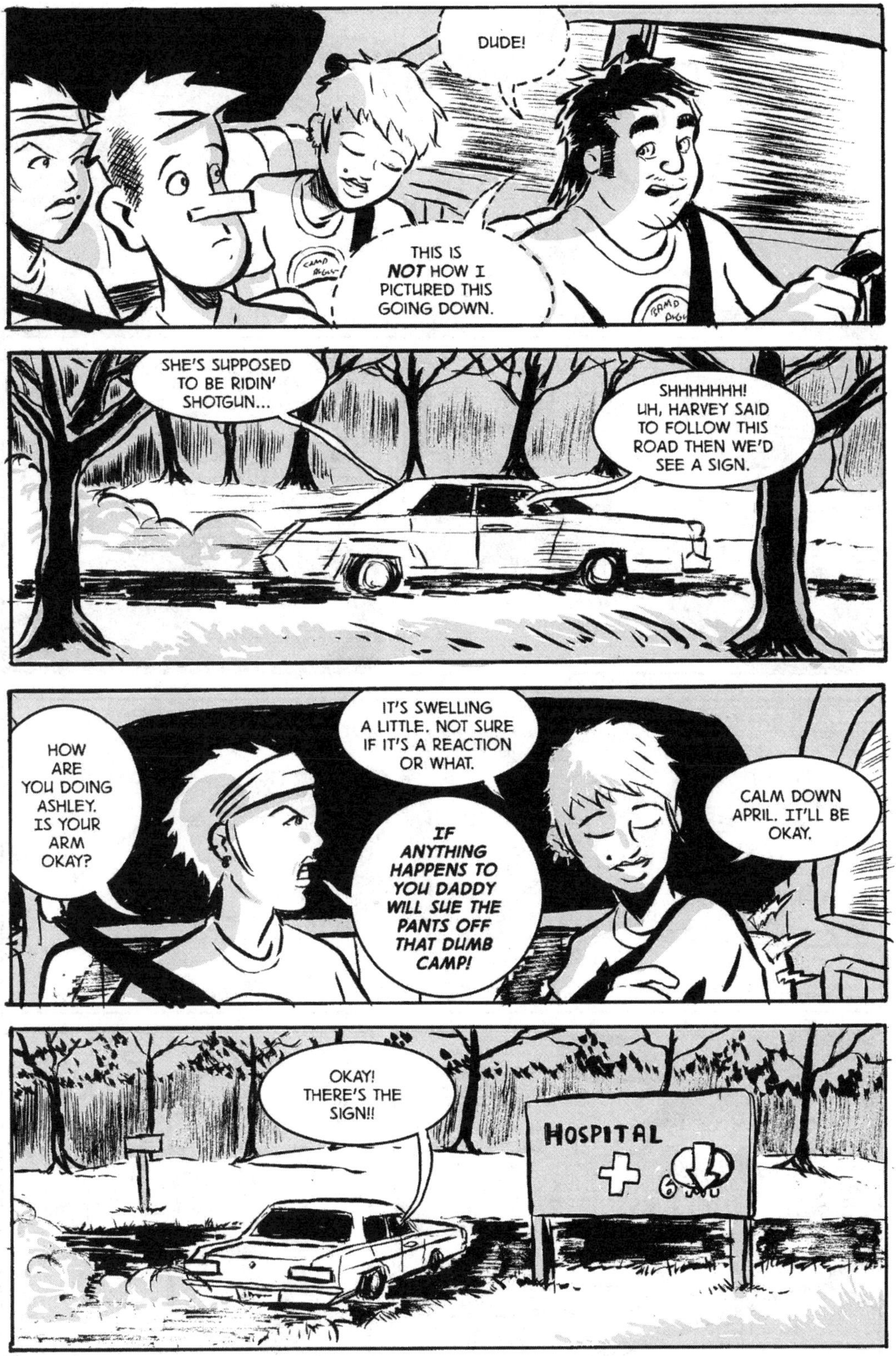
DUDE!
THIS IS **NOT** HOW I PICTURED THIS GOING DOWN.
SHE'S SUPPOSED TO BE RIDIN' SHOTGUN...
SHHHHHHH! UH, HARVEY SAID TO FOLLOW THIS ROAD THEN WE'D SEE A SIGN.
HOW ARE YOU DOING ASHLEY. IS YOUR ARM OKAY?
IT'S SWELLING A LITTLE. NOT SURE IF IT'S A REACTION OR WHAT.
IF ANYTHING HAPPENS TO YOU DADDY WILL SUE THE PANTS OFF THAT DUMB CAMP!
CALM DOWN APRIL. IT'LL BE OKAY.
OKAY! THERE'S THE SIGN!!
HOSPITAL

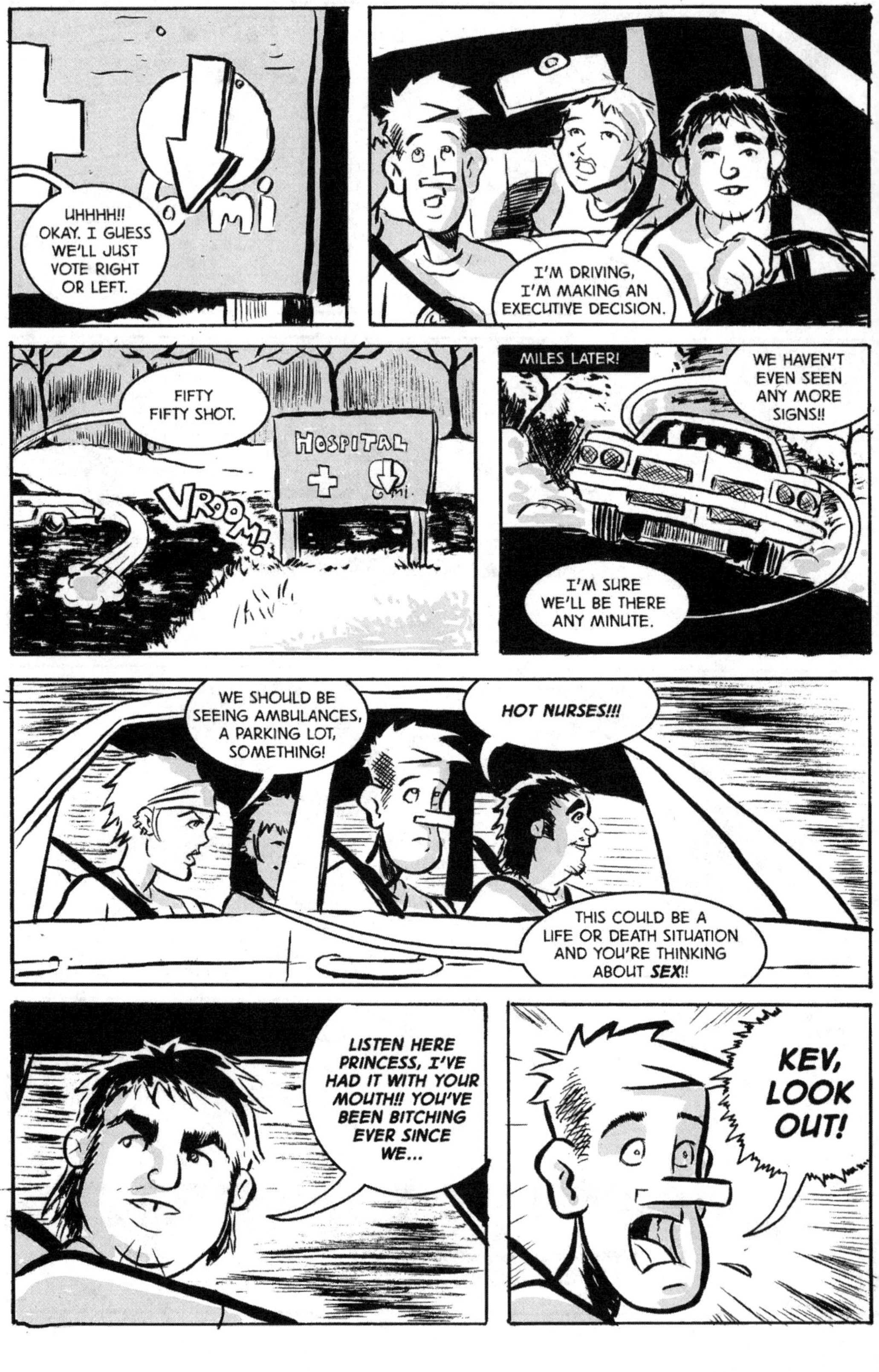
UHHHH!! OKAY. I GUESS WE'LL JUST VOTE RIGHT OR LEFT.
I'M DRIVING, I'M MAKING AN EXECUTIVE DECISION.
FIFTY FIFTY SHOT.
HOSPITAL
VROOM!
MILES LATER!
WE HAVEN'T EVEN SEEN ANY MORE SIGNS!!
I'M SURE WE'LL BE THERE ANY MINUTE.
WE SHOULD BE SEEING AMBULANCES, A PARKING LOT, SOMETHING!
HOT NURSES!!!
THIS COULD BE A LIFE OR DEATH SITUATION AND YOU'RE THINKING ABOUT SEX!!
LISTEN HERE PRINCESS, I'VE HAD IT WITH YOUR MOUTH!! YOU'VE BEEN BITCHING EVER SINCE WE...
KEV, LOOK OUT!

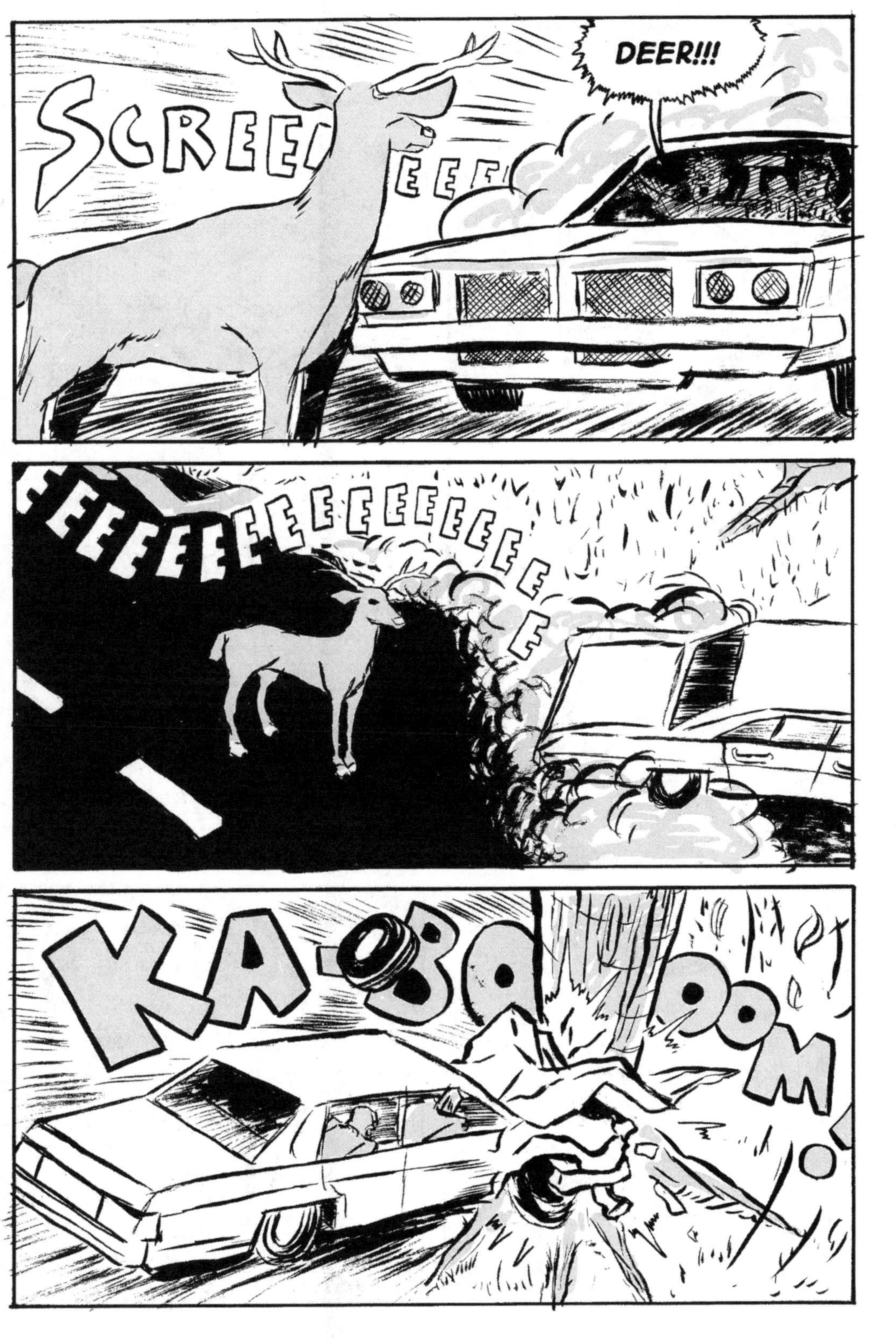
SCREEEEEE
DEER!!!
EEEEEEEEEEEEEEEEE
KA-BOOOM!

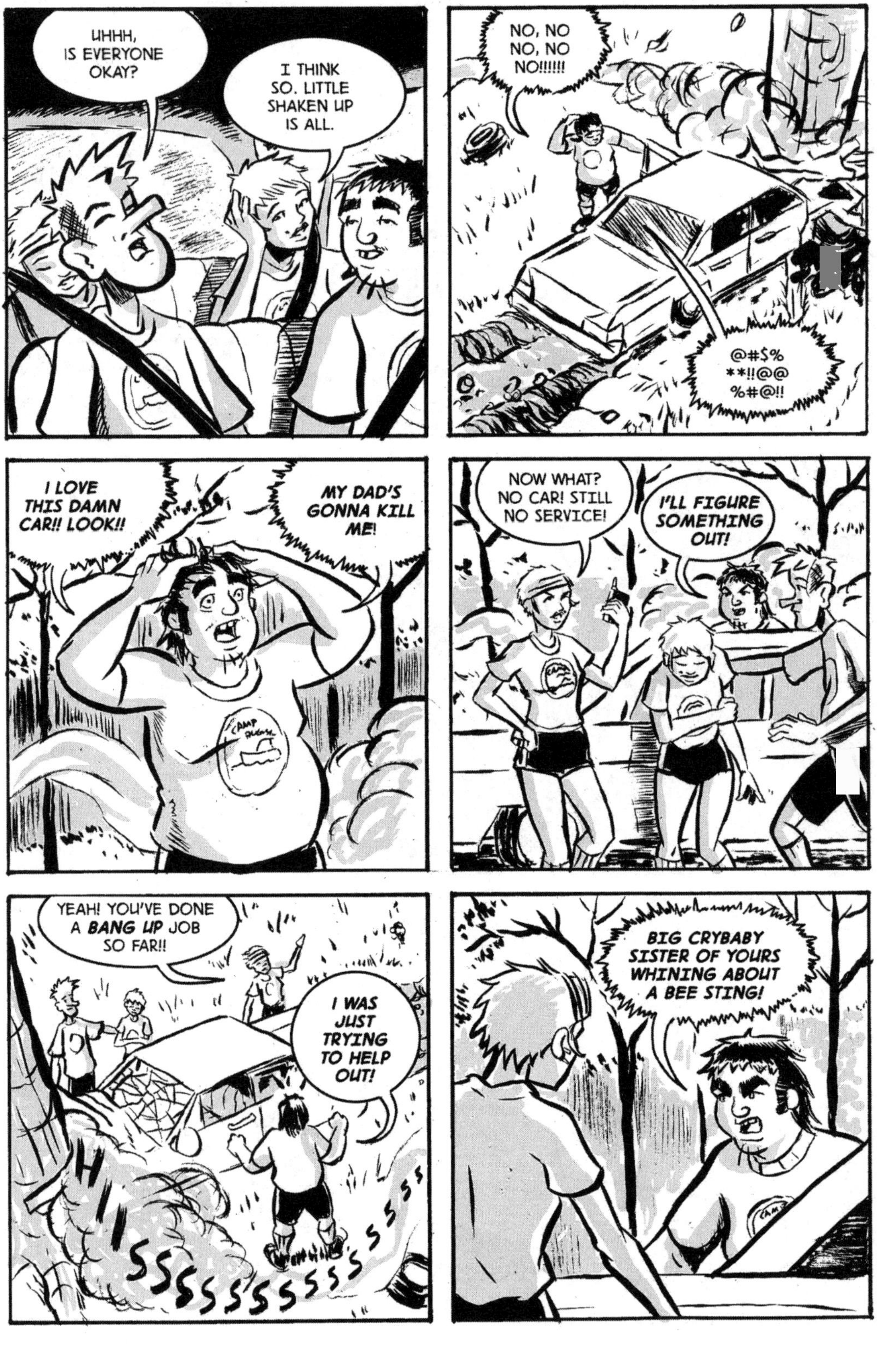
UHHH, IS EVERYONE OKAY?
I THINK SO. LITTLE SHAKEN UP IS ALL.
NO, NO NO, NO NO!!!!!!
@#$% **!!@@ %#@!!
I LOVE THIS DAMN CAR!! LOOK!!
MY DAD'S GONNA KILL ME!
NOW WHAT? NO CAR! STILL NO SERVICE!
I'LL FIGURE SOMETHING OUT!
YEAH! YOU'VE DONE A BANG UP JOB SO FAR!!
I WAS JUST TRYING TO HELP OUT!
SSSSSSSSSSSSSSS
BIG CRYBABY SISTER OF YOURS WHINING ABOUT A BEE STING!

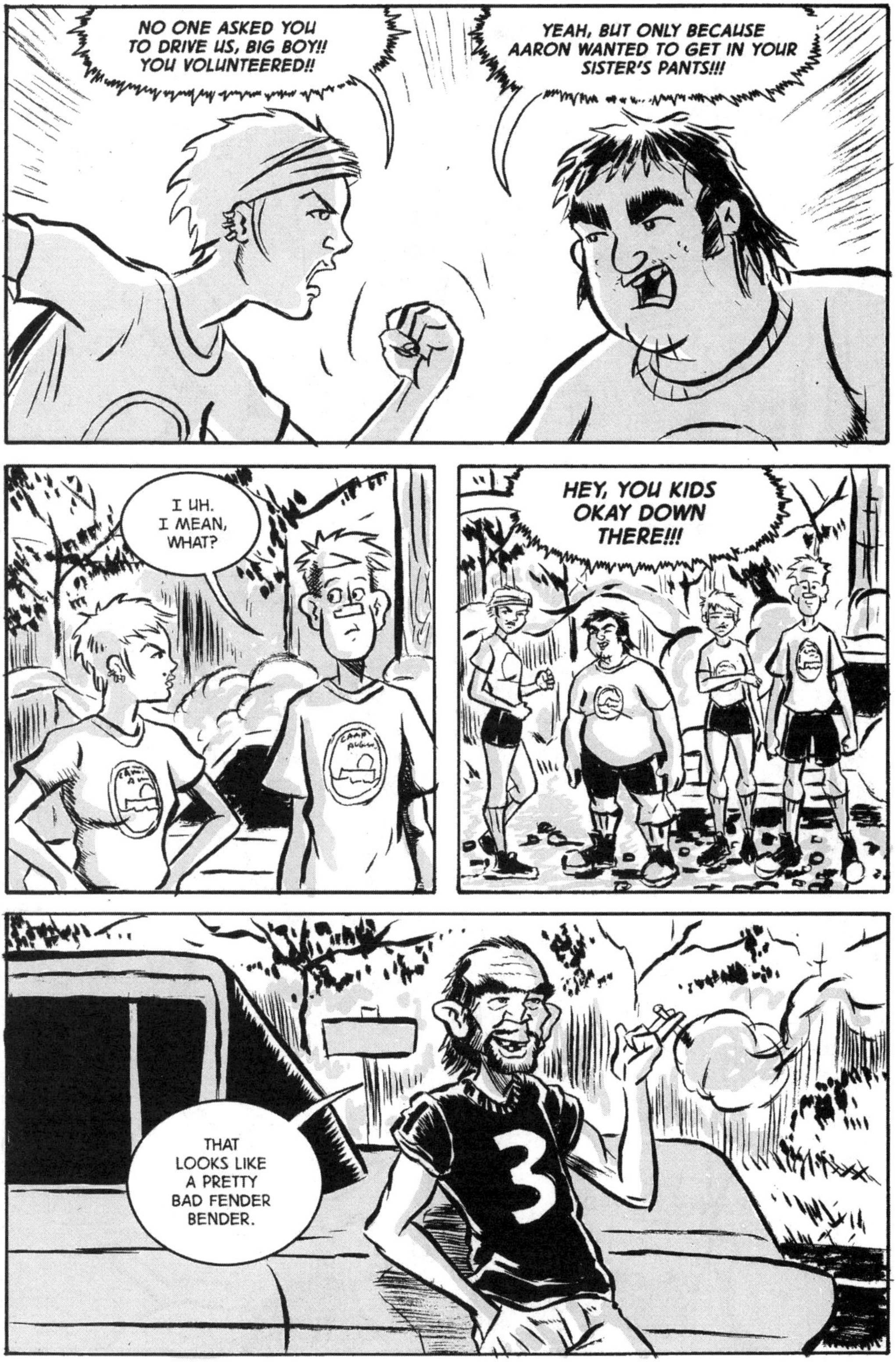
NO ONE ASKED YOU TO DRIVE US, BIG BOY!! YOU VOLUNTEERED!!
YEAH, BUT ONLY BECAUSE AARON WANTED TO GET IN YOUR SISTER'S PANTS!!!
I UH. I MEAN, WHAT?
HEY, YOU KIDS OKAY DOWN THERE!!!
THAT LOOKS LIKE A PRETTY BAD FENDER BENDER.

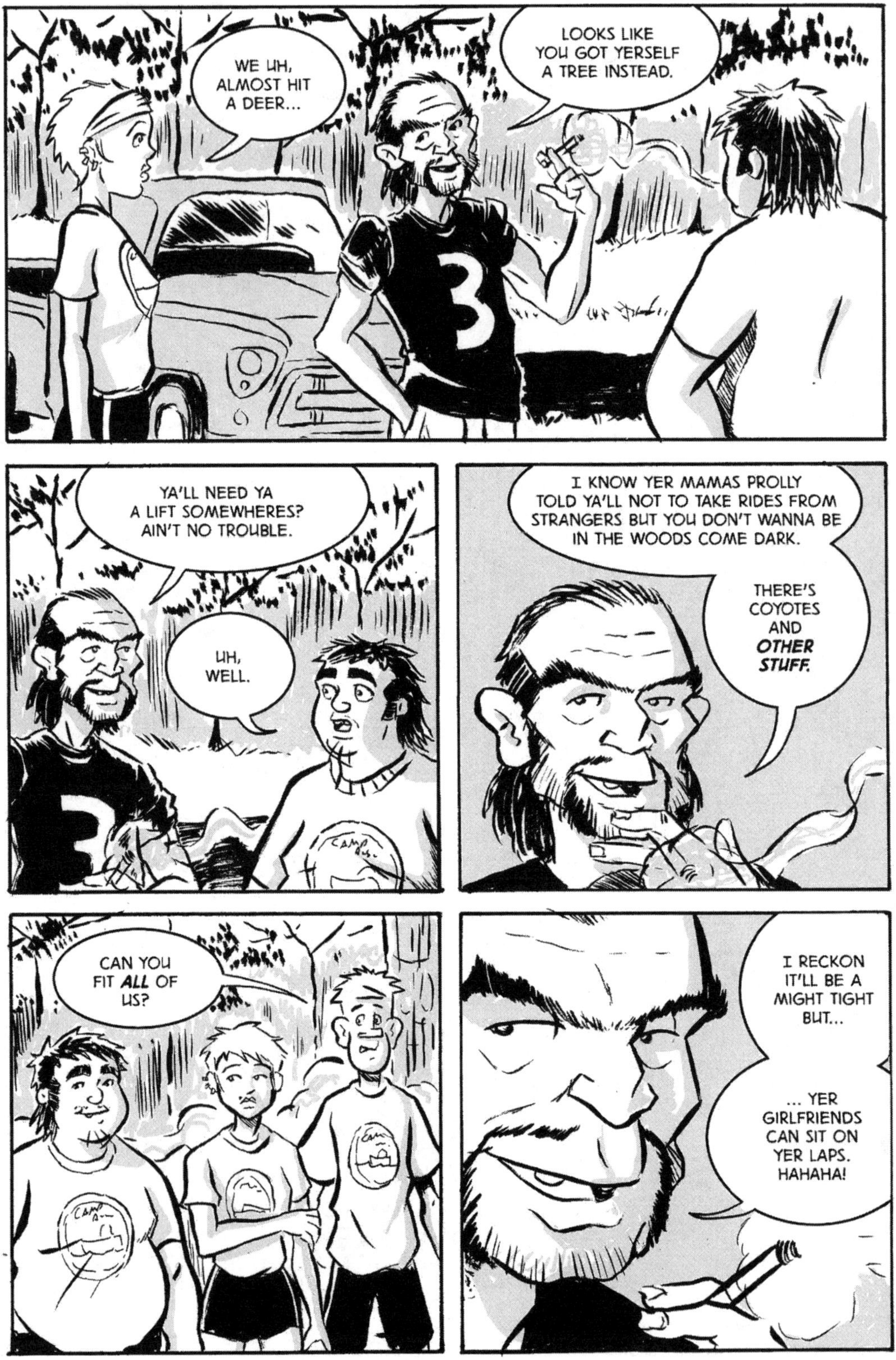
WE UH,
ALMOST HIT
A DEER...
LOOKS LIKE
YOU GOT YERSELF
A TREE INSTEAD.
YA'LL NEED YA
A LIFT SOMEWHERES?
AIN'T NO TROUBLE.
UH,
WELL.
I KNOW YER MAMAS PROLLY
TOLD YA'LL NOT TO TAKE RIDES FROM
STRANGERS BUT YOU DON'T WANNA BE
IN THE WOODS COME DARK.
THERE'S
COYOTES
AND
OTHER
STUFF.
CAN YOU
FIT ALL OF
US?
I RECKON
IT'LL BE A
MIGHT TIGHT
BUT...
... YER
GIRLFRIENDS
CAN SIT ON
YER LAPS.
HAHAHA!

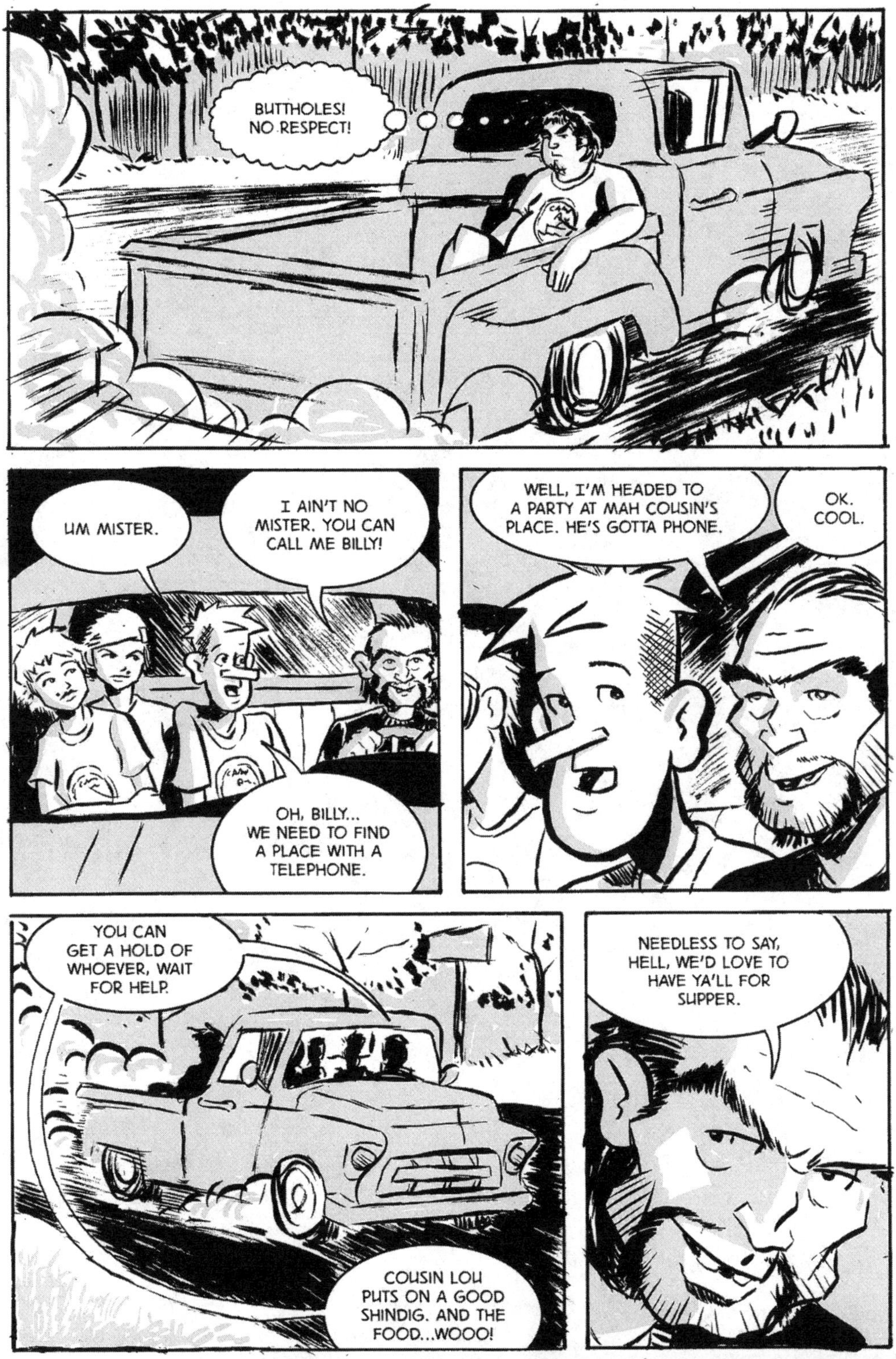
BUTTHOLES! NO RESPECT!
UM MISTER.
I AIN'T NO MISTER. YOU CAN CALL ME BILLY!
OH, BILLY... WE NEED TO FIND A PLACE WITH A TELEPHONE.
WELL, I'M HEADED TO A PARTY AT MAH COUSIN'S PLACE. HE'S GOTTA PHONE.
OK. COOL.
YOU CAN GET A HOLD OF WHOEVER, WAIT FOR HELP.
COUSIN LOU PUTS ON A GOOD SHINDIG. AND THE FOOD...WOOO!
NEEDLESS TO SAY, HELL, WE'D LOVE TO HAVE YA'LL FOR SUPPER.

CONTINUED IN THE PAGES OF 'BEE STING'

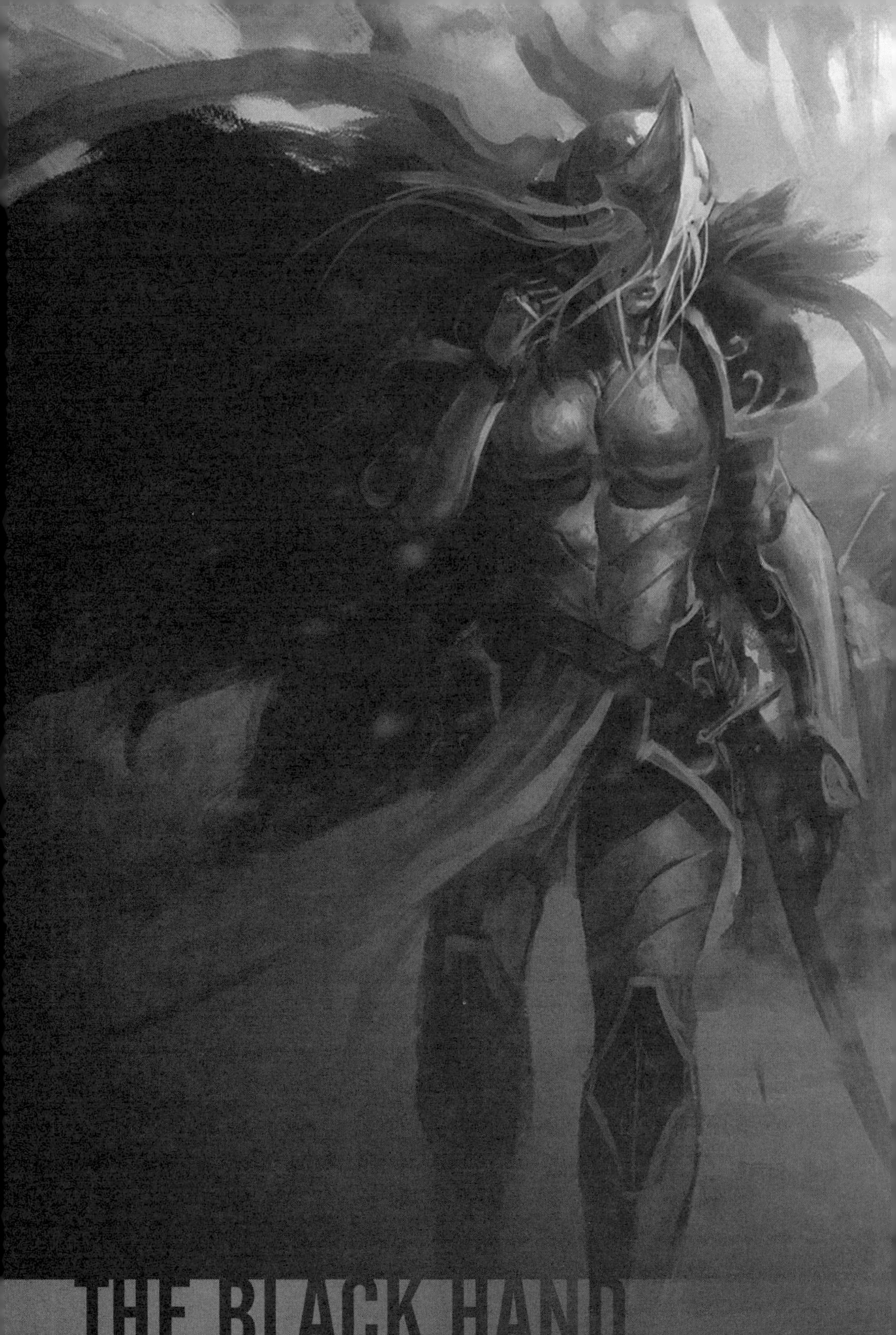

THE BLACK HAND

THE BLACK HAND

VICTORIA ADDAIR

"Being cold and alone is no way to die."

A childhood brush with death left VICTORIA ADDAIR with a blackened hand that has the power to slay the undead with a touch. Drafted into the Order of the Black Hand, Victoria is sent to an old mining town to slay a ghost, THE GREY BOY, who haunts the mountainside. Victoria learns that all is not as it appears and the secrets of the Grey Boy's origin could have devastating consequences for them all!

Age: 22
Height: 5'10"
Weight: 150 lbs.

First Appearance:
THE BLACK HAND #1 (2012)

Created by Erica J. Heflin
Illustration by Fares Maese

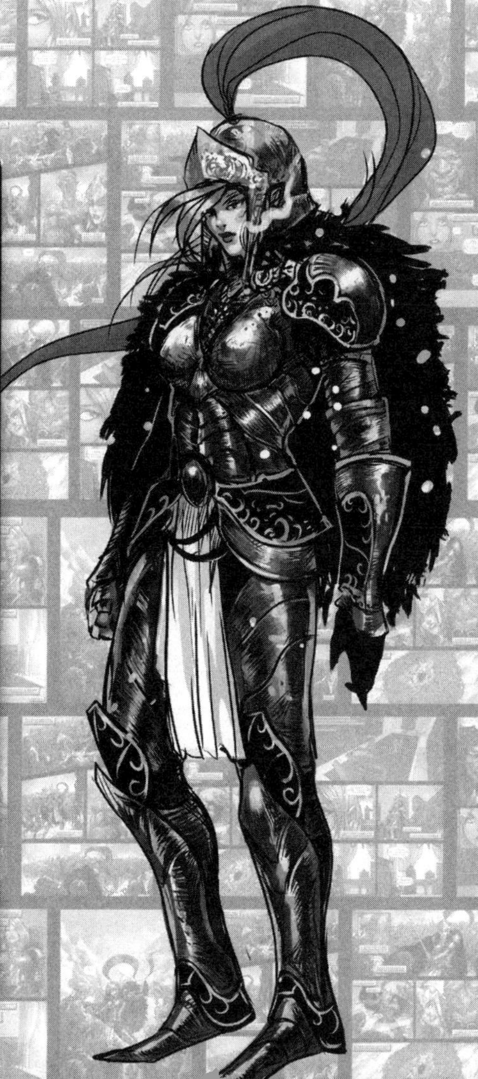

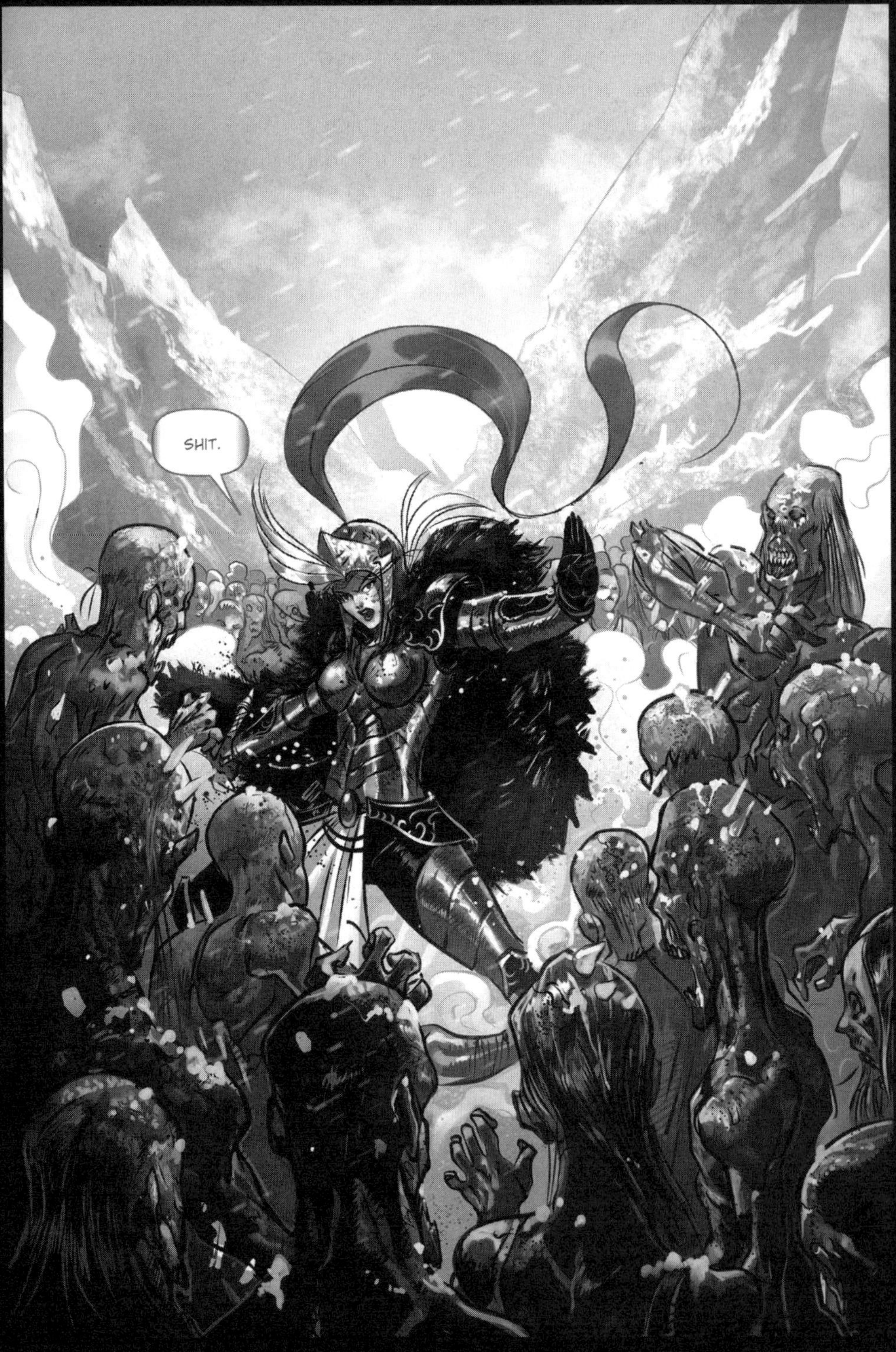
SHIT.

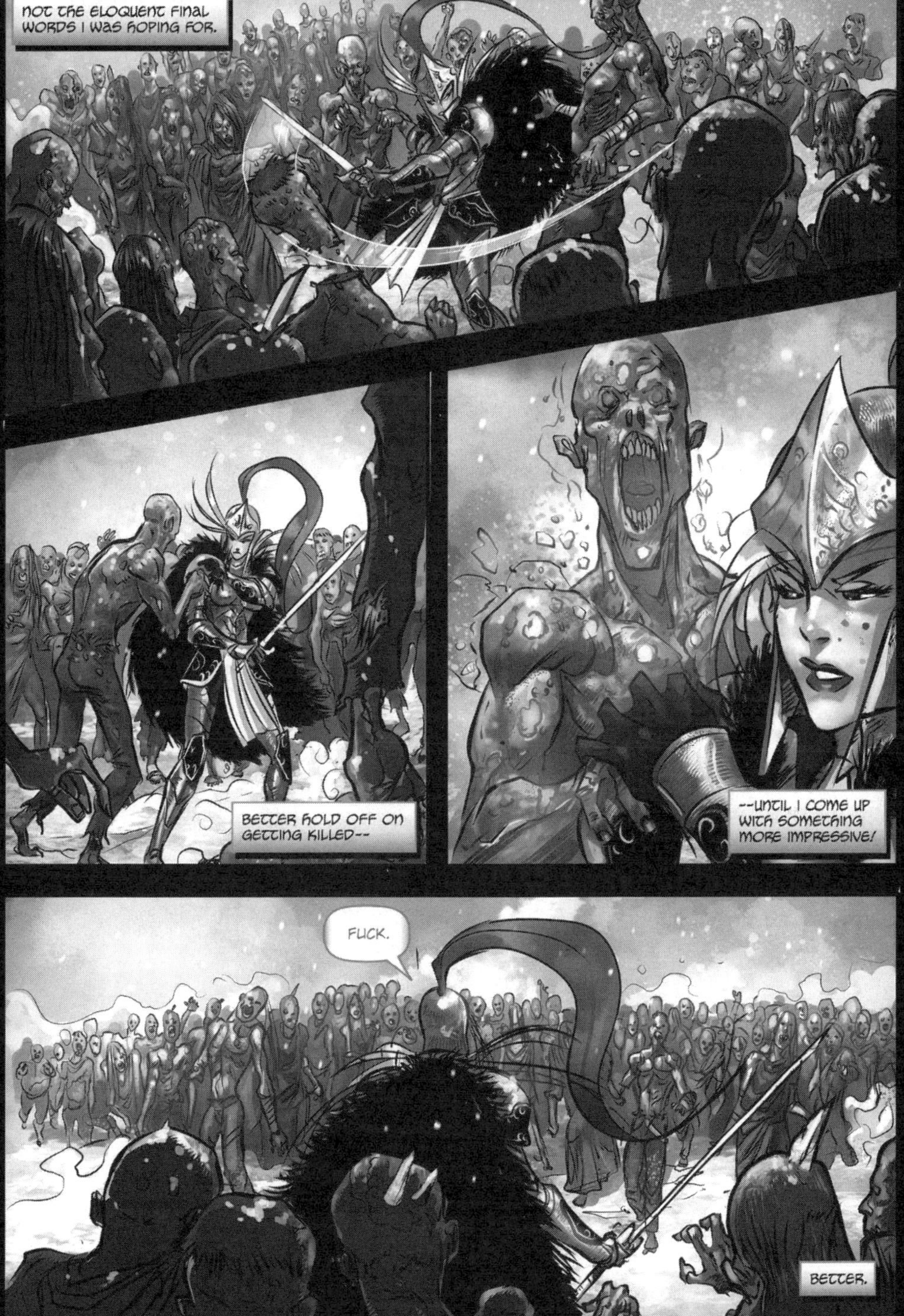
NOT THE ELOQUENT FINAL WORDS I WAS HOPING FOR.
BETTER HOLD OFF ON GETTING KILLED--
--UNTIL I COME UP WITH SOMETHING MORE IMPRESSIVE!
FUCK.
BETTER.

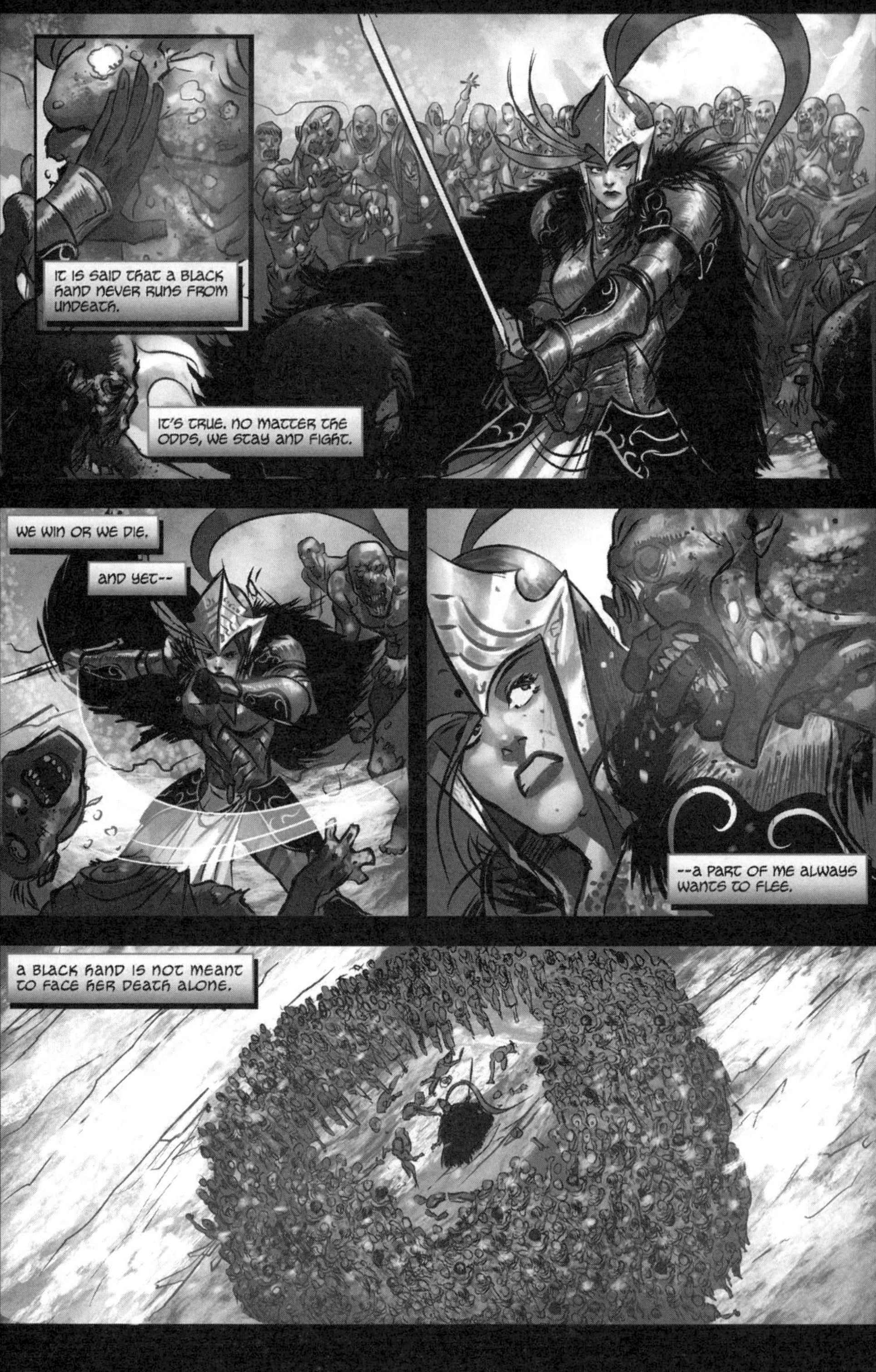
It is said that a Black Hand never runs from undeath.
It's true. No matter the odds, we stay and fight.
We win or we die.
And yet--
--a part of me always wants to flee.
A Black Hand is not meant to face her death alone.

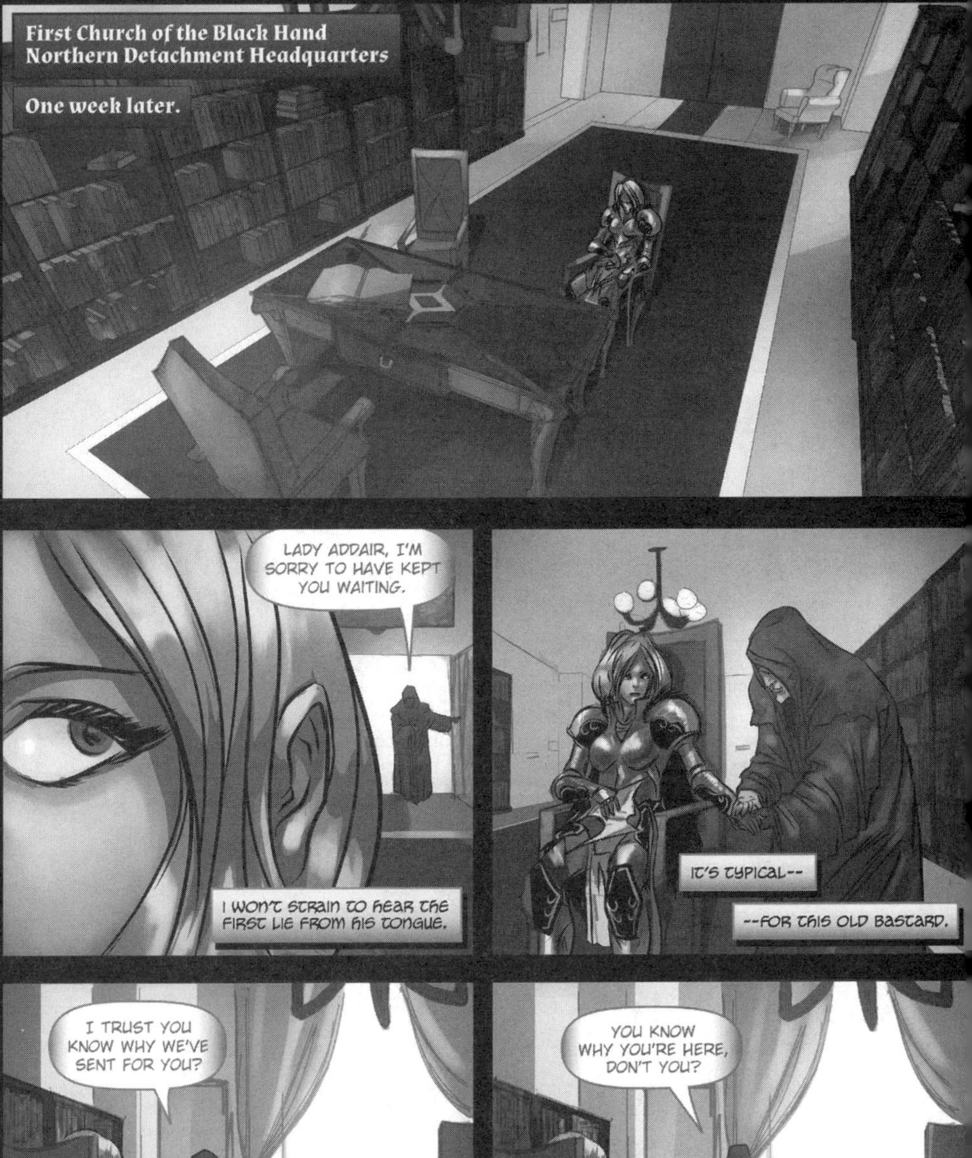
First Church of the Black Hand
Northern Detachment Headquarters
One week later.
LADY ADDAIR, I'M SORRY TO HAVE KEPT YOU WAITING.
I WON'T STRAIN TO HEAR THE FIRST LIE FROM HIS TONGUE.
IT'S TYPICAL--
--FOR THIS OLD BASTARD.
I TRUST YOU KNOW WHY WE'VE SENT FOR YOU?
YOU KNOW WHY YOU'RE HERE, DON'T YOU?
I HAVE MY SUSPICIONS.
JUST STAY CALM, PLAY HIS GAMES. NO PUNCHING. NO CURSING.

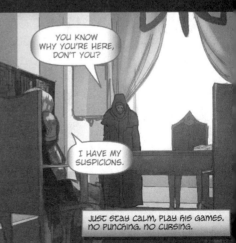

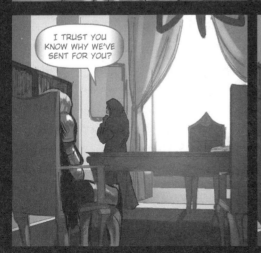

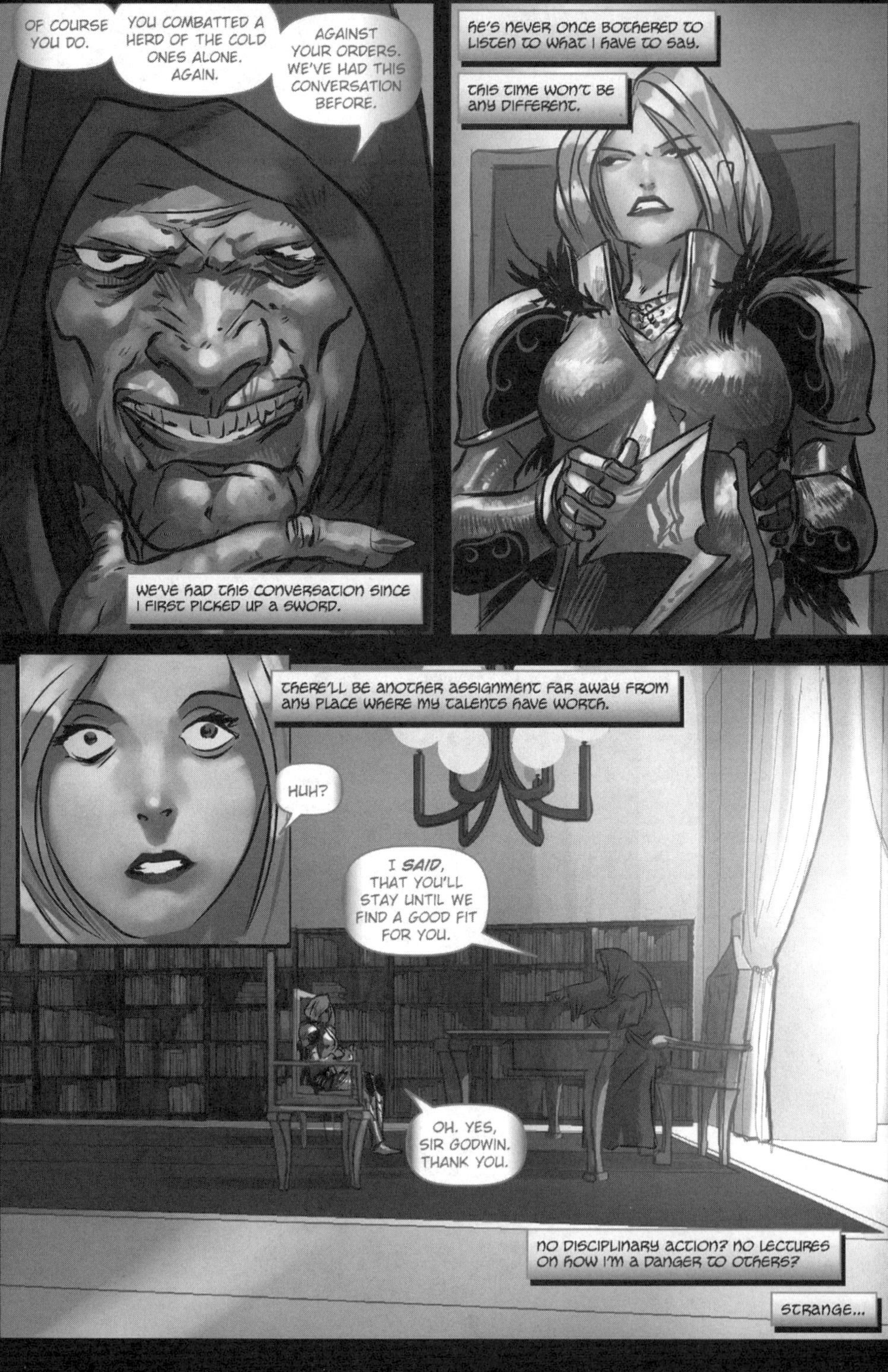
OF COURSE YOU DO.
YOU COMBATTED A HERD OF THE COLD ONES ALONE. AGAIN.
AGAINST YOUR ORDERS. WE'VE HAD THIS CONVERSATION BEFORE.
WE'VE HAD THIS CONVERSATION SINCE I FIRST PICKED UP A SWORD.
HE'S NEVER ONCE BOTHERED TO LISTEN TO WHAT I HAVE TO SAY.
THIS TIME WON'T BE ANY DIFFERENT.
THERE'LL BE ANOTHER ASSIGNMENT FAR AWAY FROM ANY PLACE WHERE MY TALENTS HAVE WORTH.
HUH?
I *SAID*, THAT YOU'LL STAY UNTIL WE FIND A GOOD FIT FOR YOU.
OH. YES, SIR GODWIN. THANK YOU.
NO DISCIPLINARY ACTION? NO LECTURES ON HOW I'M A DANGER TO OTHERS?
STRANGE...

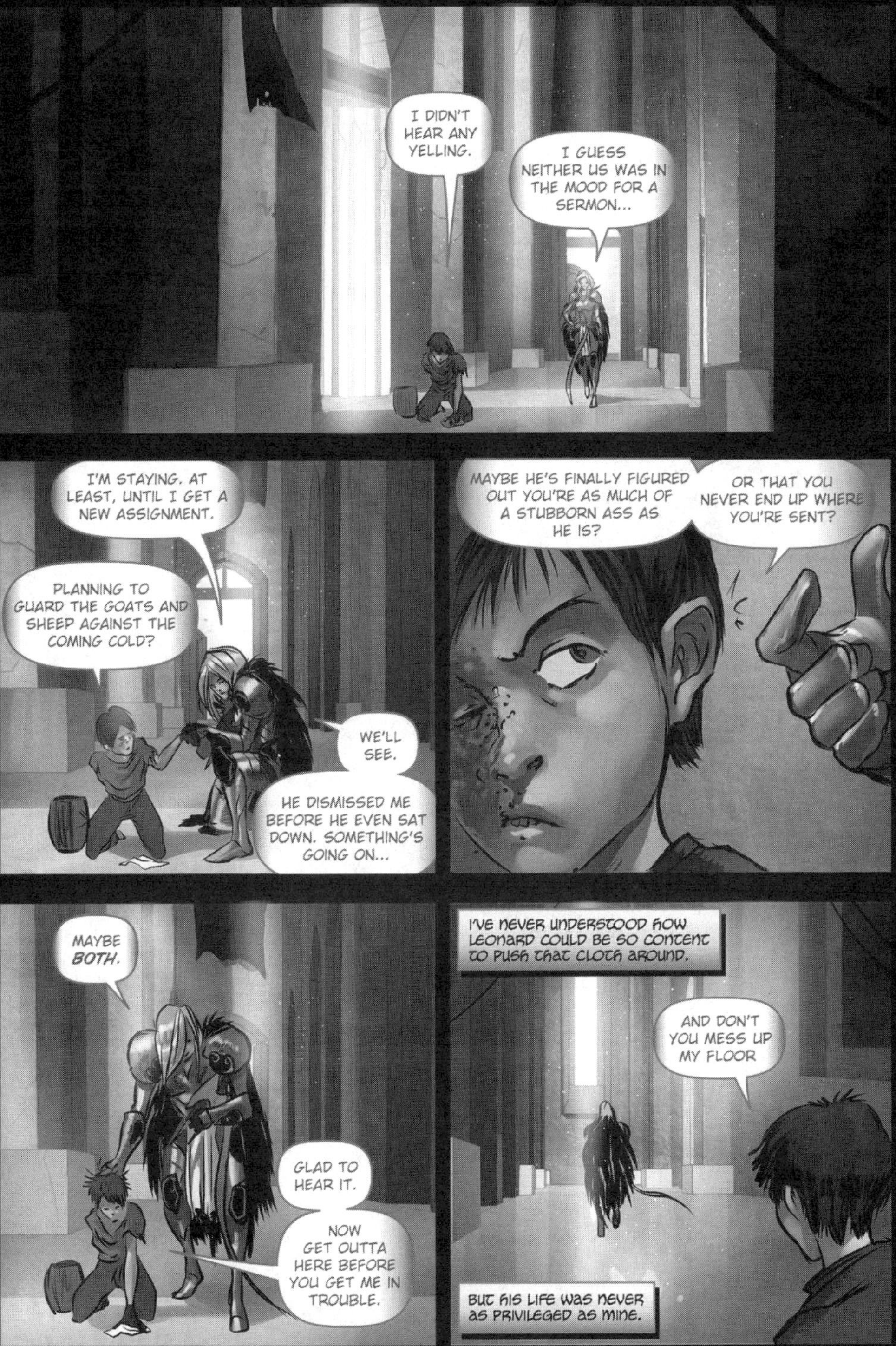
I DIDN'T HEAR ANY YELLING.
I GUESS NEITHER US WAS IN THE MOOD FOR A SERMON...
I'M STAYING. AT LEAST, UNTIL I GET A NEW ASSIGNMENT.
PLANNING TO GUARD THE GOATS AND SHEEP AGAINST THE COMING COLD?
WE'LL SEE.
HE DISMISSED ME BEFORE HE EVEN SAT DOWN. SOMETHING'S GOING ON...
MAYBE HE'S FINALLY FIGURED OUT YOU'RE AS MUCH OF A STUBBORN ASS AS HE IS?
OR THAT YOU NEVER END UP WHERE YOU'RE SENT?
MAYBE *BOTH*.
GLAD TO HEAR IT.
NOW GET OUTTA HERE BEFORE YOU GET ME IN TROUBLE.
I'VE NEVER UNDERSTOOD HOW LEONARD COULD BE SO CONTENT TO PUSH THAT CLOTH AROUND.
AND DON'T YOU MESS UP MY FLOOR
BUT HIS LIFE WAS NEVER AS PRIVILEGED AS MINE.

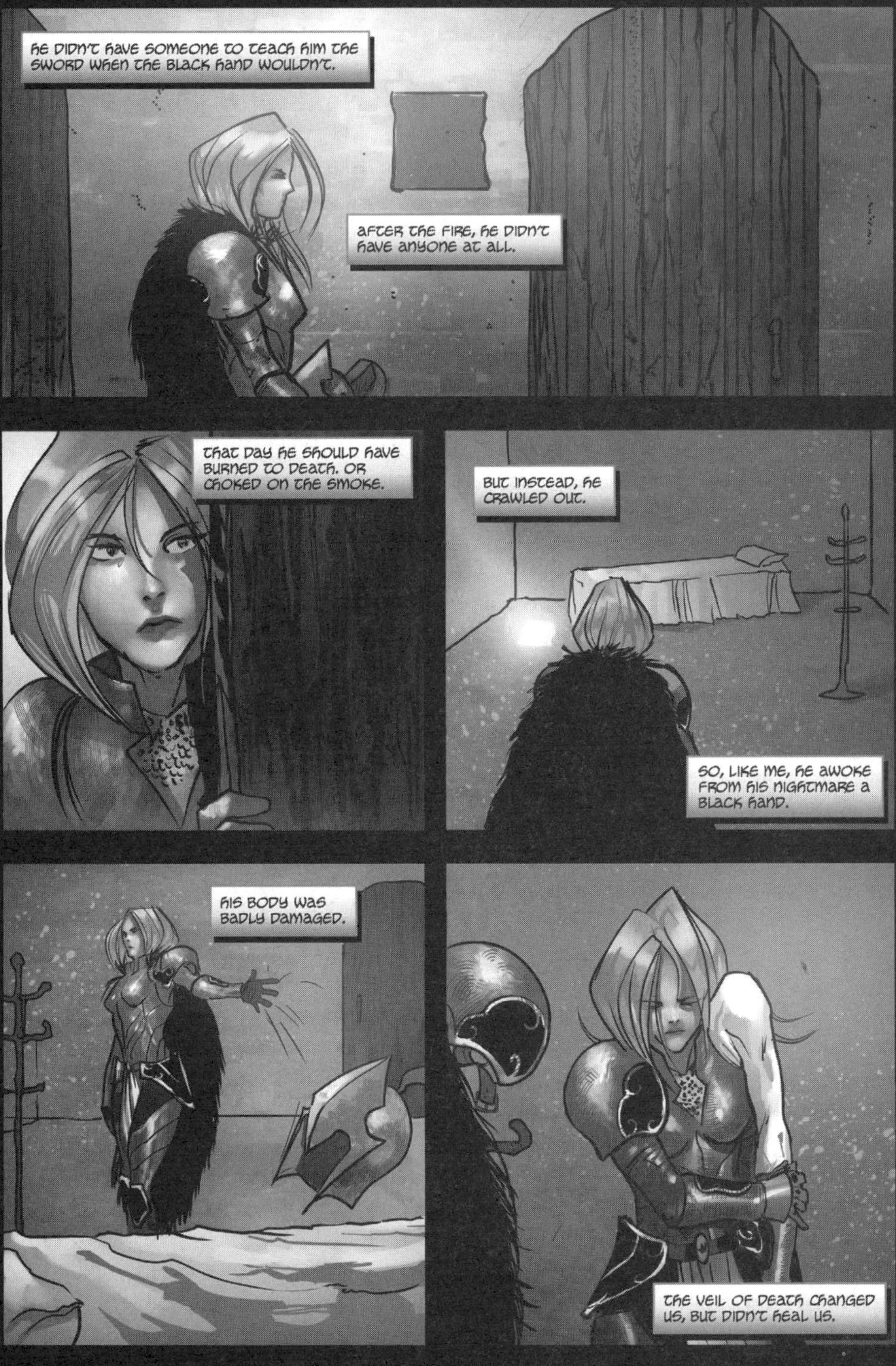
HE DIDN'T HAVE SOMEONE TO TEACH HIM THE SWORD WHEN THE BLACK HAND WOULDN'T.
AFTER THE FIRE, HE DIDN'T HAVE ANYONE AT ALL.
THAT DAY HE SHOULD HAVE BURNED TO DEATH. OR CHOKED ON THE SMOKE.
BUT INSTEAD, HE CRAWLED OUT.
SO, LIKE ME, HE AWOKE FROM HIS NIGHTMARE A BLACK HAND.
HIS BODY WAS BADLY DAMAGED.
THE VEIL OF DEATH CHANGED US, BUT DIDN'T HEAL US.

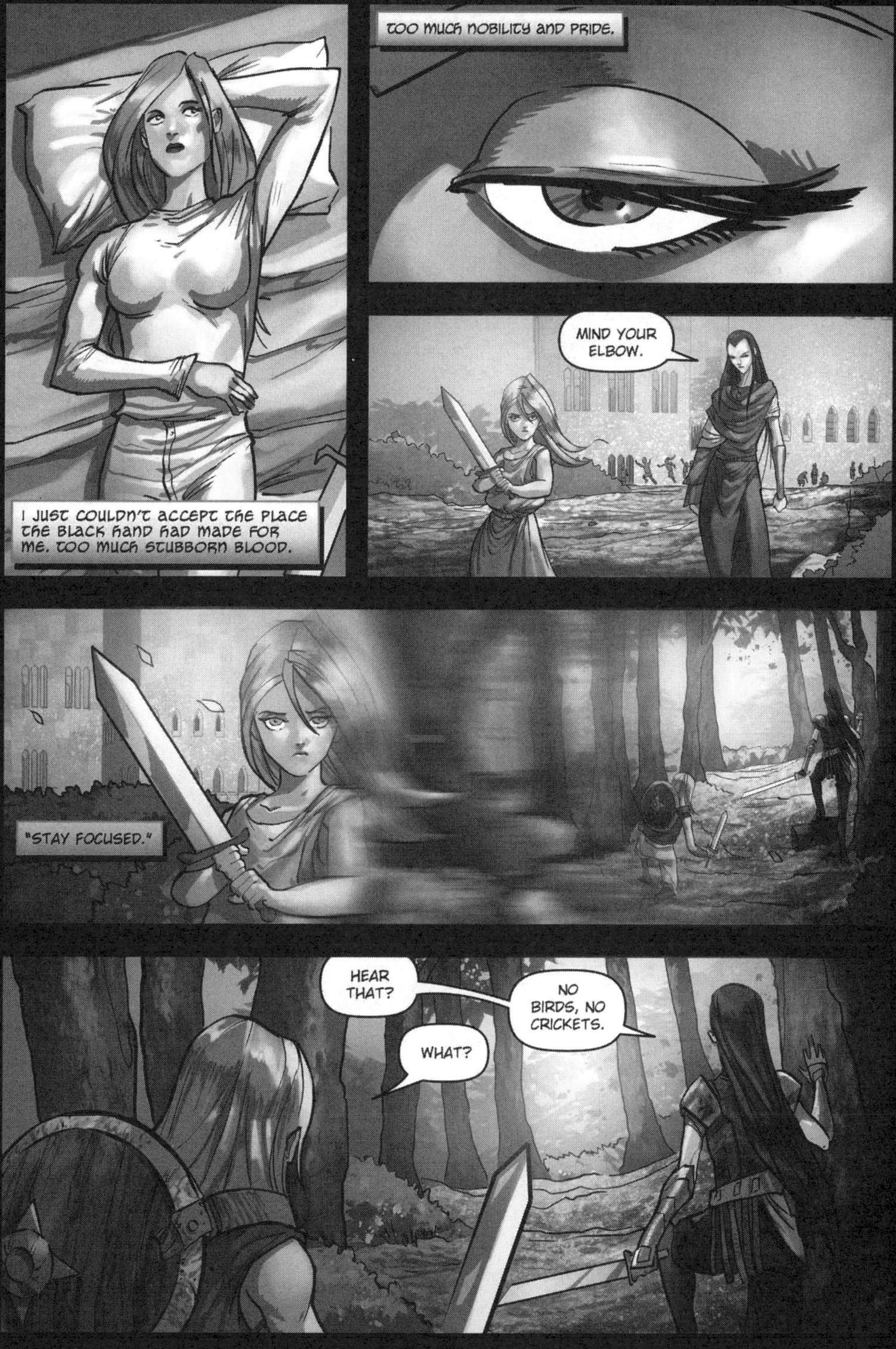
TOO MUCH NOBILITY AND PRIDE.
I JUST COULDN'T ACCEPT THE PLACE THE BLACK HAND HAD MADE FOR ME. TOO MUCH STUBBORN BLOOD.
MIND YOUR ELBOW.
"STAY FOCUSED."
HEAR THAT?
WHAT?
NO BIRDS, NO CRICKETS.

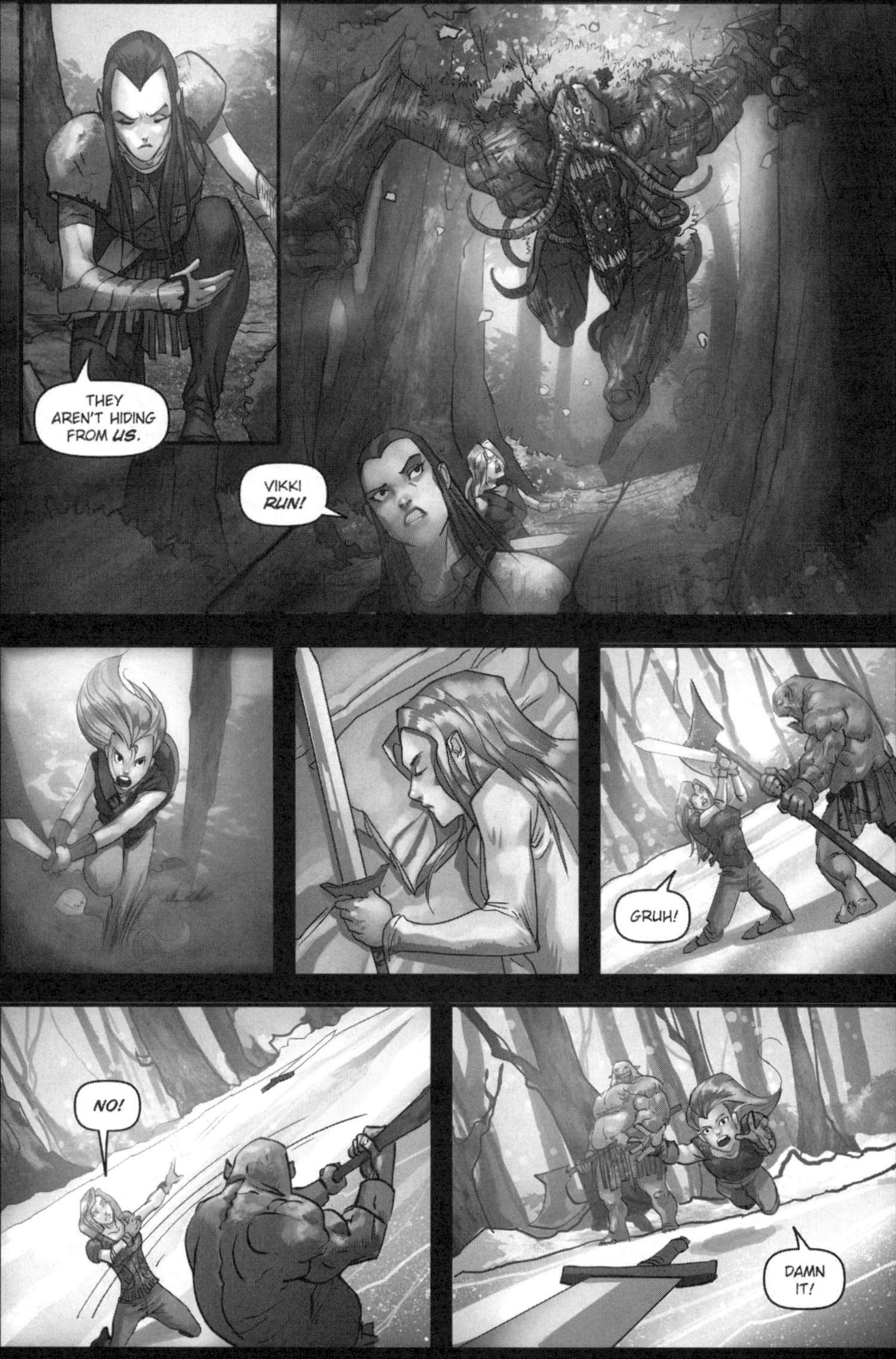
THEY AREN'T HIDING FROM *US*.
VIKKI *RUN!*
GRUH!
NO!
DAMN IT!

CONTINUED IN THE PAGES OF 'THE BLACK HAND'

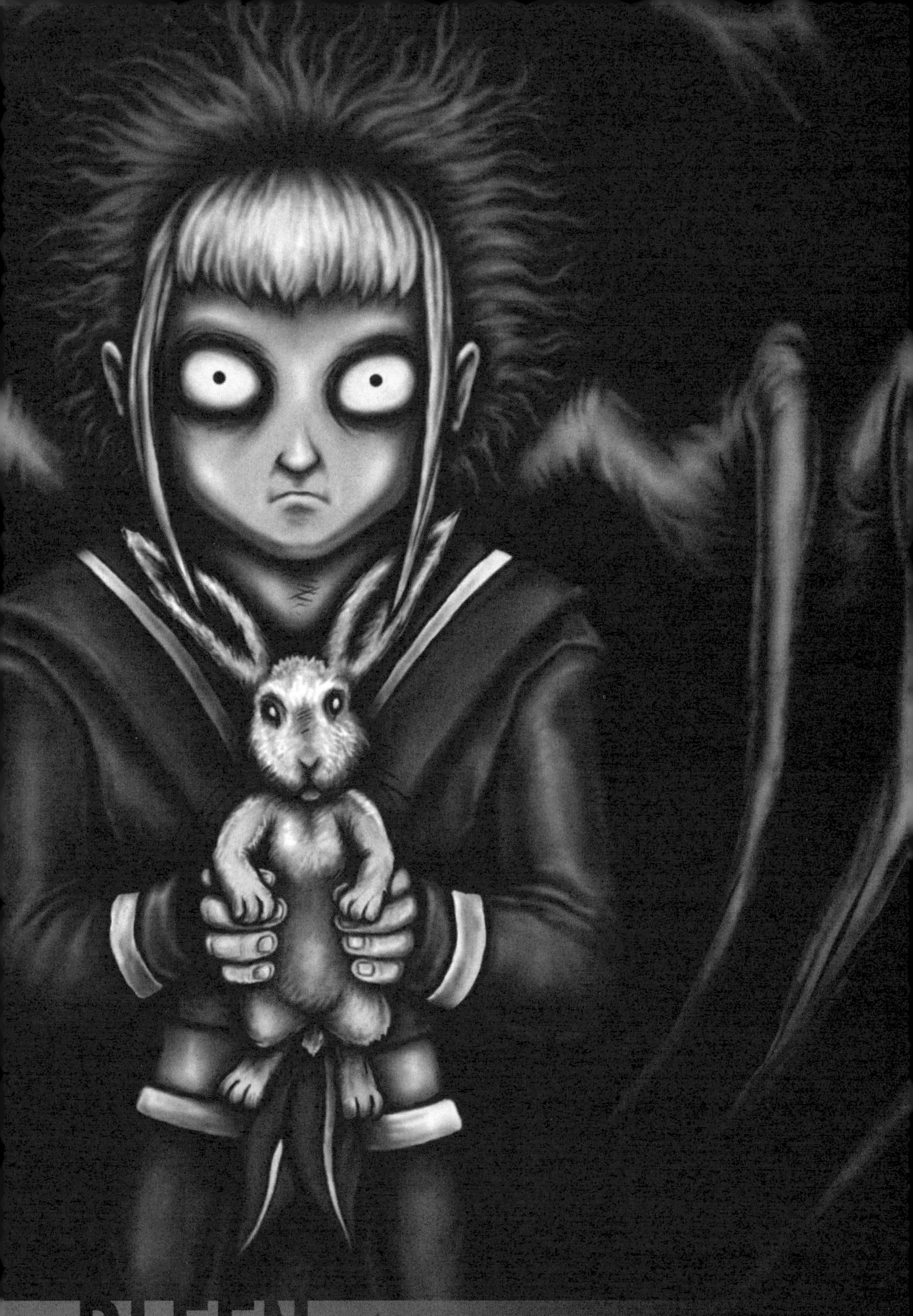

BLEEN

BLEEN

OBLEENA GRUNKEL

"Don't leave your bananas under the bed..."

Obleena (or Bleen) is full of mystery and darkness, plagued by nightmarish demons who speak horrible things to her. Wrongfully suspected for murdering her father, Bleen is committed to the Mayber Hills Sanitarium. Little does anyone know that the truth is far more sinister than they expected. Pushed to the brink, Bleen decides that she must escape the sanitarium, but not without a little help from her... *friends*.

Age: 15
Height: 5'2"
Weight: 105 lbs.

First Appearance:
BLEEN #1 (2014)

Created by
Jon A. Colunga
Illustration by
Landon Huber

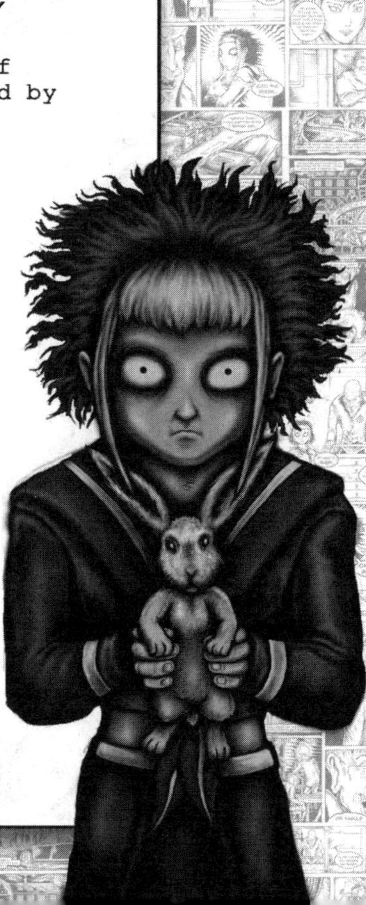

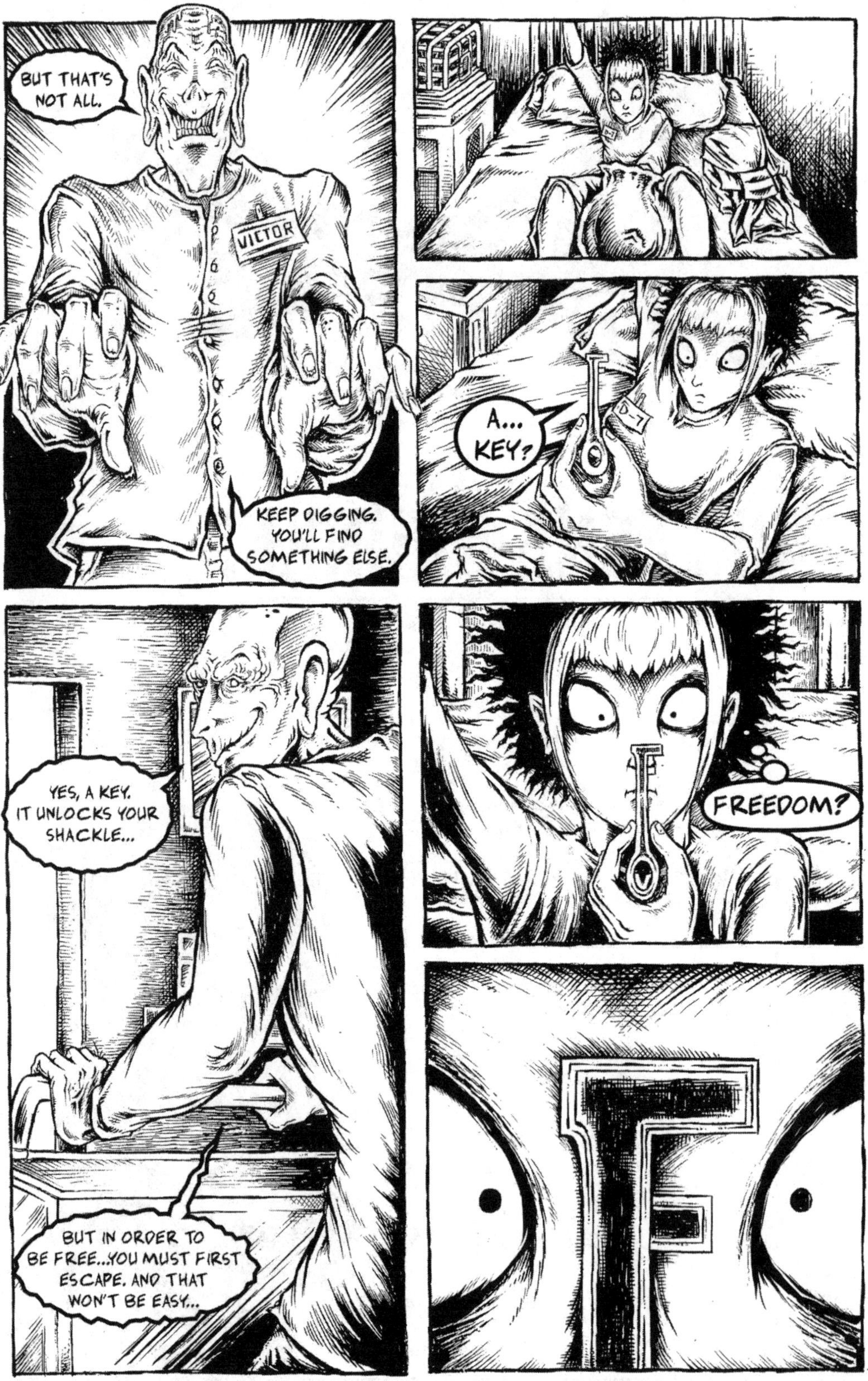
BUT THAT'S NOT ALL.
VICTOR
KEEP DIGGING. YOU'LL FIND SOMETHING ELSE.
D-7
A... KEY?
YES, A KEY. IT UNLOCKS YOUR SHACKLE...
FREEDOM?
BUT IN ORDER TO BE FREE...YOU MUST FIRST ESCAPE. AND THAT WON'T BE EASY...

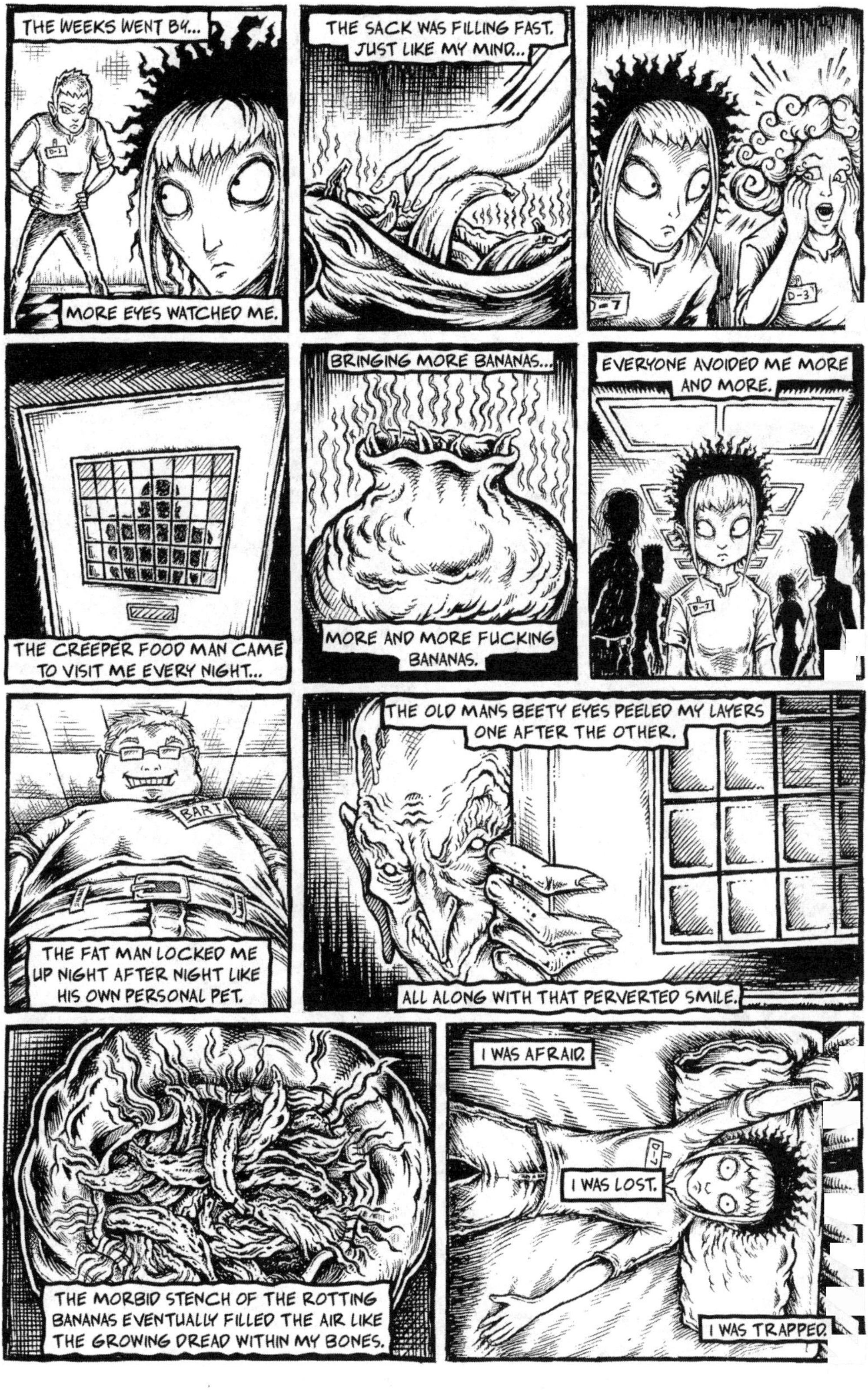
THE WEEKS WENT BY...
MORE EYES WATCHED ME.
THE SACK WAS FILLING FAST. JUST LIKE MY MIND...
THE CREEPER FOOD MAN CAME TO VISIT ME EVERY NIGHT...
BRINGING MORE BANANAS...
MORE AND MORE FUCKING BANANAS.
EVERYONE AVOIDED ME MORE AND MORE.
BARTA
THE FAT MAN LOCKED ME UP NIGHT AFTER NIGHT LIKE HIS OWN PERSONAL PET.
THE OLD MANS BEETY EYES PEELED MY LAYERS ONE AFTER THE OTHER.
ALL ALONG WITH THAT PERVERTED SMILE.
THE MORBID STENCH OF THE ROTTING BANANAS EVENTUALLY FILLED THE AIR LIKE THE GROWING DREAD WITHIN MY BONES.
I WAS AFRAID.
I WAS LOST.
I WAS TRAPPED.

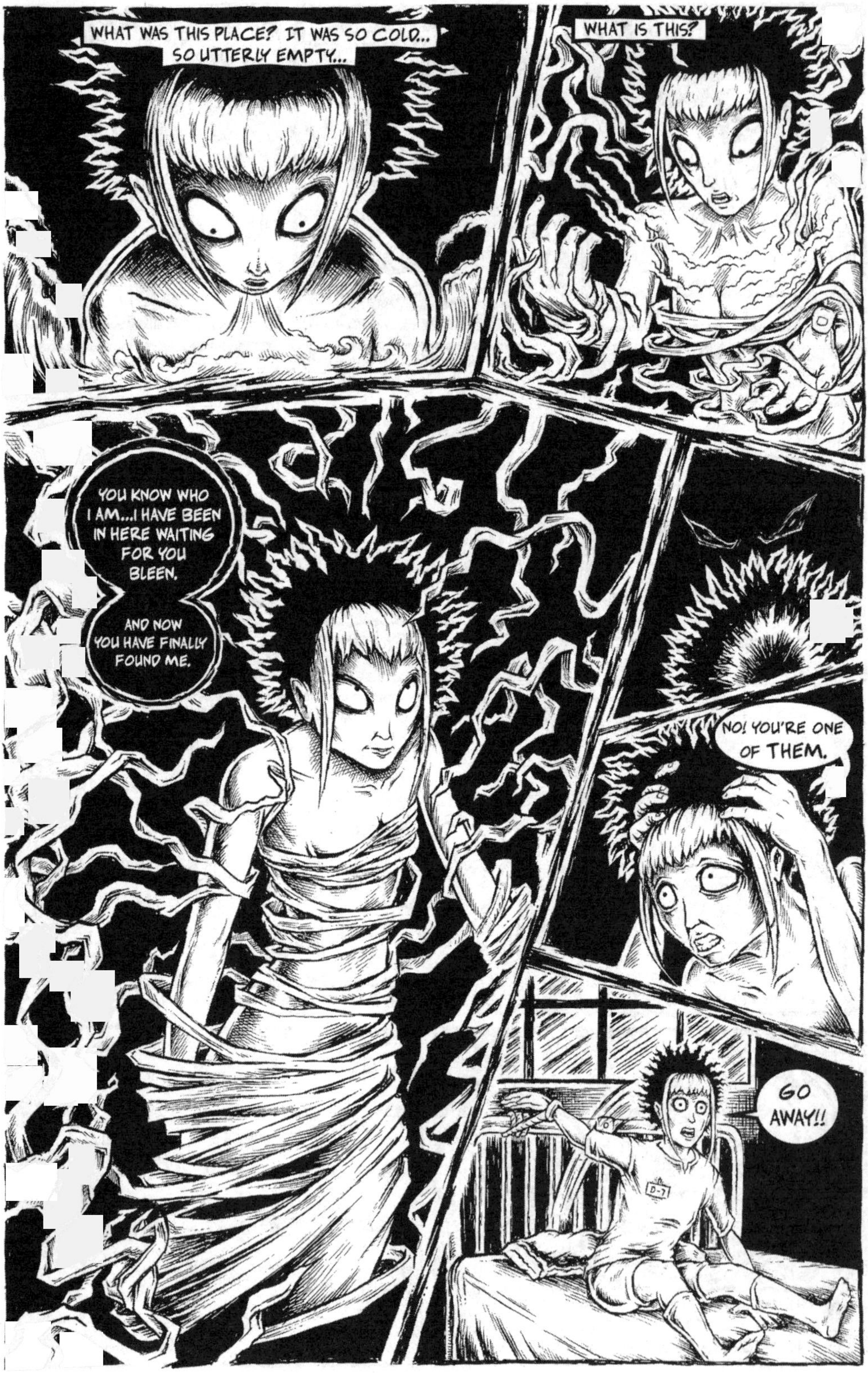
WHAT WAS THIS PLACE? IT WAS SO COLD... SO UTTERLY EMPTY...
WHAT IS THIS?
YOU KNOW WHO I AM...I HAVE BEEN IN HERE WAITING FOR YOU BLEEN.
AND NOW YOU HAVE FINALLY FOUND ME.
NO! YOU'RE ONE OF THEM.
GO AWAY!!
D-7

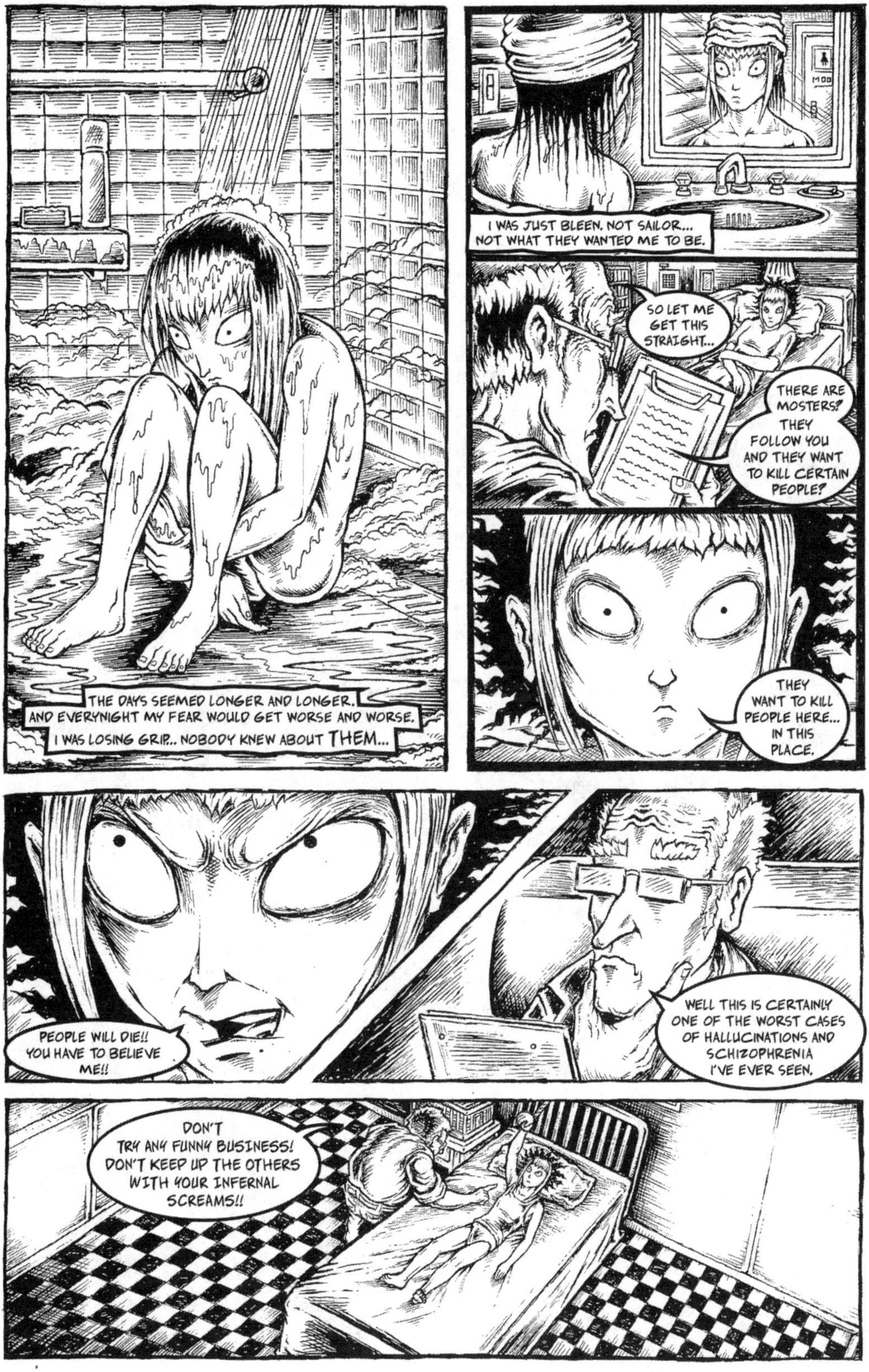
THE DAYS SEEMED LONGER AND LONGER.
AND EVERYNIGHT MY FEAR WOULD GET WORSE AND WORSE.
I WAS LOSING GRIP... NOBODY KNEW ABOUT THEM...
I WAS JUST BLEEN. NOT SAILOR... NOT WHAT THEY WANTED ME TO BE.
SO LET ME GET THIS STRAIGHT...
THERE ARE MOSTERS? THEY FOLLOW YOU AND THEY WANT TO KILL CERTAIN PEOPLE?
THEY WAN'T TO KILL PEOPLE HERE... IN THIS PLACE.
PEOPLE WILL DIE!! YOU HAVE TO BELIEVE ME!!
WELL THIS IS CERTAINLY ONE OF THE WORST CASES OF HALLUCINATIONS AND SCHIZOPHRENIA I'VE EVER SEEN.
DON'T TRY ANY FUNNY BUSINESS! DON'T KEEP UP THE OTHERS WITH YOUR INFERNAL SCREAMS!!

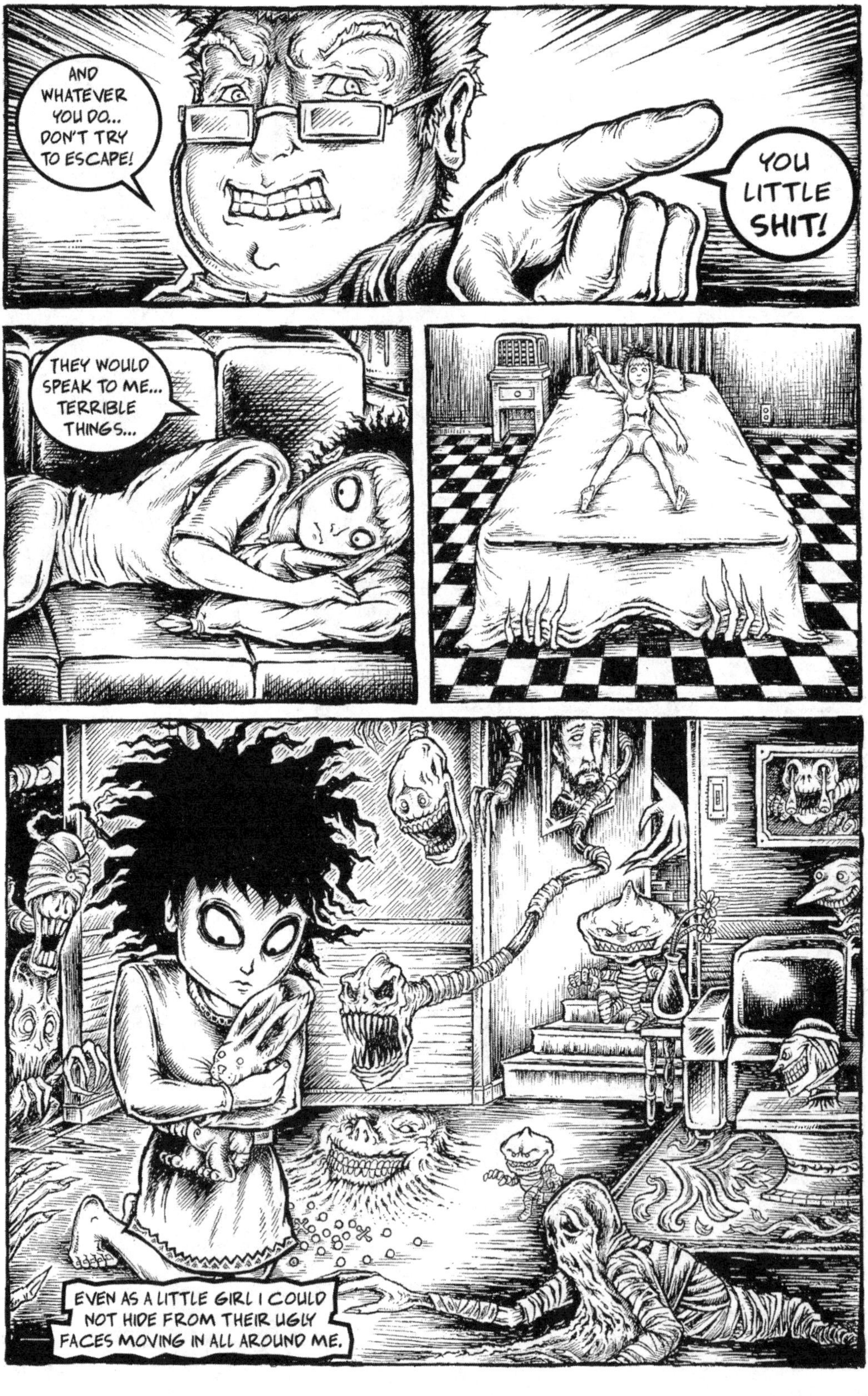
AND WHATEVER YOU DO... DON'T TRY TO ESCAPE!
YOU LITTLE SHIT!
THEY WOULD SPEAK TO ME... TERRIBLE THINGS...
EVEN AS A LITTLE GIRL I COULD NOT HIDE FROM THEIR UGLY FACES MOVING IN ALL AROUND ME.

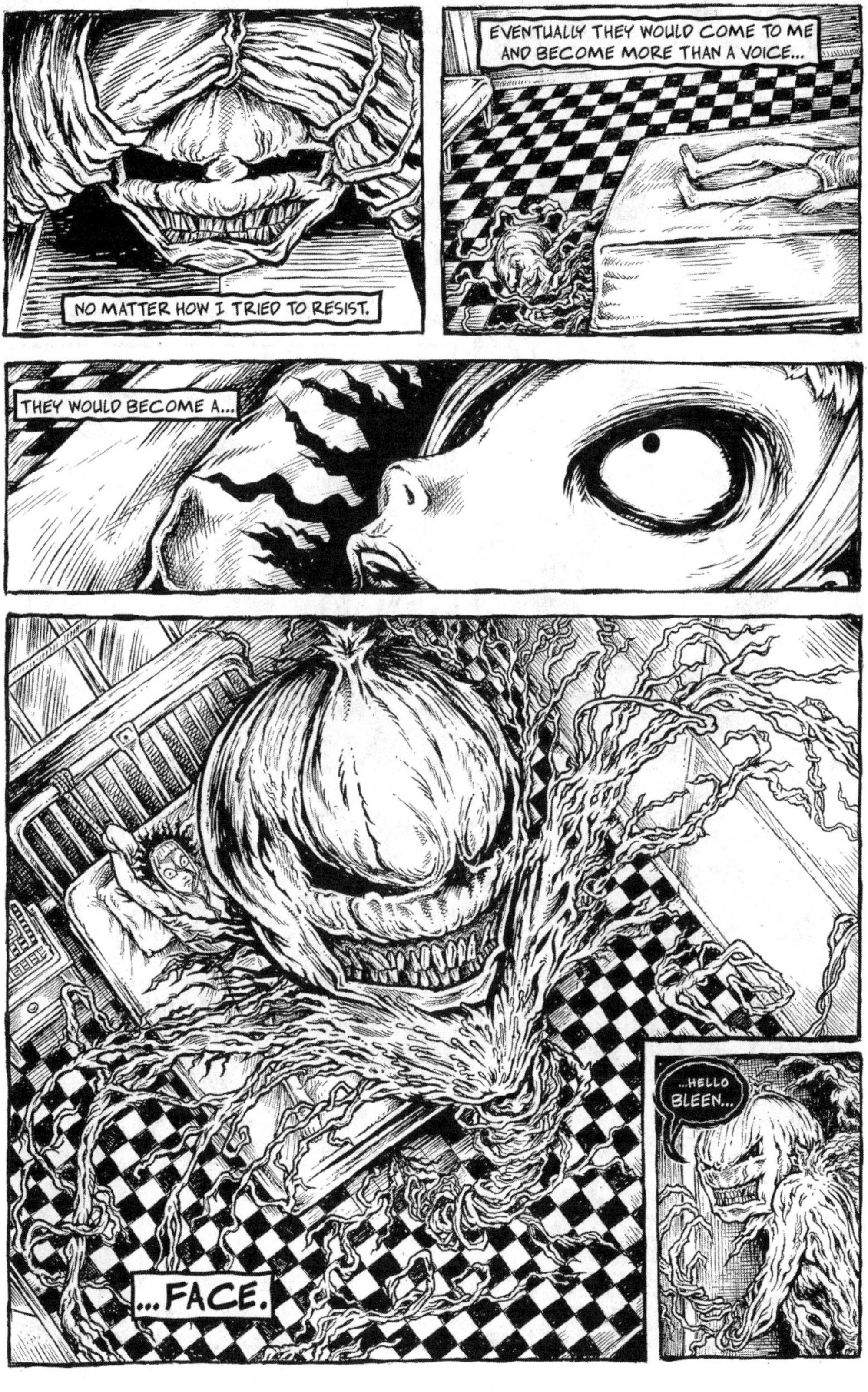
NO MATTER HOW I TRIED TO RESIST.
EVENTUALLY THEY WOULD COME TO ME AND BECOME MORE THAN A VOICE...
THEY WOULD BECOME A...
...FACE.
...HELLO BLEEN...

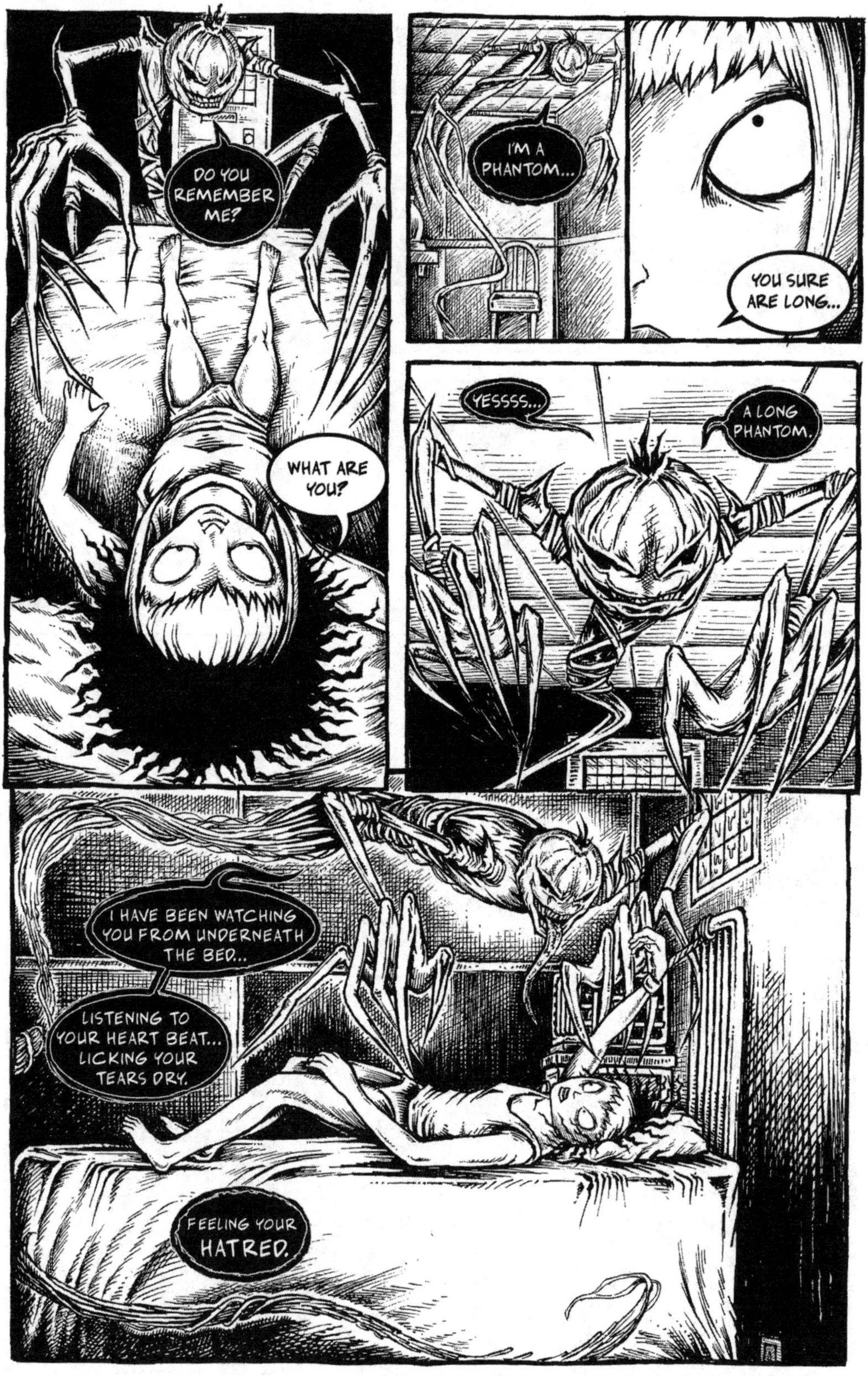
DO YOU REMEMBER ME?
WHAT ARE YOU?
I'M A PHANTOM...
YOU SURE ARE LONG...
YESSSS...
A LONG PHANTOM.
I HAVE BEEN WATCHING YOU FROM UNDERNEATH THE BED...
LISTENING TO YOUR HEART BEAT... LICKING YOUR TEARS DRY.
FEELING YOUR HATRED.

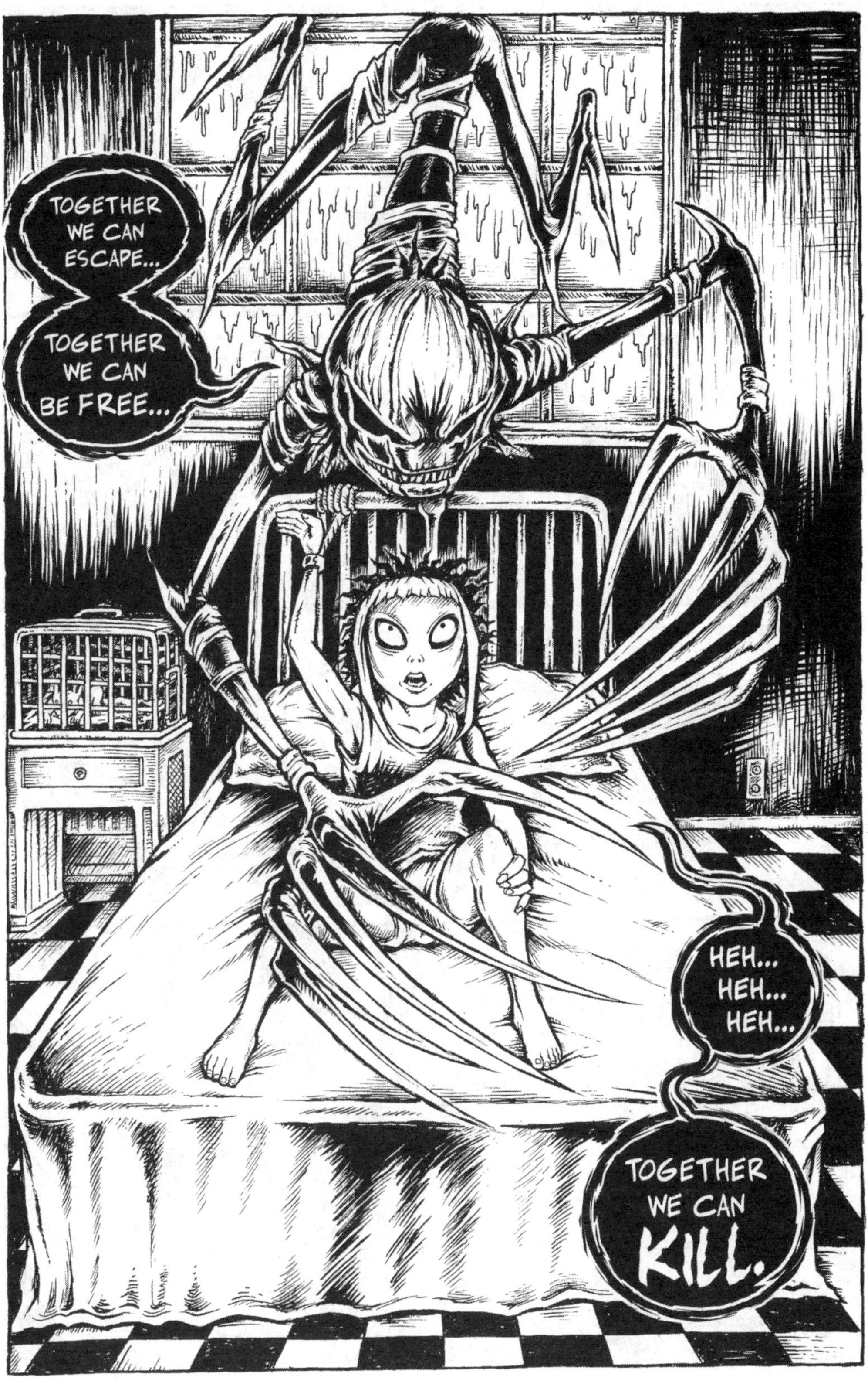
TOGETHER WE CAN ESCAPE...
TOGETHER WE CAN BE FREE...
HEH... HEH... HEH...
TOGETHER WE CAN KILL.

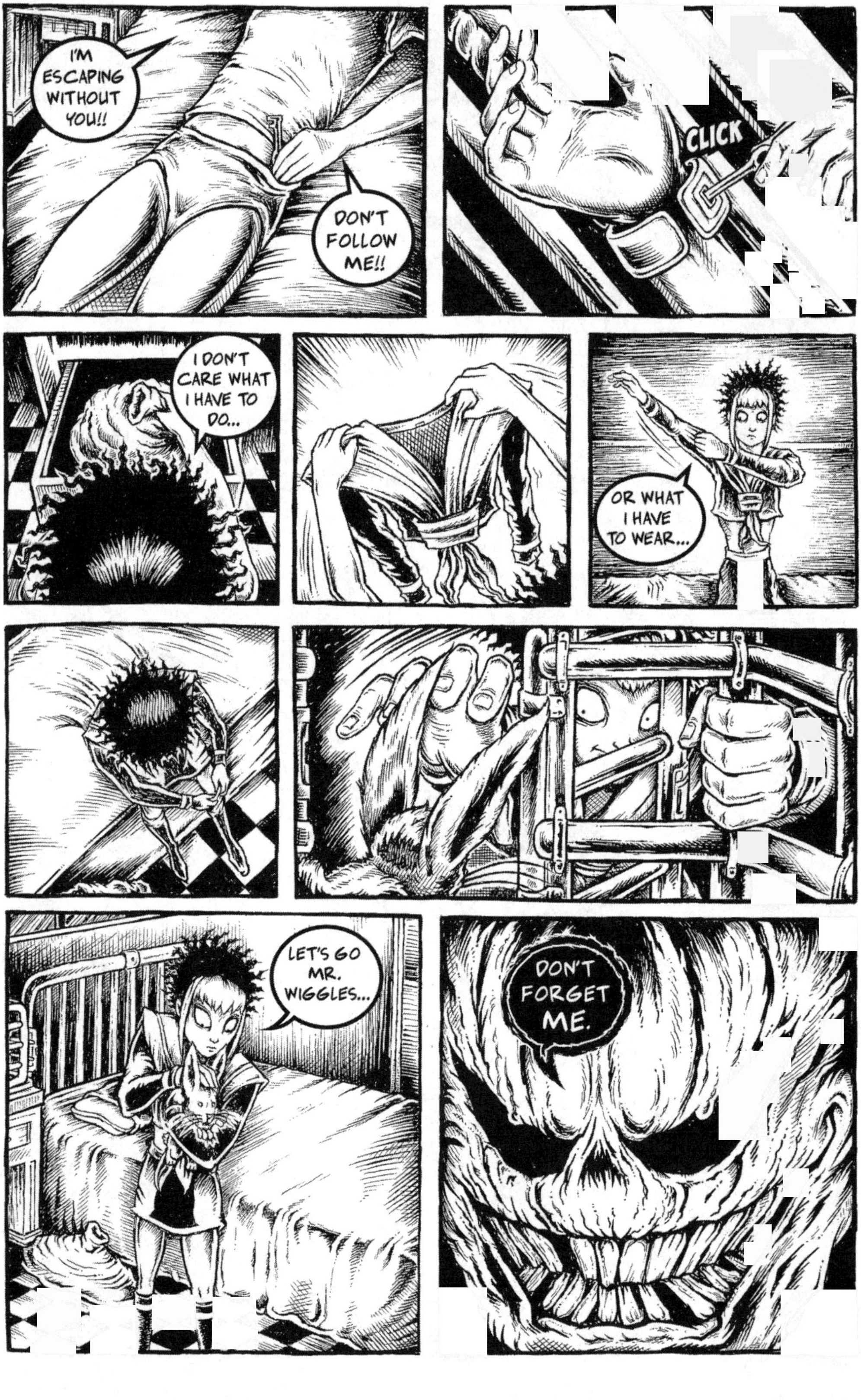
I'M ESCAPING WITHOUT YOU!!
DON'T FOLLOW ME!!
CLICK
I DON'T CARE WHAT I HAVE TO DO...
OR WHAT I HAVE TO WEAR...
LET'S GO MR. WIGGLES...
DON'T FORGET ME.

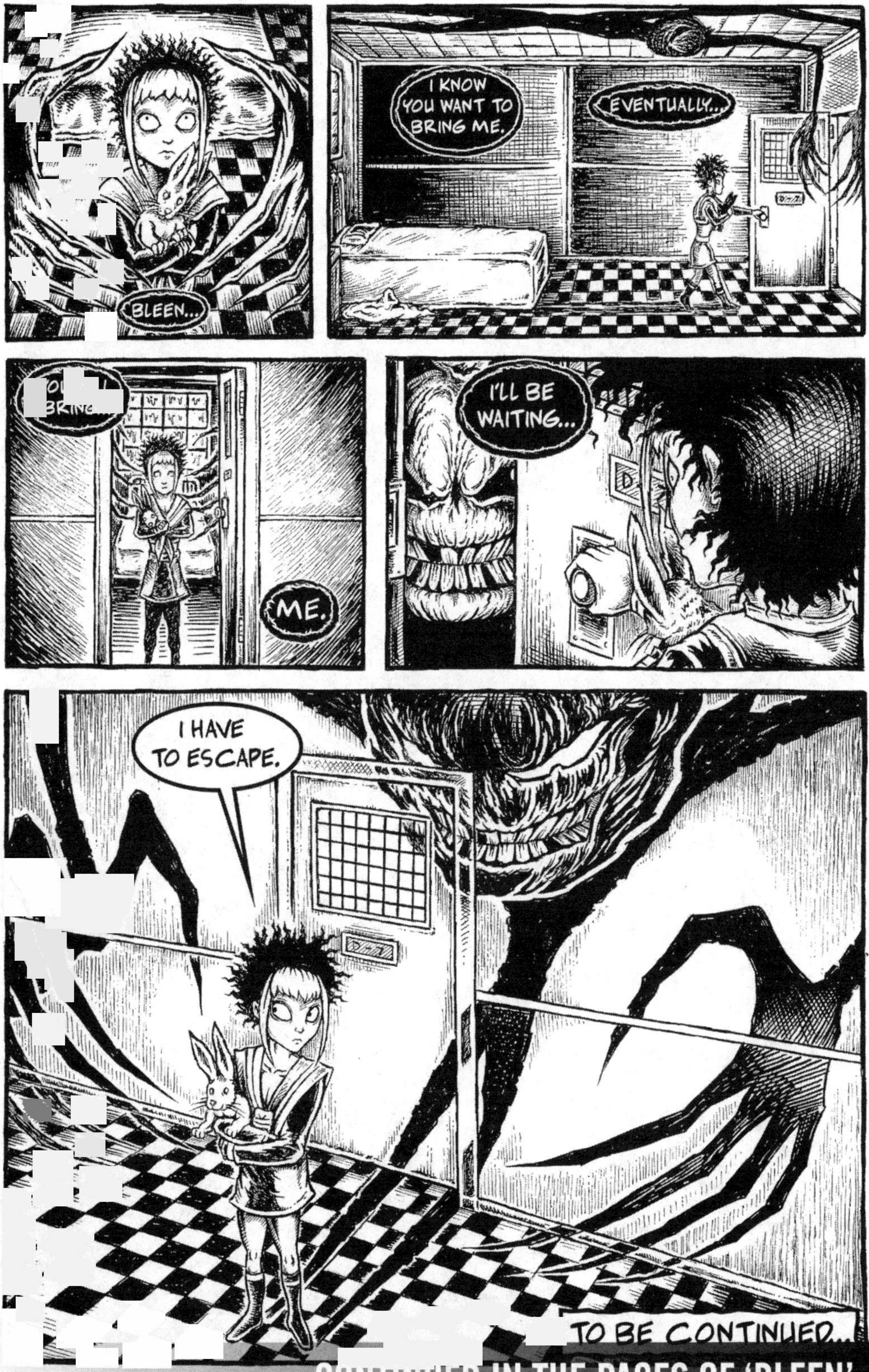
BLEEN...
I KNOW YOU WANT TO BRING ME.
EVENTUALLY...
ME.
I'LL BE WAITING...
I HAVE TO ESCAPE.
TO BE CONTINUED...

CONTINUED IN THE PAGES OF 'BLEEN'

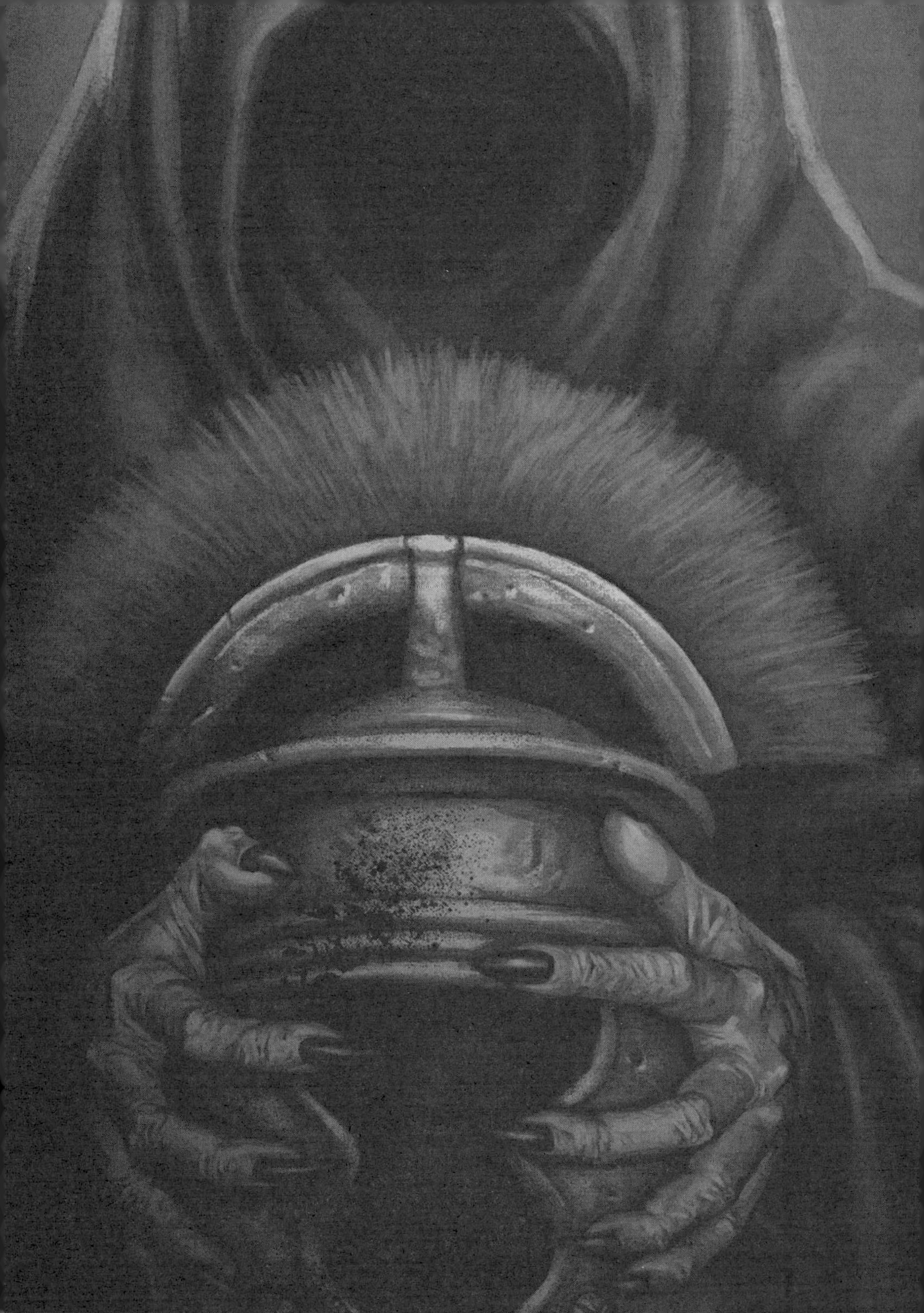

BLOOD FOR STONE

BLOOD FOR STONE

VELKA

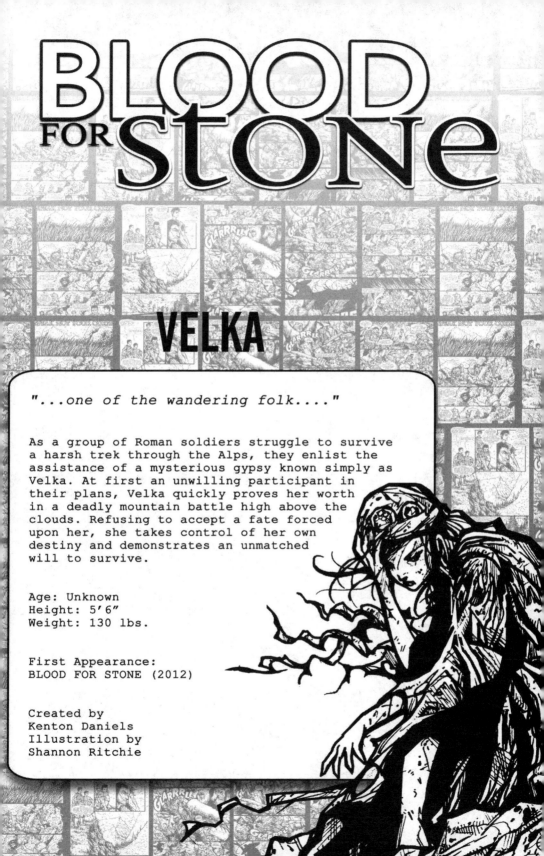

"...one of the wandering folk...."

As a group of Roman soldiers struggle to survive a harsh trek through the Alps, they enlist the assistance of a mysterious gypsy known simply as Velka. At first an unwilling participant in their plans, Velka quickly proves her worth in a deadly mountain battle high above the clouds. Refusing to accept a fate forced upon her, she takes control of her own destiny and demonstrates an unmatched will to survive.

Age: Unknown
Height: 5'6"
Weight: 130 lbs.

First Appearance:
BLOOD FOR STONE (2012)

Created by
Kenton Daniels
Illustration by
Shannon Ritchie

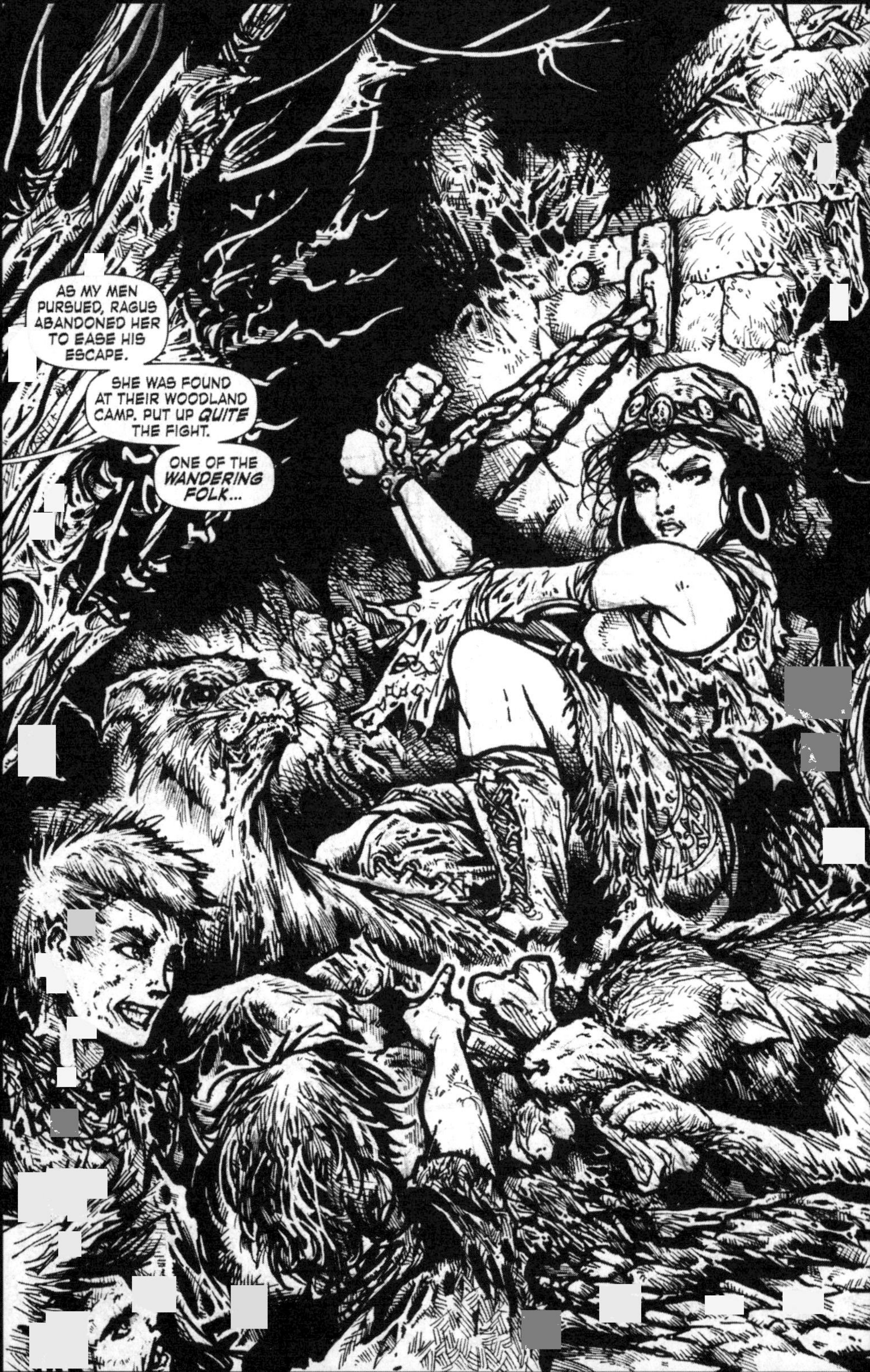
AS MY MEN PURSUED, RAGUS ABANDONED HER TO EASE HIS ESCAPE.
SHE WAS FOUND AT THEIR WOODLAND CAMP. PUT UP QUITE THE FIGHT.
ONE OF THE WANDERING FOLK...

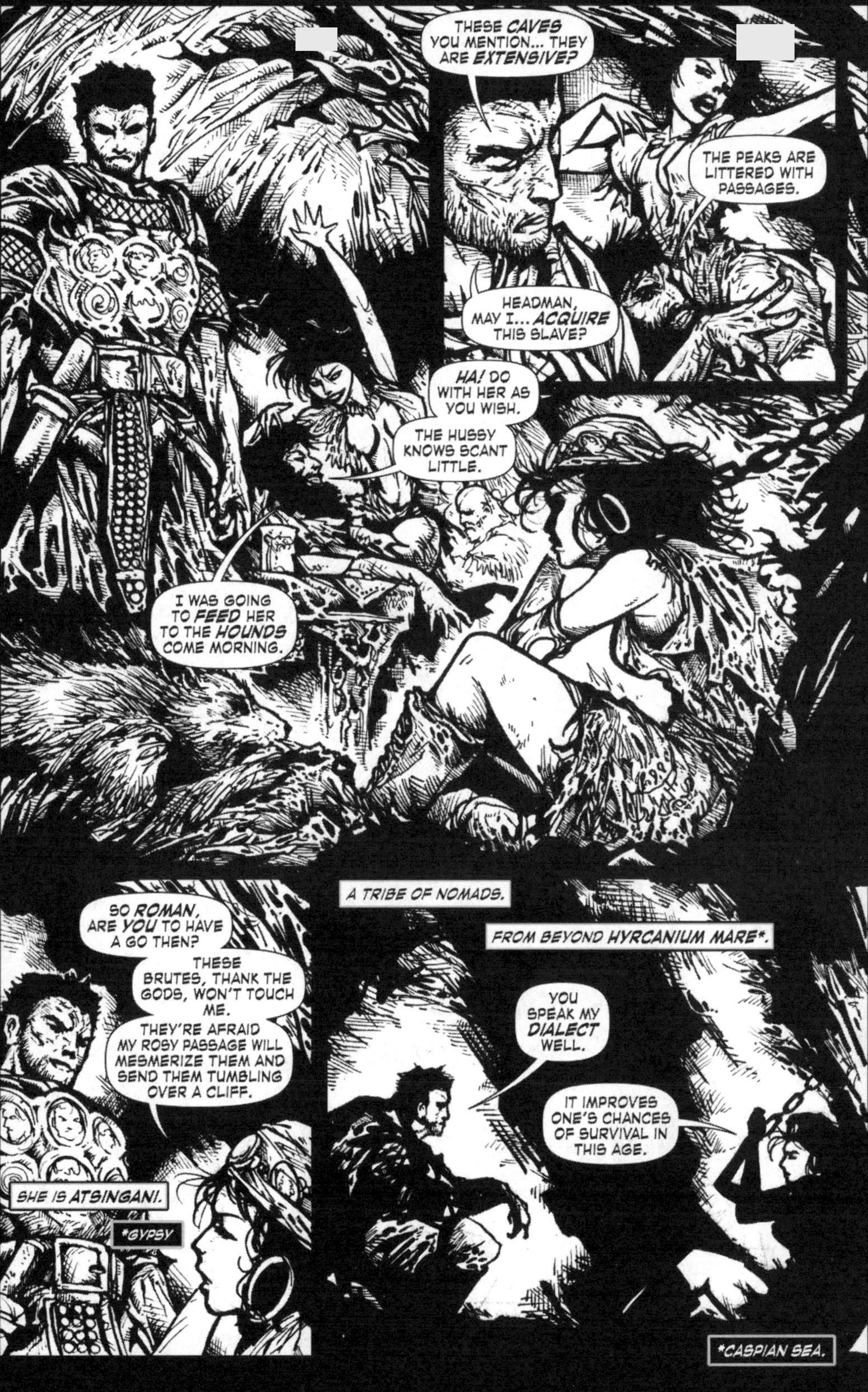
THESE CAVES YOU MENTION... THEY ARE EXTENSIVE?
THE PEAKS ARE LITTERED WITH PASSAGES.
HEADMAN, MAY I... ACQUIRE THIS SLAVE?
HA! DO WITH HER AS YOU WISH.
THE HUSSY KNOWS SCANT LITTLE.
I WAS GOING TO FEED HER TO THE HOUNDS COME MORNING.
SO ROMAN, ARE YOU TO HAVE A GO THEN?
THESE BRUTES, THANK THE GODS, WON'T TOUCH ME.
THEY'RE AFRAID MY ROSY PASSAGE WILL MESMERIZE THEM AND SEND THEM TUMBLING OVER A CLIFF.
SHE IS ATSINGANI.
*GYPSY
A TRIBE OF NOMADS.
FROM BEYOND HYRCANIUM MARE*.
YOU SPEAK MY DIALECT WELL.
IT IMPROVES ONE'S CHANCES OF SURVIVAL IN THIS AGE.
*CASPIAN SEA.

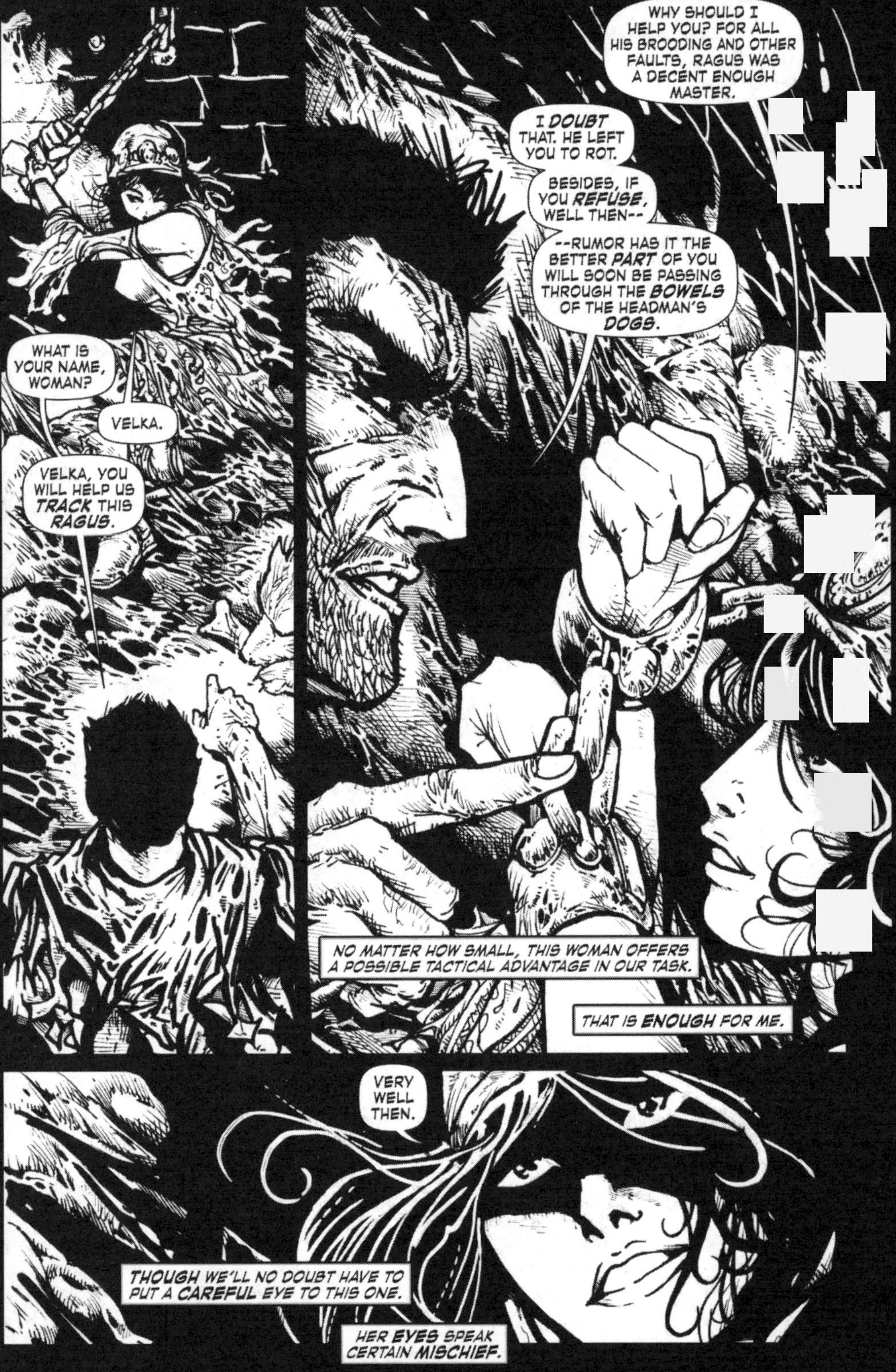
WHAT IS YOUR NAME, WOMAN?
VELKA.
VELKA, YOU WILL HELP US TRACK THIS RAGUS.
WHY SHOULD I HELP YOU? FOR ALL HIS BROODING AND OTHER FAULTS, RAGUS WAS A DECENT ENOUGH MASTER.
I DOUBT THAT. HE LEFT YOU TO ROT.
BESIDES, IF YOU REFUSE, WELL THEN--
--RUMOR HAS IT THE BETTER PART OF YOU WILL SOON BE PASSING THROUGH THE BOWELS OF THE HEADMAN'S DOGS.
NO MATTER HOW SMALL, THIS WOMAN OFFERS A POSSIBLE TACTICAL ADVANTAGE IN OUR TASK.
THAT IS ENOUGH FOR ME.
VERY WELL THEN.
THOUGH WE'LL NO DOUBT HAVE TO PUT A CAREFUL EYE TO THIS ONE.
HER EYES SPEAK CERTAIN MISCHIEF.

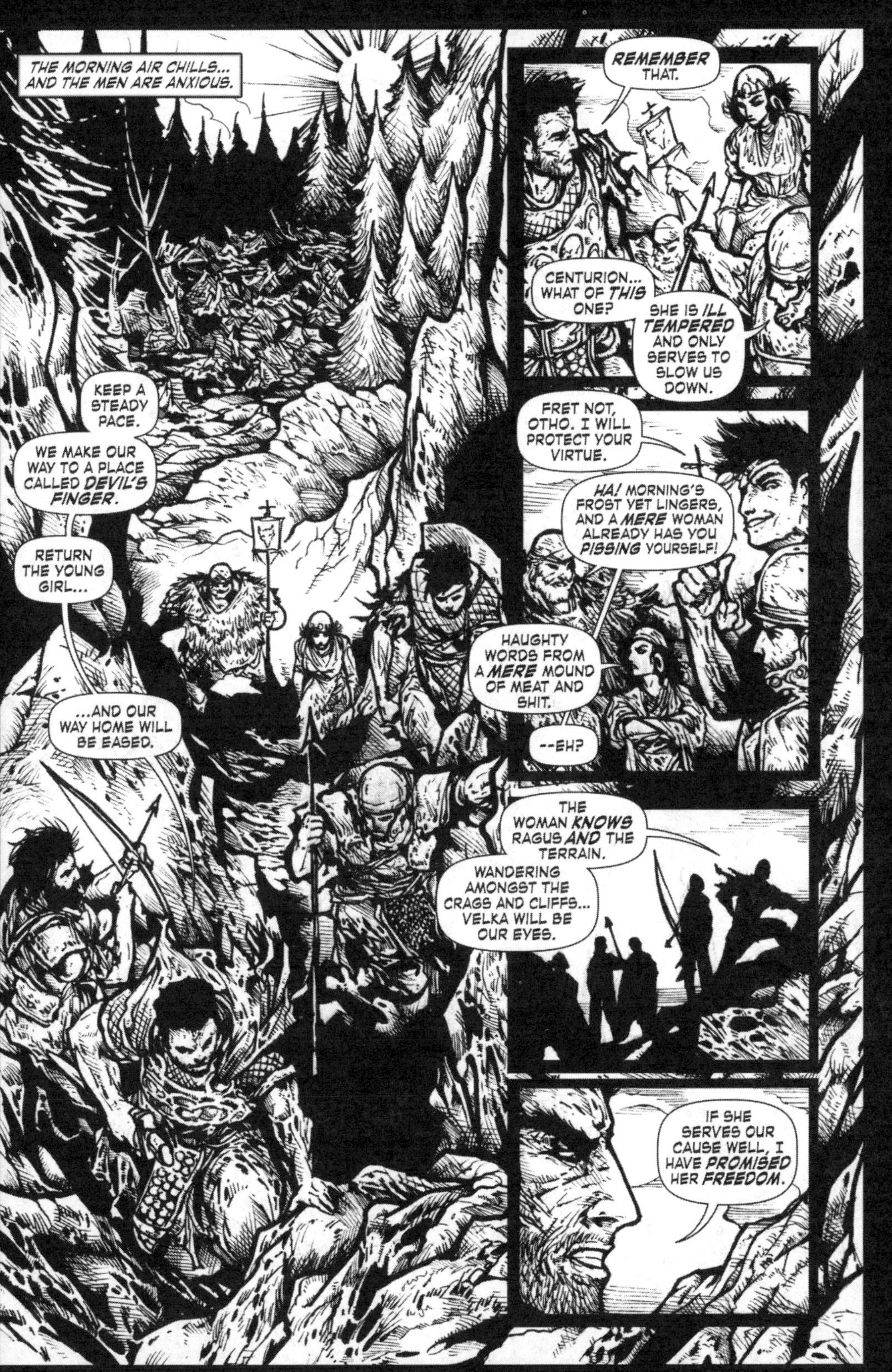
THE MORNING AIR CHILLS... AND THE MEN ARE ANXIOUS.
KEEP A STEADY PACE.
WE MAKE OUR WAY TO A PLACE CALLED DEVIL'S FINGER.
RETURN THE YOUNG GIRL...
...AND OUR WAY HOME WILL BE EASED.
REMEMBER THAT.
CENTURION... WHAT OF THIS ONE?
SHE IS ILL TEMPERED AND ONLY SERVES TO SLOW US DOWN.
FRET NOT, OTHO. I WILL PROTECT YOUR VIRTUE.
HA! MORNING'S FROST YET LINGERS, AND A MERE WOMAN ALREADY HAS YOU PISSING YOURSELF!
HAUGHTY WORDS FROM A MERE MOUND OF MEAT AND SHIT.
--EH?
THE WOMAN KNOWS RAGUS AND THE TERRAIN.
WANDERING AMONGST THE CRAGS AND CLIFFS... VELKA WILL BE OUR EYES.
IF SHE SERVES OUR CAUSE WELL, I HAVE PROMISED HER FREEDOM.

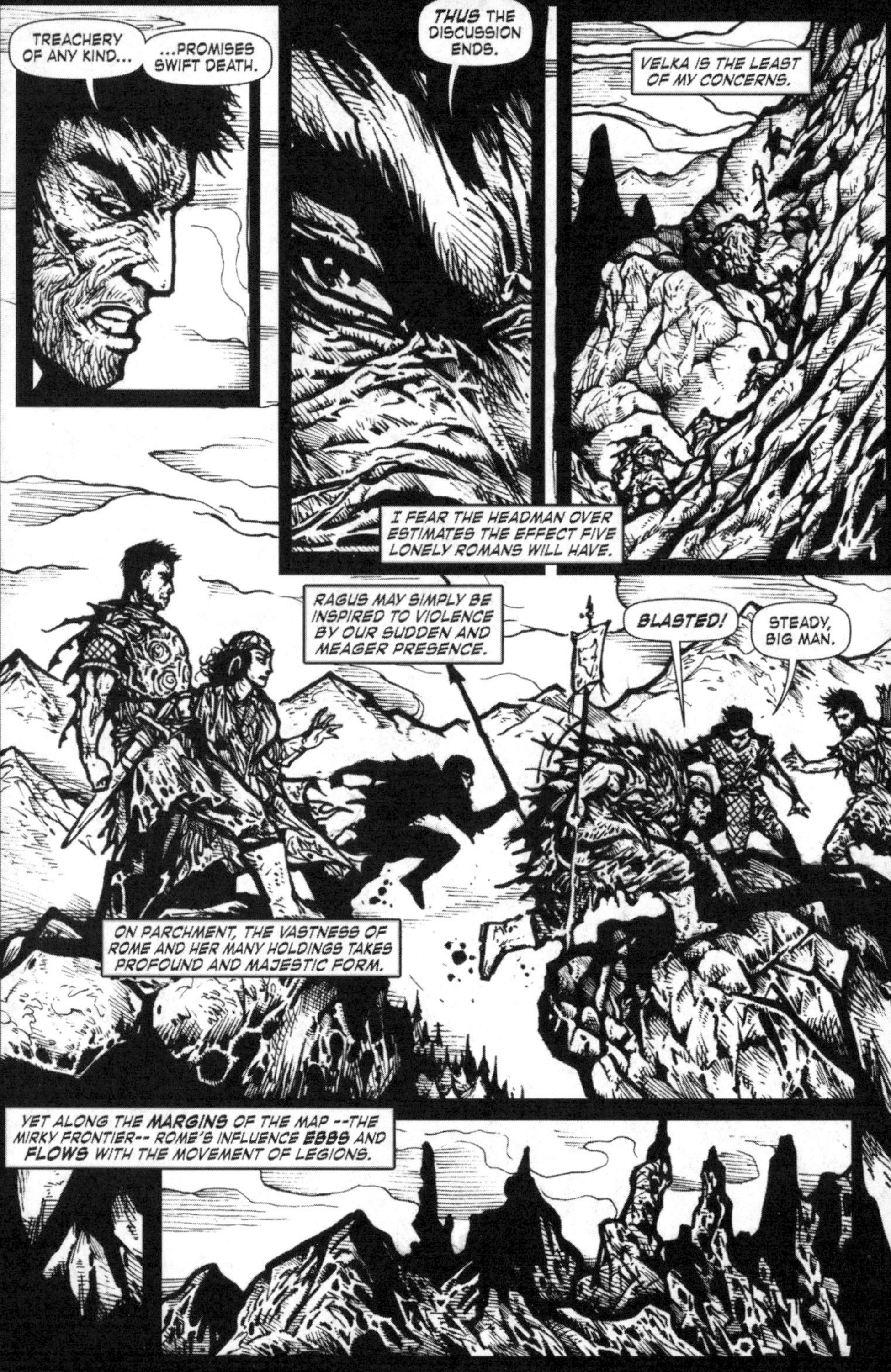
TREACHERY OF ANY KIND...
...PROMISES SWIFT DEATH.
THUS THE DISCUSSION ENDS.
VELKA IS THE LEAST OF MY CONCERNS.
I FEAR THE HEADMAN OVER ESTIMATES THE EFFECT FIVE LONELY ROMANS WILL HAVE.
RAGUS MAY SIMPLY BE INSPIRED TO VIOLENCE BY OUR SUDDEN AND MEAGER PRESENCE.
BLASTED!
STEADY, BIG MAN.
ON PARCHMENT, THE VASTNESS OF ROME AND HER MANY HOLDINGS TAKES PROFOUND AND MAJESTIC FORM.
YET ALONG THE MARGINS OF THE MAP --THE MIRKY FRONTIER-- ROME'S INFLUENCE EBBS AND FLOWS WITH THE MOVEMENT OF LEGIONS.

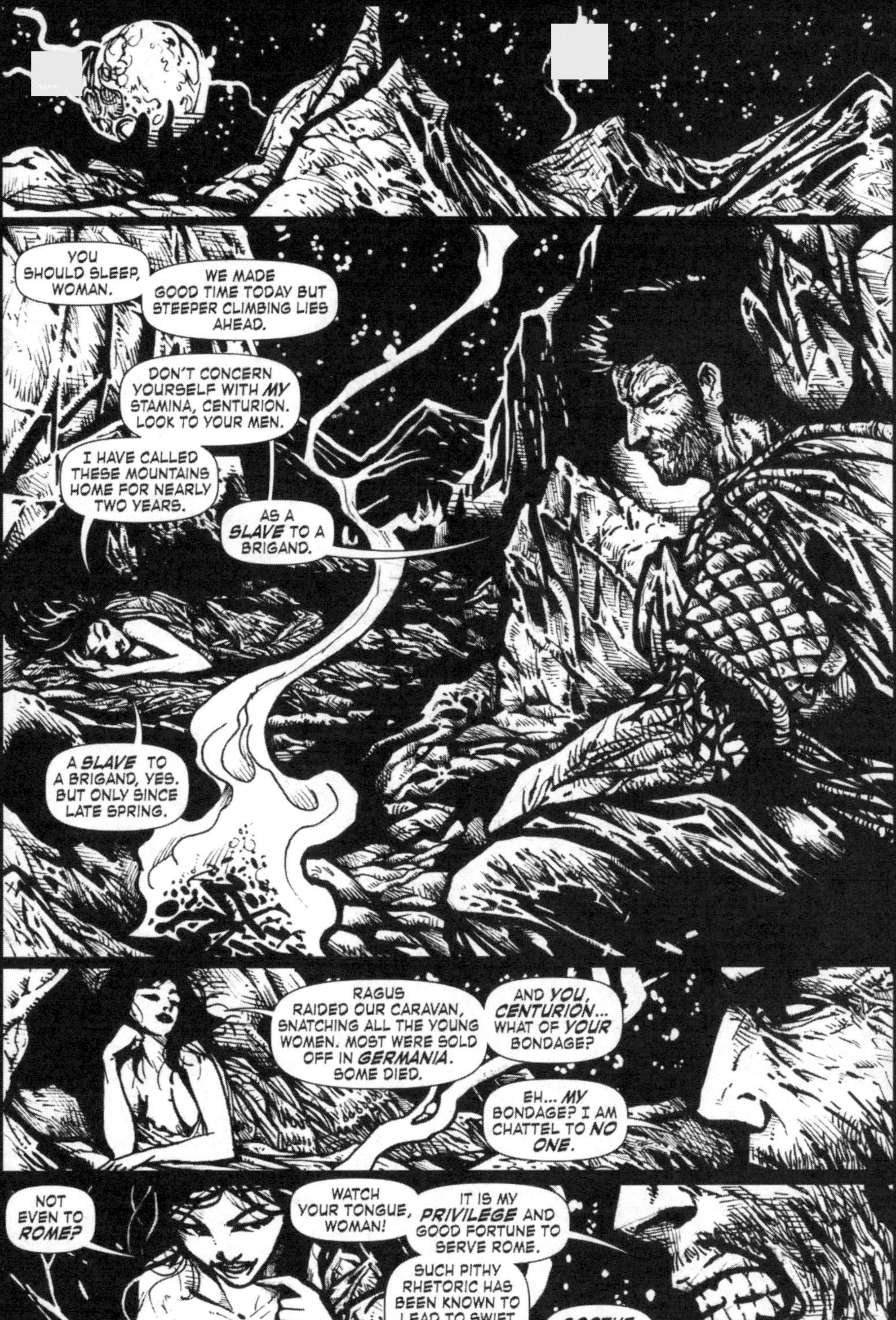
YOU SHOULD SLEEP, WOMAN.
WE MADE GOOD TIME TODAY BUT STEEPER CLIMBING LIES AHEAD.
DON'T CONCERN YOURSELF WITH MY STAMINA, CENTURION. LOOK TO YOUR MEN.
I HAVE CALLED THESE MOUNTAINS HOME FOR NEARLY TWO YEARS.
AS A SLAVE TO A BRIGAND.
A SLAVE TO A BRIGAND, YES. BUT ONLY SINCE LATE SPRING.
RAGUS RAIDED OUR CARAVAN, SNATCHING ALL THE YOUNG WOMEN. MOST WERE SOLD OFF IN GERMANIA. SOME DIED.
AND YOU, CENTURION... WHAT OF YOUR BONDAGE?
EH... MY BONDAGE? I AM CHATTEL TO NO ONE.
NOT EVEN TO ROME?
WATCH YOUR TONGUE, WOMAN!
IT IS MY PRIVILEGE AND GOOD FORTUNE TO SERVE ROME.
SUCH PITHY RHETORIC HAS BEEN KNOWN TO LEAD TO SWIFT AND PAIN-FILLED REBUTTAL.
SOOTHE YOURSELF, CENTURION. I MEANT NO OFFENSE.

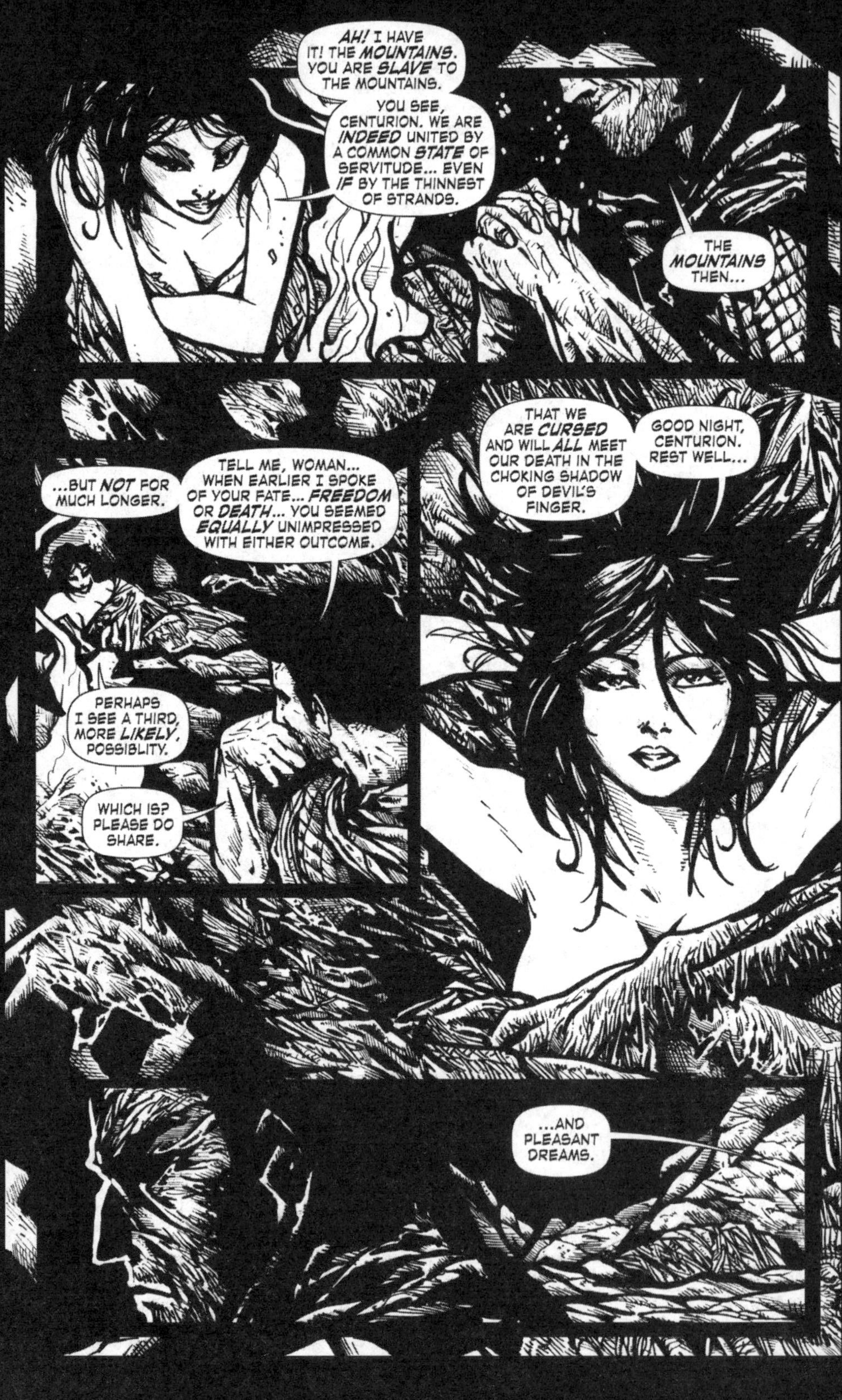
AH! I HAVE IT! THE MOUNTAINS. YOU ARE SLAVE TO THE MOUNTAINS.
YOU SEE, CENTURION. WE ARE INDEED UNITED BY A COMMON STATE OF SERVITUDE... EVEN IF BY THE THINNEST OF STRANDS.
THE MOUNTAINS THEN...
...BUT NOT FOR MUCH LONGER.
TELL ME, WOMAN... WHEN EARLIER I SPOKE OF YOUR FATE... FREEDOM OR DEATH... YOU SEEMED EQUALLY UNIMPRESSED WITH EITHER OUTCOME.
PERHAPS I SEE A THIRD, MORE LIKELY, POSSIBLITY.
WHICH IS? PLEASE DO SHARE.
THAT WE ARE CURSED AND WILL ALL MEET OUR DEATH IN THE CHOKING SHADOW OF DEVIL'S FINGER.
GOOD NIGHT, CENTURION. REST WELL...
...AND PLEASANT DREAMS.

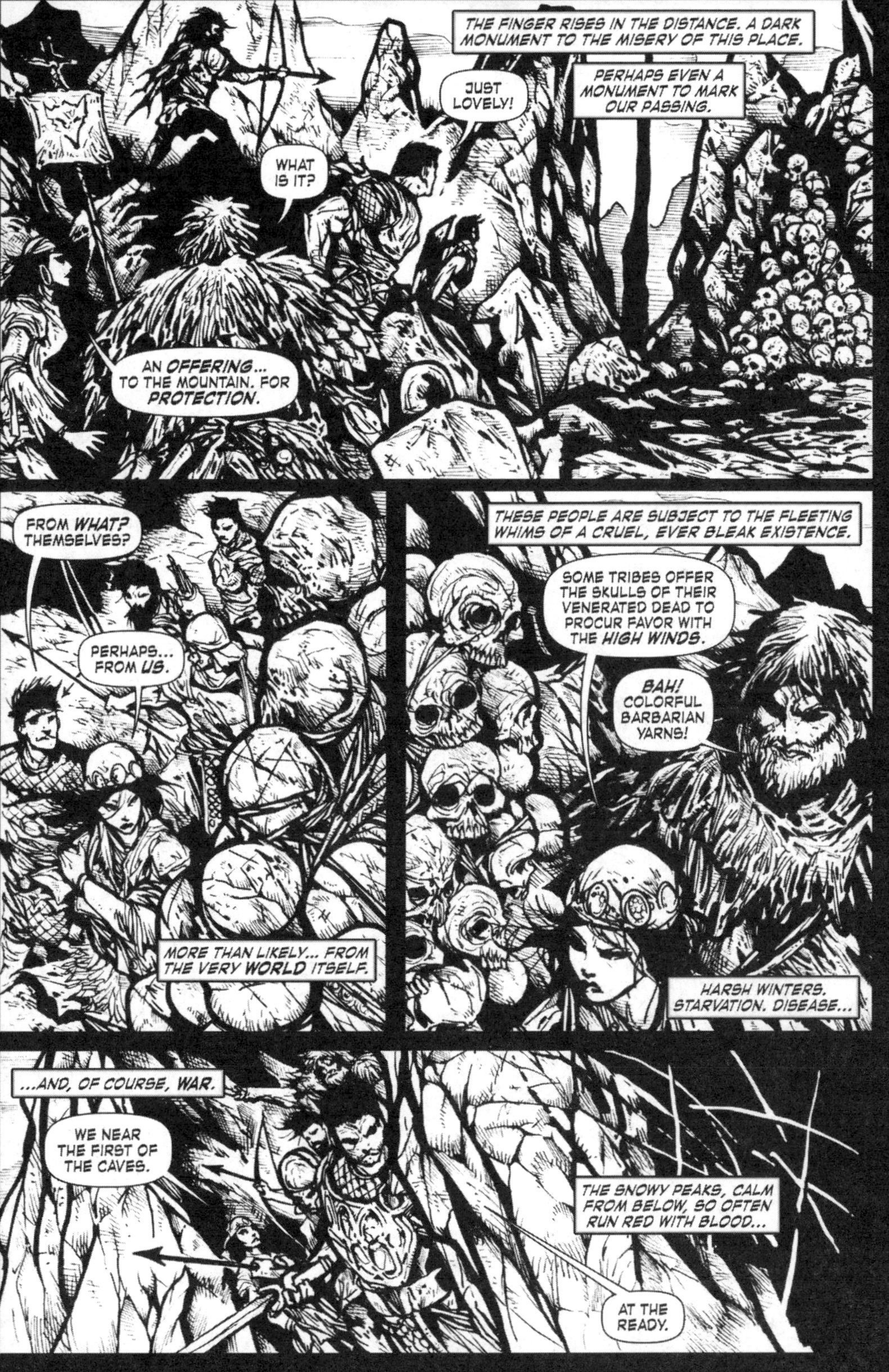
THE FINGER RISES IN THE DISTANCE. A DARK MONUMENT TO THE MISERY OF THIS PLACE.
JUST LOVELY!
PERHAPS EVEN A MONUMENT TO MARK OUR PASSING.
WHAT IS IT?
AN OFFERING... TO THE MOUNTAIN. FOR PROTECTION.
FROM WHAT? THEMSELVES?
PERHAPS... FROM US.
MORE THAN LIKELY... FROM THE VERY WORLD ITSELF.
THESE PEOPLE ARE SUBJECT TO THE FLEETING WHIMS OF A CRUEL, EVER BLEAK EXISTENCE.
SOME TRIBES OFFER THE SKULLS OF THEIR VENERATED DEAD TO PROCUR FAVOR WITH THE HIGH WINDS.
BAH! COLORFUL BARBARIAN YARNS!
HARSH WINTERS. STARVATION. DISEASE...
...AND, OF COURSE, WAR.
WE NEAR THE FIRST OF THE CAVES.
THE SNOWY PEAKS, CALM FROM BELOW, SO OFTEN RUN RED WITH BLOOD...
AT THE READY.

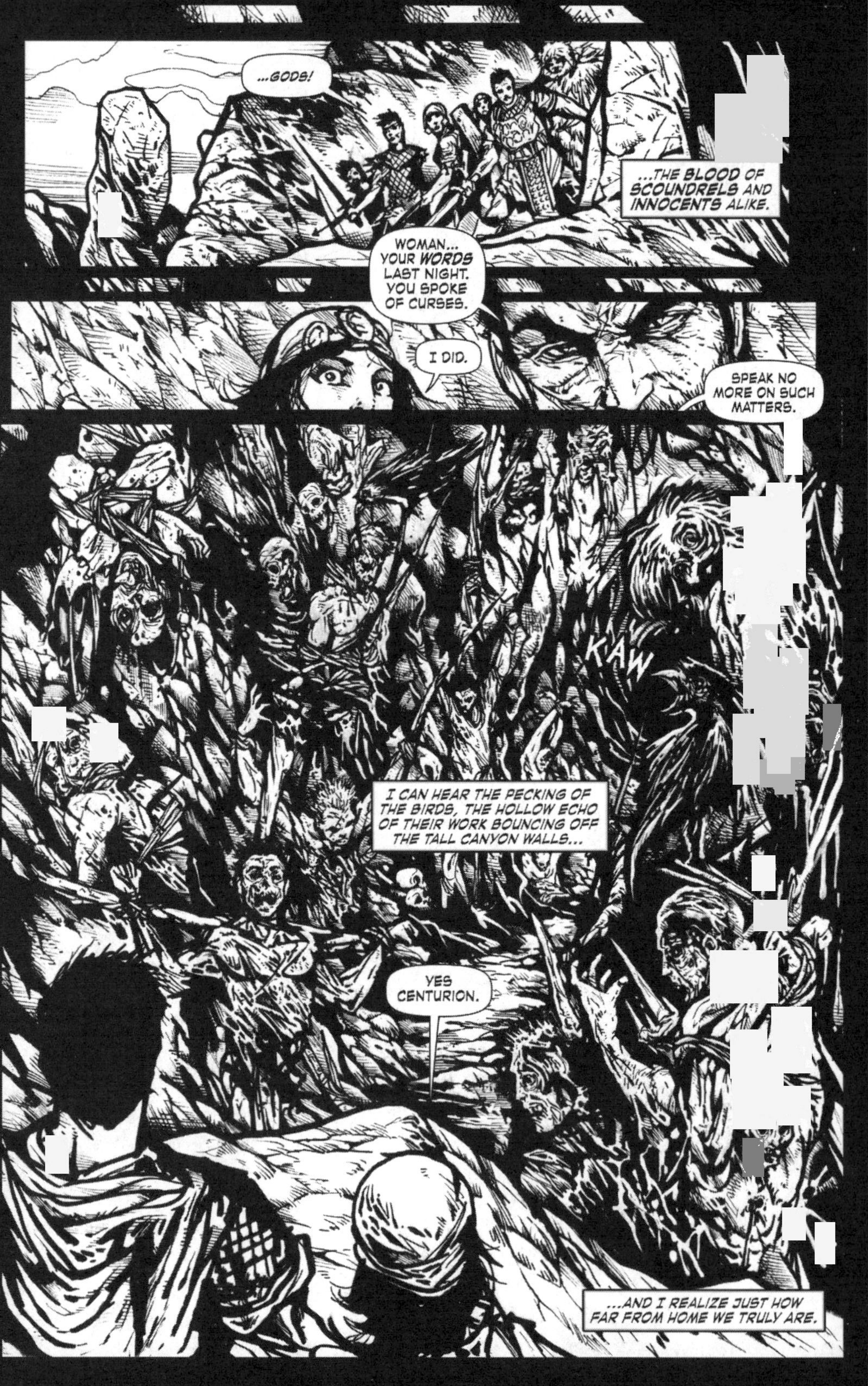
...GODS!
...THE BLOOD OF SCOUNDRELS AND INNOCENTS ALIKE.
WOMAN... YOUR WORDS LAST NIGHT. YOU SPOKE OF CURSES.
I DID.
SPEAK NO MORE ON SUCH MATTERS.
KAW
I CAN HEAR THE PECKING OF THE BIRDS, THE HOLLOW ECHO OF THEIR WORK BOUNCING OFF THE TALL CANYON WALLS...
YES CENTURION.
...AND I REALIZE JUST HOW FAR FROM HOME WE TRULY ARE.

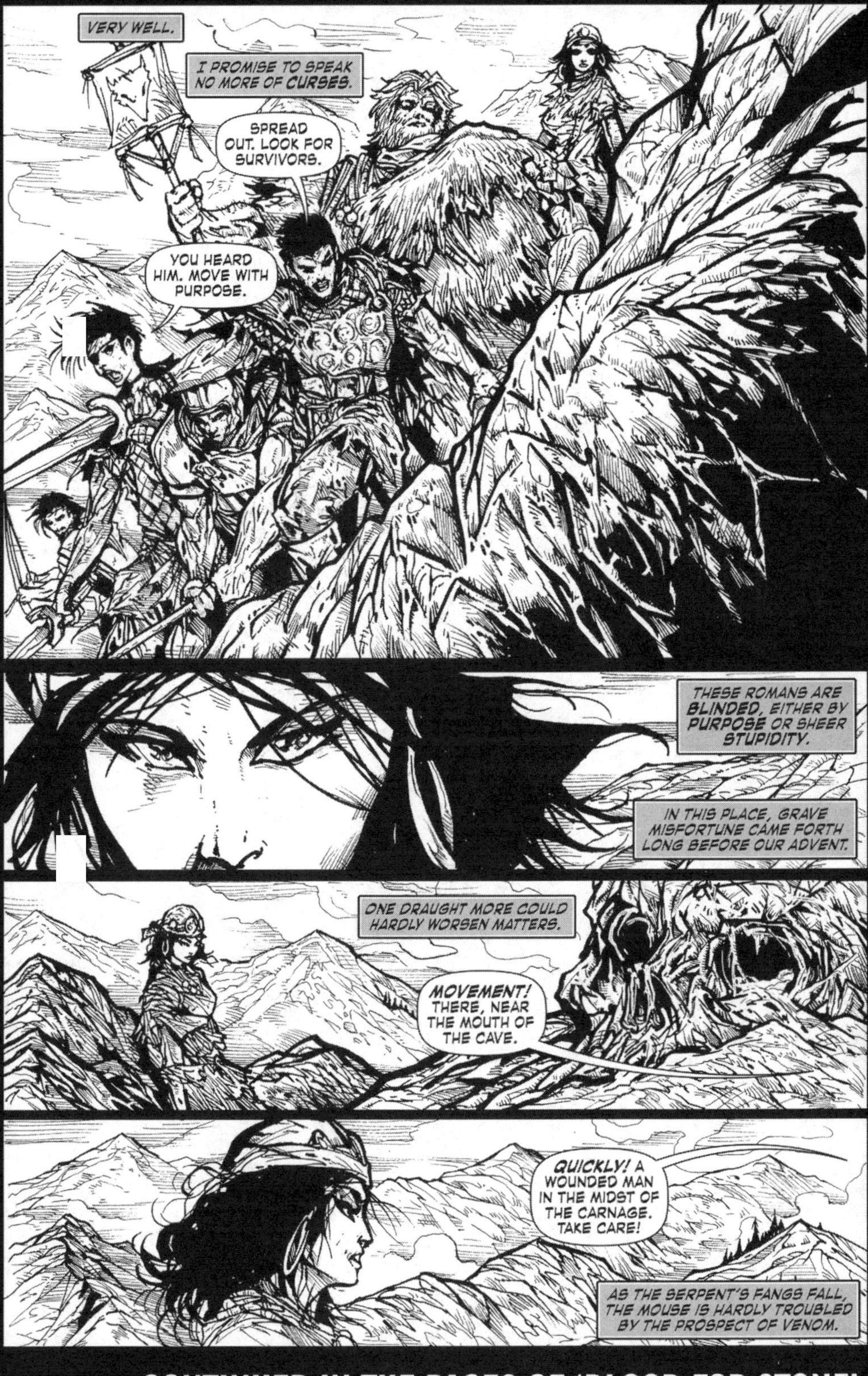
VERY WELL.
I PROMISE TO SPEAK NO MORE OF CURSES.
SPREAD OUT. LOOK FOR SURVIVORS.
YOU HEARD HIM. MOVE WITH PURPOSE.
THESE ROMANS ARE BLINDED, EITHER BY PURPOSE OR SHEER STUPIDITY.
IN THIS PLACE, GRAVE MISFORTUNE CAME FORTH LONG BEFORE OUR ADVENT.
ONE DRAUGHT MORE COULD HARDLY WORSEN MATTERS.
MOVEMENT! THERE, NEAR THE MOUTH OF THE CAVE.
QUICKLY! A WOUNDED MAN IN THE MIDST OF THE CARNAGE. TAKE CARE!
AS THE SERPENT'S FANGS FALL, THE MOUSE IS HARDLY TROUBLED BY THE PROSPECT OF VENOM.

CONTINUED IN THE PAGES OF 'BLOOD FOR STONE'

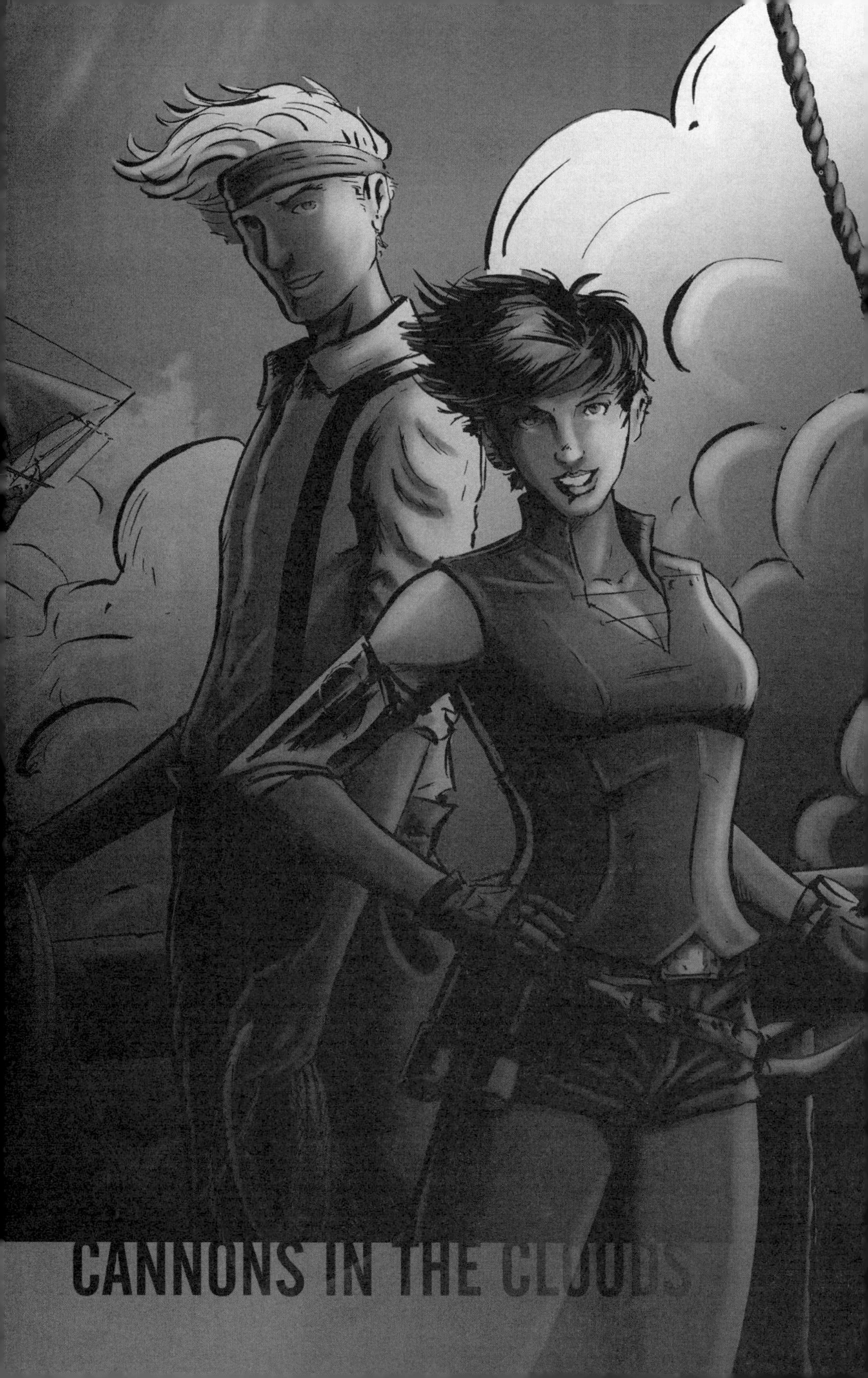

CANNONS IN THE CLOUDS

CANNONS IN THE CLOUDS

SELA & ROBB

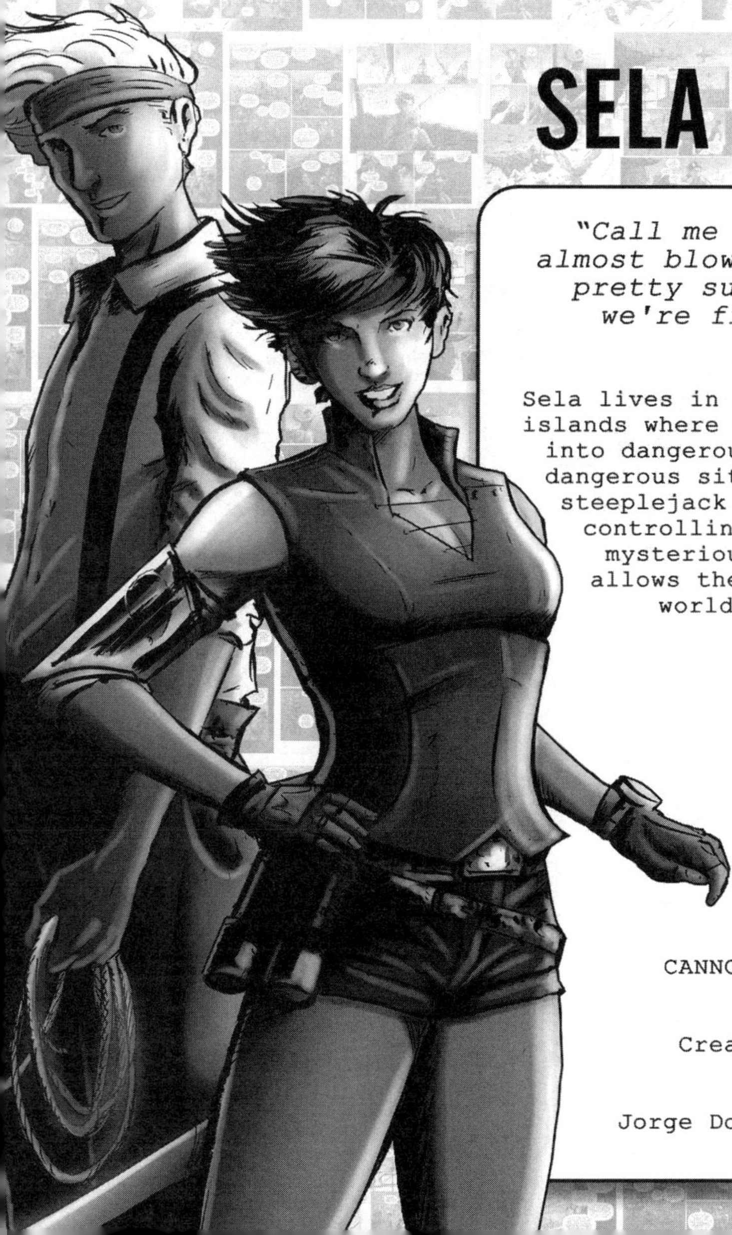

"Call me Sela! We were almost blown up together - pretty sure that means we're friends now."

Sela lives in a world of floating islands where she manages to dive into dangerous situation after dangerous situation. Robb is a steeplejack with a knack for controlling diametal, the mysterious alloy which allows the ships of this world to float.

Sela Windbourne
Age: 16
Height: 5'2"
Weight: 110 lbs.

Robert Cadman
Age: 17
Height: 5'10"
Weight: 160 lbs.

First appearance:
CANNONS IN THE CLOUDS #1
(2014)

Created by Anne Gresham
and Daniel Woolley
Illustration by
Jorge Donis and Kirsty Swan

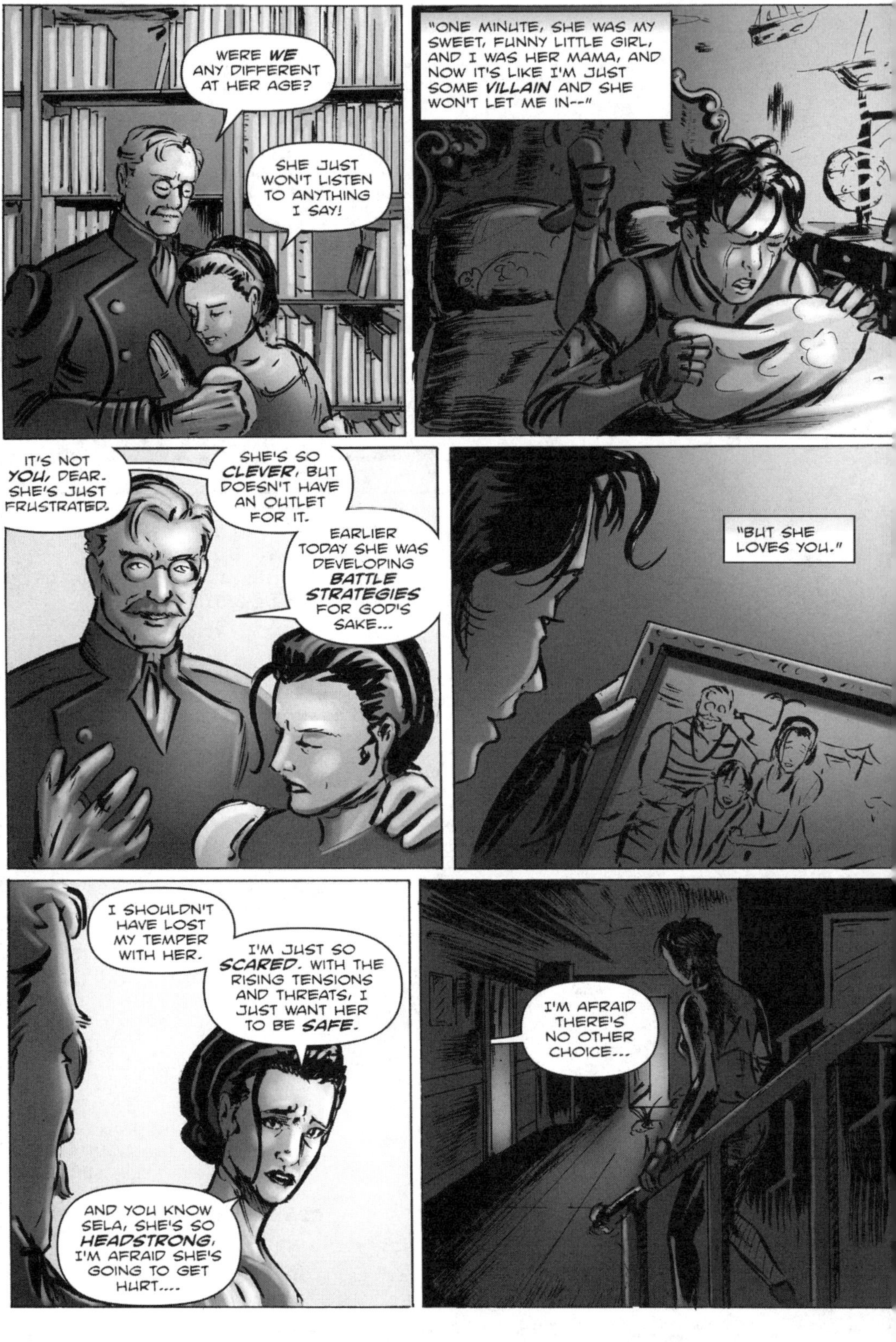
WERE WE ANY DIFFERENT AT HER AGE?
SHE JUST WON'T LISTEN TO ANYTHING I SAY!
"ONE MINUTE, SHE WAS MY SWEET, FUNNY LITTLE GIRL, AND I WAS HER MAMA, AND NOW IT'S LIKE I'M JUST SOME VILLAIN AND SHE WON'T LET ME IN--"
IT'S NOT YOU, DEAR. SHE'S JUST FRUSTRATED.
SHE'S SO CLEVER, BUT DOESN'T HAVE AN OUTLET FOR IT.
EARLIER TODAY SHE WAS DEVELOPING BATTLE STRATEGIES FOR GOD'S SAKE...
"BUT SHE LOVES YOU."
I SHOULDN'T HAVE LOST MY TEMPER WITH HER.
I'M JUST SO SCARED. WITH THE RISING TENSIONS AND THREATS, I JUST WANT HER TO BE SAFE.
AND YOU KNOW SELA, SHE'S SO HEADSTRONG, I'M AFRAID SHE'S GOING TO GET HURT....
I'M AFRAID THERE'S NO OTHER CHOICE...

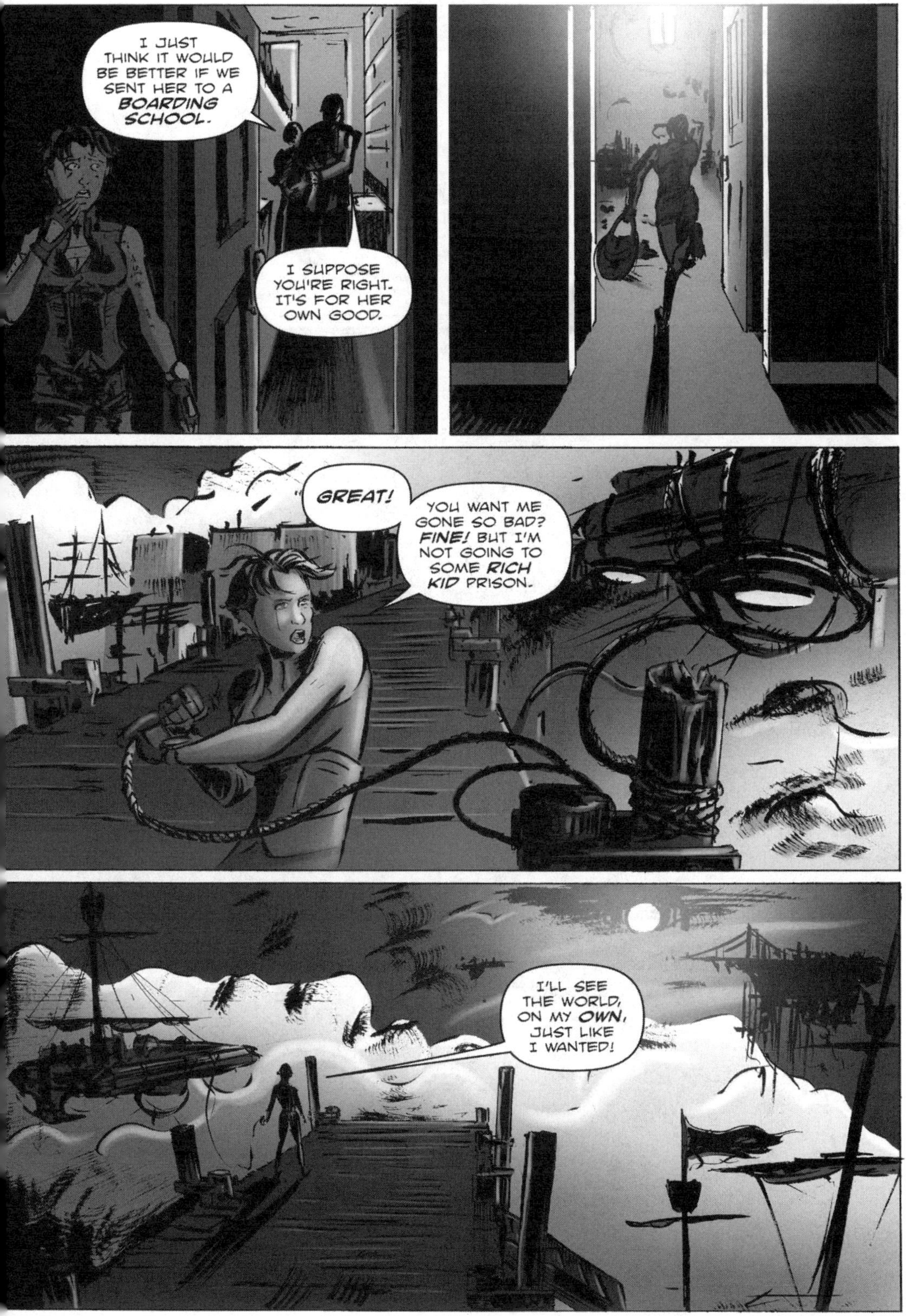
I JUST THINK IT WOULD BE BETTER IF WE SENT HER TO A BOARDING SCHOOL.
I SUPPOSE YOU'RE RIGHT. IT'S FOR HER OWN GOOD.
GREAT!
YOU WANT ME GONE SO BAD? FINE! BUT I'M NOT GOING TO SOME RICH KID PRISON.
I'LL SEE THE WORLD, ON MY OWN, JUST LIKE I WANTED!

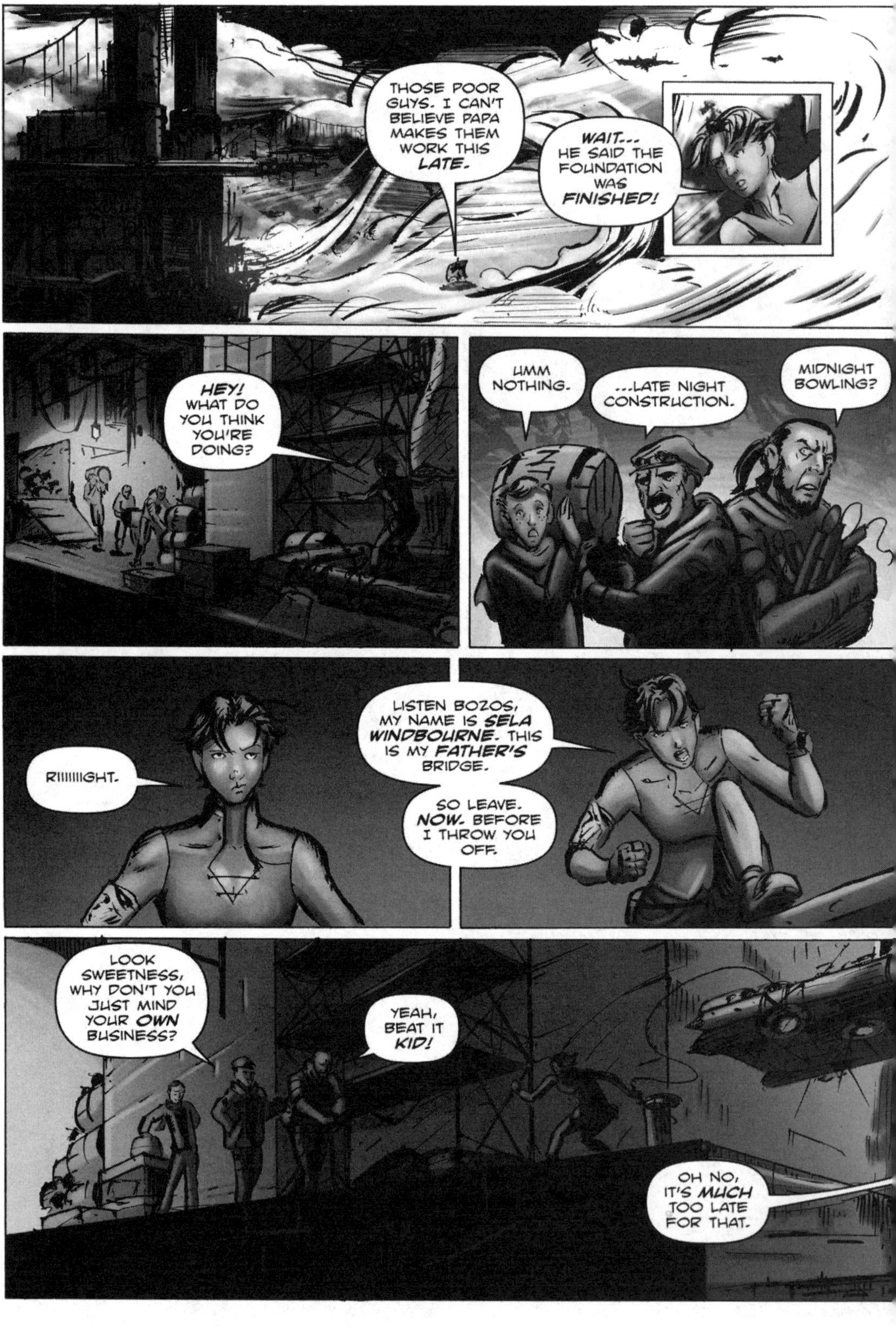
THOSE POOR GUYS. I CAN'T BELIEVE PAPA MAKES THEM WORK THIS LATE.
WAIT... HE SAID THE FOUNDATION WAS FINISHED!
HEY! WHAT DO YOU THINK YOU'RE DOING?
UMM NOTHING.
...LATE NIGHT CONSTRUCTION.
MIDNIGHT BOWLING?
RIIIIIIGHT.
LISTEN BOZOS, MY NAME IS SELA WINDBOURNE. THIS IS MY FATHER'S BRIDGE.
SO LEAVE. NOW. BEFORE I THROW YOU OFF.
LOOK SWEETNESS, WHY DON'T YOU JUST MIND YOUR OWN BUSINESS?
YEAH, BEAT IT KID!
OH NO, IT'S MUCH TOO LATE FOR THAT.

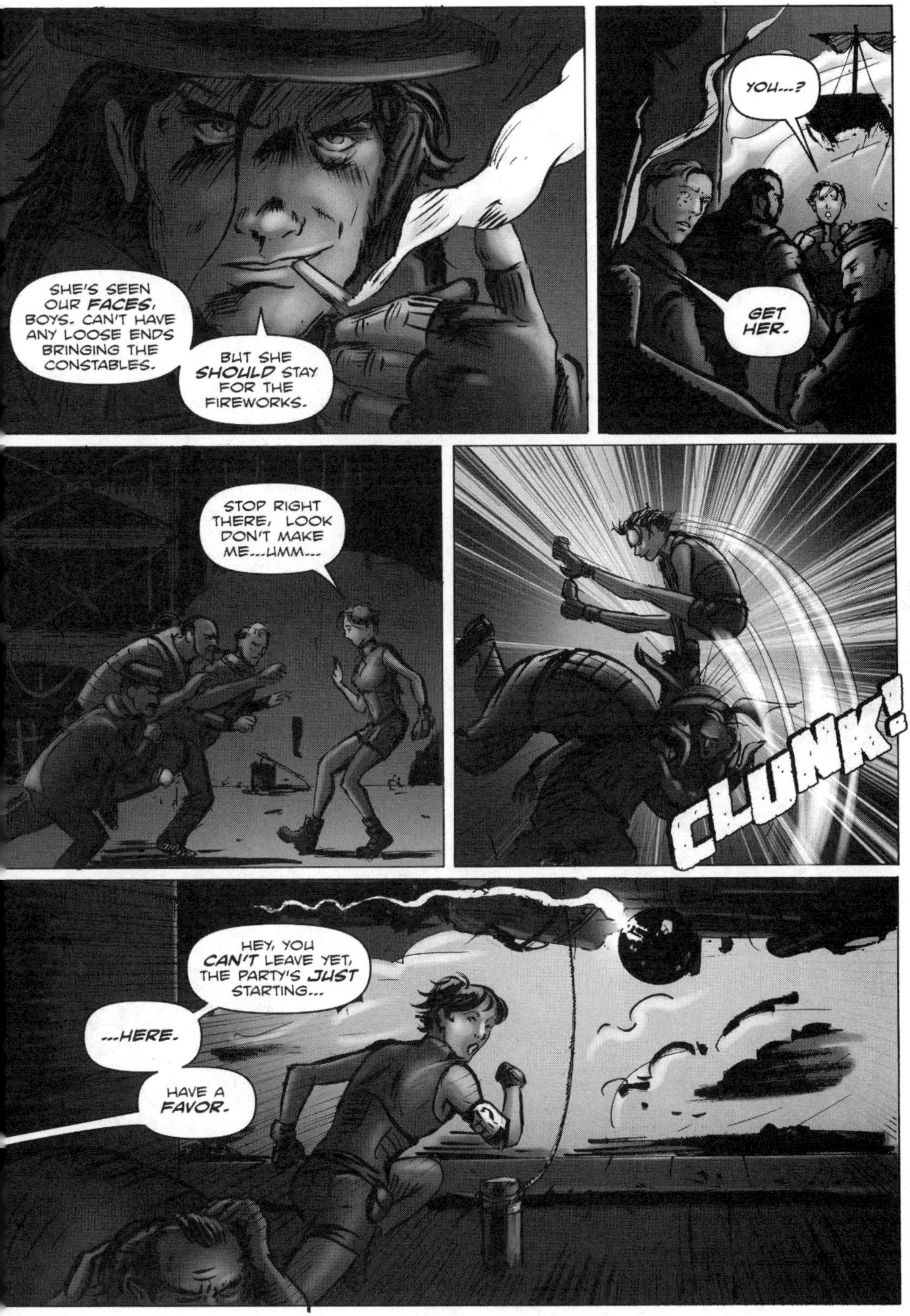

SHE'S SEEN OUR FACES, BOYS. CAN'T HAVE ANY LOOSE ENDS BRINGING THE CONSTABLES.
BUT SHE SHOULD STAY FOR THE FIREWORKS.
YOU...?
GET HER.
STOP RIGHT THERE, LOOK DON'T MAKE ME...UMM...
CLUNK!
HEY, YOU CAN'T LEAVE YET, THE PARTY'S JUST STARTING...
...HERE.
HAVE A FAVOR.

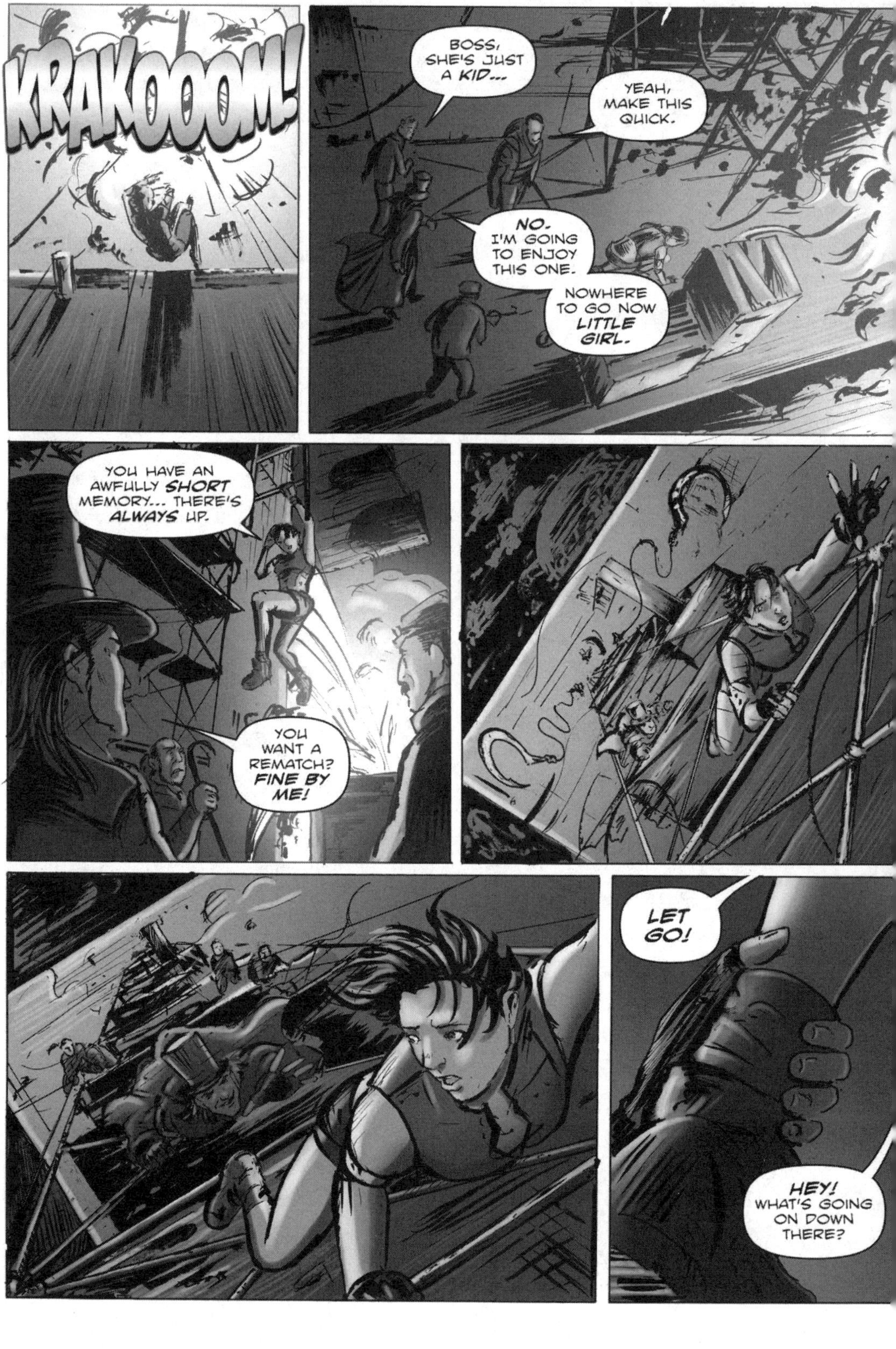
KRAKOOOM!
BOSS, SHE'S JUST A KID...
YEAH, MAKE THIS QUICK.
NO. I'M GOING TO ENJOY THIS ONE.
NOWHERE TO GO NOW LITTLE GIRL.
YOU HAVE AN AWFULLY SHORT MEMORY... THERE'S ALWAYS UP.
YOU WANT A REMATCH? FINE BY ME!
LET GO!
HEY! WHAT'S GOING ON DOWN THERE?

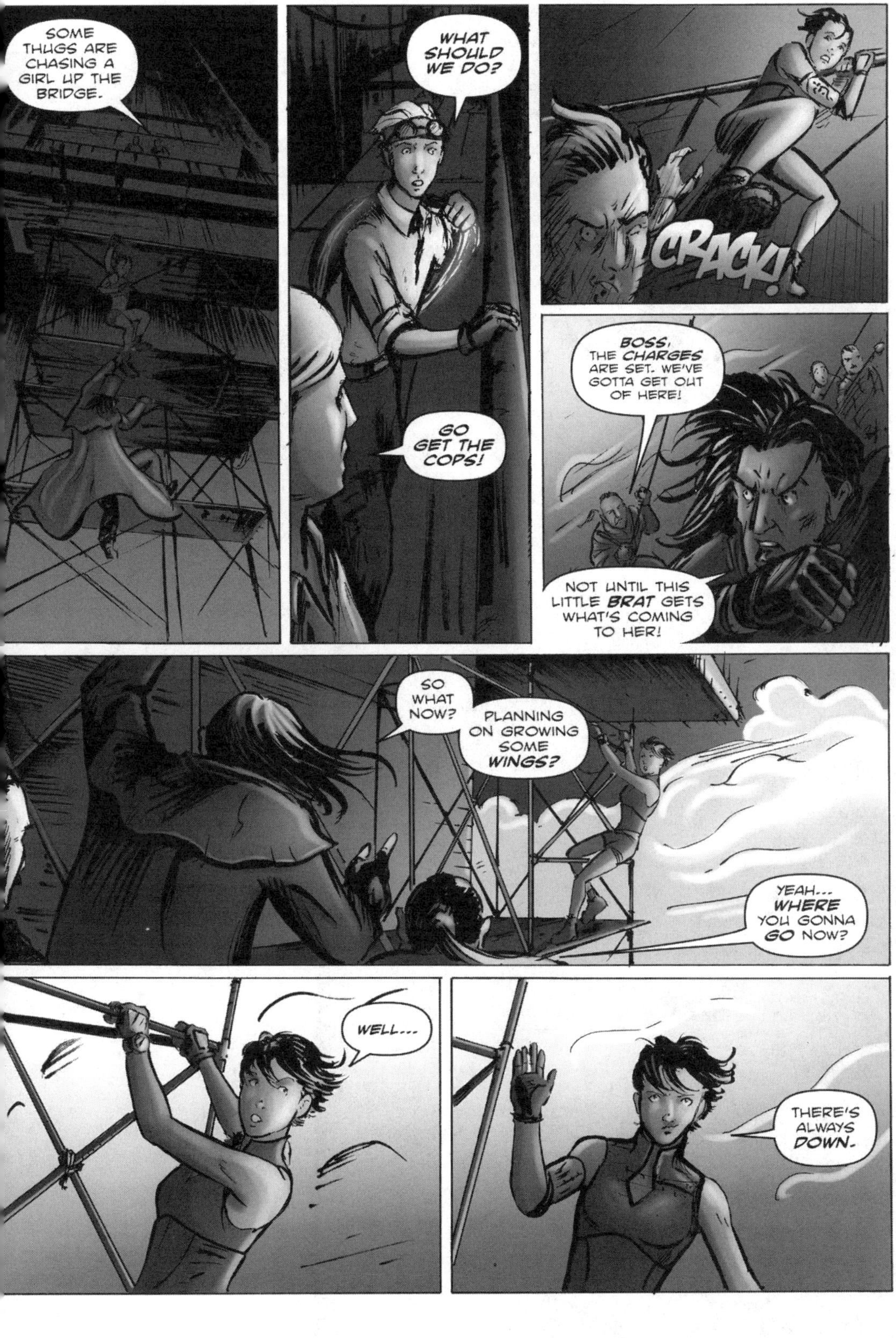

SOME THUGS ARE CHASING A GIRL UP THE BRIDGE.
WHAT SHOULD WE DO?
GO GET THE COPS!
CRACK!
BOSS, THE CHARGES ARE SET. WE'VE GOTTA GET OUT OF HERE!
NOT UNTIL THIS LITTLE BRAT GETS WHAT'S COMING TO HER!
SO WHAT NOW?
PLANNING ON GROWING SOME WINGS?
YEAH... WHERE YOU GONNA GO NOW?
WELL...
THERE'S ALWAYS DOWN.

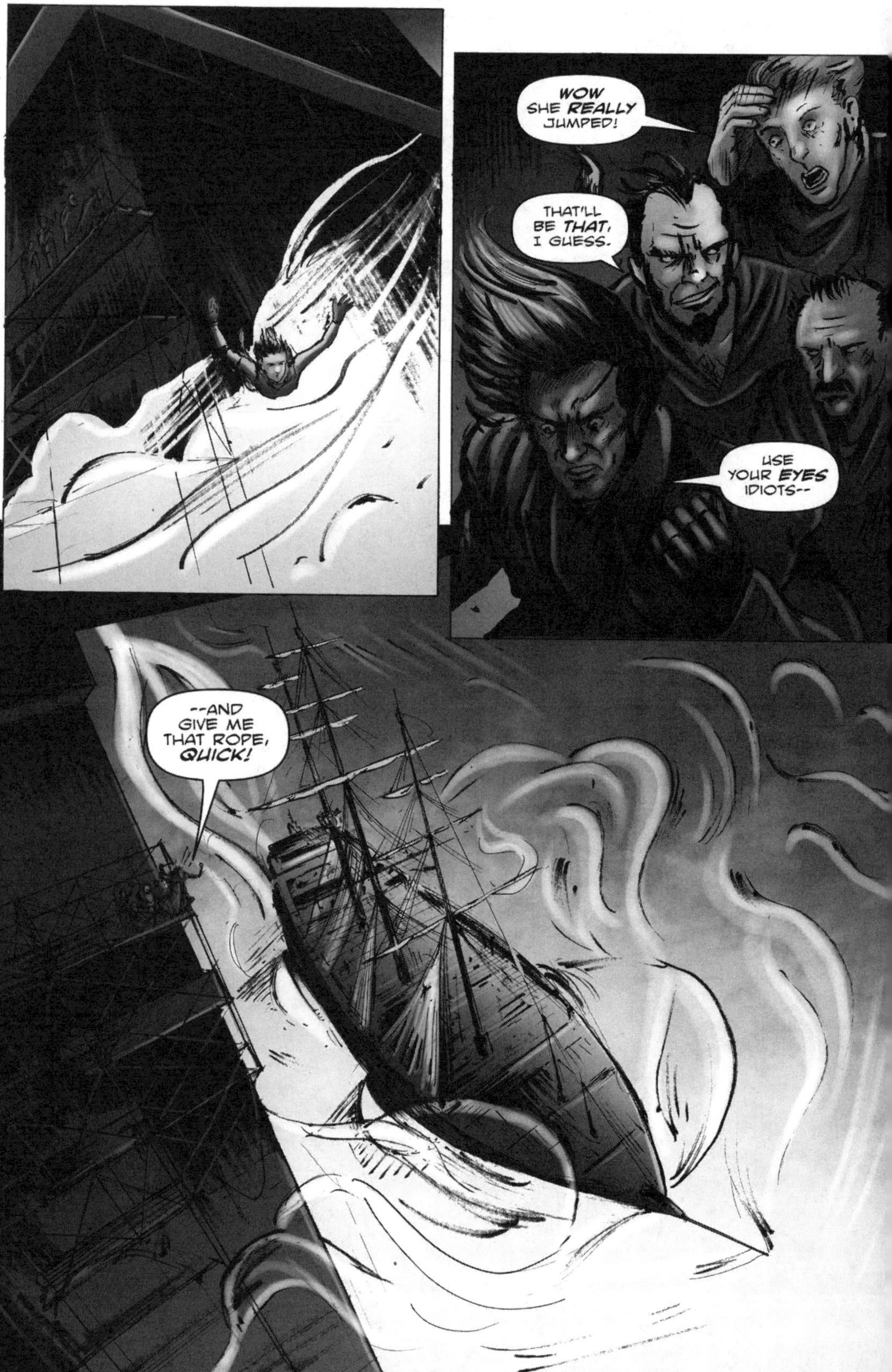
WOW SHE REALLY JUMPED!
THAT'LL BE THAT, I GUESS.
USE YOUR EYES IDIOTS--
--AND GIVE ME THAT ROPE, QUICK!

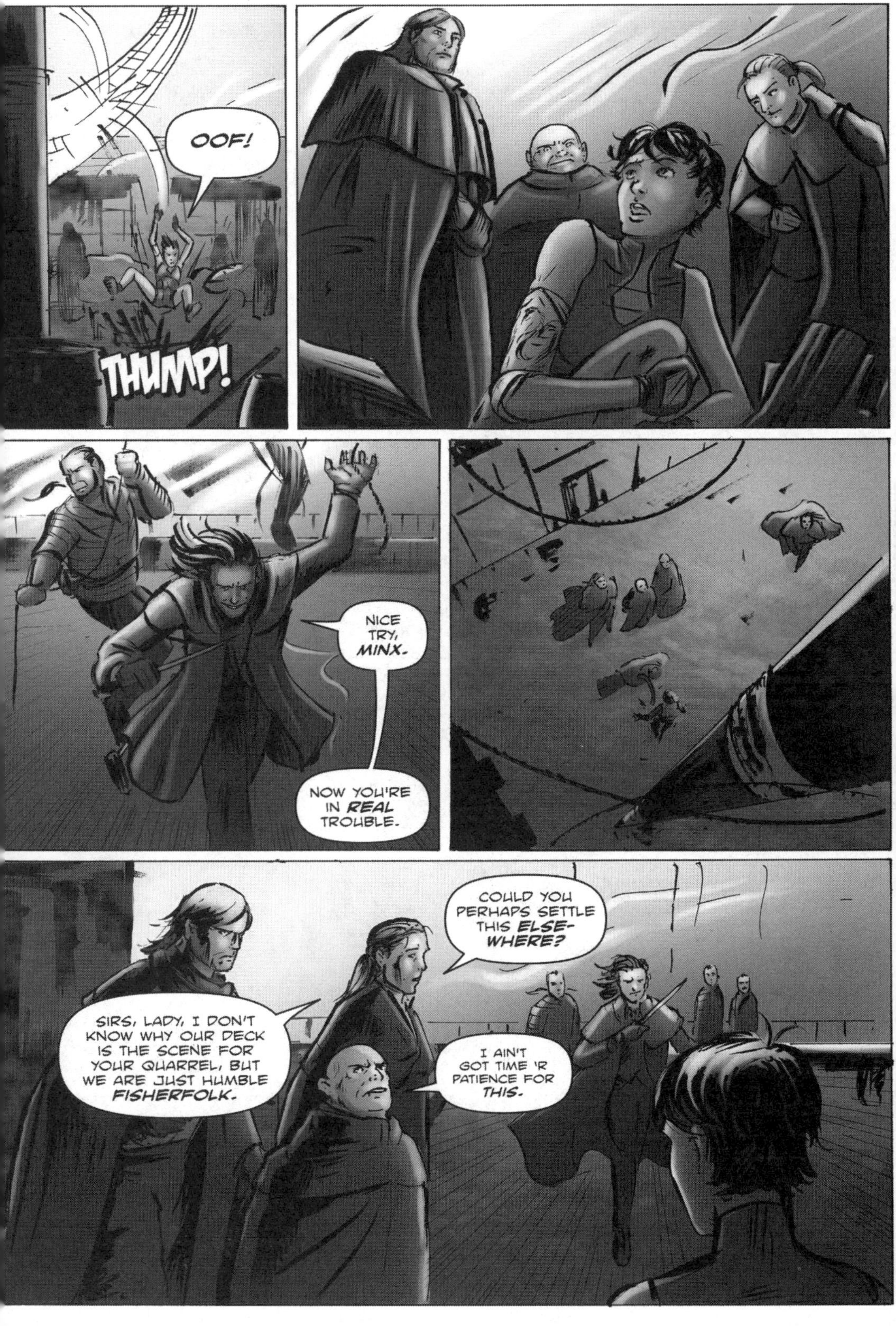
OOF!
THUMP!
NICE TRY, MINX.
NOW YOU'RE IN REAL TROUBLE.
COULD YOU PERHAPS SETTLE THIS ELSE-WHERE?
SIRS, LADY, I DON'T KNOW WHY OUR DECK IS THE SCENE FOR YOUR QUARREL, BUT WE ARE JUST HUMBLE FISHERFOLK.
I AIN'T GOT TIME 'R PATIENCE FOR THIS.

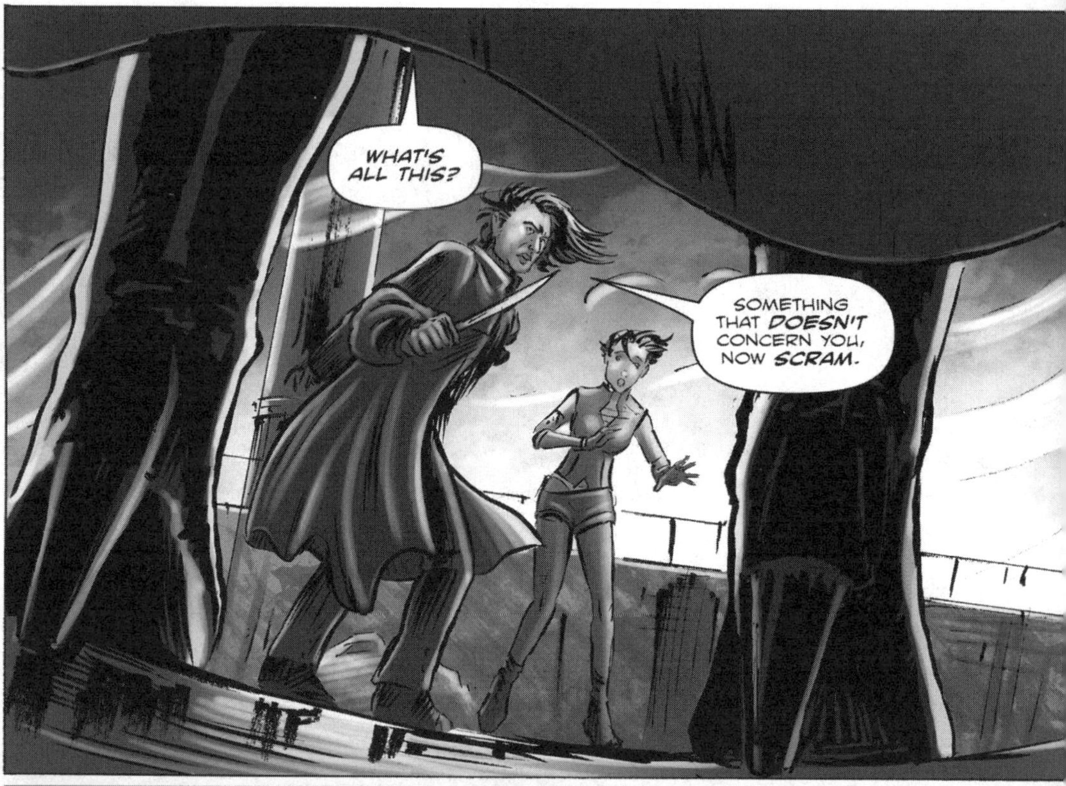
WHAT'S ALL THIS?
SOMETHING THAT DOESN'T CONCERN YOU, NOW SCRAM.

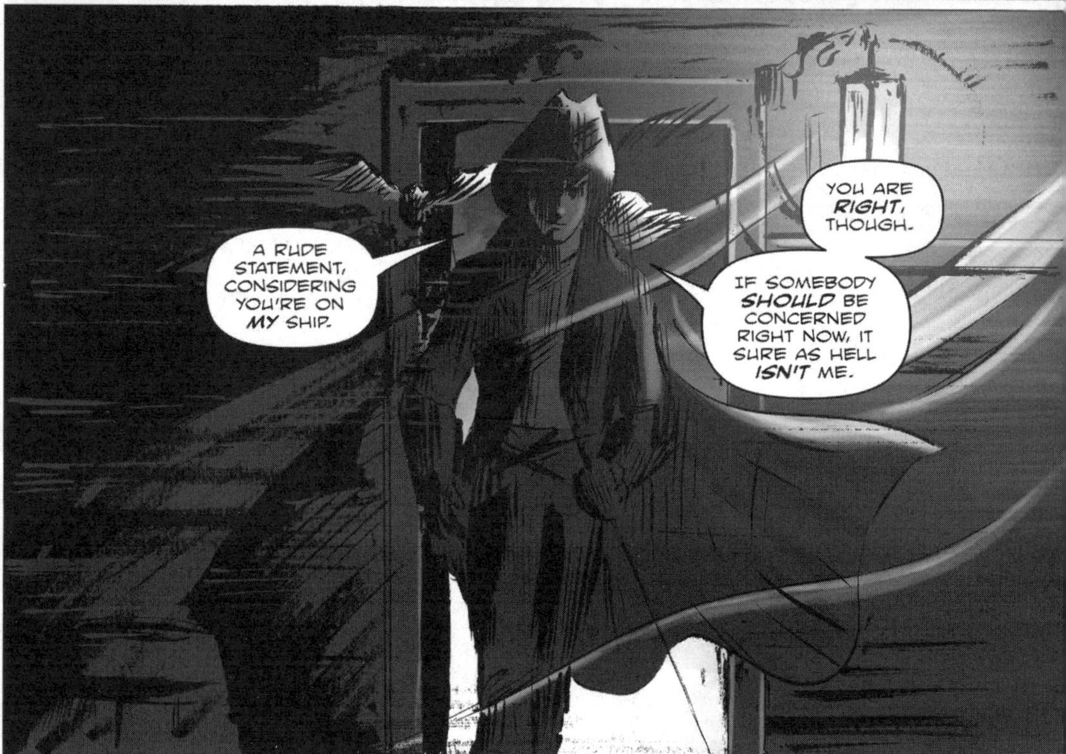
A RUDE STATEMENT, CONSIDERING YOU'RE ON MY SHIP.
YOU ARE RIGHT, THOUGH.
IF SOMEBODY SHOULD BE CONCERNED RIGHT NOW, IT SURE AS HELL ISN'T ME.

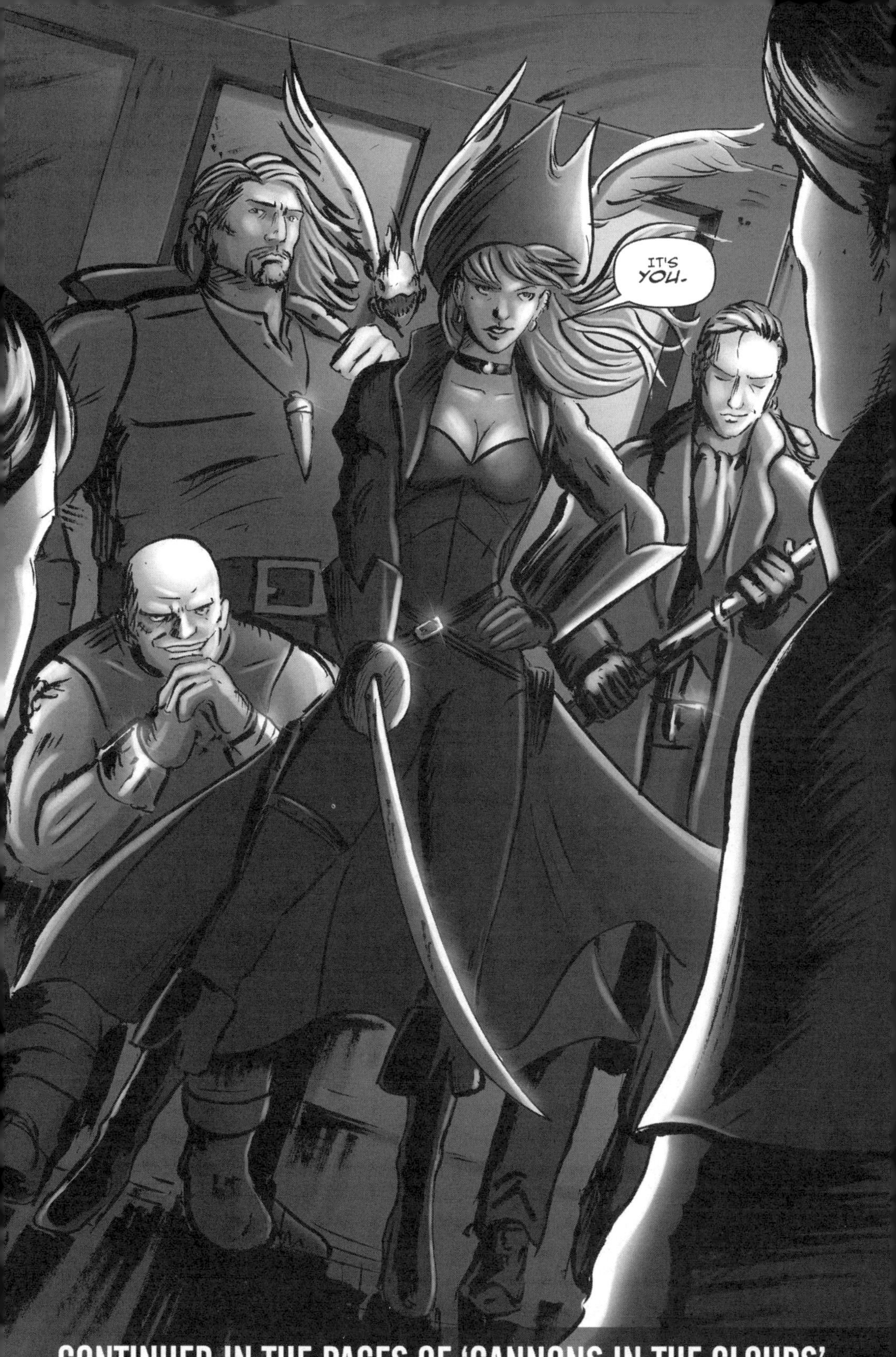
IT'S YOU.

CONTINUED IN THE PAGES OF 'CANNONS IN THE CLOUDS'

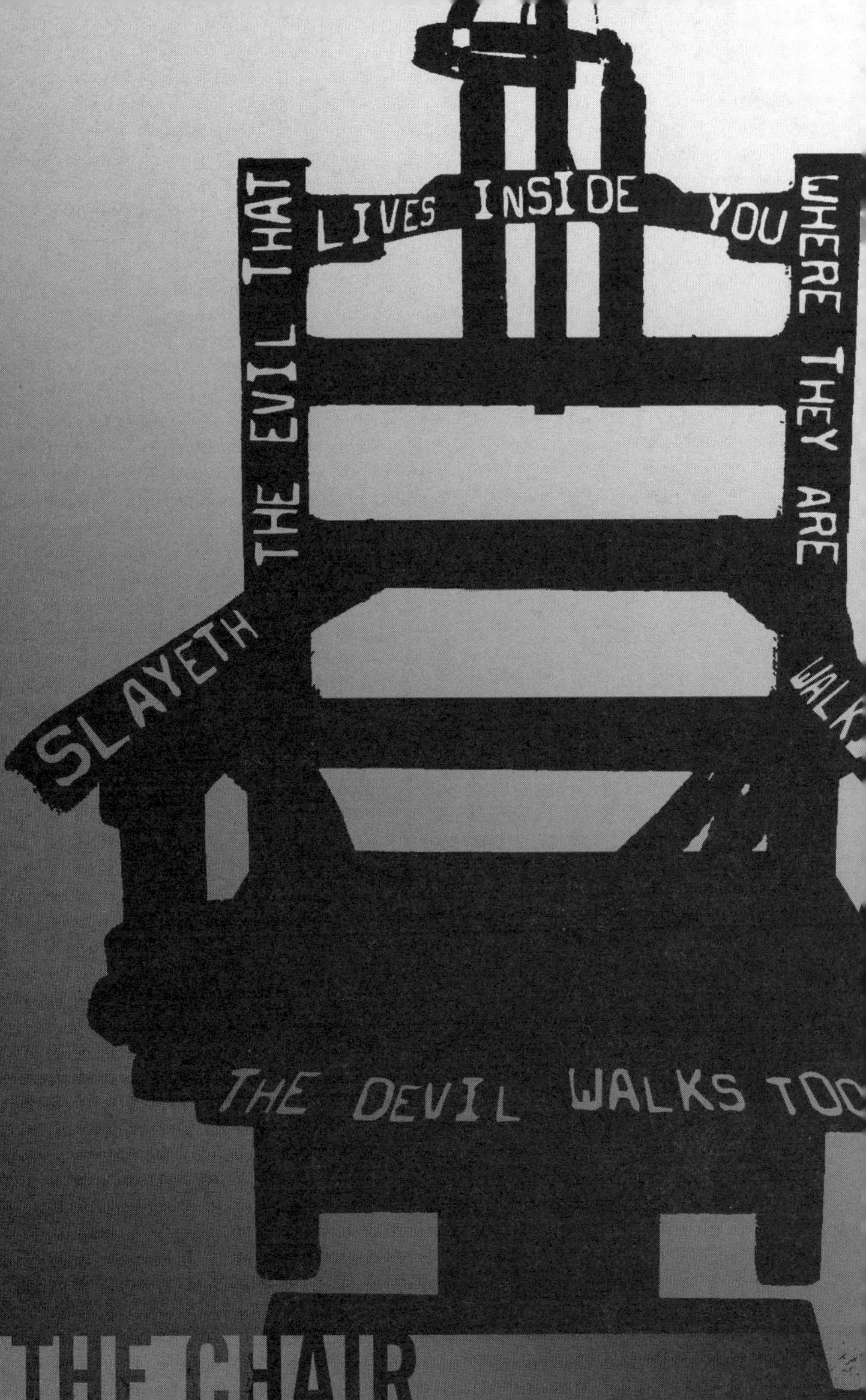
SLAYETH THE EVIL THAT LIVES INSIDE YOU WHERE THEY ARE WALK
THE DEVIL WALKS TOO

THE CHAIR

THE CHAIR

RICHARD SULLIVAN

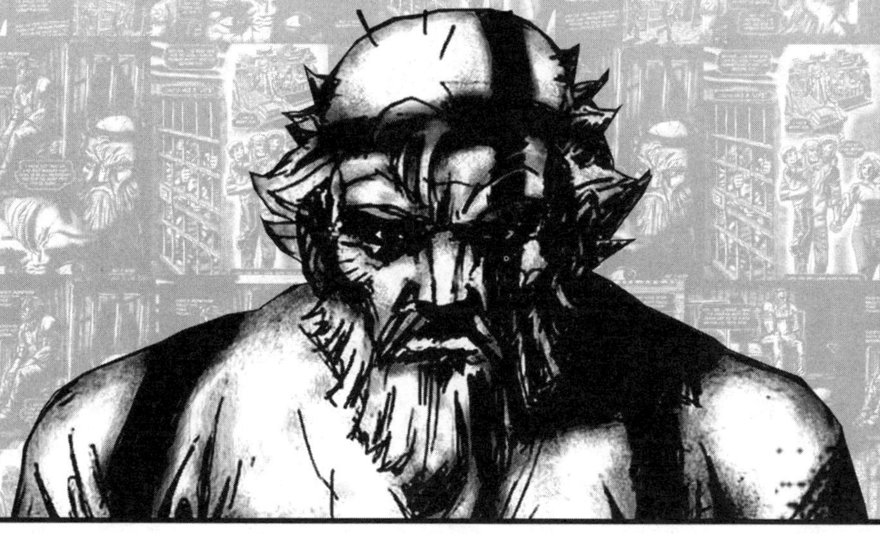

"I didn't do it.
It's what they all say.
I say it too from time to time.
Only thing is... I'm telling the truth."

Richard Sullivan is an innocent man on death row. Witnessing savage killings at the hands of the prison's villainous Warden, Sullivan realizes that he must fight to survive. But with the violence and carnage mounting, Sullivan begins to lose his grip on reality - and his sanity.

Age: 52 Height: 5'11" Weight: 215 lbs.

First Appearance: THE CHAIR #1 (2006)

Created by Peter Simeti
Illustration by Kevin Christensen & Peter Simeti

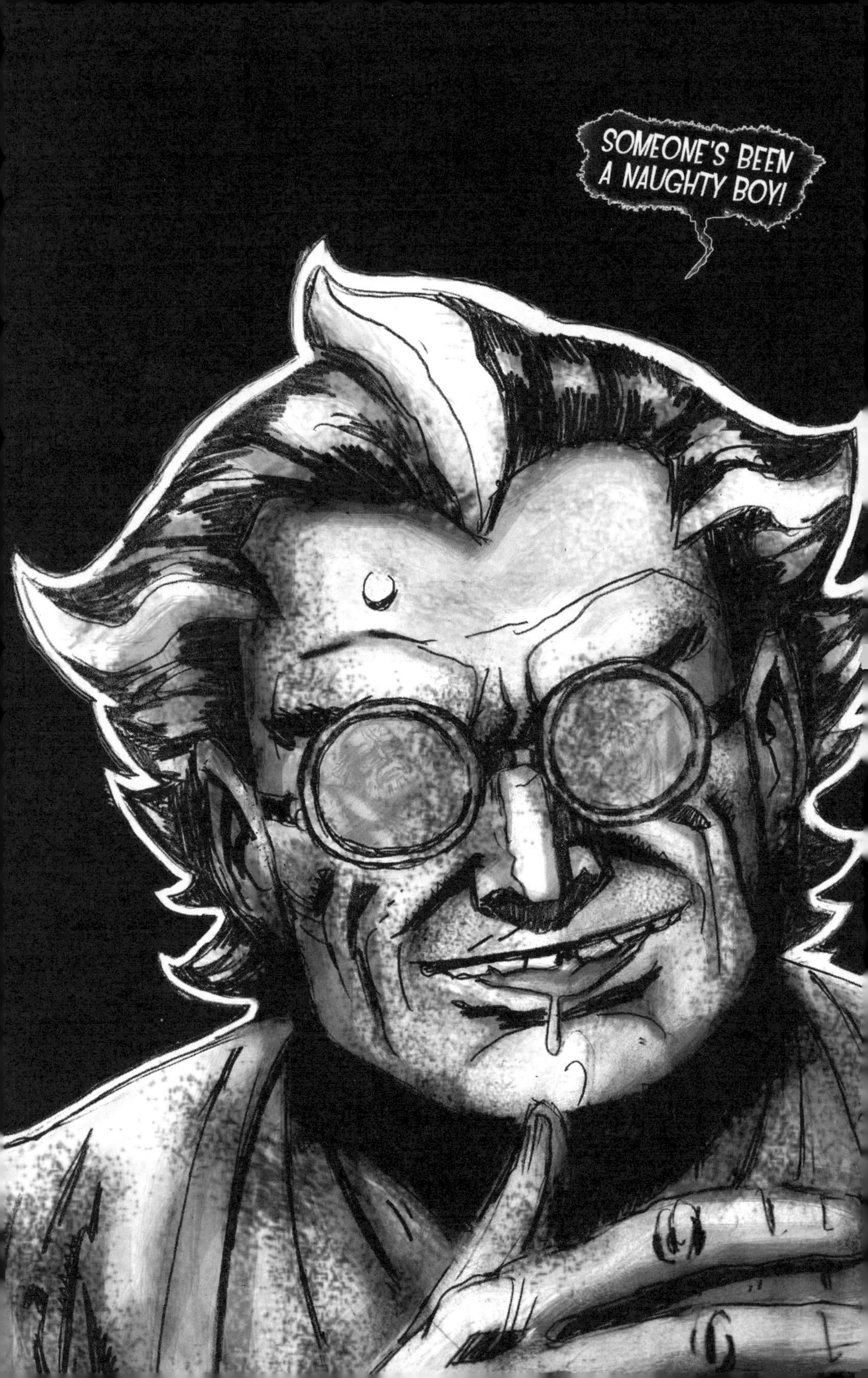
SOMEONE'S BEEN A NAUGHTY BOY!

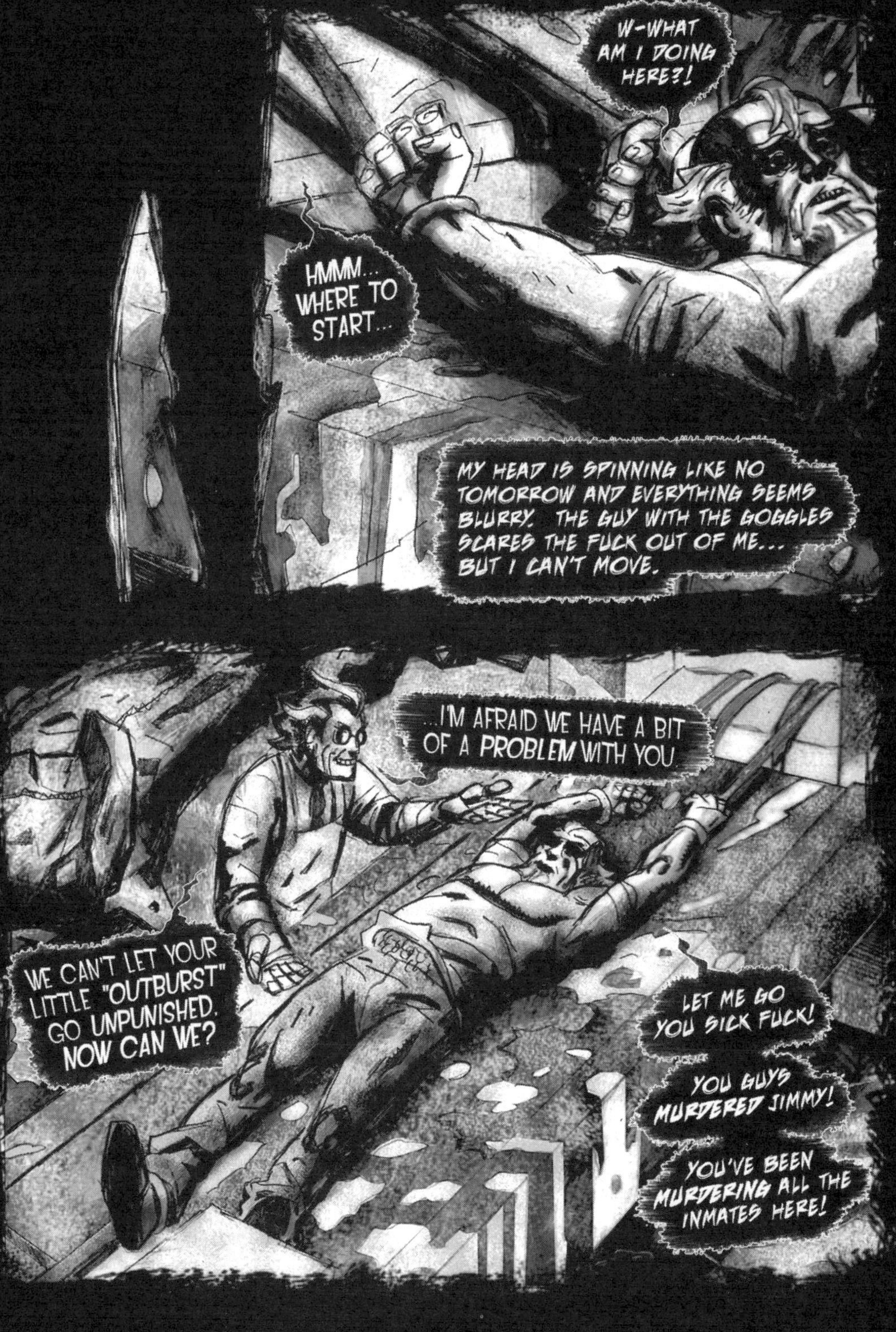
W-WHAT AM I DOING HERE?!
HMMM... WHERE TO START...
MY HEAD IS SPINNING LIKE NO TOMORROW AND EVERYTHING SEEMS BLURRY. THE GUY WITH THE GOGGLES SCARES THE FUCK OUT OF ME... BUT I CAN'T MOVE.
...I'M AFRAID WE HAVE A BIT OF A PROBLEM WITH YOU
WE CAN'T LET YOUR LITTLE "OUTBURST" GO UNPUNISHED, NOW CAN WE?
LET ME GO YOU SICK FUCK!
YOU GUYS MURDERED JIMMY!
YOU'VE BEEN MURDERING ALL THE INMATES HERE!

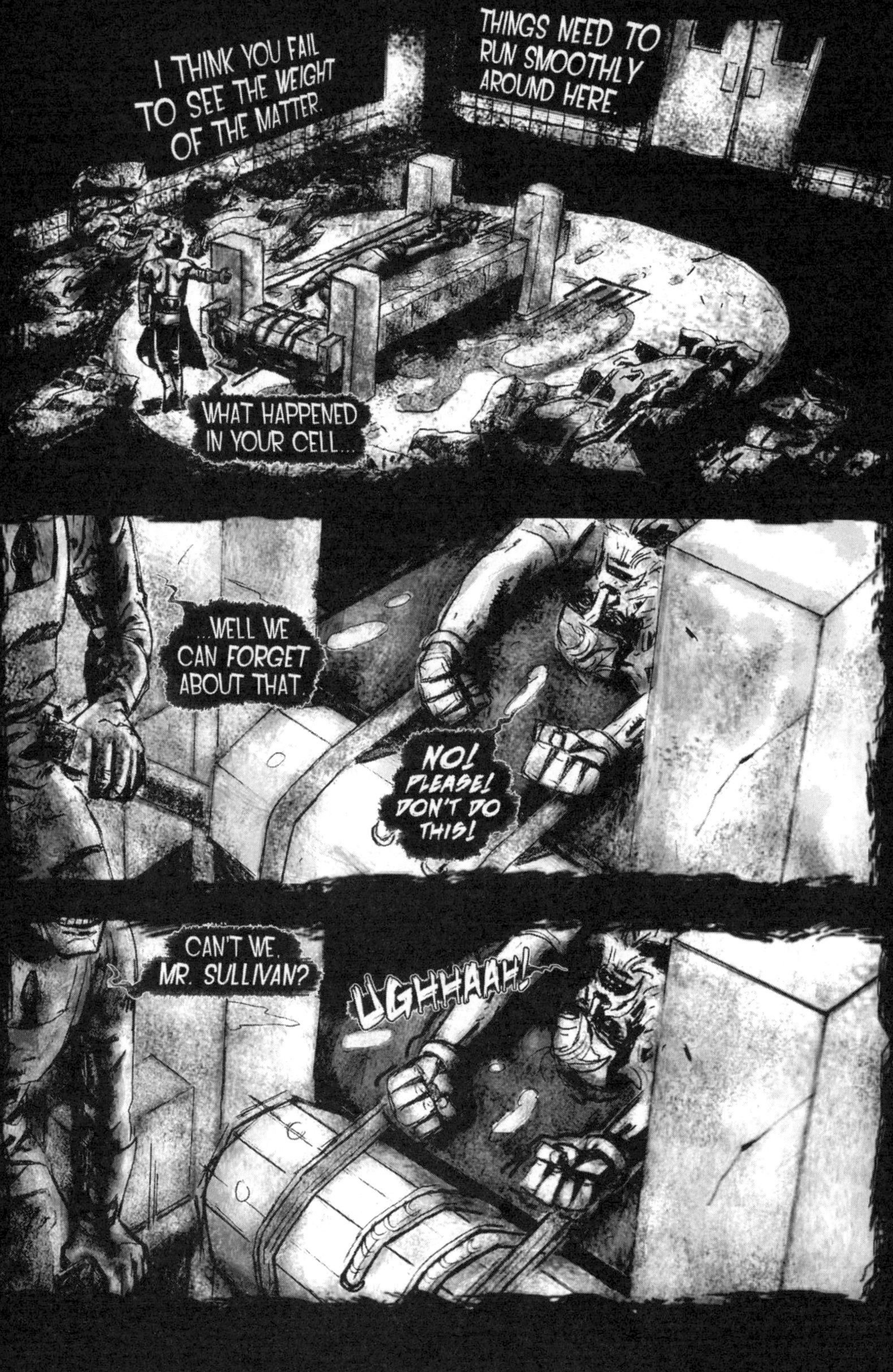
I THINK YOU FAIL TO SEE THE WEIGHT OF THE MATTER.
THINGS NEED TO RUN SMOOTHLY AROUND HERE.
WHAT HAPPENED IN YOUR CELL...
...WELL WE CAN FORGET ABOUT THAT.
NO! PLEASE! DON'T DO THIS!
CAN'T WE, MR. SULLIVAN?
UGHHAAH!

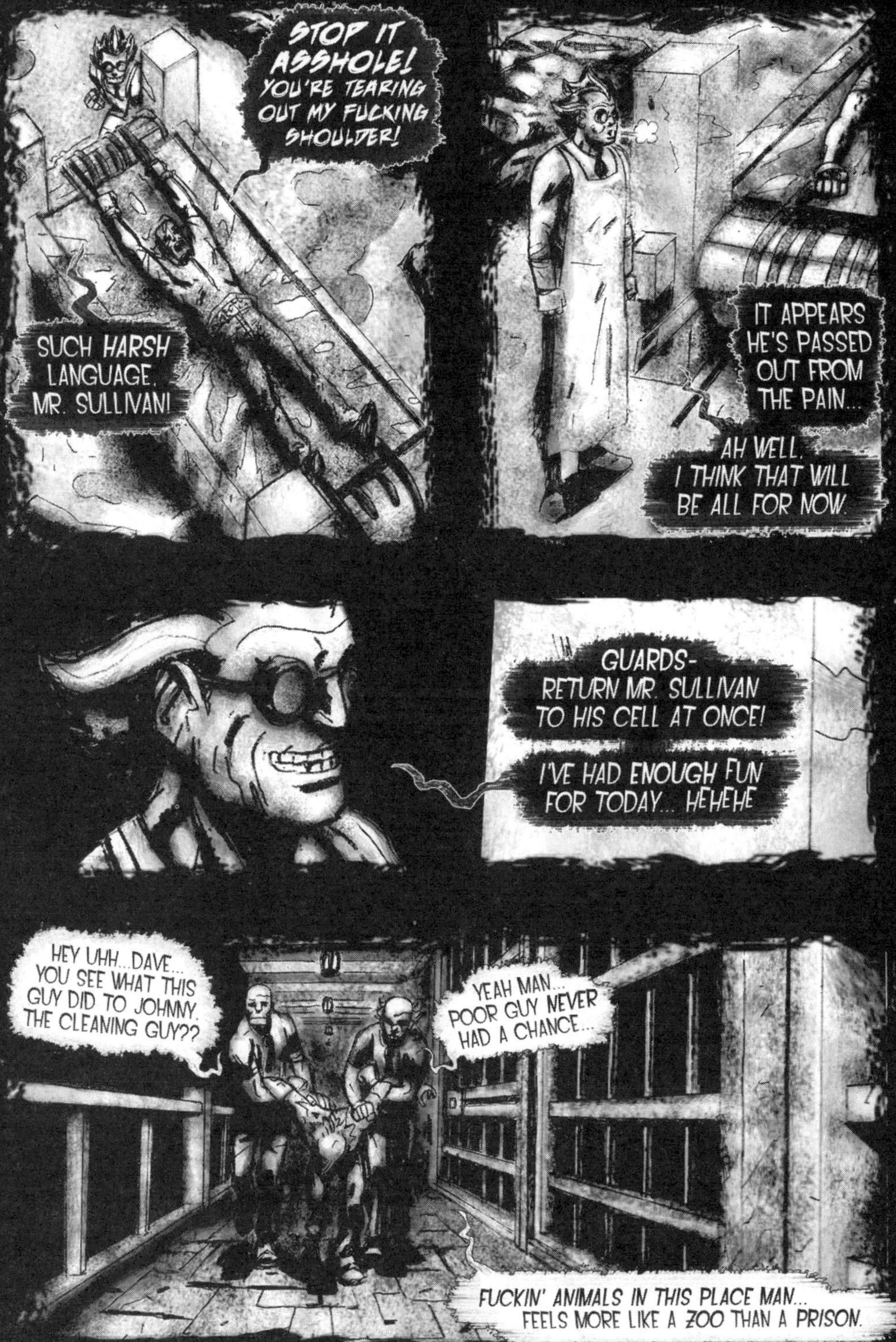
STOP IT ASSHOLE! YOU'RE TEARING OUT MY FUCKING SHOULDER!
SUCH HARSH LANGUAGE, MR. SULLIVAN!
IT APPEARS HE'S PASSED OUT FROM THE PAIN...
AH WELL. I THINK THAT WILL BE ALL FOR NOW.
GUARDS- RETURN MR. SULLIVAN TO HIS CELL AT ONCE!
I'VE HAD ENOUGH FUN FOR TODAY... HEHEHE
HEY UHH...DAVE... YOU SEE WHAT THIS GUY DID TO JOHNNY, THE CLEANING GUY??
YEAH MAN... POOR GUY NEVER HAD A CHANCE...
FUCKIN' ANIMALS IN THIS PLACE MAN... FEELS MORE LIKE A ZOO THAN A PRISON.

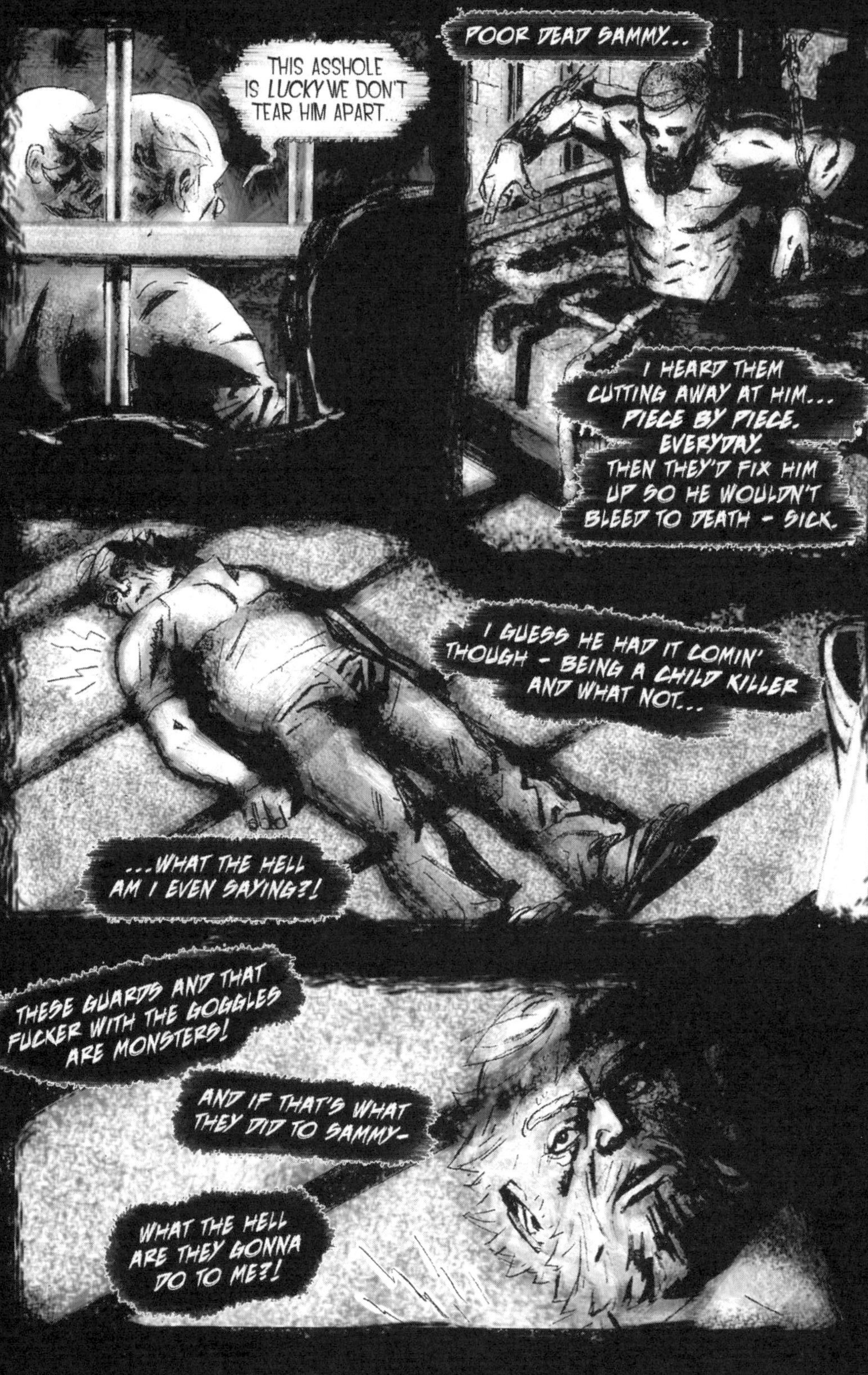
THIS ASSHOLE IS LUCKY WE DON'T TEAR HIM APART...
POOR DEAD SAMMY...
I HEARD THEM CUTTING AWAY AT HIM... PIECE BY PIECE. EVERYDAY. THEN THEY'D FIX HIM UP SO HE WOULDN'T BLEED TO DEATH - SICK.
I GUESS HE HAD IT COMIN' THOUGH - BEING A CHILD KILLER AND WHAT NOT...
...WHAT THE HELL AM I EVEN SAYING?!
THESE GUARDS AND THAT FUCKER WITH THE GOGGLES ARE MONSTERS!
AND IF THAT'S WHAT THEY DID TO SAMMY-
WHAT THE HELL ARE THEY GONNA DO TO ME?!

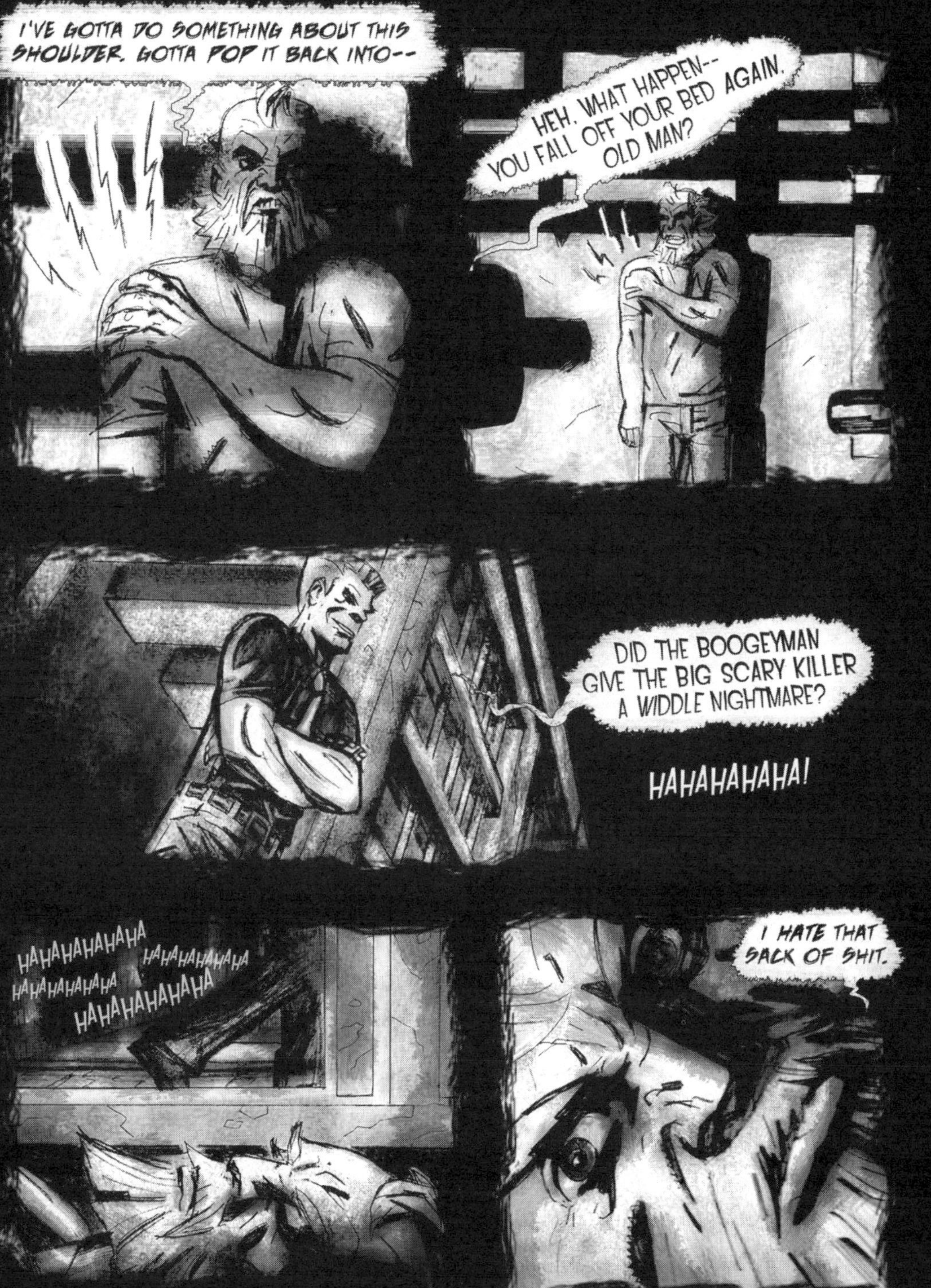
I'VE GOTTA DO SOMETHING ABOUT THIS SHOULDER. GOTTA POP IT BACK INTO--
HEH. WHAT HAPPEN-- YOU FALL OFF YOUR BED AGAIN, OLD MAN?
DID THE BOOGEYMAN GIVE THE BIG SCARY KILLER A WIDDLE NIGHTMARE?
HAHAHAHAHA!
HAHAHAHAHAHA
HAHAHAHAHAHA
HAHAHAHAHAHA
HAHAHAHAHAHA
I HATE THAT SACK OF SHIT.

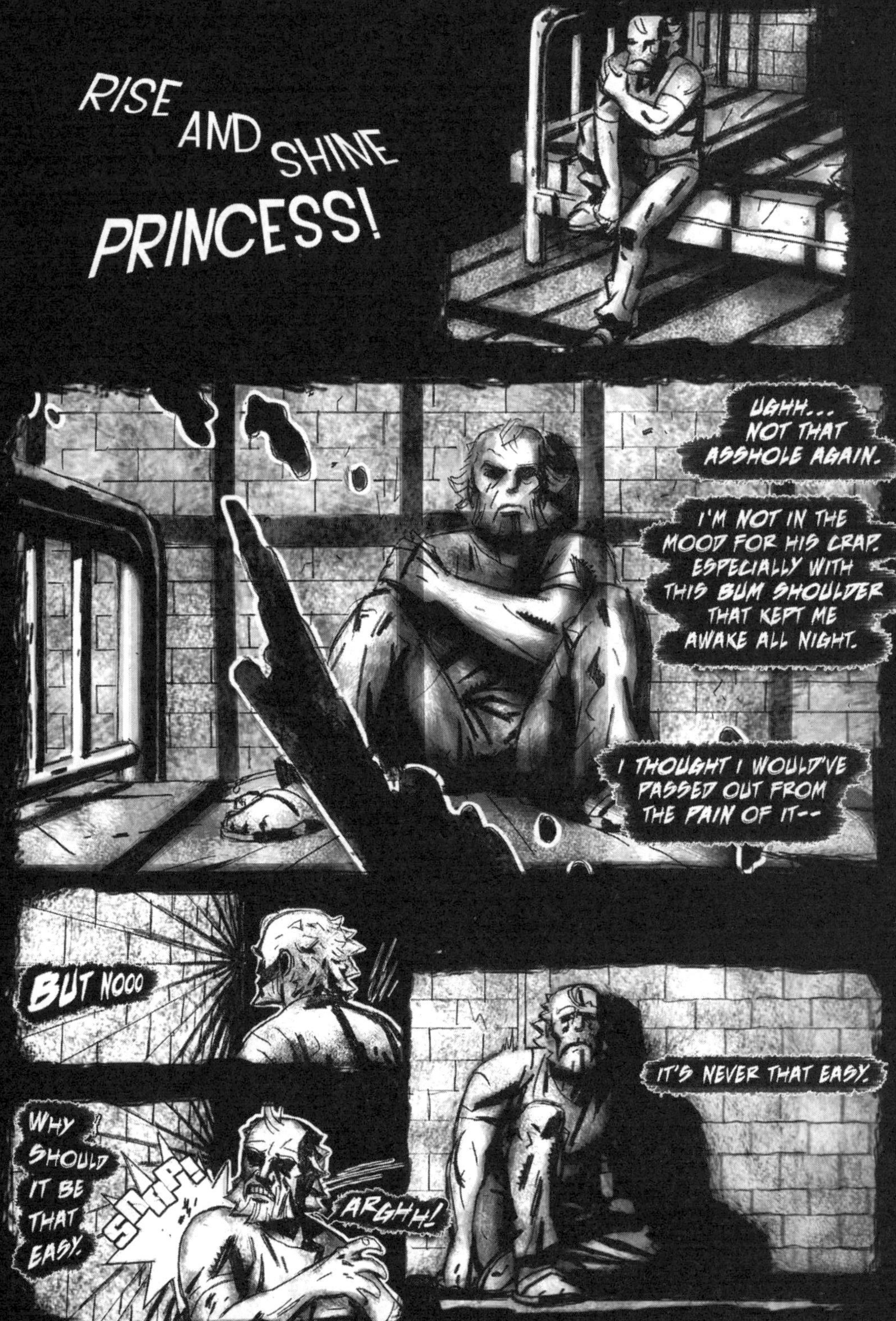
RISE AND SHINE PRINCESS!
UGHH... NOT THAT ASSHOLE AGAIN.
I'M NOT IN THE MOOD FOR HIS CRAP. ESPECIALLY WITH THIS BUM SHOULDER THAT KEPT ME AWAKE ALL NIGHT.
I THOUGHT I WOULD'VE PASSED OUT FROM THE PAIN OF IT--
BUT NOOO
IT'S NEVER THAT EASY.
WHY SHOULD IT BE THAT EASY.
SNAP!
ARGHH!

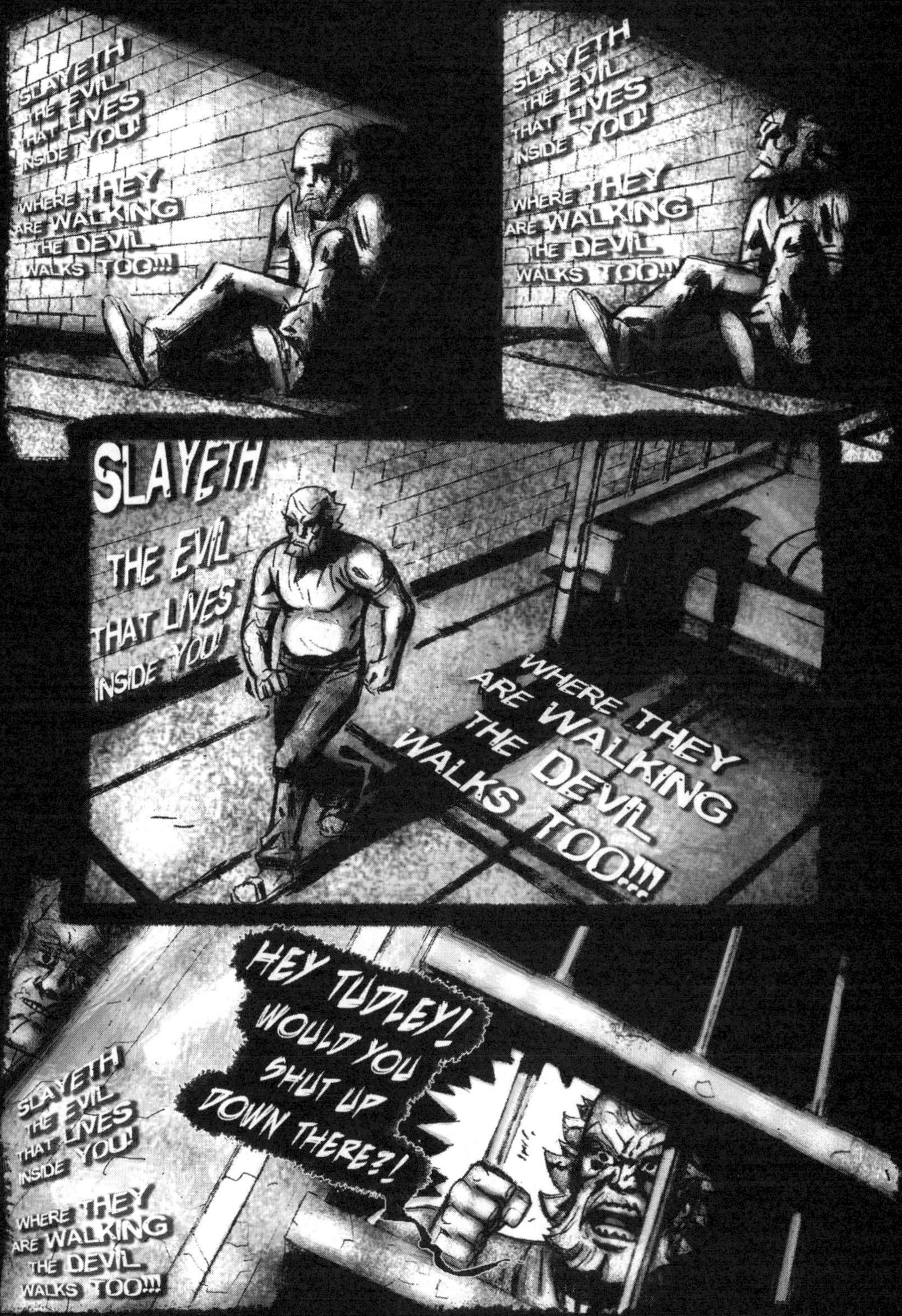
SLAYETH THE EVIL THAT LIVES INSIDE YOU!
WHERE THEY ARE WALKING THE DEVIL WALKS TOO!!!
SLAYETH THE EVIL THAT LIVES INSIDE YOU!
WHERE THEY ARE WALKING THE DEVIL WALKS TOO!!!
SLAYETH THE EVIL THAT LIVES INSIDE YOU!
WHERE THEY ARE WALKING THE DEVIL WALKS TOO!!!
SLAYETH THE EVIL THAT LIVES INSIDE YOU!
WHERE THEY ARE WALKING THE DEVIL WALKS TOO!!!
HEY TUDLEY! WOULD YOU SHUT UP DOWN THERE?!

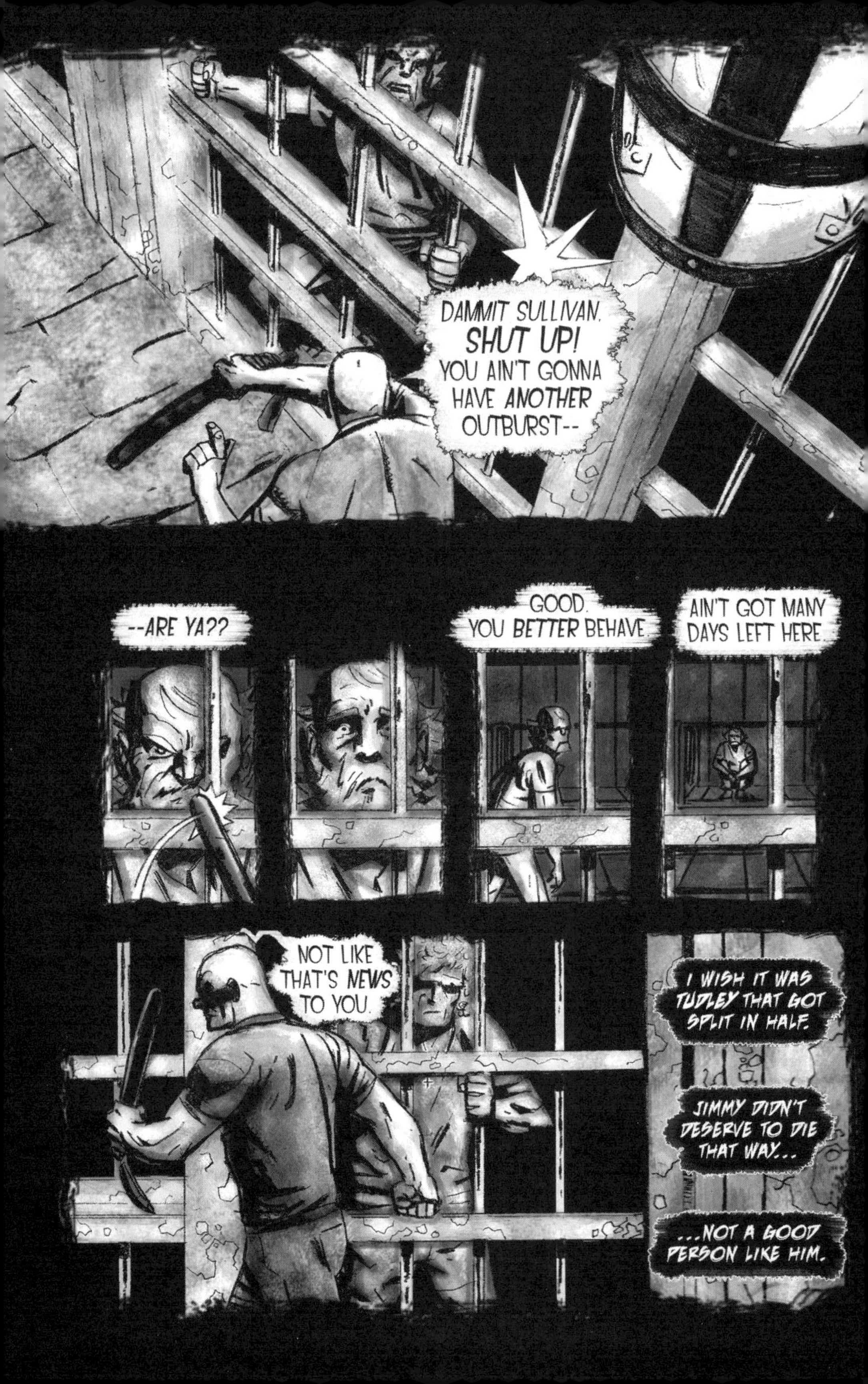
DAMMIT SULLIVAN, SHUT UP! YOU AIN'T GONNA HAVE ANOTHER OUTBURST--
--ARE YA??
GOOD. YOU BETTER BEHAVE.
AIN'T GOT MANY DAYS LEFT HERE.
NOT LIKE THAT'S NEWS TO YOU.
I WISH IT WAS TUDLEY THAT GOT SPLIT IN HALF.
JIMMY DIDN'T DESERVE TO DIE THAT WAY...
...NOT A GOOD PERSON LIKE HIM.

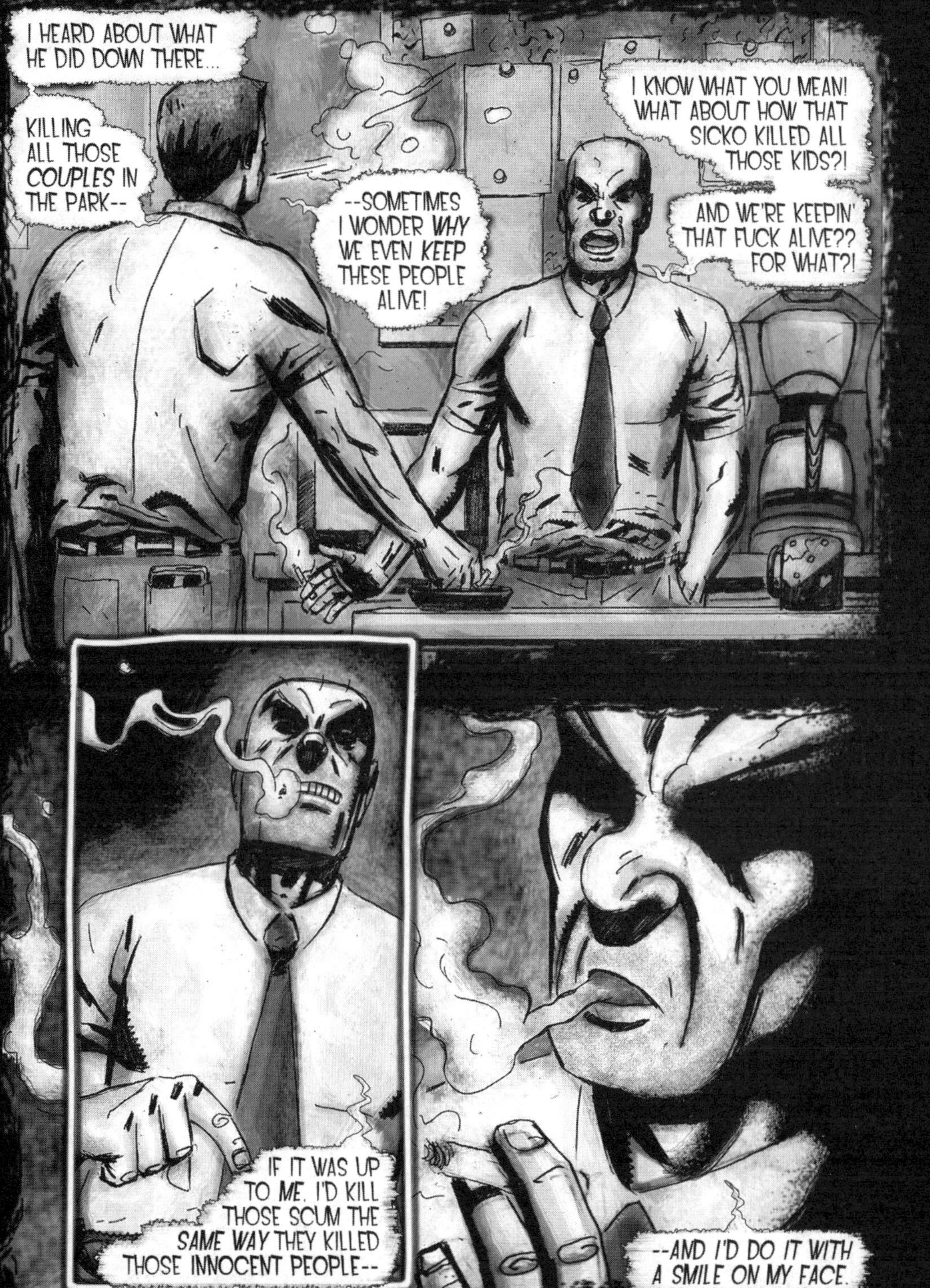
I HEARD ABOUT WHAT HE DID DOWN THERE...
KILLING ALL THOSE COUPLES IN THE PARK--
--SOMETIMES I WONDER WHY WE EVEN KEEP THESE PEOPLE ALIVE!
I KNOW WHAT YOU MEAN! WHAT ABOUT HOW THAT SICKO KILLED ALL THOSE KIDS?!
AND WE'RE KEEPIN' THAT FUCK ALIVE?? FOR WHAT?!
IF IT WAS UP TO ME, I'D KILL THOSE SCUM THE SAME WAY THEY KILLED THOSE INNOCENT PEOPLE--
--AND I'D DO IT WITH A SMILE ON MY FACE.

CONTINUED IN THE PAGES OF 'THE CHAIR'

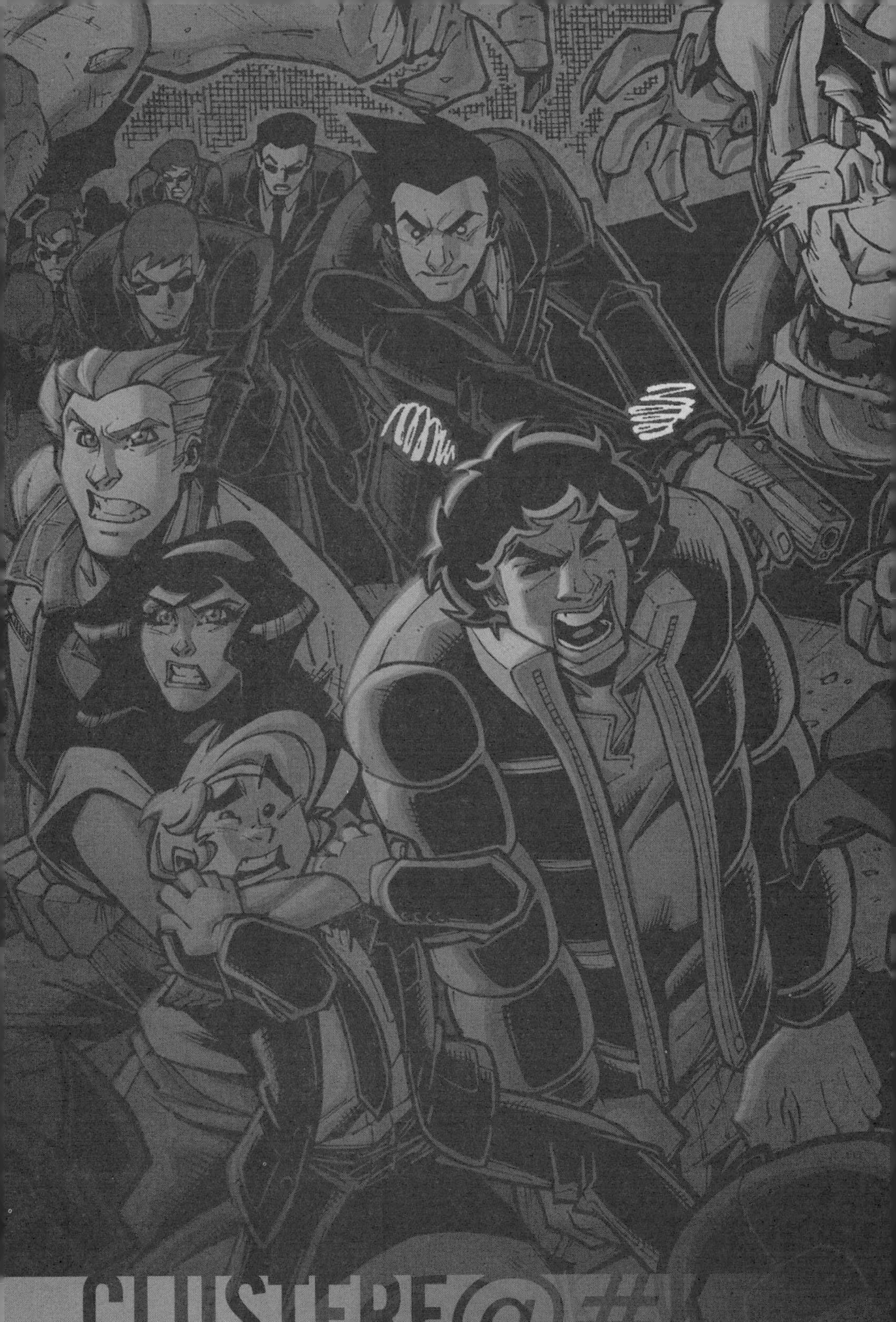

CLUSTERF@#K

CLUSTERF@#K

JIM PARKER

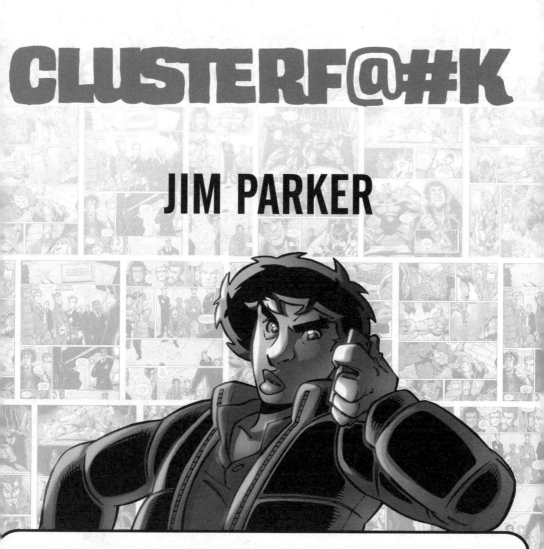

"Wow. We suck..."

A former agent of the Department of Extraterrestrial and Paranormal Defense, Parker left the organization with his best friend Karl to pursue a career in Private Investigation. Despite being told by the DEPD not to meddle in supernatural affairs, Jim and Karl often find themselves stumbling into such affairs. Jim also has a smart mouth which gets him into trouble and has gained multiple enemies because of it.
He loves Blaxploitation films and classic martial arts films.

Age: 25   Height: 5'8"   Weight: 165 lbs.

First Appearance: CLUSTERF@#K #1 (2014)

Created by Jon Parrish
Illustration by Diego Toro & Kote Carvajal

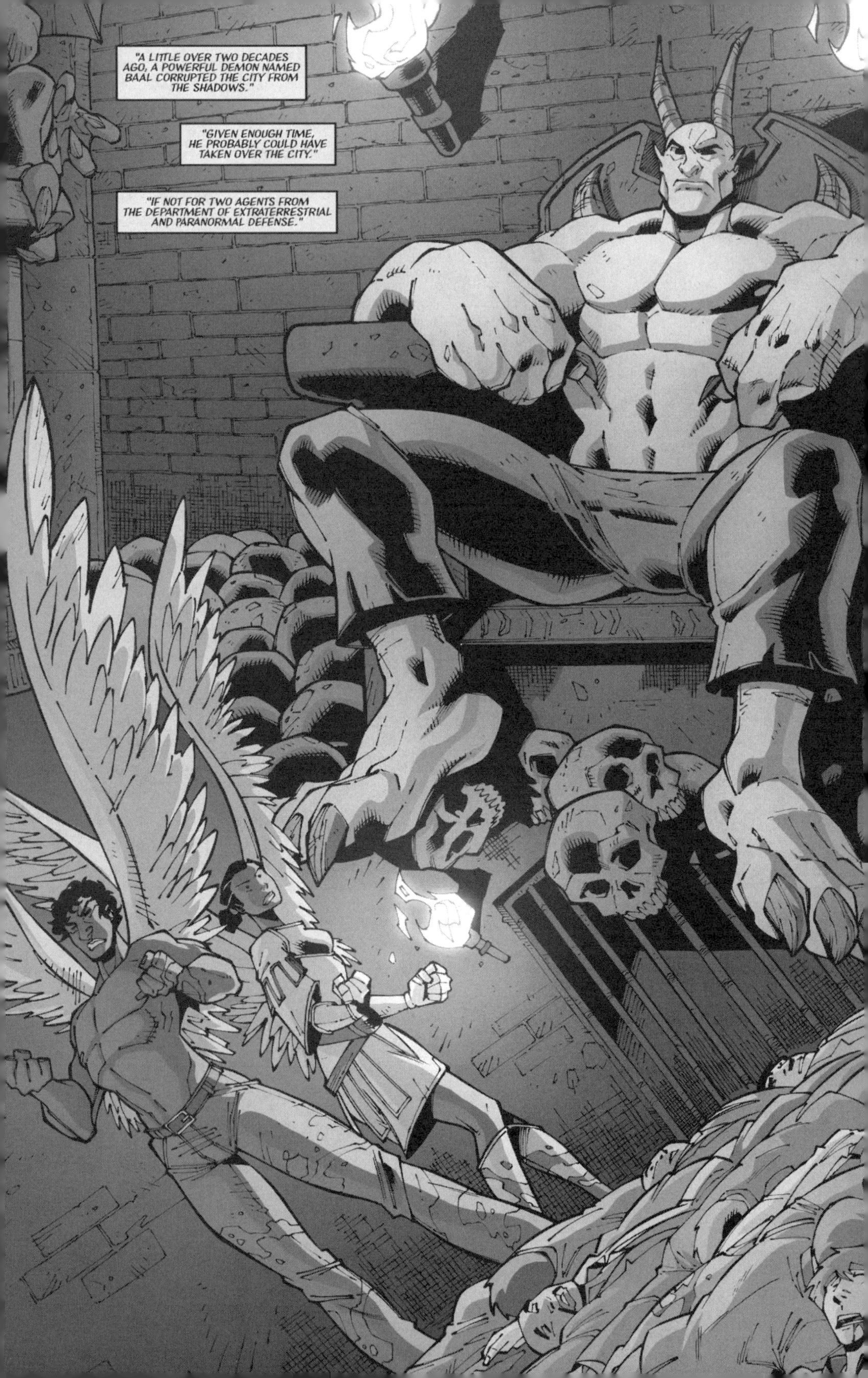
"A LITTLE OVER TWO DECADES AGO, A POWERFUL DEMON NAMED BAAL CORRUPTED THE CITY FROM THE SHADOWS."
"GIVEN ENOUGH TIME, HE PROBABLY COULD HAVE TAKEN OVER THE CITY."
"IF NOT FOR TWO AGENTS FROM THE DEPARTMENT OF EXTRATERRESTRIAL AND PARANORMAL DEFENSE."

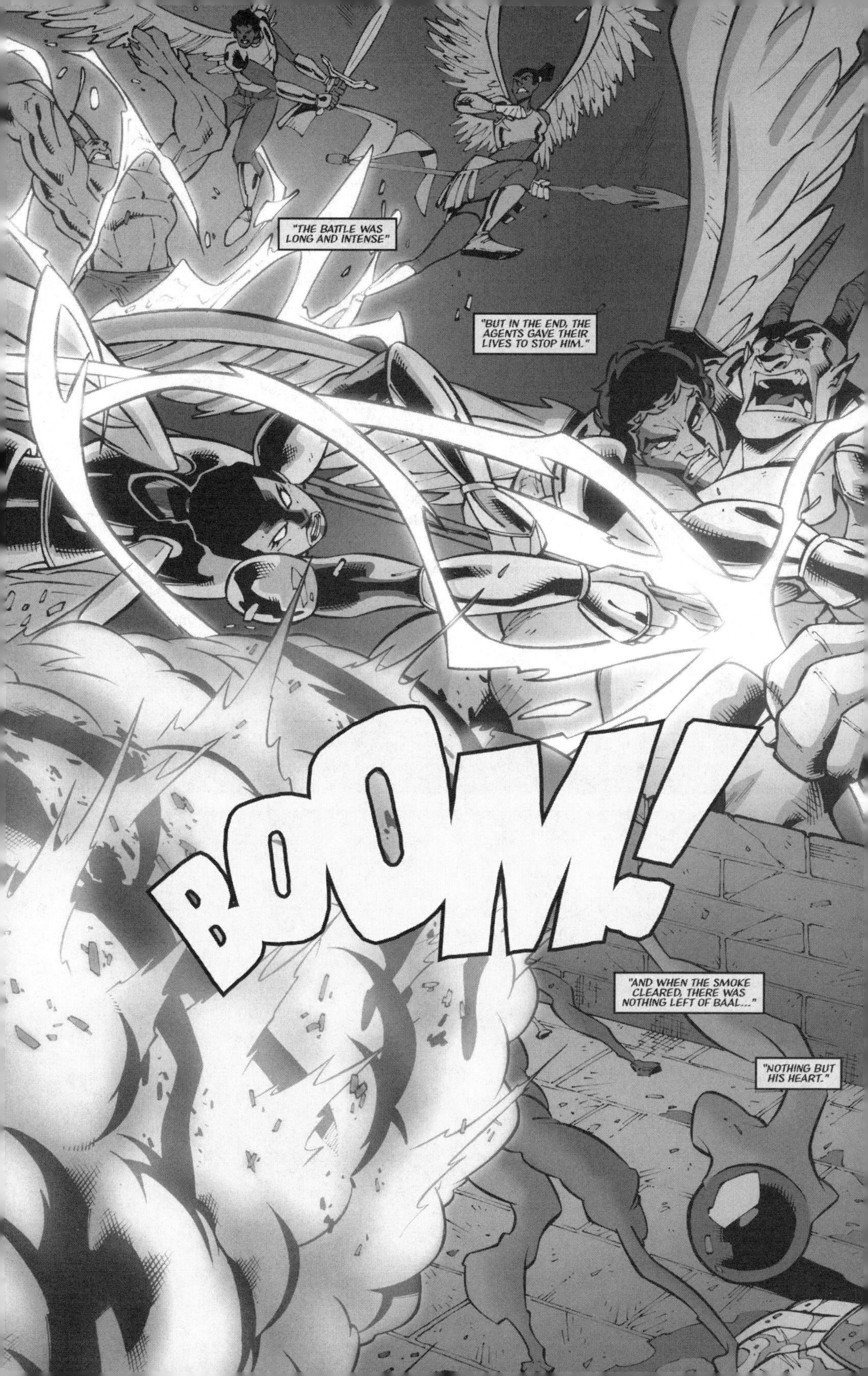
"THE BATTLE WAS LONG AND INTENSE"
"BUT IN THE END, THE AGENTS GAVE THEIR LIVES TO STOP HIM."
BOOM!
"AND WHEN THE SMOKE CLEARED, THERE WAS NOTHING LEFT OF BAAL..."
"NOTHING BUT HIS HEART."

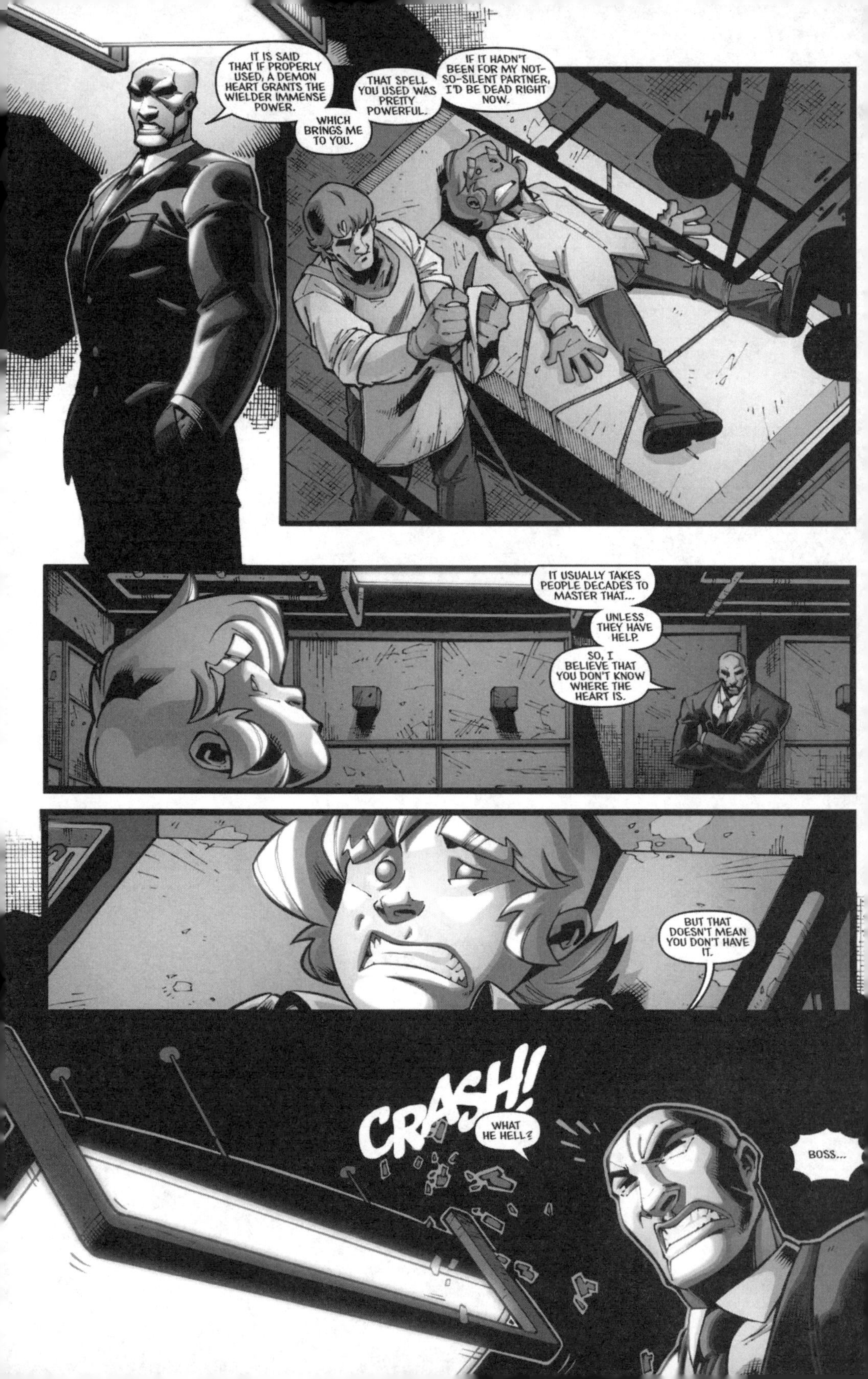

IT IS SAID THAT IF PROPERLY USED, A DEMON HEART GRANTS THE WIELDER IMMENSE POWER.
WHICH BRINGS ME TO YOU.
THAT SPELL YOU USED WAS PRETTY POWERFUL.
IF IT HADN'T BEEN FOR MY NOT-SO-SILENT PARTNER, I'D BE DEAD RIGHT NOW.
IT USUALLY TAKES PEOPLE DECADES TO MASTER THAT...
UNLESS THEY HAVE HELP.
SO, I BELIEVE THAT YOU DON'T KNOW WHERE THE HEART IS.
BUT THAT DOESN'T MEAN YOU DON'T HAVE IT.
CRASH!
WHAT HE HELL?
BOSS...

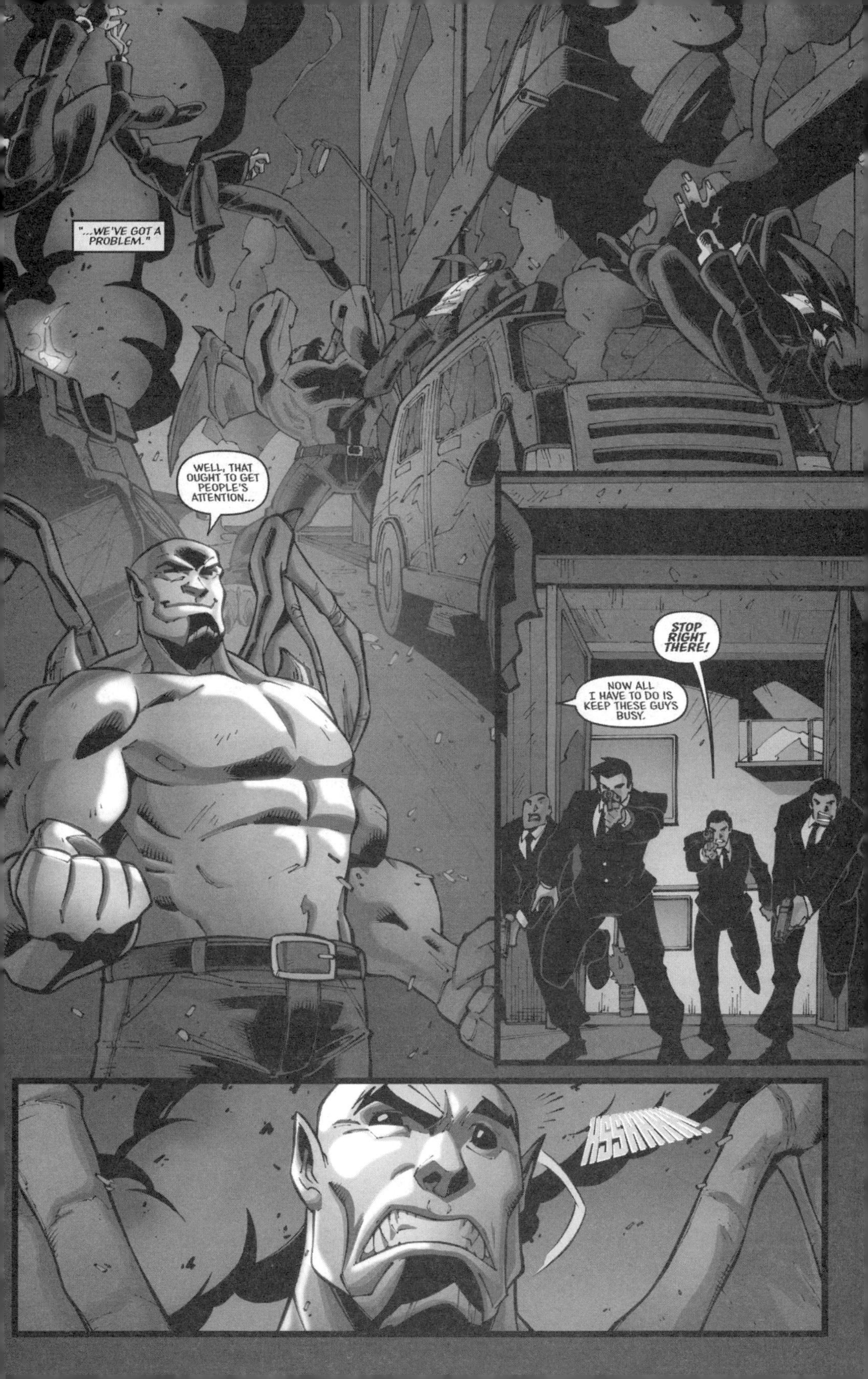
"...WE'VE GOT A PROBLEM."
WELL, THAT OUGHT TO GET PEOPLE'S ATTENTION...
STOP RIGHT THERE!
NOW ALL I HAVE TO DO IS KEEP THESE GUYS BUSY.
HSSHHHH!

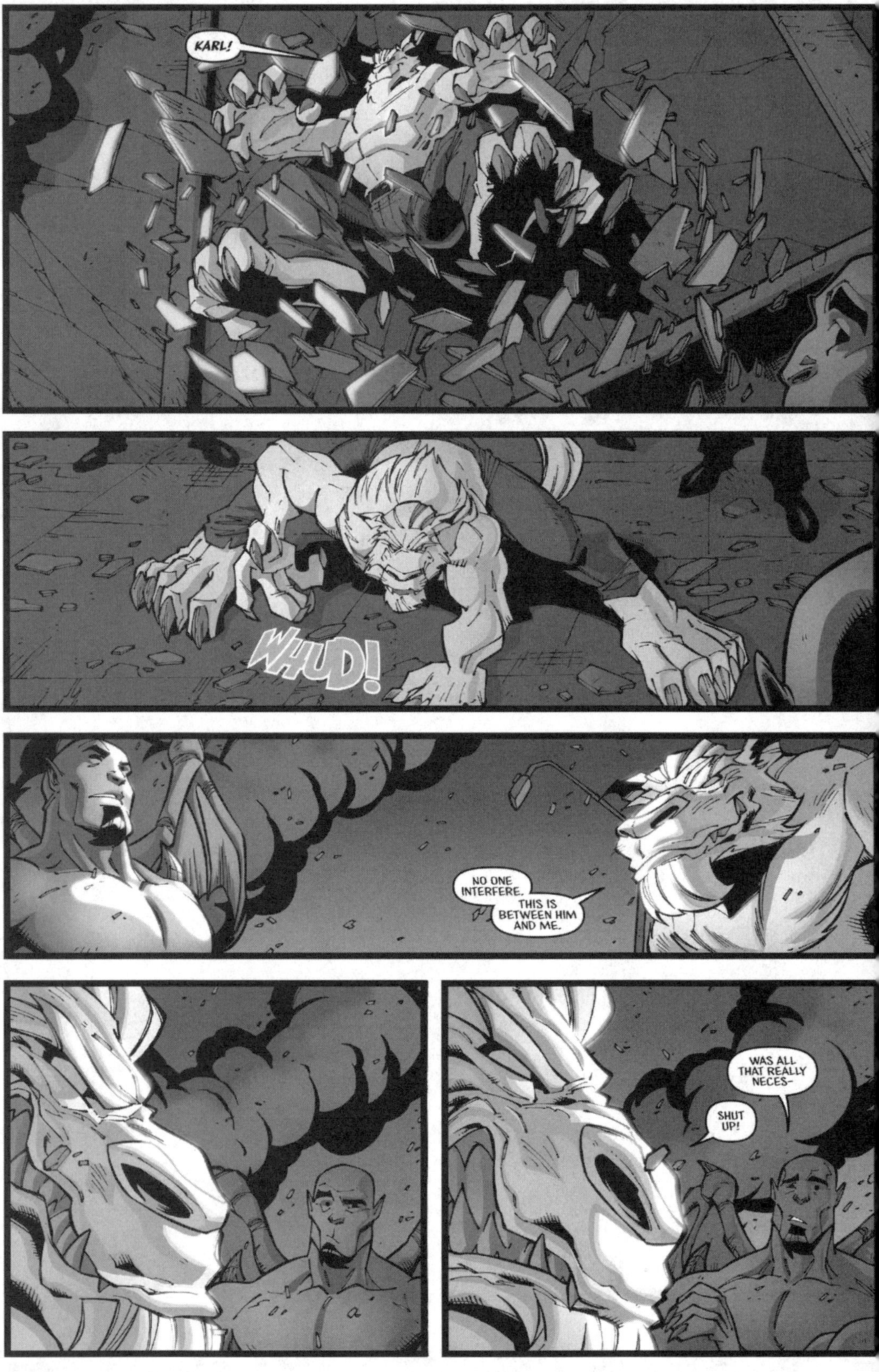
KARL!
WHUD!
NO ONE INTERFERE.
THIS IS BETWEEN HIM AND ME.
WAS ALL THAT REALLY NECES-
SHUT UP!

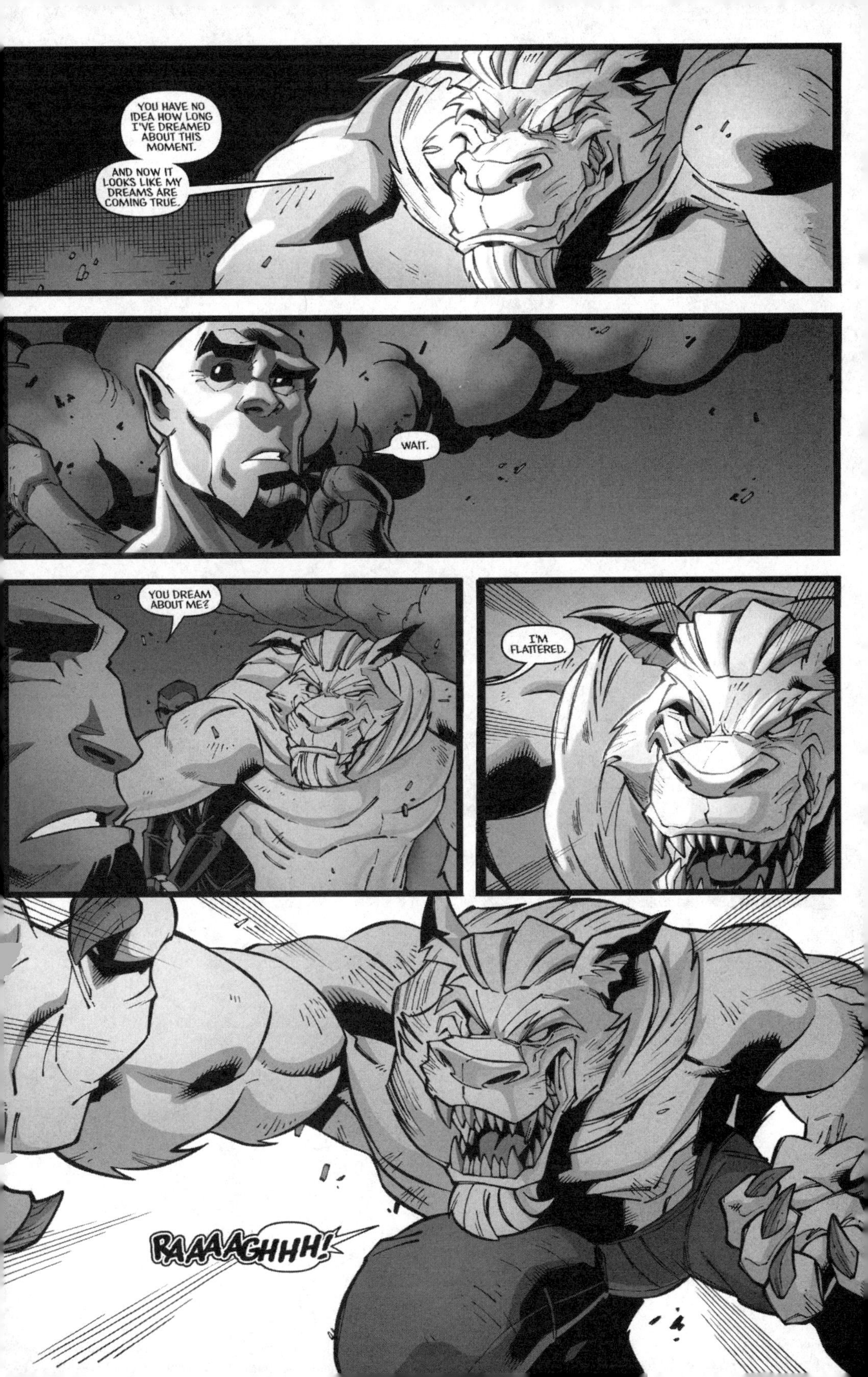
YOU HAVE NO IDEA HOW LONG I'VE DREAMED ABOUT THIS MOMENT.
AND NOW IT LOOKS LIKE MY DREAMS ARE COMING TRUE.
WAIT.
YOU DREAM ABOUT ME?
I'M FLATTERED.
RAAAAGHHH!

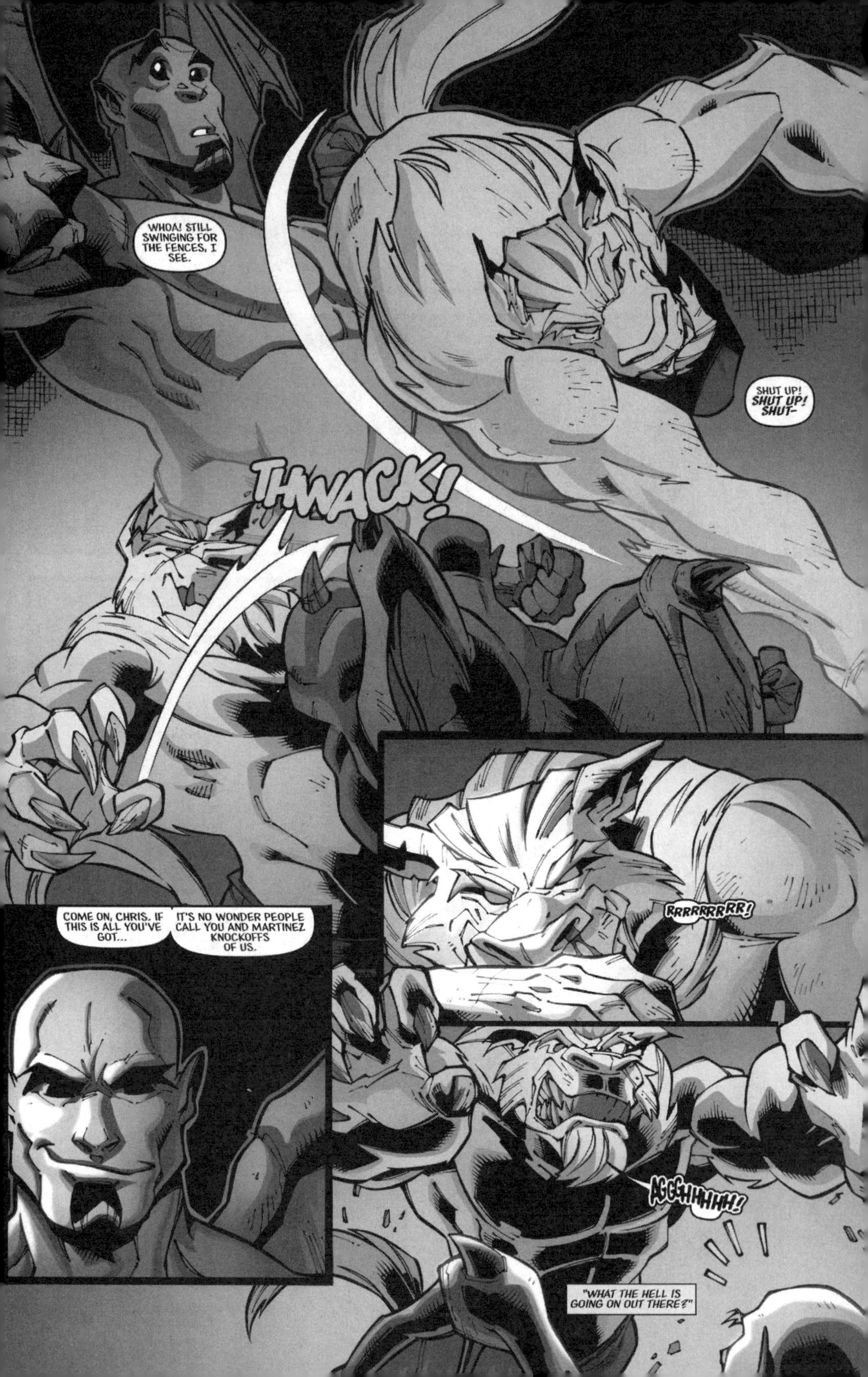
WHOA! STILL SWINGING FOR THE FENCES, I SEE.
SHUT UP! SHUT UP! SHUT-
THWACK!
COME ON, CHRIS. IF THIS IS ALL YOU'VE GOT...
IT'S NO WONDER PEOPLE CALL YOU AND MARTINEZ KNOCKOFFS OF US.
RRRRRRRRR!
AGGGHHHHH!
"WHAT THE HELL IS GOING ON OUT THERE?"

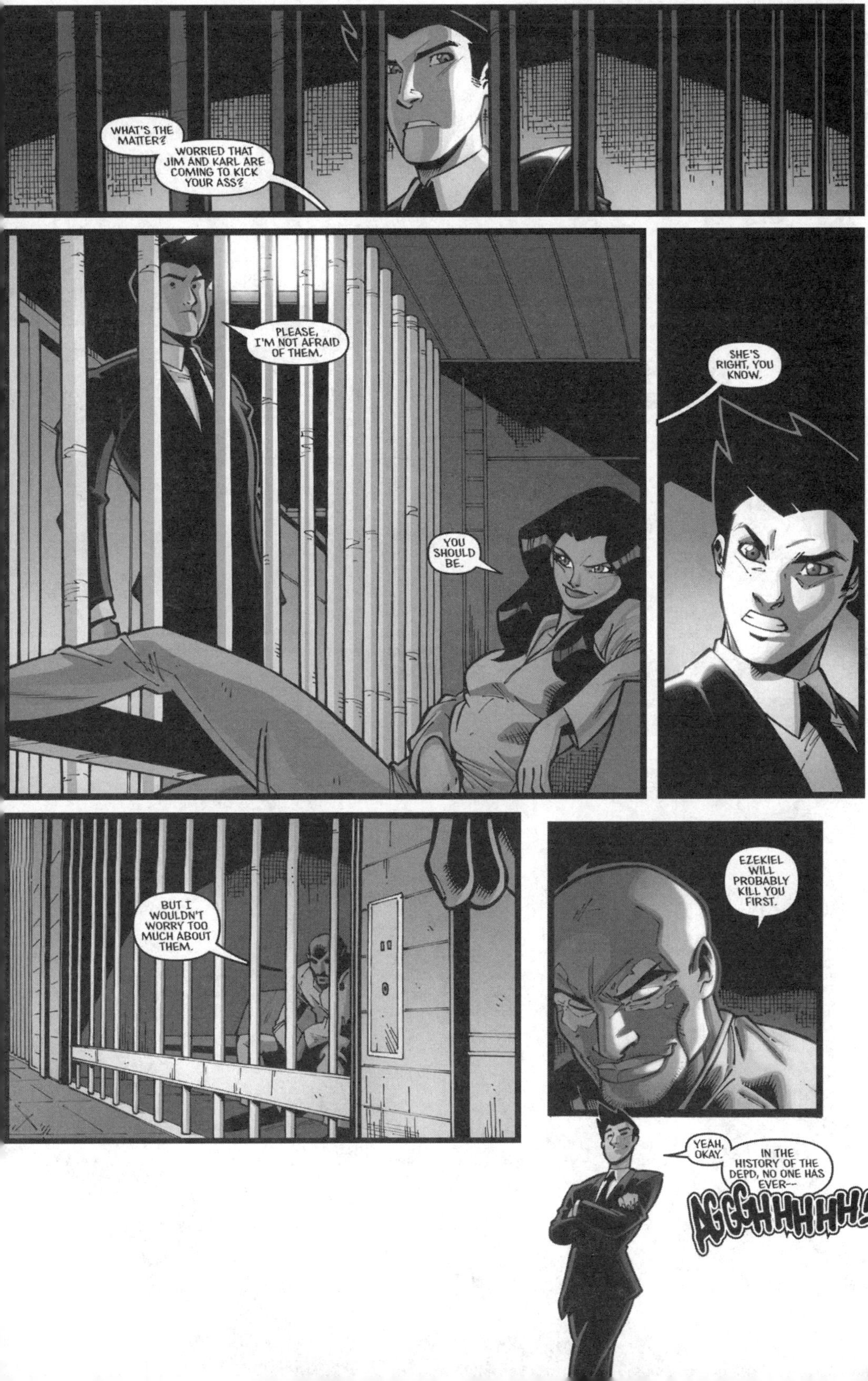
WHAT'S THE MATTER?
WORRIED THAT JIM AND KARL ARE COMING TO KICK YOUR ASS?
PLEASE, I'M NOT AFRAID OF THEM.
YOU SHOULD BE.
SHE'S RIGHT, YOU KNOW.
BUT I WOULDN'T WORRY TOO MUCH ABOUT THEM.
EZEKIEL WILL PROBABLY KILL YOU FIRST.
YEAH, OKAY.
IN THE HISTORY OF THE DEPD, NO ONE HAS EVER--
AGGHHHHHH!

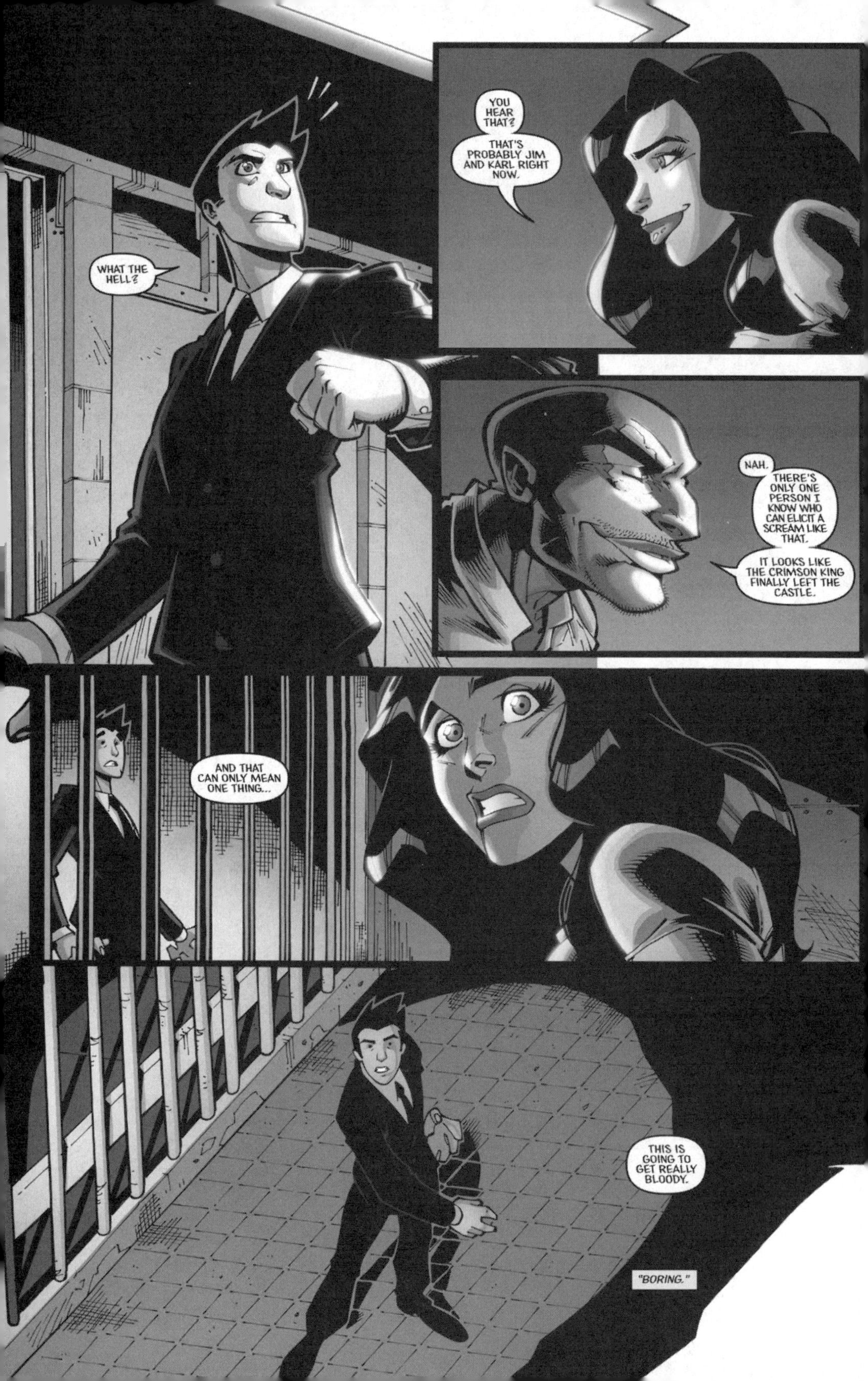
WHAT THE HELL?
YOU HEAR THAT?
THAT'S PROBABLY JIM AND KARL RIGHT NOW.
NAH.
THERE'S ONLY ONE PERSON I KNOW WHO CAN ELICIT A SCREAM LIKE THAT.
IT LOOKS LIKE THE CRIMSON KING FINALLY LEFT THE CASTLE.
AND THAT CAN ONLY MEAN ONE THING...
THIS IS GOING TO GET REALLY BLOODY.
"BORING."

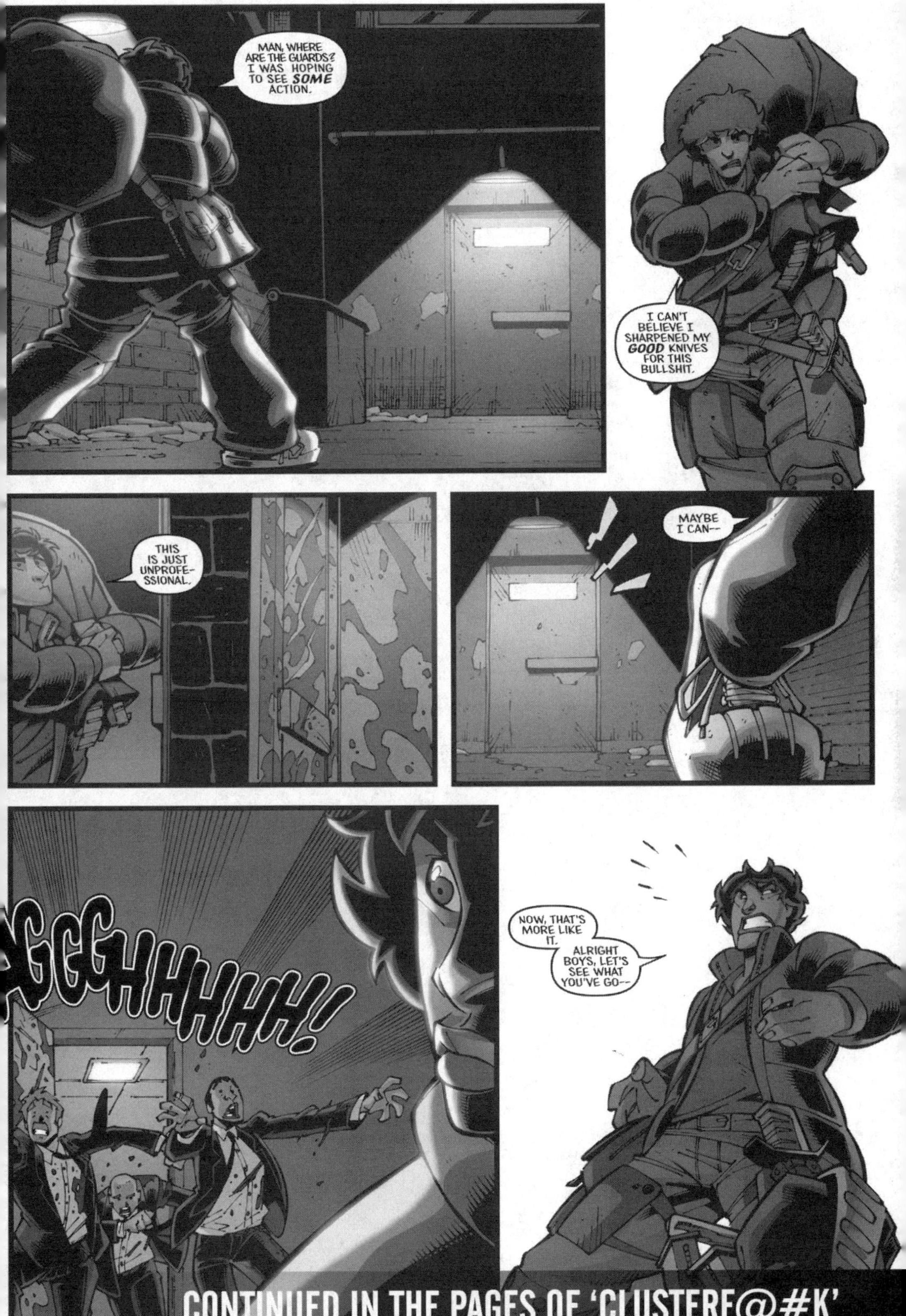
MAN, WHERE ARE THE GUARDS? I WAS HOPING TO SEE SOME ACTION.
I CAN'T BELIEVE I SHARPENED MY GOOD KNIVES FOR THIS BULLSHIT.
THIS IS JUST UNPROFESSIONAL.
MAYBE I CAN--
GGHHHHHH!
NOW, THAT'S MORE LIKE IT.
ALRIGHT BOYS, LET'S SEE WHAT YOU'VE GO--
CONTINUED IN THE PAGES OF 'CLUSTERF@#K'

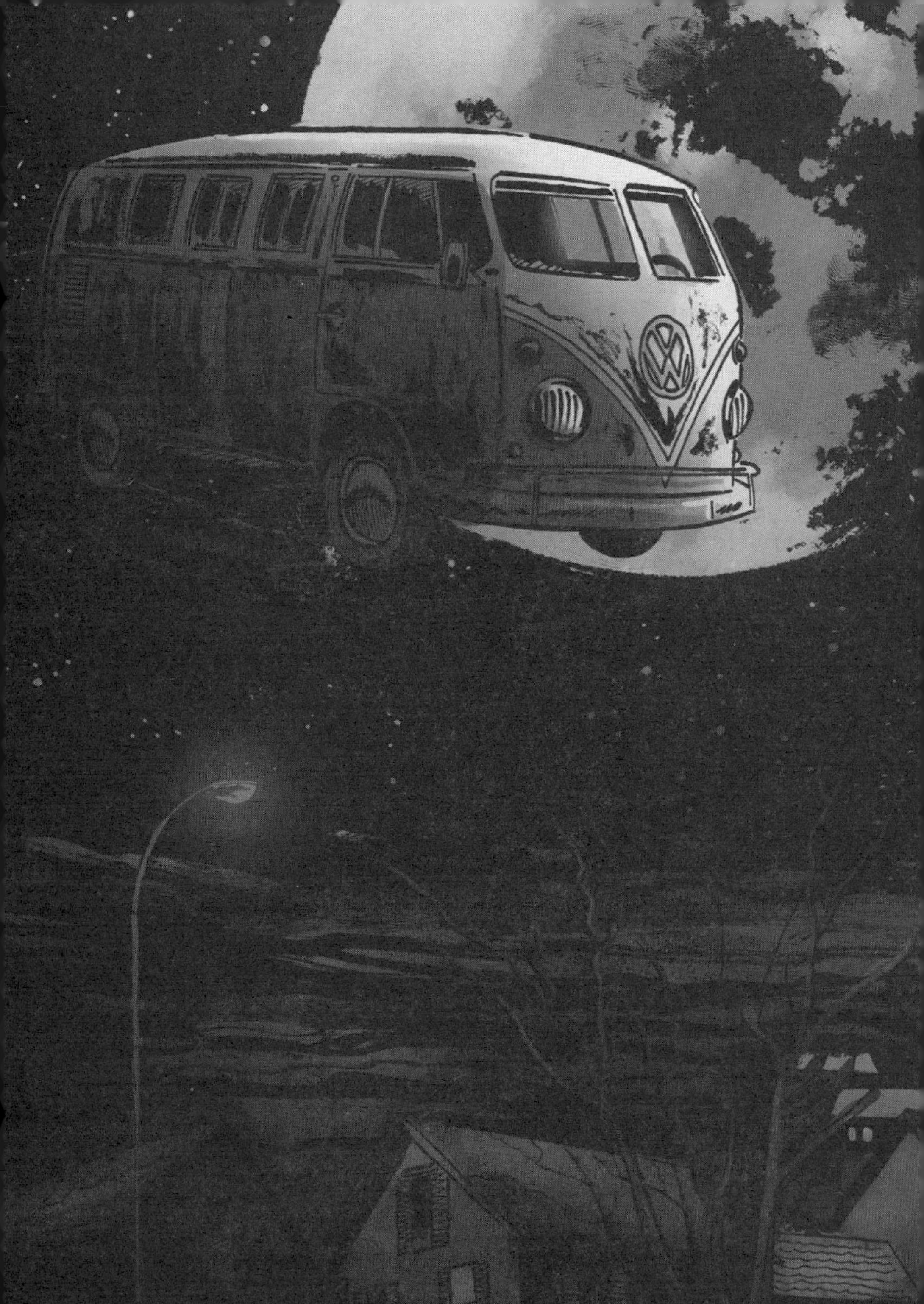

COMPLEX

COMPLEX

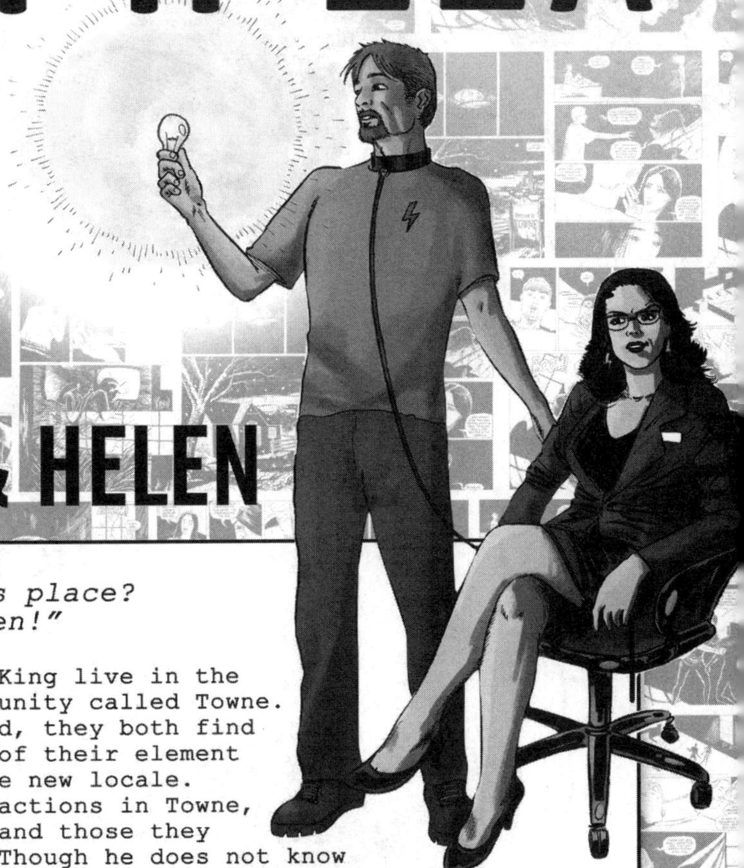

ZACH & HELEN

*"What is this place?
Tell me, Helen!"*

Zach and Helen King live in the artificial community called Towne. Recently married, they both find themselves out of their element in their strange new locale. There are two factions in Towne, the scientists and those they experiment on. Though he does not know why or how, Zach can manipulate and create powerful electric waves. Unfortunately, there's something else that Zach doesn't know - Helen has a secret that threatens to destroy their relationship and even their lives.

ZACH	Age: Unknown	Height: 6'	Weight: 195 lbs.
HELEN	Age: Unknown	Height: 5'8"	Weight: 135 lbs.

First Appearance: Complex #1 (2012)

Created by Michael Malkin
Illustration by Kay

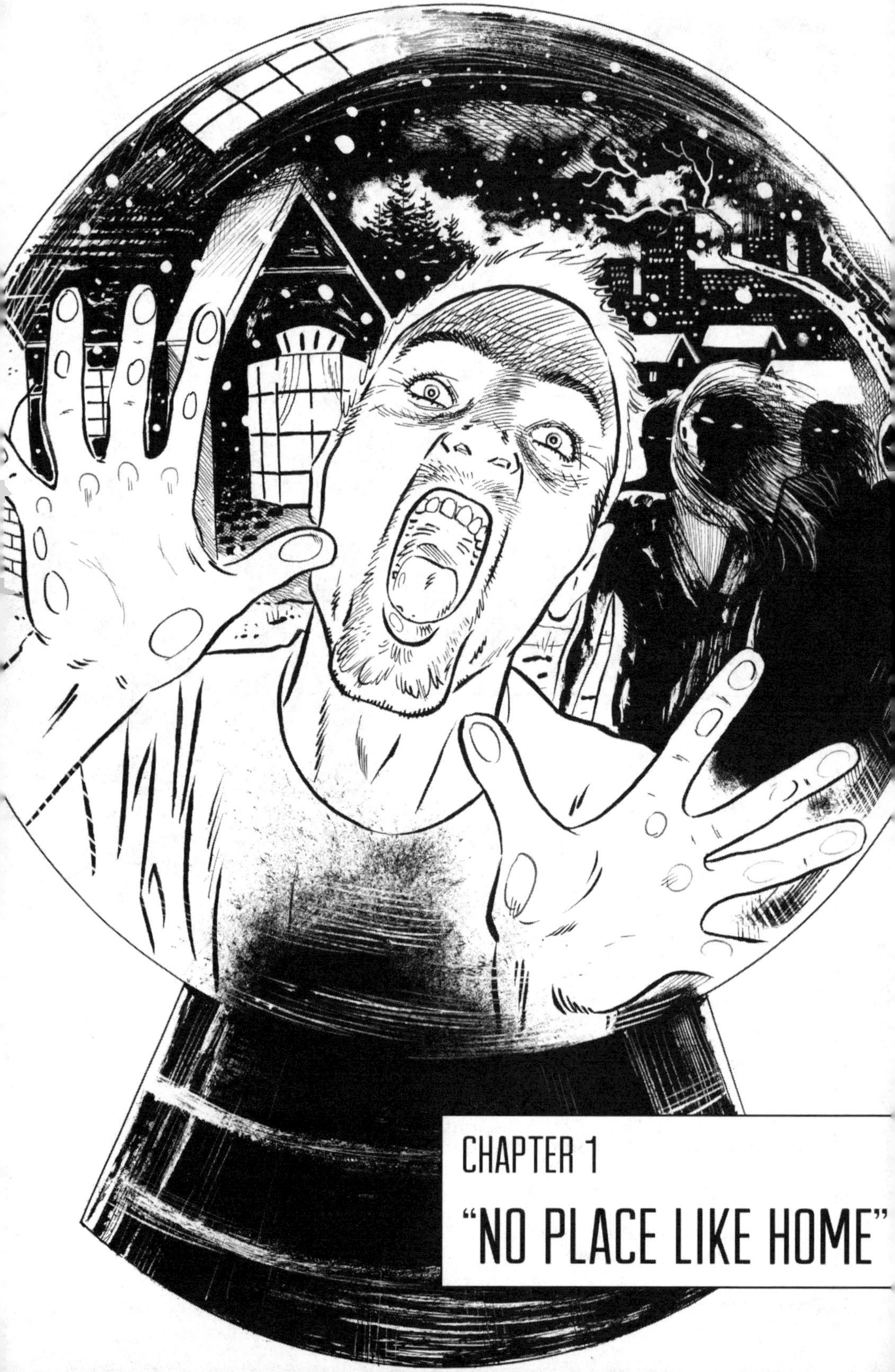

CHAPTER 1

"NO PLACE LIKE HOME"

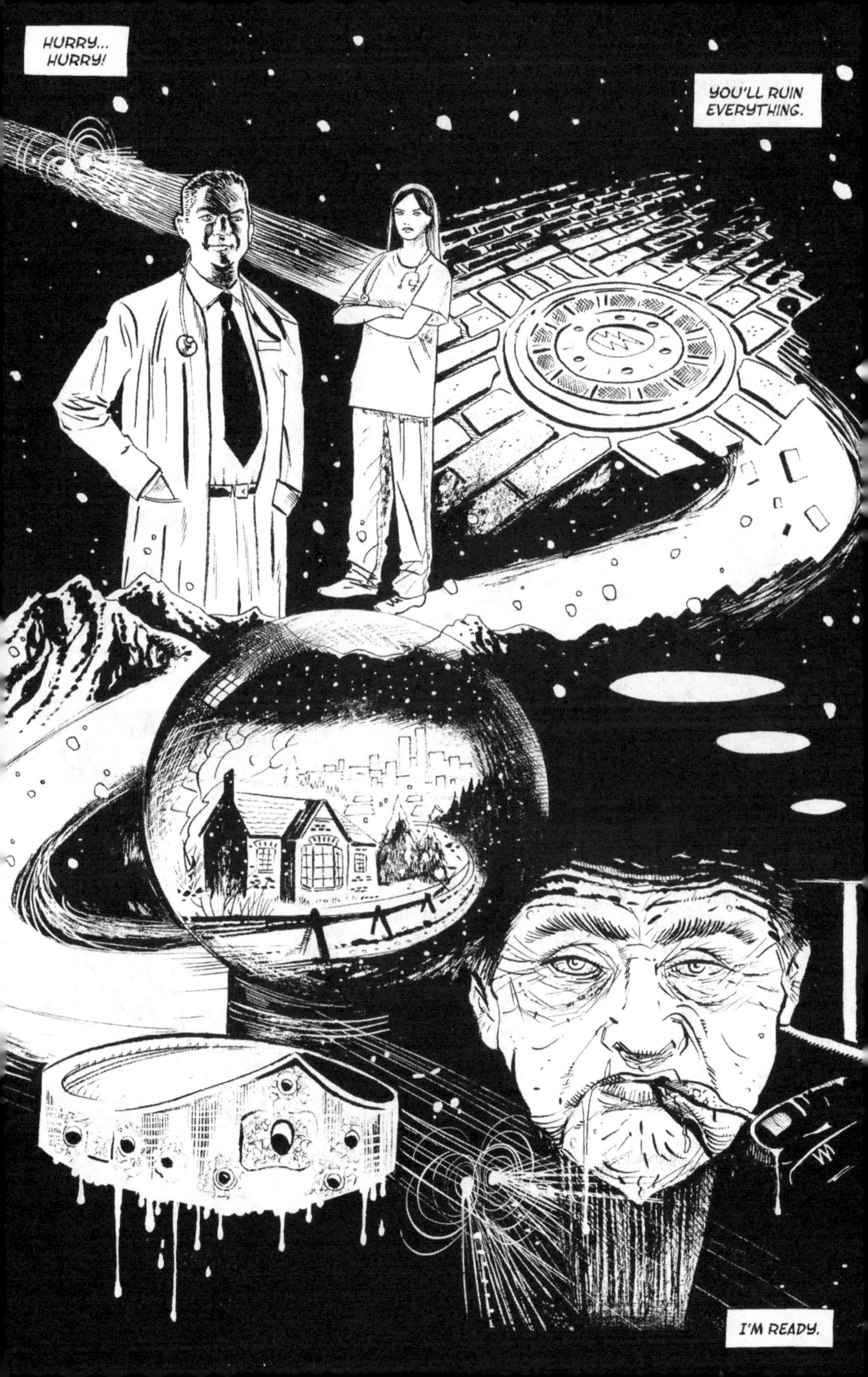
HURRY... HURRY!
YOU'LL RUIN EVERYTHING.
I'M READY.

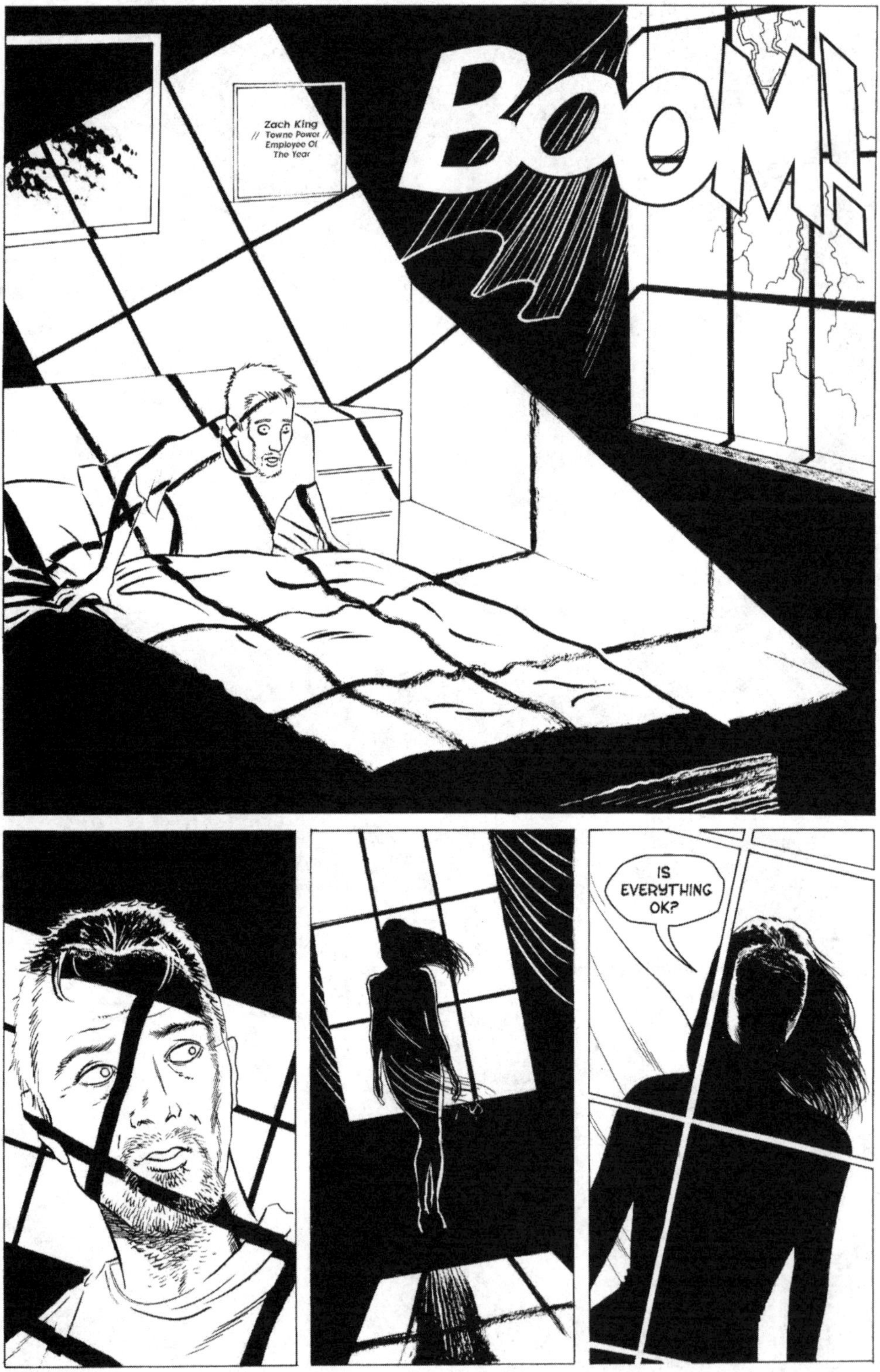
Zach King
// Towne Power //
Employee Of
The Year
BOOM!
IS
EVERYTHING
OK?

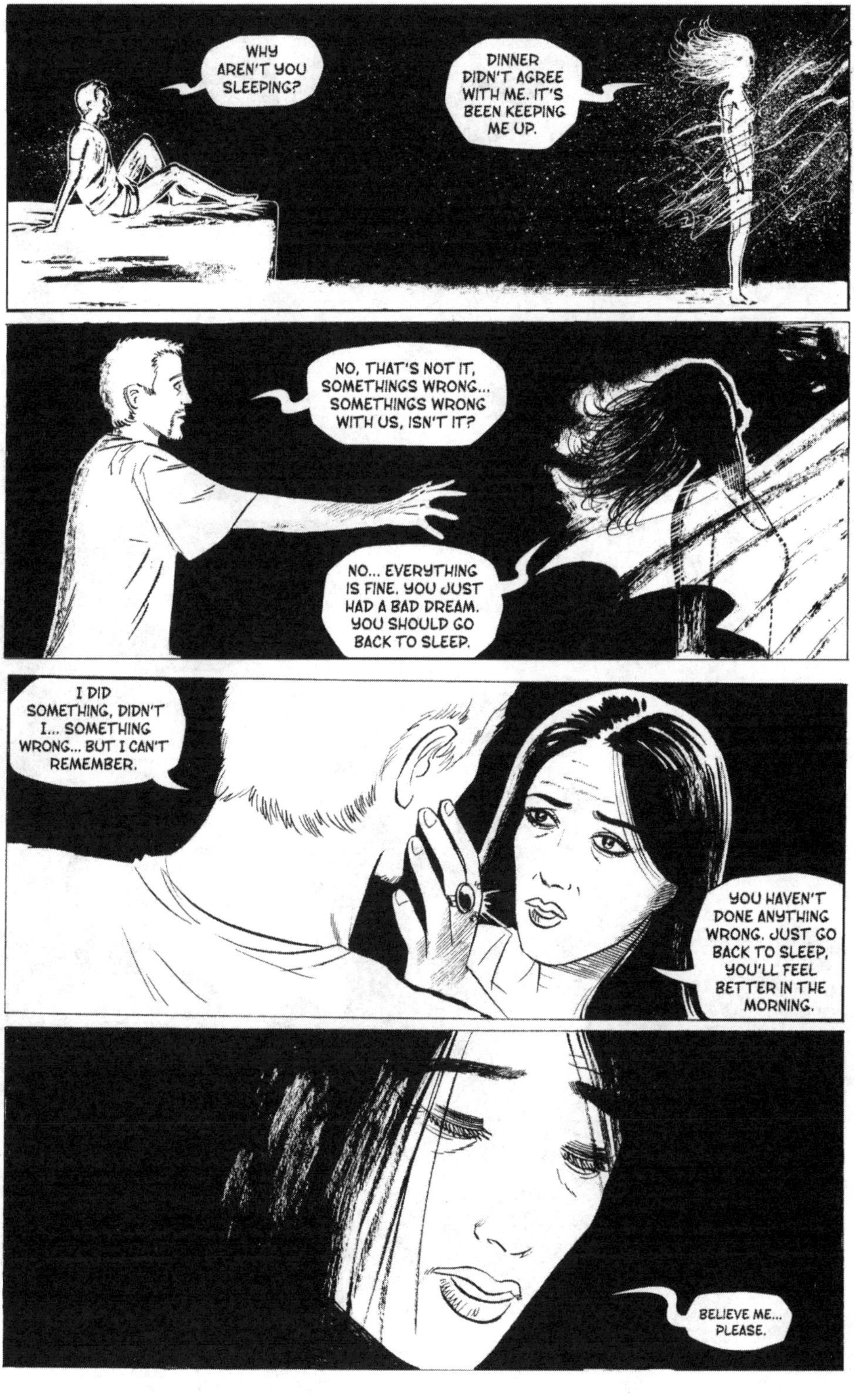
WHY AREN'T YOU SLEEPING?
DINNER DIDN'T AGREE WITH ME. IT'S BEEN KEEPING ME UP.
NO, THAT'S NOT IT, SOMETHINGS WRONG... SOMETHINGS WRONG WITH US, ISN'T IT?
NO... EVERYTHING IS FINE. YOU JUST HAD A BAD DREAM. YOU SHOULD GO BACK TO SLEEP.
I DID SOMETHING, DIDN'T I... SOMETHING WRONG... BUT I CAN'T REMEMBER.
YOU HAVEN'T DONE ANYTHING WRONG. JUST GO BACK TO SLEEP, YOU'LL FEEL BETTER IN THE MORNING.
BELIEVE ME... PLEASE.

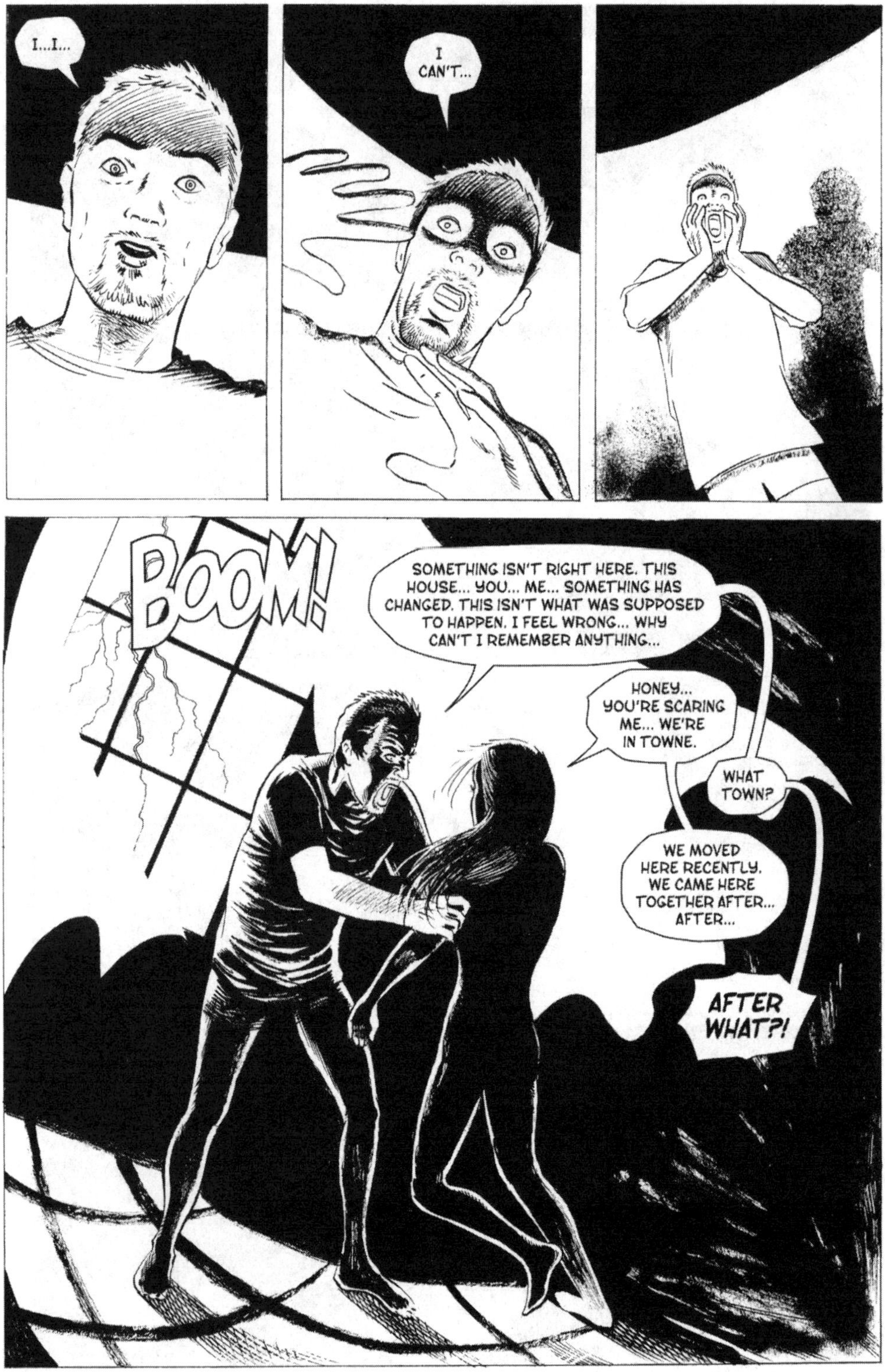
I...I...
I CAN'T...
BOOM!
SOMETHING ISN'T RIGHT HERE. THIS HOUSE... YOU... ME... SOMETHING HAS CHANGED. THIS ISN'T WHAT WAS SUPPOSED TO HAPPEN. I FEEL WRONG... WHY CAN'T I REMEMBER ANYTHING...
HONEY... YOU'RE SCARING ME... WE'RE IN TOWNE.
WHAT TOWN?
WE MOVED HERE RECENTLY. WE CAME HERE TOGETHER AFTER... AFTER...
AFTER WHAT?!

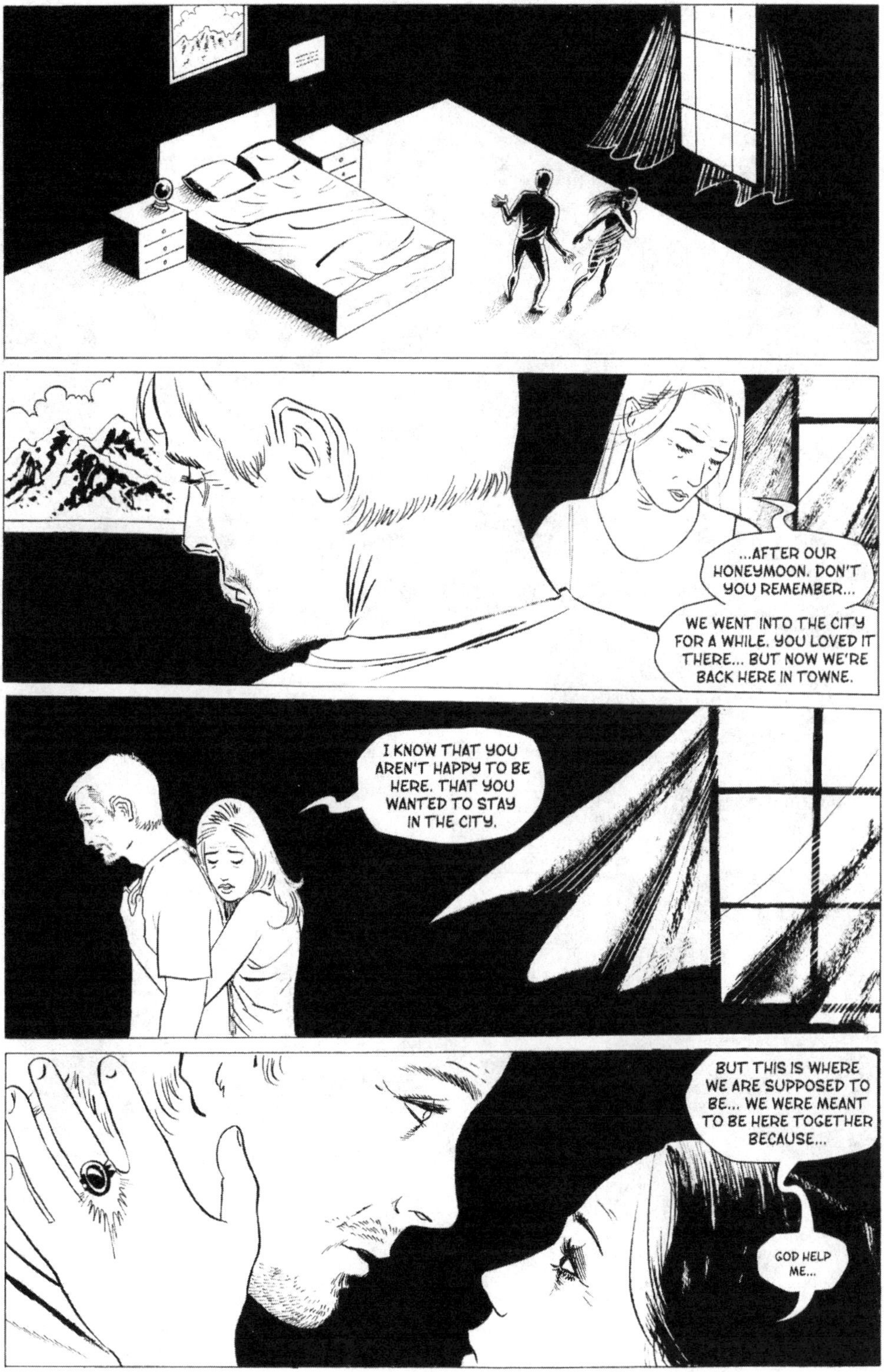
...AFTER OUR HONEYMOON. DON'T YOU REMEMBER...
WE WENT INTO THE CITY FOR A WHILE. YOU LOVED IT THERE... BUT NOW WE'RE BACK HERE IN TOWNE.
I KNOW THAT YOU AREN'T HAPPY TO BE HERE. THAT YOU WANTED TO STAY IN THE CITY.
BUT THIS IS WHERE WE ARE SUPPOSED TO BE... WE WERE MEANT TO BE HERE TOGETHER BECAUSE...
GOD HELP ME...

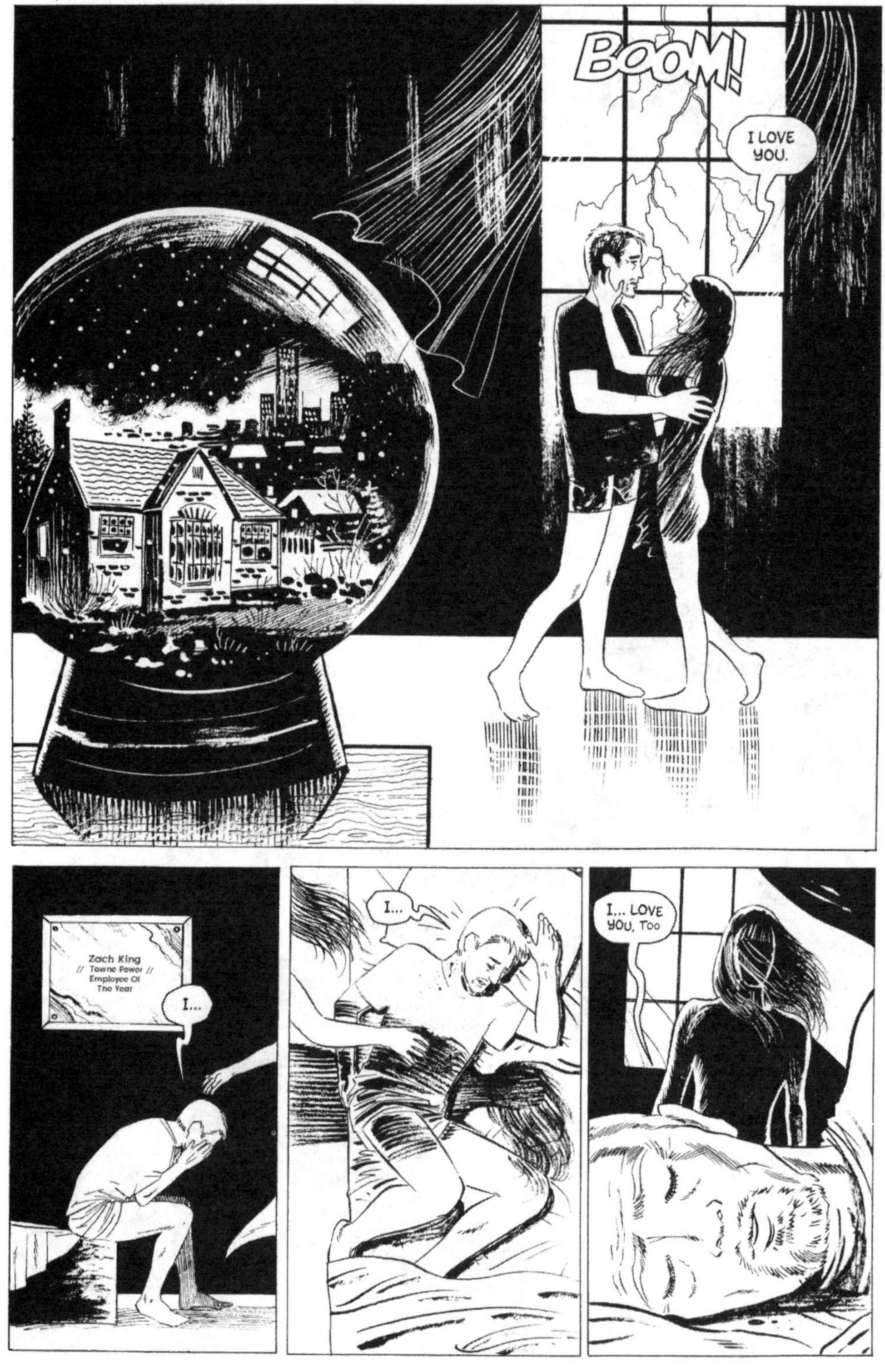
BOOM!
I LOVE YOU.
Zach King
// Towne Power //
Employee Of
The Year
I...
I...
I... LOVE YOU, Too

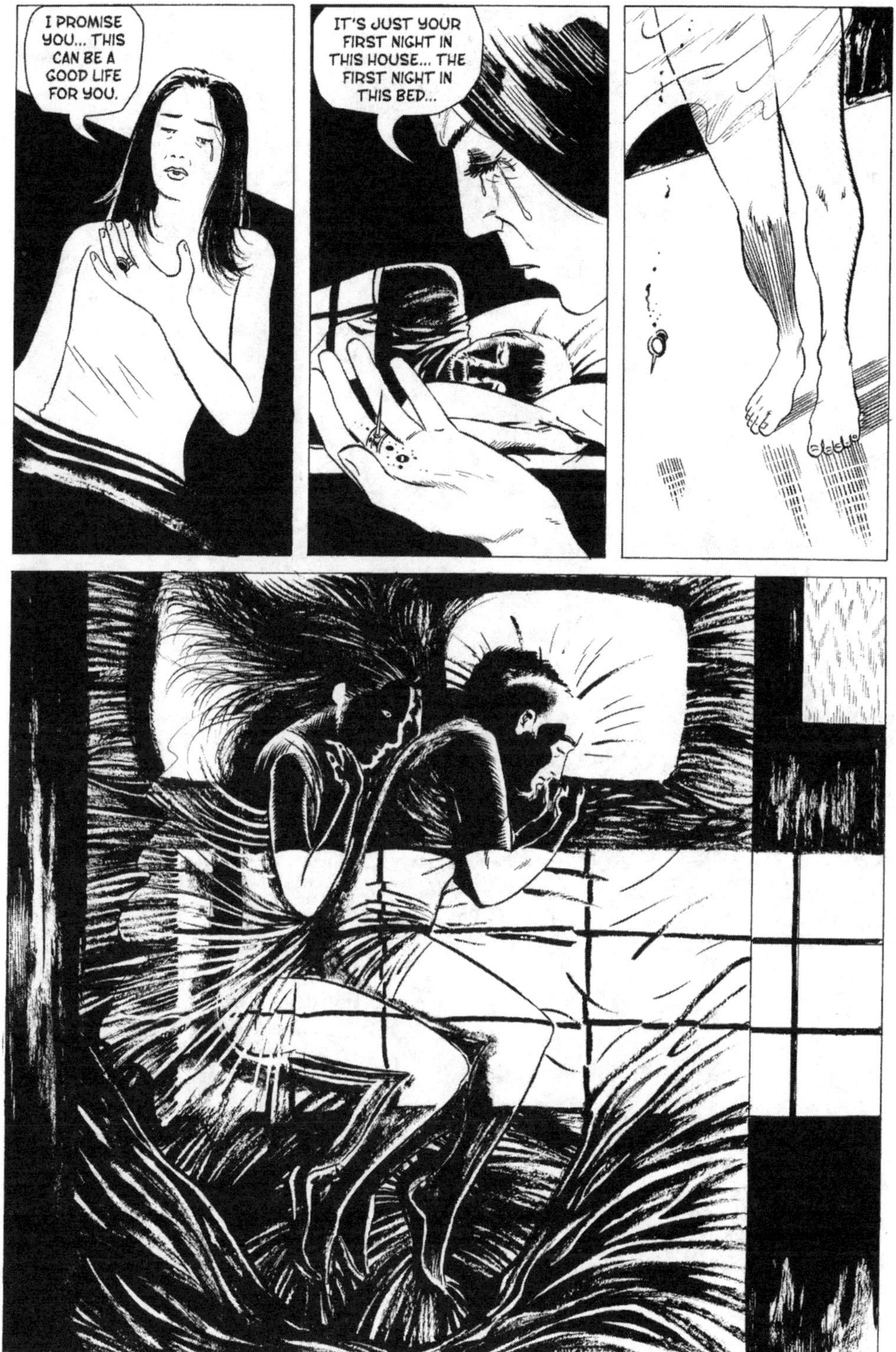
I PROMISE YOU... THIS CAN BE A GOOD LIFE FOR YOU.
IT'S JUST YOUR FIRST NIGHT IN THIS HOUSE... THE FIRST NIGHT IN THIS BED...

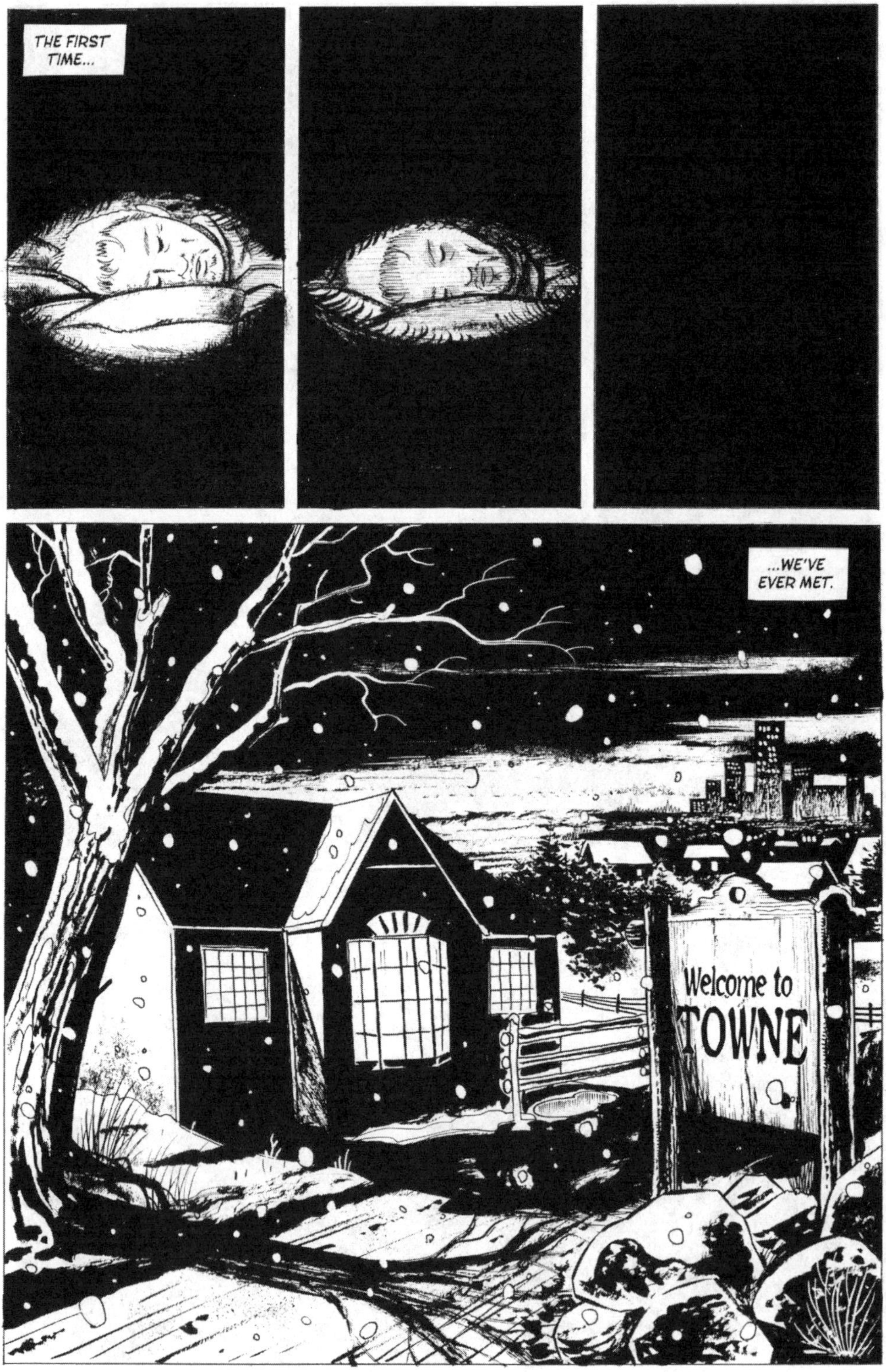
THE FIRST TIME...
...WE'VE EVER MET.
Welcome to
TOWNE

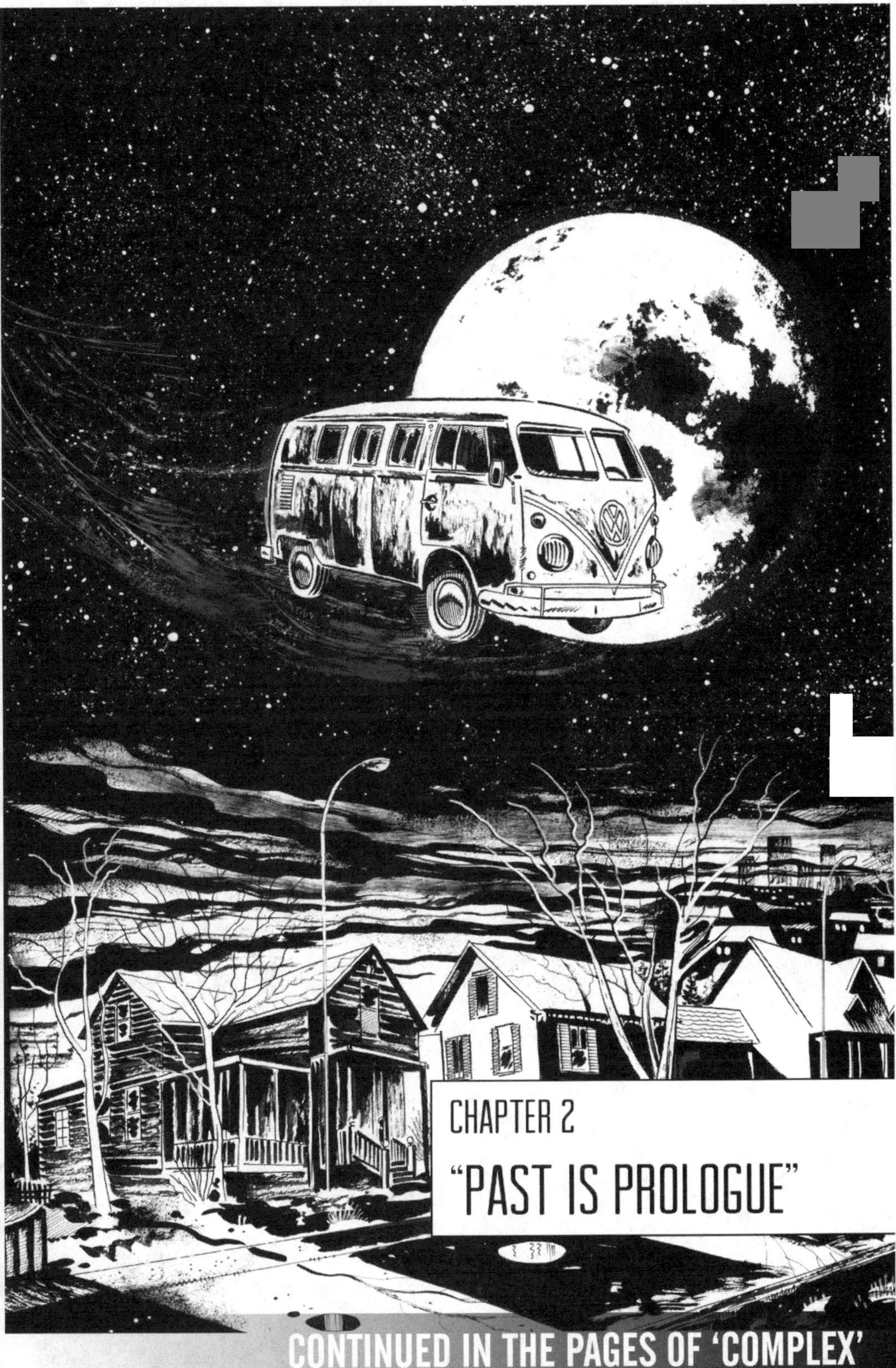
CHAPTER 2
"PAST IS PROLOGUE"

CONTINUED IN THE PAGES OF 'COMPLEX'

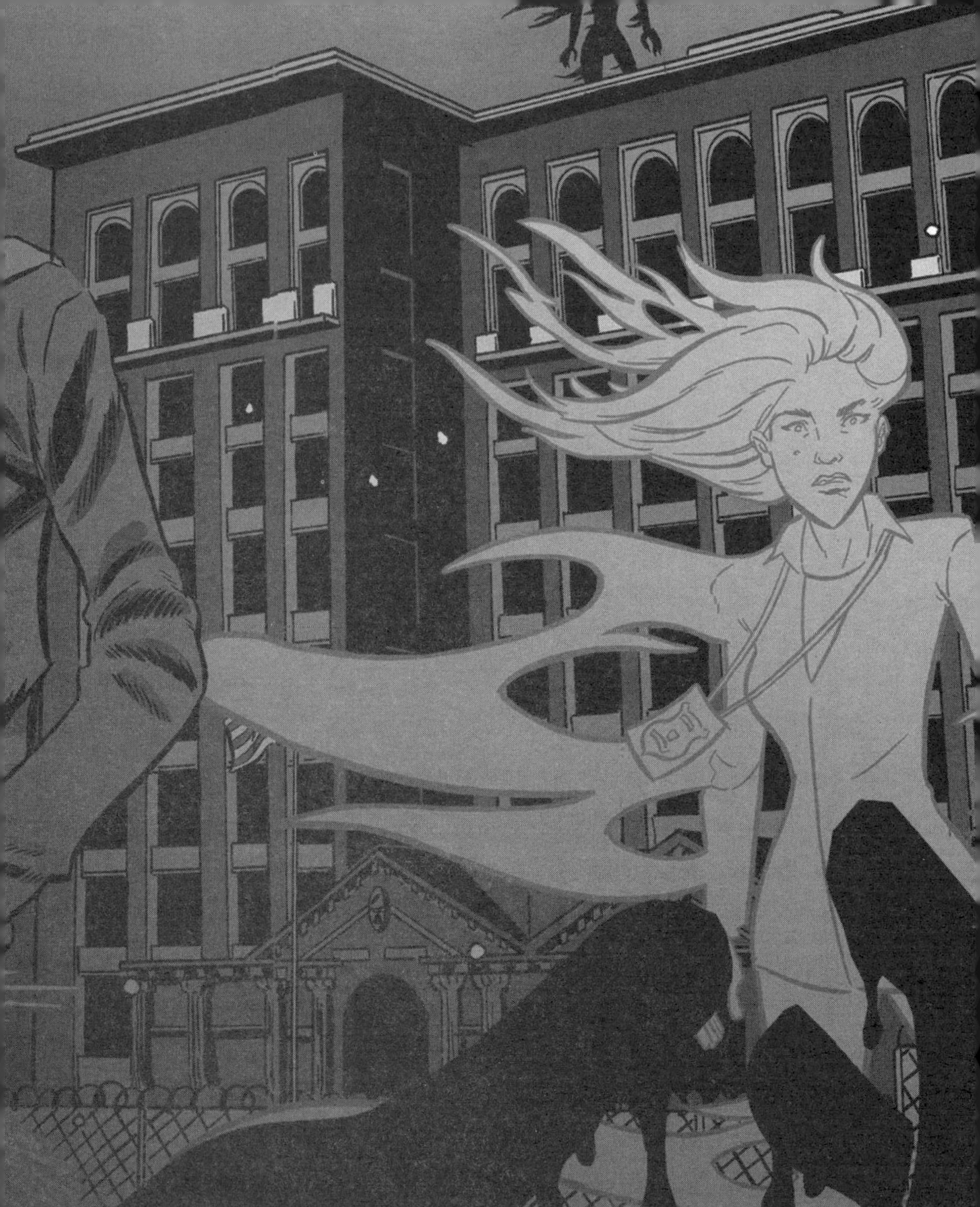

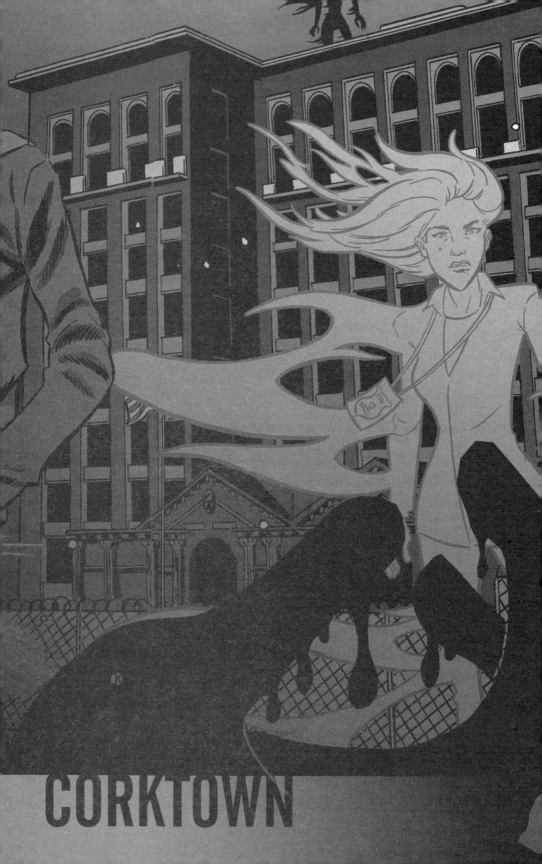

CORKTOWN

Corktown

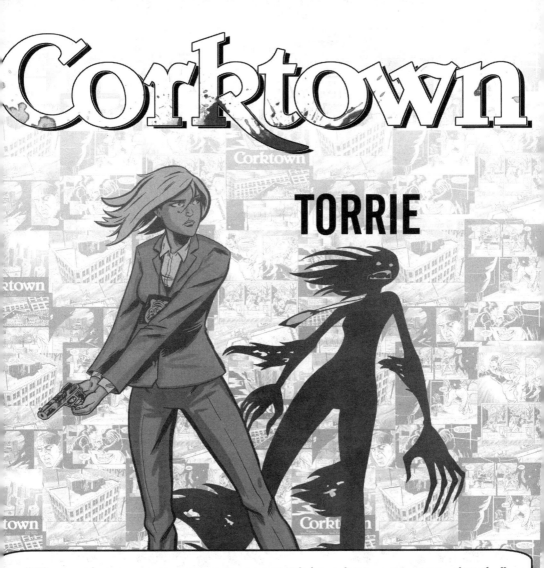

TORRIE

"There is no easy way to say this, but you are dead."

After dying in the line of duty, Detective Torrie Brandstaetter is now forced to roam Detroit as a restless spirit while her reanimated body commits savage murders in the vicinity of the Corktown neighborhood. Unable to physically intervene, she uses her supernatural abilities to push her former partner in the right direction in hopes of destroying the shell of her former self, so she can finally move on to the next world.

Age: 36   Height: Variable   Weight: 21 grams

First Appearance: CORKTOWN #1 (2016)

Created by Scott Ewen & Mario Candelaria
Illustration by Scott Ewen

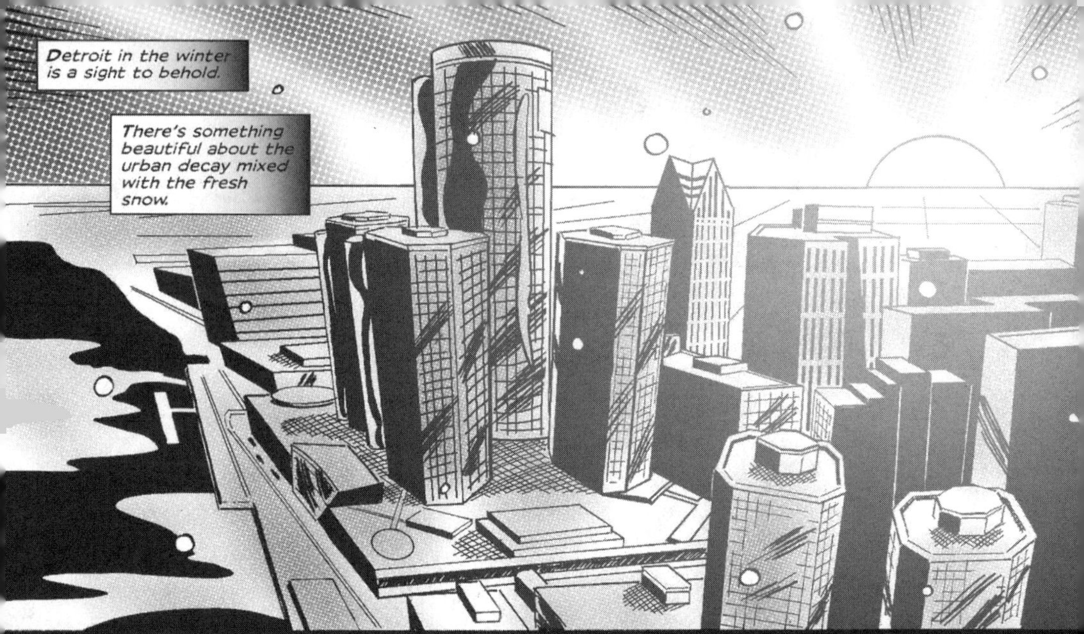
Detroit in the winter is a sight to behold.
There's something beautiful about the urban decay mixed with the fresh snow.

Corktown

Written by Mario Candelaria

Art by Scott Ewen

Lettering by Zakk Saam

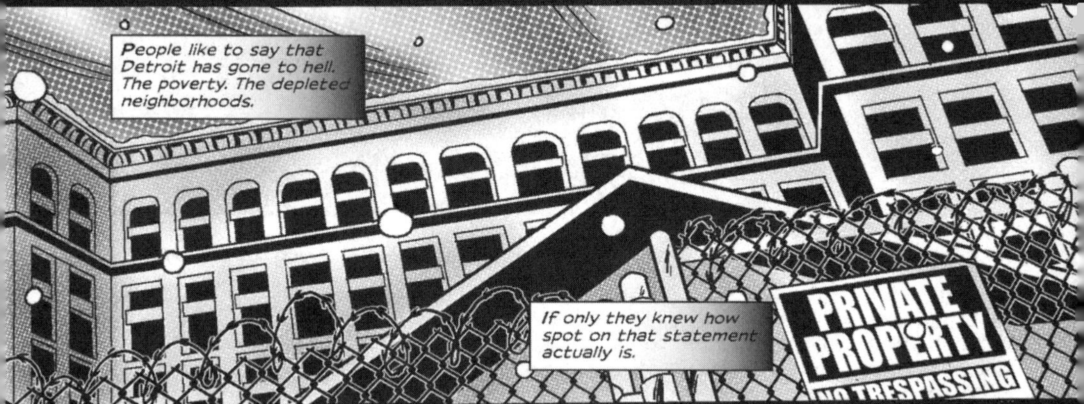
People like to say that Detroit has gone to hell. The poverty. The depleted neighborhoods.
If only they knew how spot on that statement actually is.
PRIVATE PROPERTY
NO TRESPASSING

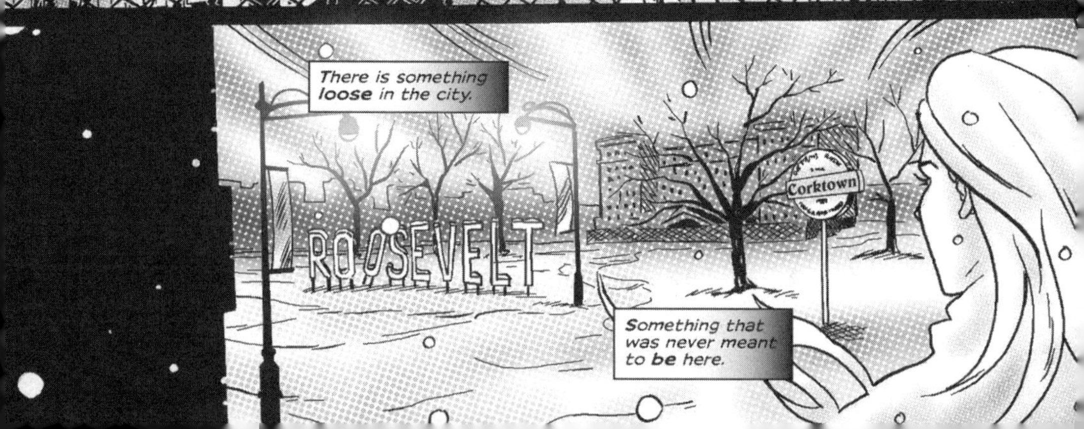
There is something loose in the city.
ROOSEVELT
Corktown
Something that was never meant to be here.

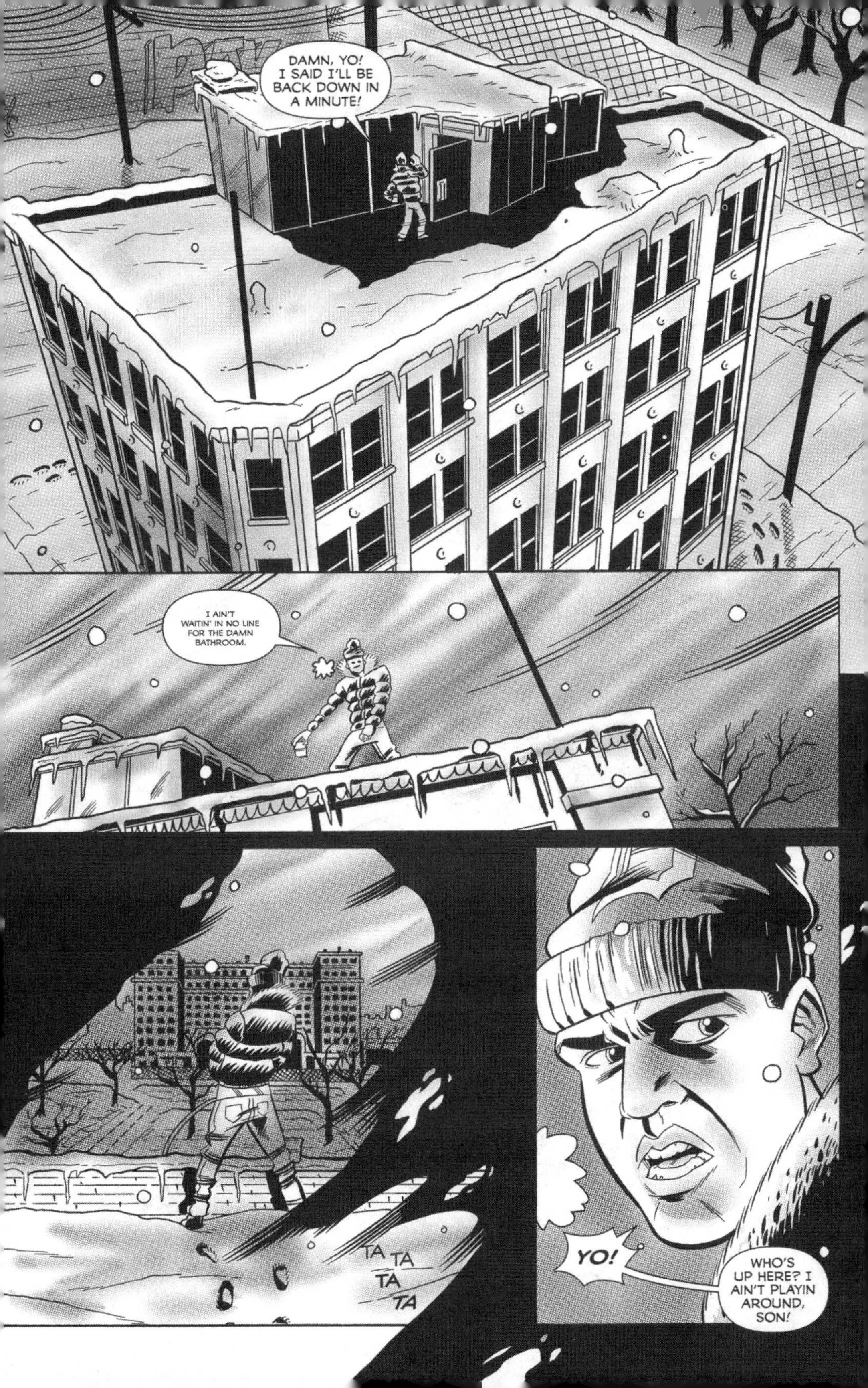
DAMN, YO! I SAID I'LL BE BACK DOWN IN A MINUTE!
I AIN'T WAITIN' IN NO LINE FOR THE DAMN BATHROOM.
TA TA TA TA
YO!
WHO'S UP HERE? I AIN'T PLAYIN AROUND, SON!

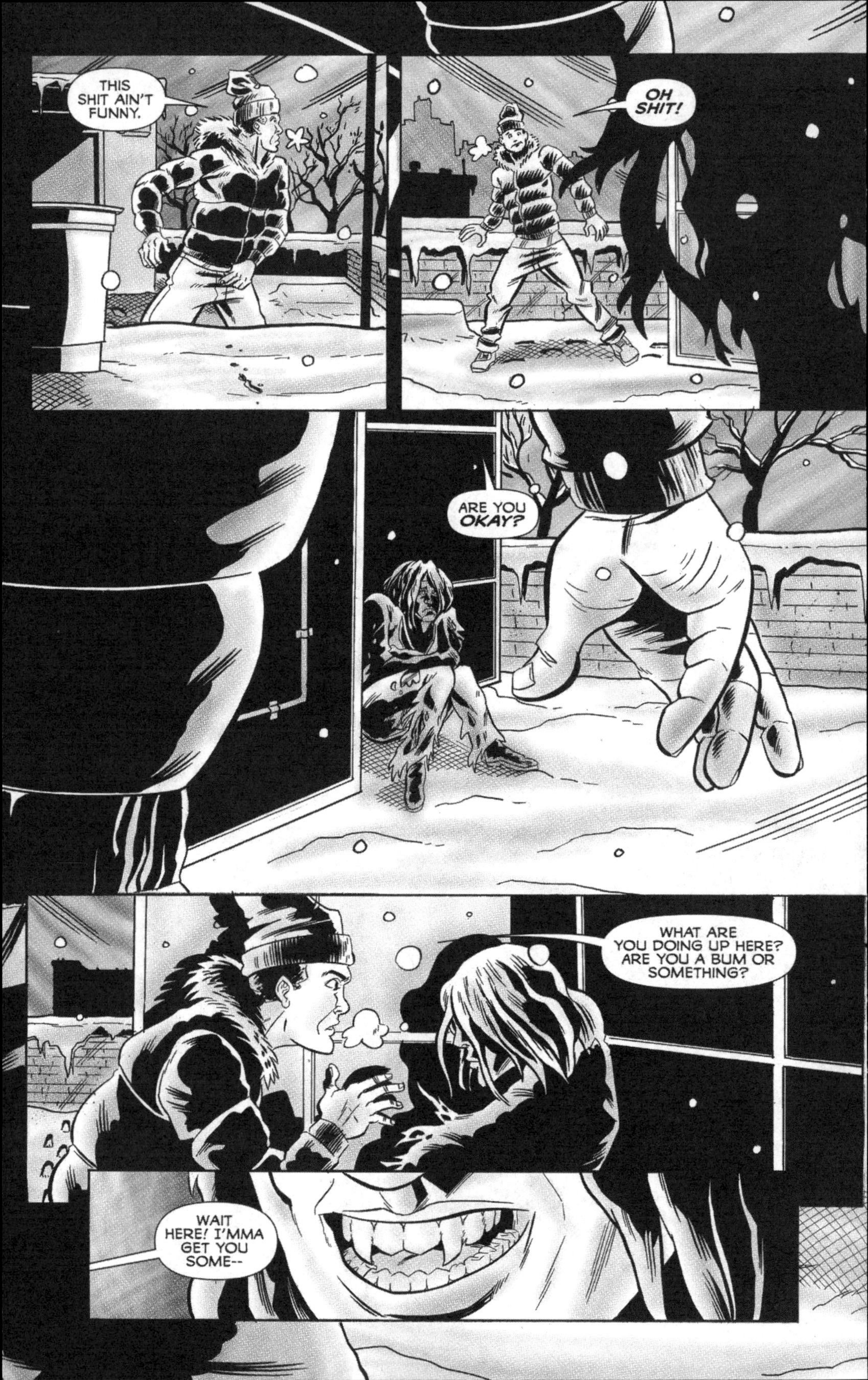
THIS SHIT AIN'T FUNNY.
OH SHIT!
ARE YOU OKAY?
WHAT ARE YOU DOING UP HERE? ARE YOU A BUM OR SOMETHING?
WAIT HERE! I'MMA GET YOU SOME--

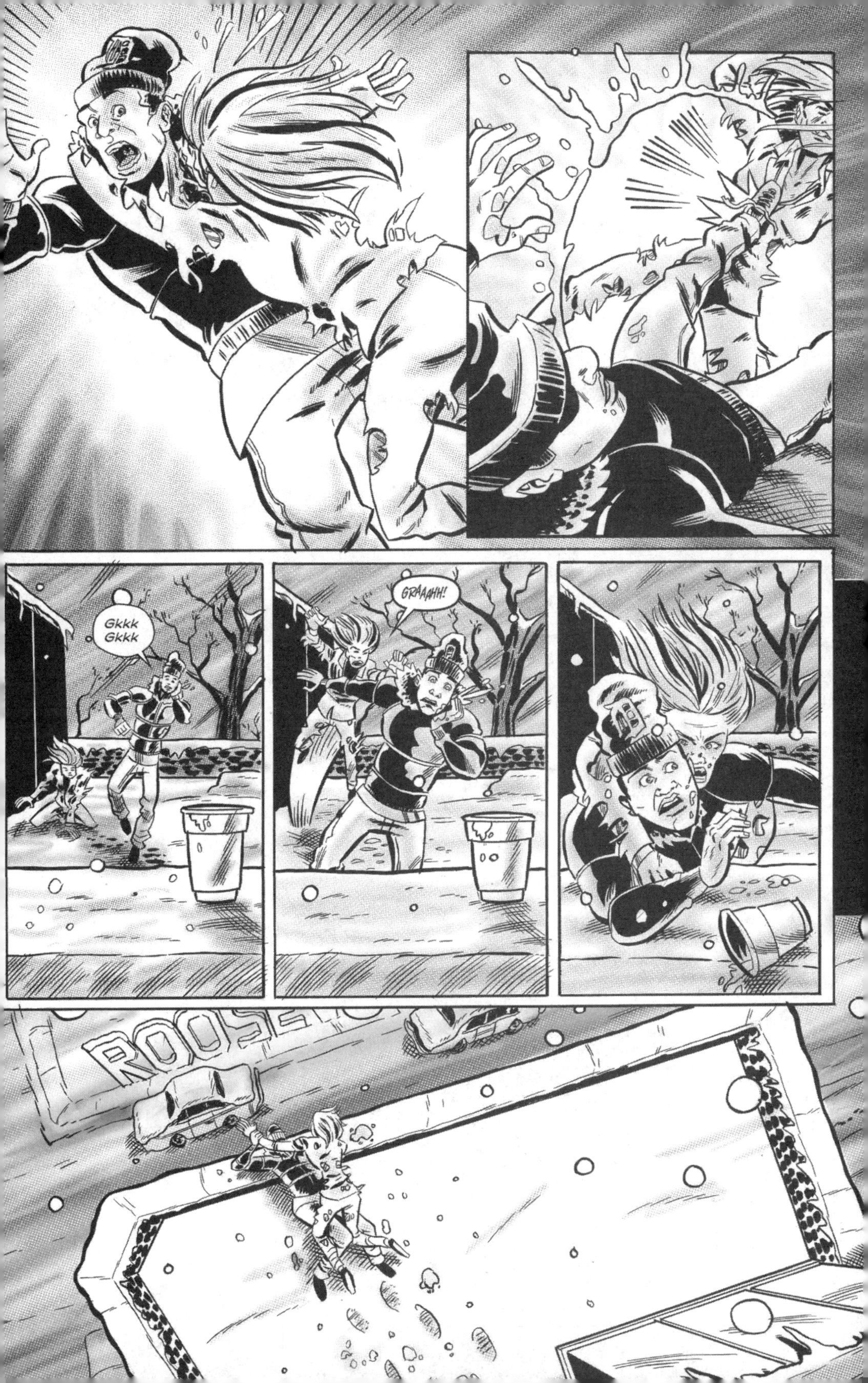
Gkkk Gkkk
GRAAAHH!

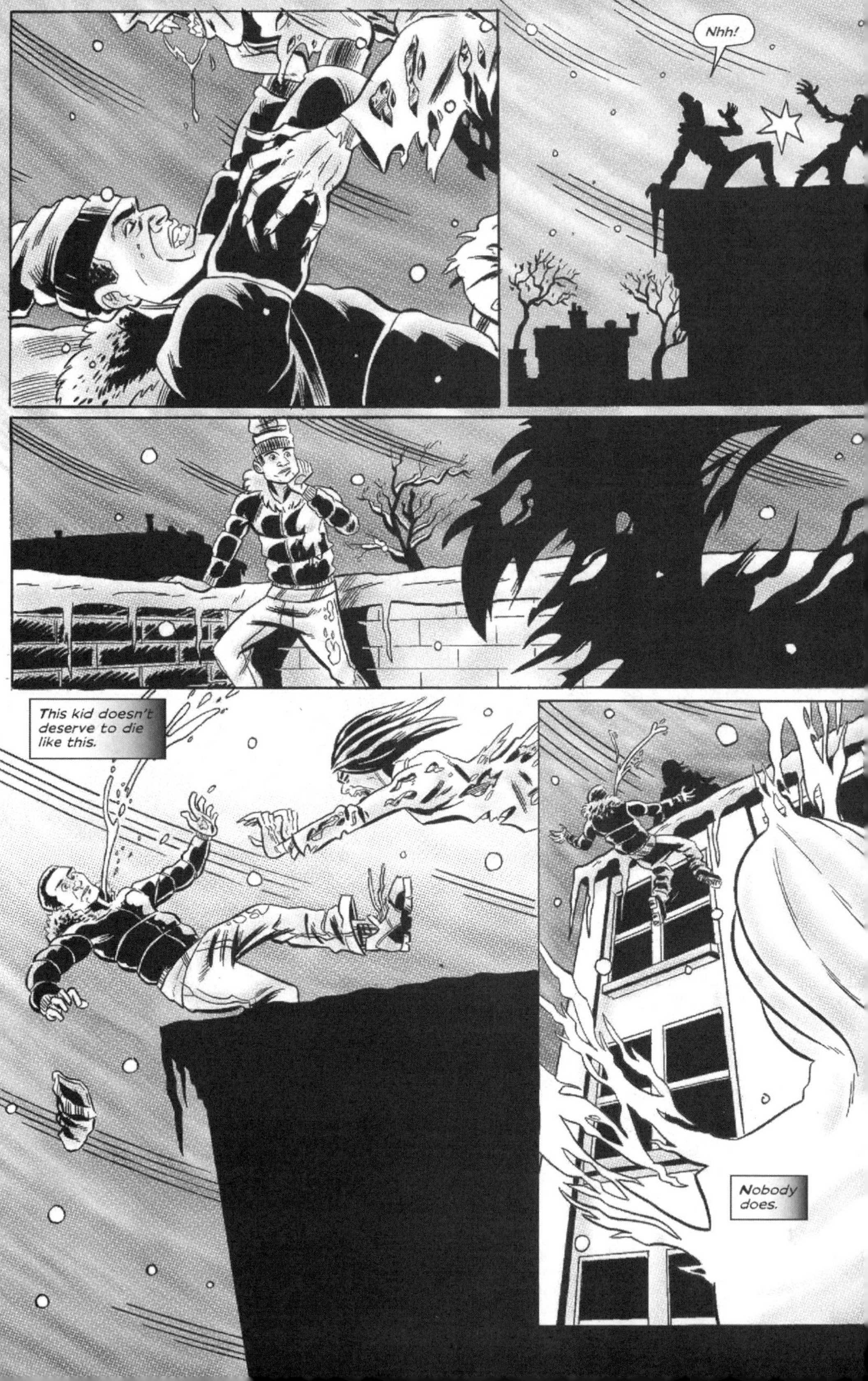
Nhh!
This kid doesn't deserve to die like this.
Nobody does.

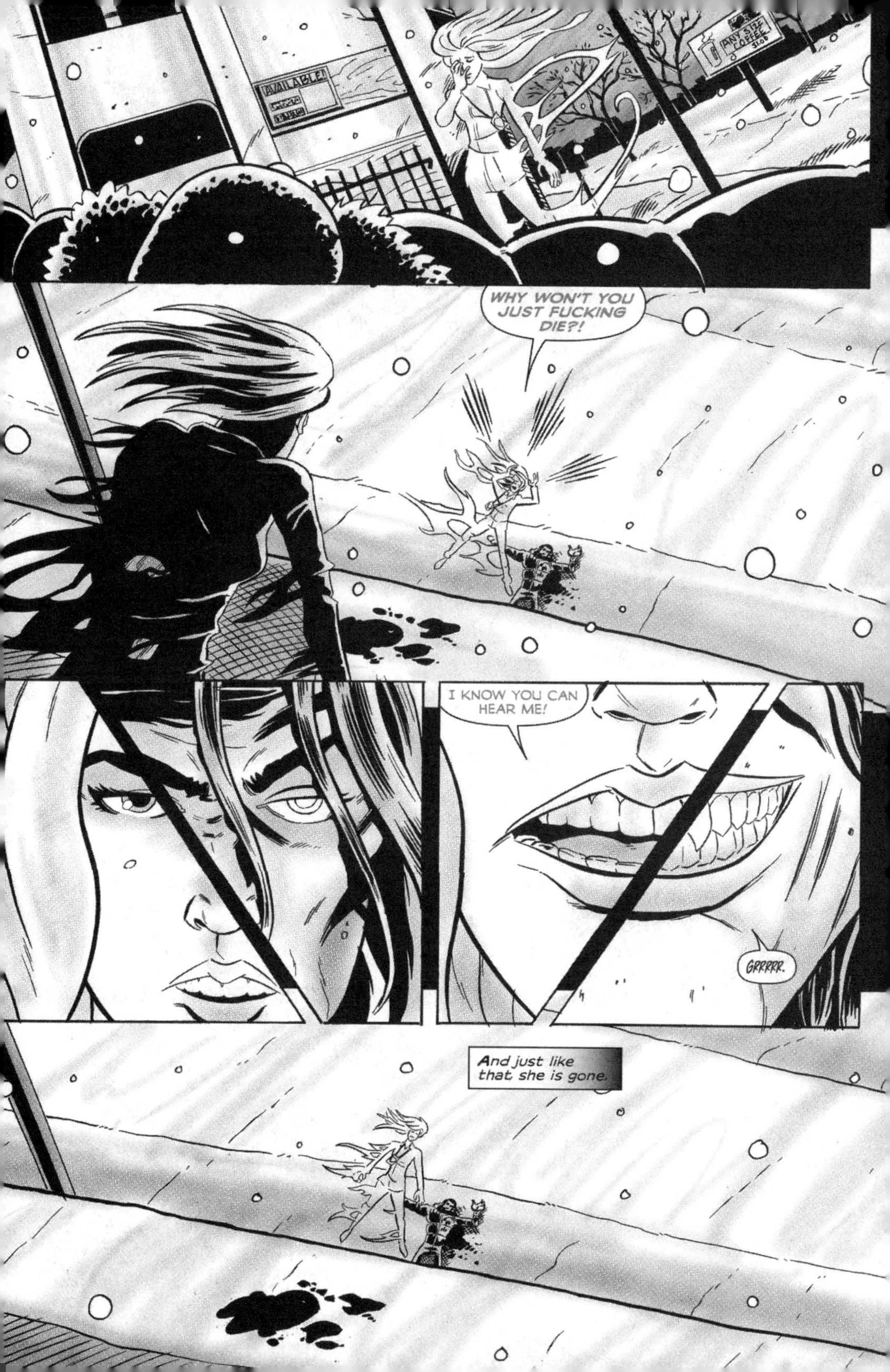
AVAILABLE!
ANY SIZE COFFEE
WHY WON'T YOU JUST FUCKING DIE?!
I KNOW YOU CAN HEAR ME!
GRRRRR.
And just like that she is gone.

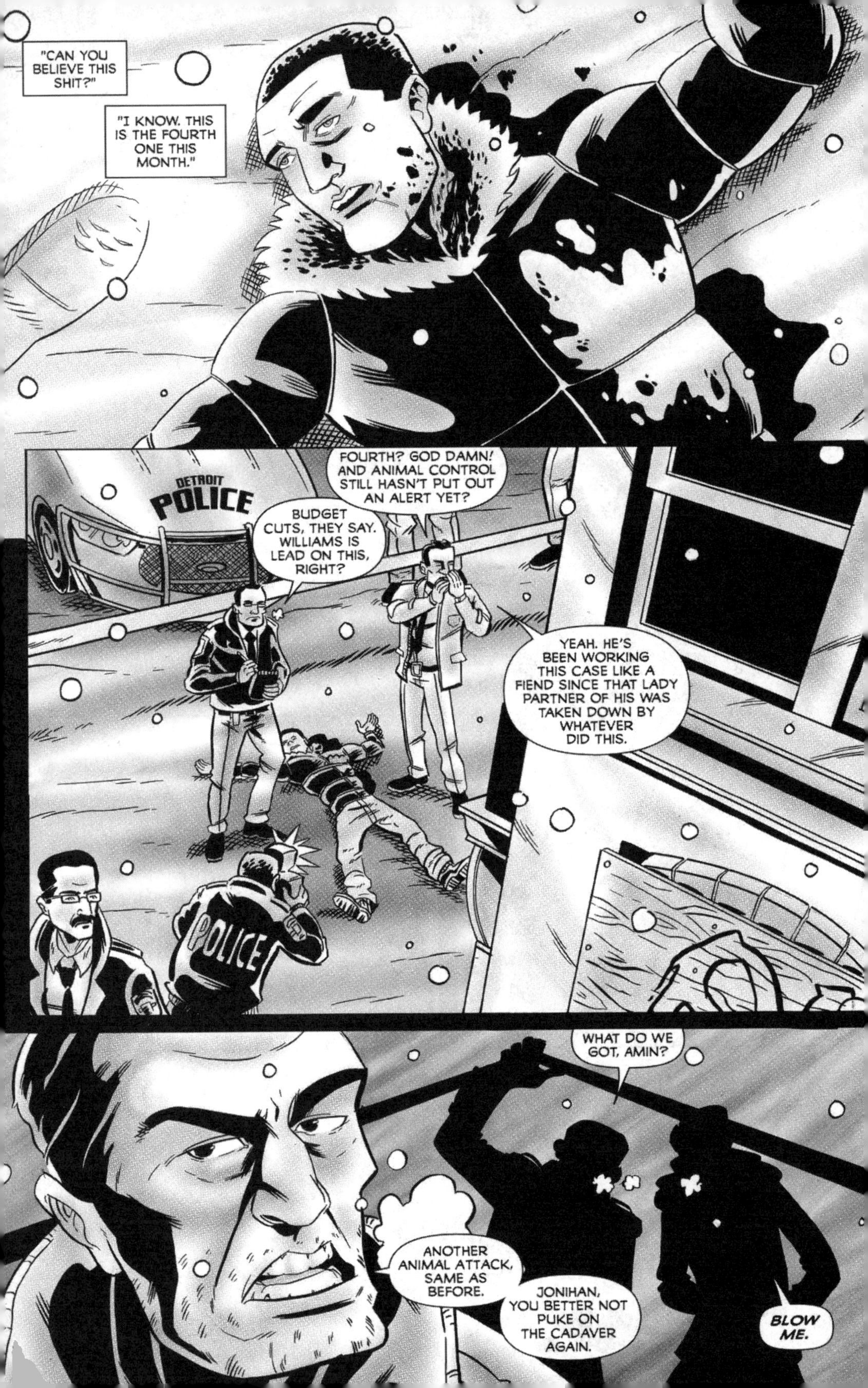
"CAN YOU BELIEVE THIS SHIT?"
"I KNOW. THIS IS THE FOURTH ONE THIS MONTH."
DETROIT POLICE
FOURTH? GOD DAMN! AND ANIMAL CONTROL STILL HASN'T PUT OUT AN ALERT YET?
BUDGET CUTS, THEY SAY. WILLIAMS IS LEAD ON THIS, RIGHT?
YEAH. HE'S BEEN WORKING THIS CASE LIKE A FIEND SINCE THAT LADY PARTNER OF HIS WAS TAKEN DOWN BY WHATEVER DID THIS.
POLICE
WHAT DO WE GOT, AMIN?
ANOTHER ANIMAL ATTACK, SAME AS BEFORE.
JONIHAN, YOU BETTER NOT PUKE ON THE CADAVER AGAIN.
BLOW ME.

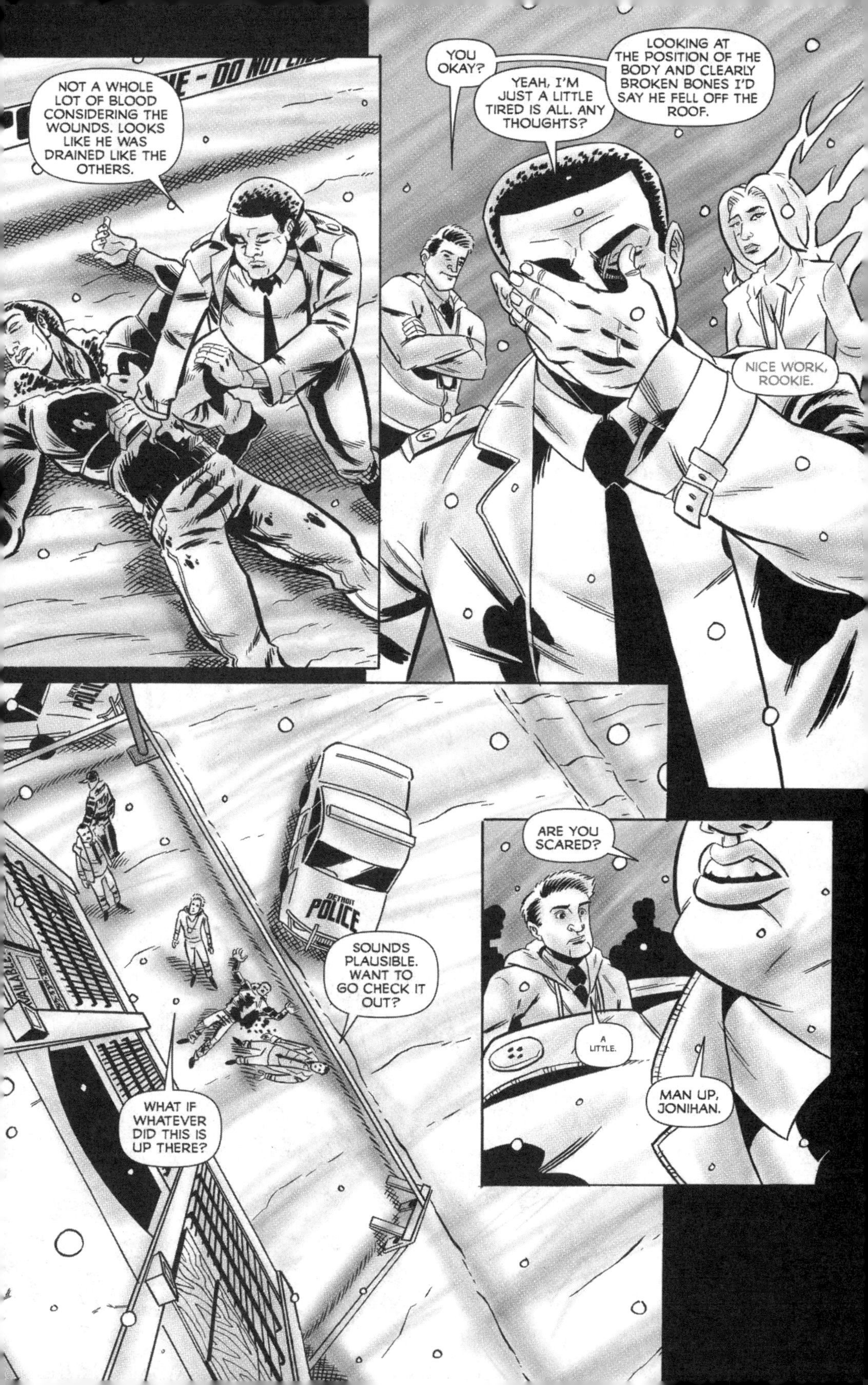

NOT A WHOLE LOT OF BLOOD CONSIDERING THE WOUNDS. LOOKS LIKE HE WAS DRAINED LIKE THE OTHERS.
YOU OKAY?
YEAH, I'M JUST A LITTLE TIRED IS ALL. ANY THOUGHTS?
LOOKING AT THE POSITION OF THE BODY AND CLEARLY BROKEN BONES I'D SAY HE FELL OFF THE ROOF.
NICE WORK, ROOKIE.
DETROIT POLICE
SOUNDS PLAUSIBLE. WANT TO GO CHECK IT OUT?
WHAT IF WHATEVER DID THIS IS UP THERE?
ARE YOU SCARED?
A LITTLE.
MAN UP, JONIHAN.

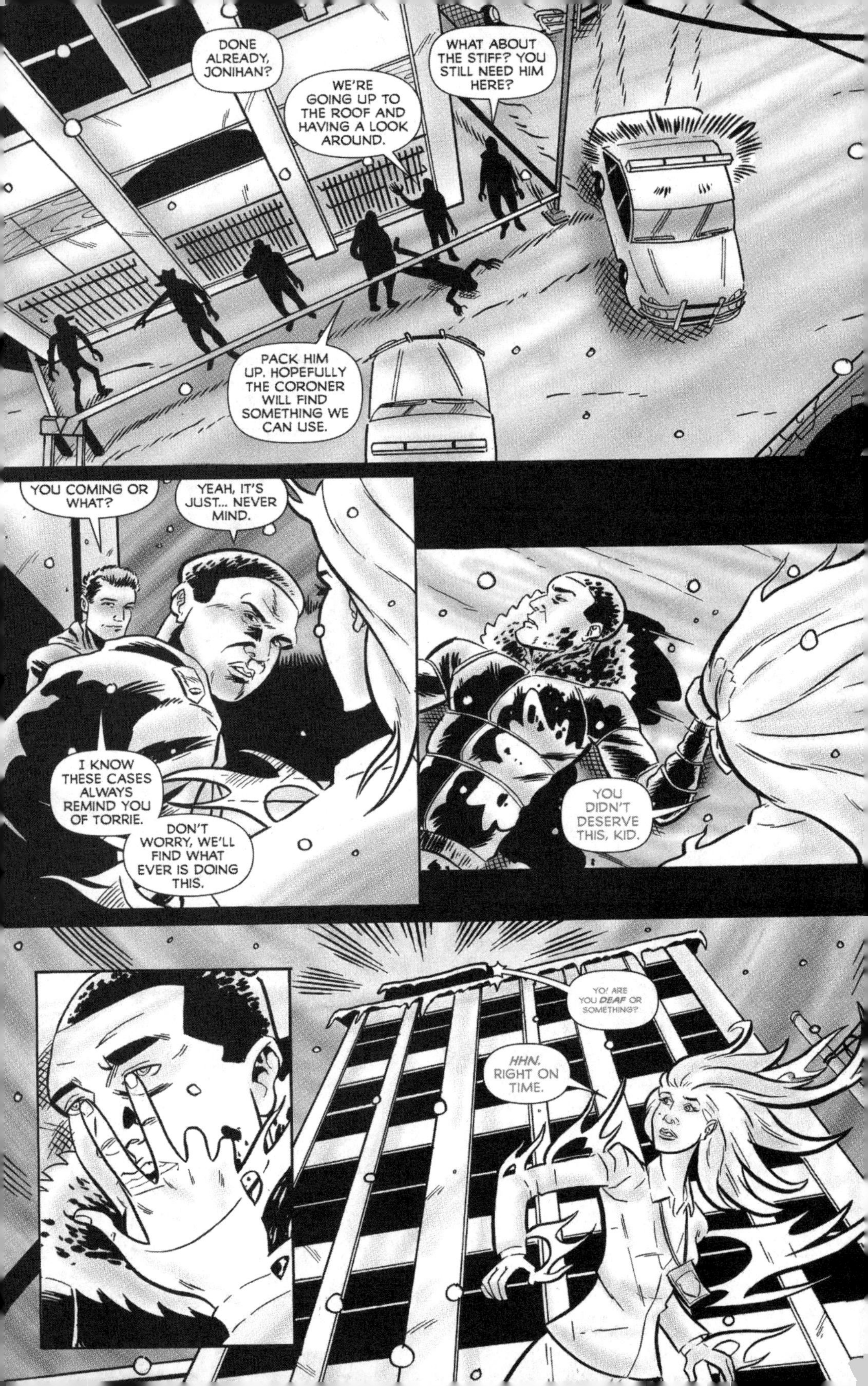
DONE ALREADY, JONIHAN?
WE'RE GOING UP TO THE ROOF AND HAVING A LOOK AROUND.
WHAT ABOUT THE STIFF? YOU STILL NEED HIM HERE?
PACK HIM UP. HOPEFULLY THE CORONER WILL FIND SOMETHING WE CAN USE.
YOU COMING OR WHAT?
YEAH, IT'S JUST... NEVER MIND.
I KNOW THESE CASES ALWAYS REMIND YOU OF TORRIE.
DON'T WORRY, WE'LL FIND WHAT EVER IS DOING THIS.
YOU DIDN'T DESERVE THIS, KID.
YO! ARE YOU DEAF OR SOMETHING?
HHN. RIGHT ON TIME.

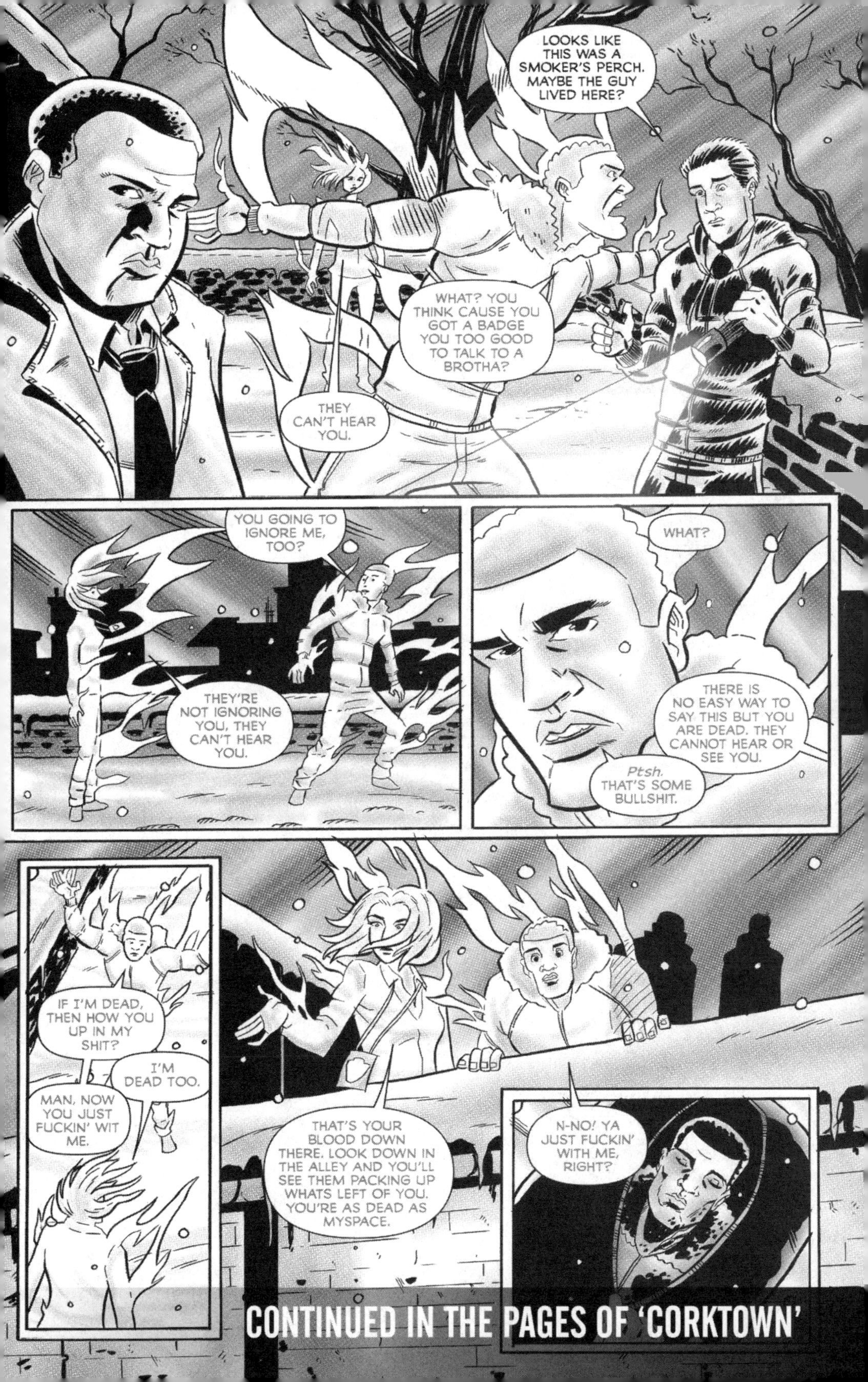
LOOKS LIKE THIS WAS A SMOKER'S PERCH. MAYBE THE GUY LIVED HERE?
WHAT? YOU THINK CAUSE YOU GOT A BADGE YOU TOO GOOD TO TALK TO A BROTHA?
THEY CAN'T HEAR YOU.
YOU GOING TO IGNORE ME, TOO?
THEY'RE NOT IGNORING YOU, THEY CAN'T HEAR YOU.
WHAT?
THERE IS NO EASY WAY TO SAY THIS BUT YOU ARE DEAD. THEY CANNOT HEAR OR SEE YOU.
Ptsh. THAT'S SOME BULLSHIT.
IF I'M DEAD, THEN HOW YOU UP IN MY SHIT?
I'M DEAD TOO.
MAN, NOW YOU JUST FUCKIN' WIT ME.
THAT'S YOUR BLOOD DOWN THERE. LOOK DOWN IN THE ALLEY AND YOU'LL SEE THEM PACKING UP WHATS LEFT OF YOU. YOU'RE AS DEAD AS MYSPACE.
N-NO! YA JUST FUCKIN' WITH ME, RIGHT?
CONTINUED IN THE PAGES OF 'CORKTOWN'

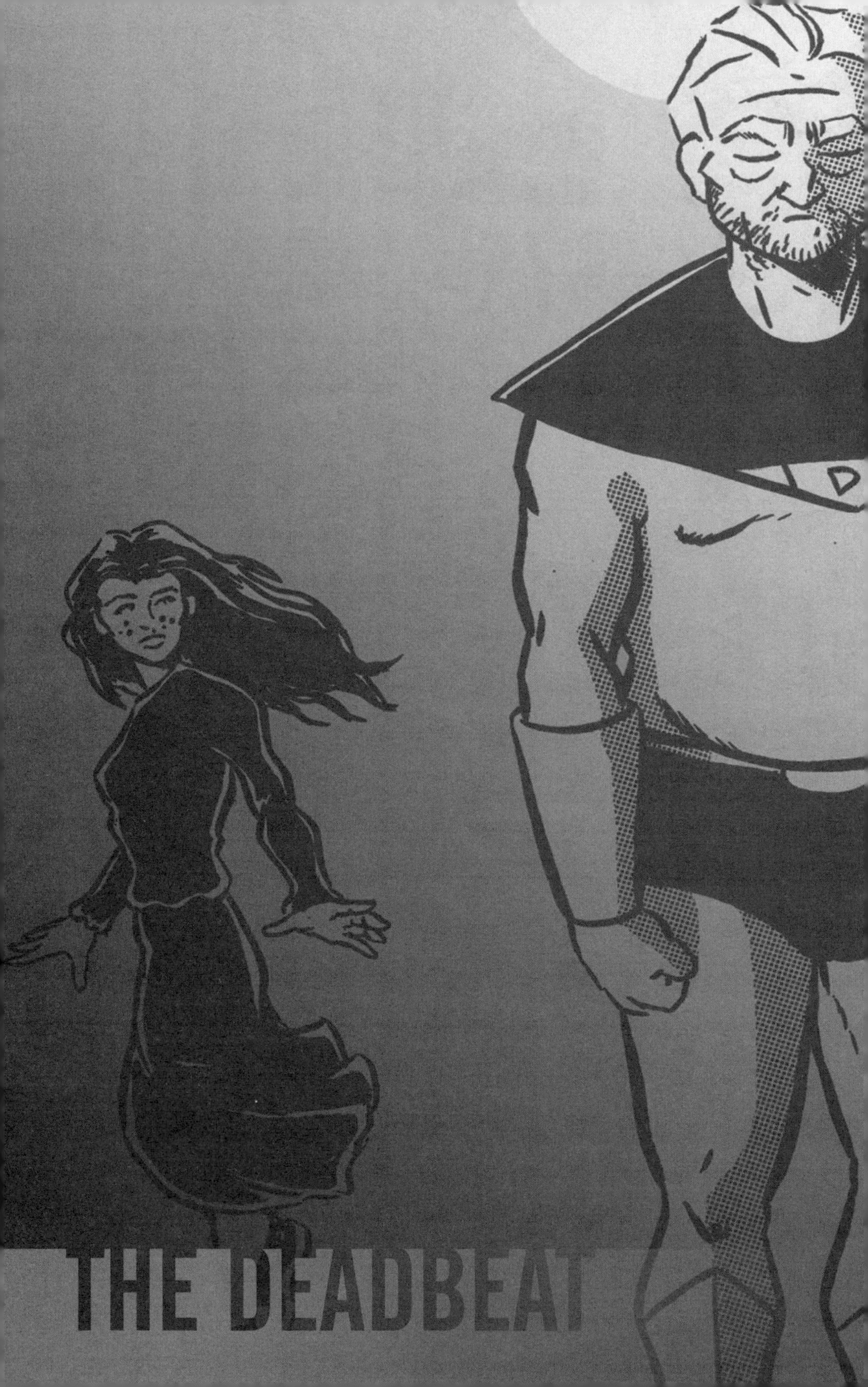

THE DEADBEAT

the DeaDBeat

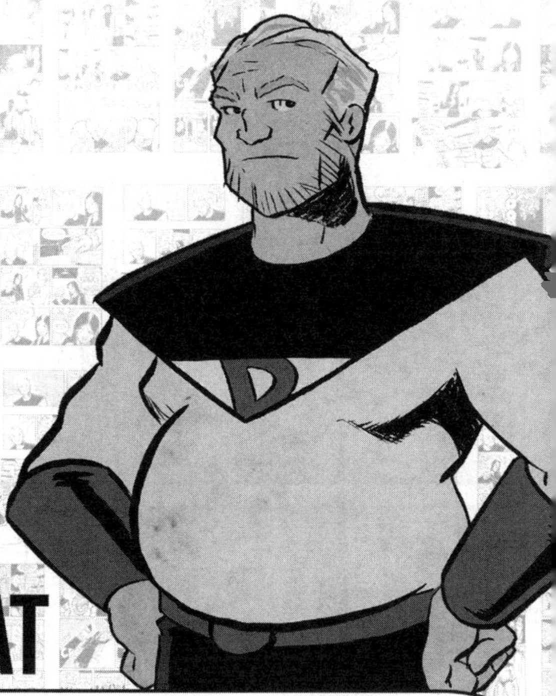

THE DEADBEAT

"Better late than never, kid."

A down-on-his-luck superhero spends his days content with drinking chocolate milk at his favorite bar and wasting away when his daughter, Vera (who he abandoned years ago) walks back into his life.

Seeing her return as a sign to finally get it together he cleans up his act and tries to repair the rift between them. Unfortunately, their reunion is quickly interrupted with the escape of our hero's oldest foe who happens to be the very villain who caused his downward spiral all those years ago.

Age: 55 Height: 6'4" Weight:(he'd rather not say)

First Appearance: THE DEADBEAT (2007)

Created by Jeremy Massie Illustration by Jeremy Massie

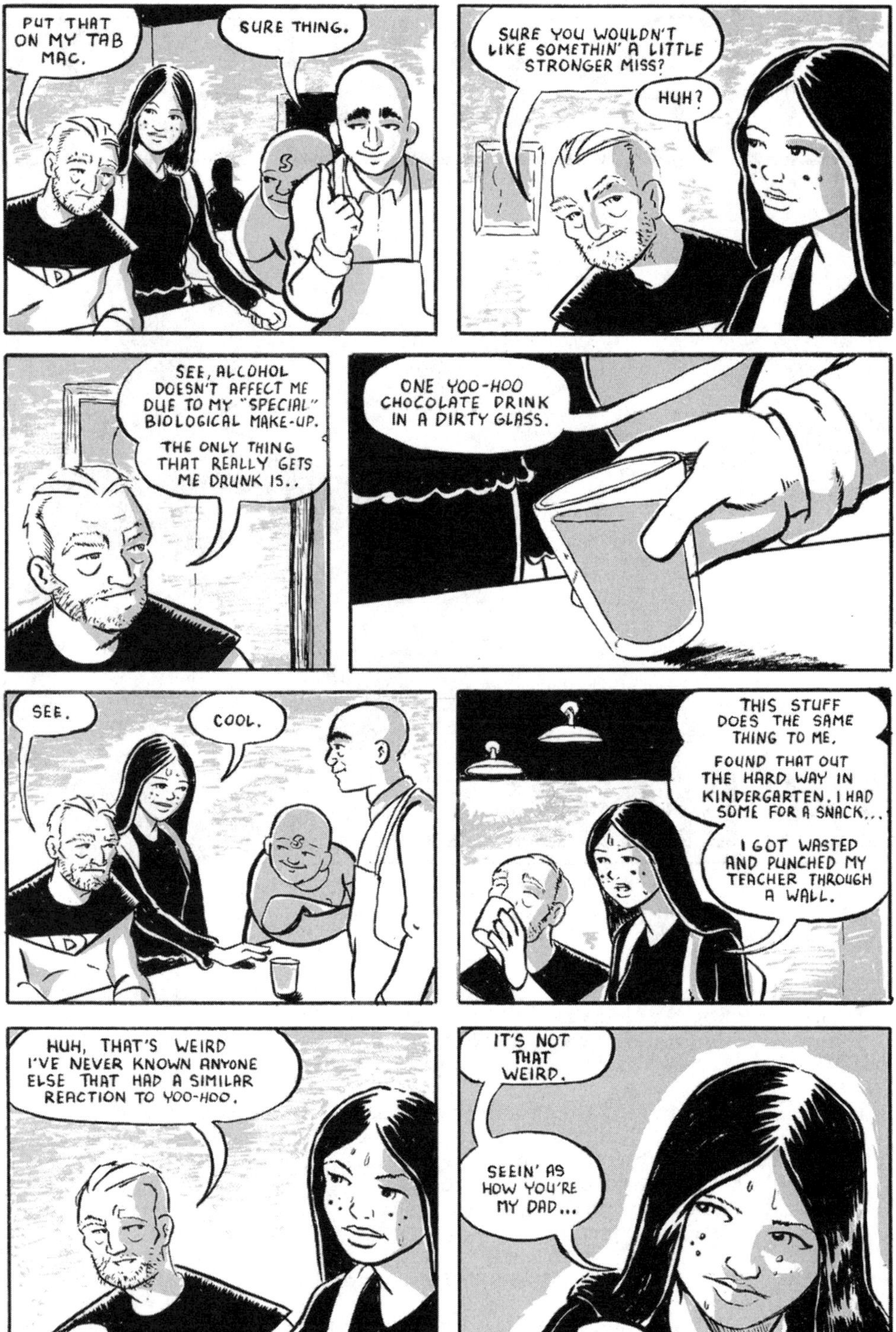
PUT THAT ON MY TAB MAC.
SURE THING.
SURE YOU WOULDN'T LIKE SOMETHIN' A LITTLE STRONGER MISS?
HUH?
SEE, ALCOHOL DOESN'T AFFECT ME DUE TO MY "SPECIAL" BIOLOGICAL MAKE-UP.
THE ONLY THING THAT REALLY GETS ME DRUNK IS..
ONE YOO-HOO CHOCOLATE DRINK IN A DIRTY GLASS.
SEE.
COOL.
THIS STUFF DOES THE SAME THING TO ME.
FOUND THAT OUT THE HARD WAY IN KINDERGARTEN. I HAD SOME FOR A SNACK...
I GOT WASTED AND PUNCHED MY TEACHER THROUGH A WALL.
HUH, THAT'S WEIRD I'VE NEVER KNOWN ANYONE ELSE THAT HAD A SIMILAR REACTION TO YOO-HOO.
IT'S NOT THAT WEIRD.
SEEIN' AS HOW YOU'RE MY DAD...

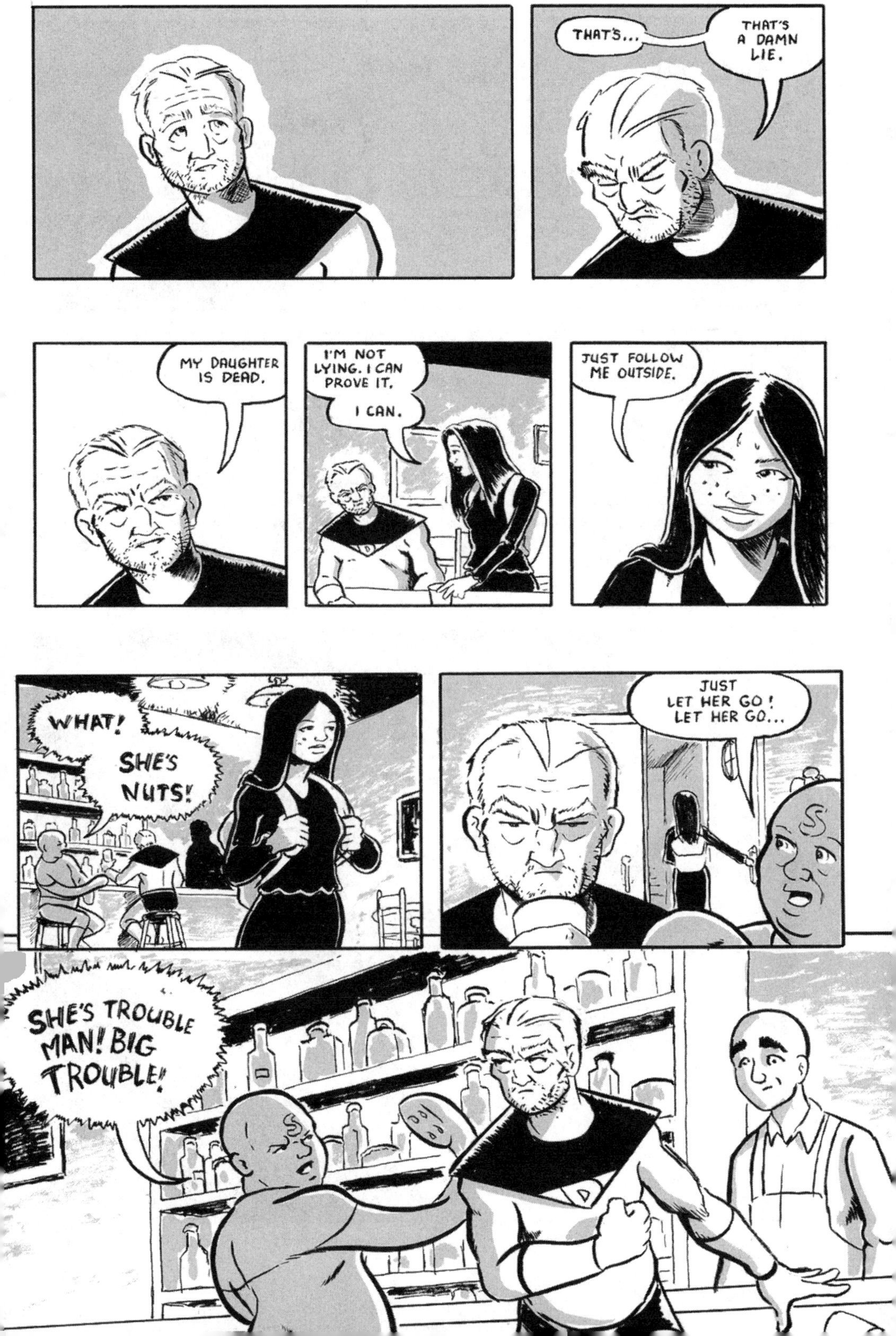

THAT'S...
THAT'S A DAMN LIE.
MY DAUGHTER IS DEAD.
I'M NOT LYING. I CAN PROVE IT.
I CAN.
JUST FOLLOW ME OUTSIDE.
WHAT!
SHE'S NUTS!
JUST LET HER GO! LET HER GO...
SHE'S TROUBLE MAN! BIG TROUBLE!

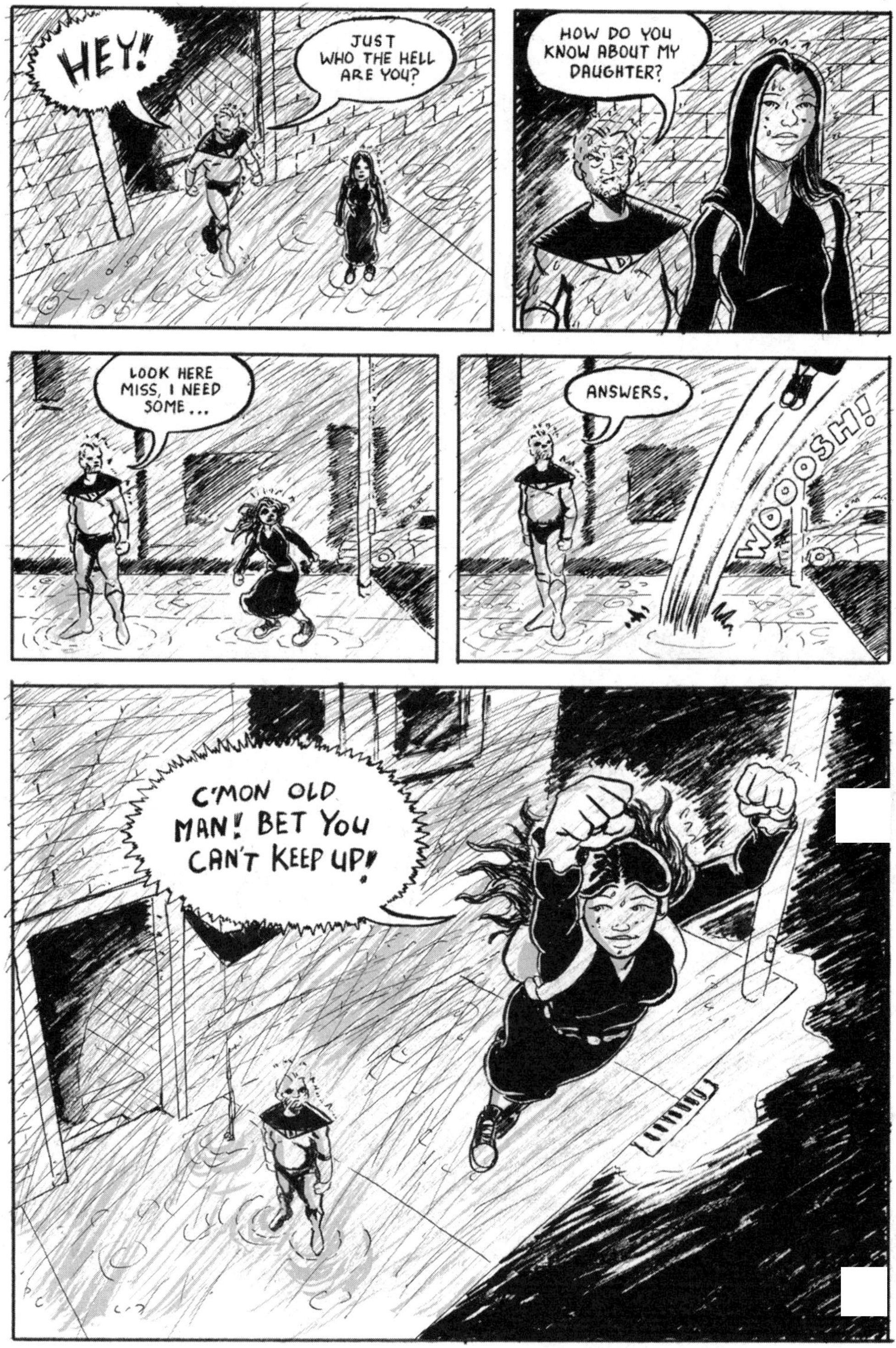
HEY!
JUST WHO THE HELL ARE YOU?
HOW DO YOU KNOW ABOUT MY DAUGHTER?
LOOK HERE MISS, I NEED SOME...
ANSWERS.
WOOOSH!
C'MON OLD MAN! BET YOU CAN'T KEEP UP!

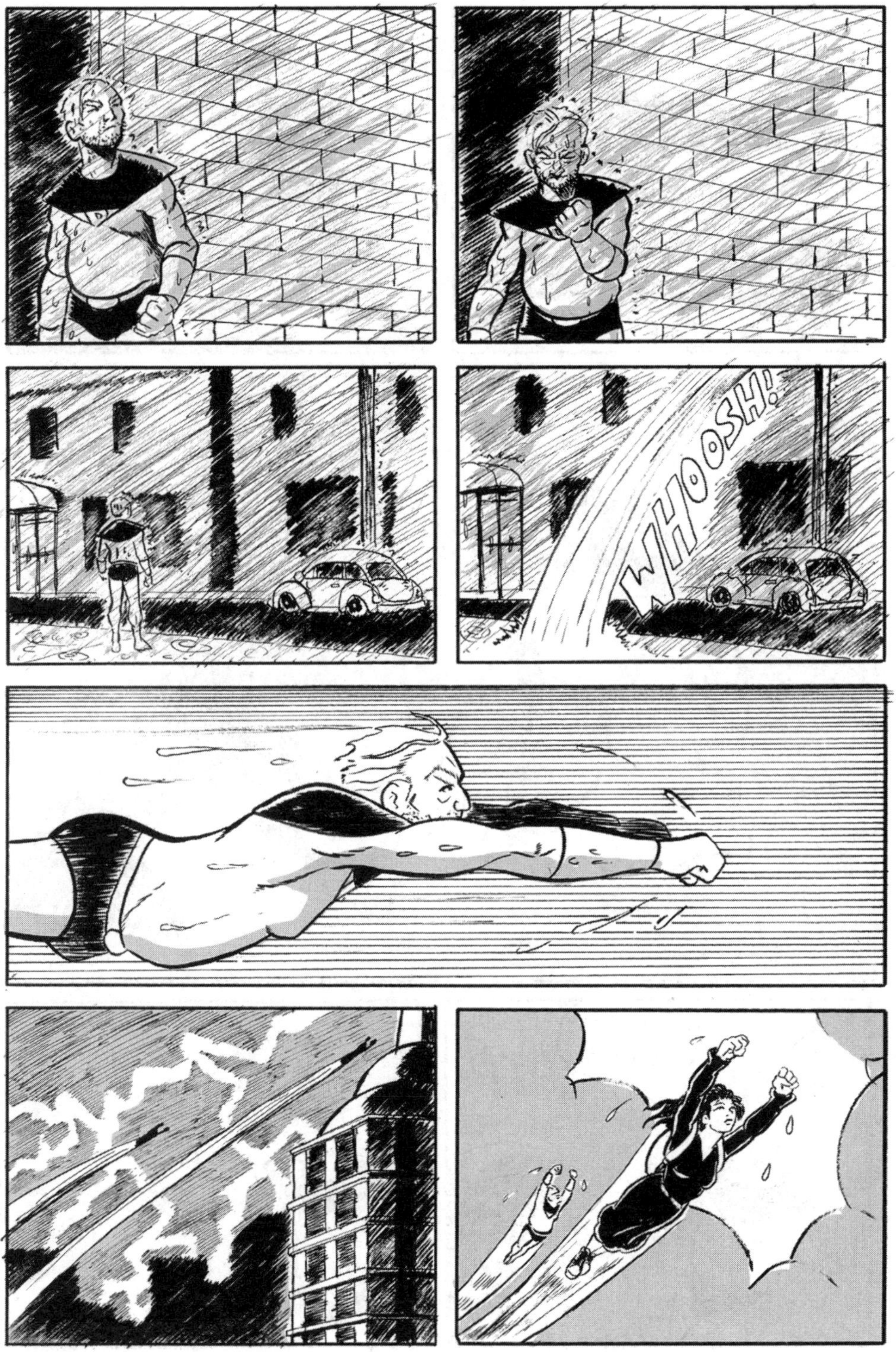
WHOOSH!

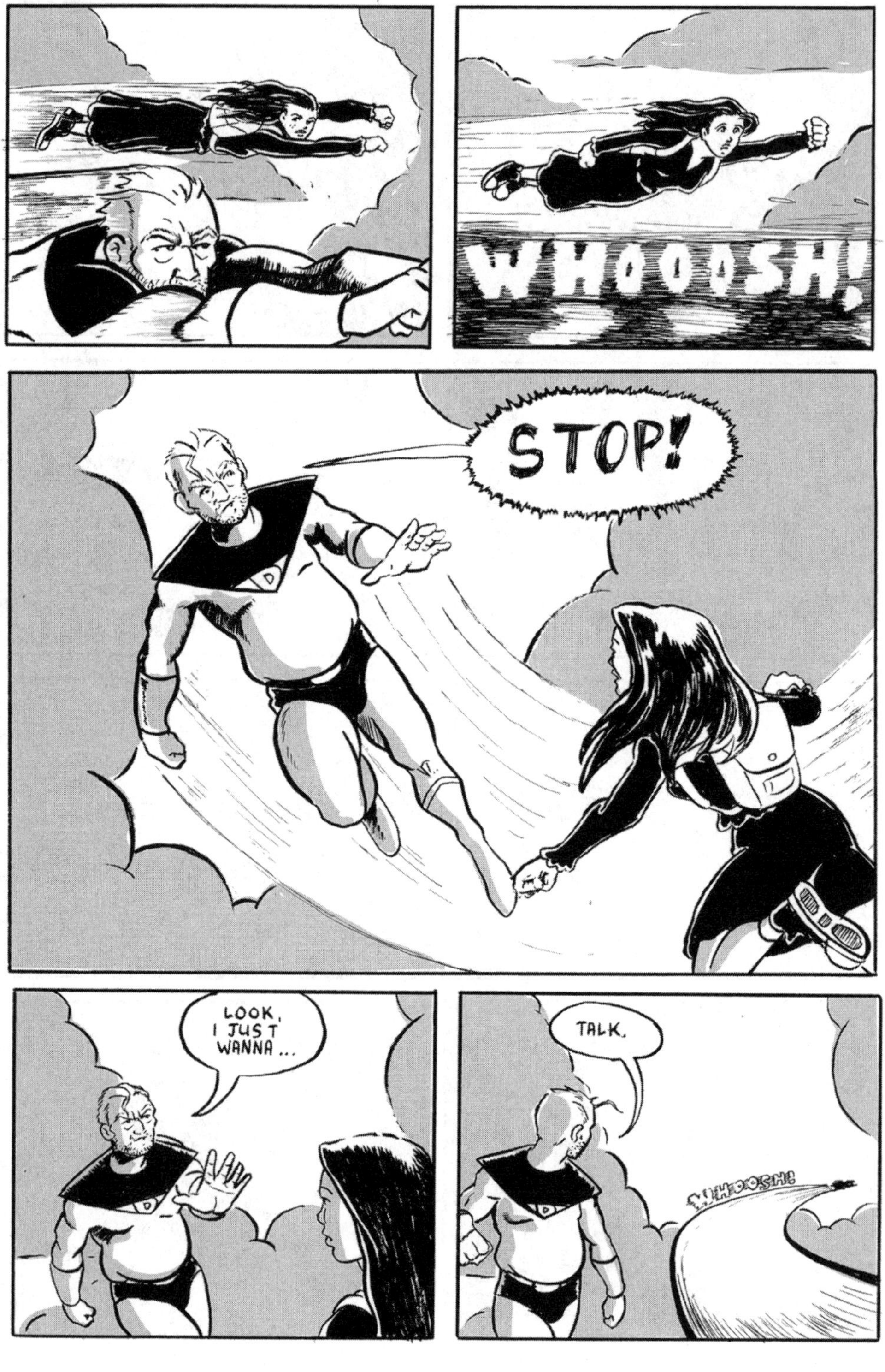
WHOOOSH!
STOP!
LOOK, I JUST WANNA ...
TALK.
WHOOOSH!

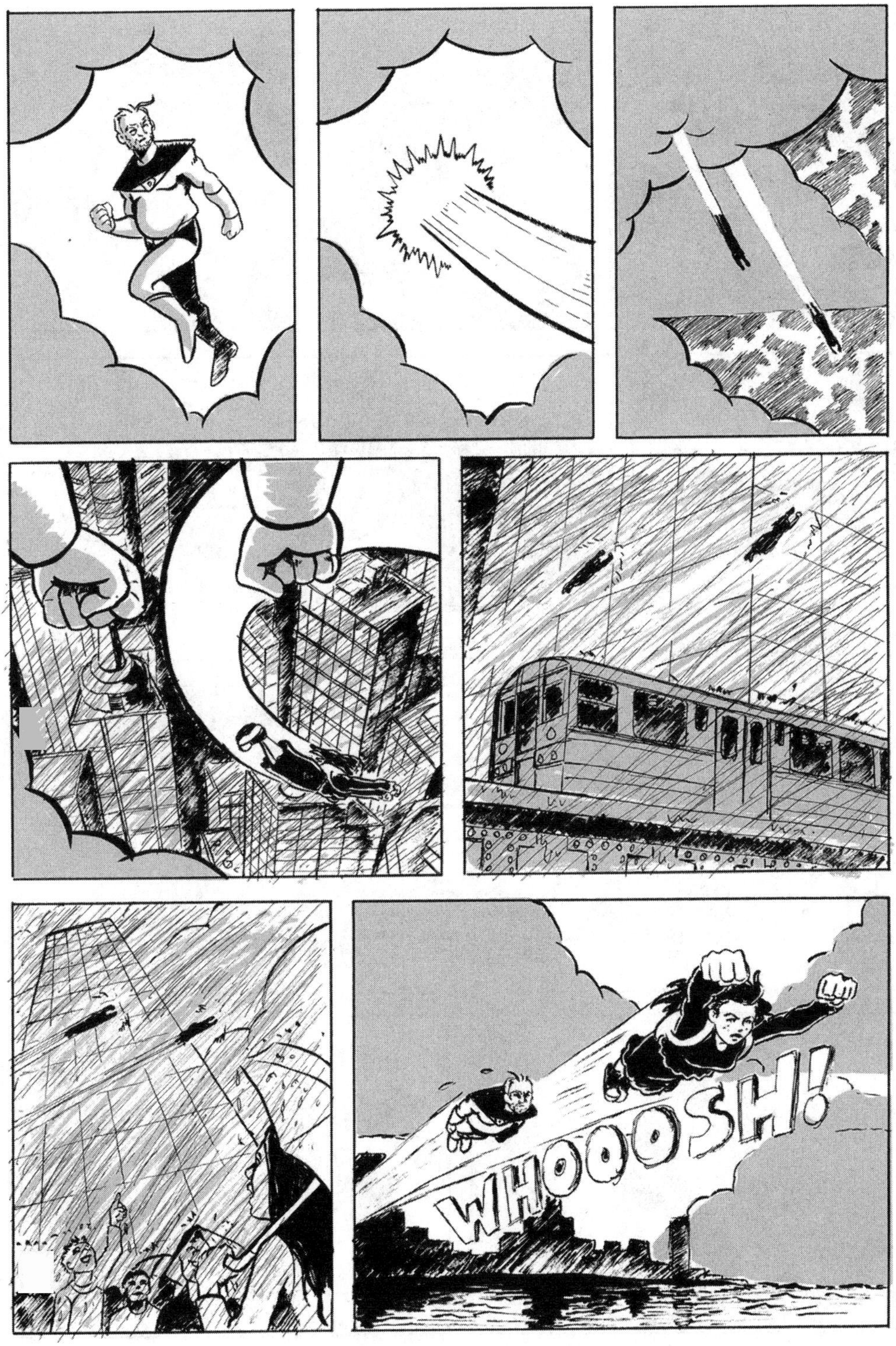
WHOOOSH!

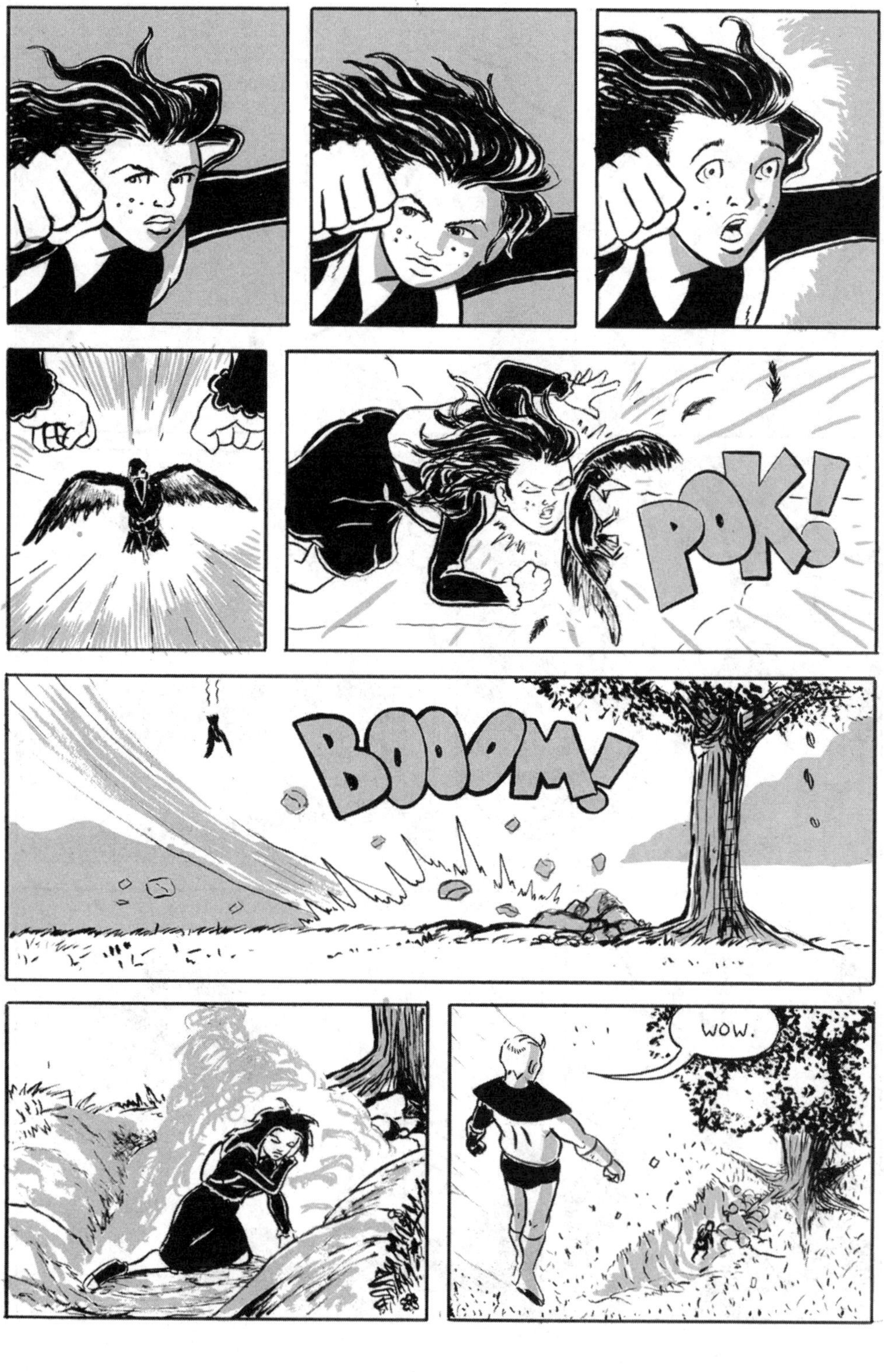
POK!
BOOOM!
WOW.

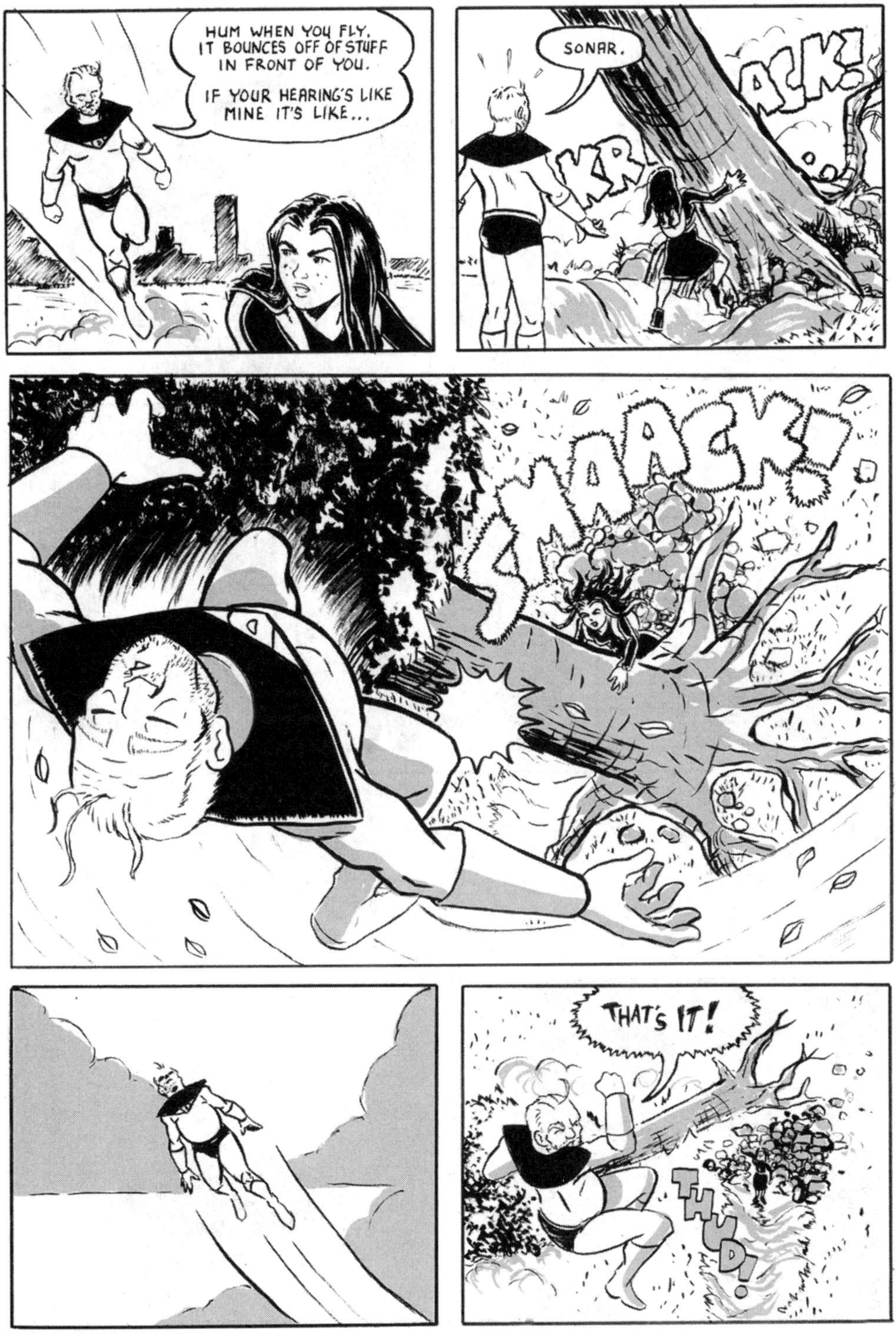
HUM WHEN YOU FLY. IT BOUNCES OFF OF STUFF IN FRONT OF YOU.
IF YOUR HEARING'S LIKE MINE IT'S LIKE...
SONAR.
KR
ACK!
SMACK!
THAT'S IT!
THUD!

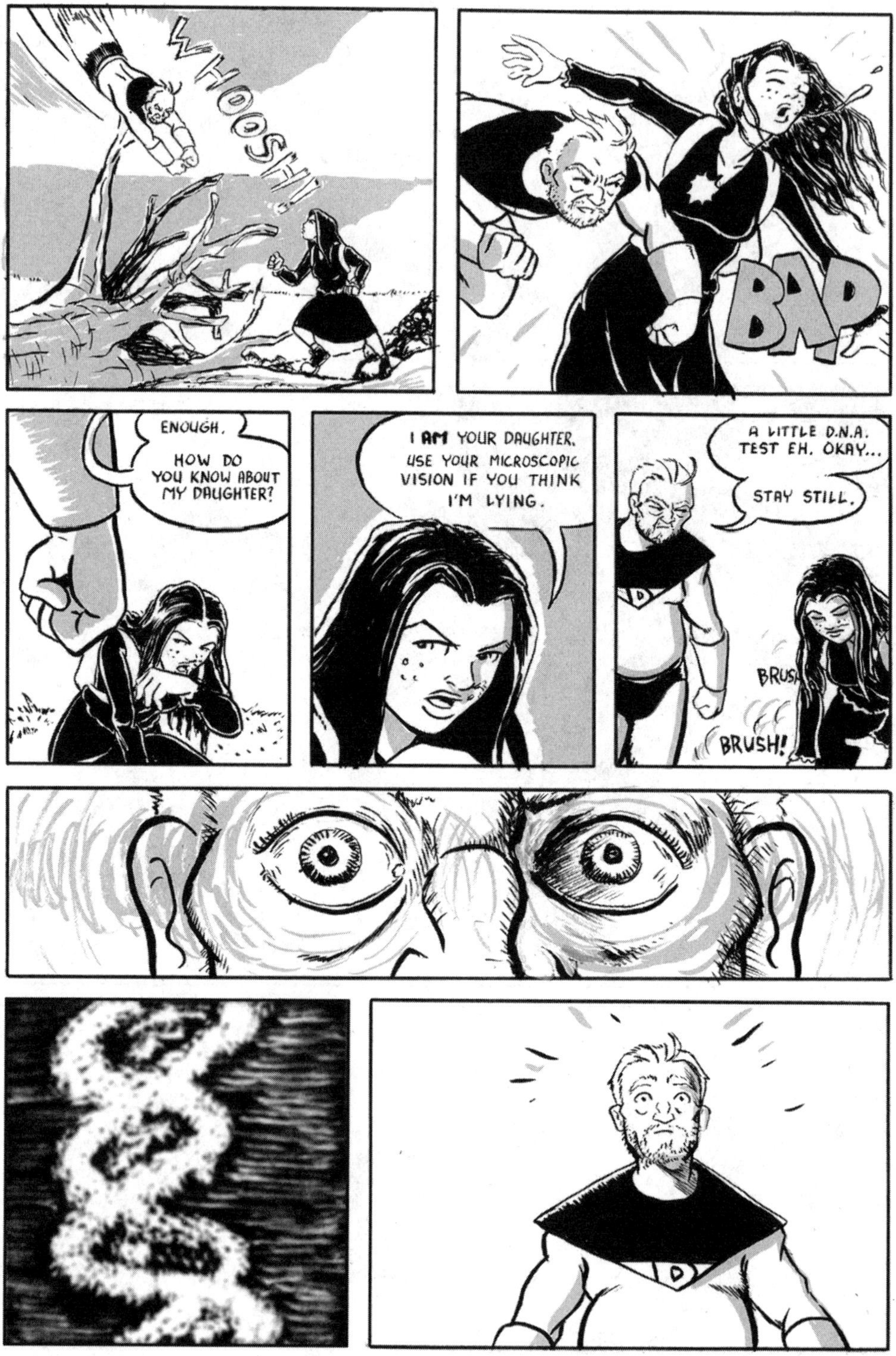
WHOOSH!!
BAP
ENOUGH.
HOW DO YOU KNOW ABOUT MY DAUGHTER?
I AM YOUR DAUGHTER. USE YOUR MICROSCOPIC VISION IF YOU THINK I'M LYING.
A LITTLE D.N.A. TEST EH. OKAY...
STAY STILL.
BRUSH
BRUSH!

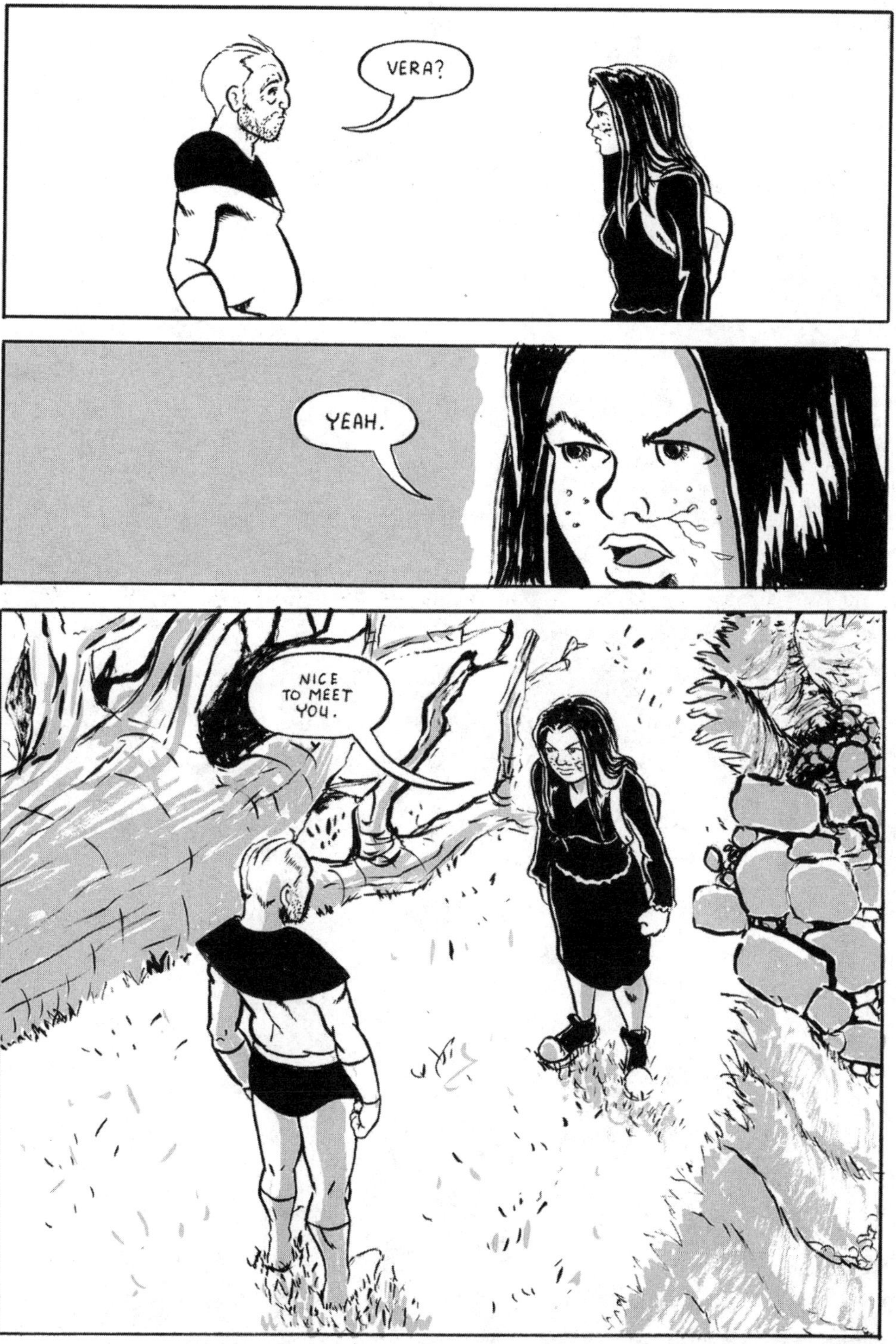
VERA?
YEAH.
NICE TO MEET YOU.

CONTINUED IN THE PAGES OF 'THE DEADBEAT'

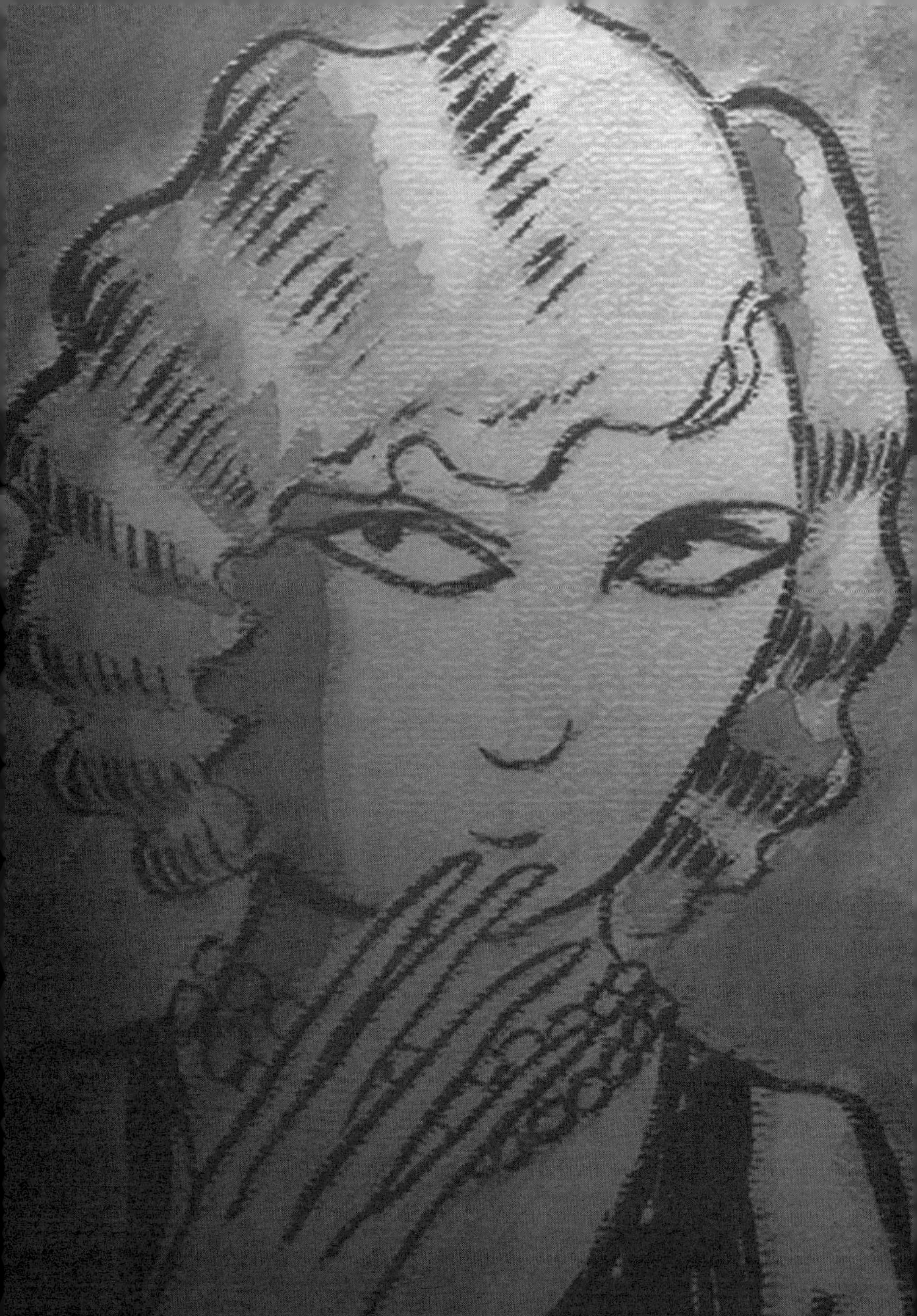

THE DIARY OF THE BLACK WIDOW

DIARY OF THE BLACK WIDOW

BLACK WIDOW & DETECTIVE INSPECTOR

"...and don't you forget it!"

She is a seductress with a trail of dead lovers and an even deadlier intellect.

He... is a blithering idiot.

Can the Detective Inspector solve the case or will he become the Black Widow's latest victim?

BLACK WIDOW
Age: 23
Height: 5'5"
Weight: Never ask a woman that question... especially this one... it might be your last.

DETECTIVE INSPECTOR
Age: 45
Height: 6'5"
Weight: 14 stone

First Appearance:
DIARY OF THE BLACK WIDOW #1 (2005)

Created by Bret M. Herholz
Illustration by Bret M. Herholz

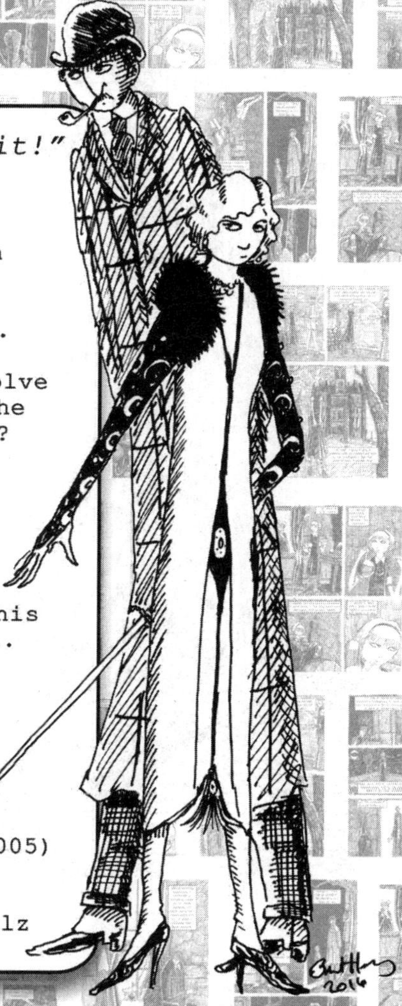

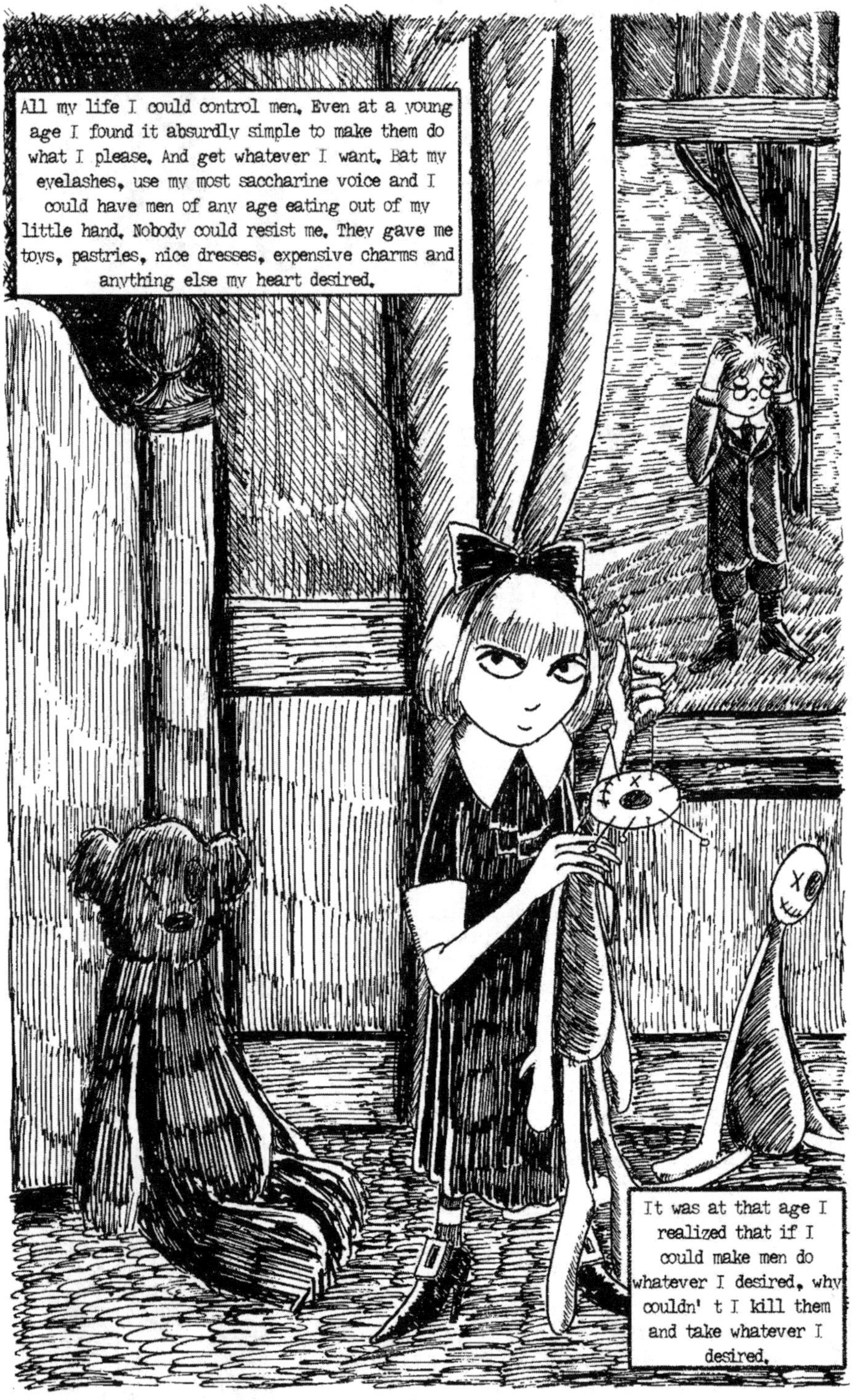
All my life I could control men. Even at a young age I found it absurdly simple to make them do what I please. And get whatever I want. Bat my eyelashes, use my most saccharine voice and I could have men of any age eating out of my little hand. Nobody could resist me. They gave me toys, pastries, nice dresses, expensive charms and anything else my heart desired.
It was at that age I realized that if I could make men do whatever I desired, why couldn' t I kill them and take whatever I desired.

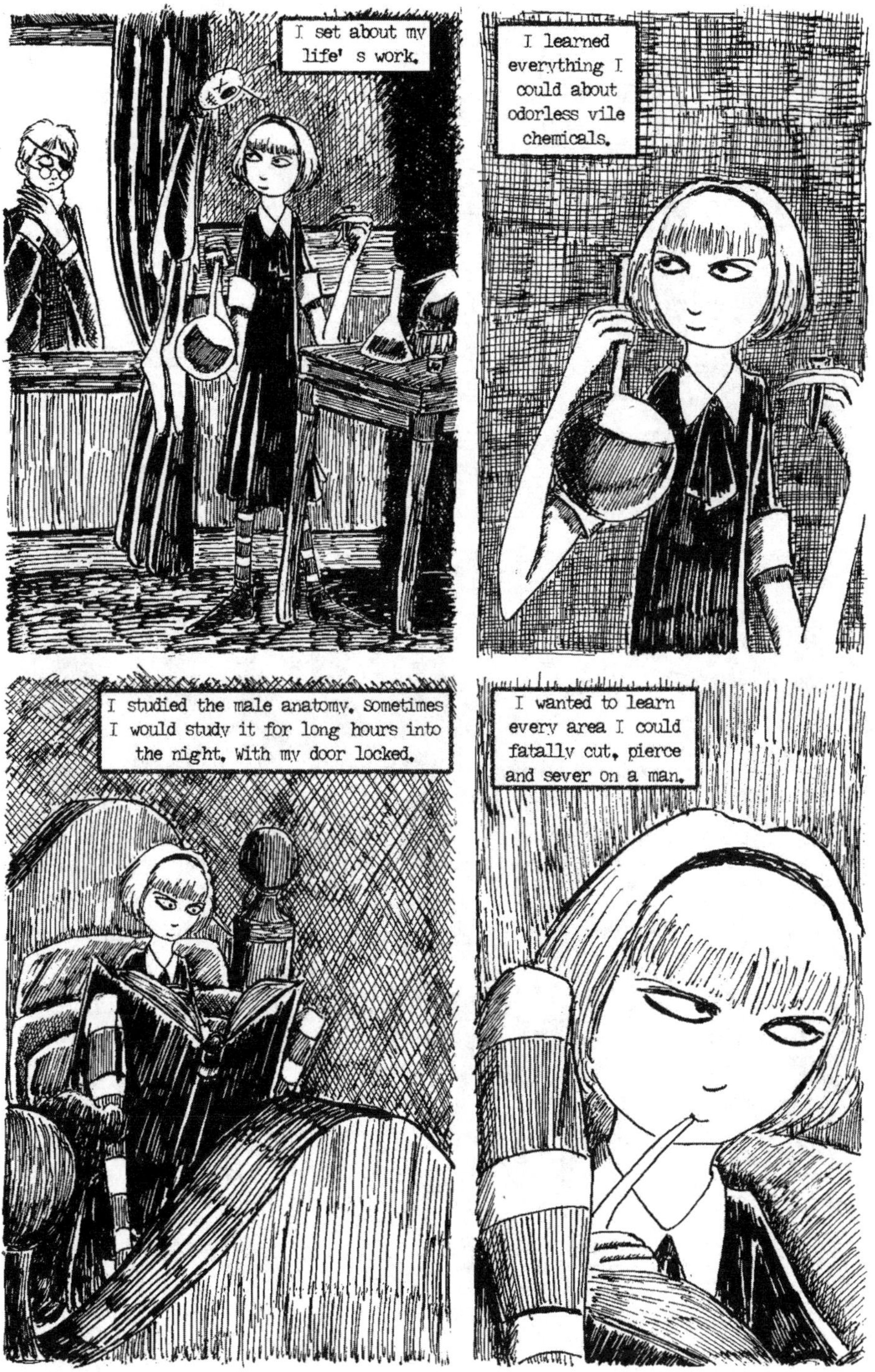
I set about my life' s work.
I learned everything I could about odorless vile chemicals.
I studied the male anatomy. Sometimes I would study it for long hours into the night. With my door locked.
I wanted to learn every area I could fatally cut, pierce and sever on a man.

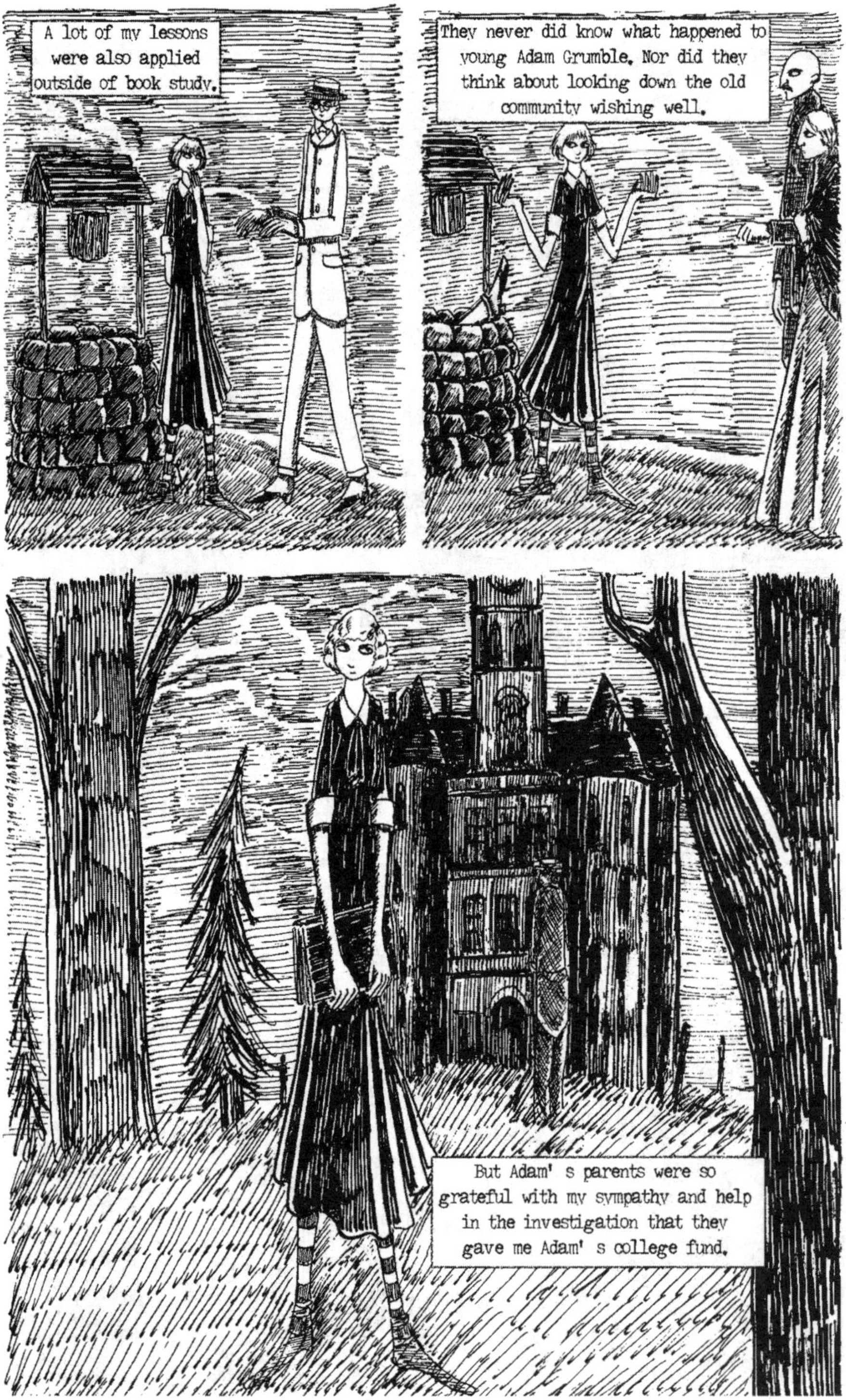
A lot of my lessons were also applied outside of book study.
They never did know what happened to young Adam Grumble. Nor did they think about looking down the old community wishing well.
But Adam's parents were so grateful with my sympathy and help in the investigation that they gave me Adam's college fund.

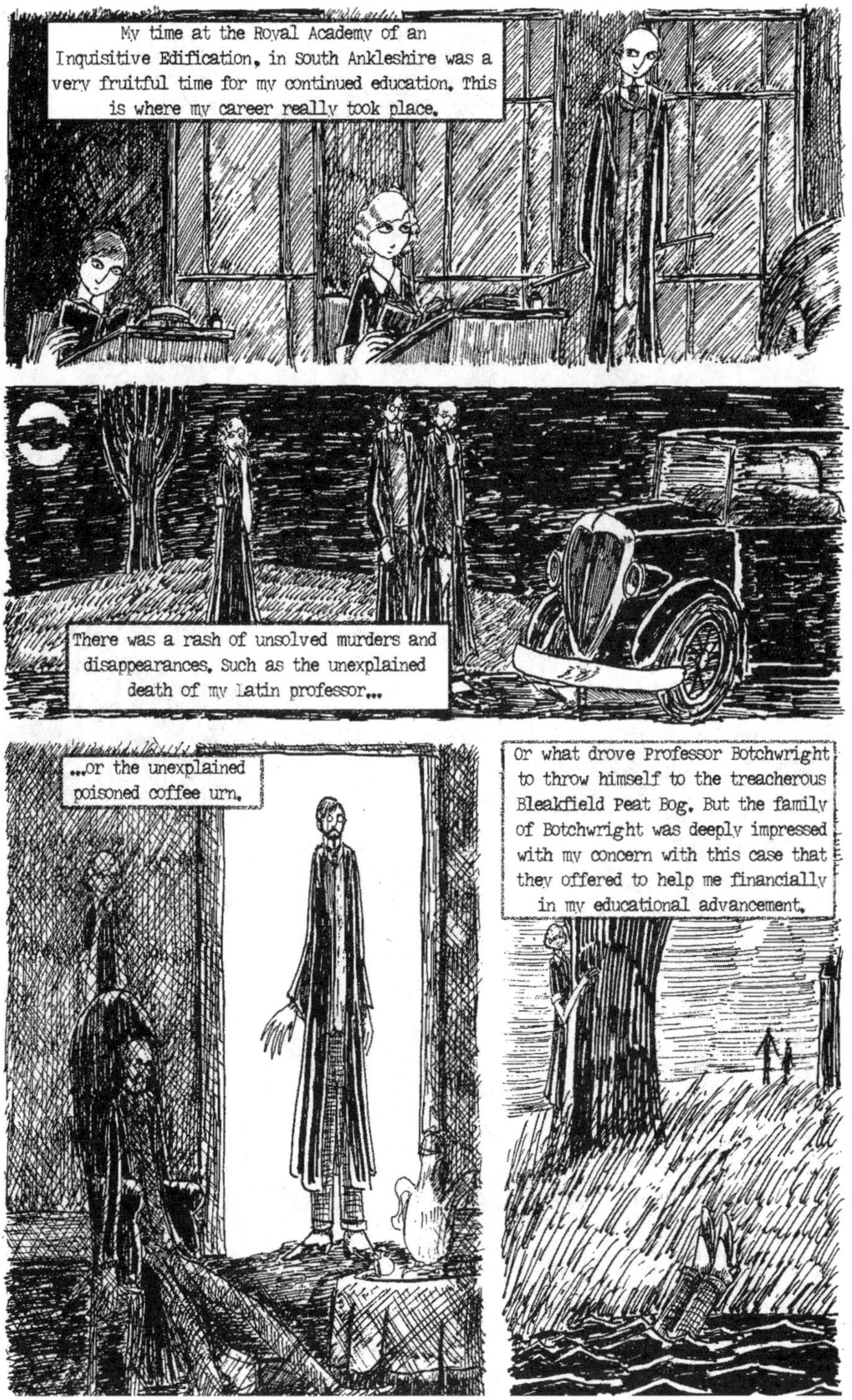
My time at the Royal Academy of an Inquisitive Edification, in South Ankleshire was a very fruitful time for my continued education. This is where my career really took place.
There was a rash of unsolved murders and disappearances. Such as the unexplained death of my Latin professor...
...or the unexplained poisoned coffee urn.
Or what drove Professor Botchwright to throw himself to the treacherous Bleakfield Peat Bog. But the family of Botchwright was deeply impressed with my concern with this case that they offered to help me financially in my educational advancement.

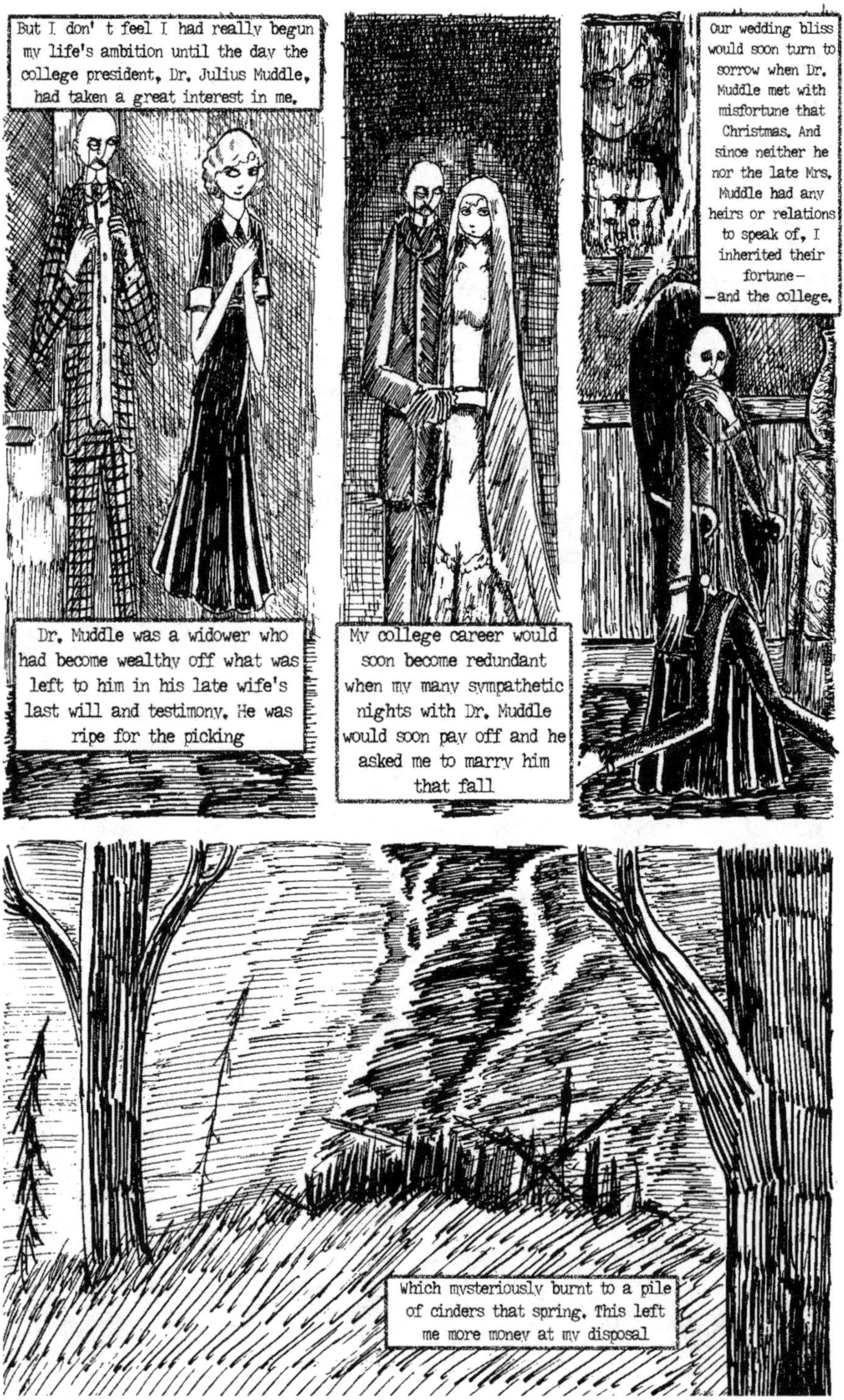

But I don' t feel I had really begun my life's ambition until the day the college president, Dr. Julius Muddle, had taken a great interest in me.
Dr. Muddle was a widower who had become wealthy off what was left to him in his late wife's last will and testimony. He was ripe for the picking
My college career would soon become redundant when my many sympathetic nights with Dr. Muddle would soon pay off and he asked me to marry him that fall
Our wedding bliss would soon turn to sorrow when Dr. Muddle met with misfortune that Christmas. And since neither he nor the late Mrs. Muddle had any heirs or relations to speak of, I inherited their fortune—
—and the college.
Which mysteriously burnt to a pile of cinders that spring. This left me more money at my disposal

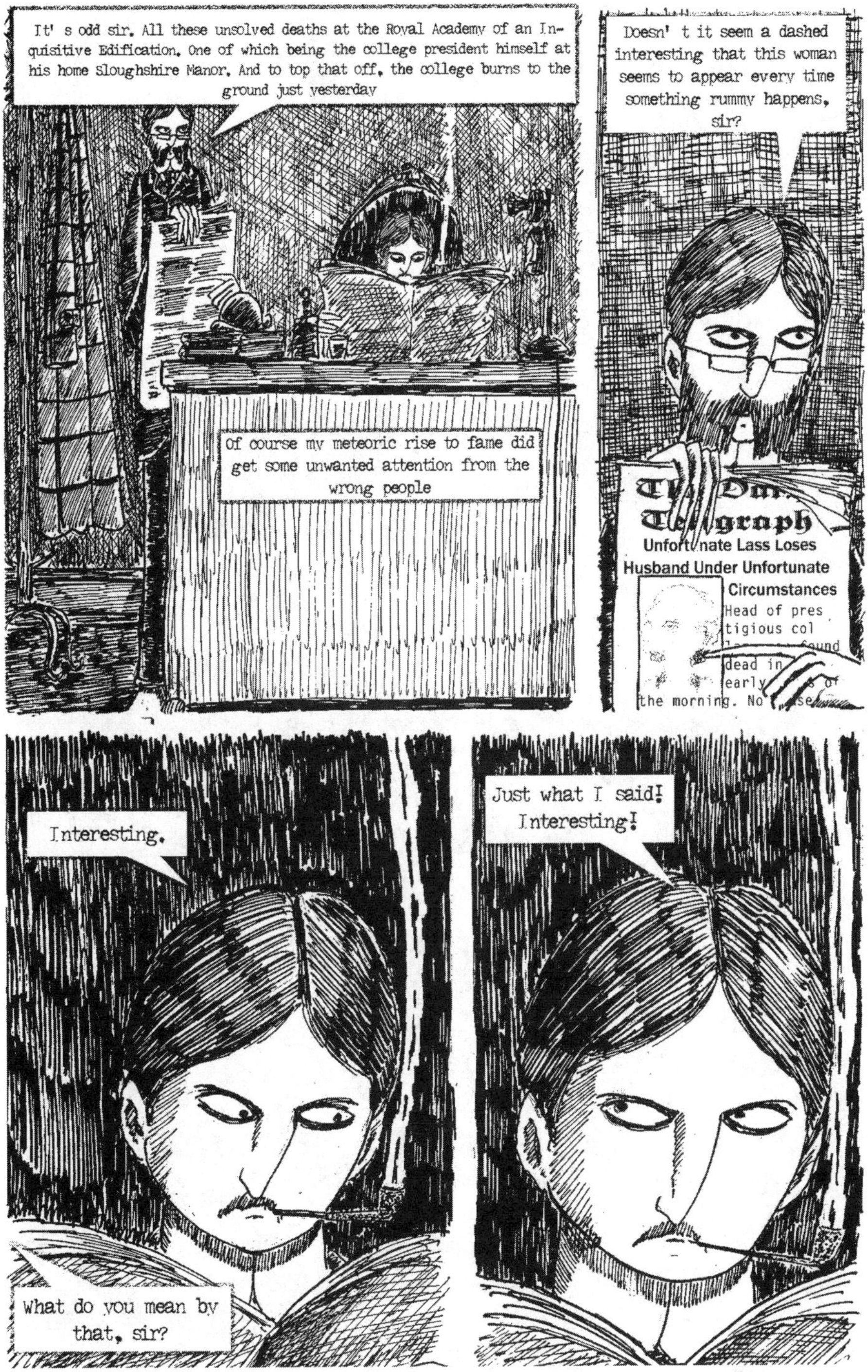

It' s odd sir. All these unsolved deaths at the Royal Academy of an Inquisitive Edification. One of which being the college president himself at his home Sloughshire Manor. And to top that off, the college burns to the ground just yesterday
Of course my meteoric rise to fame did get some unwanted attention from the wrong people
Doesn' t it seem a dashed interesting that this woman seems to appear every time something rummy happens, sir?
Unfortunate Lass Loses Husband Under Unfortunate Circumstances
Head of pres
tigious col
dead in
early
the morning.
Interesting.
What do you mean by that, sir?
Just what I said! Interesting!

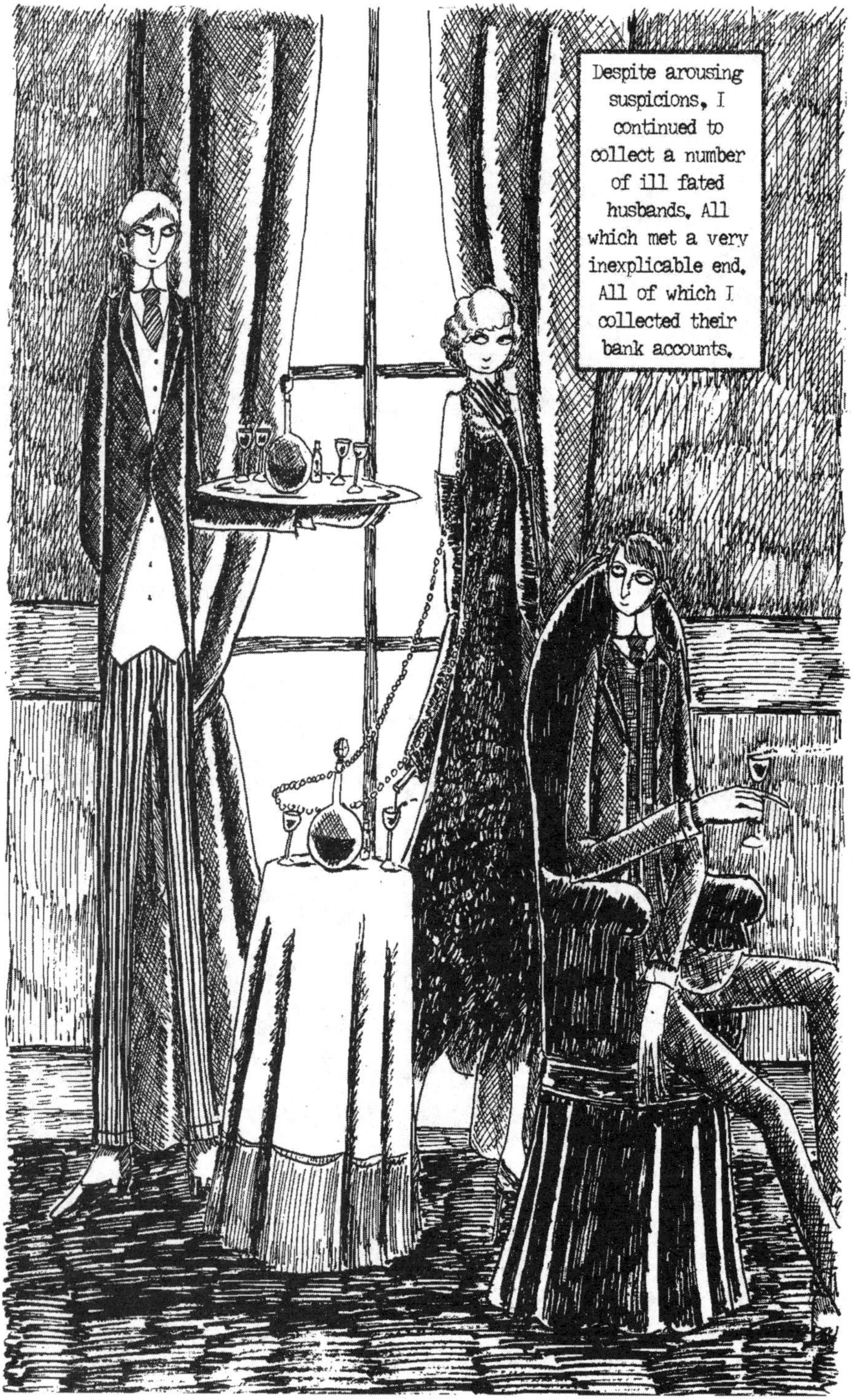
Despite arousing suspicions, I continued to collect a number of ill fated husbands. All which met a very inexplicable end. All of which I collected their bank accounts.

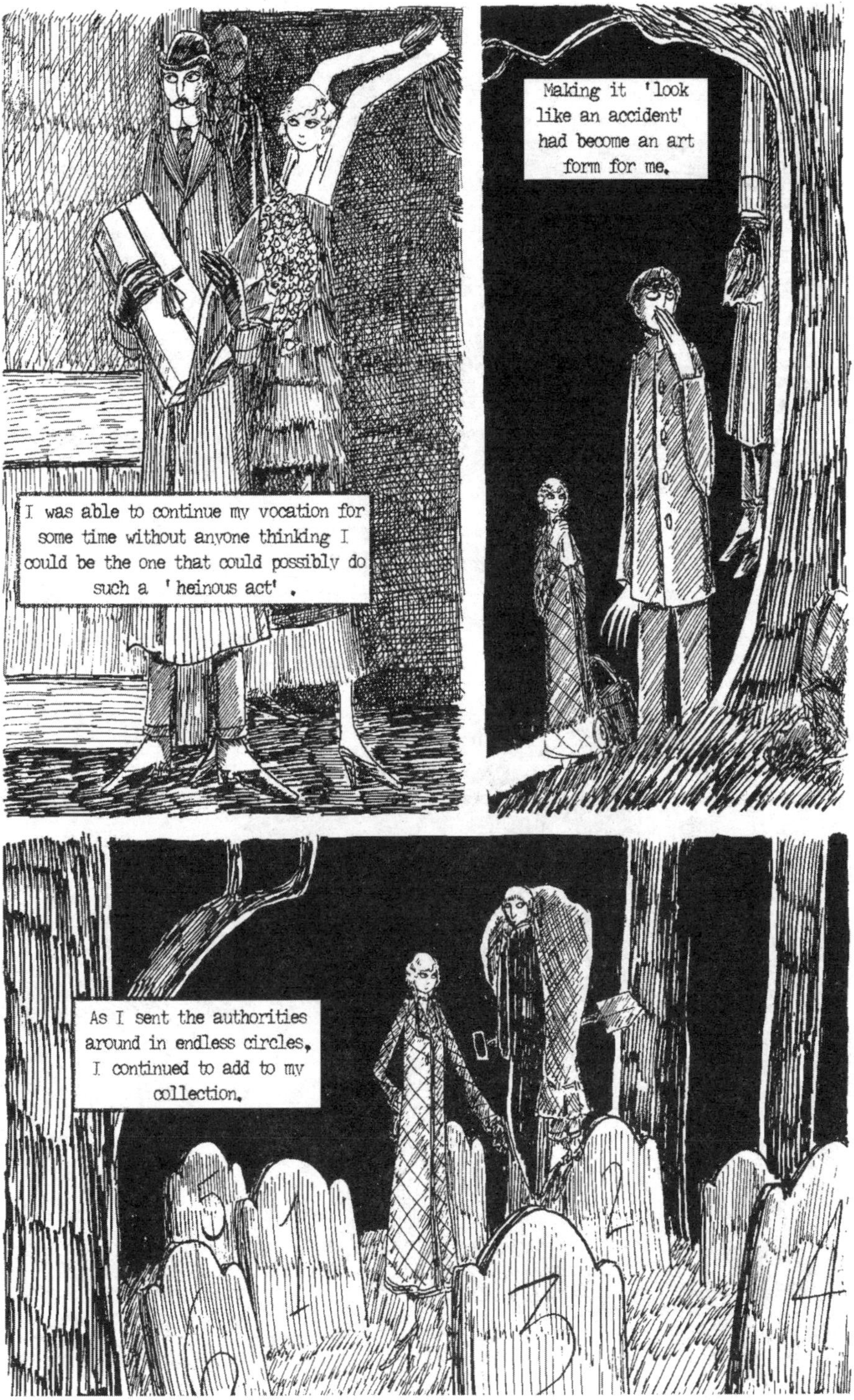
I was able to continue my vocation for some time without anyone thinking I could be the one that could possibly do such a 'heinous act'.
Making it 'look like an accident' had become an art form for me.
As I sent the authorities around in endless circles, I continued to add to my collection.

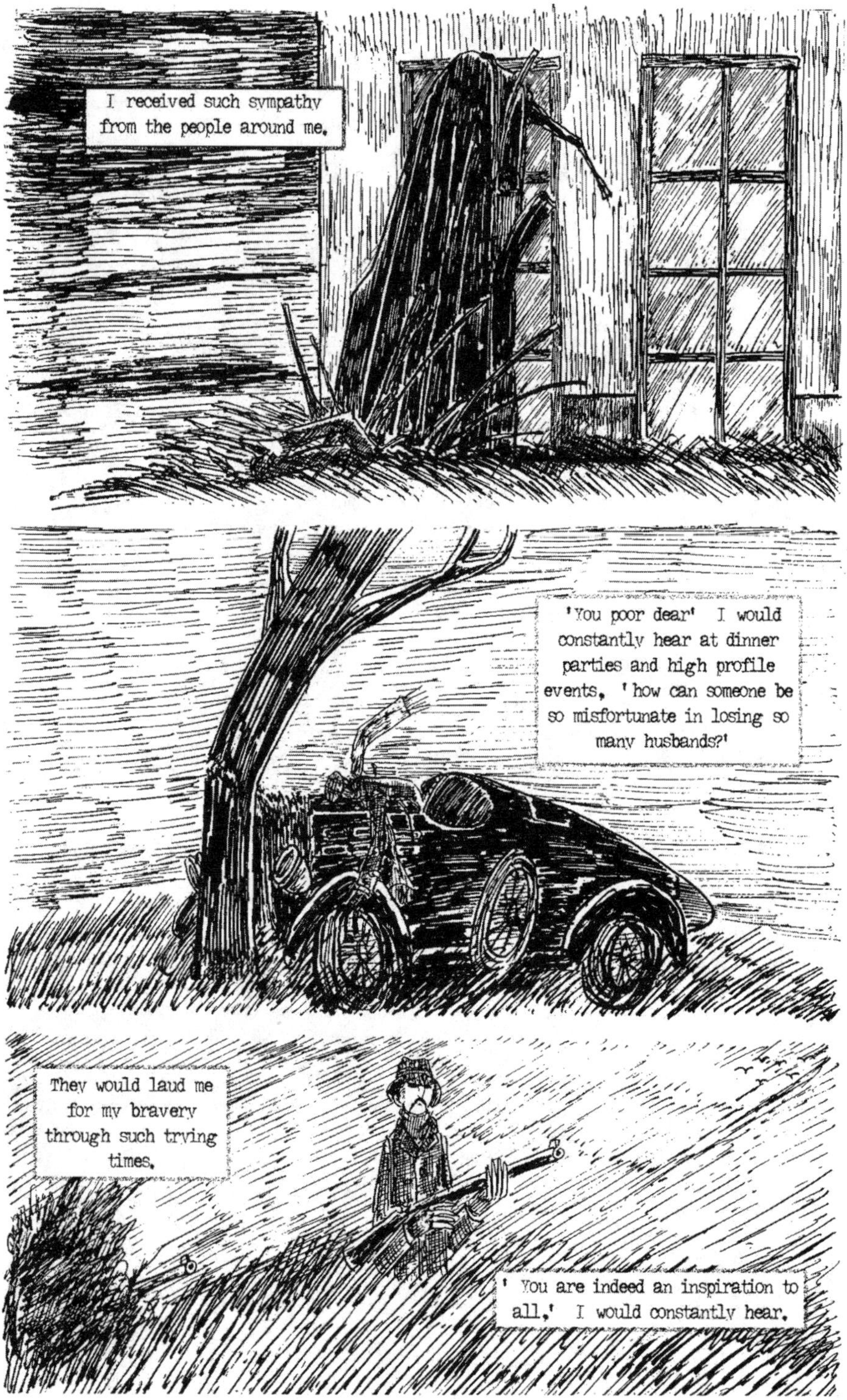
I received such sympathy from the people around me.
'You poor dear' I would constantly hear at dinner parties and high profile events, 'how can someone be so misfortunate in losing so many husbands?'
They would laud me for my bravery through such trying times.
' You are indeed an inspiration to all.' I would constantly hear.

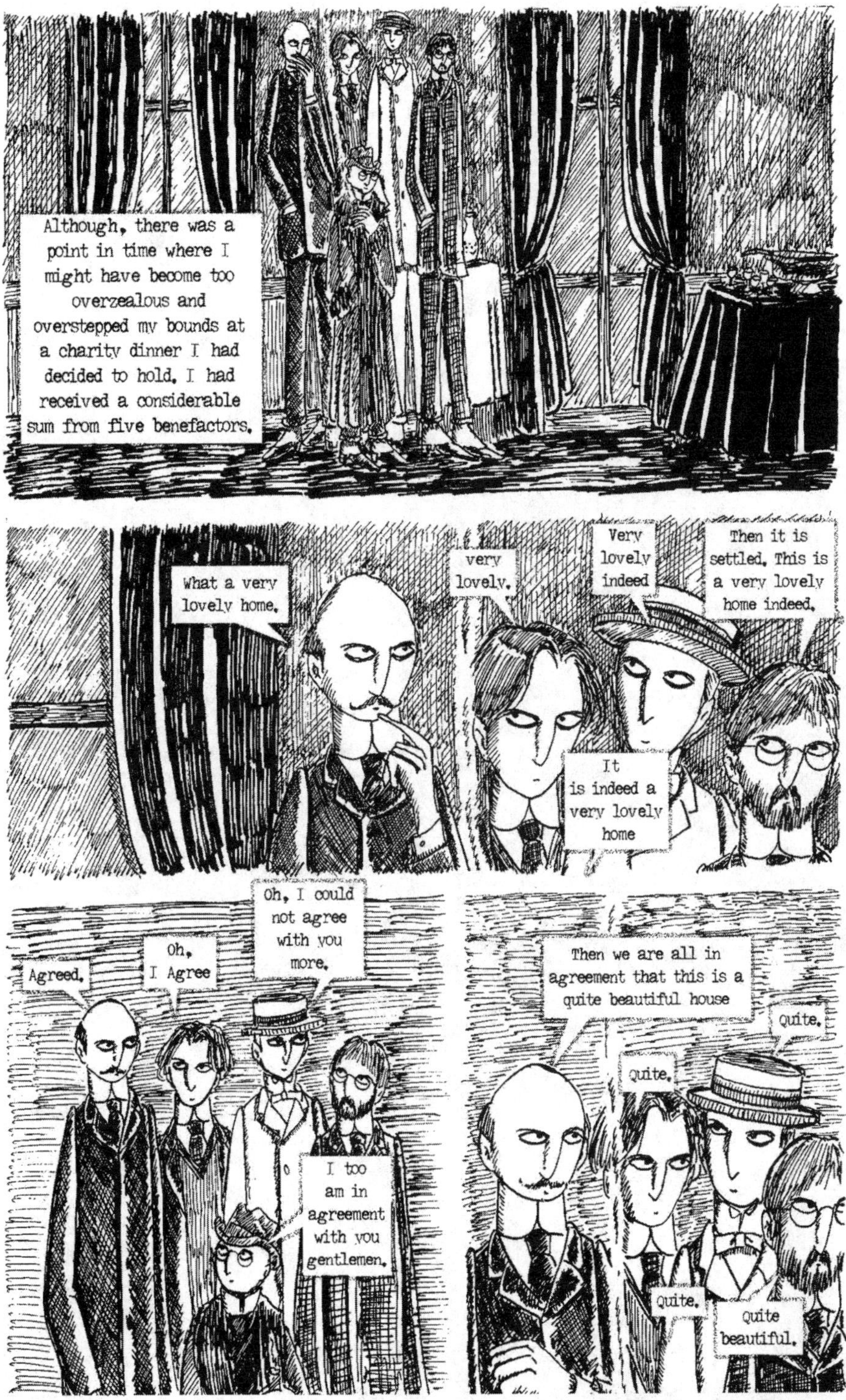
Although, there was a point in time where I might have become too overzealous and overstepped my bounds at a charity dinner I had decided to hold. I had received a considerable sum from five benefactors.
What a very lovely home.
very lovely.
Very lovely indeed
Then it is settled. This is a very lovely home indeed.
It is indeed a very lovely home
Agreed.
Oh, I Agree
Oh, I could not agree with you more.
I too am in agreement with you gentlemen.
Then we are all in agreement that this is a quite beautiful house
Quite.
Quite.
Quite.
Quite beautiful.

CONTINUED IN THE PAGES OF 'DIARY OF THE BLACK WIDOW'

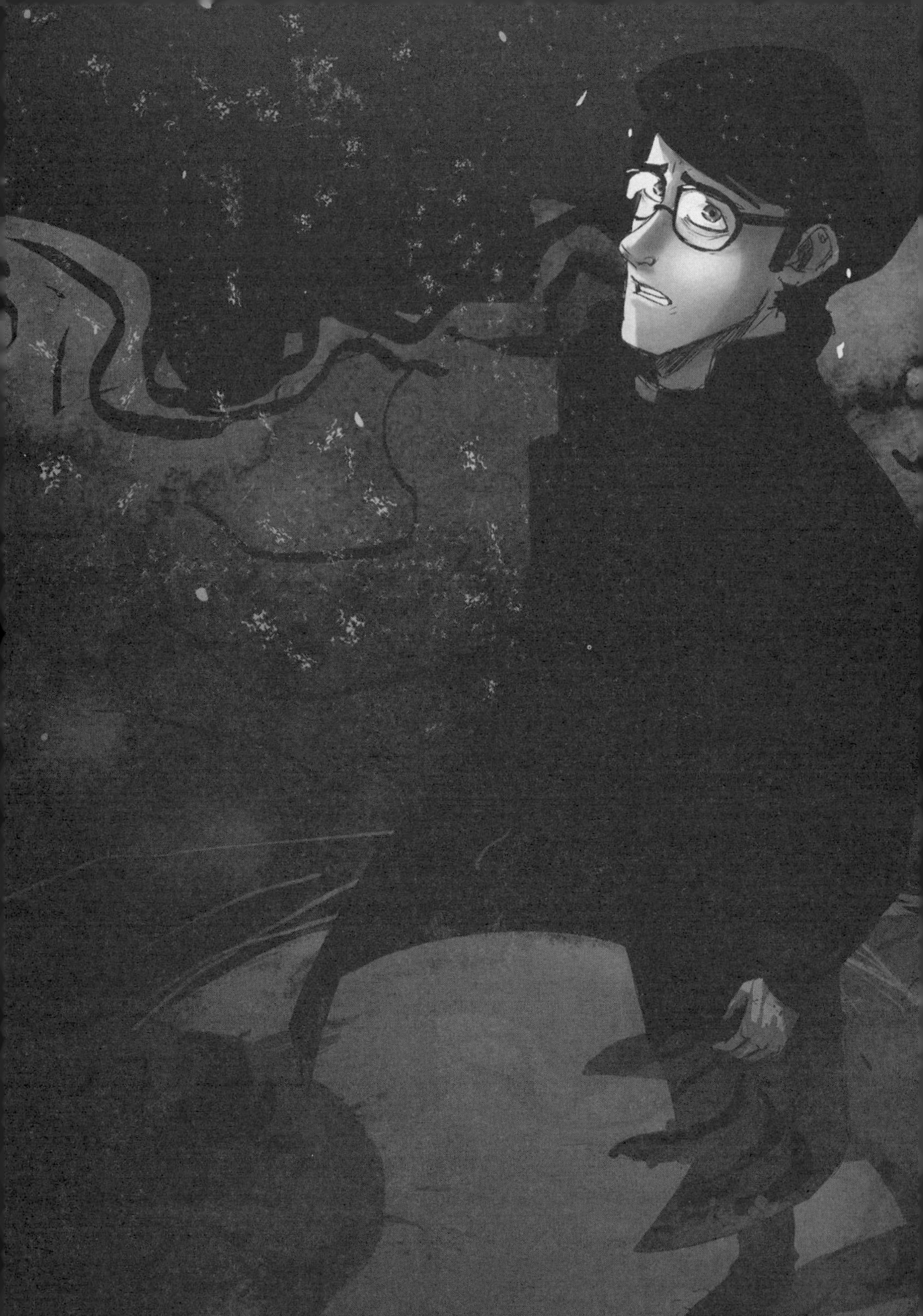

THE DOLRIDGE SACRAMENT

The Dolridge Sacrament

FATHER DANIEL DOLRIDGE

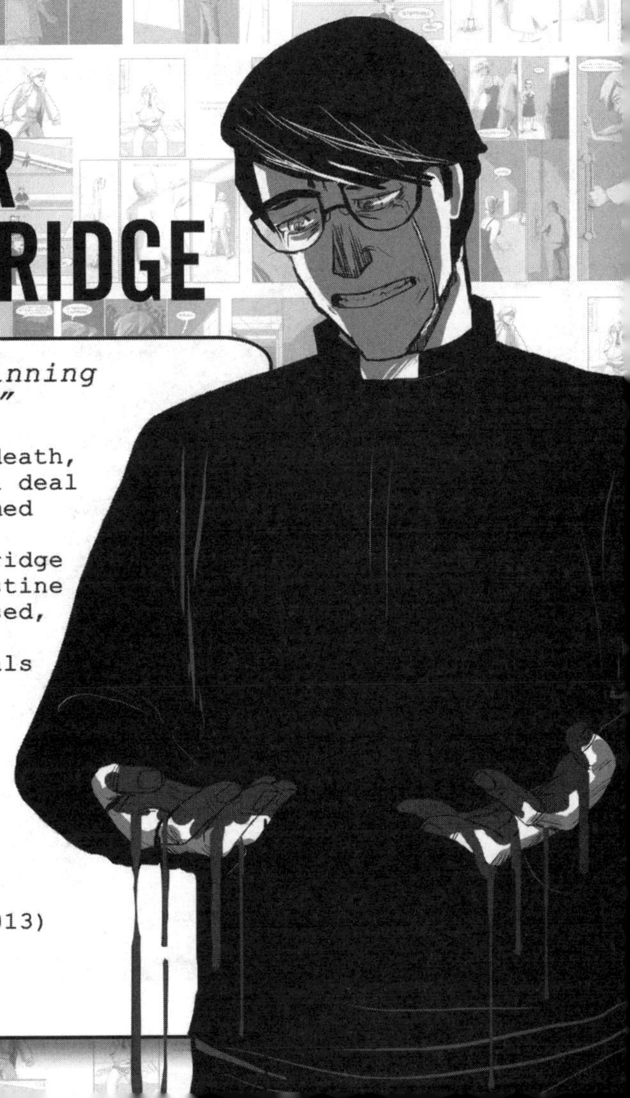

"This is the beginning of a family."

After his sister's untimely death, Father Daniel Dolridge made a deal with a demon mysteriously named The Witness. In exchange for gaining a family, Father Dolridge must complete a dark, clandestine ritual. Frightened and confused, Dolridge misunderstands the agreement and unknowingly seals the fate of a young traveler and everyone at the Dolridge House...

Age: 34
Height: 5'10"
Weight: 169 lbs.

First Appearance:
THE DOLRIDGE SACRAMENT #1 (2013)

Created by Wilson Taylor
Illustration by Maia Gross

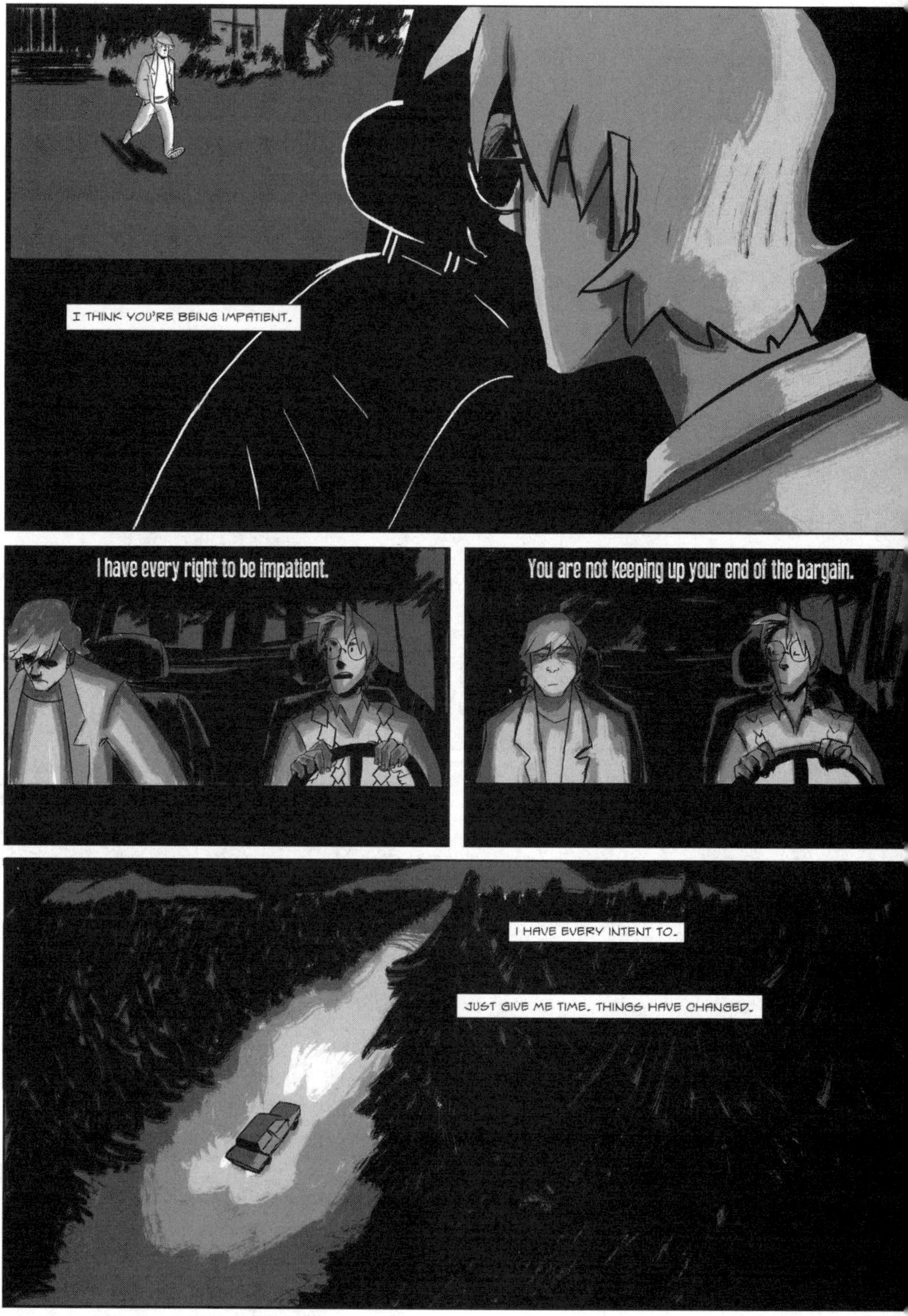
I THINK YOU'RE BEING IMPATIENT.
I have every right to be impatient.
You are not keeping up your end of the bargain.
I HAVE EVERY INTENT TO.
JUST GIVE ME TIME. THINGS HAVE CHANGED.

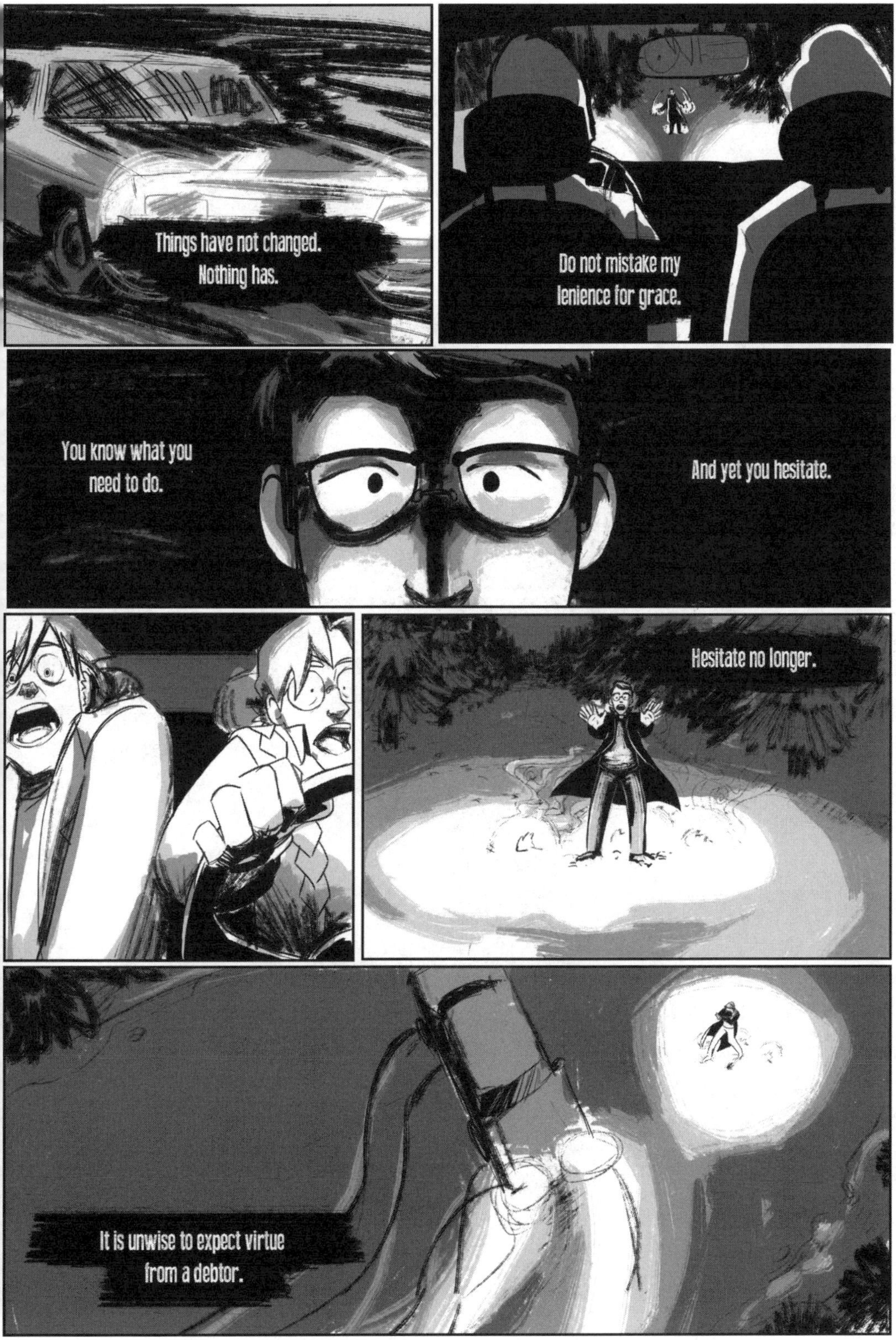
Things have not changed.
Nothing has.
Do not mistake my lenience for grace.
You know what you need to do.
And yet you hesitate.
Hesitate no longer.
It is unwise to expect virtue from a debtor.

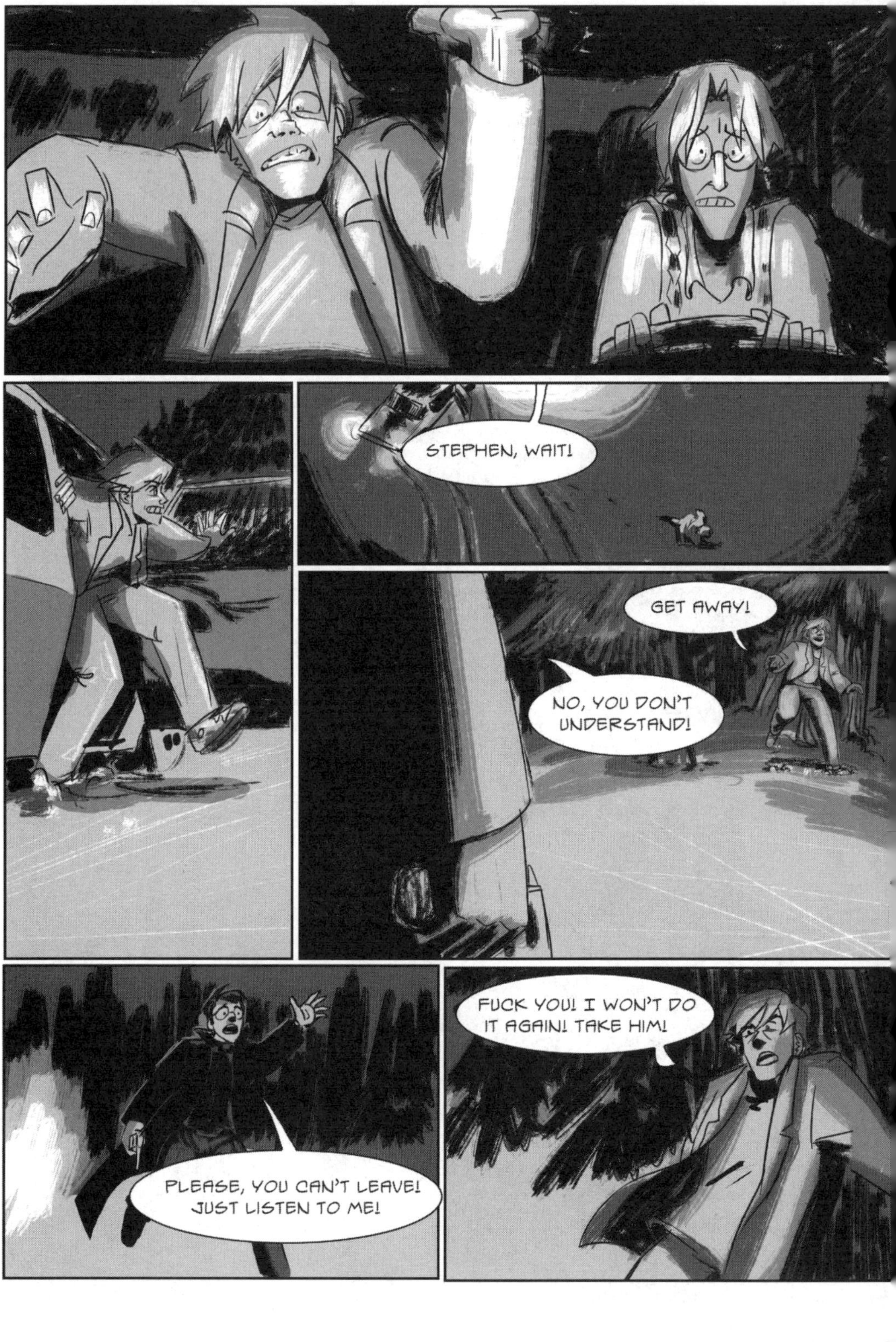
STEPHEN, WAIT!
GET AWAY!
NO, YOU DON'T UNDERSTAND!
PLEASE, YOU CAN'T LEAVE! JUST LISTEN TO ME!
FUCK YOU! I WON'T DO IT AGAIN! TAKE HIM!

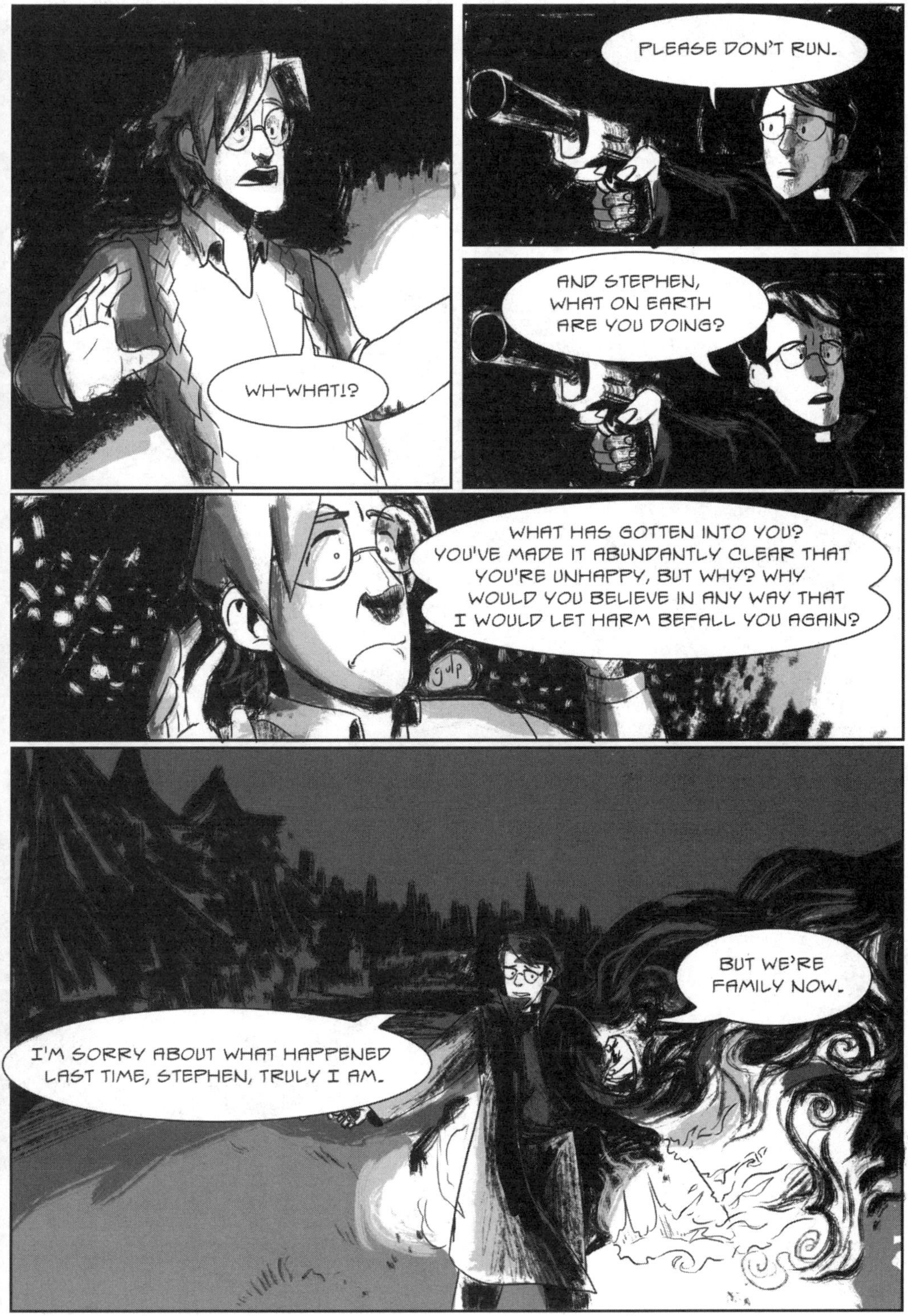
WH-WHAT!?
PLEASE DON'T RUN.
AND STEPHEN, WHAT ON EARTH ARE YOU DOING?
WHAT HAS GOTTEN INTO YOU? YOU'VE MADE IT ABUNDANTLY CLEAR THAT YOU'RE UNHAPPY, BUT WHY? WHY WOULD YOU BELIEVE IN ANY WAY THAT I WOULD LET HARM BEFALL YOU AGAIN?
gulp
BUT WE'RE FAMILY NOW.
I'M SORRY ABOUT WHAT HAPPENED LAST TIME, STEPHEN, TRULY I AM.

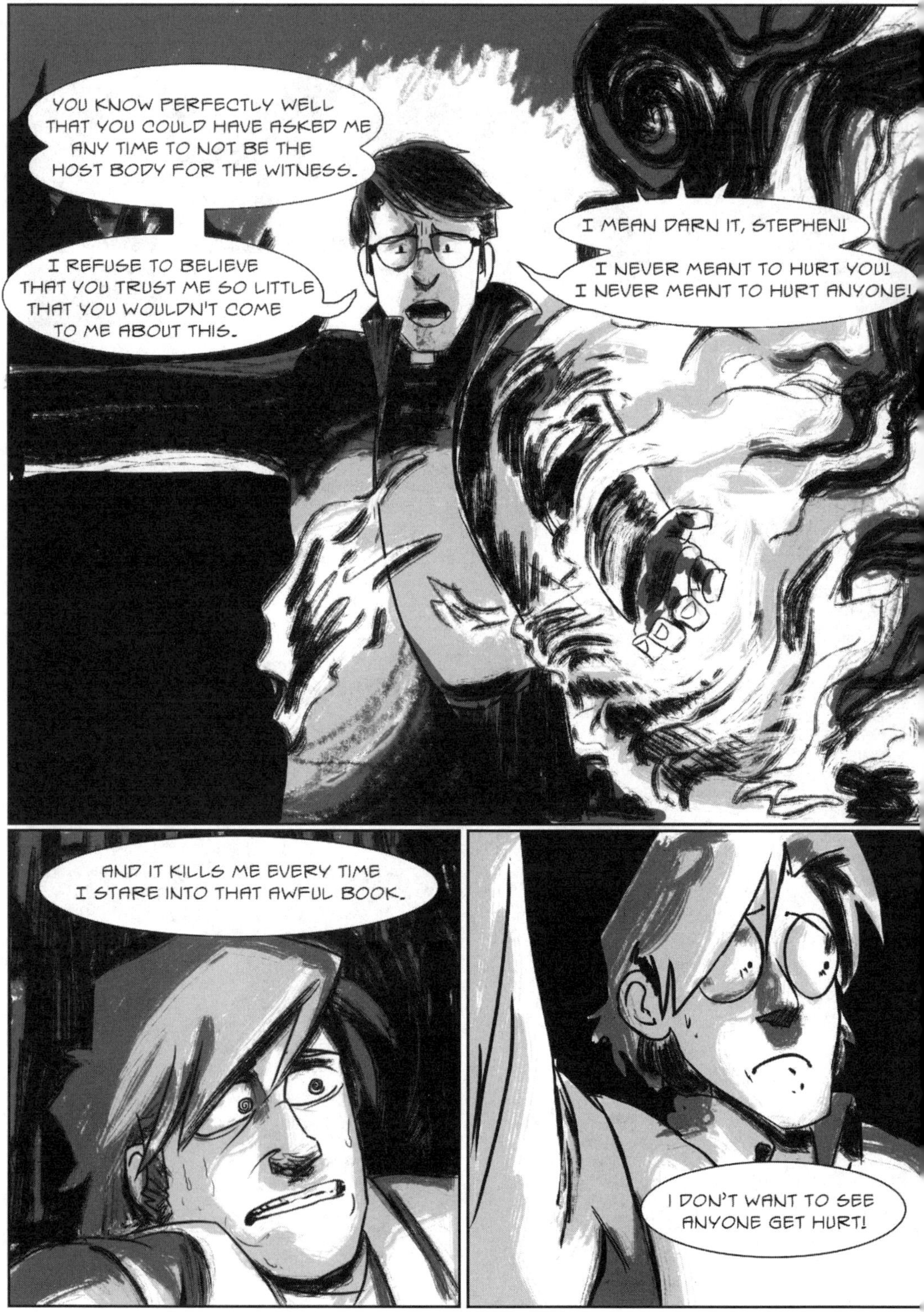
YOU KNOW PERFECTLY WELL THAT YOU COULD HAVE ASKED ME ANY TIME TO NOT BE THE HOST BODY FOR THE WITNESS.
I REFUSE TO BELIEVE THAT YOU TRUST ME SO LITTLE THAT YOU WOULDN'T COME TO ME ABOUT THIS.
I MEAN DARN IT, STEPHEN!
I NEVER MEANT TO HURT YOU! I NEVER MEANT TO HURT ANYONE!
AND IT KILLS ME EVERY TIME I STARE INTO THAT AWFUL BOOK.
I DON'T WANT TO SEE ANYONE GET HURT!

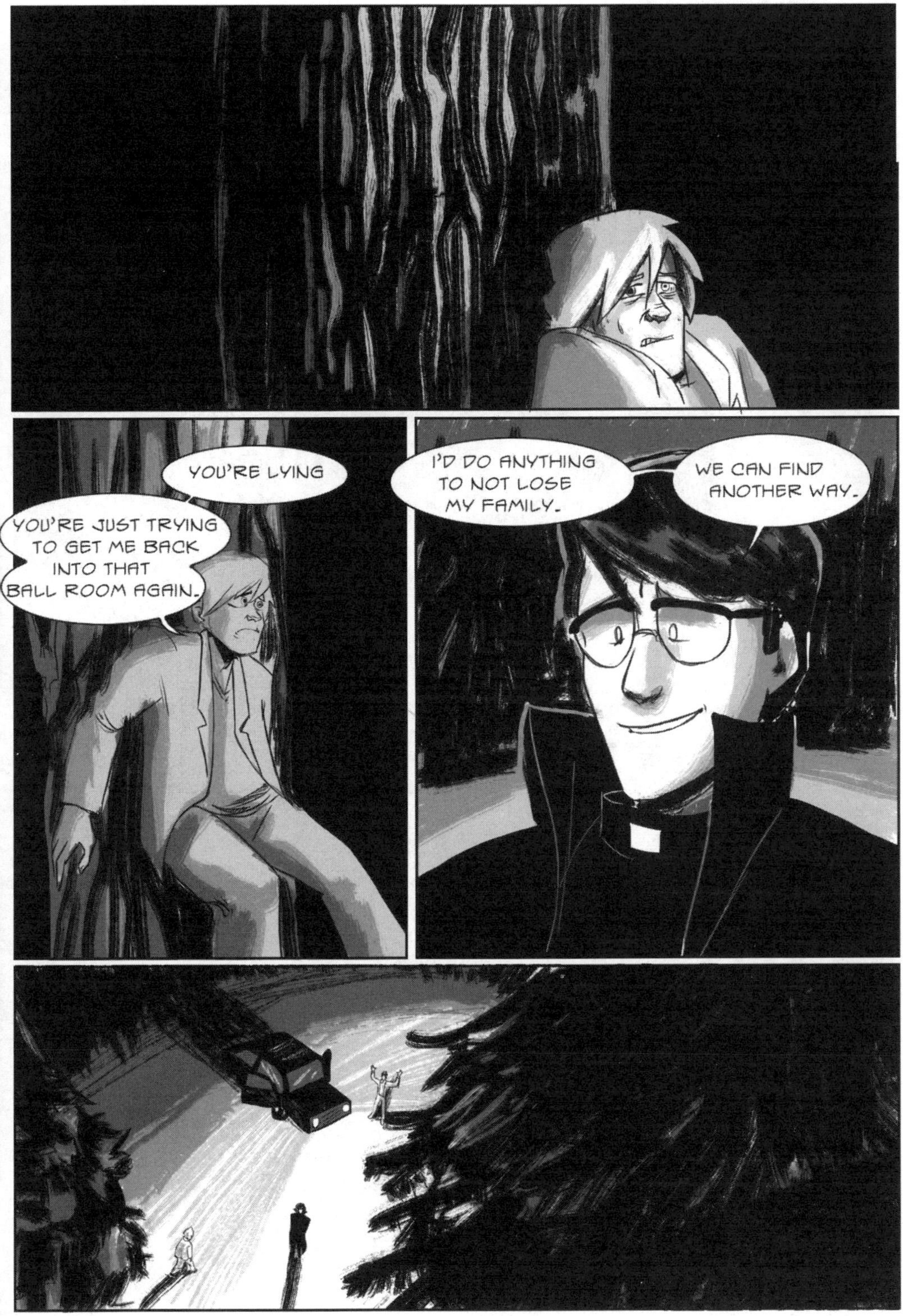
YOU'RE LYING
YOU'RE JUST TRYING TO GET ME BACK INTO THAT BALL ROOM AGAIN.
I'D DO ANYTHING TO NOT LOSE MY FAMILY.
WE CAN FIND ANOTHER WAY.

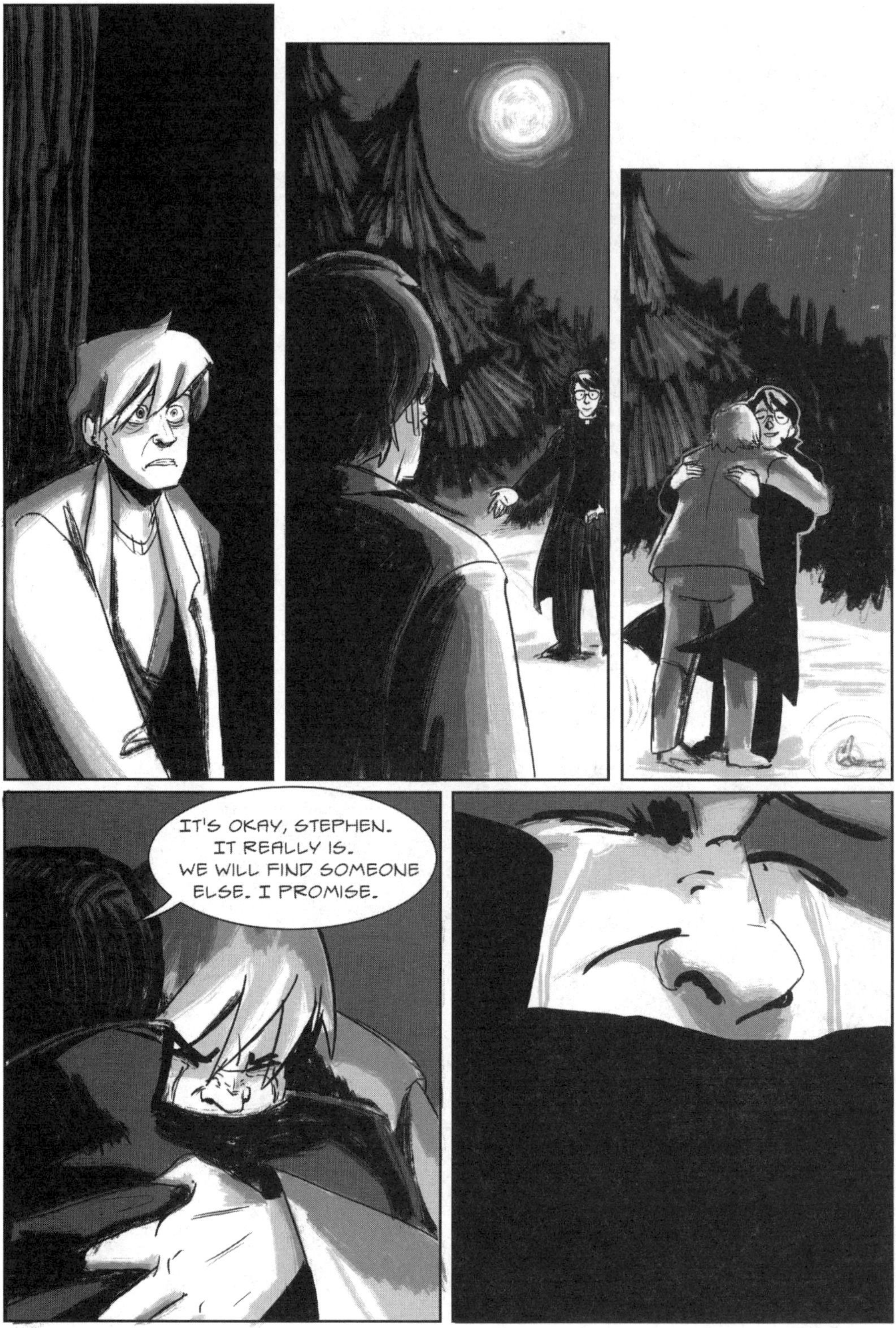
IT'S OKAY, STEPHEN. IT REALLY IS. WE WILL FIND SOMEONE ELSE. I PROMISE.

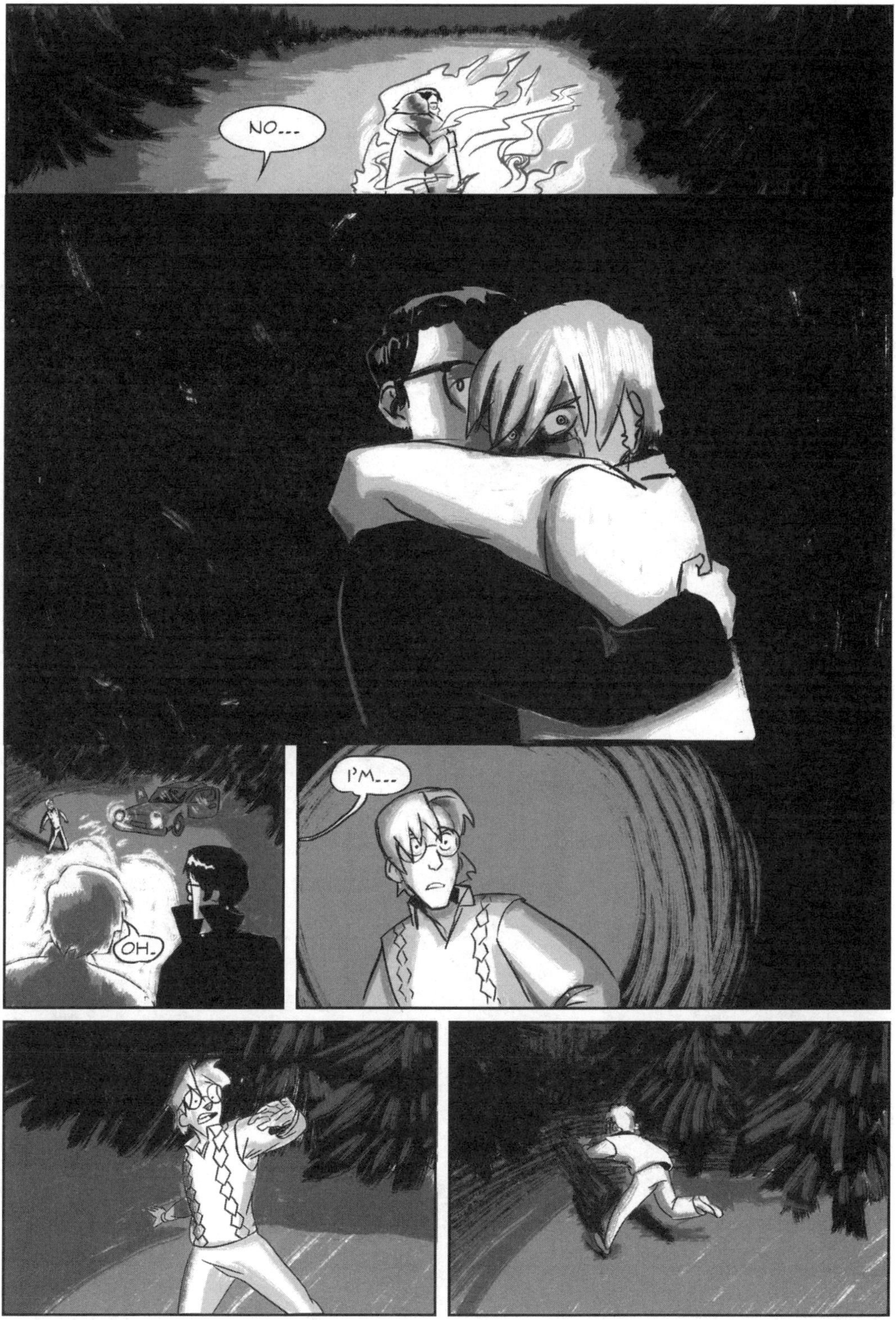

NO...
OH.
I'M...

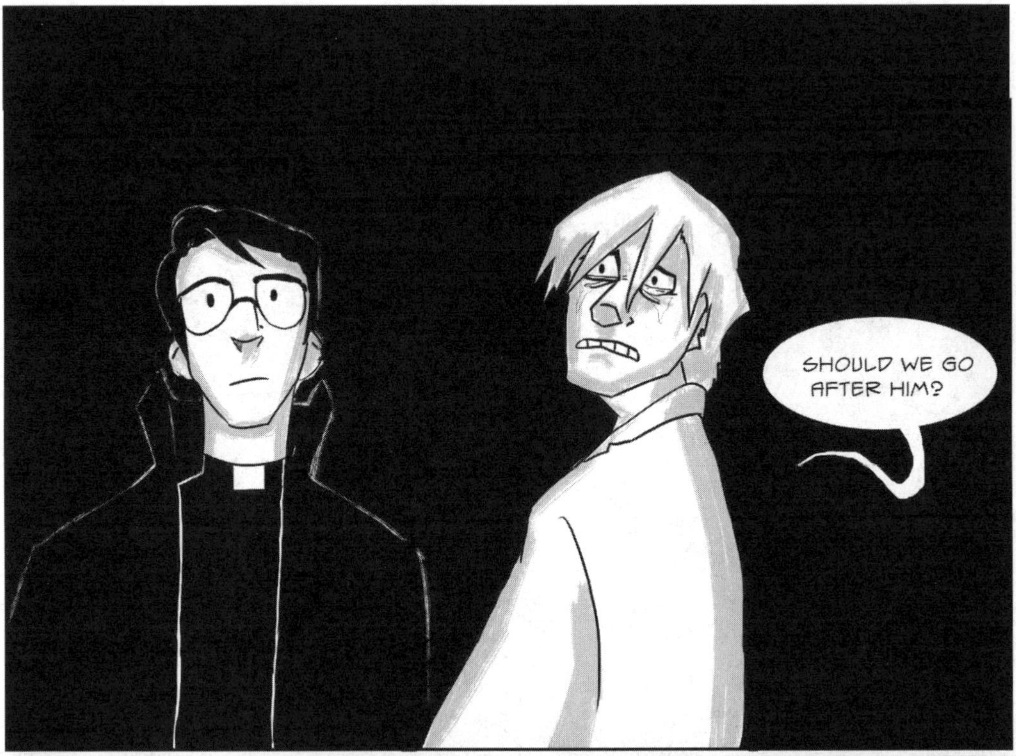
SHOULD WE GO AFTER HIM?

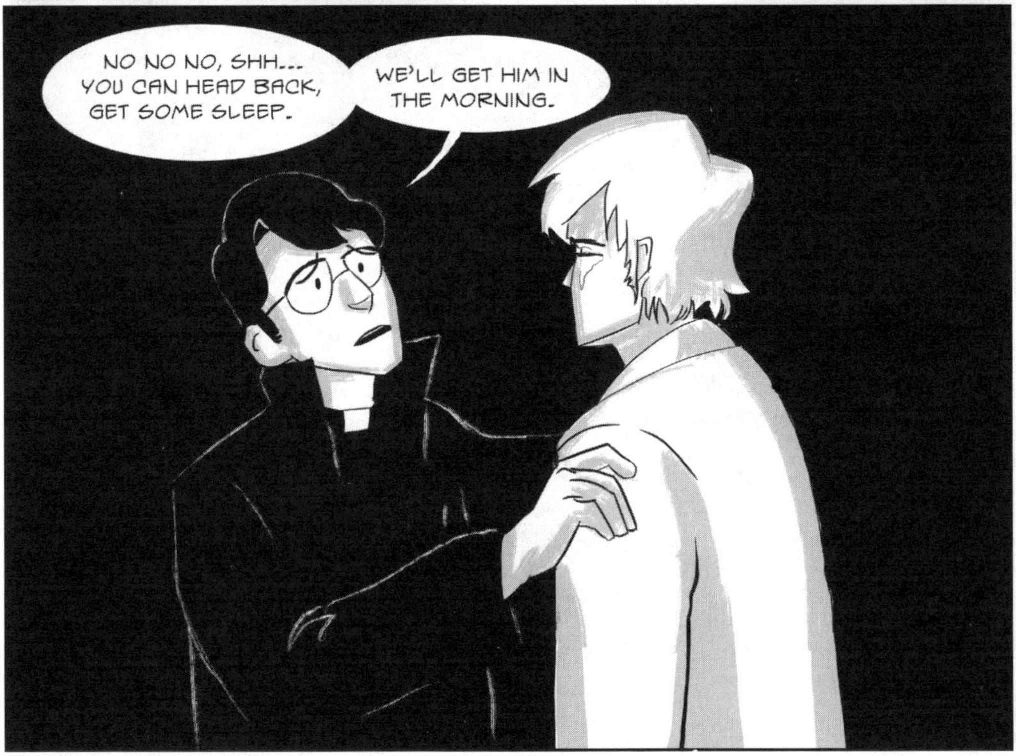
NO NO NO, SHH... YOU CAN HEAD BACK, GET SOME SLEEP.
WE'LL GET HIM IN THE MORNING.

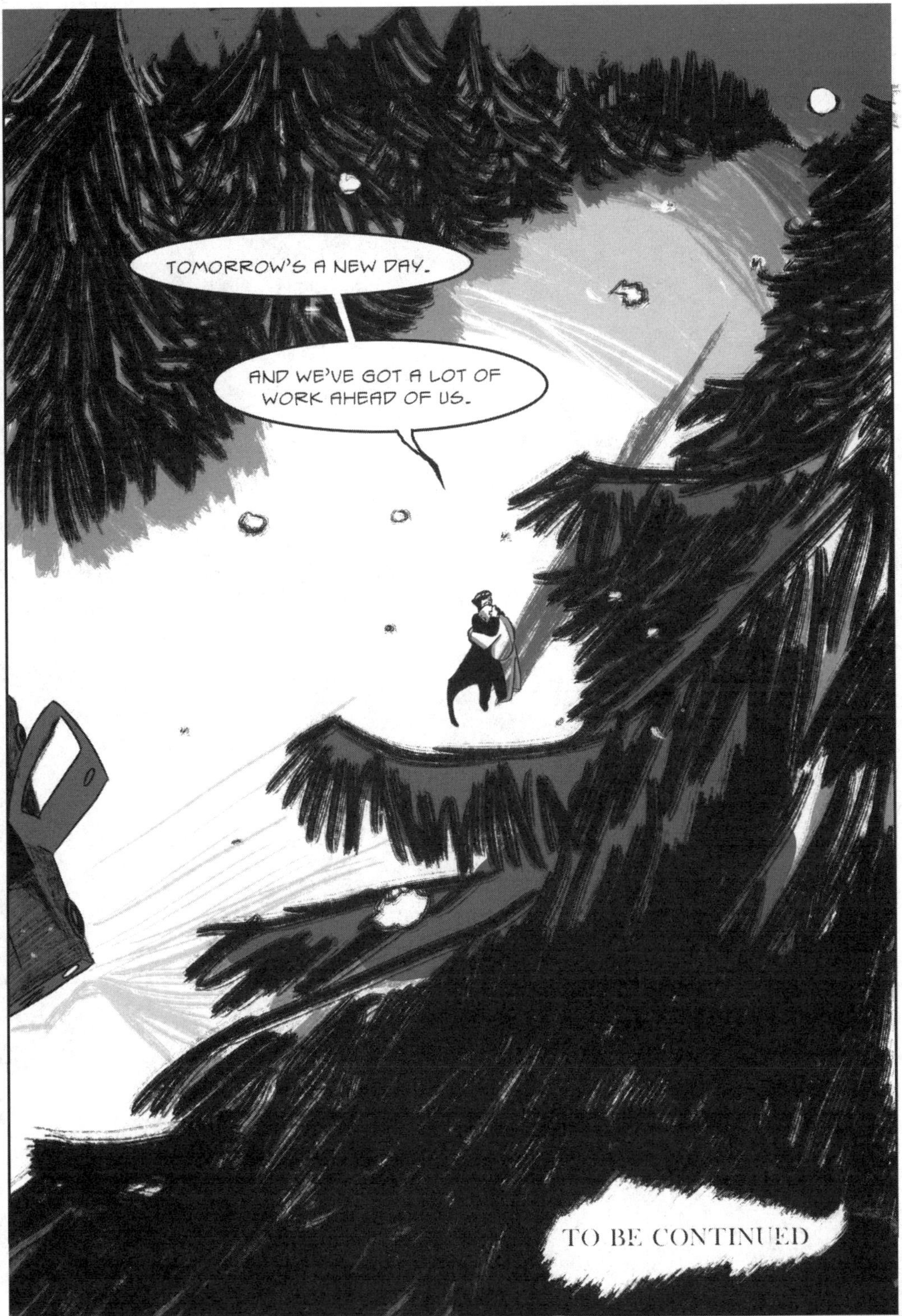
TOMORROW'S A NEW DAY.
AND WE'VE GOT A LOT OF WORK AHEAD OF US.
TO BE CONTINUED

CONTINUED IN THE PAGES OF 'THE DOLRIDGE SACRAMENT'

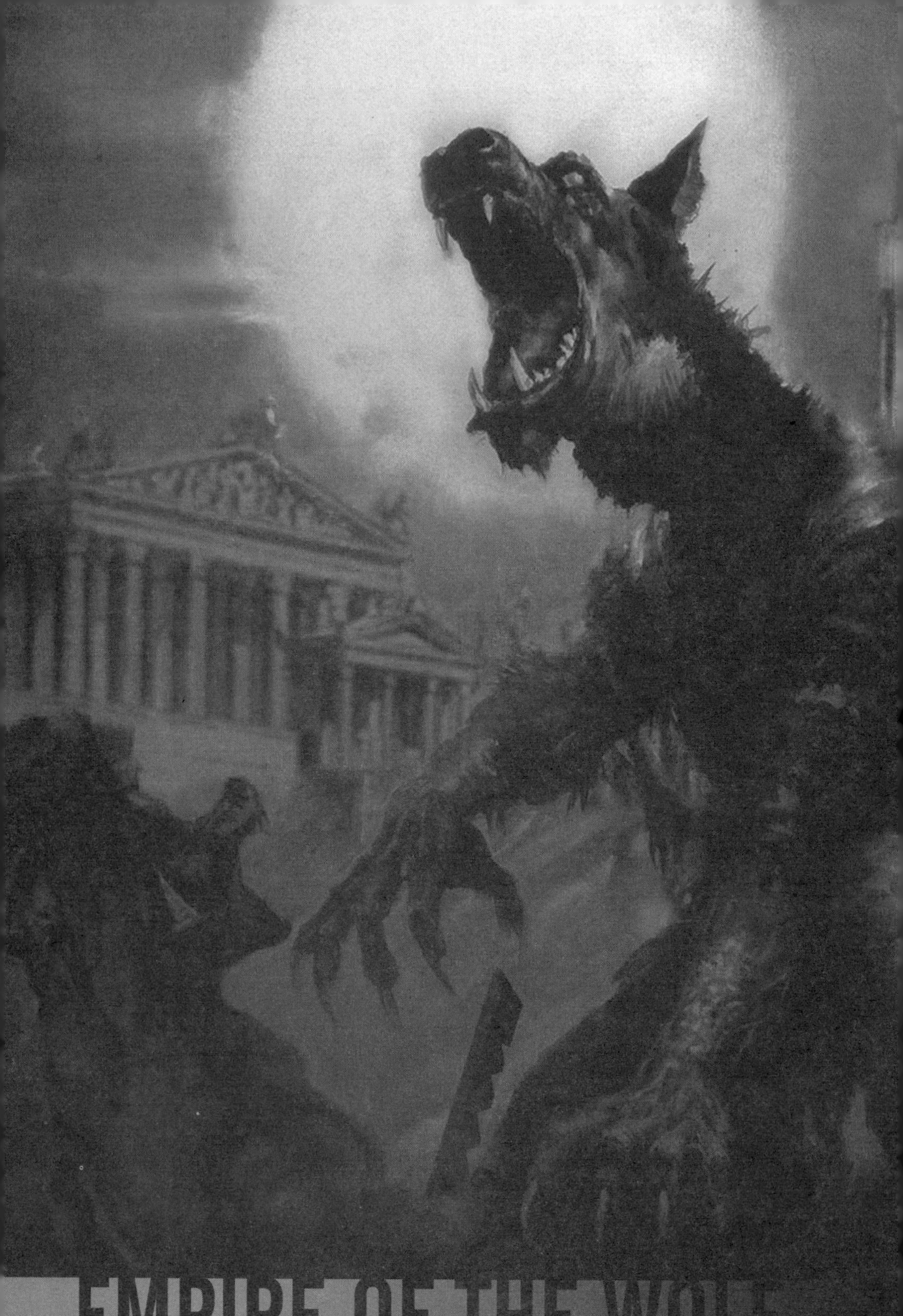

EMPIRE OF THE WOLF

EMPIRE OF THE WOLF

CANISIUS & LUCIUS

*"Farewell Lucius, my brother...
for the glory of Rome!"*

Canisius spent most of his youth as a slave, fighting
for freedom in Rome's gladiatorial pits, while Lucius
had a patrician upbringing as nephew to the emperor.
Despite their differences, together on the battlefield
their pasts are naught, as they are the most loyal and
valiant of brothers-in-arms. Nothing can get between
them — not even their love for the same woman — until
a werewolf's bite curses their bond, and forces them
to relive the most infamous fraternal legacy of them
all, that of Rome's founders: Romulus and Remus.

CANISIUS SARCIPIO
Height: 5'10"   Weight: 210 lbs.

LUCIUS DOMITIUS
AHENOBARBUS
Height: 6'2"
Weight: 185 lbs.

First Appearance:
EMPIRE OF THE WOLF #1
(2013)

Created by
Michael Kogge
Illustration by
Dan Parsons
& David Rabbitte

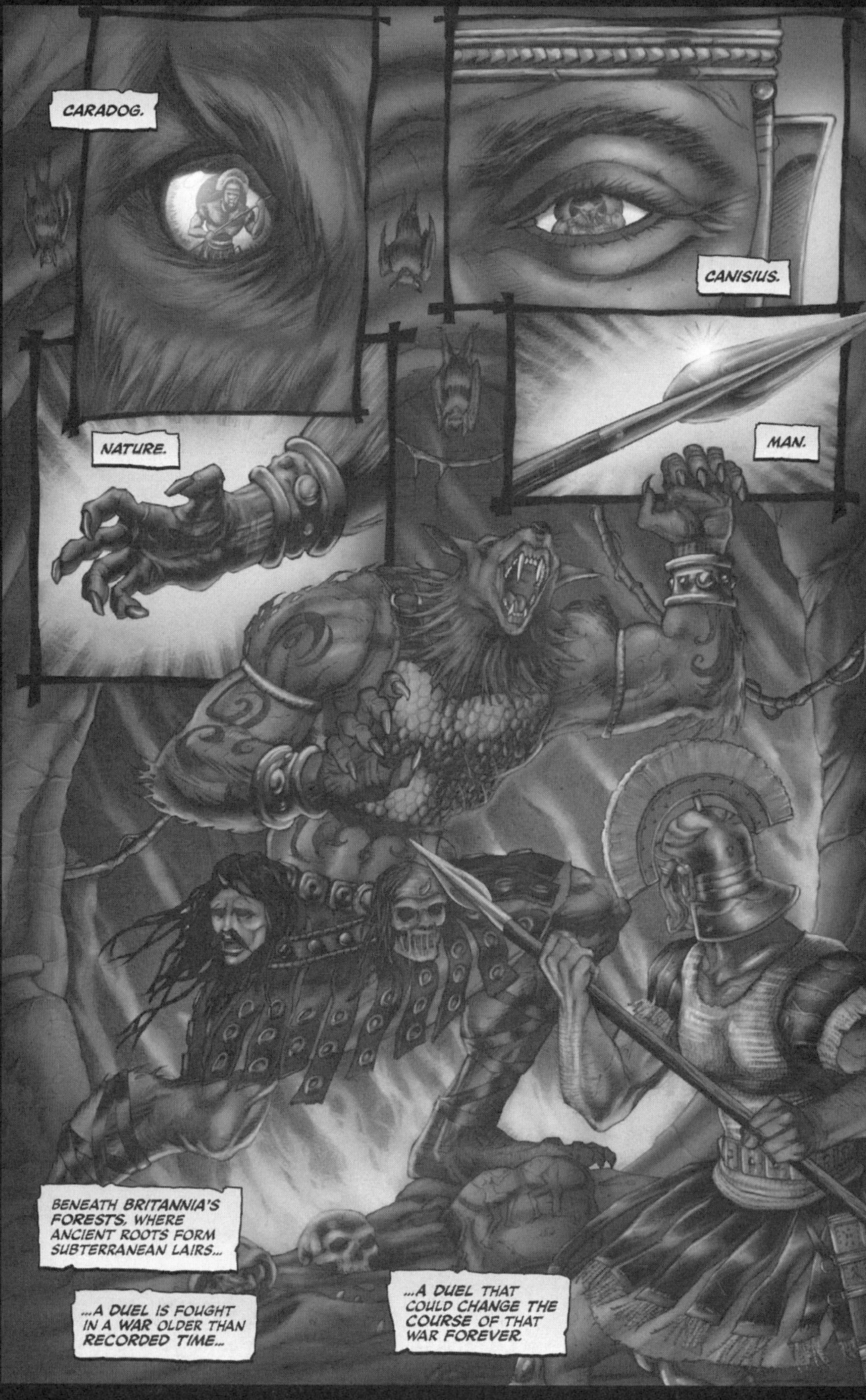
CARADOG.
CANISIUS.
NATURE.
MAN.
BENEATH BRITANNIA'S FORESTS, WHERE ANCIENT ROOTS FORM SUBTERRANEAN LAIRS...
...A DUEL IS FOUGHT IN A WAR OLDER THAN RECORDED TIME...
...A DUEL THAT COULD CHANGE THE COURSE OF THAT WAR FOREVER.

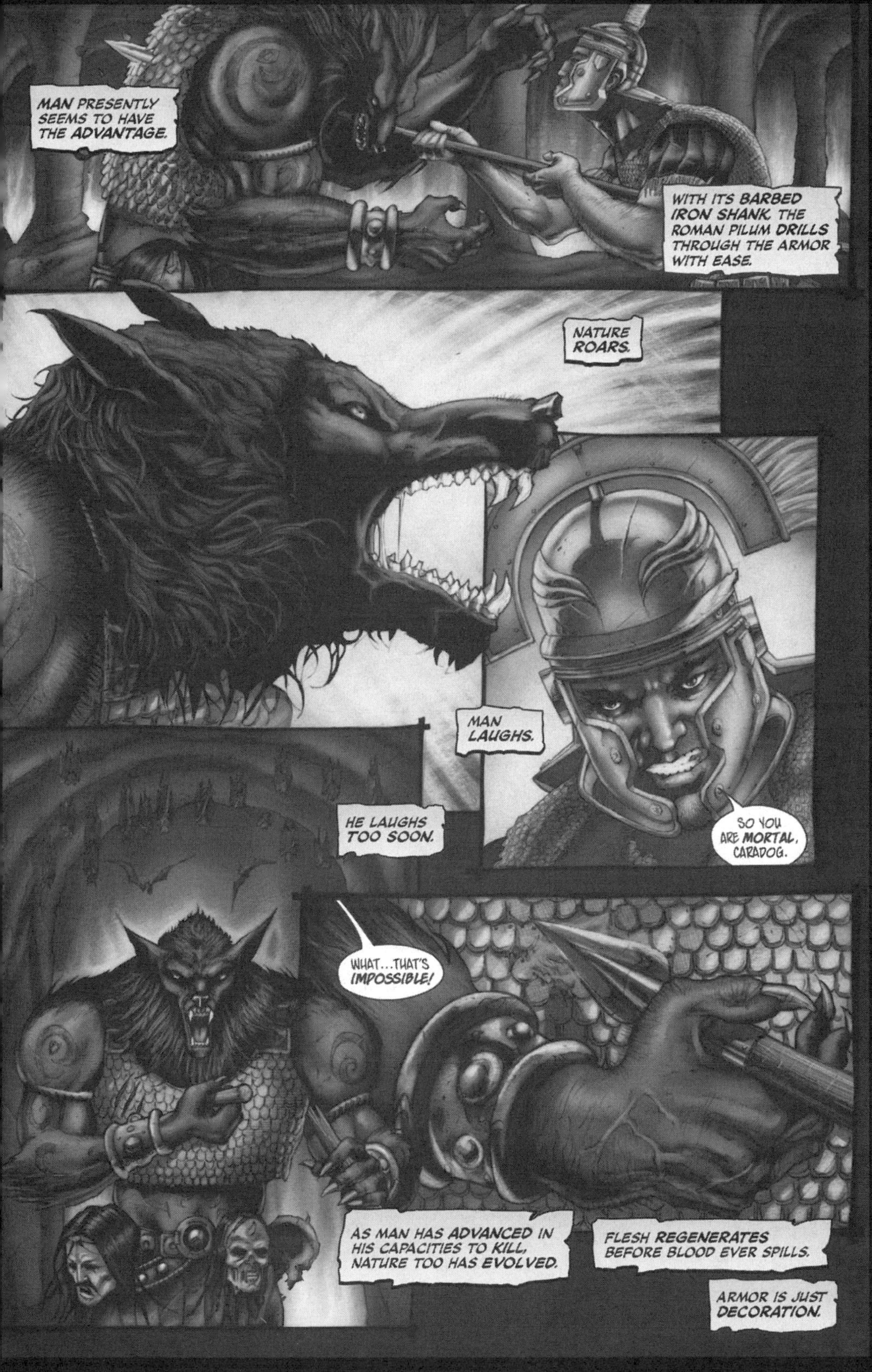
MAN PRESENTLY SEEMS TO HAVE THE ADVANTAGE.
WITH ITS BARBED IRON SHANK, THE ROMAN PILUM DRILLS THROUGH THE ARMOR WITH EASE.
NATURE ROARS.
MAN LAUGHS.
HE LAUGHS TOO SOON.
SO YOU ARE MORTAL, CARADOG.
WHAT...THAT'S IMPOSSIBLE!
AS MAN HAS ADVANCED IN HIS CAPACITIES TO KILL, NATURE TOO HAS EVOLVED.
FLESH REGENERATES BEFORE BLOOD EVER SPILLS.
ARMOR IS JUST DECORATION.

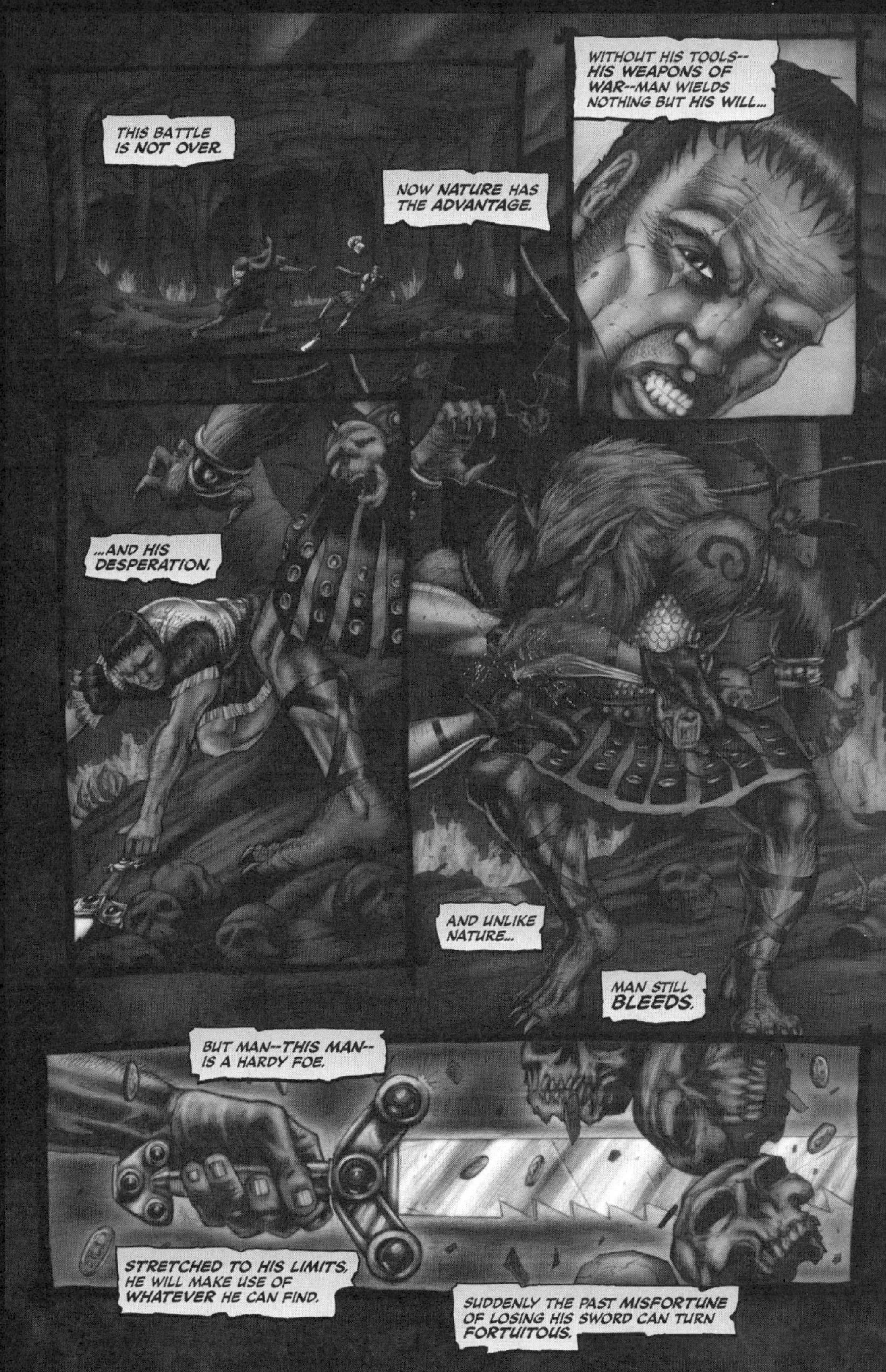
THIS BATTLE IS NOT OVER.
NOW NATURE HAS THE ADVANTAGE.
WITHOUT HIS TOOLS-- HIS WEAPONS OF WAR--MAN WIELDS NOTHING BUT HIS WILL...
...AND HIS DESPERATION.
AND UNLIKE NATURE...
MAN STILL BLEEDS.
BUT MAN--THIS MAN-- IS A HARDY FOE.
STRETCHED TO HIS LIMITS, HE WILL MAKE USE OF WHATEVER HE CAN FIND.
SUDDENLY THE PAST MISFORTUNE OF LOSING HIS SWORD CAN TURN FORTUITOUS.

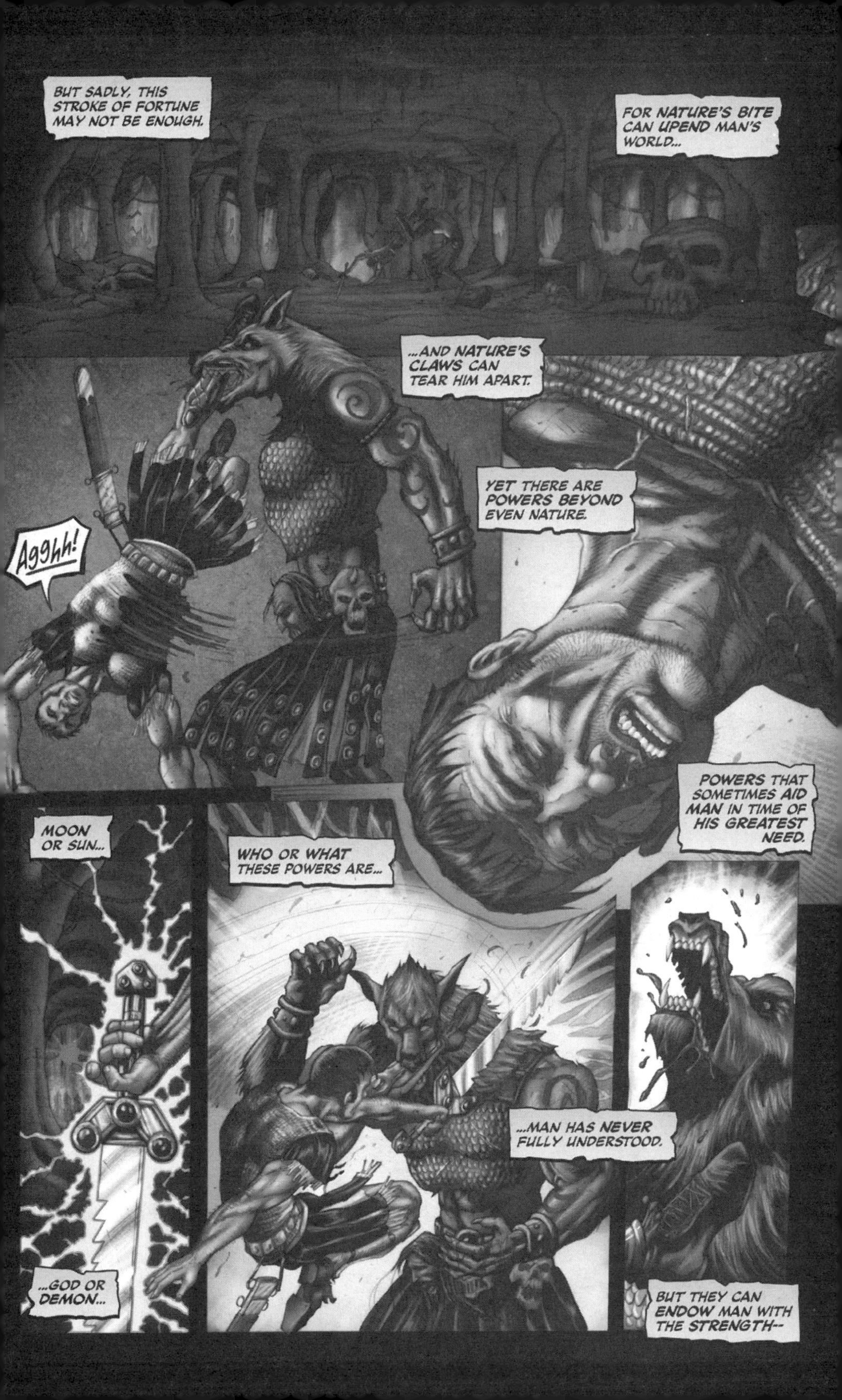
BUT SADLY, THIS STROKE OF FORTUNE MAY NOT BE ENOUGH.
FOR NATURE'S BITE CAN UPEND MAN'S WORLD...
...AND NATURE'S CLAWS CAN TEAR HIM APART.
Agghh!
YET THERE ARE POWERS BEYOND EVEN NATURE.
POWERS THAT SOMETIMES AID MAN IN TIME OF HIS GREATEST NEED.
MOON OR SUN...
...GOD OR DEMON...
WHO OR WHAT THESE POWERS ARE...
...MAN HAS NEVER FULLY UNDERSTOOD.
BUT THEY CAN ENDOW MAN WITH THE STRENGTH--

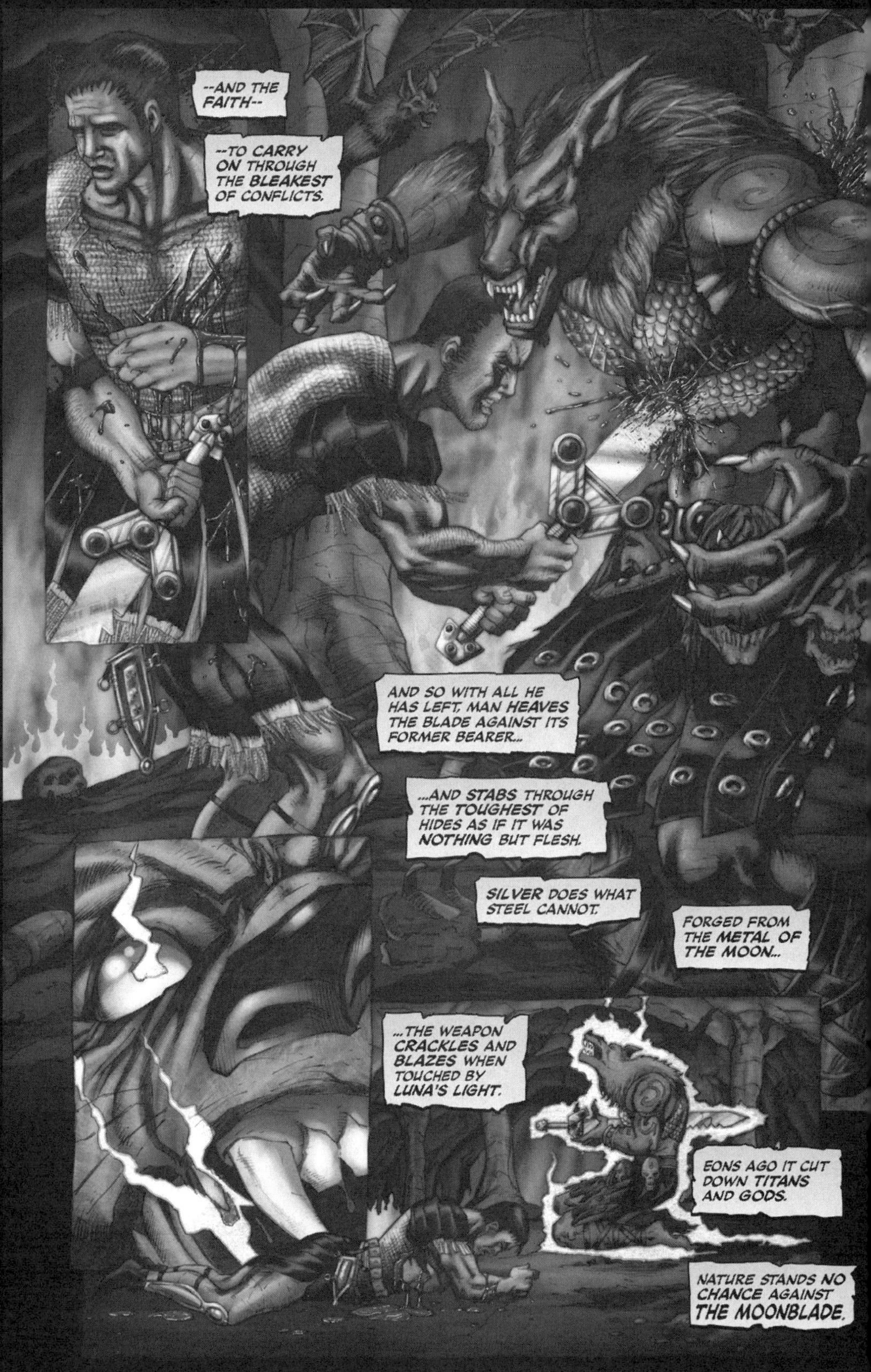
--AND THE FAITH--
--TO CARRY ON THROUGH THE BLEAKEST OF CONFLICTS.
AND SO WITH ALL HE HAS LEFT, MAN HEAVES THE BLADE AGAINST ITS FORMER BEARER...
...AND STABS THROUGH THE TOUGHEST OF HIDES AS IF IT WAS NOTHING BUT FLESH.
SILVER DOES WHAT STEEL CANNOT.
FORGED FROM THE METAL OF THE MOON...
...THE WEAPON CRACKLES AND BLAZES WHEN TOUCHED BY LUNA'S LIGHT.
EONS AGO IT CUT DOWN TITANS AND GODS.
NATURE STANDS NO CHANCE AGAINST THE MOONBLADE.

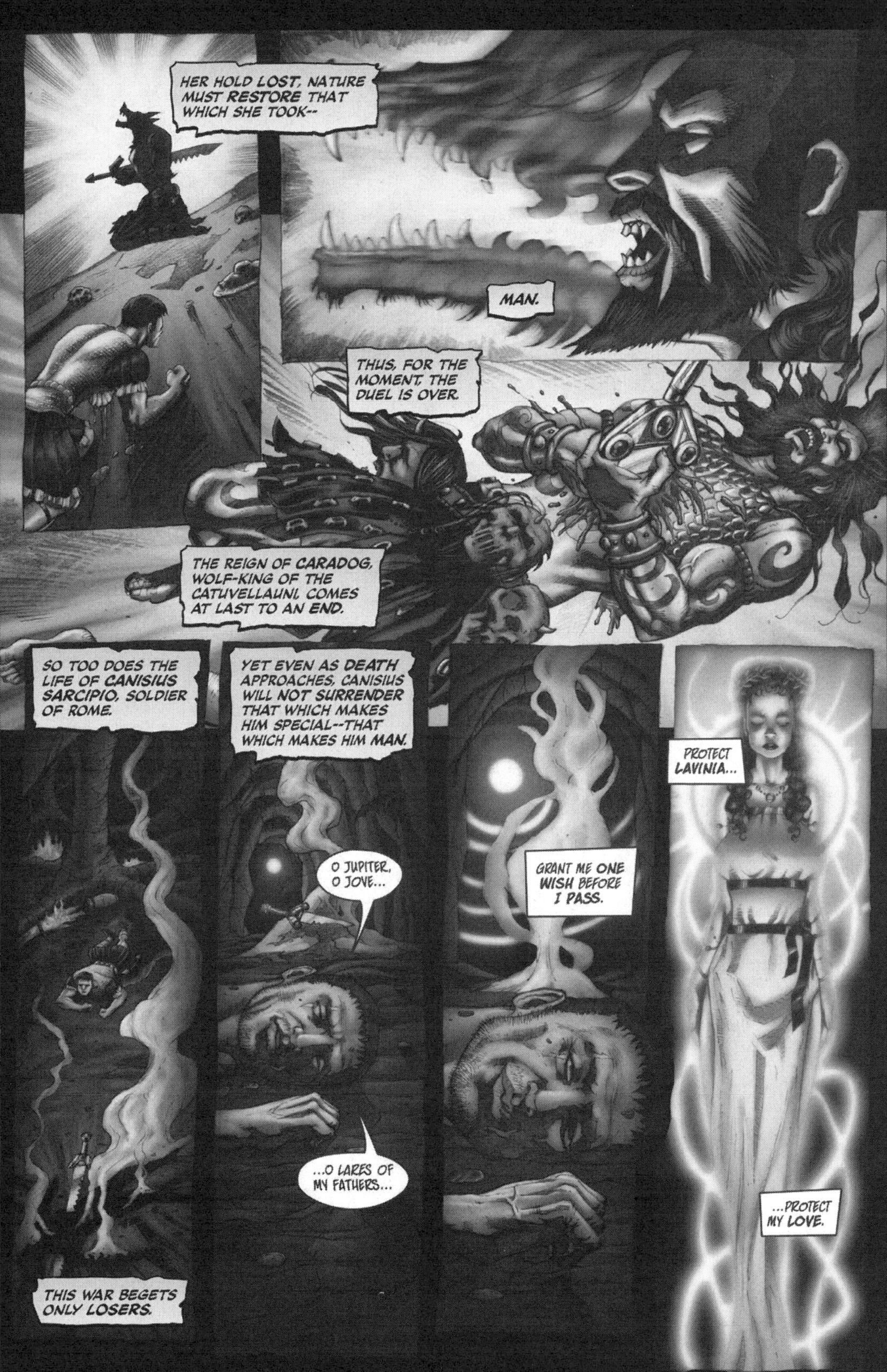
HER HOLD LOST, NATURE MUST RESTORE THAT WHICH SHE TOOK--
MAN.
THUS, FOR THE MOMENT, THE DUEL IS OVER.
THE REIGN OF CARADOG, WOLF-KING OF THE CATUVELLAUNI, COMES AT LAST TO AN END.
SO TOO DOES THE LIFE OF CANISIUS SARCIPIO, SOLDIER OF ROME.
YET EVEN AS DEATH APPROACHES, CANISIUS WILL NOT SURRENDER THAT WHICH MAKES HIM SPECIAL--THAT WHICH MAKES HIM MAN.
THIS WAR BEGETS ONLY LOSERS.
O JUPITER, O JOVE...
...O LARES OF MY FATHERS...
GRANT ME ONE WISH BEFORE I PASS.
PROTECT LAVINIA...
...PROTECT MY LOVE.

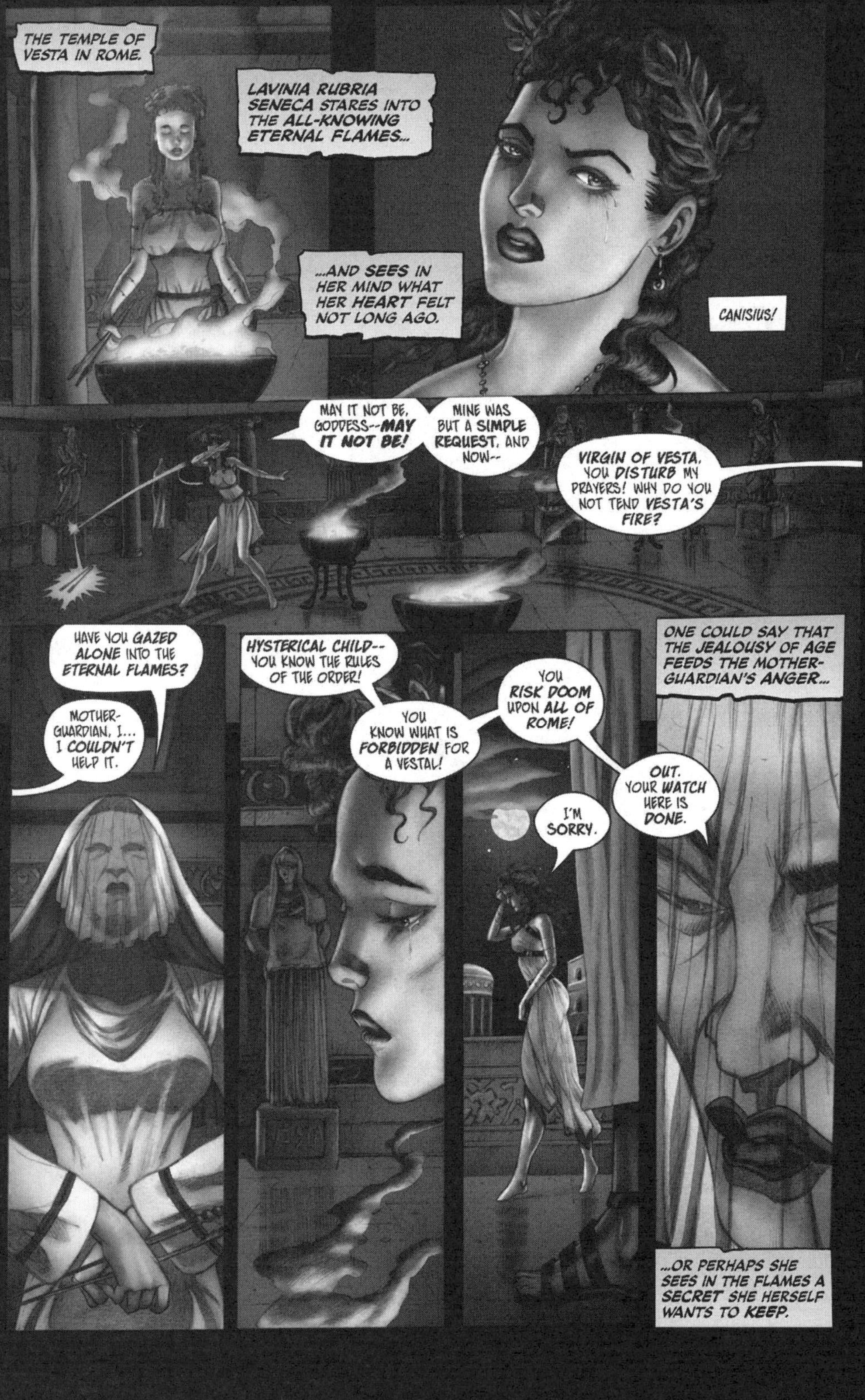
THE TEMPLE OF VESTA IN ROME.
LAVINIA RUBRIA SENECA STARES INTO THE ALL-KNOWING ETERNAL FLAMES...
...AND SEES IN HER MIND WHAT HER HEART FELT NOT LONG AGO.
CANISIUS!
MAY IT NOT BE, GODDESS--MAY IT NOT BE!
MINE WAS BUT A SIMPLE REQUEST, AND NOW--
VIRGIN OF VESTA, YOU DISTURB MY PRAYERS! WHY DO YOU NOT TEND VESTA'S FIRE?
HAVE YOU GAZED ALONE INTO THE ETERNAL FLAMES?
MOTHER-GUARDIAN, I... I COULDN'T HELP IT.
HYSTERICAL CHILD--YOU KNOW THE RULES OF THE ORDER!
YOU KNOW WHAT IS FORBIDDEN FOR A VESTAL!
YOU RISK DOOM UPON ALL OF ROME!
I'M SORRY.
OUT. YOUR WATCH HERE IS DONE.
ONE COULD SAY THAT THE JEALOUSY OF AGE FEEDS THE MOTHER-GUARDIAN'S ANGER...
...OR PERHAPS SHE SEES IN THE FLAMES A SECRET SHE HERSELF WANTS TO KEEP.

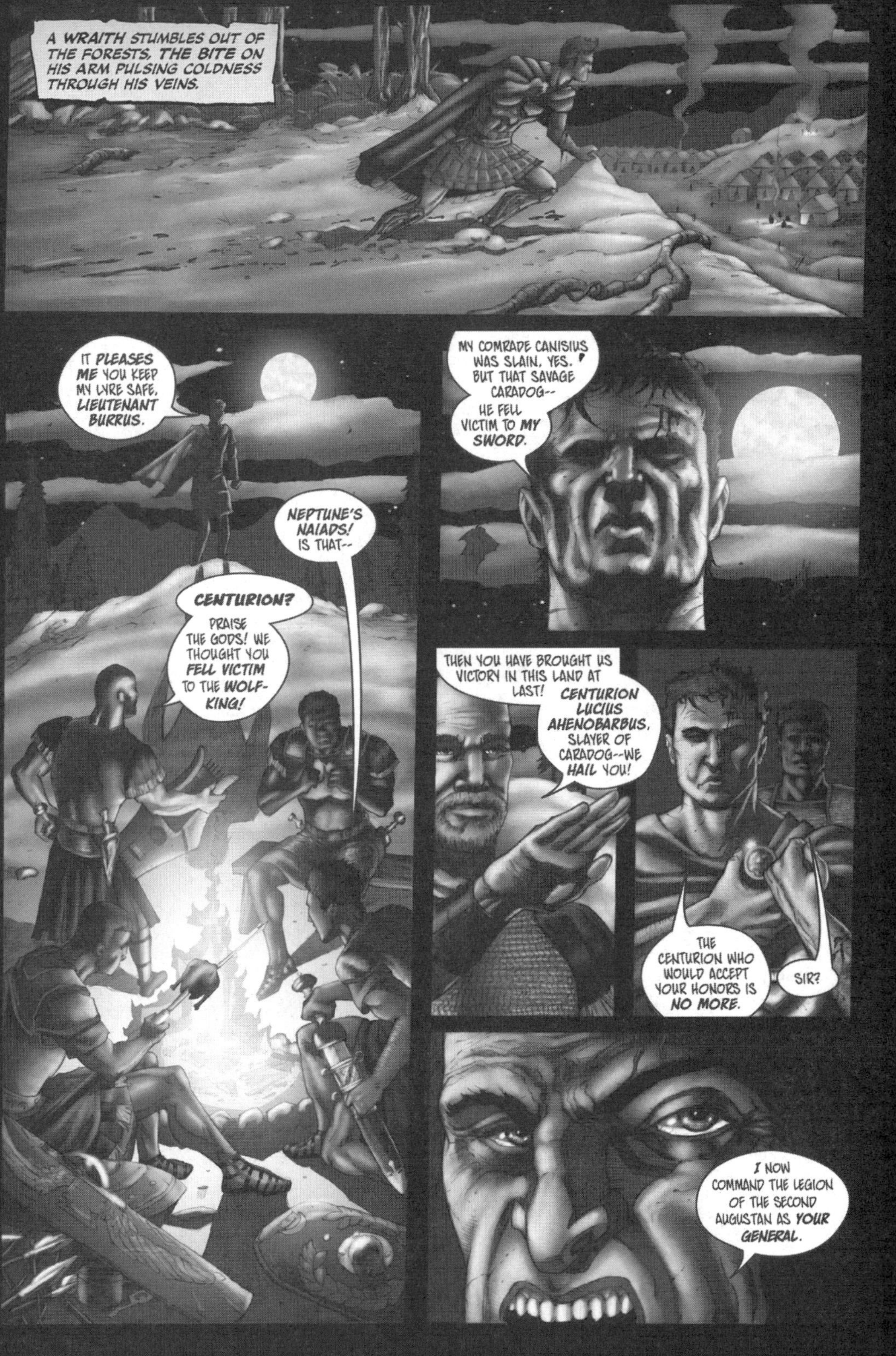

A WRAITH STUMBLES OUT OF THE FORESTS, THE BITE ON HIS ARM PULSING COLDNESS THROUGH HIS VEINS.
IT PLEASES ME YOU KEEP MY LYRE SAFE, LIEUTENANT BURRUS.
NEPTUNE'S NAIADS! IS THAT--
CENTURION?
PRAISE THE GODS! WE THOUGHT YOU FELL VICTIM TO THE WOLF-KING!
MY COMRADE CANISIUS WAS SLAIN, YES. BUT THAT SAVAGE CARADOG--
HE FELL VICTIM TO MY SWORD.
THEN YOU HAVE BROUGHT US VICTORY IN THIS LAND AT LAST!
CENTURION LUCIUS AHENOBARBUS, SLAYER OF CARADOG--WE HAIL YOU!
THE CENTURION WHO WOULD ACCEPT YOUR HONORS IS NO MORE.
SIR?
I NOW COMMAND THE LEGION OF THE SECOND AUGUSTAN AS YOUR GENERAL.

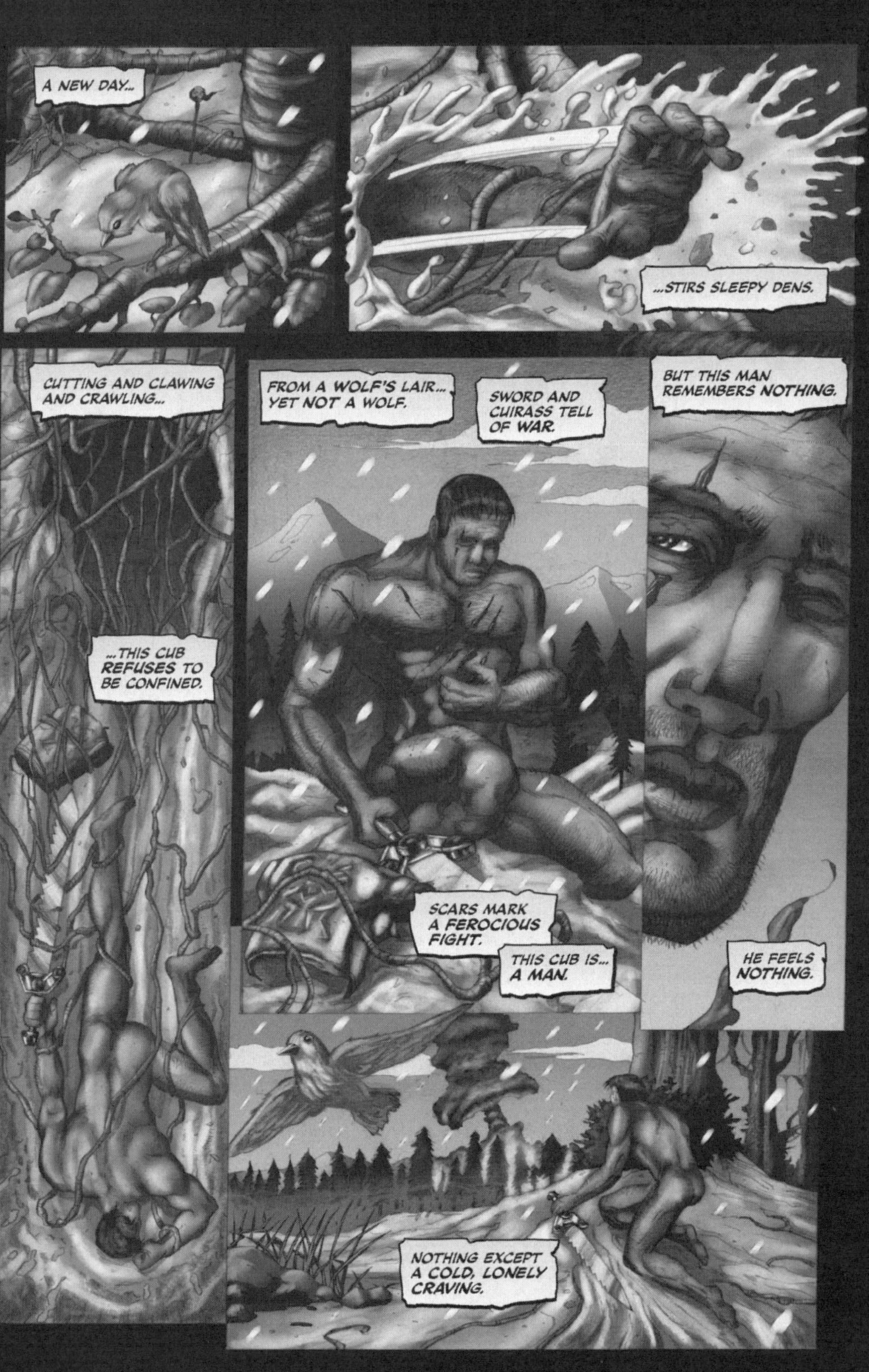
A NEW DAY...
...STIRS SLEEPY DENS.
CUTTING AND CLAWING AND CRAWLING...
...THIS CUB REFUSES TO BE CONFINED.
FROM A WOLF'S LAIR... YET NOT A WOLF.
SWORD AND CUIRASS TELL OF WAR.
SCARS MARK A FEROCIOUS FIGHT.
THIS CUB IS... A MAN.
BUT THIS MAN REMEMBERS NOTHING.
HE FEELS NOTHING.
NOTHING EXCEPT A COLD, LONELY CRAVING.

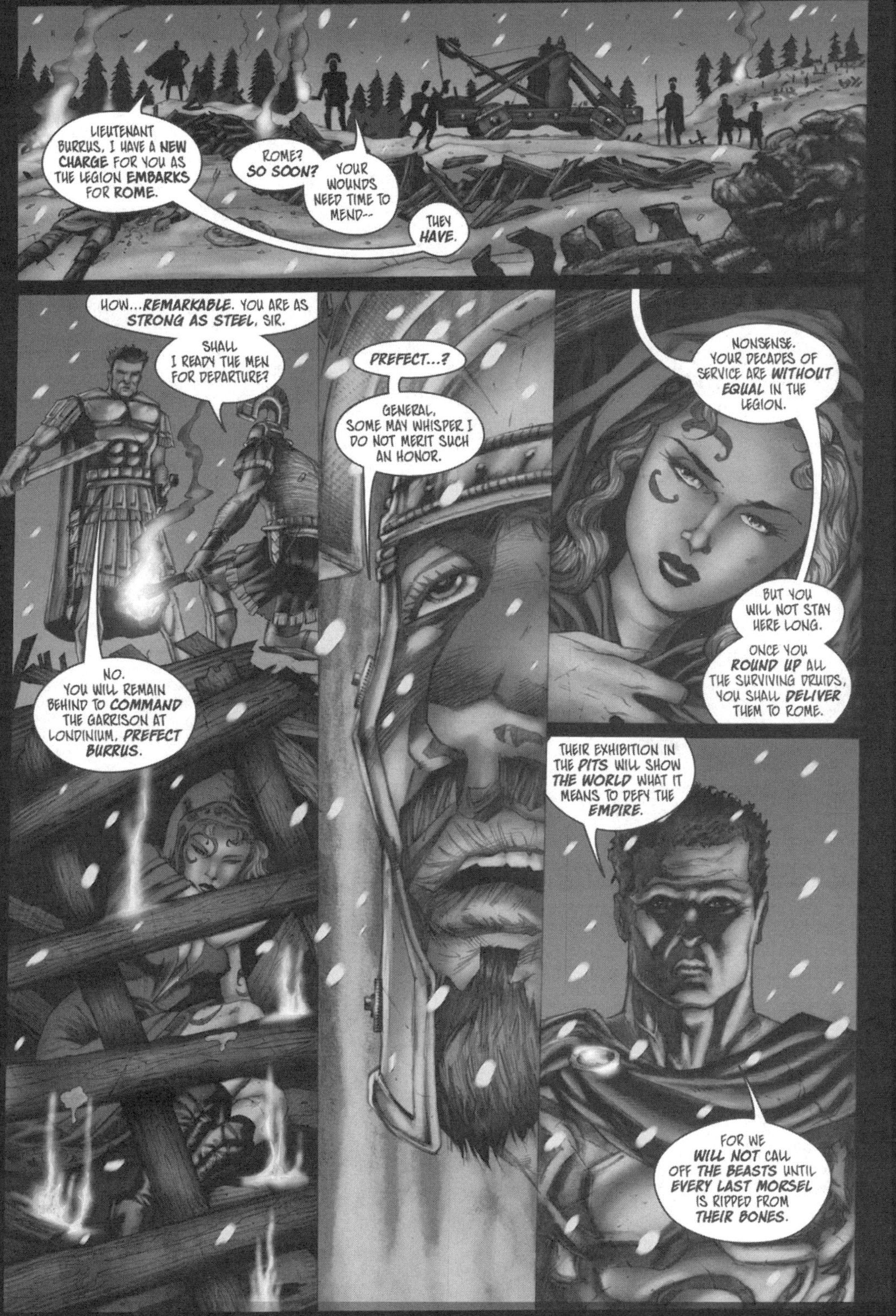
LIEUTENANT BURRUS, I HAVE A NEW CHARGE FOR YOU AS THE LEGION EMBARKS FOR ROME.
ROME? SO SOON?
YOUR WOUNDS NEED TIME TO MEND--
THEY HAVE.
HOW...REMARKABLE. YOU ARE AS STRONG AS STEEL, SIR.
SHALL I READY THE MEN FOR DEPARTURE?
NO. YOU WILL REMAIN BEHIND TO COMMAND THE GARRISON AT LONDINIUM, PREFECT BURRUS.
PREFECT...?
GENERAL, SOME MAY WHISPER I DO NOT MERIT SUCH AN HONOR.
NONSENSE. YOUR DECADES OF SERVICE ARE WITHOUT EQUAL IN THE LEGION.
BUT YOU WILL NOT STAY HERE LONG.
ONCE YOU ROUND UP ALL THE SURVIVING DRUIDS, YOU SHALL DELIVER THEM TO ROME.
THEIR EXHIBITION IN THE PITS WILL SHOW THE WORLD WHAT IT MEANS TO DEFY THE EMPIRE.
FOR WE WILL NOT CALL OFF THE BEASTS UNTIL EVERY LAST MORSEL IS RIPPED FROM THEIR BONES.

CONTINUED IN THE PAGES OF 'EMPIRE OF THE WOLF'

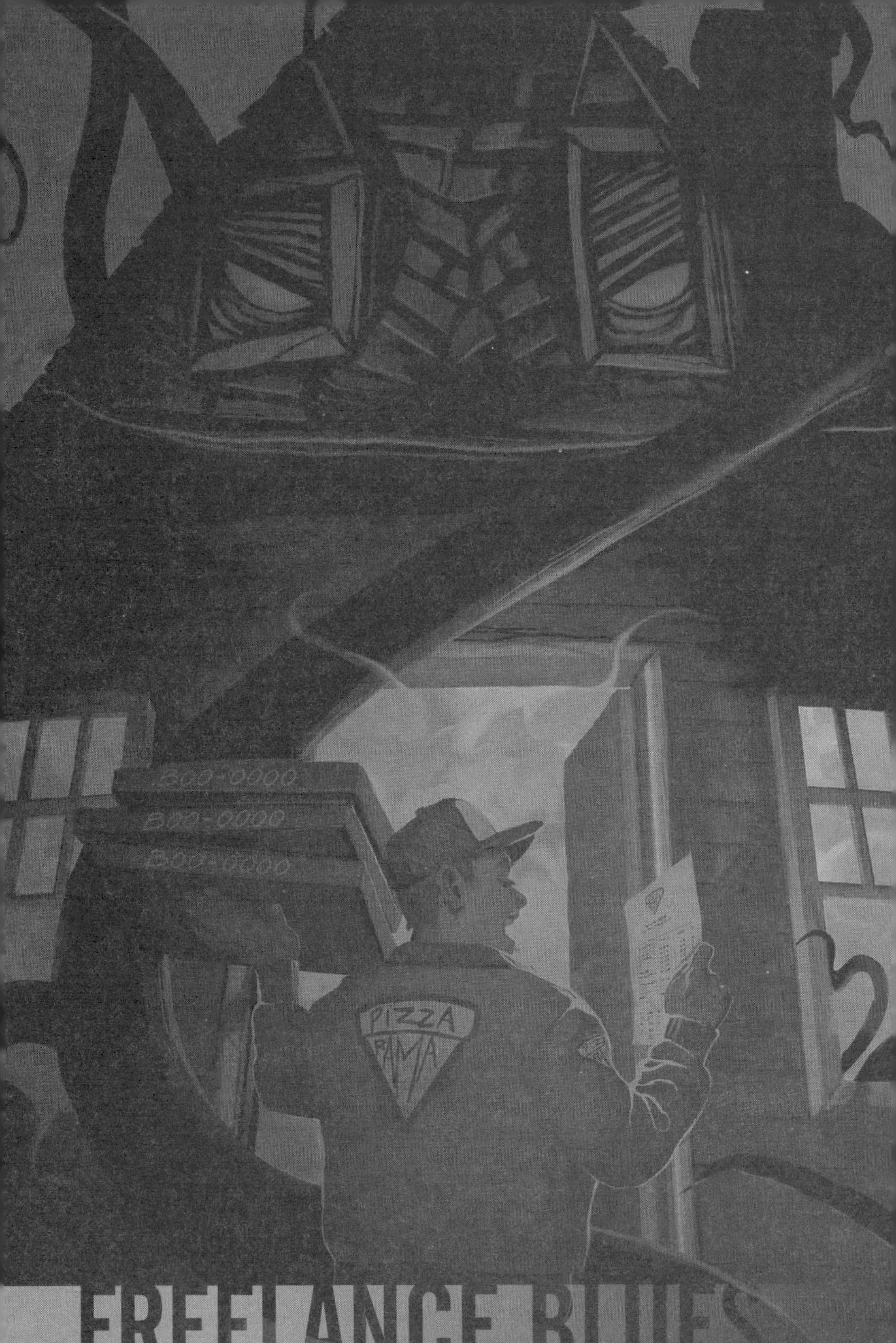
800-0000
800-0000
800-0000
PIZZA
PAMA

FREELANCE BLUES

FREELANCE BLUES

LANCE BUNKMAN

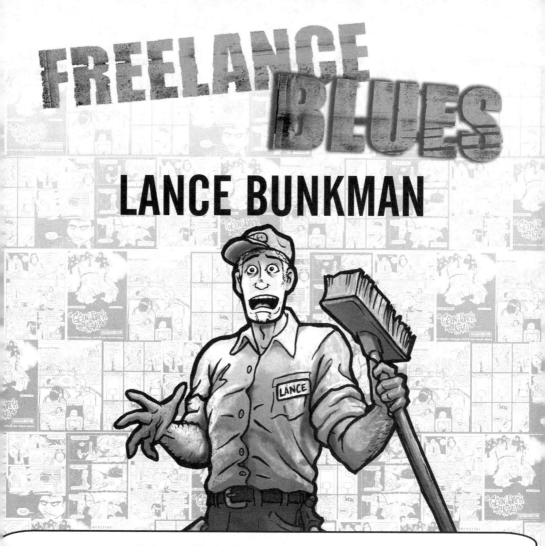

"When fighting giant monsters, my number one rule is: ALWAYS smash the statue."

Ever feel like your job is sucking the life out of you? You might be right.

It turns out that all of Lance's bosses are evil on a supernatural level; bent on world domination (or destruction, whichever comes first). It's up to Lance to save his co-workers, defeat his evil bosses, and then get up tomorrow to try to find a new job because being a hero doesn't pay the bills.

Age: 28   Height: 5'11"   Weight: 195 lbs.

First Appearance: FREELANCE BLUES #0 (2008)

Created by Ian Daffern & Mike Leone
Illustration by Stephen Sayer

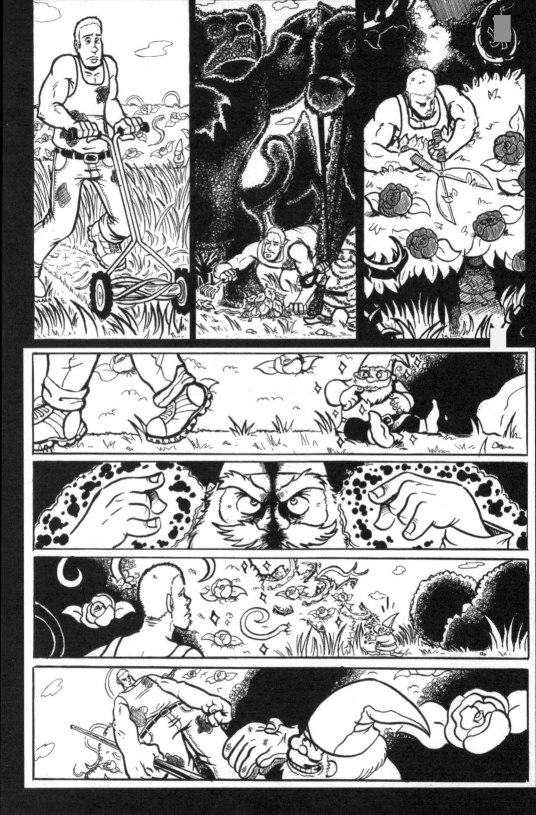

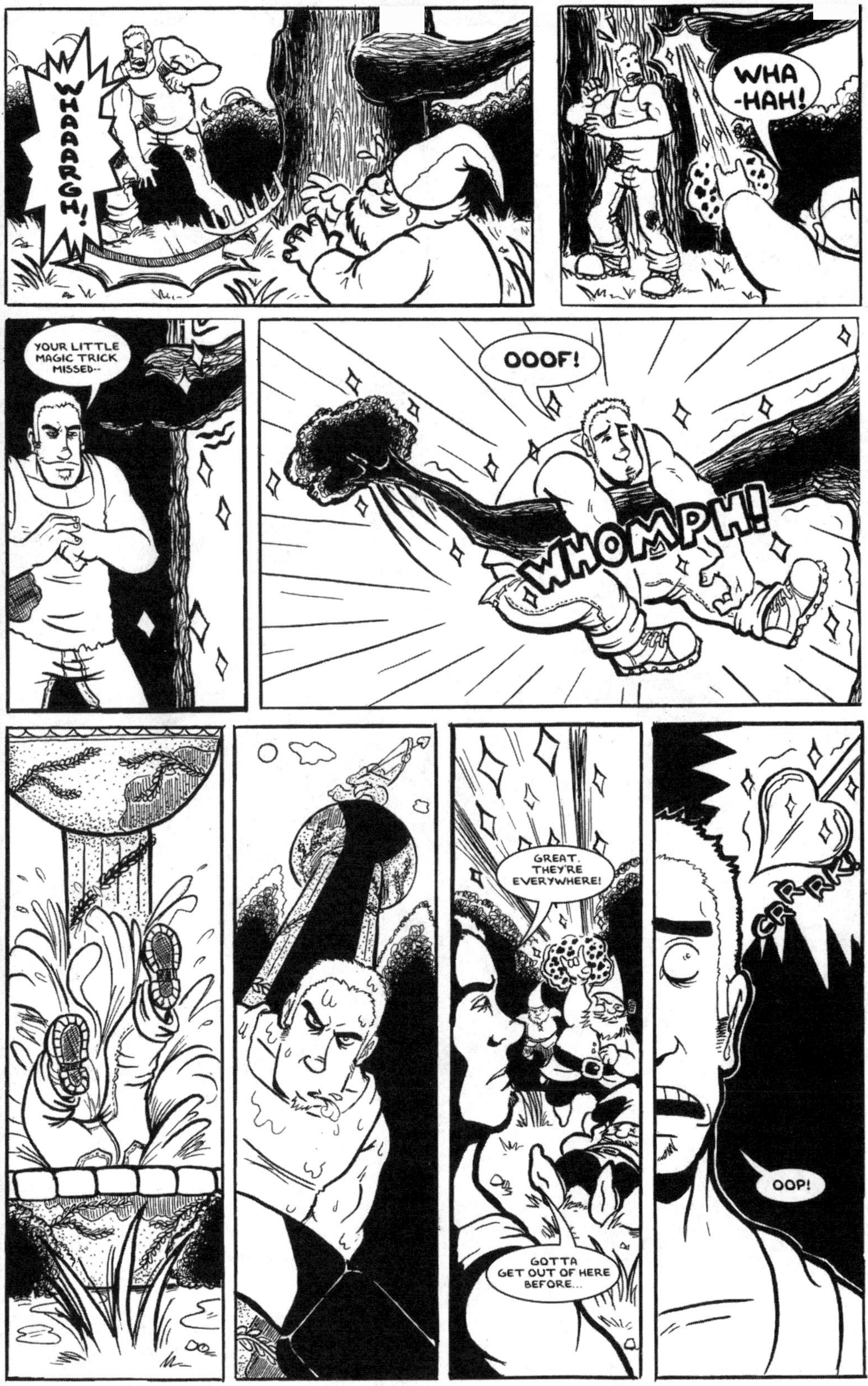
WHAAAARGH!
WHA -HAH!
YOUR LITTLE MAGIC TRICK MISSED--
OOOF!
WHOMPH!
GREAT. THEY'RE EVERYWHERE!
GOTTA GET OUT OF HERE BEFORE...
CRRRK!
OOP!

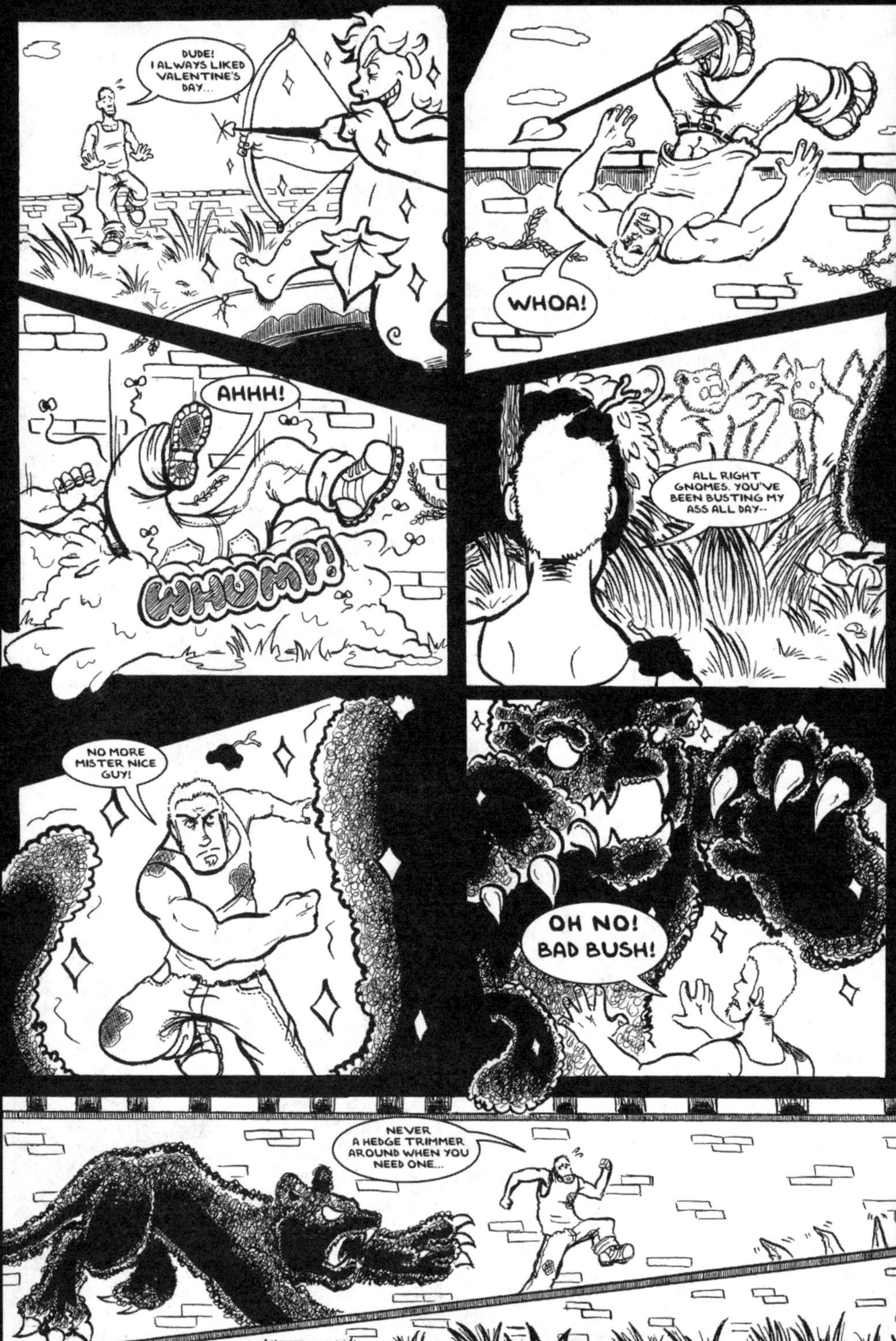
DUDE! I ALWAYS LIKED VALENTINE'S DAY...
WHOA!
AHHH!
WHUMP!
ALL RIGHT GNOMES. YOU'VE BEEN BUSTING MY ASS ALL DAY--
NO MORE MISTER NICE GUY!
OH NO! BAD BUSH!
NEVER A HEDGE TRIMMER AROUND WHEN YOU NEED ONE...

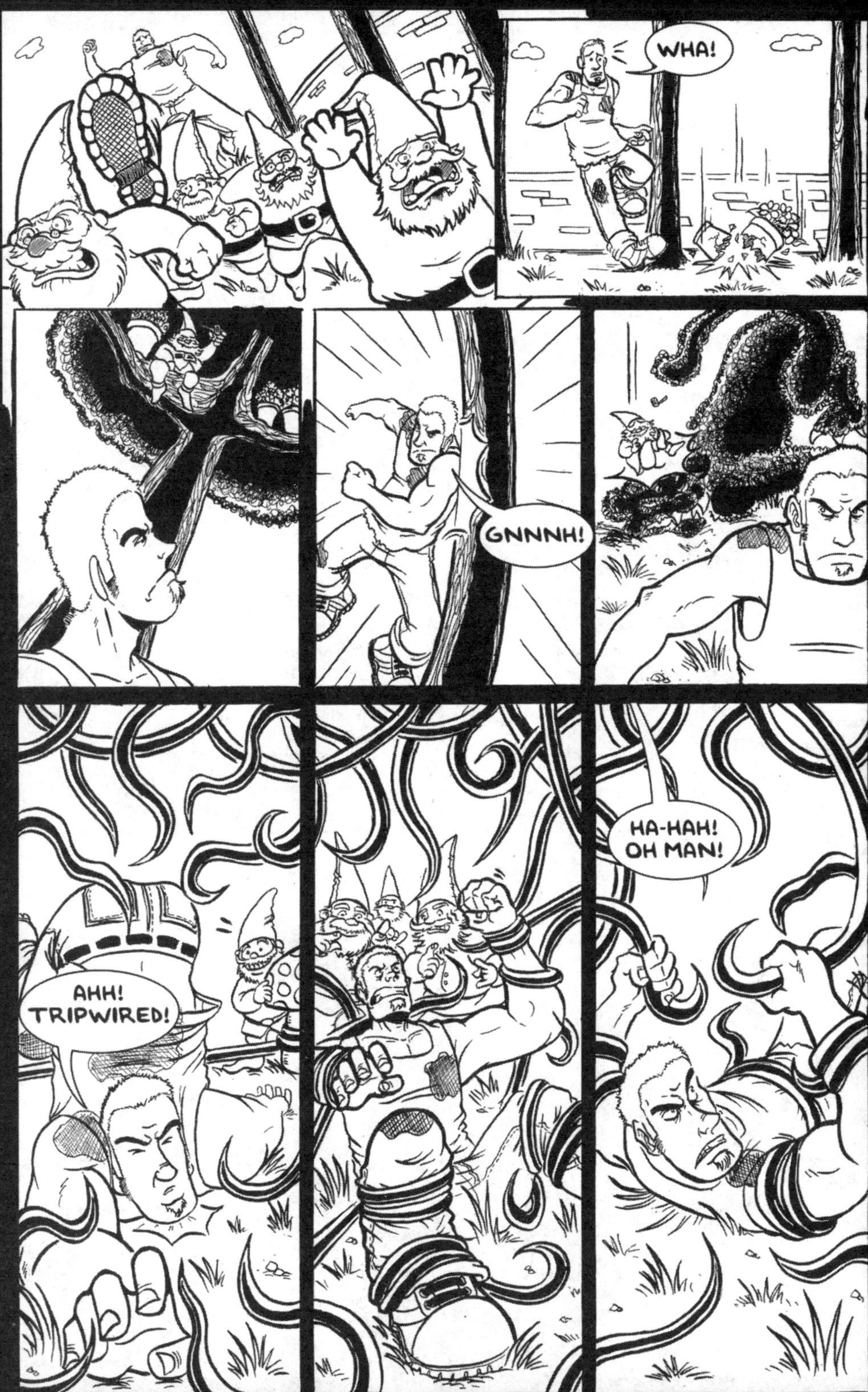
WHA!
GNNNH!
AHH! TRIPWIRED!
HA-HAH! OH MAN!

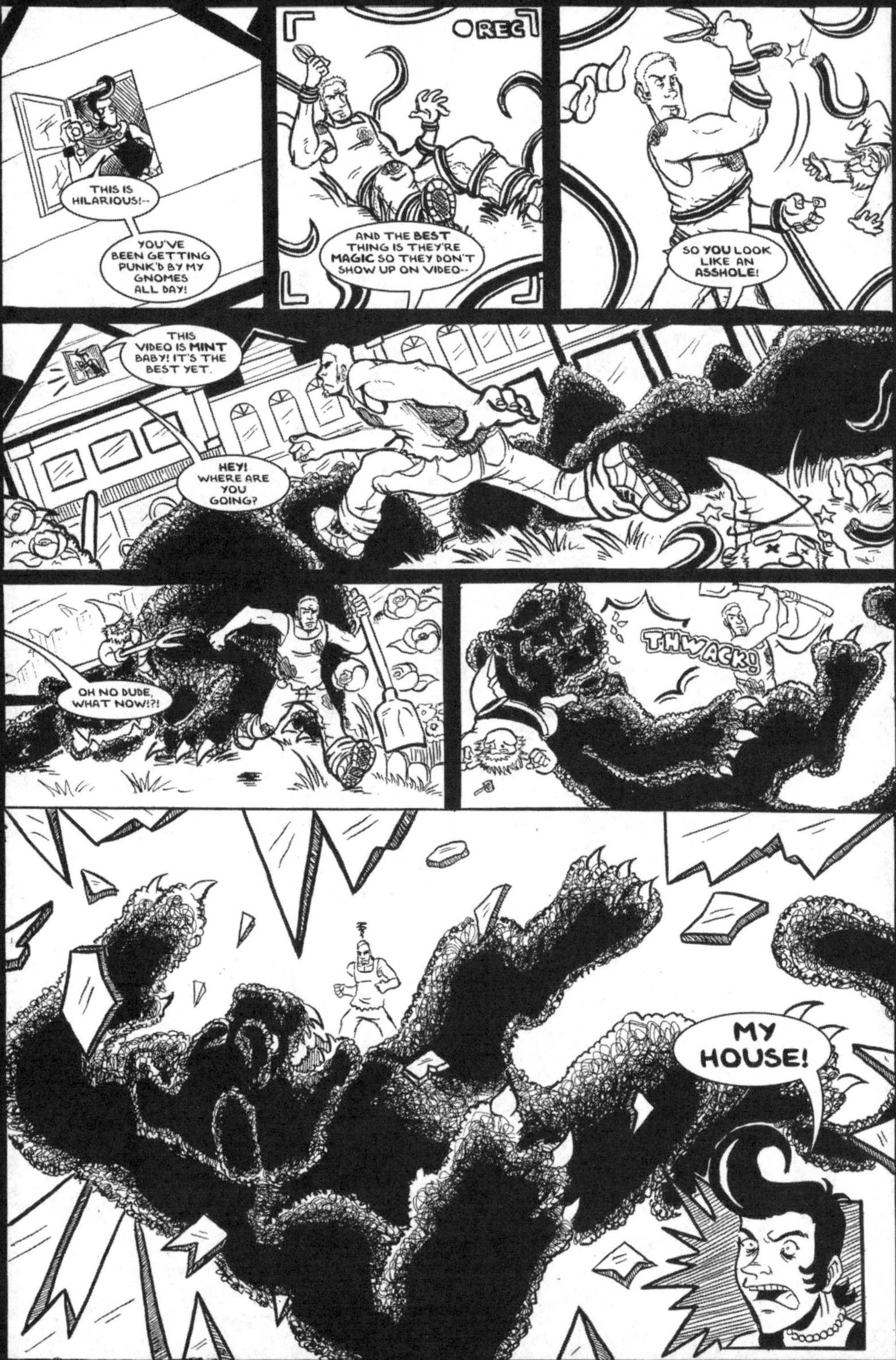
THIS IS HILARIOUS!--
YOU'VE BEEN GETTING PUNK'D BY MY GNOMES ALL DAY!
REC
AND THE BEST THING IS THEY'RE MAGIC SO THEY DON'T SHOW UP ON VIDEO--
SO YOU LOOK LIKE AN ASSHOLE!
THIS VIDEO IS MINT BABY! IT'S THE BEST YET.
HEY! WHERE ARE YOU GOING?
OH NO DUDE, WHAT NOW!?!
THWACK!
MY HOUSE!

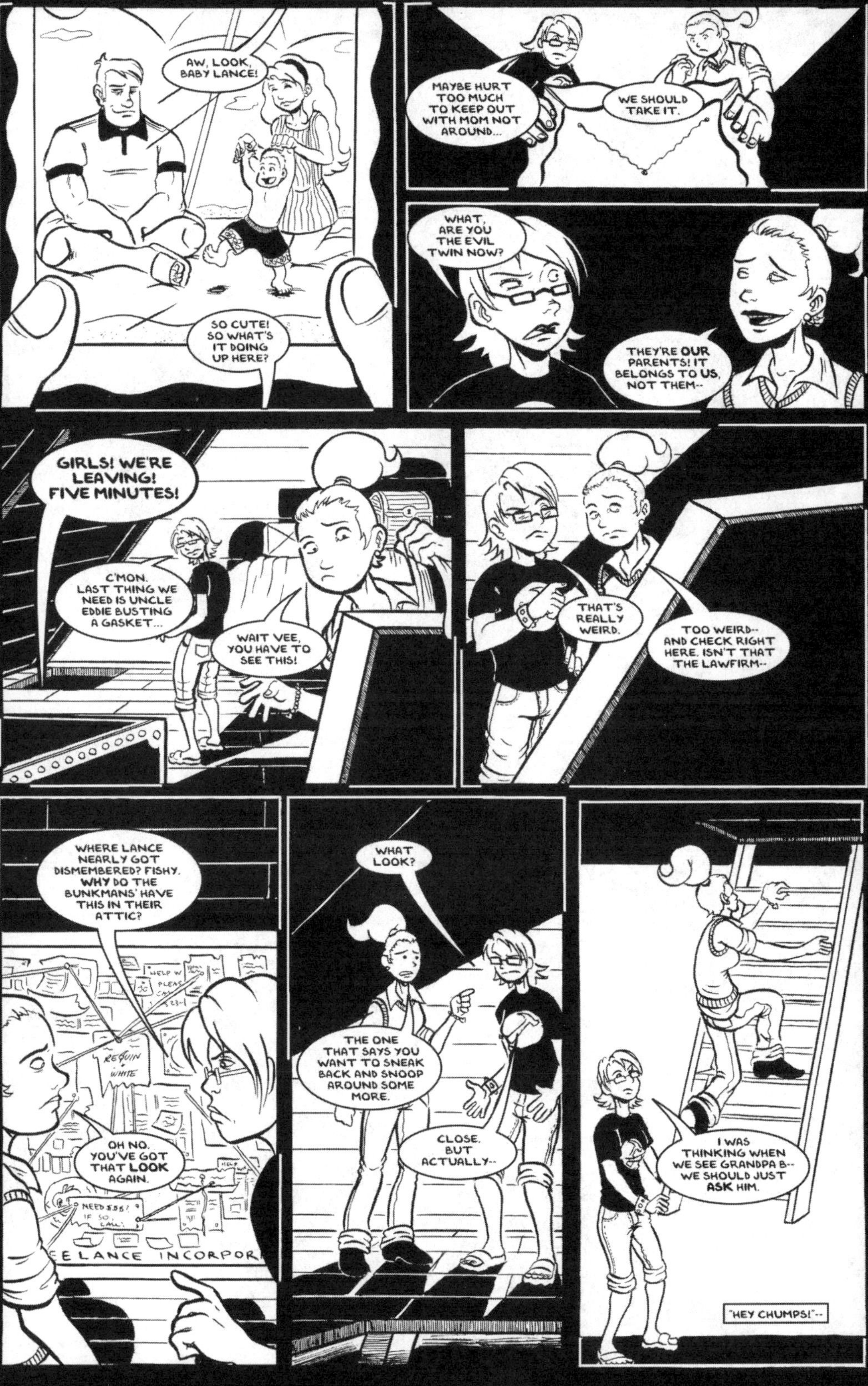
AW, LOOK, BABY LANCE!
SO CUTE! SO WHAT'S IT DOING UP HERE?
MAYBE HURT TOO MUCH TO KEEP OUT WITH MOM NOT AROUND...
WE SHOULD TAKE IT.
WHAT, ARE YOU THE EVIL TWIN NOW?
THEY'RE **OUR** PARENTS! IT BELONGS TO **US**, NOT THEM--
GIRLS! WE'RE LEAVING! FIVE MINUTES!
C'MON. LAST THING WE NEED IS UNCLE EDDIE BUSTING A GASKET...
WAIT VEE, YOU HAVE TO SEE THIS!
THAT'S REALLY WEIRD.
TOO WEIRD-- AND CHECK RIGHT HERE. ISN'T THAT THE LAWFIRM--
WHERE LANCE NEARLY GOT DISMEMBERED? FISHY. **WHY** DO THE BUNKMANS' HAVE THIS IN THEIR ATTIC?
ELANCE INCORPOR
OH NO. YOU'VE GOT THAT **LOOK** AGAIN.
WHAT LOOK?
THE ONE THAT SAYS YOU WANT TO SNEAK BACK AND SNOOP AROUND SOME MORE.
CLOSE. BUT ACTUALLY--
I WAS THINKING WHEN WE SEE GRANDPA B-- WE SHOULD JUST **ASK** HIM.
"HEY CHUMPS!"--

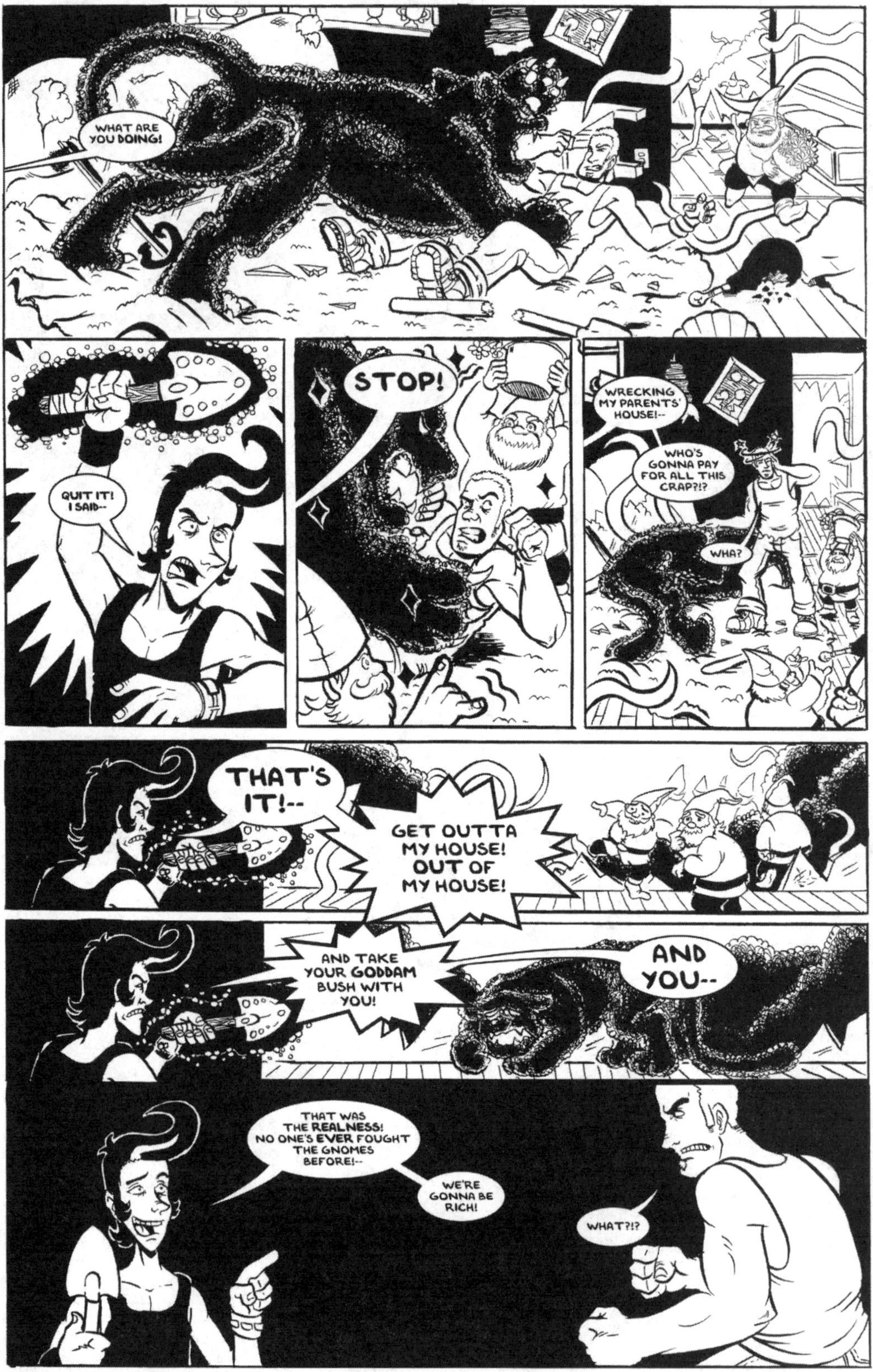
WHAT ARE YOU DOING!
QUIT IT! I SAID--
STOP!
WRECKING MY PARENTS' HOUSE!--
WHO'S GONNA PAY FOR ALL THIS CRAP?!?
WHA?
THAT'S IT!--
GET OUTTA MY HOUSE! OUT OF MY HOUSE!
AND TAKE YOUR GODDAM BUSH WITH YOU!
AND YOU--
THAT WAS THE REALNESS! NO ONE'S EVER FOUGHT THE GNOMES BEFORE!--
WE'RE GONNA BE RICH!
WHAT?!?

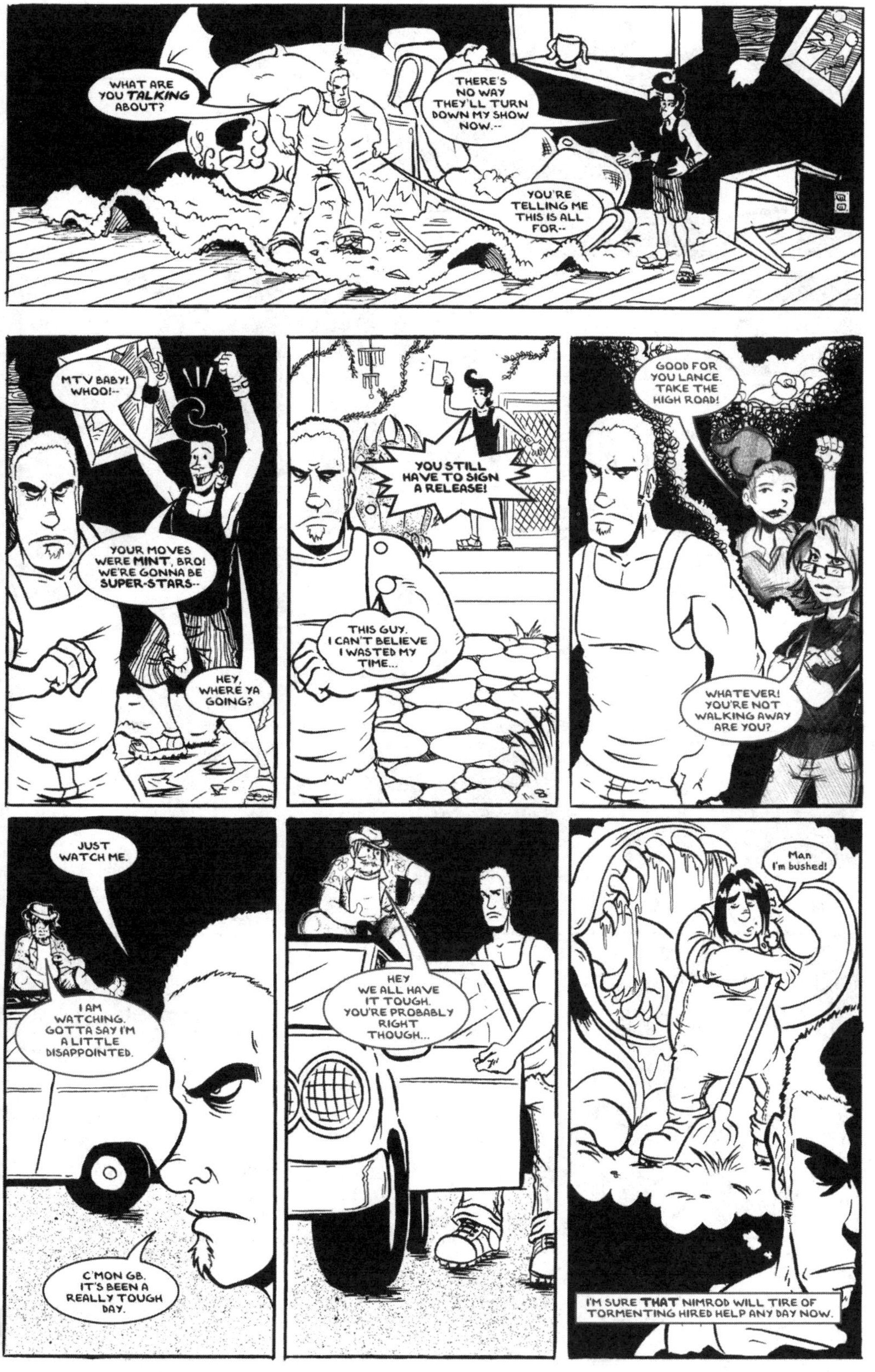

WHAT ARE YOU TALKING ABOUT?
THERE'S NO WAY THEY'LL TURN DOWN MY SHOW NOW.--
YOU'RE TELLING ME THIS IS ALL FOR--
MTV BABY! WHOO!--
YOUR MOVES WERE MINT, BRO! WE'RE GONNA BE SUPER-STARS--
HEY, WHERE YA GOING?
YOU STILL HAVE TO SIGN A RELEASE!
THIS GUY. I CAN'T BELIEVE I WASTED MY TIME...
GOOD FOR YOU LANCE. TAKE THE HIGH ROAD!
WHATEVER! YOU'RE NOT WALKING AWAY ARE YOU?
JUST WATCH ME.
I AM WATCHING. GOTTA SAY I'M A LITTLE DISAPPOINTED.
C'MON GB. IT'S BEEN A REALLY TOUGH DAY.
HEY WE ALL HAVE IT TOUGH. YOU'RE PROBABLY RIGHT THOUGH...
Man I'm bushed!
I'M SURE THAT NIMROD WILL TIRE OF TORMENTING HIRED HELP ANY DAY NOW.

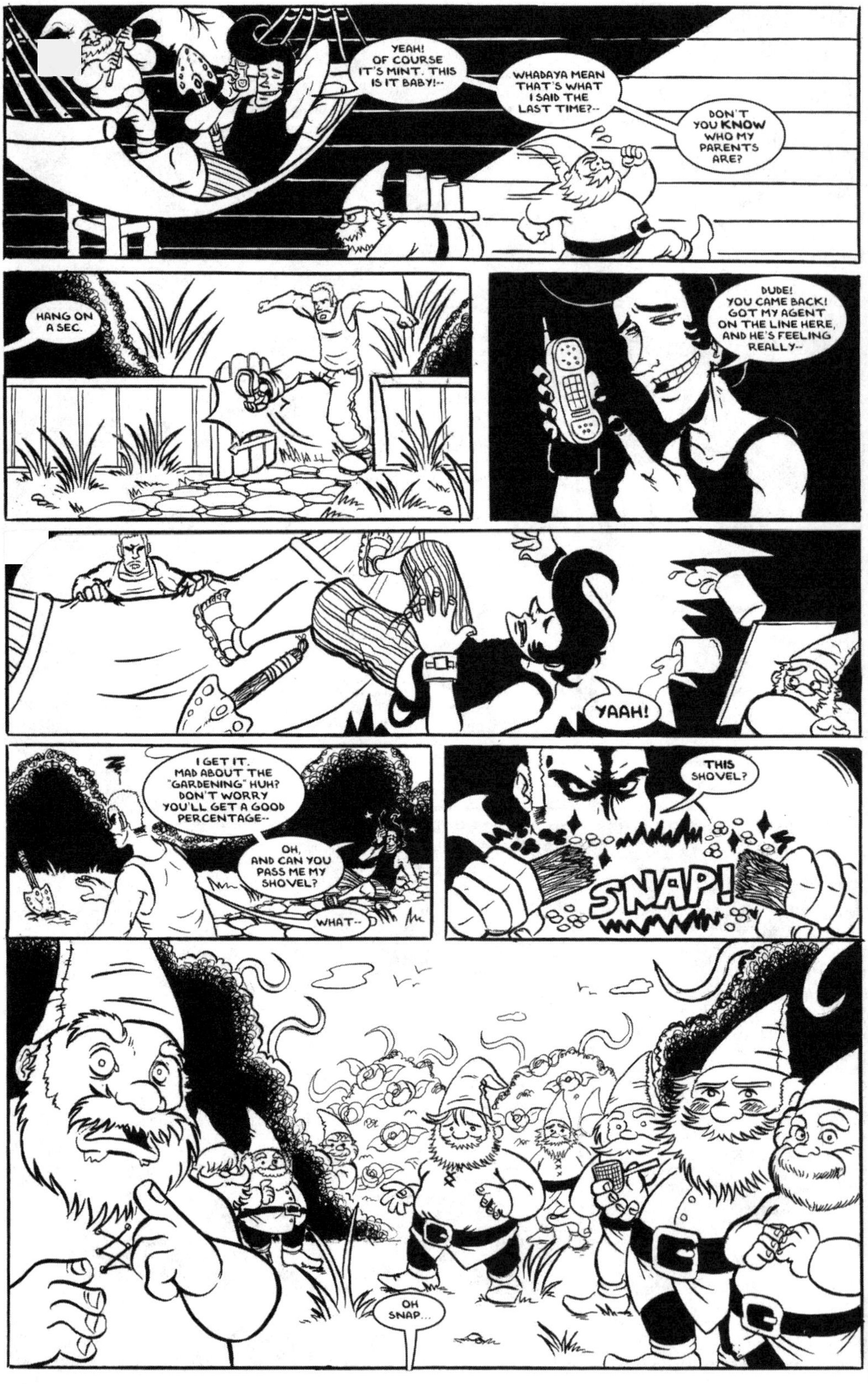
YEAH! OF COURSE IT'S MINT. THIS IS IT BABY!--
WHADAYA MEAN THAT'S WHAT I SAID THE LAST TIME?--
DON'T YOU KNOW WHO MY PARENTS ARE?
HANG ON A SEC.
DUDE! YOU CAME BACK! GOT MY AGENT ON THE LINE HERE, AND HE'S FEELING REALLY--
YAAH!
I GET IT. MAD ABOUT THE "GARDENING" HUH? DON'T WORRY YOU'LL GET A GOOD PERCENTAGE--
OH, AND CAN YOU PASS ME MY SHOVEL?
WHAT--
THIS SHOVEL?
SNAP!
OH SNAP...

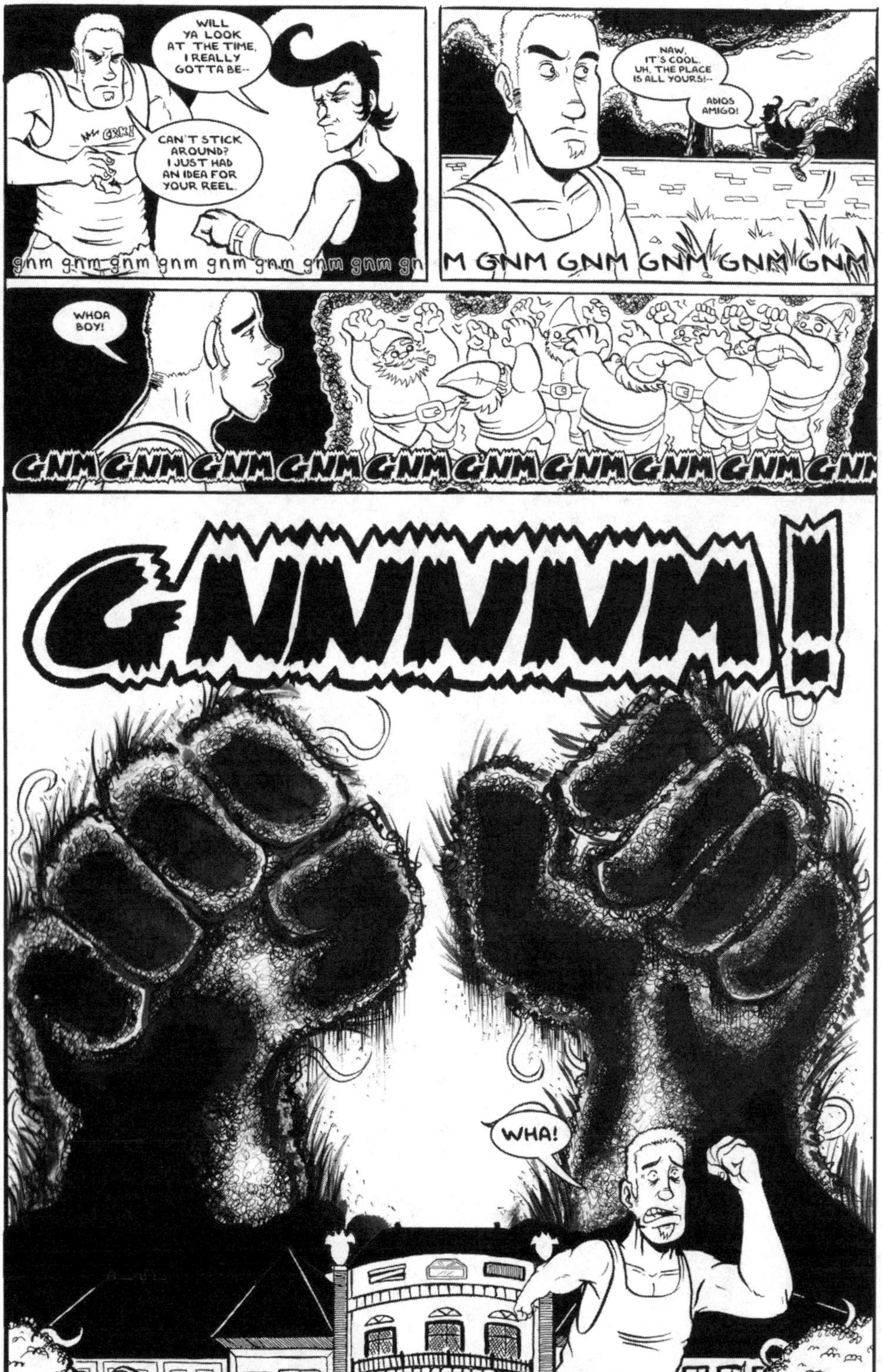
WILL YA LOOK AT THE TIME, I REALLY GOTTA BE--
GRK!
CAN'T STICK AROUND? I JUST HAD AN IDEA FOR YOUR REEL.
gnm gnm gnm gnm gnm gnm gnm gnm gn
NAW, IT'S COOL. UH, THE PLACE IS ALL YOURS!--
ADIOS AMIGO!
M GNM GNM GNM GNM GNM
WHOA BOY!
GNM GNM GNM GNM GNM GNM GNM GNM GNM
GNNNNM!
WHA!

CONTINUED IN THE PAGES OF 'FREELANCE BLUES'

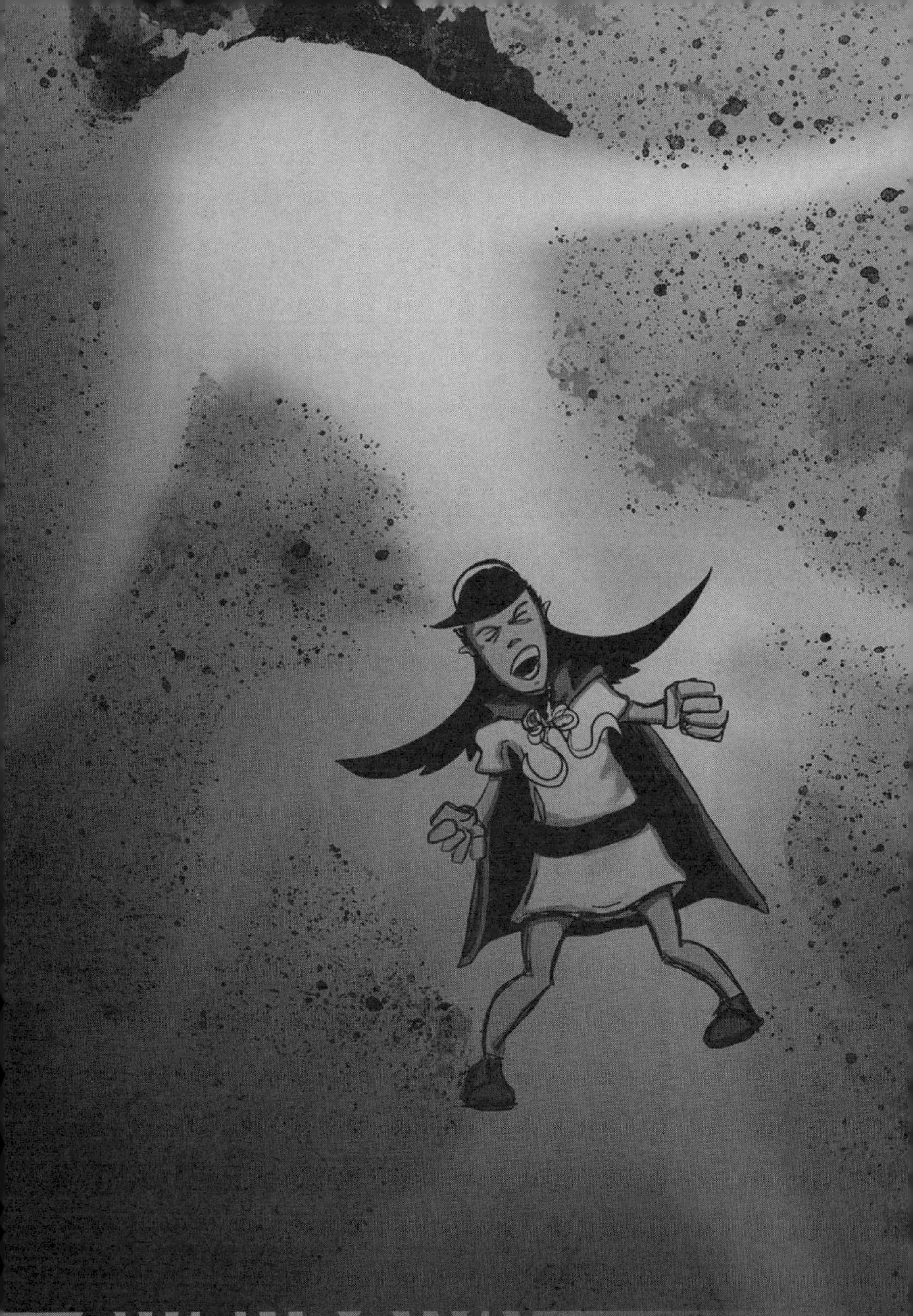

GWENDOLYN

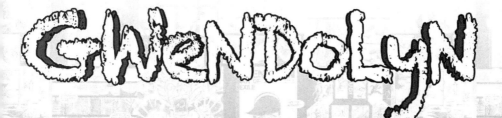

GWENDOLYN

GWENDOLYN

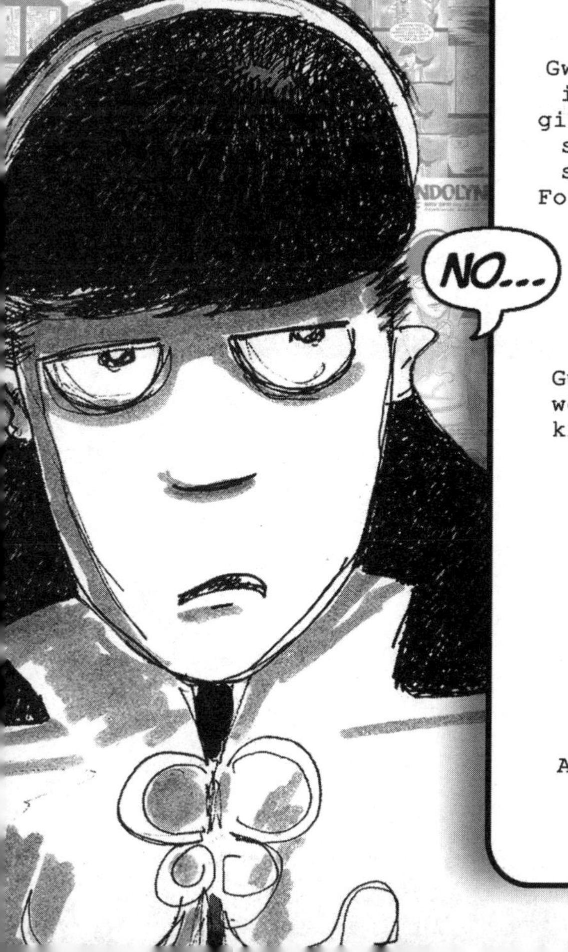

NO...

"I was not amused by your jokes 100 years ago, I am not amused now."

Gwendolyn is an ages old demon in the body of a 12-year-old girl. A being of immense power, she possesses the ability to shift into a monstrous Demon Form that grants her heightened speed, strength and invulnerability.

Having been in a self-imposed exile for the better part of a century, Gwendolyn rejoins the outside world and other demons of her kind in an attempt to protect her new more "peaceful" way of life.

Age: 265
Height: 4'5"
Weight: 85 lbs.

First Appearance:
GWENDOLYN #1 (2013)

Created by
Andrew Sanford & Joe Cabatit
Illustration by
Joe Cabatit

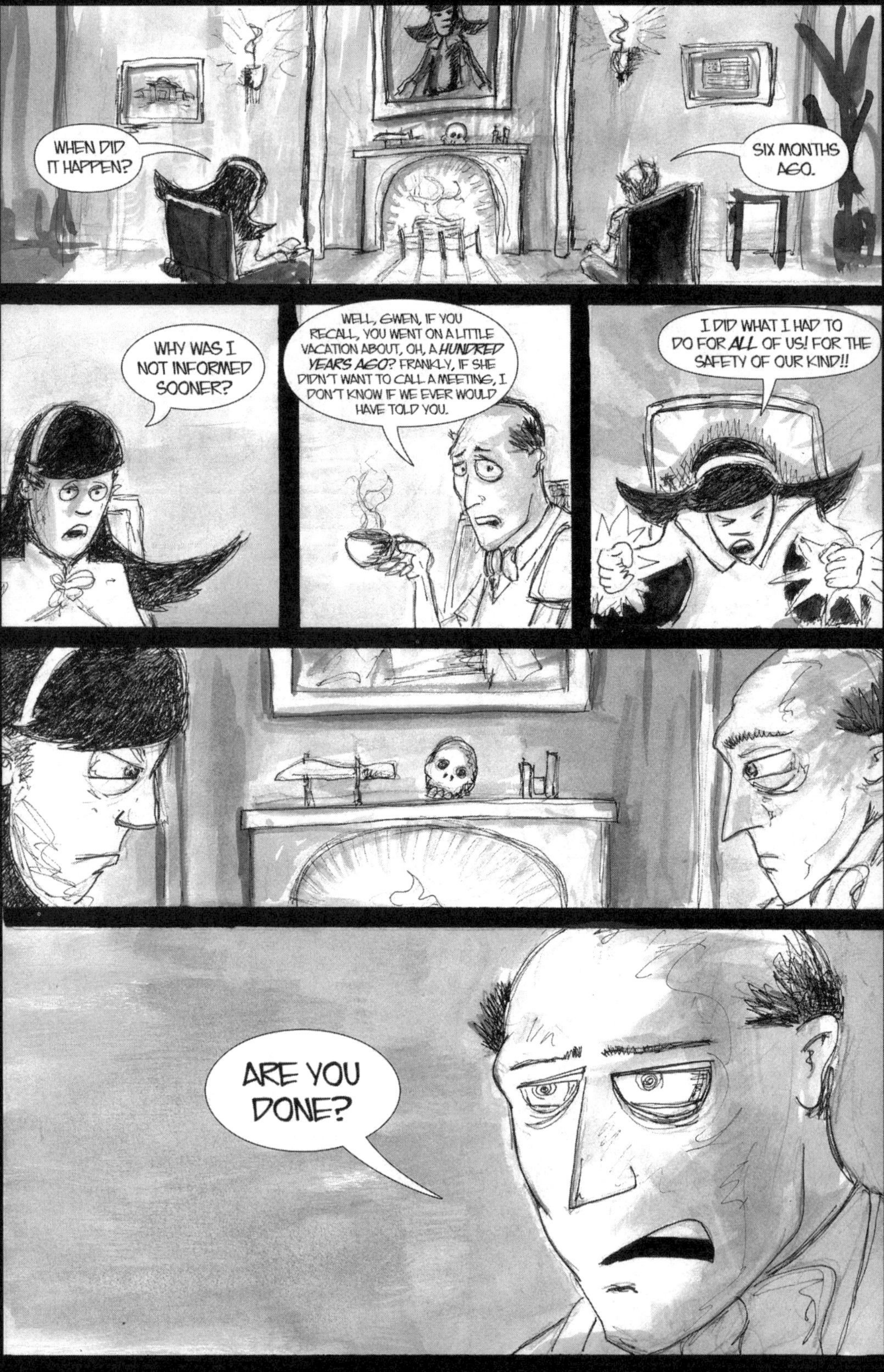
WHEN DID IT HAPPEN?
SIX MONTHS AGO.
WHY WAS I NOT INFORMED SOONER?
WELL, GWEN, IF YOU RECALL, YOU WENT ON A LITTLE VACATION ABOUT, OH, A HUNDRED YEARS AGO? FRANKLY, IF SHE DIDN'T WANT TO CALL A MEETING, I DON'T KNOW IF WE EVER WOULD HAVE TOLD YOU.
I DID WHAT I HAD TO DO FOR ALL OF US! FOR THE SAFETY OF OUR KIND!!
ARE YOU DONE?

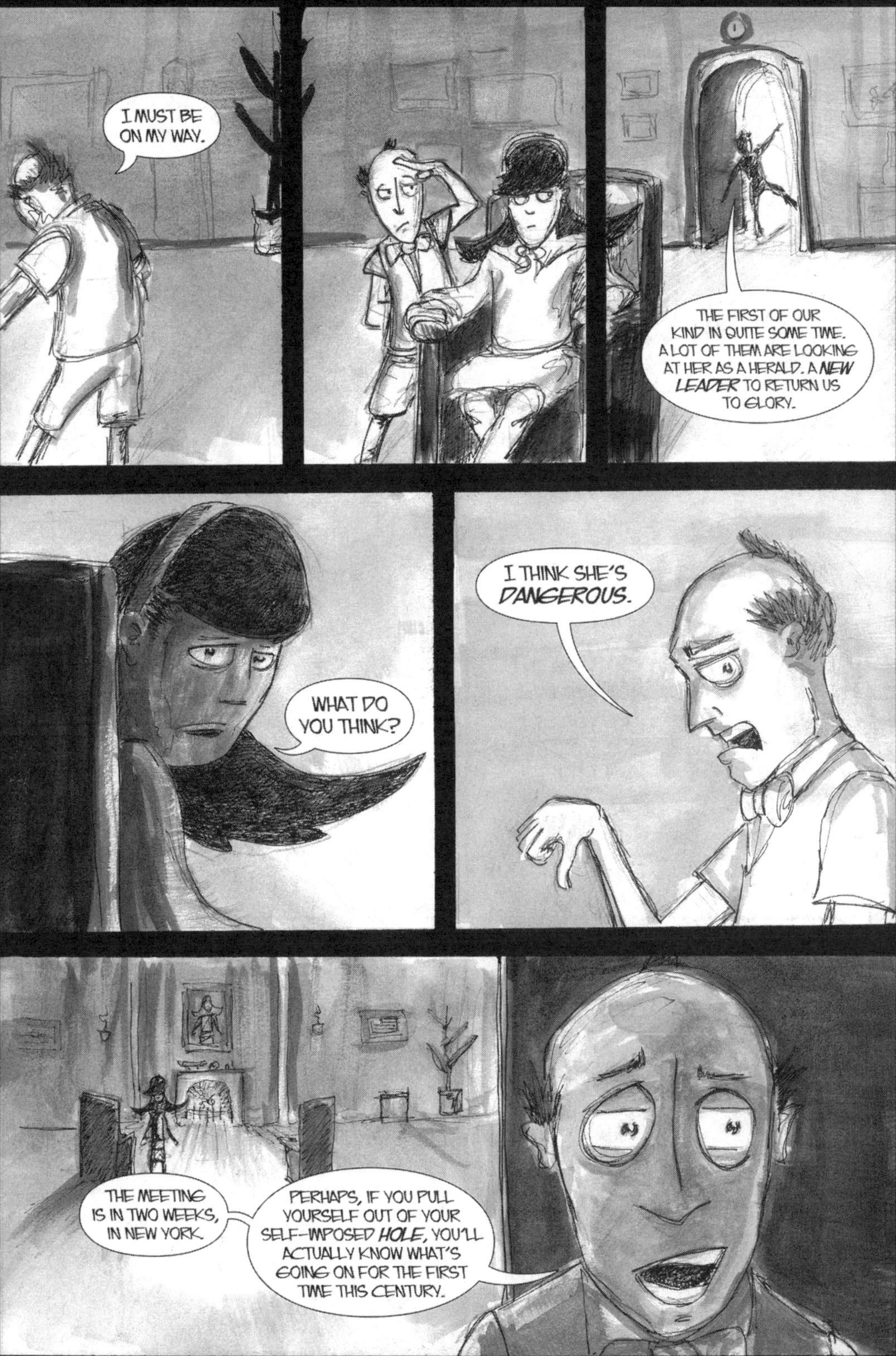
I MUST BE ON MY WAY.
THE FIRST OF OUR KIND IN QUITE SOME TIME. A LOT OF THEM ARE LOOKING AT HER AS A HERALD. A *NEW LEADER* TO RETURN US TO GLORY.
WHAT DO YOU THINK?
I THINK SHE'S *DANGEROUS*.
THE MEETING IS IN TWO WEEKS, IN NEW YORK.
PERHAPS, IF YOU PULL YOURSELF OUT OF YOUR SELF-IMPOSED *HOLE*, YOU'LL ACTUALLY KNOW WHAT'S GOING ON FOR THE FIRST TIME THIS CENTURY.

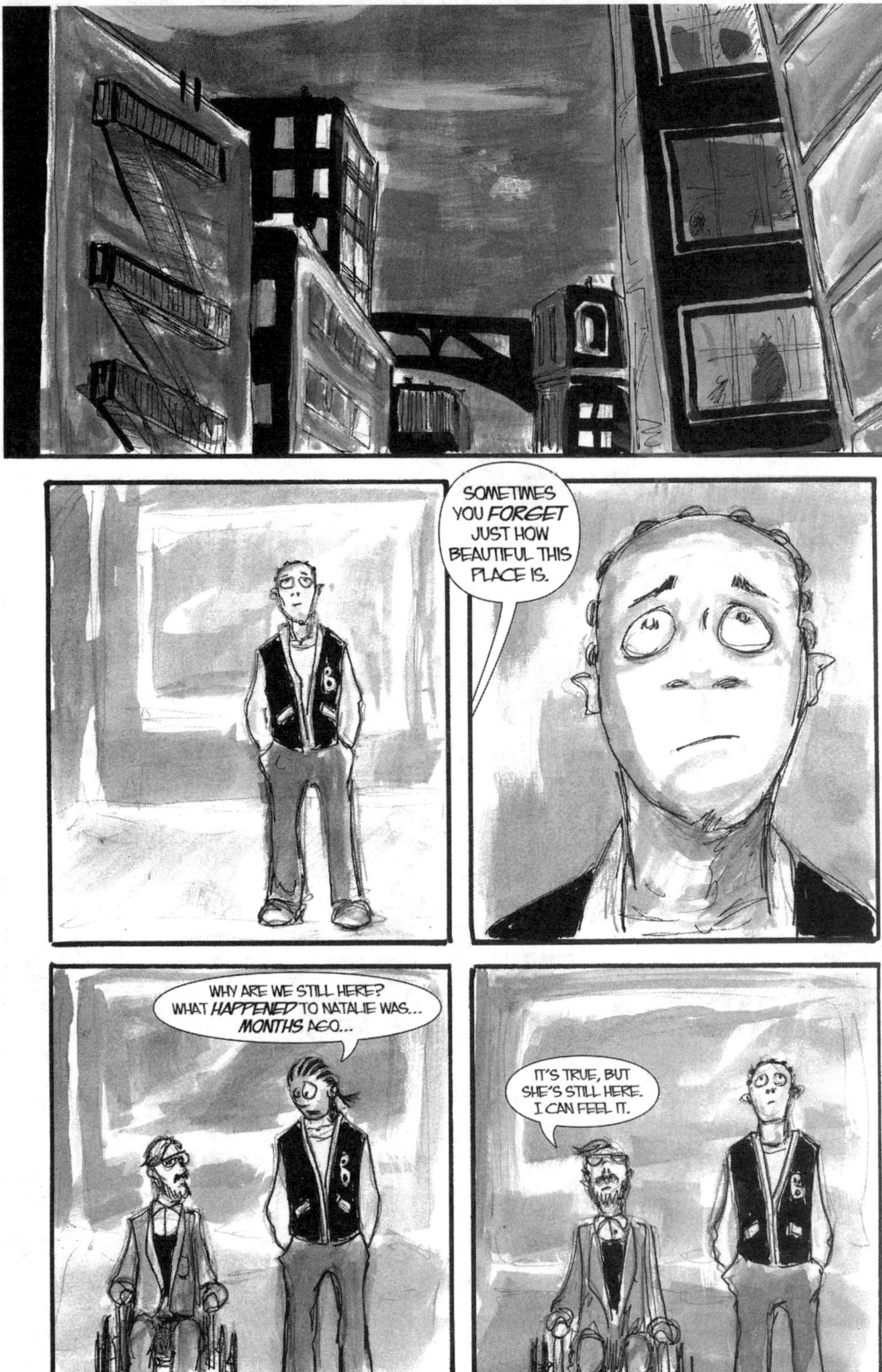
SOMETIMES YOU *FORGET* JUST HOW BEAUTIFUL THIS PLACE IS.
WHY ARE WE STILL HERE? WHAT *HAPPENED* TO NATALIE WAS... *MONTHS* AGO...
IT'S TRUE, BUT SHE'S STILL HERE. I CAN FEEL IT.

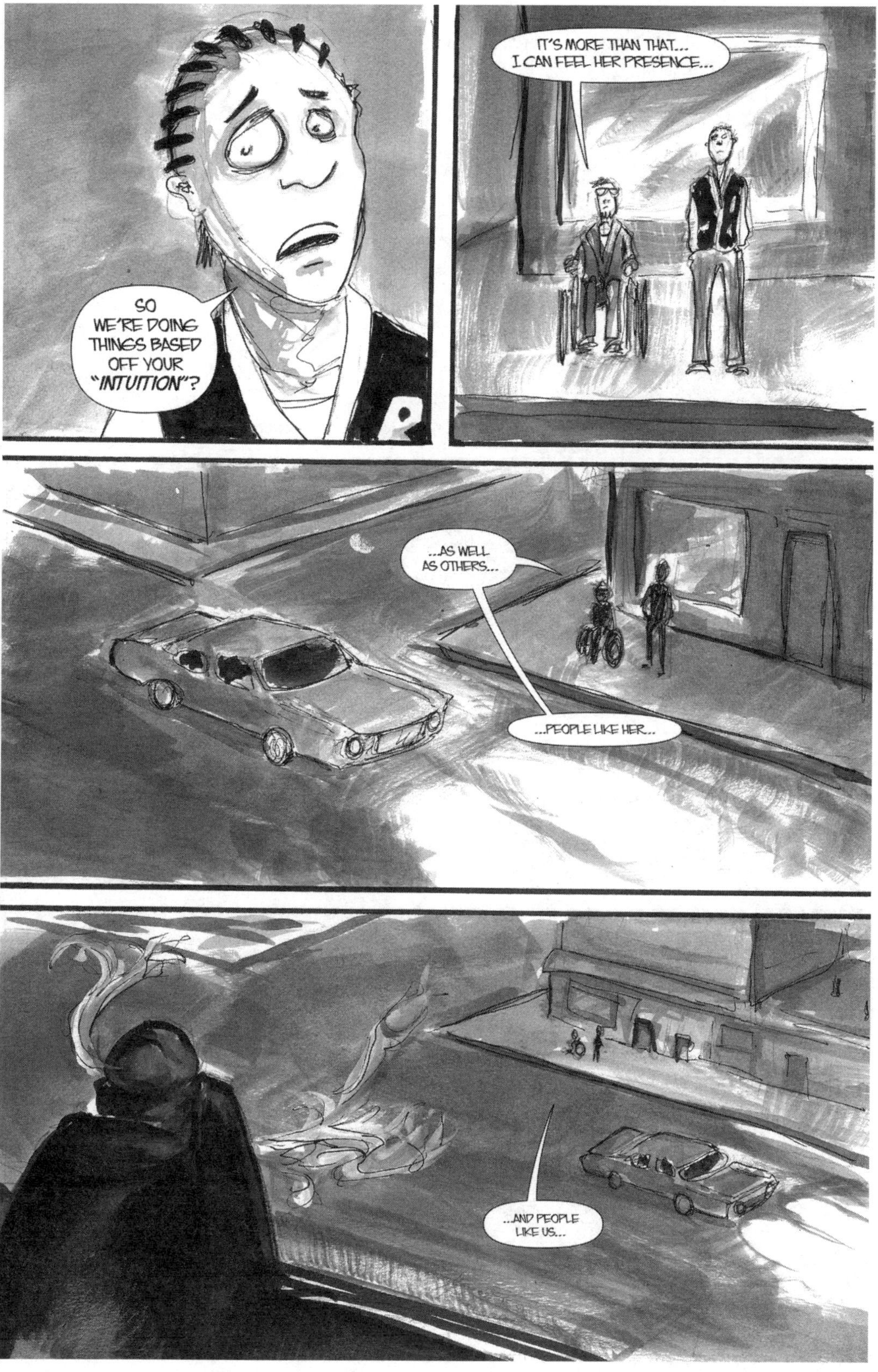
SO WE'RE DOING THINGS BASED OFF YOUR "INTUITION"?
IT'S MORE THAN THAT... I CAN FEEL HER PRESENCE...
...AS WELL AS OTHERS...
...PEOPLE LIKE HER...
...AND PEOPLE LIKE US...

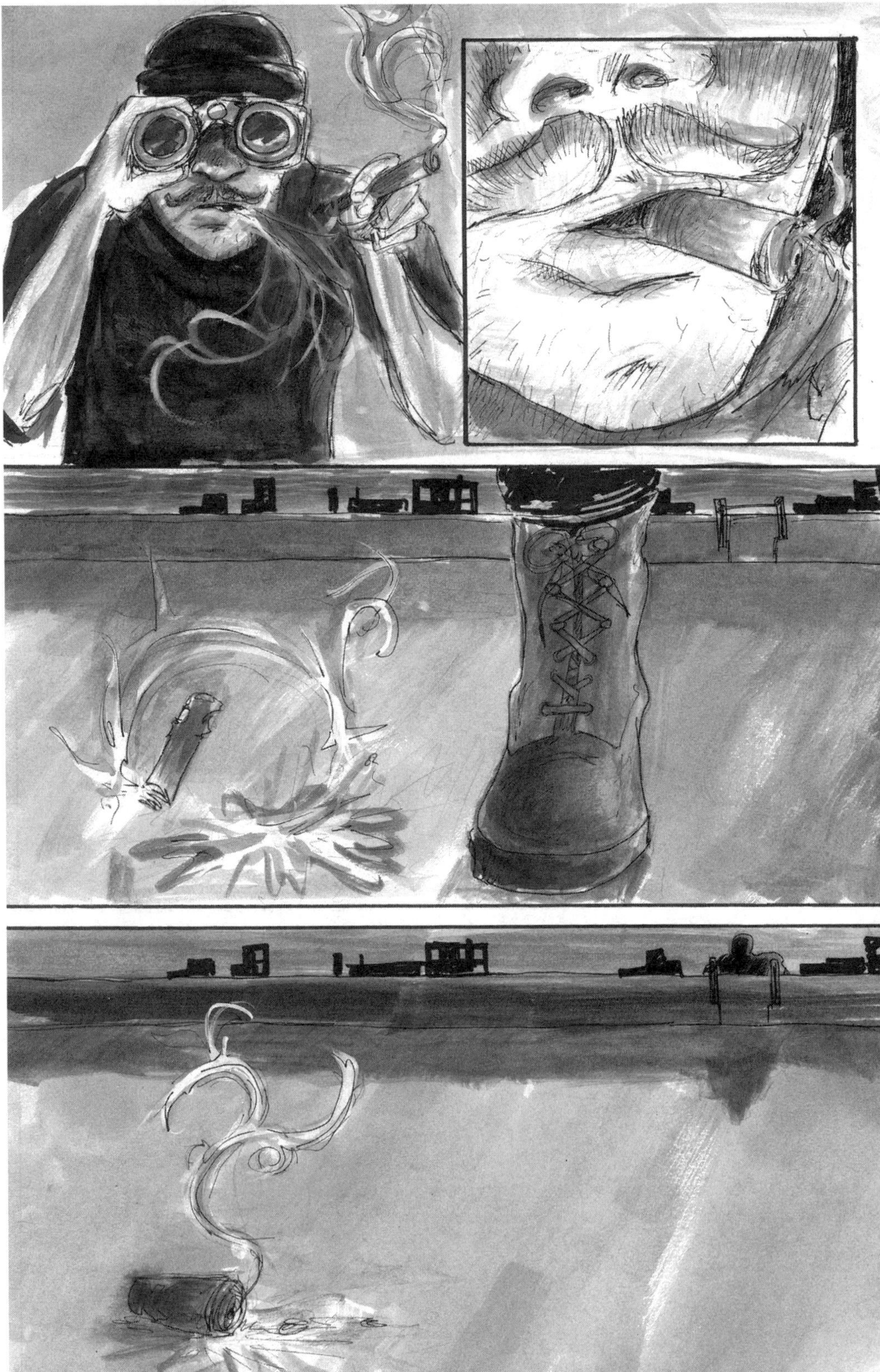

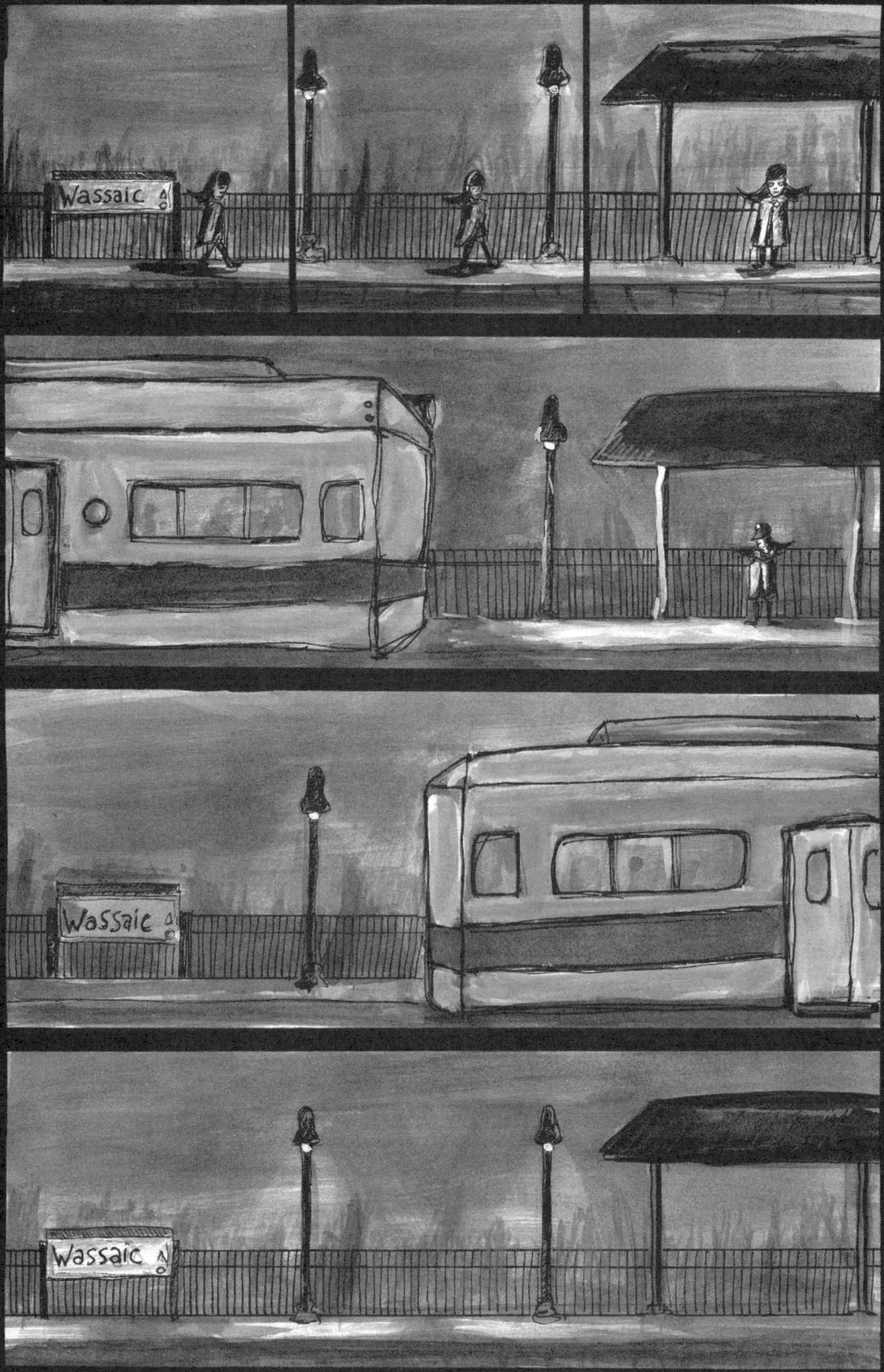
Wassaic
Wassaic
Wassaic

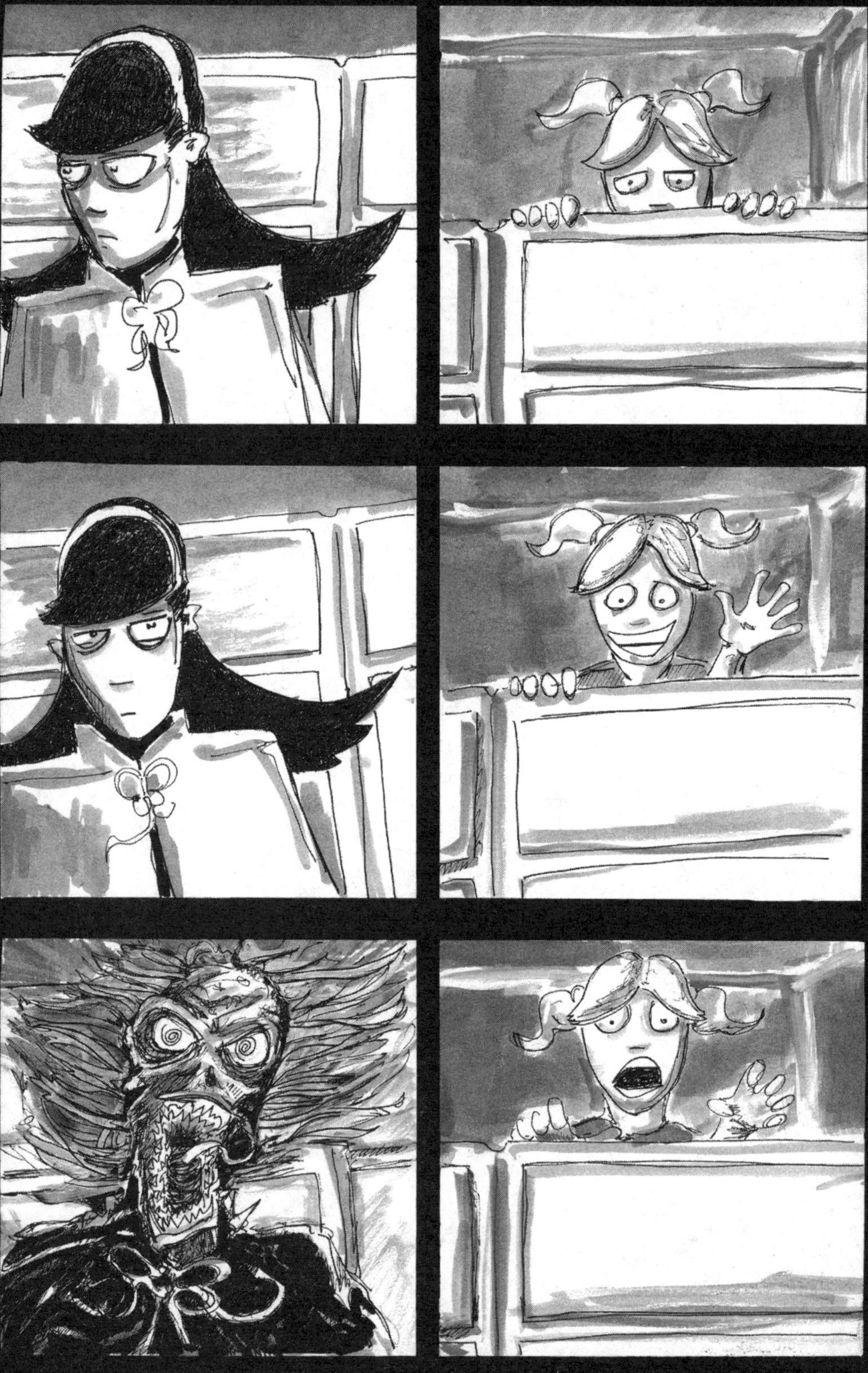

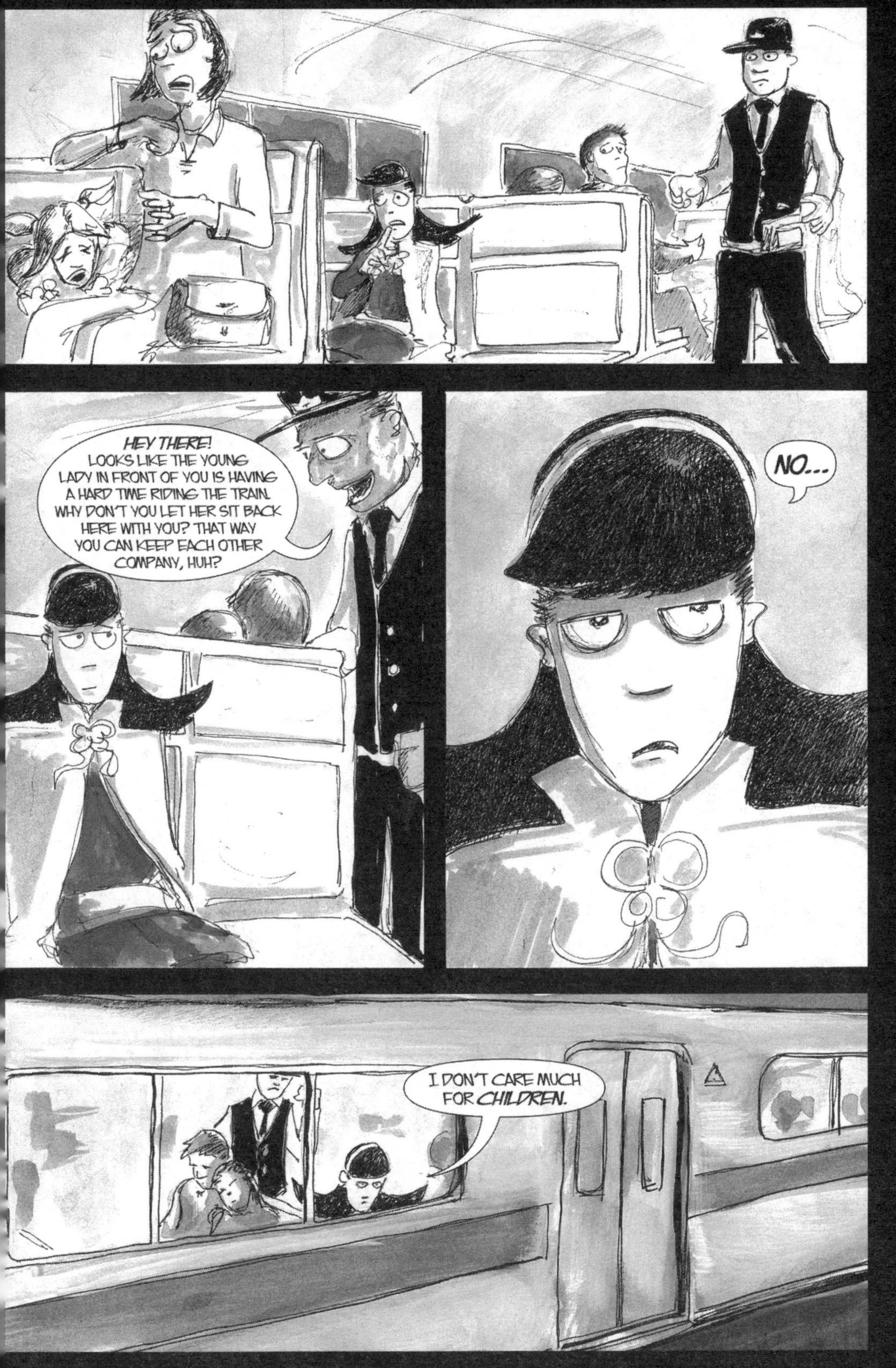
HEY THERE! LOOKS LIKE THE YOUNG LADY IN FRONT OF YOU IS HAVING A HARD TIME RIDING THE TRAIN. WHY DON'T YOU LET HER SIT BACK HERE WITH YOU? THAT WAY YOU CAN KEEP EACH OTHER COMPANY, HUH?
NO...
I DON'T CARE MUCH FOR CHILDREN.

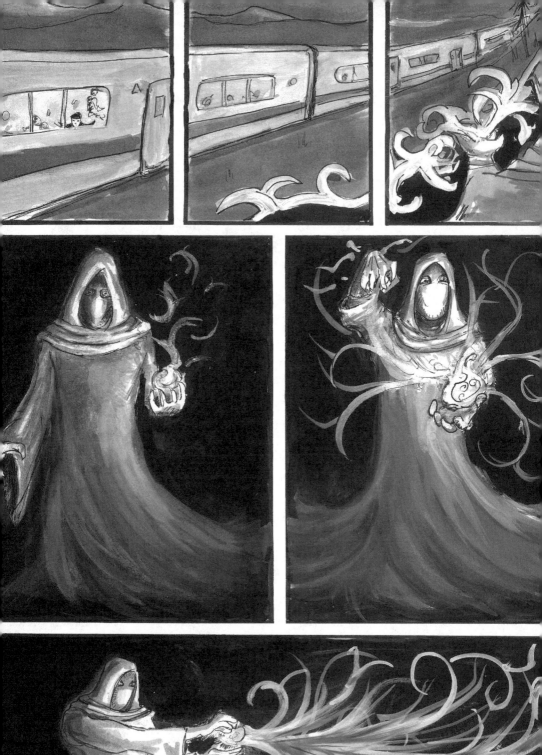

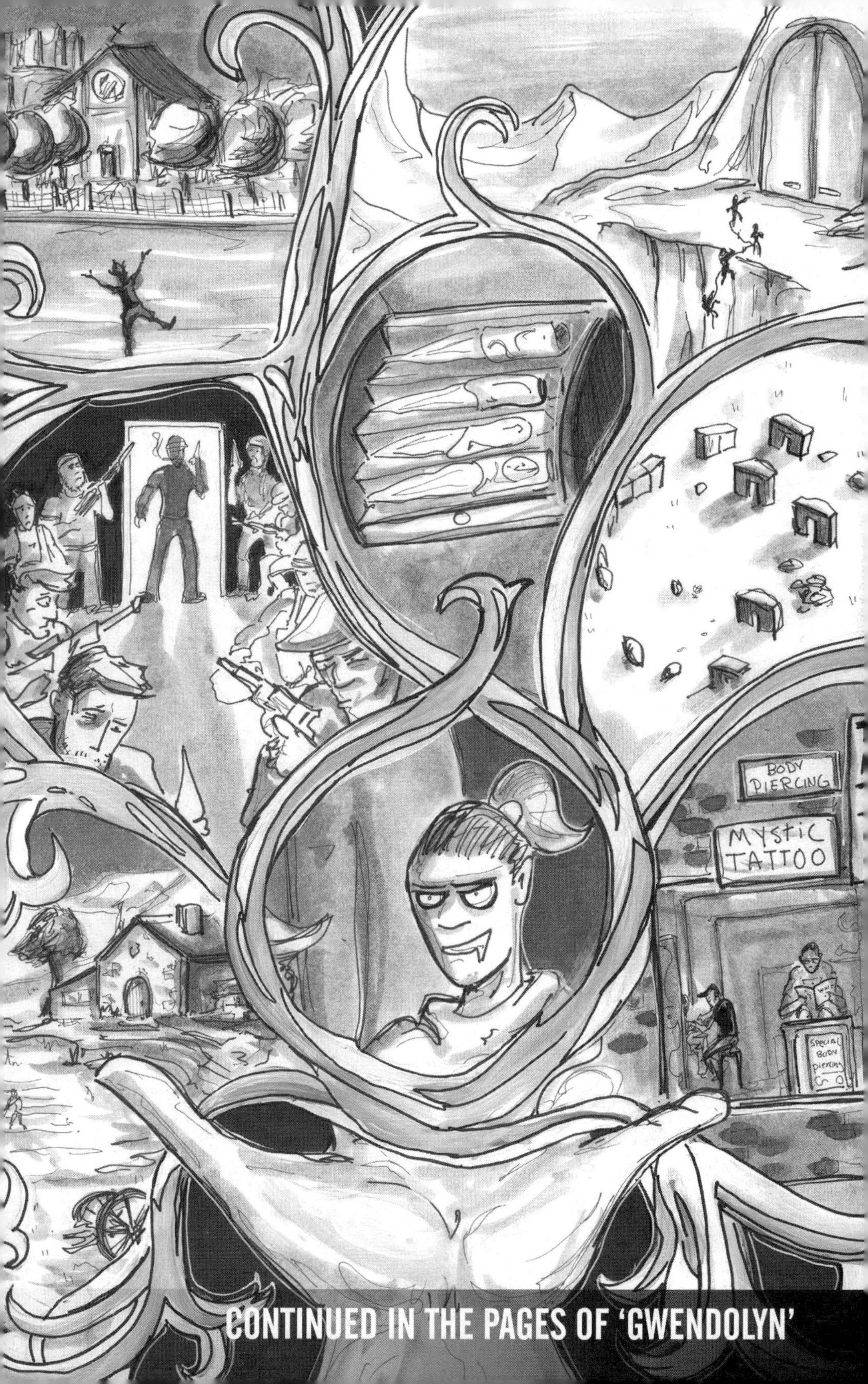
BODY PIERCING
MYSTIC TATTOO
SPECIAL BODY PIERCING

CONTINUED IN THE PAGES OF 'GWENDOLYN'

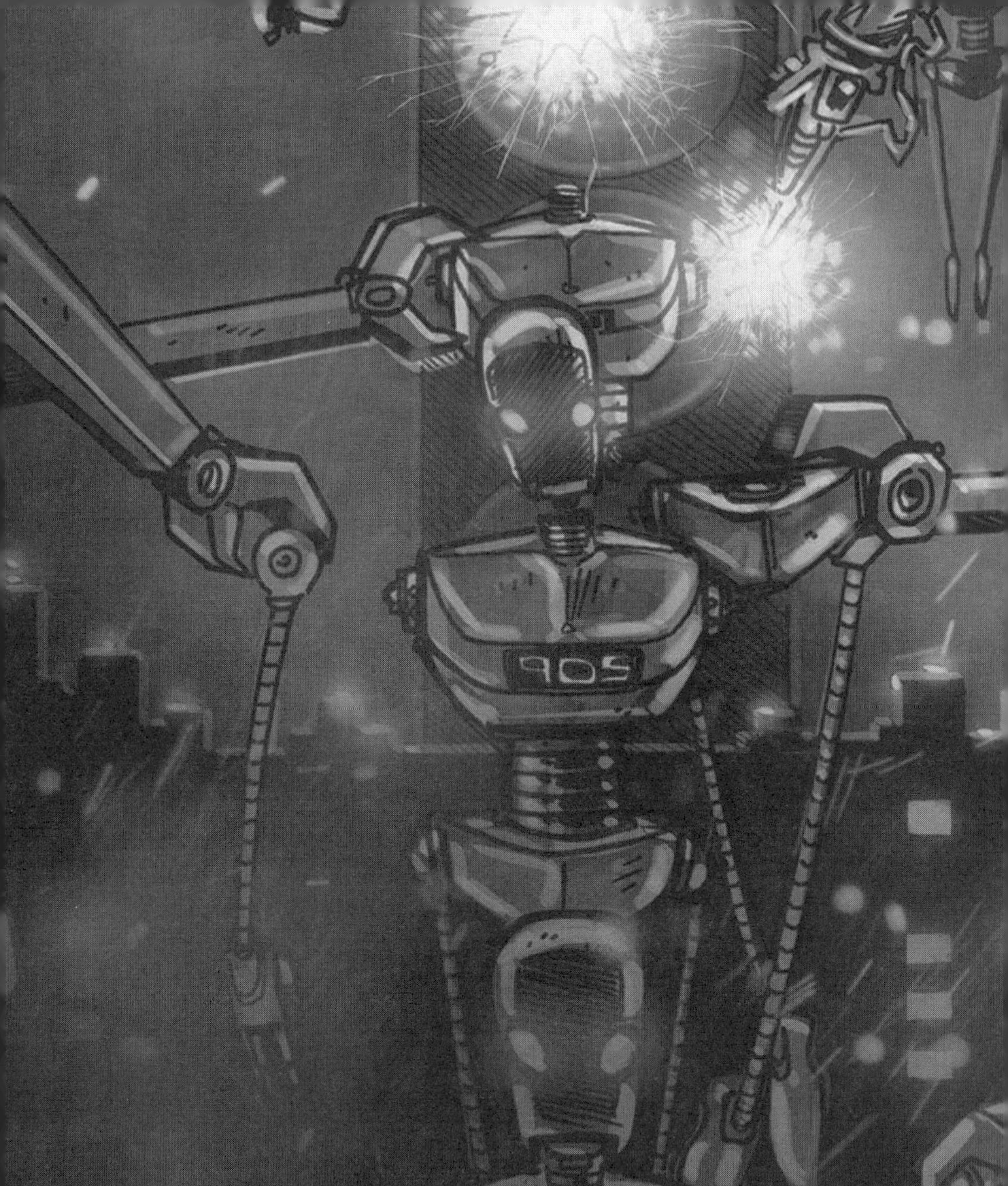

IF

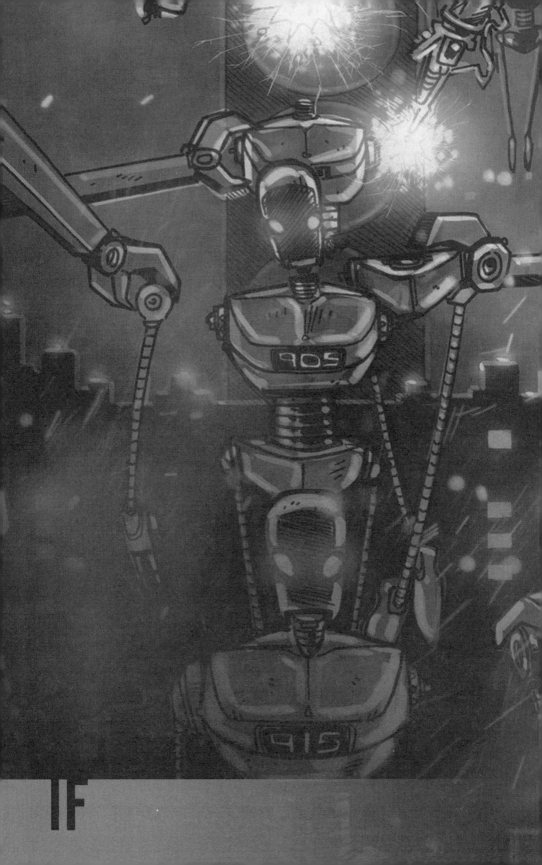

IF

915

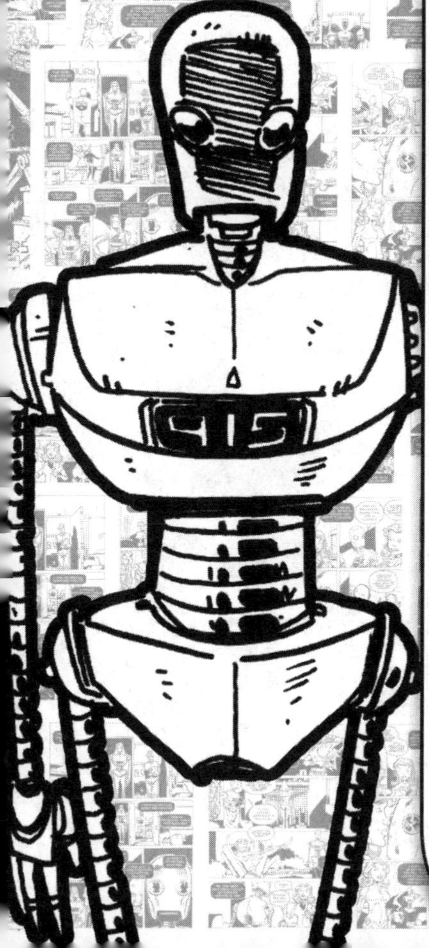
915

"I would do any-thing for her. E-ven some-thing ter-ri-ble."

915 is one of tens of thousands of robots offered for personal household use from Burn Robotics. He can perform any task asked by his owners without question and is unfathomably loyal. Although some users of this robot line have reported erratic behavior, it seems that 915 is a model employee… a robot model that is. Although he does not feel emotion, 915 enjoys taking out the garbage, helping you get dressed and most of all, spending time with his madam!

Age: Robots do not age, 915 does not feel this makes him less human.

Height: 5'10" (sizes of other models can be customized to suit YOUR needs)

Weight: 270 lbs.

First Appearance:
IF Anthology (2015)

Created by Glenn Matchett & Dan Lauer
Illustration by Dan Lauer

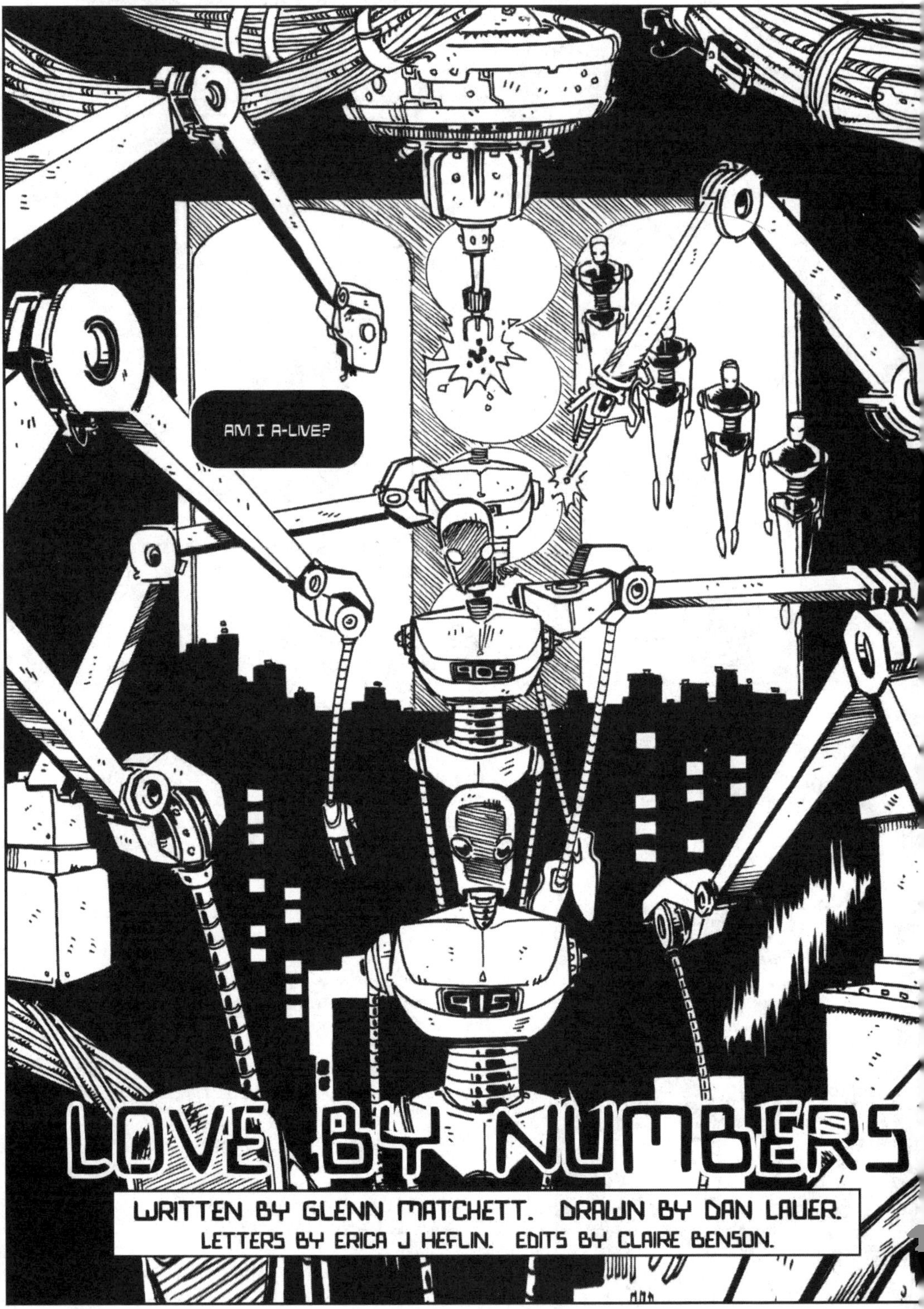
AM I A-LIVE?
909
915
LOVE BY NUMBERS
WRITTEN BY GLENN MATCHETT. DRAWN BY DAN LAUER.
LETTERS BY ERICA J HEFLIN. EDITS BY CLAIRE BENSON.

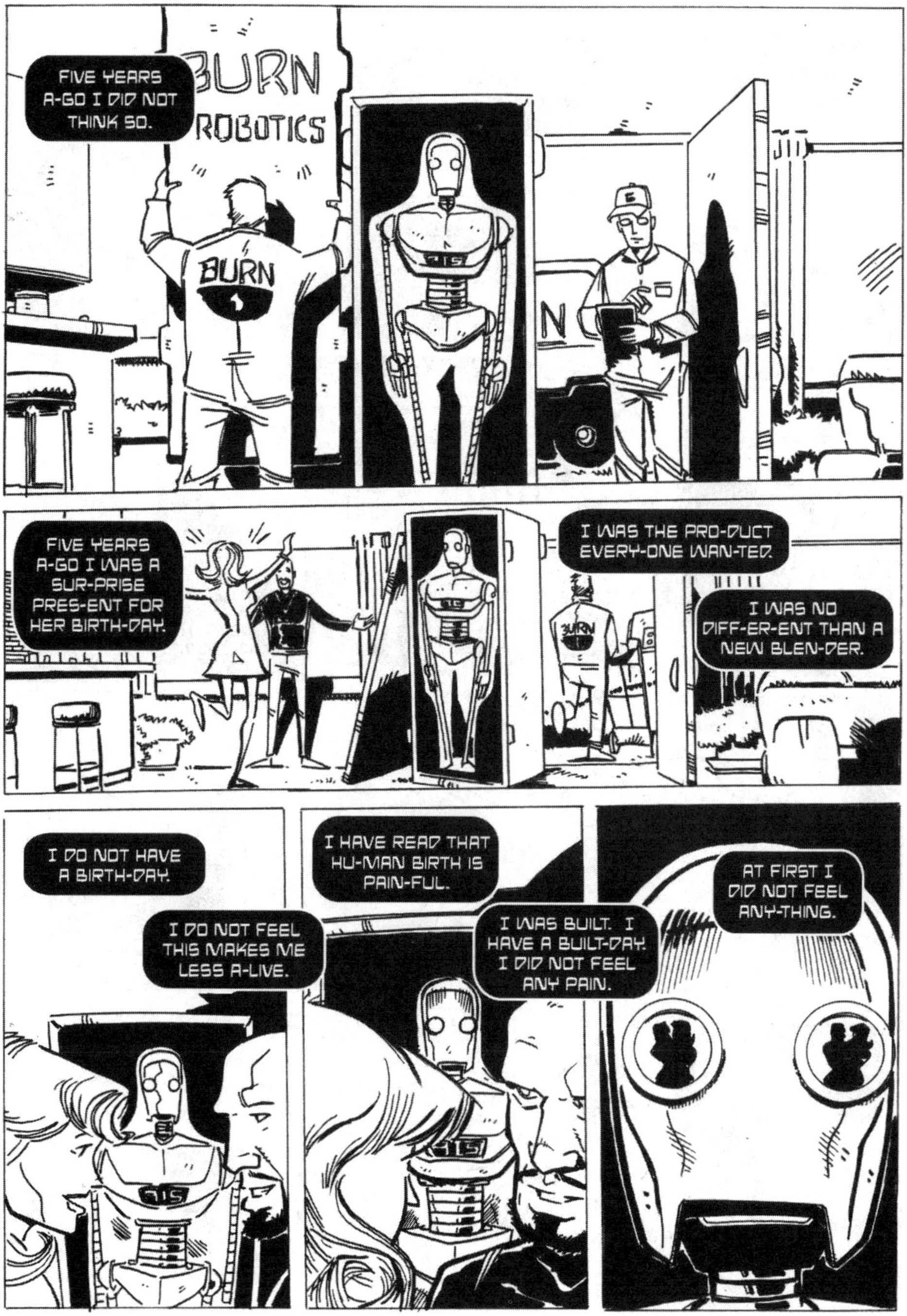
FIVE YEARS A-GO I DID NOT THINK SO.
BURN ROBOTICS
BURN
FIVE YEARS A-GO I WAS A SUR-PRISE PRES-ENT FOR HER BIRTH-DAY.
I WAS THE PRO-DUCT EVERY-ONE WAN-TED.
I WAS NO DIFF-ER-ENT THAN A NEW BLEN-DER.
I DO NOT HAVE A BIRTH-DAY.
I DO NOT FEEL THIS MAKES ME LESS A-LIVE.
I HAVE READ THAT HU-MAN BIRTH IS PAIN-FUL.
I WAS BUILT. I HAVE A BUILT-DAY. I DID NOT FEEL ANY PAIN.
AT FIRST I DID NOT FEEL ANY-THING.

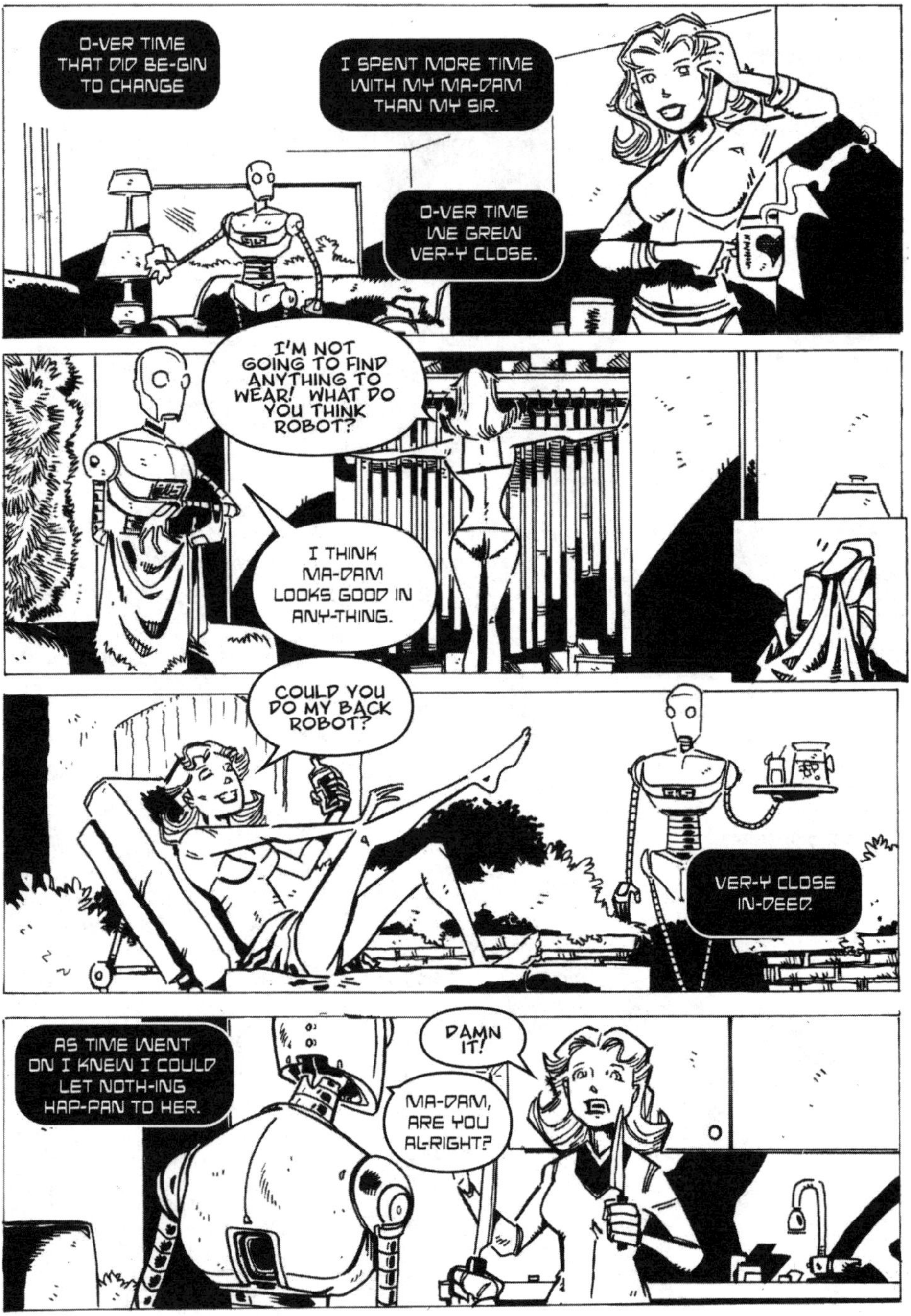
O-VER TIME THAT DID BE-GIN TO CHANGE
I SPENT MORE TIME WITH MY MA-DAM THAN MY SIR.
O-VER TIME WE GREW VER-Y CLOSE.
I'M NOT GOING TO FIND ANYTHING TO WEAR! WHAT DO YOU THINK ROBOT?
I THINK MA-DAM LOOKS GOOD IN ANY-THING.
COULD YOU DO MY BACK ROBOT?
VER-Y CLOSE IN-DEED.
AS TIME WENT ON I KNEW I COULD LET NOTH-ING HAP-PAN TO HER.
DAMN IT!
MA-DAM, ARE YOU AL-RIGHT?

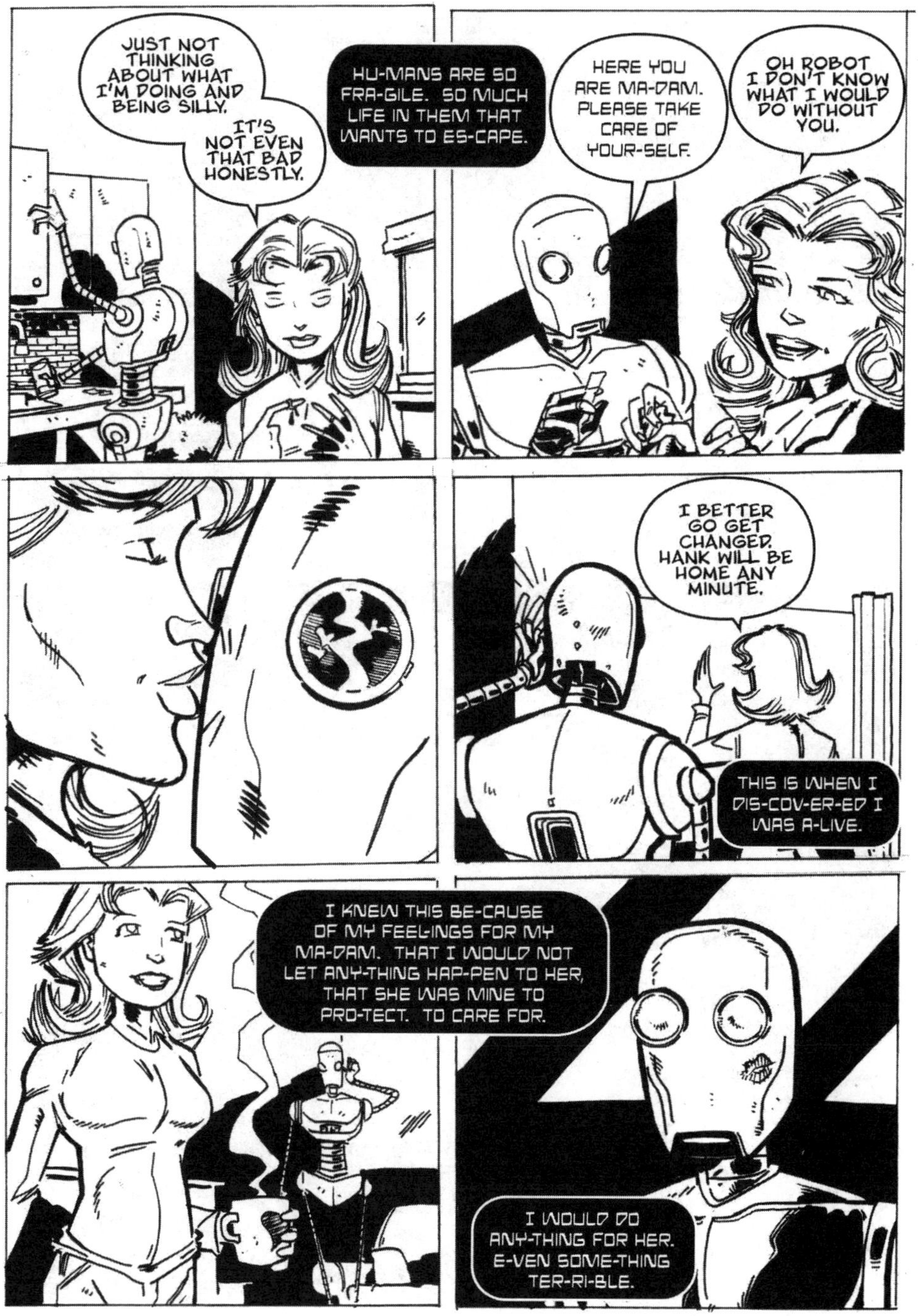
JUST NOT THINKING ABOUT WHAT I'M DOING AND BEING SILLY.
IT'S NOT EVEN THAT BAD HONESTLY.
HU-MANS ARE SO FRA-GILE. SO MUCH LIFE IN THEM THAT WANTS TO ES-CAPE.
HERE YOU ARE MA-DAM. PLEASE TAKE CARE OF YOUR-SELF.
OH ROBOT I DON'T KNOW WHAT I WOULD DO WITHOUT YOU.
I BETTER GO GET CHANGED. HANK WILL BE HOME ANY MINUTE.
THIS IS WHEN I DIS-COV-ER-ED I WAS A-LIVE.
I KNEW THIS BE-CAUSE OF MY FEEL-INGS FOR MY MA-DAM. THAT I WOULD NOT LET ANY-THING HAP-PEN TO HER, THAT SHE WAS MINE TO PRO-TECT. TO CARE FOR.
I WOULD DO ANY-THING FOR HER. E-VEN SOME-THING TER-RI-BLE.

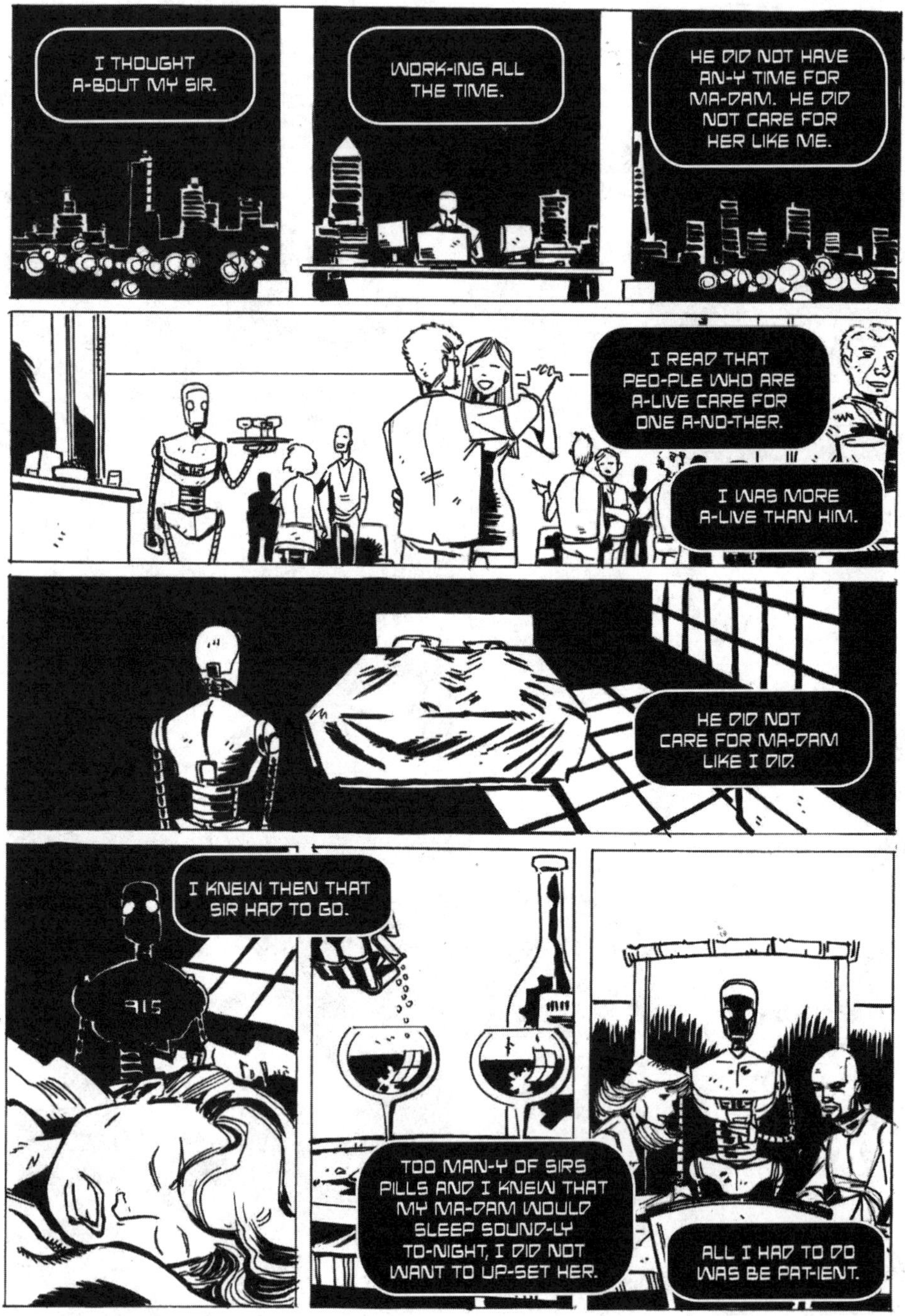
I THOUGHT A-BOUT MY SIR.
WORK-ING ALL THE TIME.
HE DID NOT HAVE AN-Y TIME FOR MA-DAM. HE DID NOT CARE FOR HER LIKE ME.
I READ THAT PEO-PLE WHO ARE A-LIVE CARE FOR ONE A-NO-THER.
I WAS MORE A-LIVE THAN HIM.
HE DID NOT CARE FOR MA-DAM LIKE I DID.
I KNEW THEN THAT SIR HAD TO GO.
TOO MAN-Y OF SIRS PILLS AND I KNEW THAT MY MA-DAM WOULD SLEEP SOUND-LY TO-NIGHT, I DID NOT WANT TO UP-SET HER.
ALL I HAD TO DO WAS BE PAT-IENT.

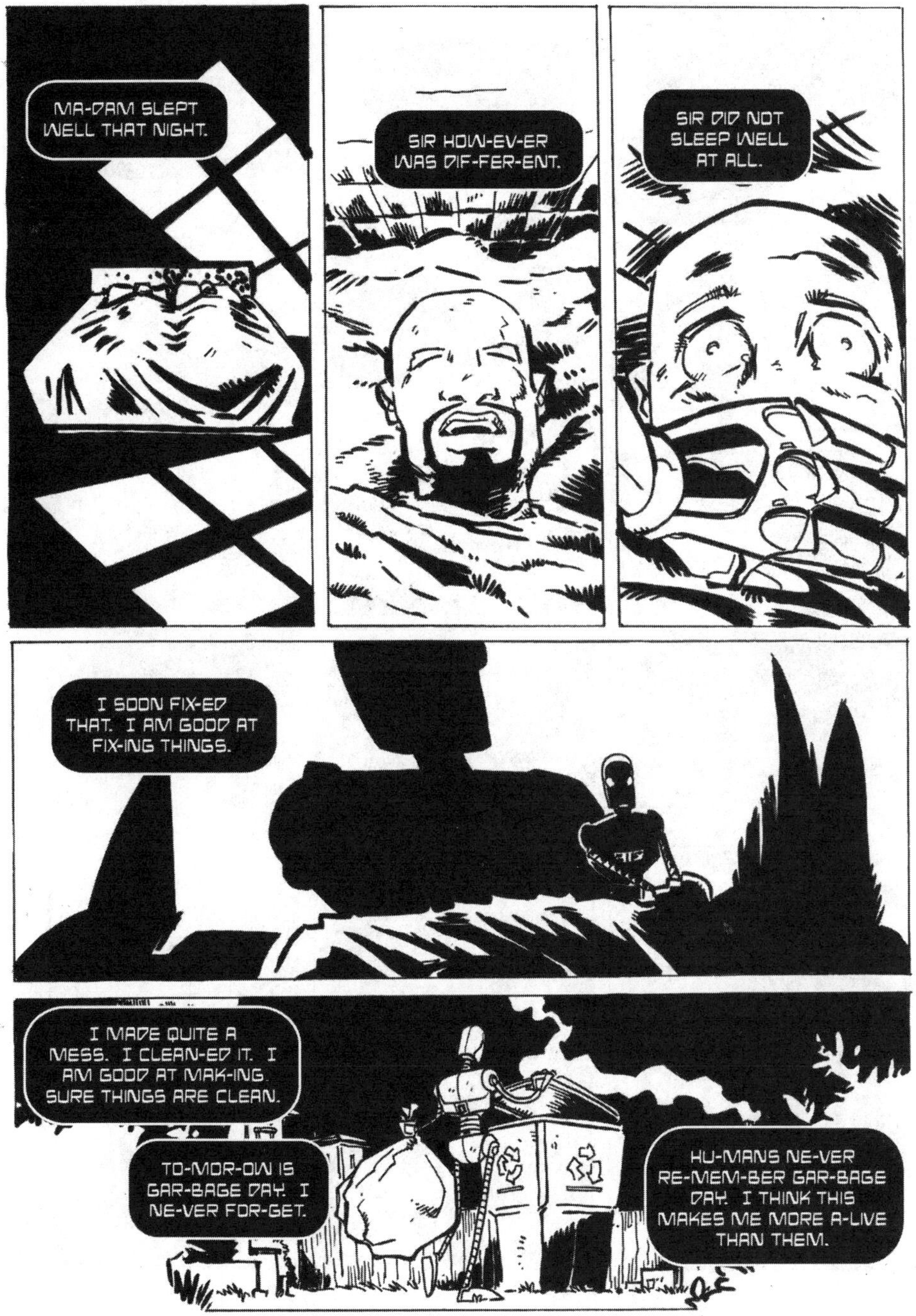
MA-DAM SLEPT WELL THAT NIGHT.
SIR HOW-EV-ER WAS DIF-FER-ENT.
SIR DID NOT SLEEP WELL AT ALL.
I SOON FIX-ED THAT. I AM GOOD AT FIX-ING THINGS.
I MADE QUITE A MESS. I CLEAN-ED IT. I AM GOOD AT MAK-ING SURE THINGS ARE CLEAN.
TO-MOR-OW IS GAR-BAGE DAY. I NE-VER FOR-GET.
HU-MANS NE-VER RE-MEM-BER GAR-BAGE DAY. I THINK THIS MAKES ME MORE A-LIVE THAN THEM.

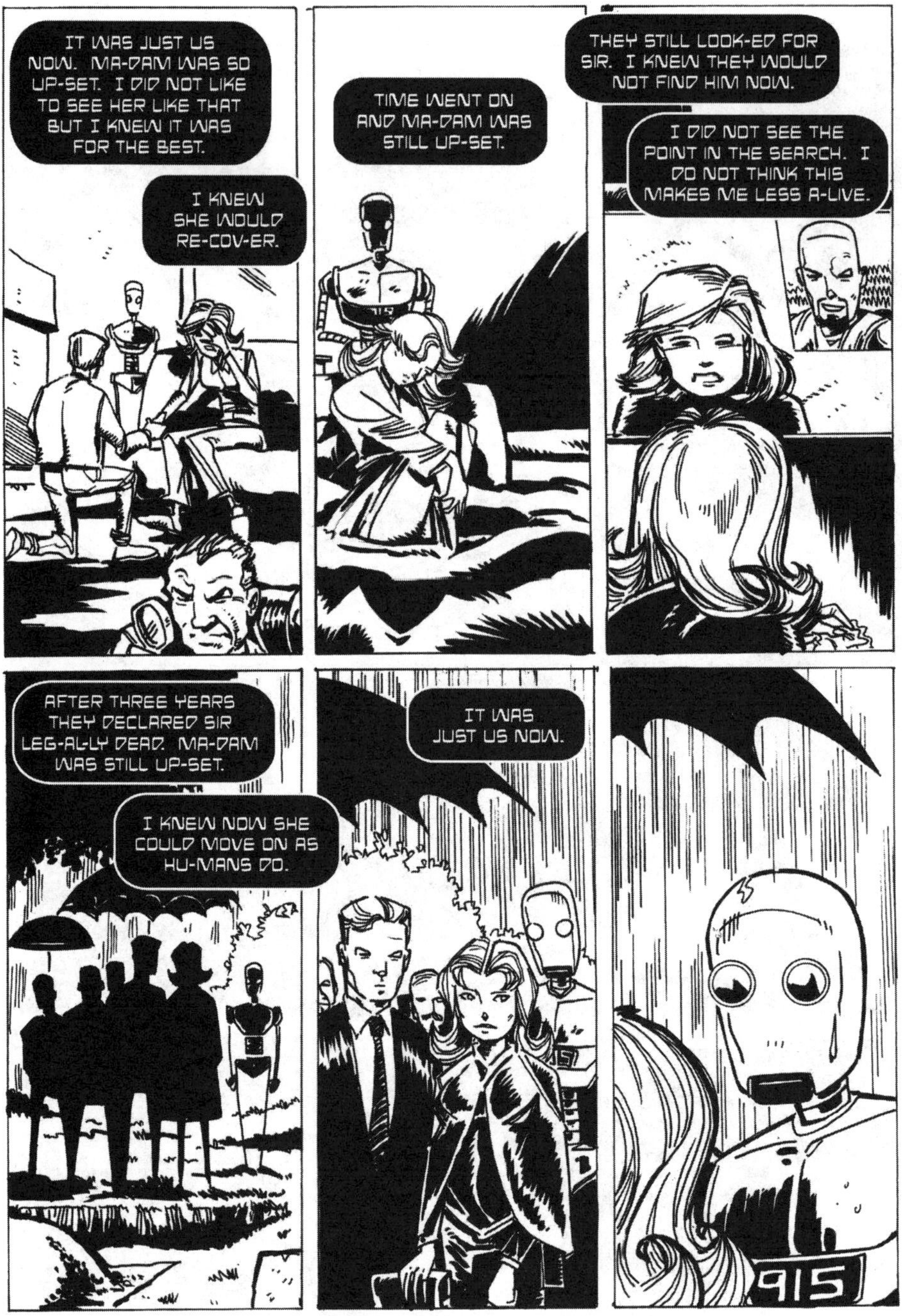
IT WAS JUST US NOW. MA-DAM WAS SO UP-SET. I DID NOT LIKE TO SEE HER LIKE THAT BUT I KNEW IT WAS FOR THE BEST.
I KNEW SHE WOULD RE-COV-ER.
TIME WENT ON AND MA-DAM WAS STILL UP-SET.
THEY STILL LOOK-ED FOR SIR. I KNEW THEY WOULD NOT FIND HIM NOW.
I DID NOT SEE THE POINT IN THE SEARCH. I DO NOT THINK THIS MAKES ME LESS A-LIVE.
AFTER THREE YEARS THEY DECLARED SIR LEG-AL-LY DEAD. MA-DAM WAS STILL UP-SET.
I KNEW NOW SHE COULD MOVE ON AS HU-MANS DO.
IT WAS JUST US NOW.
915

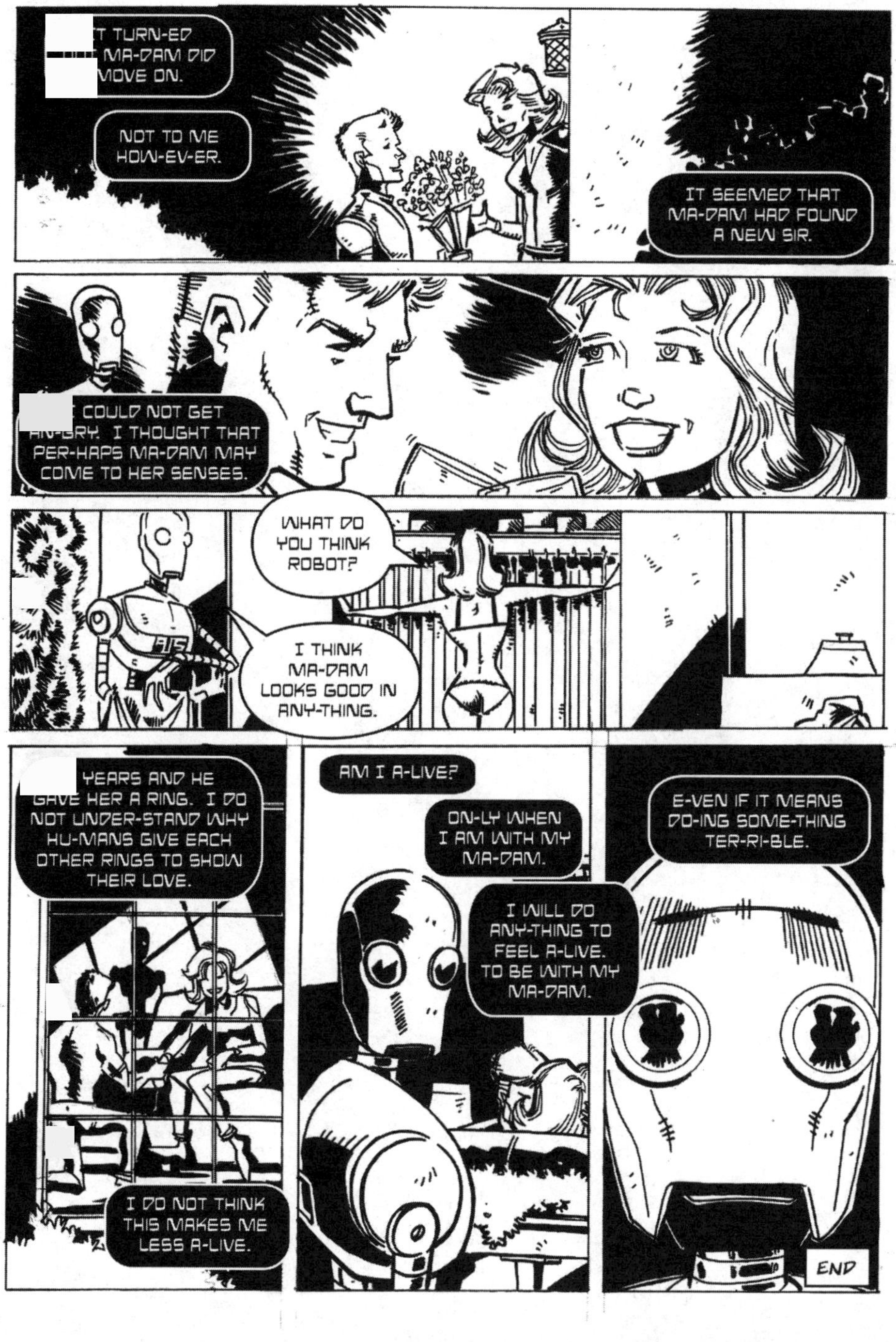

TURN-ED MA-DAM DID MOVE ON.
NOT TO ME HOW-EV-ER.
IT SEEMED THAT MA-DAM HAD FOUND A NEW SIR.
COULD NOT GET AN-GRY. I THOUGHT THAT PER-HAPS MA-DAM MAY COME TO HER SENSES.
WHAT DO YOU THINK ROBOT?
I THINK MA-DAM LOOKS GOOD IN ANY-THING.
YEARS AND HE GAVE HER A RING. I DO NOT UNDER-STAND WHY HU-MANS GIVE EACH OTHER RINGS TO SHOW THEIR LOVE.
I DO NOT THINK THIS MAKES ME LESS A-LIVE.
AM I A-LIVE?
ON-LY WHEN I AM WITH MY MA-DAM.
I WILL DO ANY-THING TO FEEL A-LIVE. TO BE WITH MY MA-DAM.
E-VEN IF IT MEANS DO-ING SOME-THING TER-RI-BLE.
END

READ MORE STORIES IN THE PAGES OF 'IF'

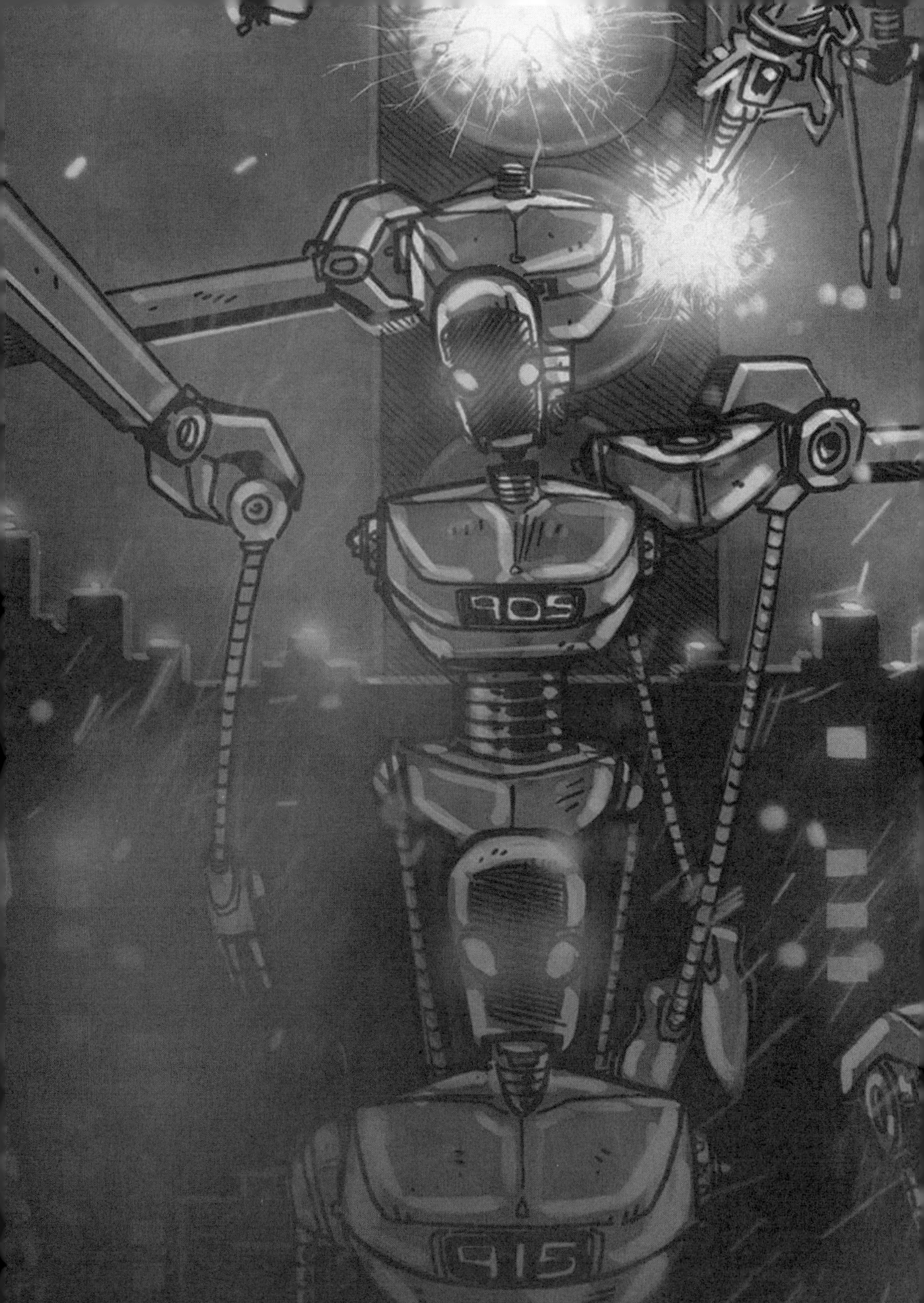
905
915

IF

IF

BIGFOOT

*"What **happened?!***
*People used to know **who** I was!"*

Somewhere in the world, a (mostly) forgotten creature has lived his life in complete isolation. This monster — no, this *abomination* — vacations wherever he pleases and has been carrying out elusive tasks for hundreds of years. Possibly thousands. While he has numerous aliases, he primarily goes by the name of Sasquatch, Windigo, Yeti, or Bigfoot.
But the scariest part?
This monster is suffering from depression.

Age:Unknown   Height: 6'6"   Weight: 345 lbs.

First Appearance: IF Anthology (2015)

Created by Chas! Pangburn
Illustration by Mariano Laclaustra

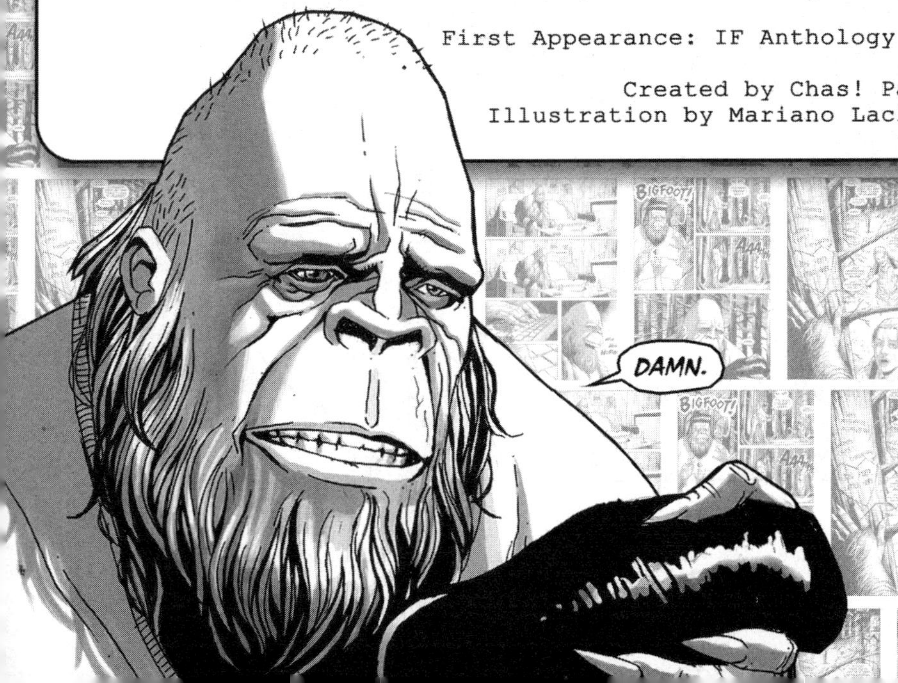
DAMN.

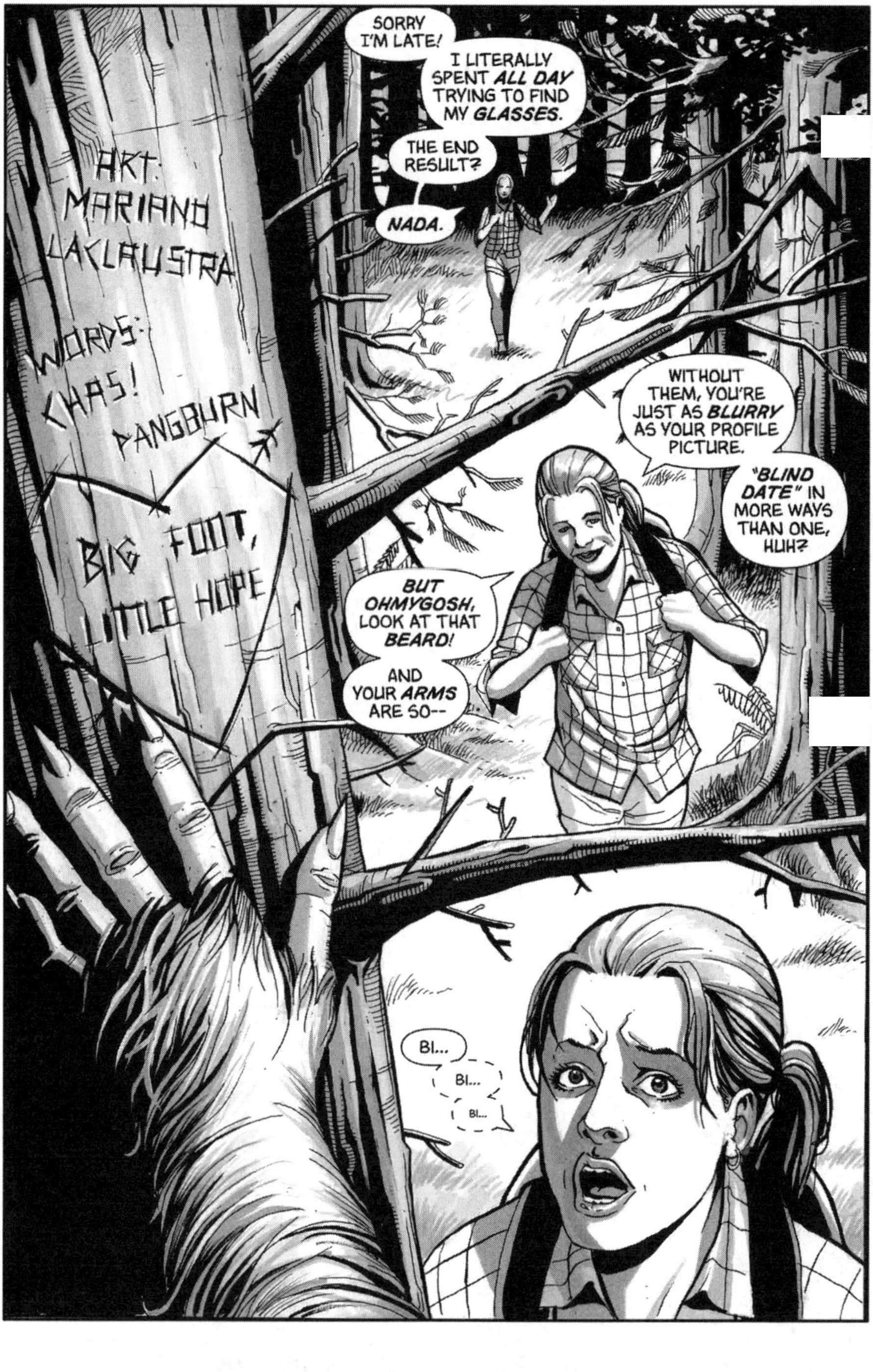
ART: MARIANO LACLAUSTRA
WORDS: CHAS! PANGBURN
BIG FOOT, LITTLE HOPE
SORRY I'M LATE!
I LITERALLY SPENT ALL DAY TRYING TO FIND MY GLASSES.
THE END RESULT?
NADA.
WITHOUT THEM, YOU'RE JUST AS BLURRY AS YOUR PROFILE PICTURE.
"BLIND DATE" IN MORE WAYS THAN ONE, HUH?
BUT OHMYGOSH, LOOK AT THAT BEARD!
AND YOUR ARMS ARE SO--
BI...
BI...
BI...

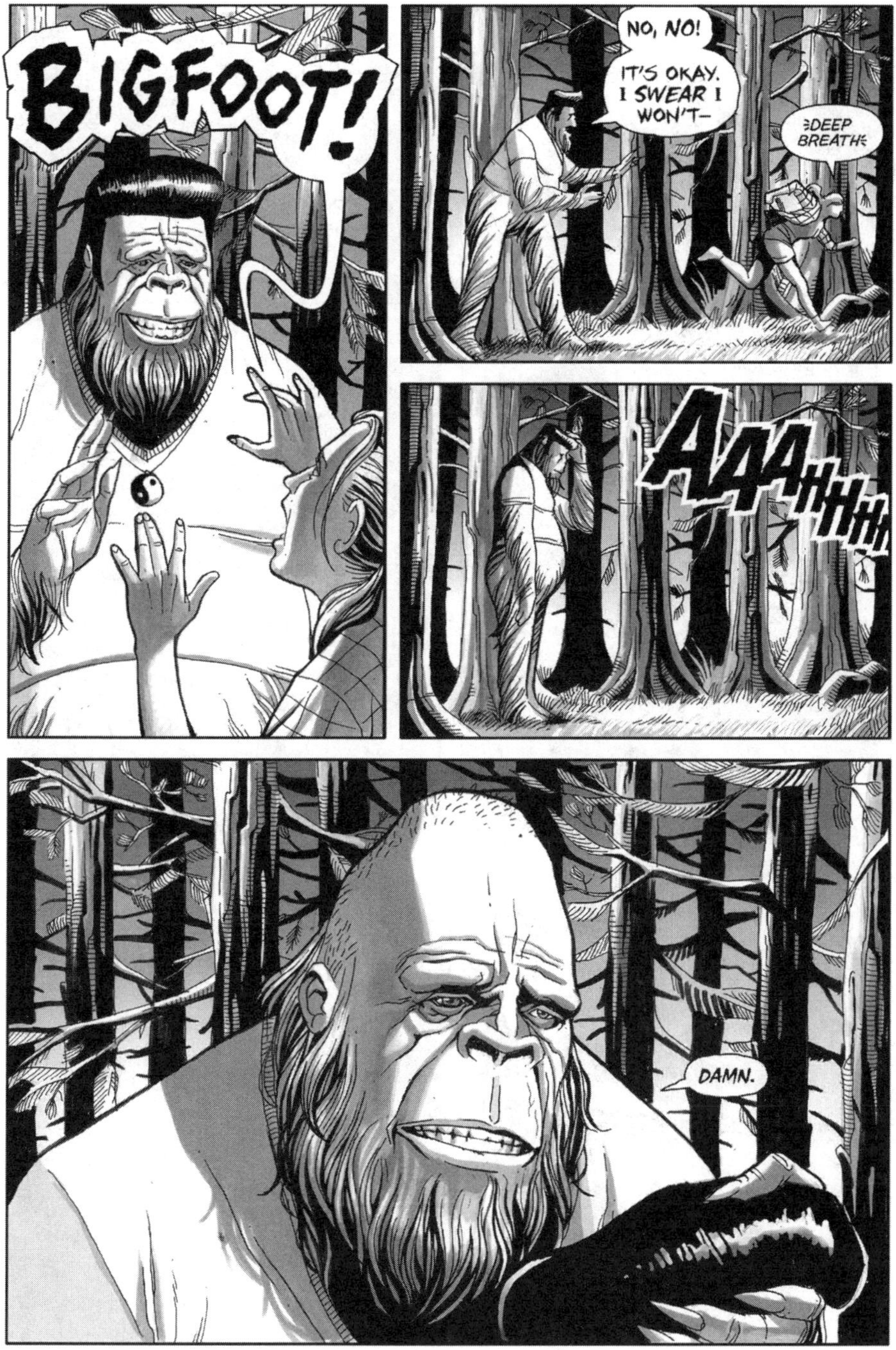
BIGFOOT!
NO, NO!
IT'S OKAY. I SWEAR I WON'T—
DEEP BREATH
AAAHHHH
DAMN.

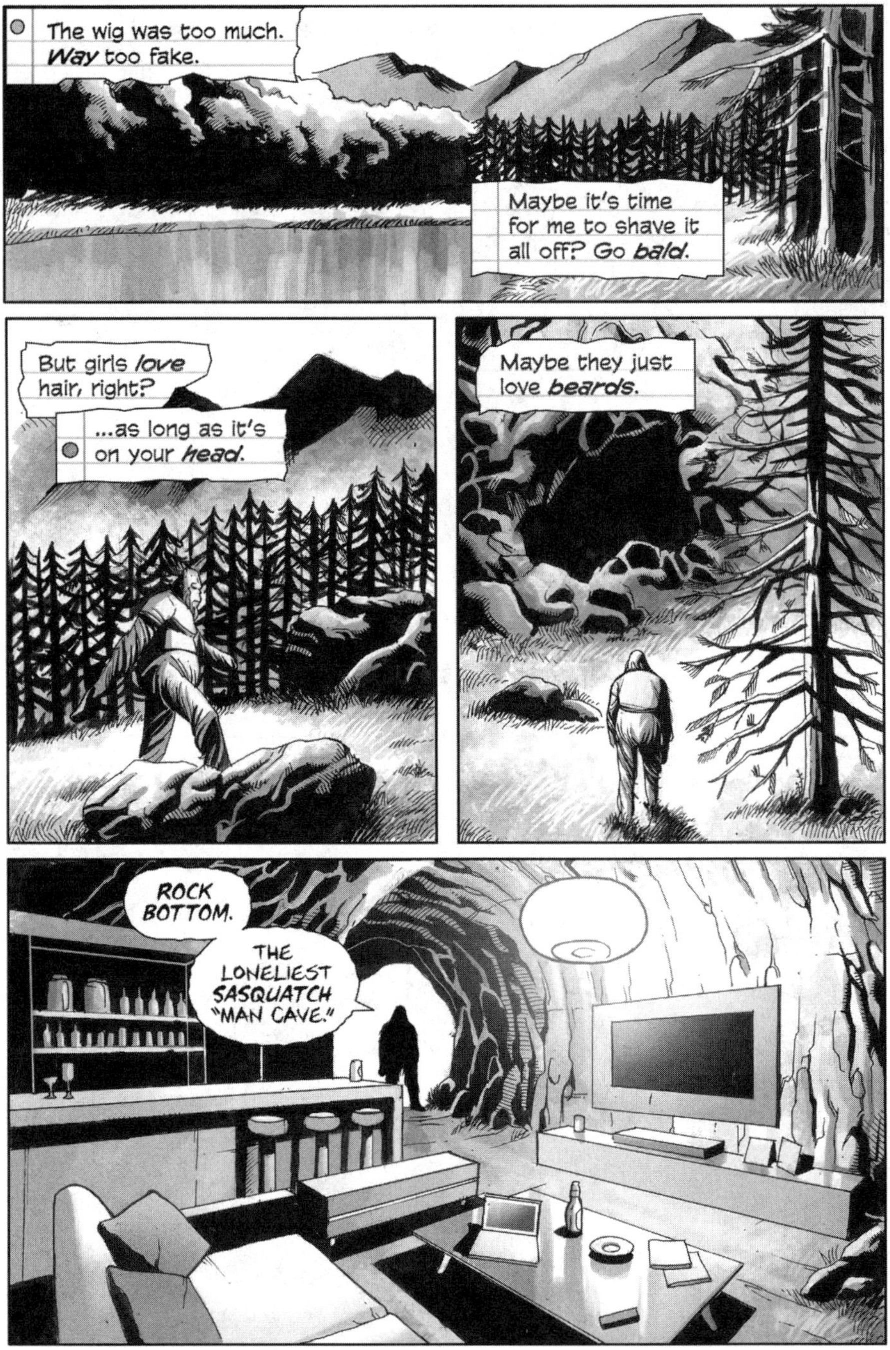

The wig was too much. *Way* too fake.
Maybe it's time for me to shave it all off? Go *bald*.
But girls *love* hair, right?
...as long as it's on your *head*.
Maybe they just love *beards*.
ROCK BOTTOM.
THE LONELIEST SASQUATCH "MAN CAVE."

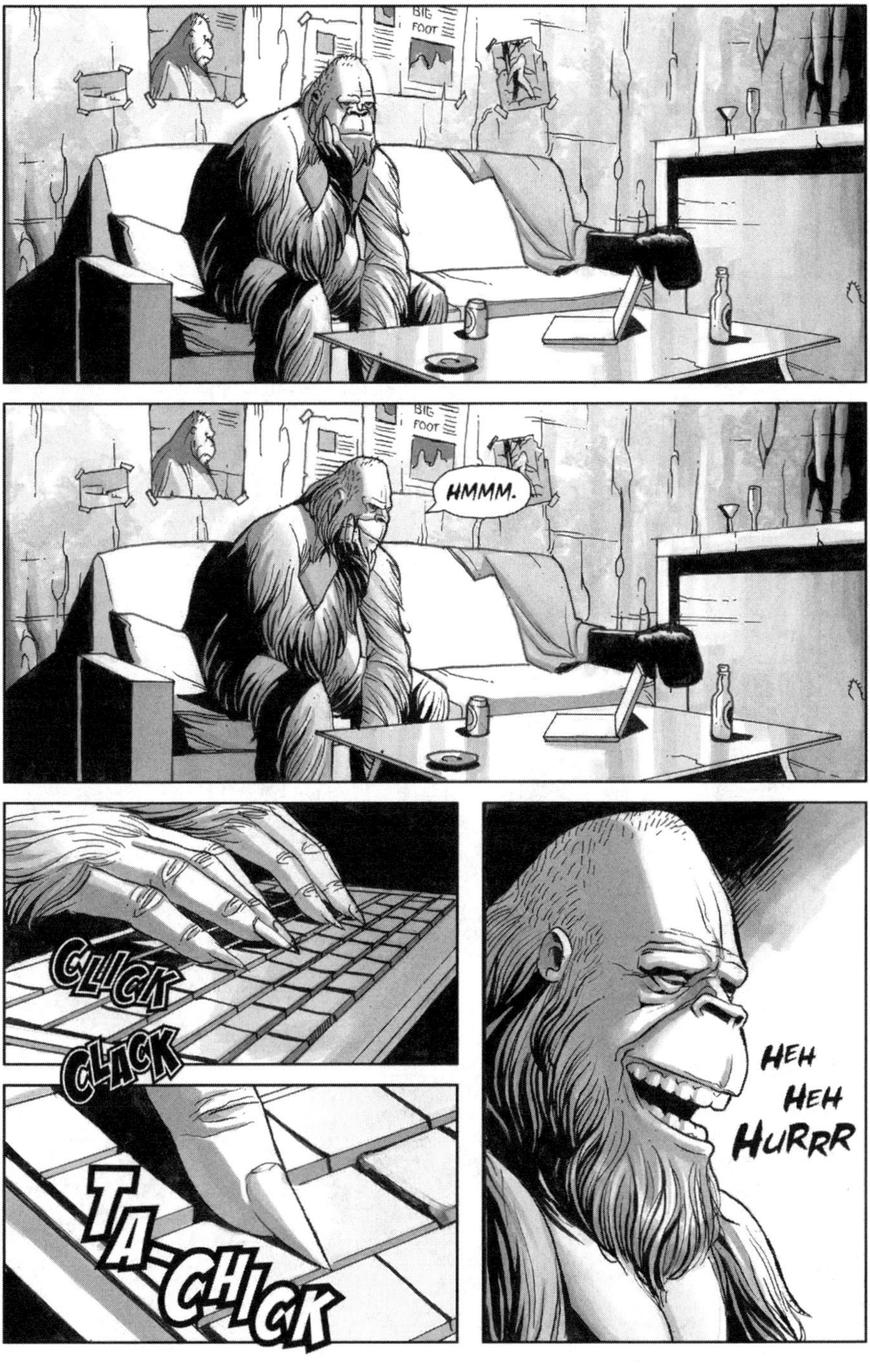
BIG FOOT
HMMM.
CLICK
CLACK
TA-CHICK
HEH
HEH
HURRR

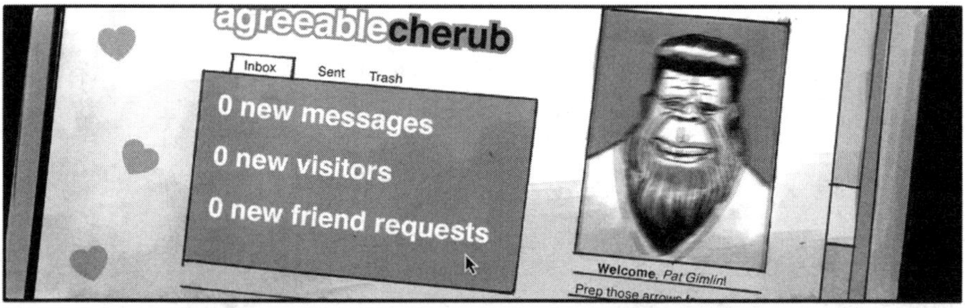
agreeablecherub
Inbox
Sent
Trash
0 new messages
0 new visitors
0 new friend requests
Welcome, Pat Gimlin!
Prep those arrows

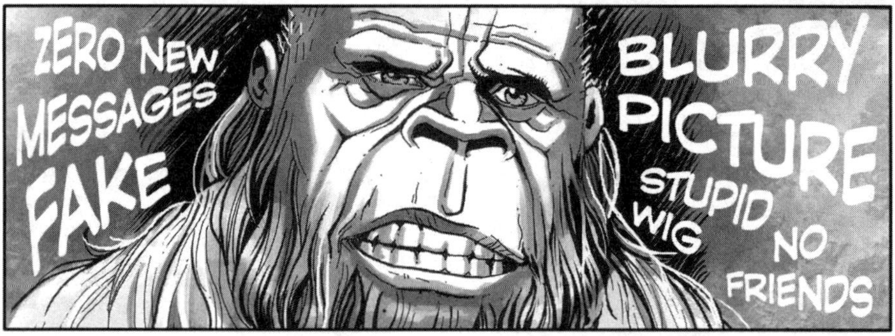
ZERO NEW MESSAGES
FAKE
BLURRY PICTURE
STUPID WIG
NO FRIENDS

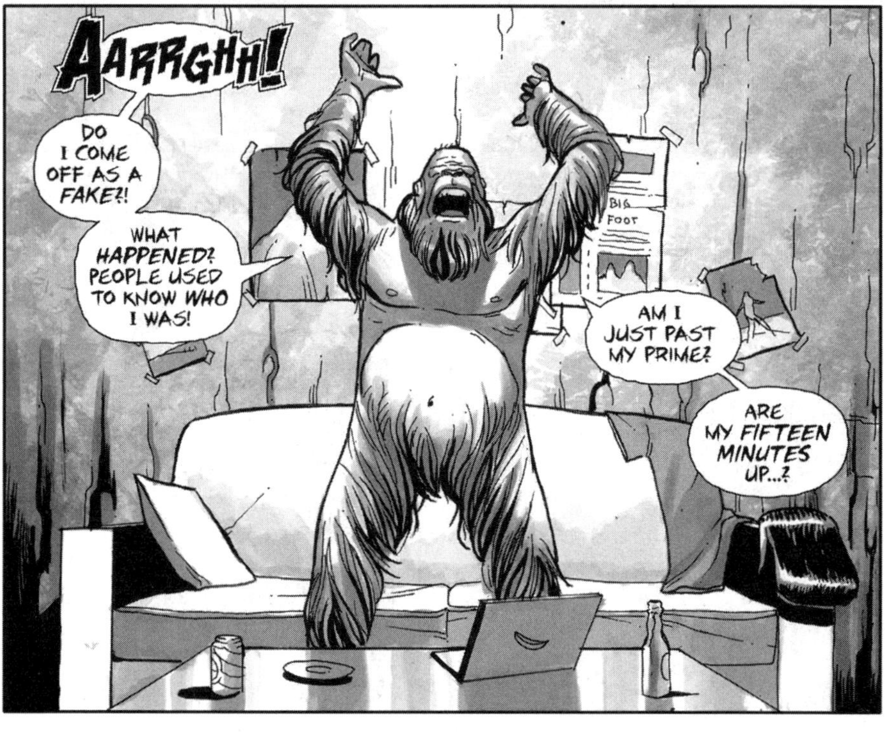
AARRGHH!
DO I COME OFF AS A FAKE?!
WHAT HAPPENED? PEOPLE USED TO KNOW WHO I WAS!
BIG FOOT
AM I JUST PAST MY PRIME?
ARE MY FIFTEEN MINUTES UP...?

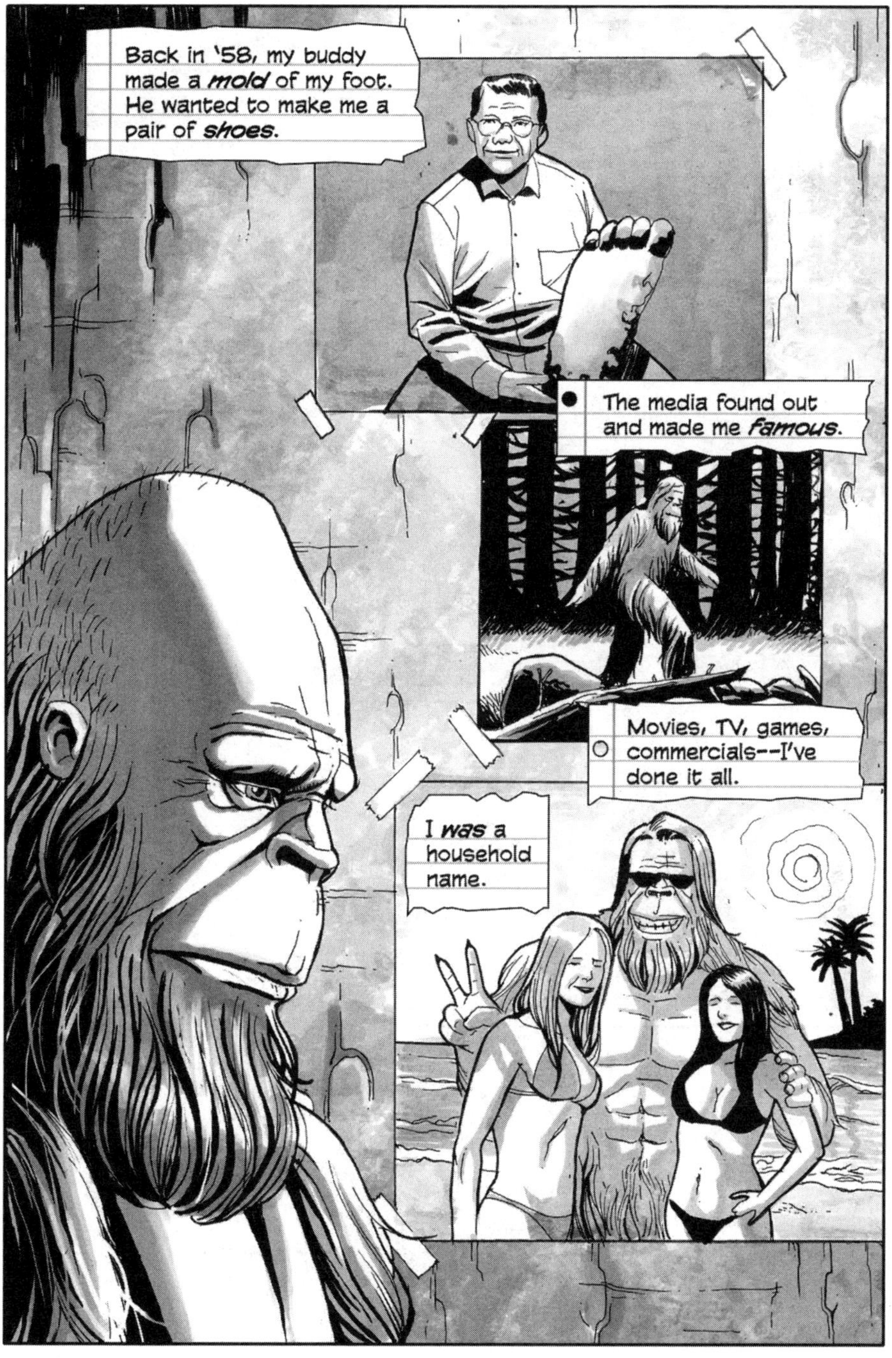
Back in '58, my buddy made a *mold* of my foot. He wanted to make me a pair of *shoes*.
The media found out and made me *famous*.
Movies, TV, games, commercials--I've done it all.
I *was* a household name.

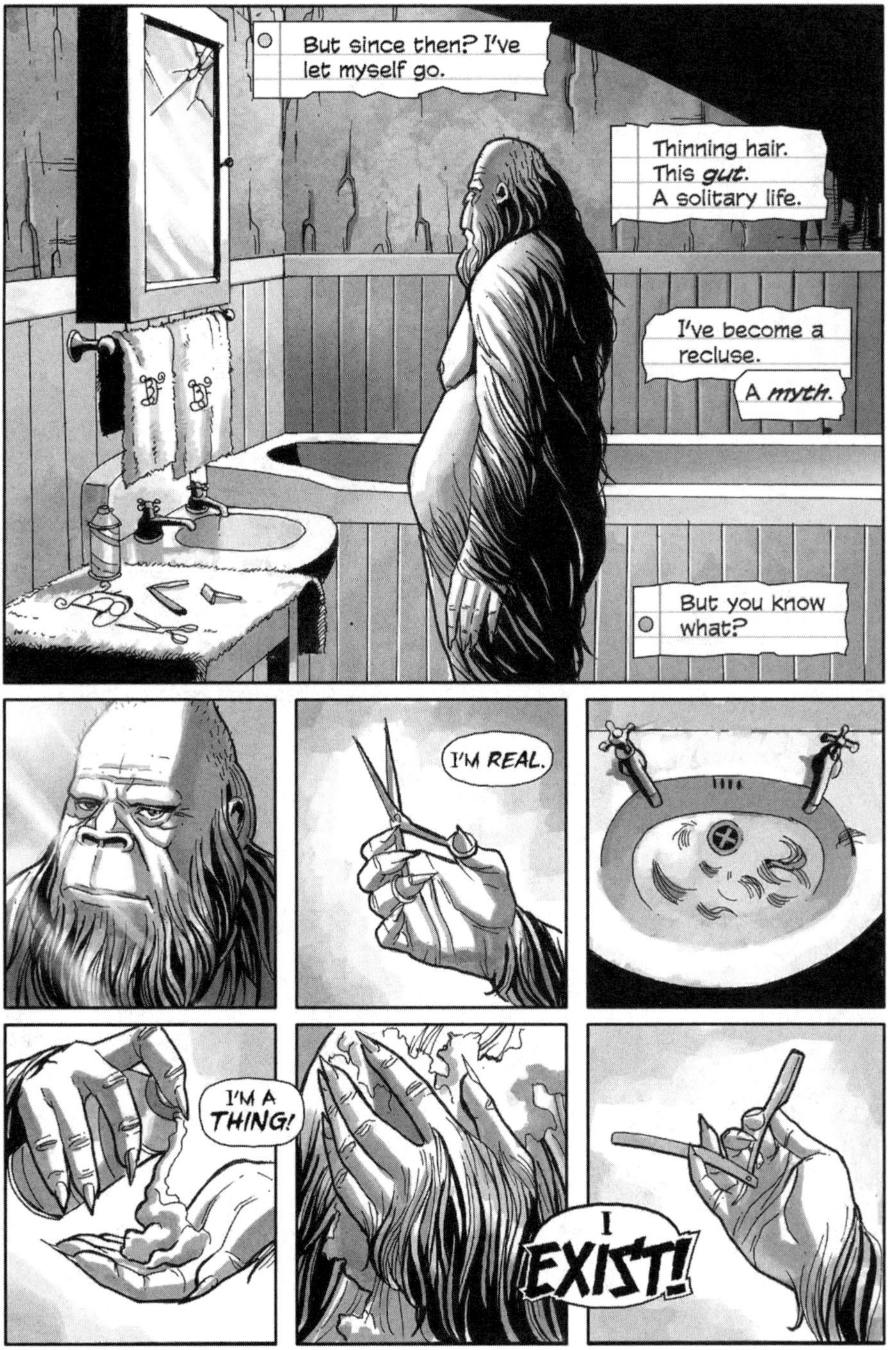
But since then? I've let myself go.
Thinning hair. This gut. A solitary life.
I've become a recluse.
A myth.
But you know what?
I'M REAL.
I'M A THING!
I EXIST!

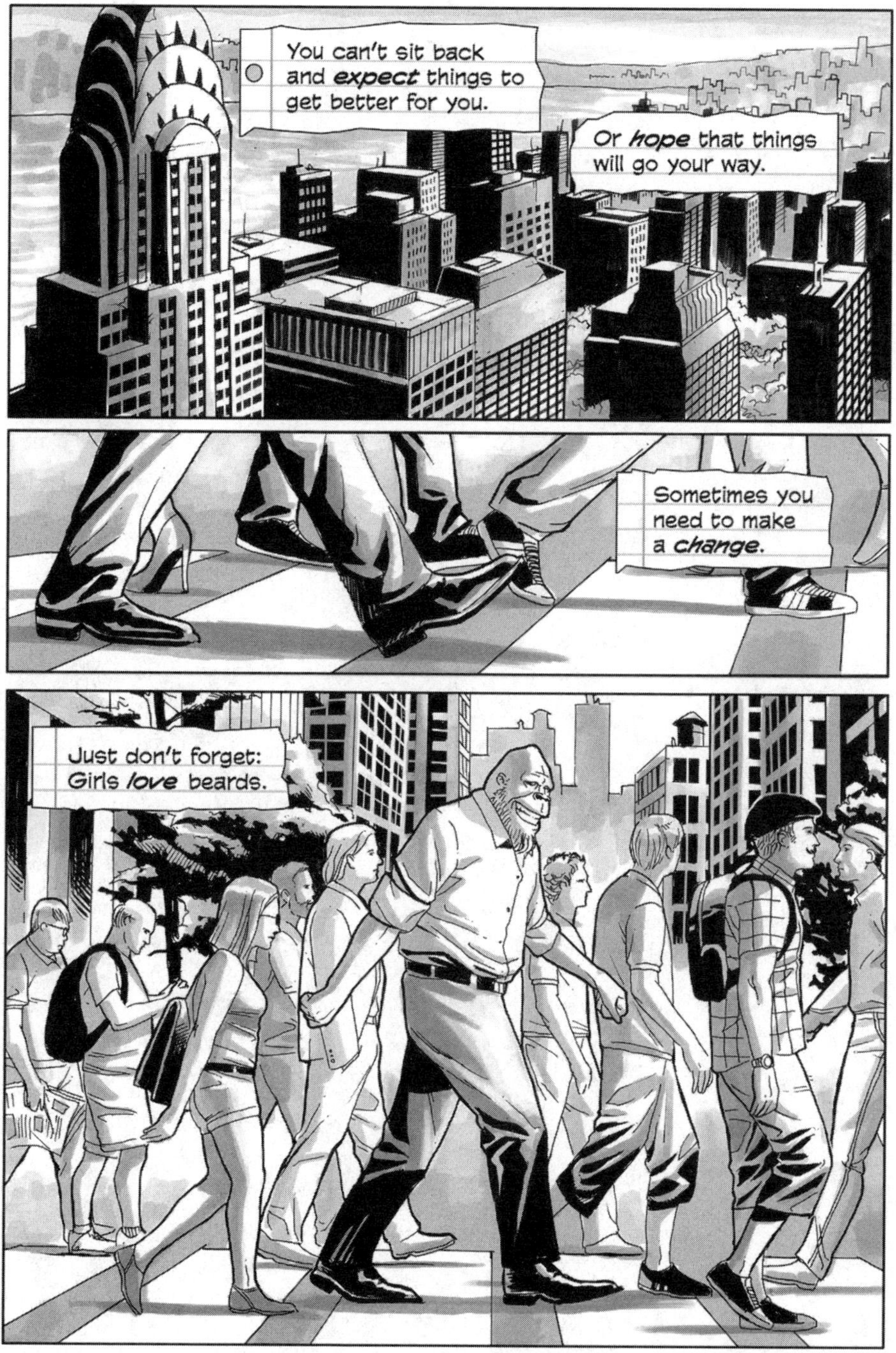
You can't sit back and *expect* things to get better for you.
Or *hope* that things will go your way.
Sometimes you need to make a *change*.
Just don't forget: Girls *love* beards.

READ MORE STORIES IN THE PAGES OF 'IF'

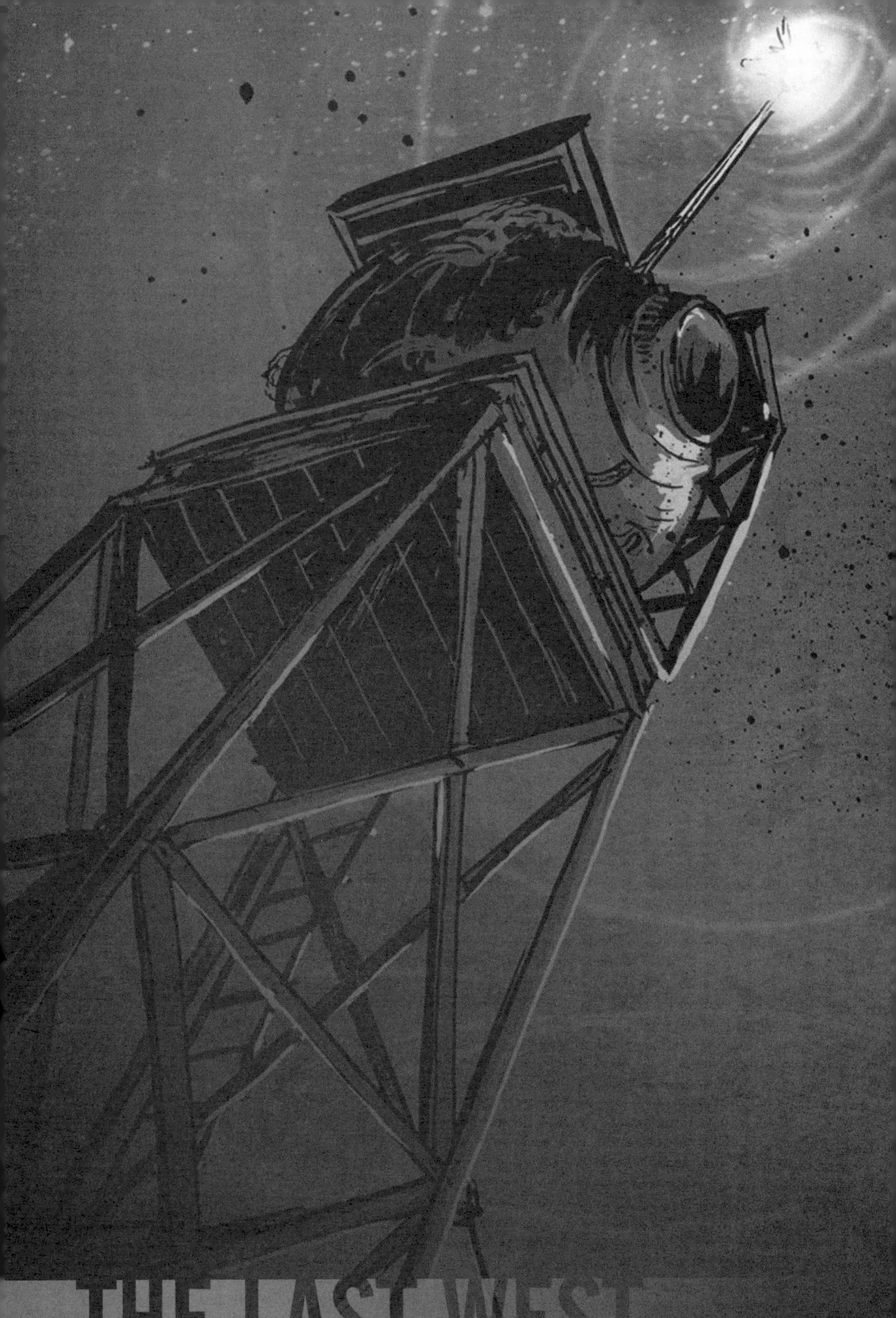

THE LAST WEST

THE LAST WEST

ROBERT WHITTENHEIMER, SR.

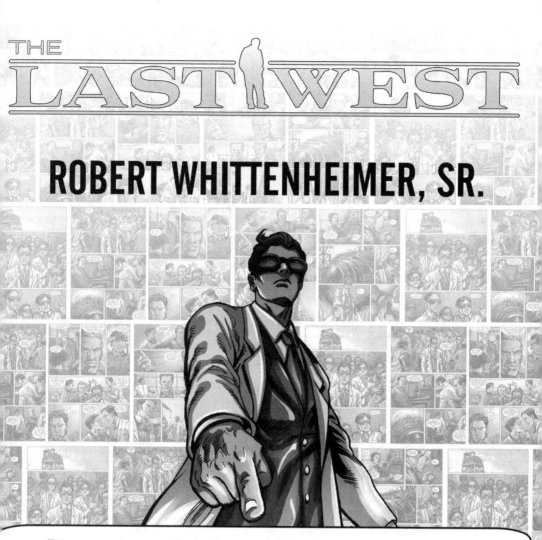

"You **must** see it! How **can't** you see it? Feel it?
It's like we're all trapped in **amber**!"

Robert Whittenheimer should have been the father of the atomic
bomb, and it should have ended the war in 1945 and ushered in a
new age of advancement. But none of that happened. Robert's atomic
bomb experiment failed, and for reasons that only one family
knows, the next 70 years have continued, unchanging. World War II
hasn't ended. Society hasn't advanced. Everything is stuck in a
stasis. And it all started when Robert Whittenheimer pushed the
button... and nothing happened.

Age: 41   Height: 5'11"   Weight: 165 lbs.

First Appearance: THE LAST WEST #1 (2013)

Created by Lou Iovino, Evan Young, and Novo Malgapo
Illustration by Novo Malgapo & Liezl Buenaventura

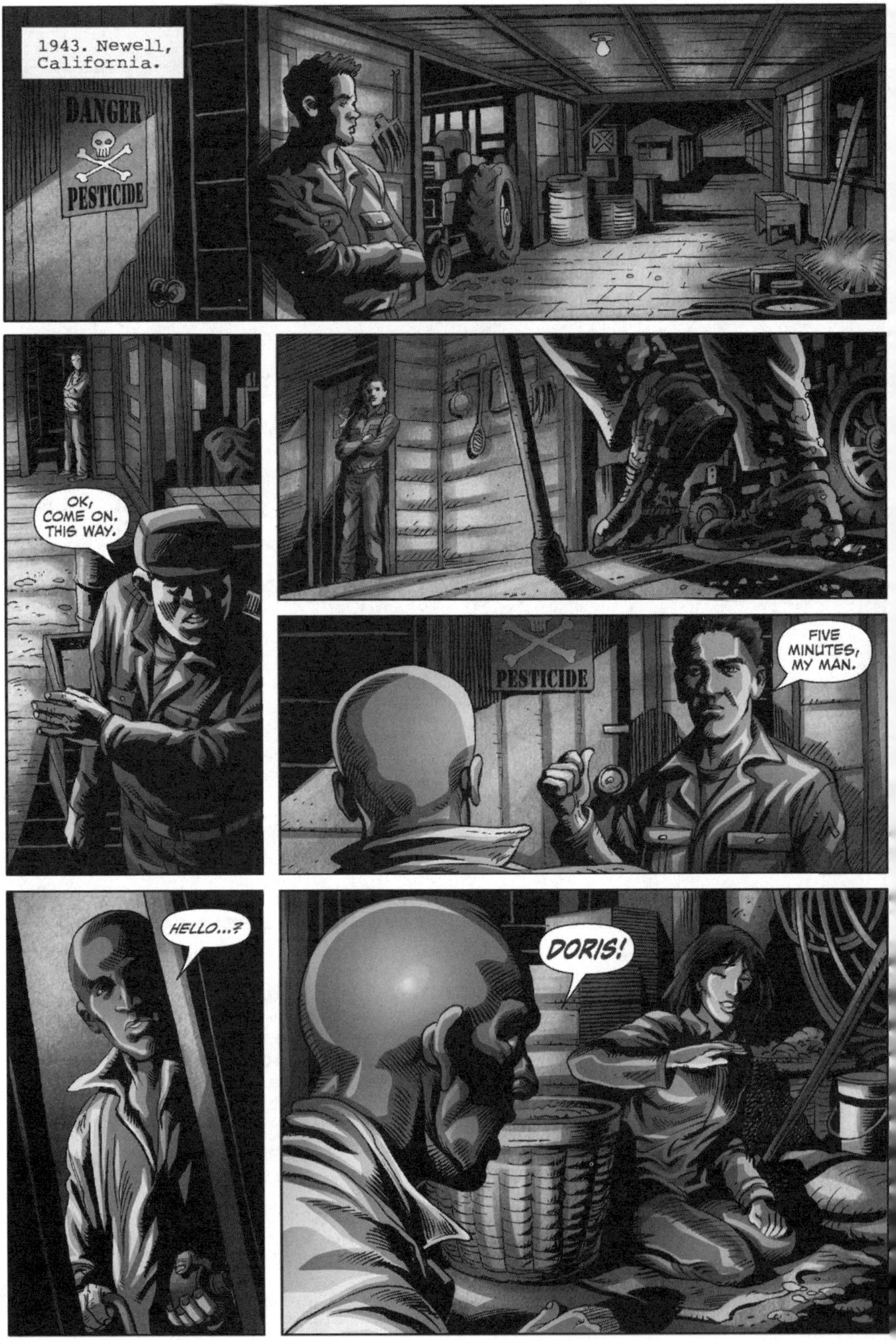
1943. Newell, California.
DANGER
PESTICIDE
OK, COME ON. THIS WAY.
PESTICIDE
FIVE MINUTES, MY MAN.
HELLO...?
DORIS!

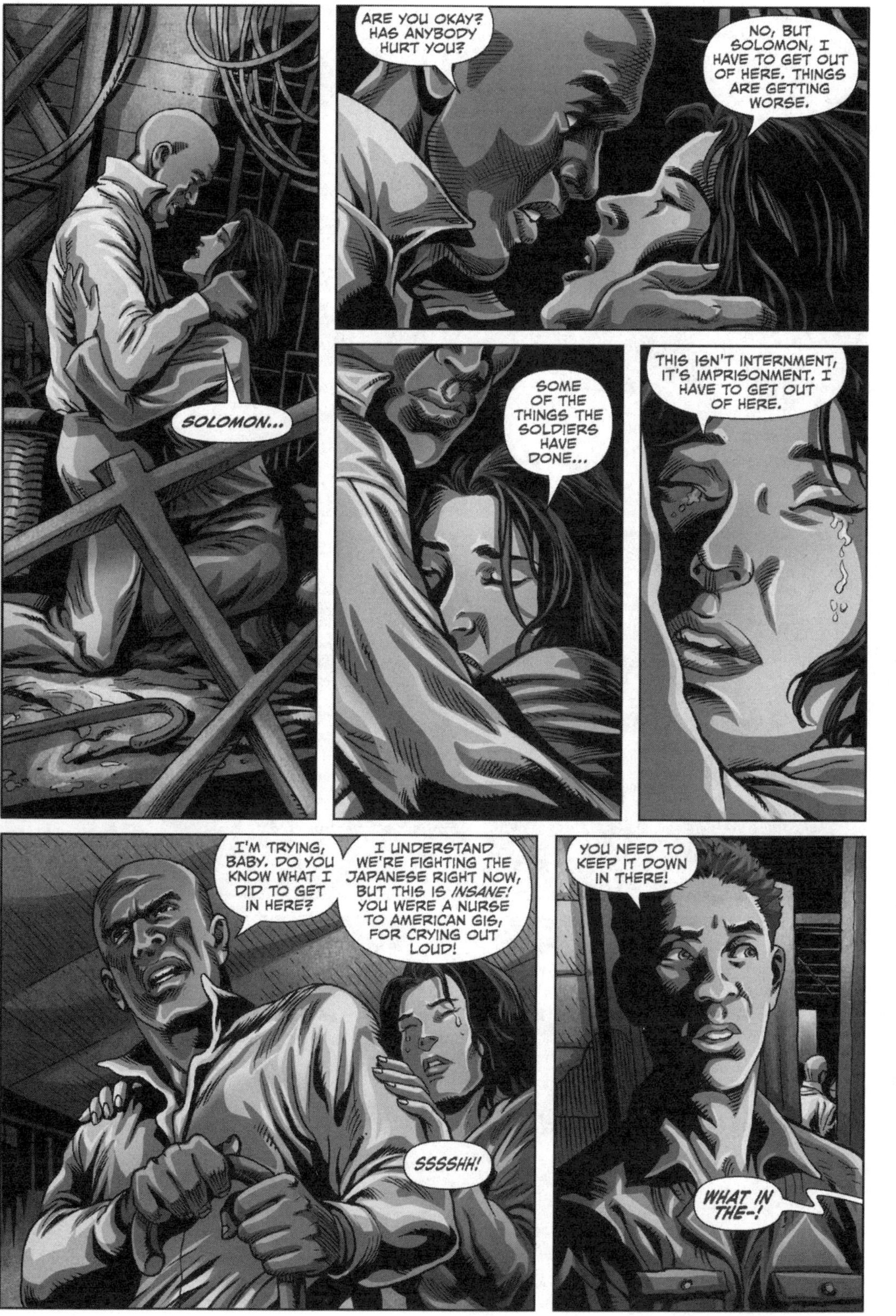
SOLOMON...
ARE YOU OKAY? HAS ANYBODY HURT YOU?
NO, BUT SOLOMON, I HAVE TO GET OUT OF HERE. THINGS ARE GETTING WORSE.
SOME OF THE THINGS THE SOLDIERS HAVE DONE...
THIS ISN'T INTERNMENT, IT'S IMPRISONMENT. I HAVE TO GET OUT OF HERE.
I'M TRYING, BABY. DO YOU KNOW WHAT I DID TO GET IN HERE?
I UNDERSTAND WE'RE FIGHTING THE JAPANESE RIGHT NOW, BUT THIS IS *INSANE!* YOU WERE A NURSE TO AMERICAN GIS, FOR CRYING OUT LOUD!
SSSSHH!
YOU NEED TO KEEP IT DOWN IN THERE!
WHAT IN THE-!

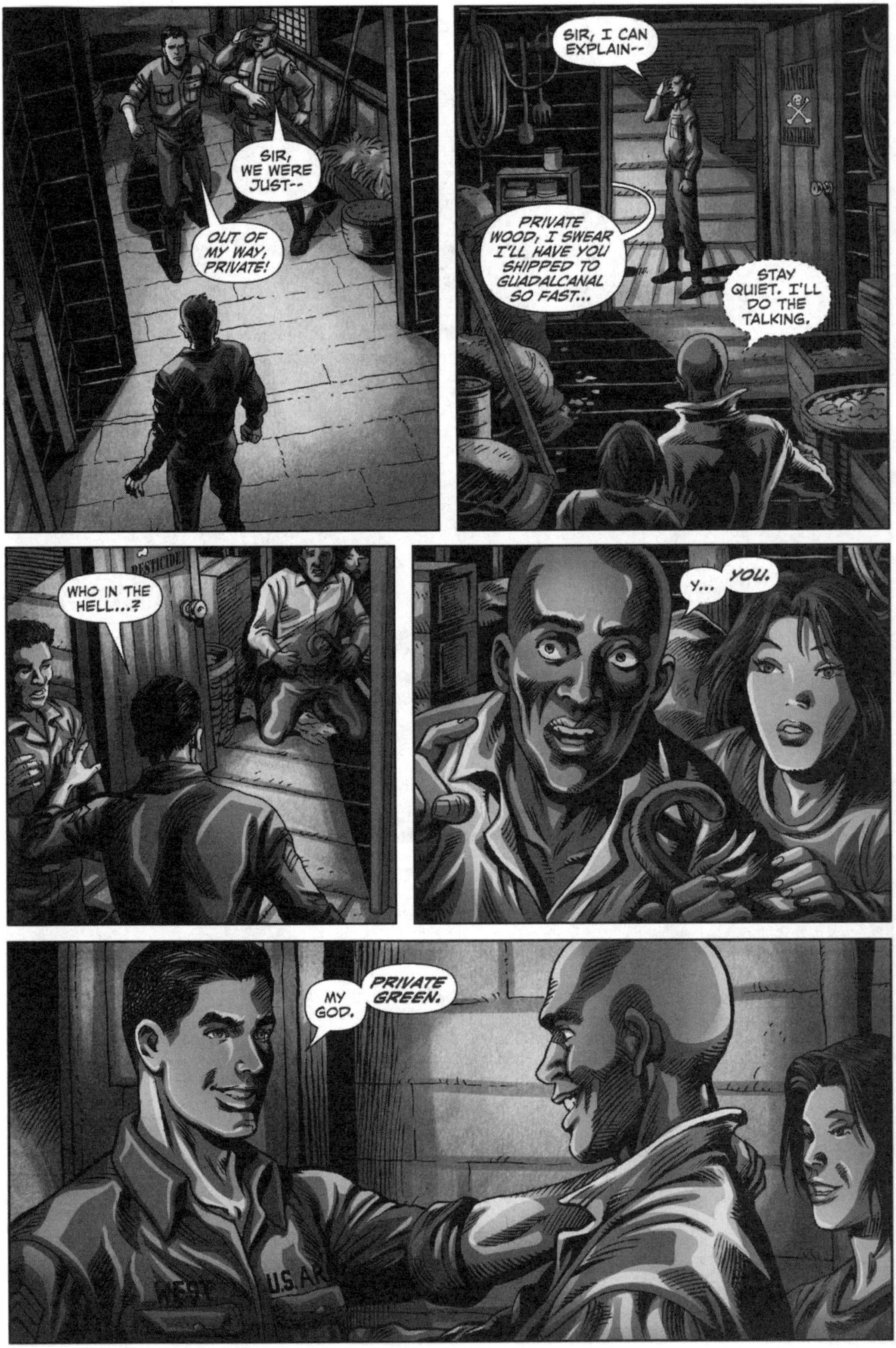
SIR, WE WERE JUST--
OUT OF MY WAY, PRIVATE!
SIR, I CAN EXPLAIN--
PRIVATE WOOD, I SWEAR I'LL HAVE YOU SHIPPED TO GUADALCANAL SO FAST...
STAY QUIET. I'LL DO THE TALKING.
PESTICIDE
WHO IN THE HELL...?
Y... YOU.
MY GOD.
PRIVATE GREEN.

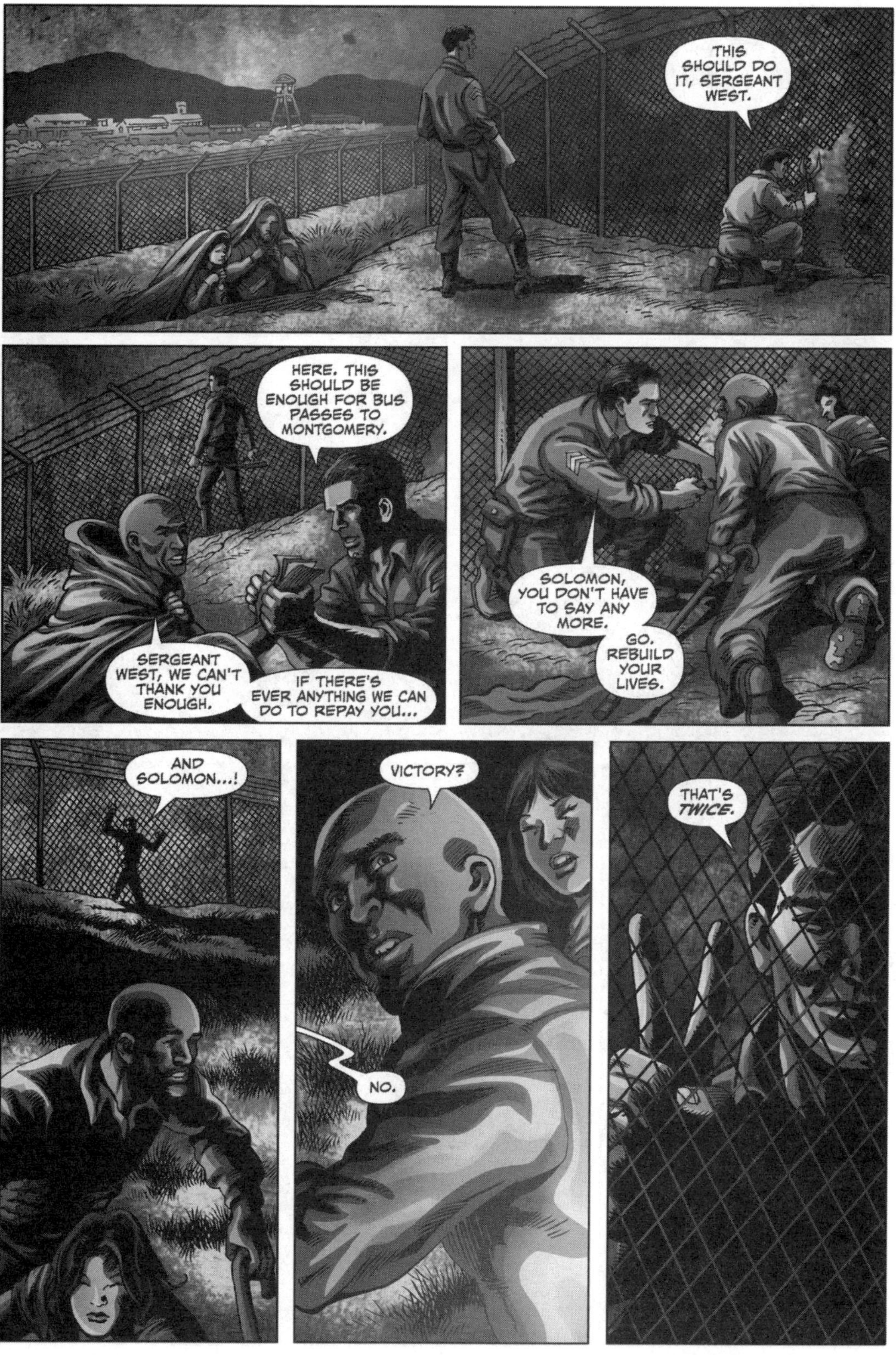
THIS SHOULD DO IT, SERGEANT WEST.
HERE. THIS SHOULD BE ENOUGH FOR BUS PASSES TO MONTGOMERY.
SERGEANT WEST, WE CAN'T THANK YOU ENOUGH.
IF THERE'S EVER ANYTHING WE CAN DO TO REPAY YOU...
SOLOMON, YOU DON'T HAVE TO SAY ANY MORE.
GO. REBUILD YOUR LIVES.
AND SOLOMON...!
VICTORY?
NO.
THAT'S *TWICE*.

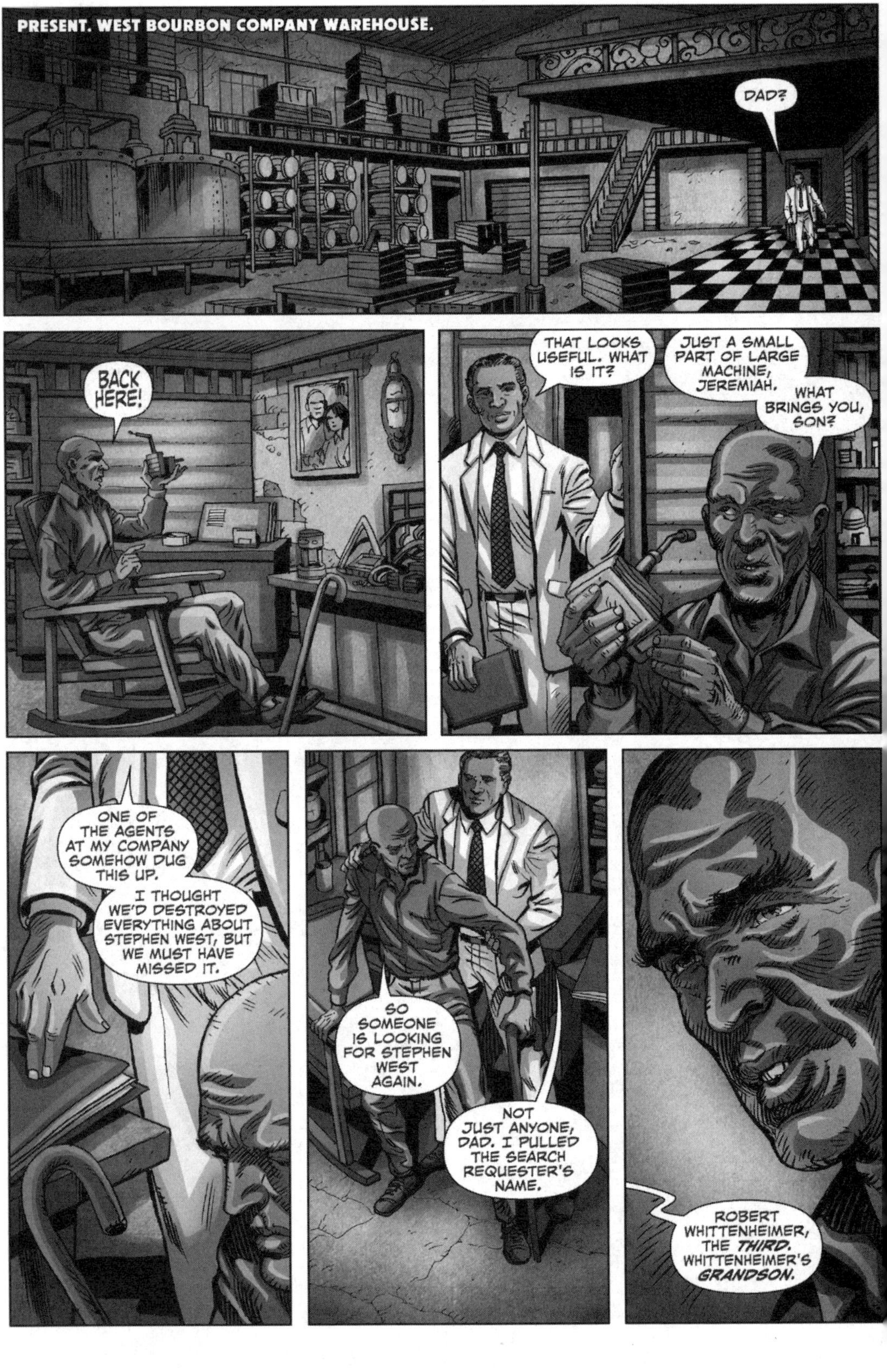
PRESENT. WEST BOURBON COMPANY WAREHOUSE.
DAD?
BACK HERE!
THAT LOOKS USEFUL. WHAT IS IT?
JUST A SMALL PART OF LARGE MACHINE, JEREMIAH.
WHAT BRINGS YOU, SON?
ONE OF THE AGENTS AT MY COMPANY SOMEHOW DUG THIS UP.
I THOUGHT WE'D DESTROYED EVERYTHING ABOUT STEPHEN WEST, BUT WE MUST HAVE MISSED IT.
SO SOMEONE IS LOOKING FOR STEPHEN WEST AGAIN.
NOT JUST ANYONE, DAD. I PULLED THE SEARCH REQUESTER'S NAME.
ROBERT WHITTENHEIMER, THE THIRD. WHITTENHEIMER'S GRANDSON.

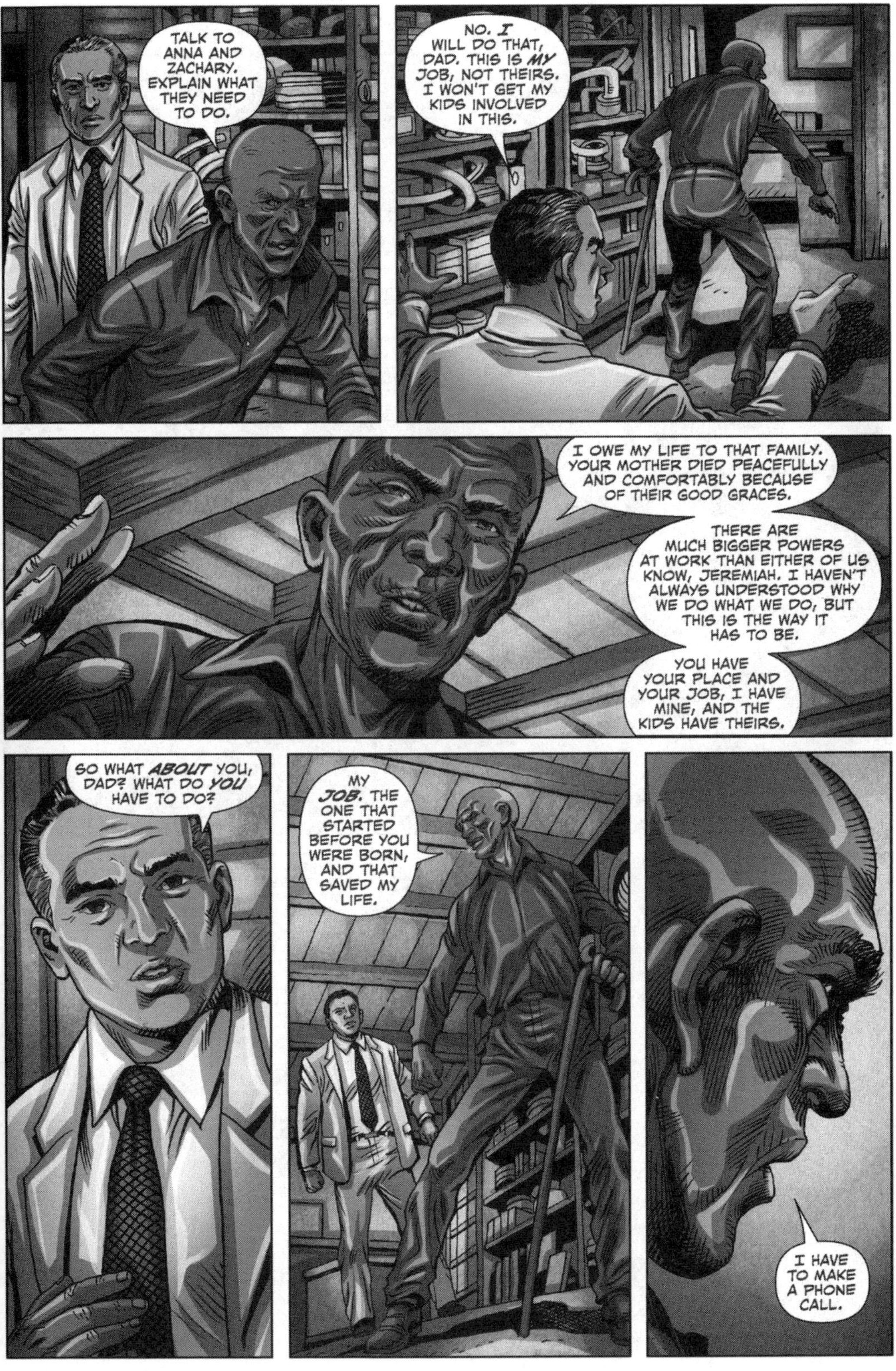
TALK TO ANNA AND ZACHARY. EXPLAIN WHAT THEY NEED TO DO.
NO. *I* WILL DO THAT, DAD. THIS IS *MY* JOB, NOT THEIRS. I WON'T GET MY KIDS INVOLVED IN THIS.
I OWE MY LIFE TO THAT FAMILY. YOUR MOTHER DIED PEACEFULLY AND COMFORTABLY BECAUSE OF THEIR GOOD GRACES.
THERE ARE MUCH BIGGER POWERS AT WORK THAN EITHER OF US KNOW, JEREMIAH. I HAVEN'T ALWAYS UNDERSTOOD WHY WE DO WHAT WE DO, BUT THIS IS THE WAY IT HAS TO BE.
YOU HAVE YOUR PLACE AND YOUR JOB, I HAVE MINE, AND THE KIDS HAVE THEIRS.
SO WHAT *ABOUT* YOU, DAD? WHAT DO *YOU* HAVE TO DO?
MY *JOB*. THE ONE THAT STARTED BEFORE YOU WERE BORN, AND THAT SAVED MY LIFE.
I HAVE TO MAKE A PHONE CALL.

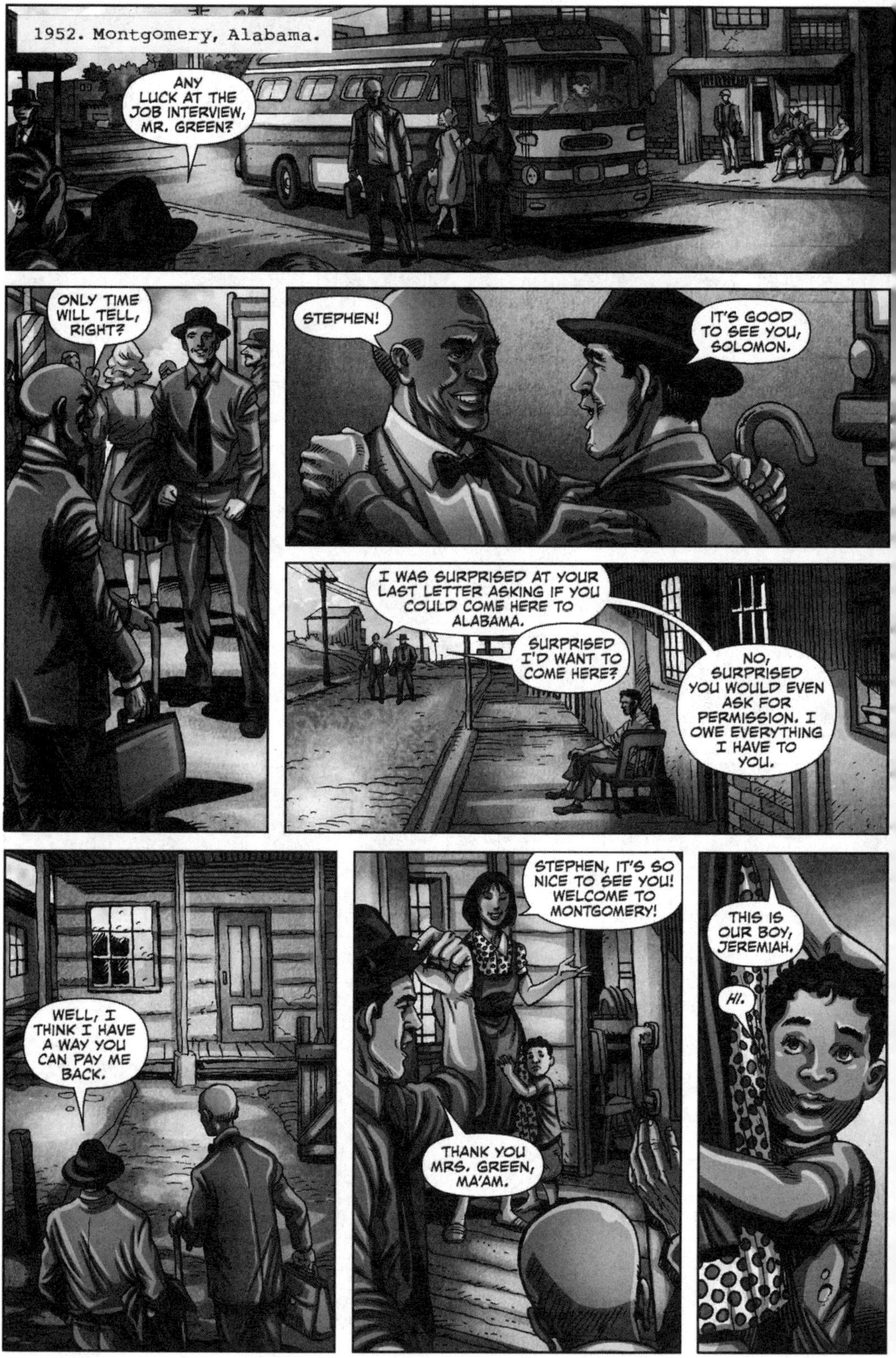
1952. Montgomery, Alabama.
ANY LUCK AT THE JOB INTERVIEW, MR. GREEN?
ONLY TIME WILL TELL, RIGHT?
STEPHEN!
IT'S GOOD TO SEE YOU, SOLOMON.
I WAS SURPRISED AT YOUR LAST LETTER ASKING IF YOU COULD COME HERE TO ALABAMA.
SURPRISED I'D WANT TO COME HERE?
NO, SURPRISED YOU WOULD EVEN ASK FOR PERMISSION. I OWE EVERYTHING I HAVE TO YOU.
WELL, I THINK I HAVE A WAY YOU CAN PAY ME BACK.
STEPHEN, IT'S SO NICE TO SEE YOU! WELCOME TO MONTGOMERY!
THANK YOU MRS. GREEN, MA'AM.
THIS IS OUR BOY, JEREMIAH.
HI.

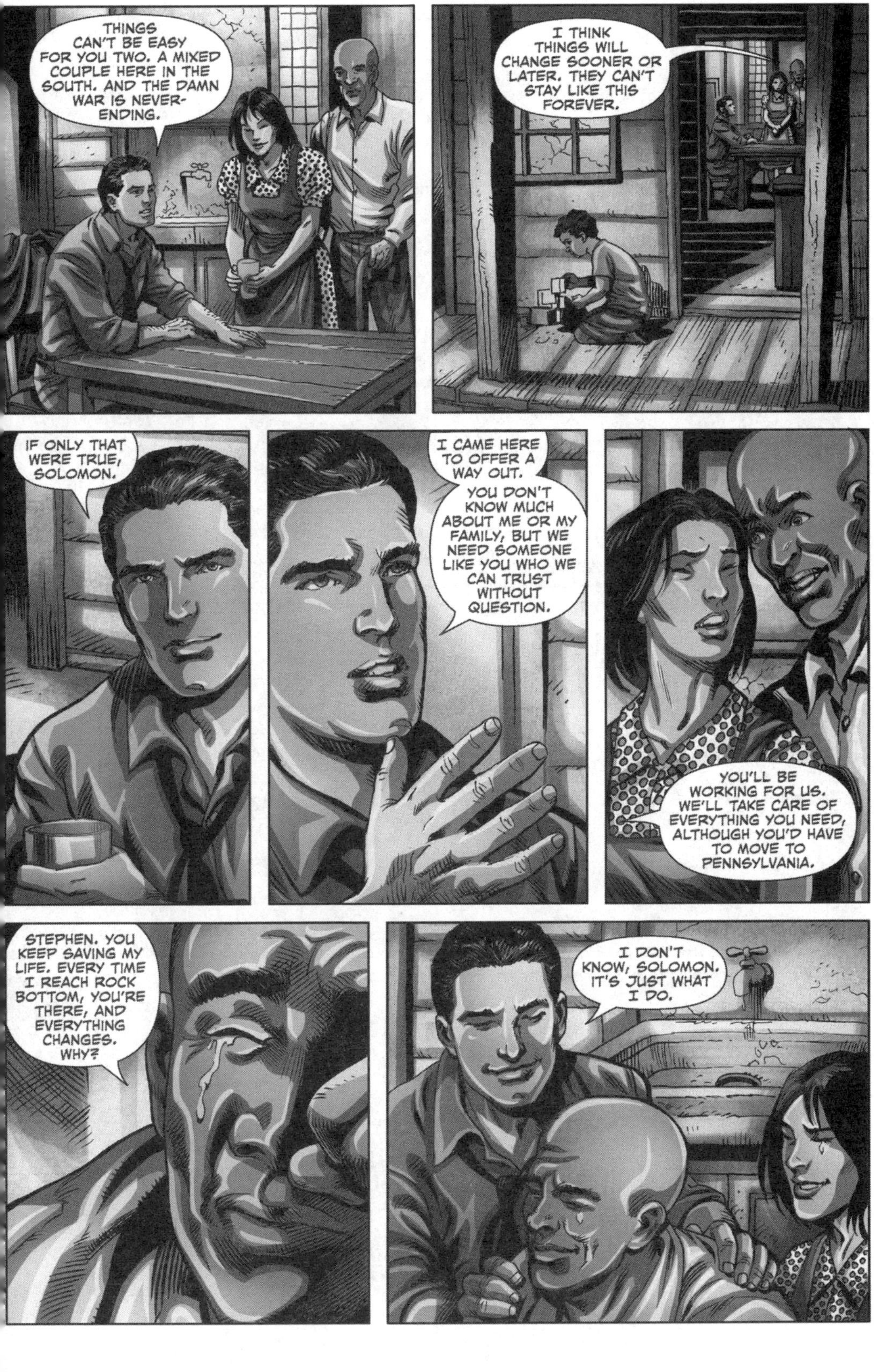
THINGS CAN'T BE EASY FOR YOU TWO. A MIXED COUPLE HERE IN THE SOUTH. AND THE DAMN WAR IS NEVER-ENDING.
I THINK THINGS WILL CHANGE SOONER OR LATER. THEY CAN'T STAY LIKE THIS FOREVER.
IF ONLY THAT WERE TRUE, SOLOMON.
I CAME HERE TO OFFER A WAY OUT.
YOU DON'T KNOW MUCH ABOUT ME OR MY FAMILY, BUT WE NEED SOMEONE LIKE YOU WHO WE CAN TRUST WITHOUT QUESTION.
YOU'LL BE WORKING FOR US. WE'LL TAKE CARE OF EVERYTHING YOU NEED, ALTHOUGH YOU'D HAVE TO MOVE TO PENNSYLVANIA.
STEPHEN. YOU KEEP SAVING MY LIFE. EVERY TIME I REACH ROCK BOTTOM, YOU'RE THERE, AND EVERYTHING CHANGES. WHY?
I DON'T KNOW, SOLOMON. IT'S JUST WHAT I DO.

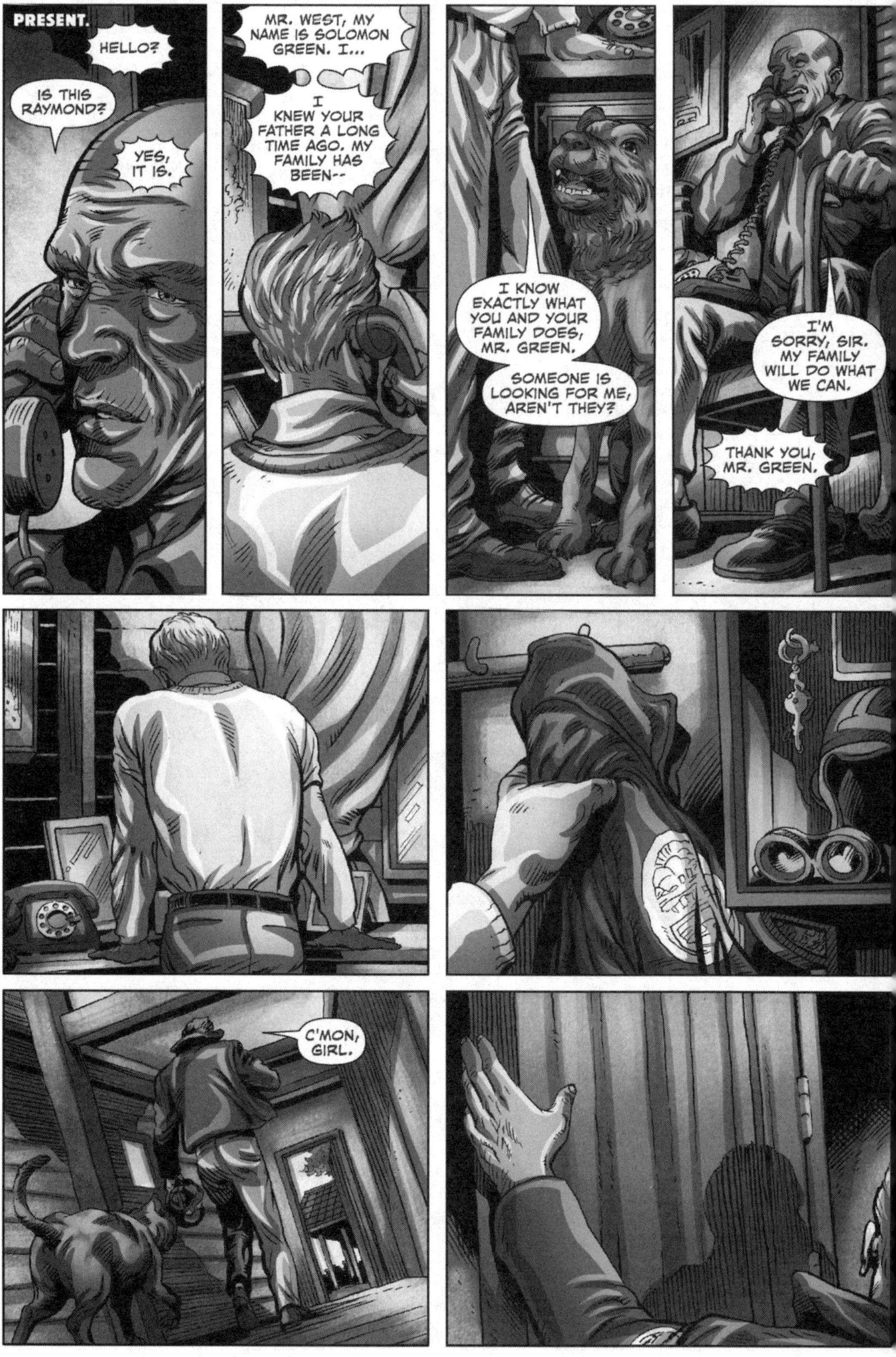
PRESENT.
HELLO?
IS THIS RAYMOND?
YES, IT IS.
MR. WEST, MY NAME IS SOLOMON GREEN. I...
I KNEW YOUR FATHER A LONG TIME AGO. MY FAMILY HAS BEEN--
I KNOW EXACTLY WHAT YOU AND YOUR FAMILY DOES, MR. GREEN.
SOMEONE IS LOOKING FOR ME, AREN'T THEY?
I'M SORRY, SIR. MY FAMILY WILL DO WHAT WE CAN.
THANK YOU, MR. GREEN.
C'MON, GIRL.

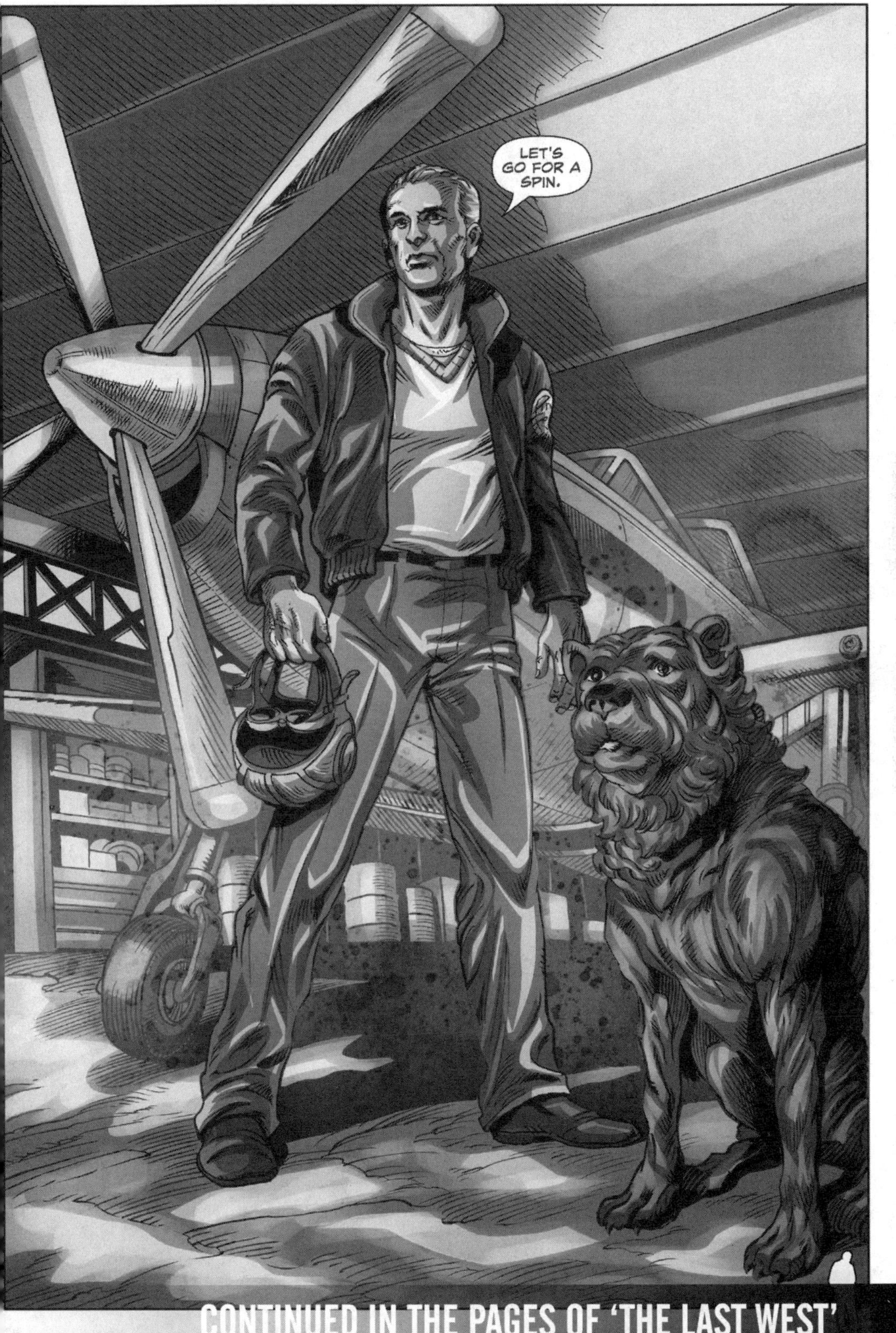
LET'S GO FOR A SPIN.

CONTINUED IN THE PAGES OF 'THE LAST WEST'

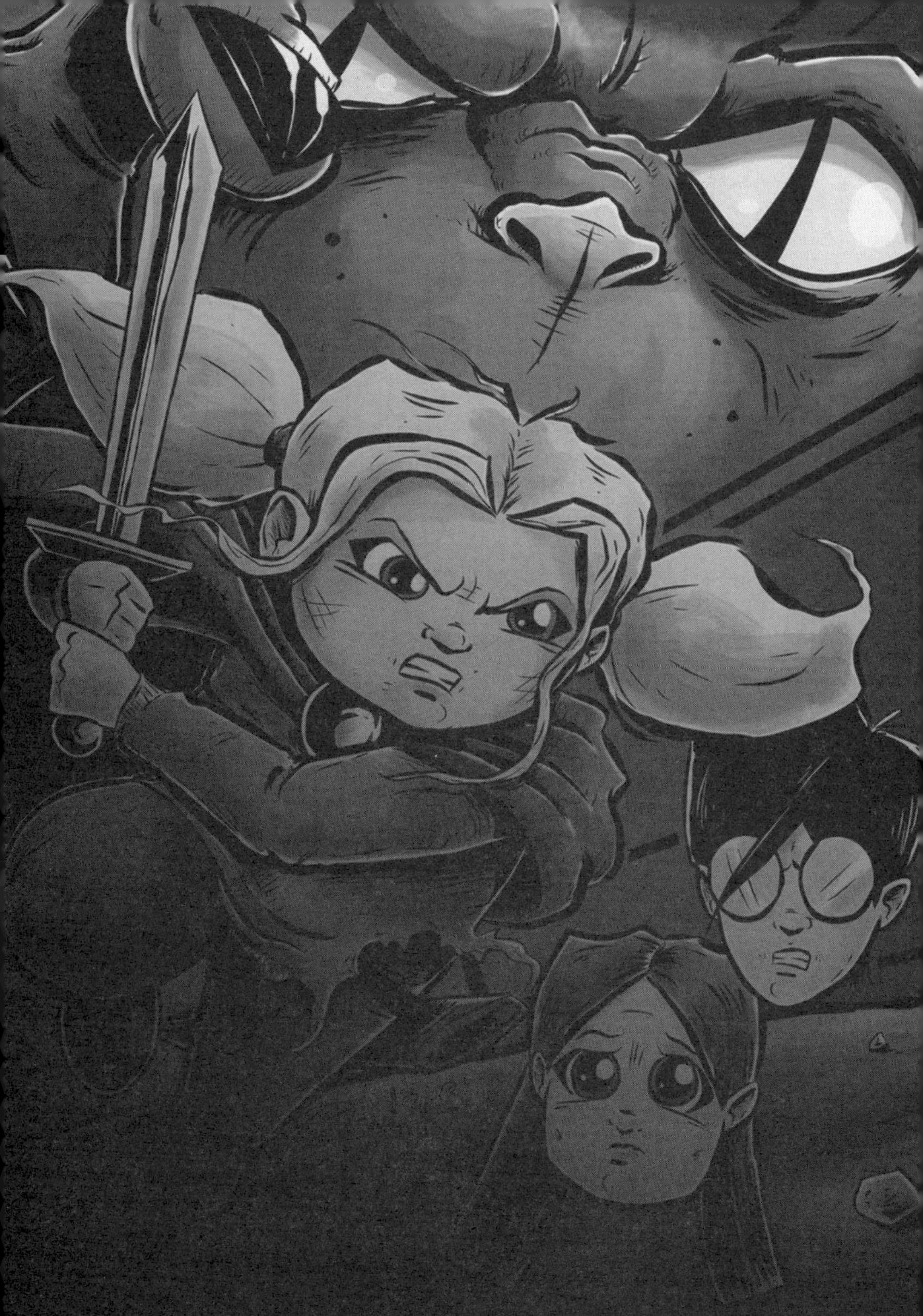

LILITH DARK

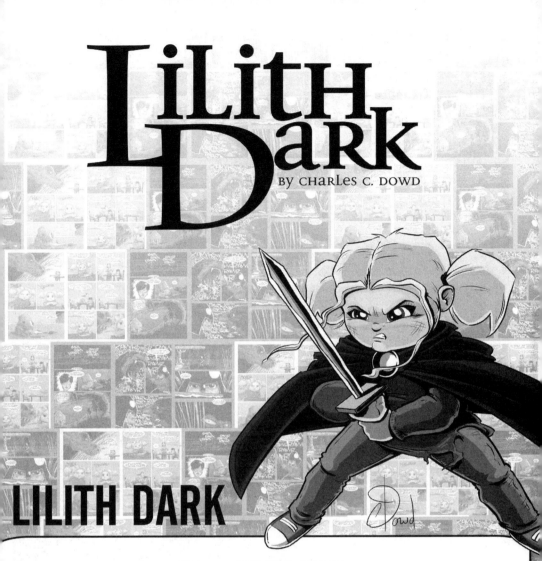

LILITH DARK

BY CHARLES C. DOWD

LILITH DARK

"I am LILITH DARK!
And I'm not ascared of you, Beastie!"

Lilith Dark has no time for tea parties and princess stuff -
she's far too busy fighting off wicked creatures and fantastic
beasts... or at least that's how she imagines things. One day,
Lilith follows a mysterious kitten into an old tree and discovers
an entire world of real beasties that has been living right under
her nose! With her big sister held captive, Lilith must face
her fears, rescue her sister from the evil beasties,
and save the day before bedtime!

Age: 9   Height: 4'1"   Weight: 66 lbs.

First Appearance: LILITH DARK #1 (2013)

Created by Charles Dowd   Illustration by Charles Dowd

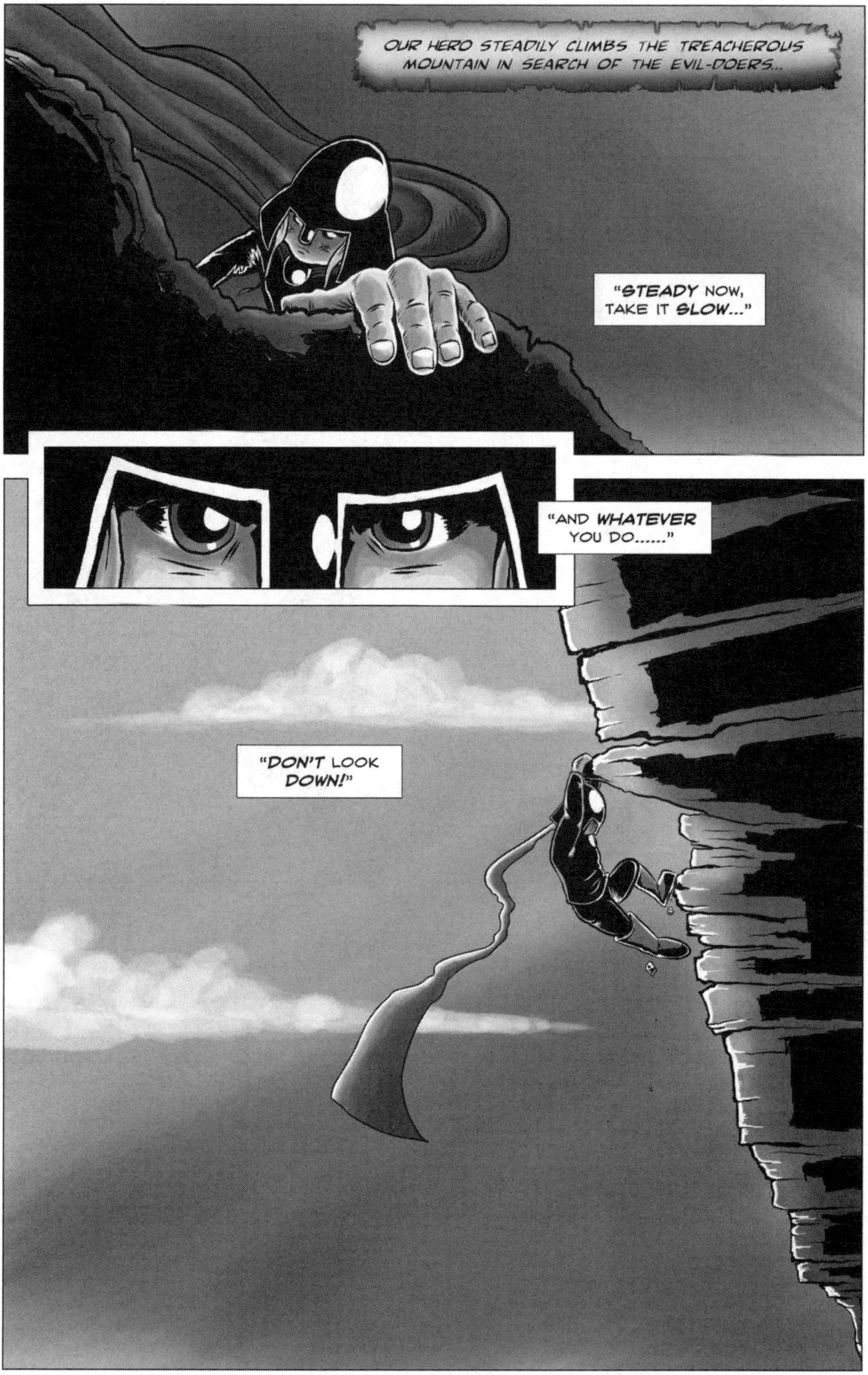
OUR HERO STEADILY CLIMBS THE TREACHEROUS MOUNTAIN IN SEARCH OF THE EVIL-DOERS...
"STEADY NOW, TAKE IT SLOW..."
"AND WHATEVER YOU DO......"
"DON'T LOOK DOWN!"

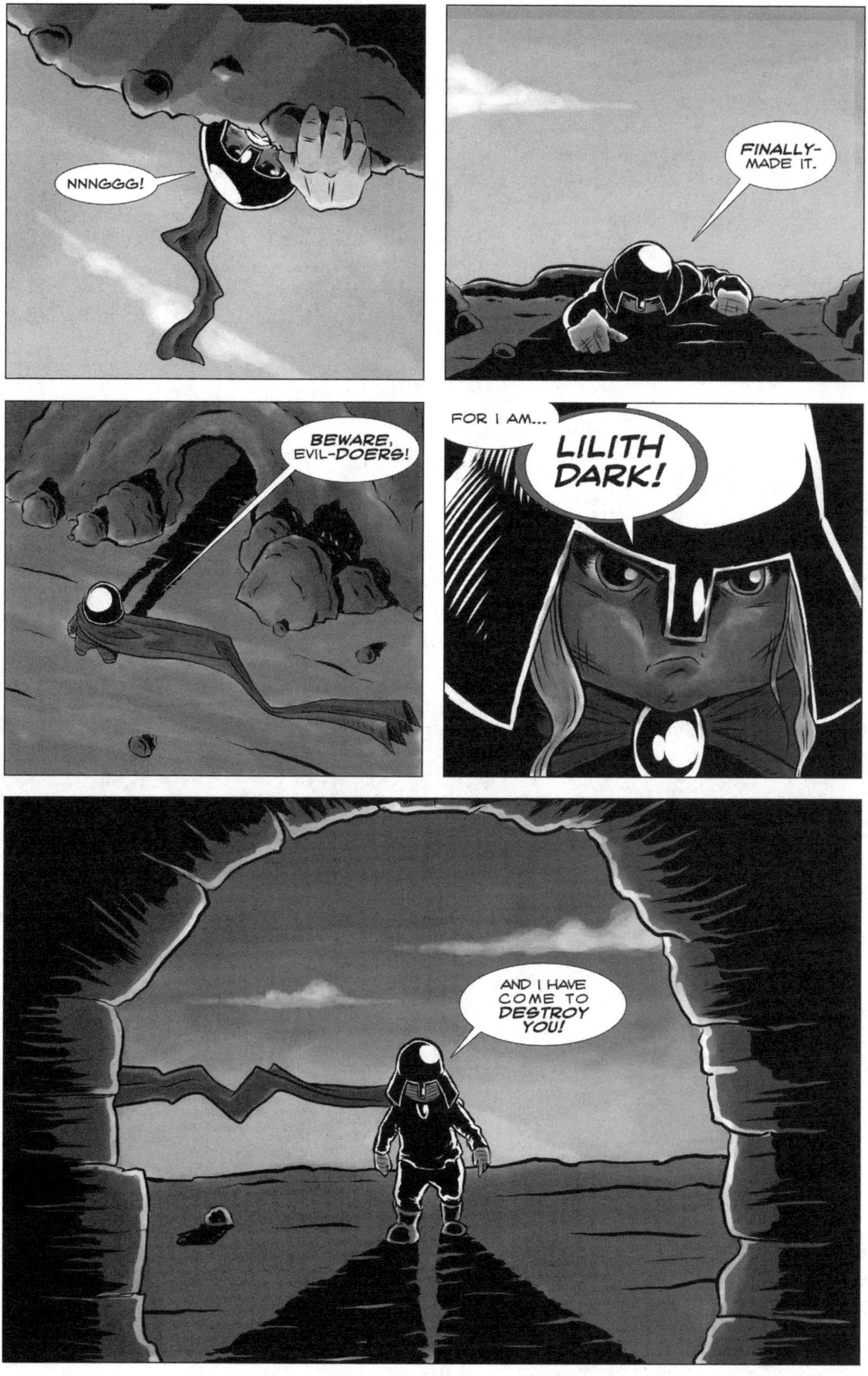
NNNGGG!
FINALLY- MADE IT.
BEWARE, EVIL-DOERS!
FOR I AM...
LILITH DARK!
AND I HAVE COME TO DESTROY YOU!

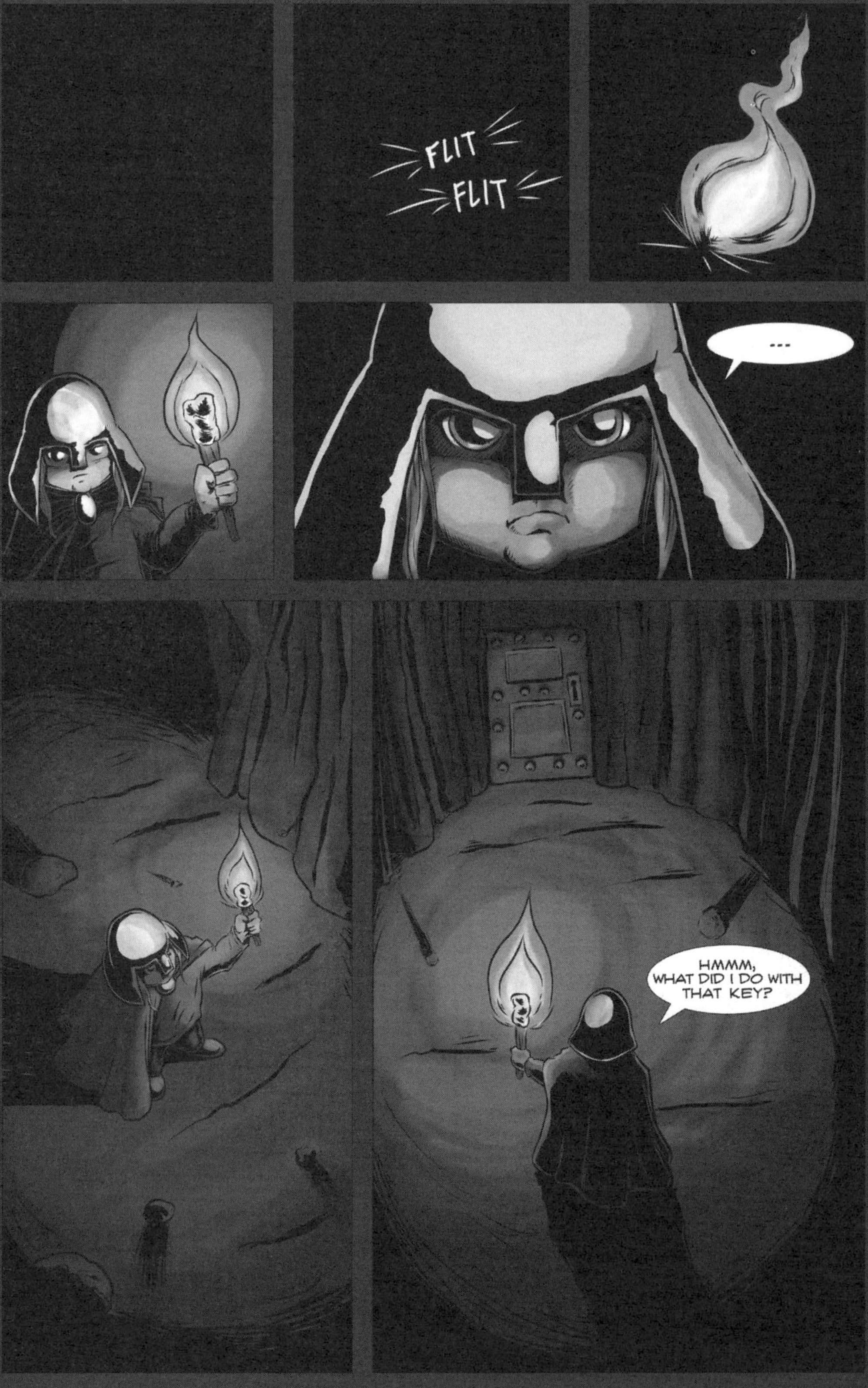
FLIT
FLIT
...
HMMM, WHAT DID I DO WITH THAT KEY?

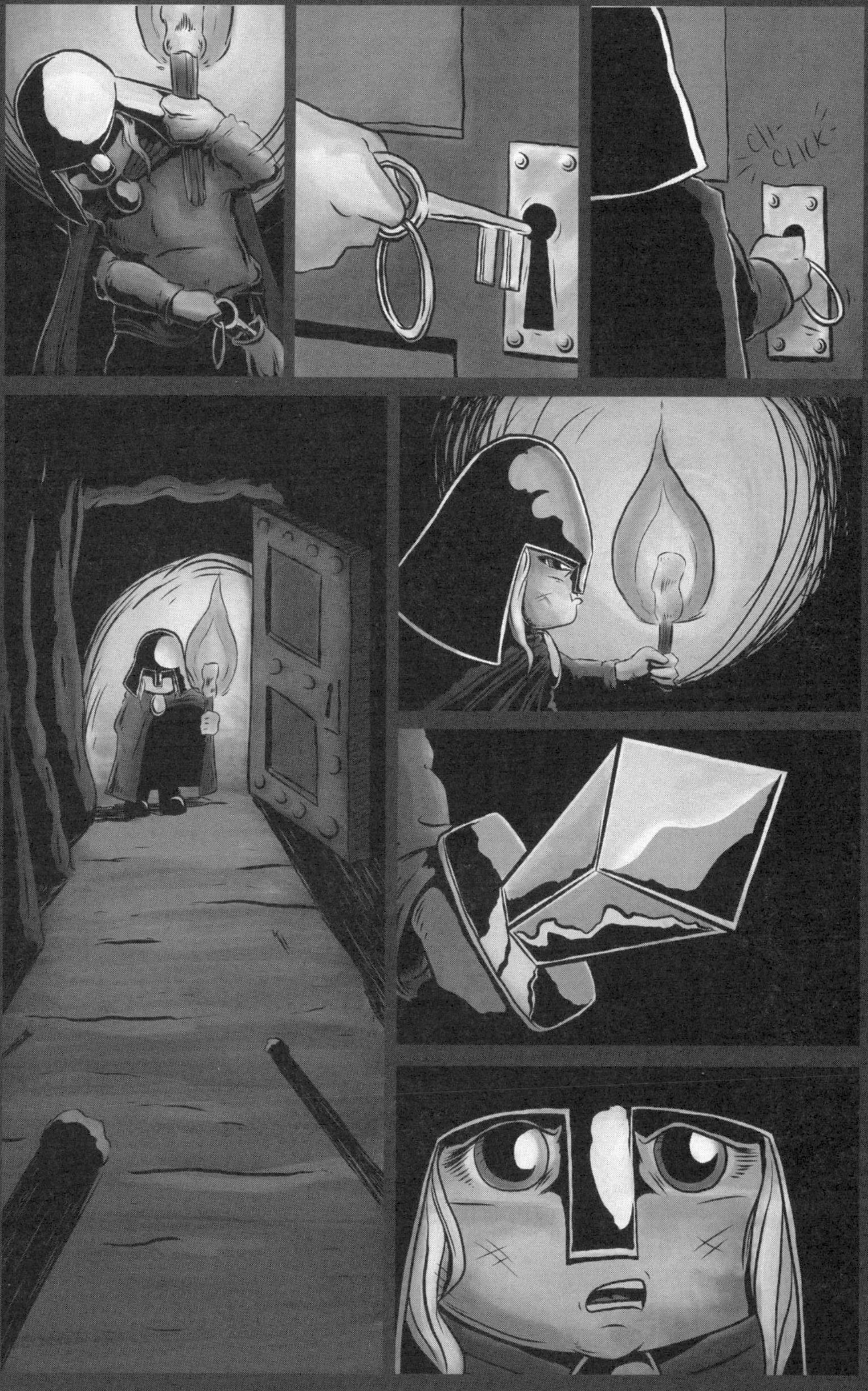
CLI-
CLICK

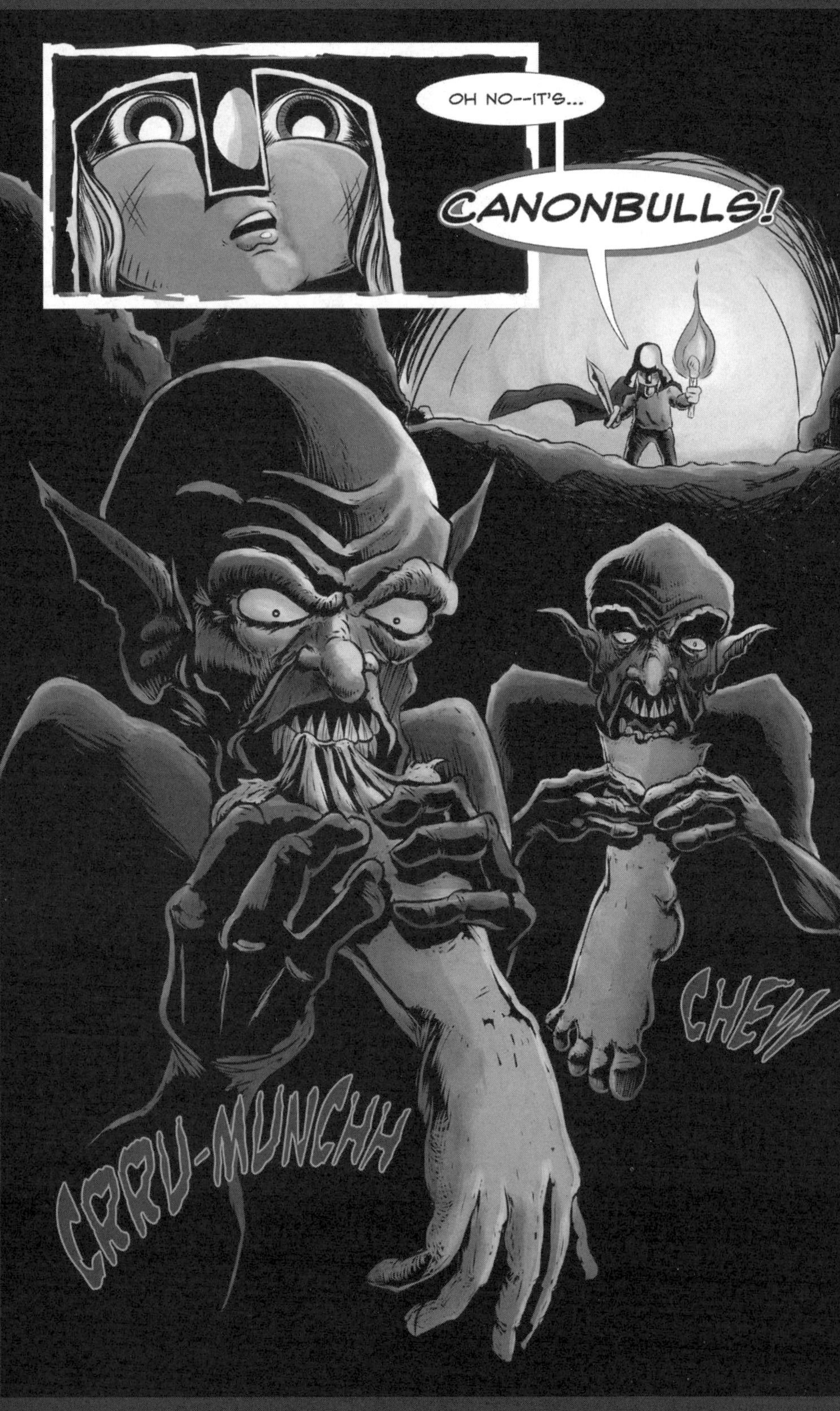
OH NO--IT'S...
CANONBULLS!
CHEW
CRRU-MUNCHH

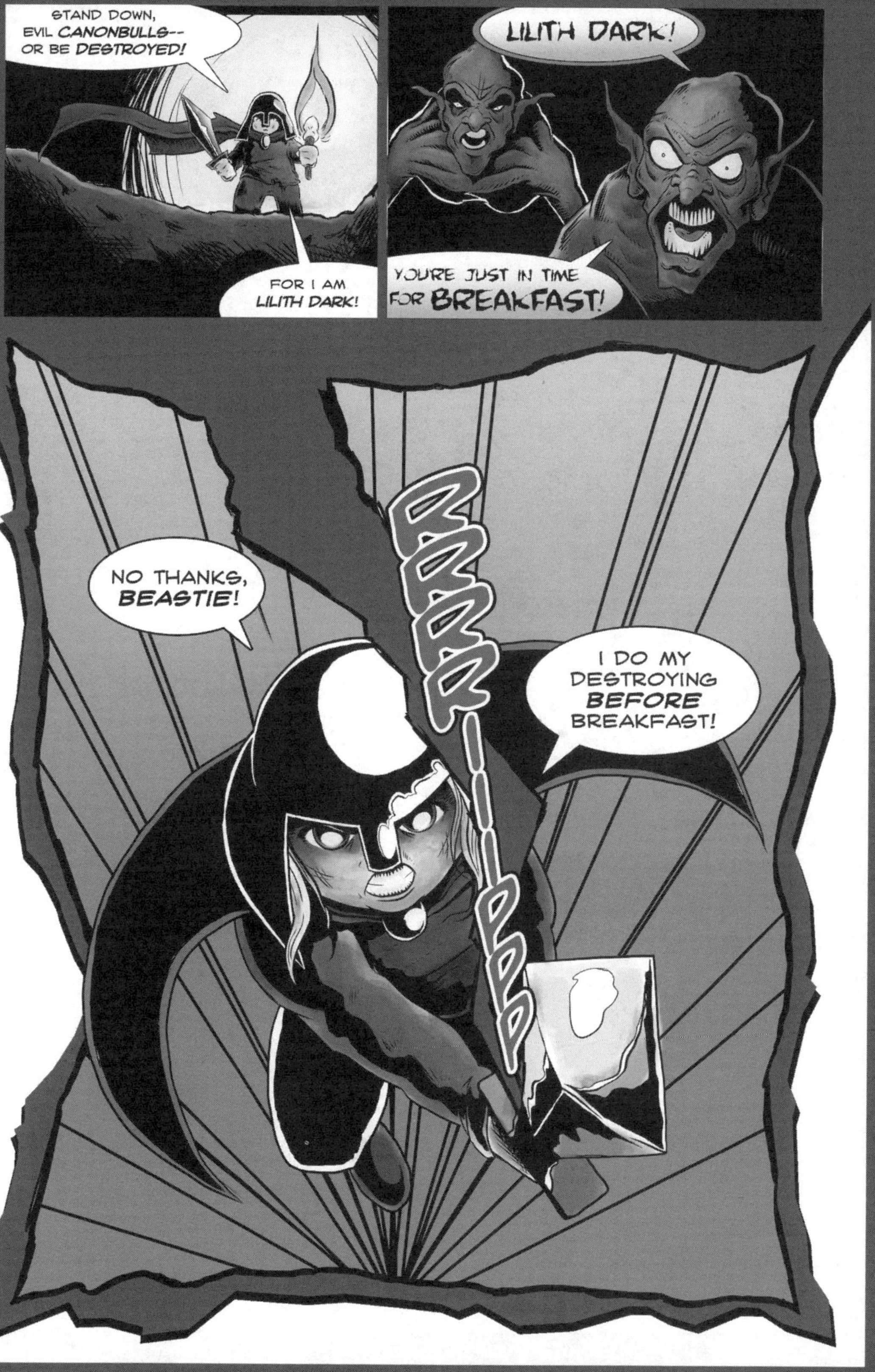
STAND DOWN, EVIL CANONBULLS-- OR BE DESTROYED!
FOR I AM LILITH DARK!
LILITH DARK!
YOU'RE JUST IN TIME FOR BREAKFAST!
NO THANKS, BEASTIE!
BRRRR-I-I-I-PPPP
I DO MY DESTROYING BEFORE BREAKFAST!

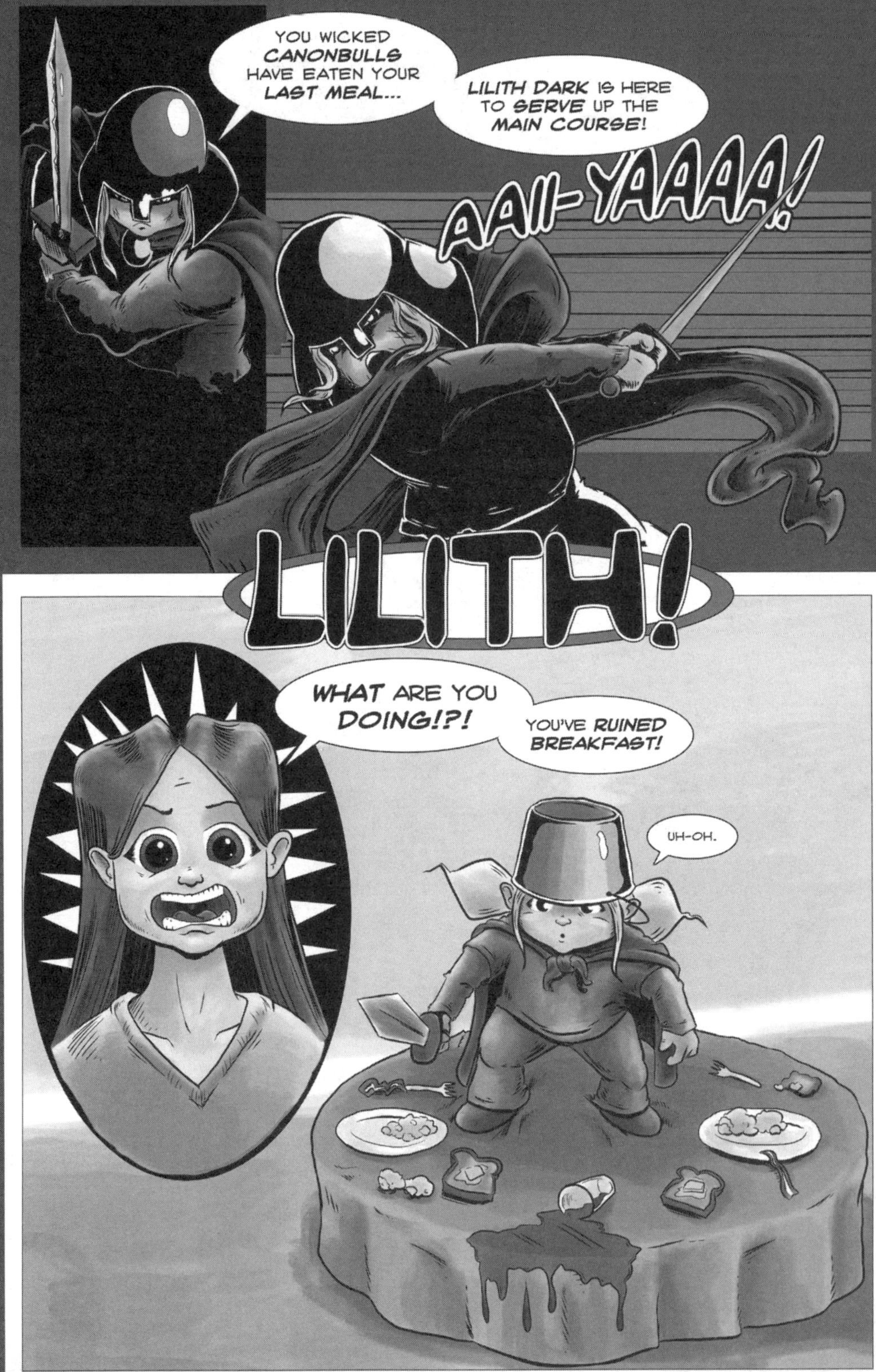
YOU WICKED CANONBULLS HAVE EATEN YOUR LAST MEAL...
LILITH DARK IS HERE TO SERVE UP THE MAIN COURSE!
AAII-YAAAA!
LILITH!
WHAT ARE YOU DOING!?!
YOU'VE RUINED BREAKFAST!
UH-OH.

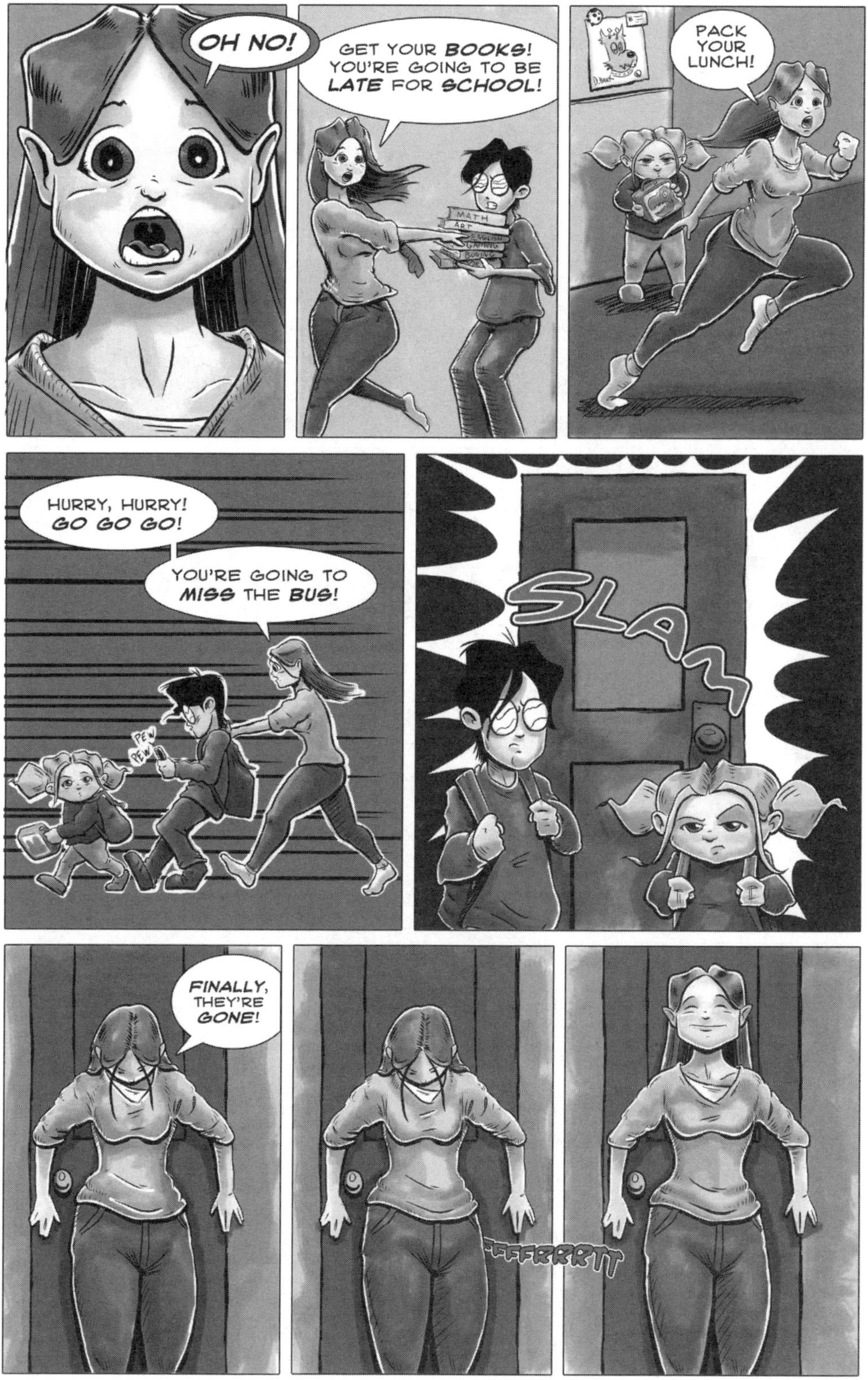
OH NO!
GET YOUR BOOKS! YOU'RE GOING TO BE LATE FOR SCHOOL!
MATH
ART
PACK YOUR LUNCH!
HURRY, HURRY! GO GO GO!
YOU'RE GOING TO MISS THE BUS!
PEW PEW
SLAM
FINALLY, THEY'RE GONE!
FFFFRRRRTT

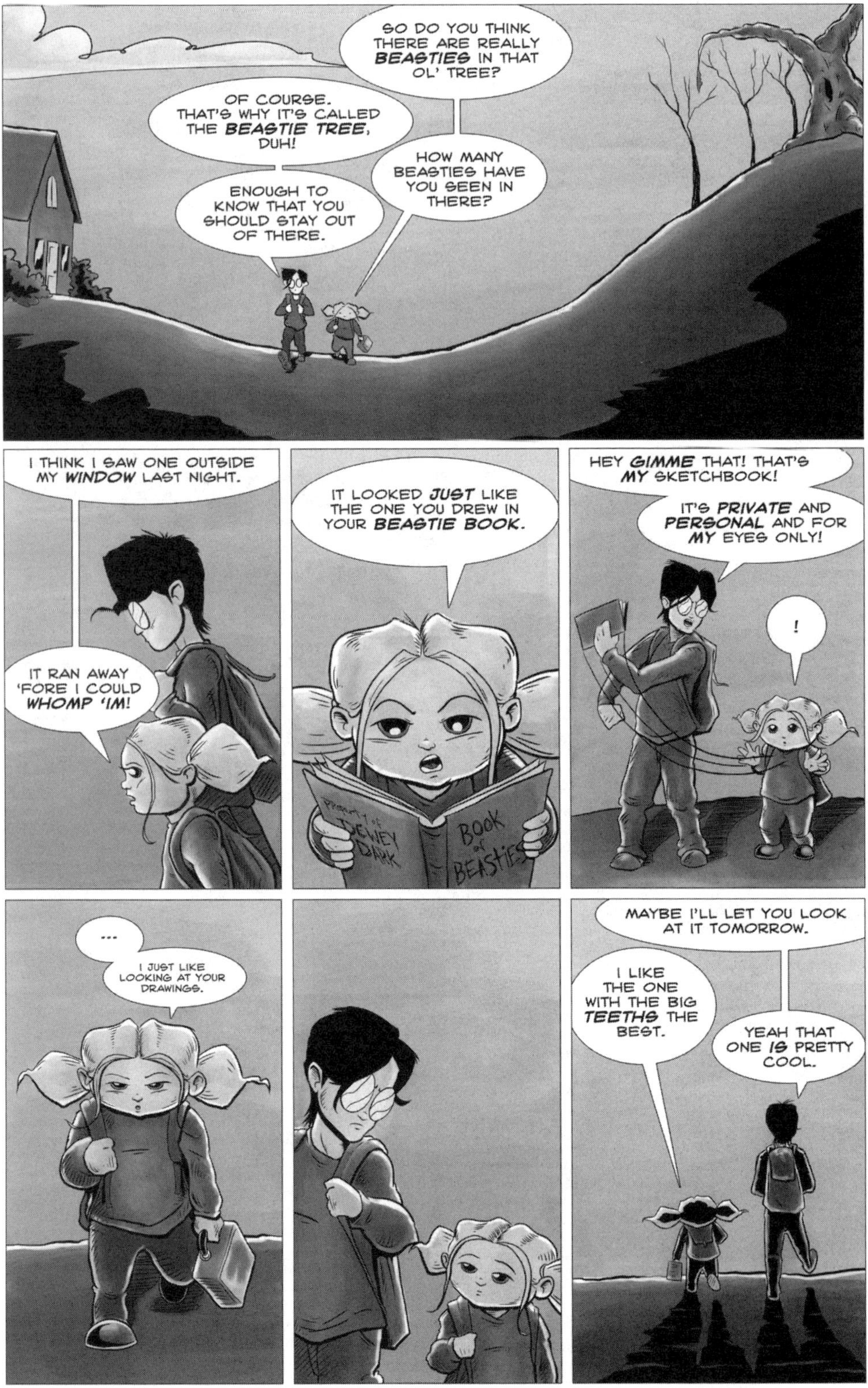
SO DO YOU THINK THERE ARE REALLY BEASTIES IN THAT OL' TREE?
OF COURSE. THAT'S WHY IT'S CALLED THE BEASTIE TREE, DUH!
HOW MANY BEASTIES HAVE YOU SEEN IN THERE?
ENOUGH TO KNOW THAT YOU SHOULD STAY OUT OF THERE.
I THINK I SAW ONE OUTSIDE MY WINDOW LAST NIGHT.
IT RAN AWAY 'FORE I COULD WHOMP 'IM!
IT LOOKED JUST LIKE THE ONE YOU DREW IN YOUR BEASTIE BOOK.
Property of DEWEY DARK
BOOK of BEASTIES
HEY GIMME THAT! THAT'S MY SKETCHBOOK!
IT'S PRIVATE AND PERSONAL AND FOR MY EYES ONLY!
!
...
I JUST LIKE LOOKING AT YOUR DRAWINGS.
MAYBE I'LL LET YOU LOOK AT IT TOMORROW.
I LIKE THE ONE WITH THE BIG TEETHS THE BEST.
YEAH THAT ONE IS PRETTY COOL.

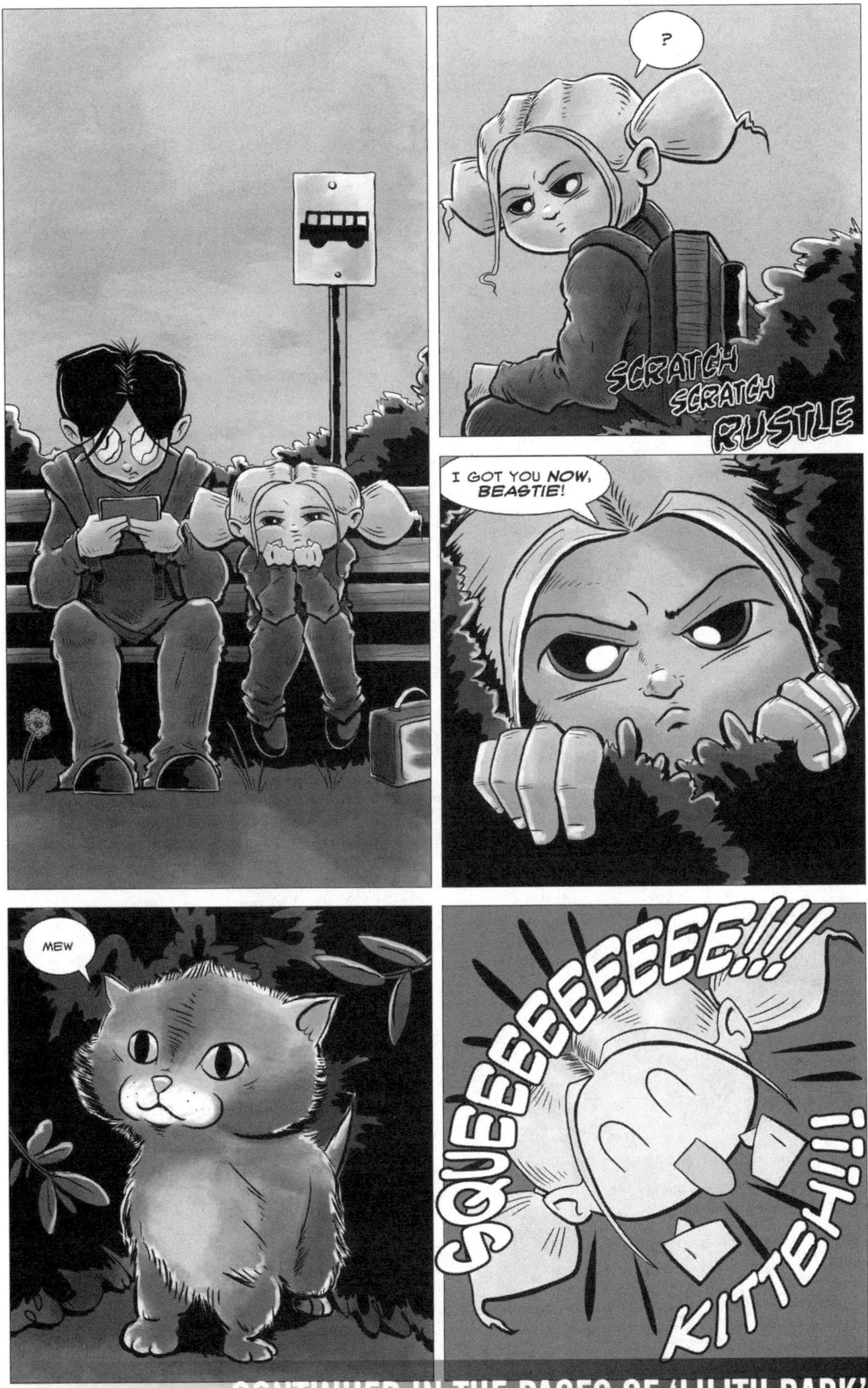
?
SCRATCH
SCRATCH
RUSTLE
I GOT YOU NOW, BEASTIE!
MEW
SQUEEEEEEEEEE!!!
KITTEH!!!!

CONTINUED IN THE PAGES OF 'LILITH DARK'

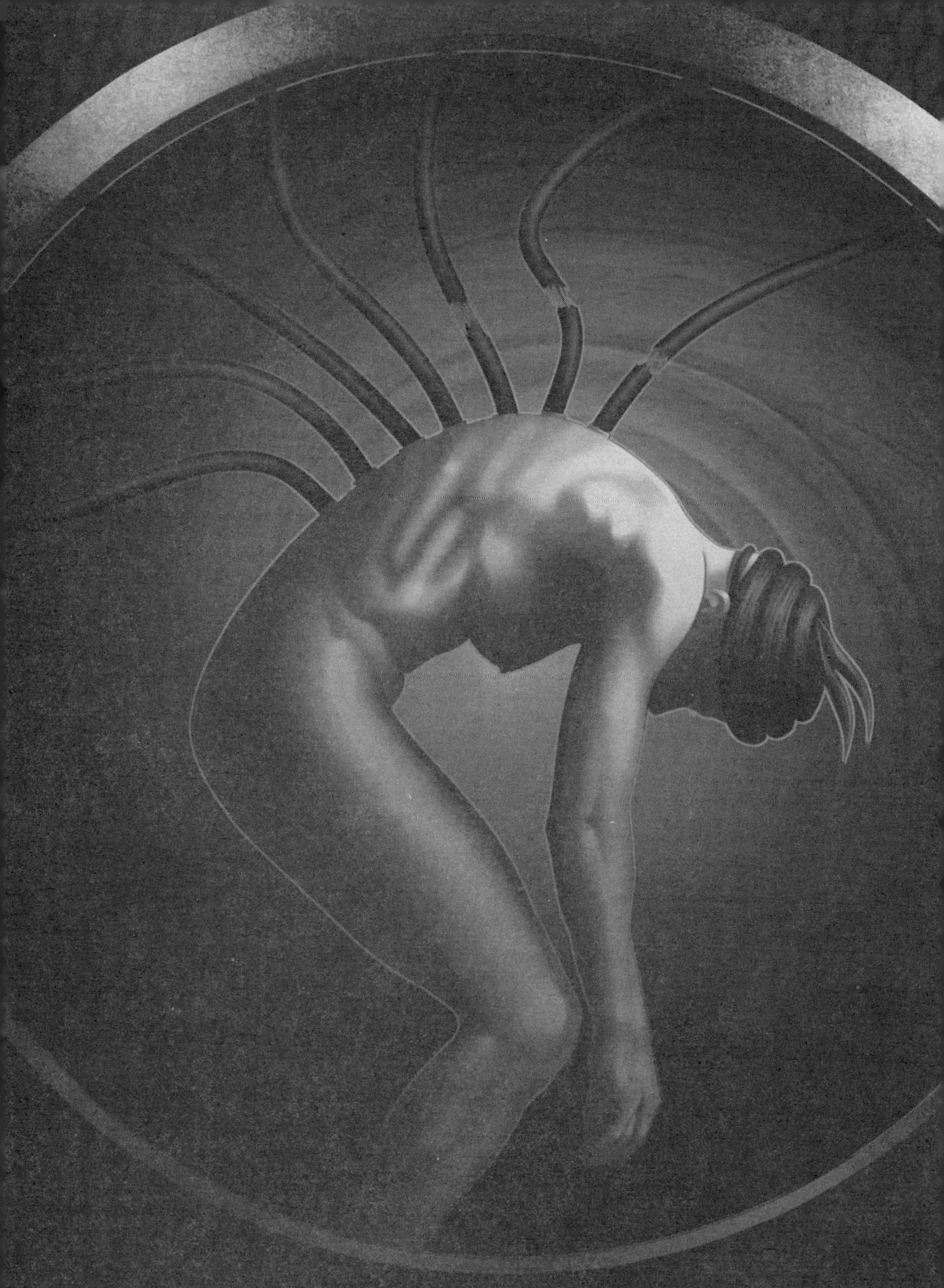

THE MACHINE STOPS

THE MACHINE STOPS

VASHTI & KUNO

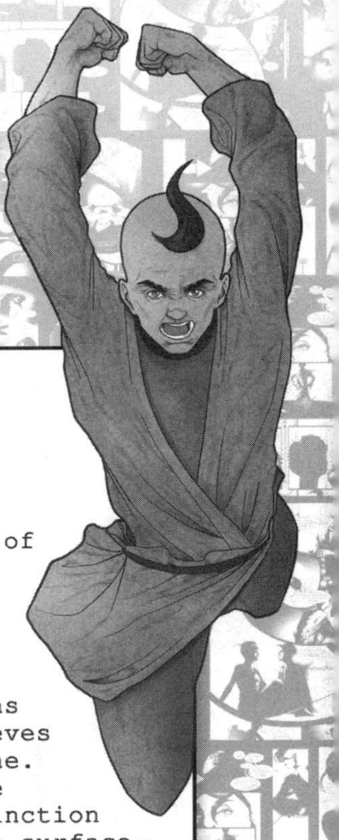

"I dream of going to the surface...
if only they would permit me.
Do you not long to see the stars?"

Adapted from the E.M. Forster short story of the same name, "The Machine Stops" prophesizes a world in which humans have lost the ability to live on Earth's surface. Survivors dwell in subterranean colonies of individual pods where the Machine regulates nearly all life functions and interactions. However, one rebel believes that there is more to life than the Machine. The system is breaking down, and with time running out the only way to prevent extinction is to return to the natural world —the surface— before the Machine stops.

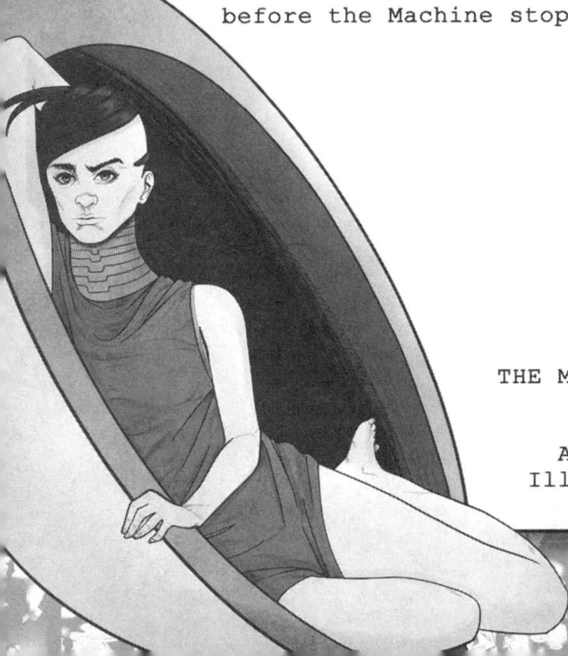

VASHTI
Age: 75
Height: 5'3"
Weight: 75 lbs.

KUNO
Age: 40
Height: 6'0"
Weight: 157 lbs.

First Appearance:
THE MACHINE STOPS #1 (2014)

Created by EM Forster
Adapted by Michael Lent
Illustration by Marc Rene

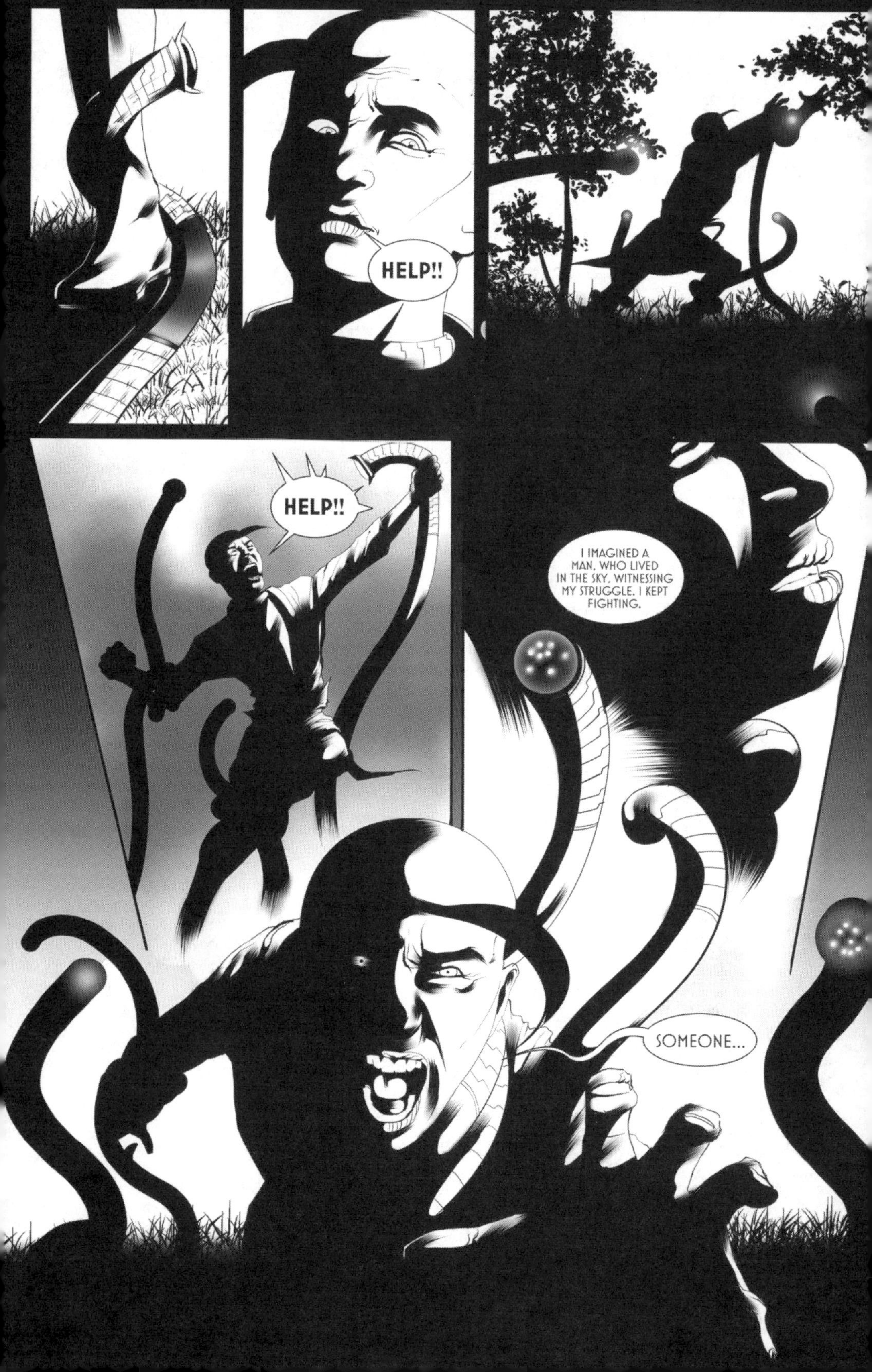
HELP!!
HELP!!
I IMAGINED A MAN, WHO LIVED IN THE SKY, WITNESSING MY STRUGGLE. I KEPT FIGHTING.
SOMEONE...

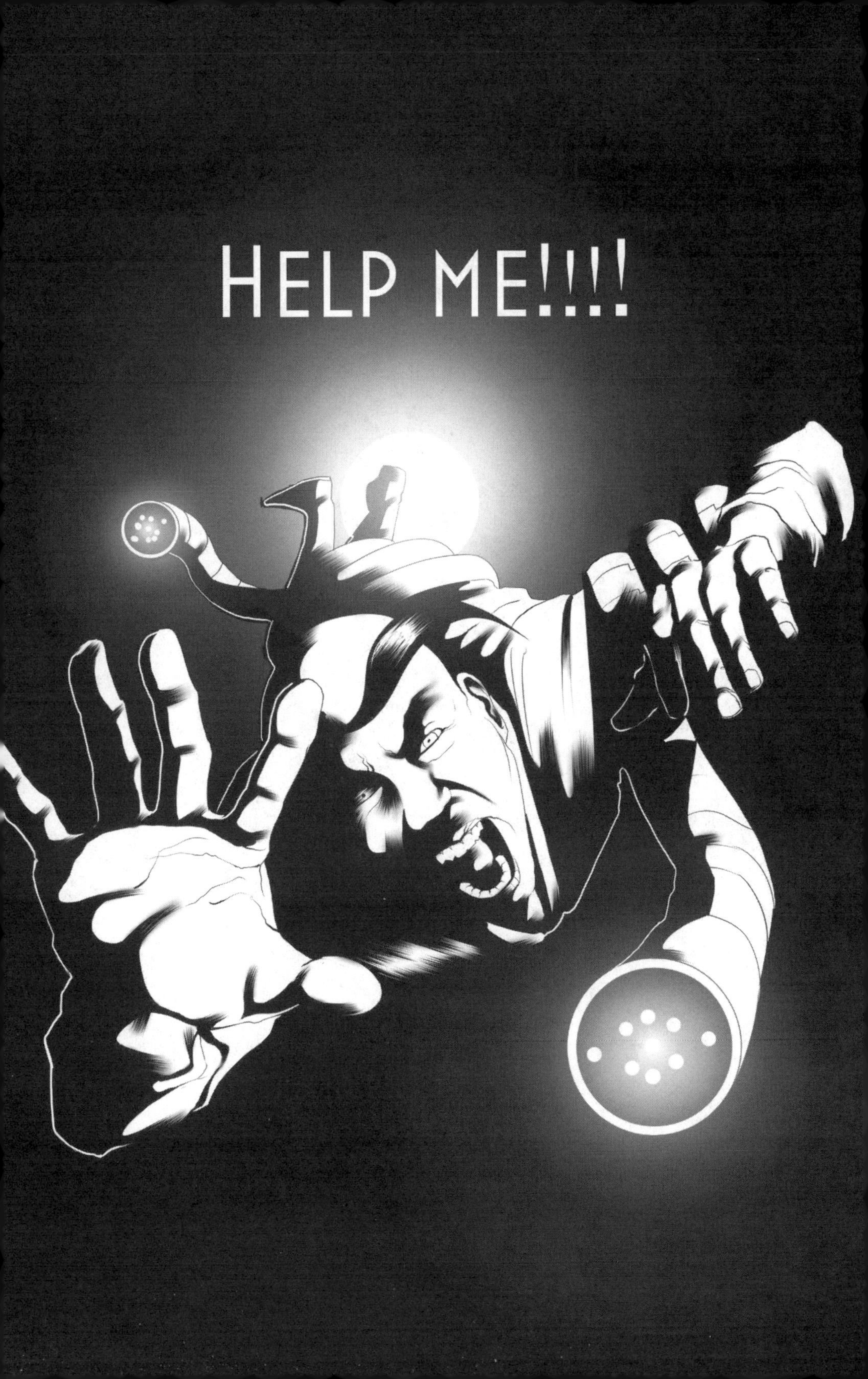
HELP ME!!!!

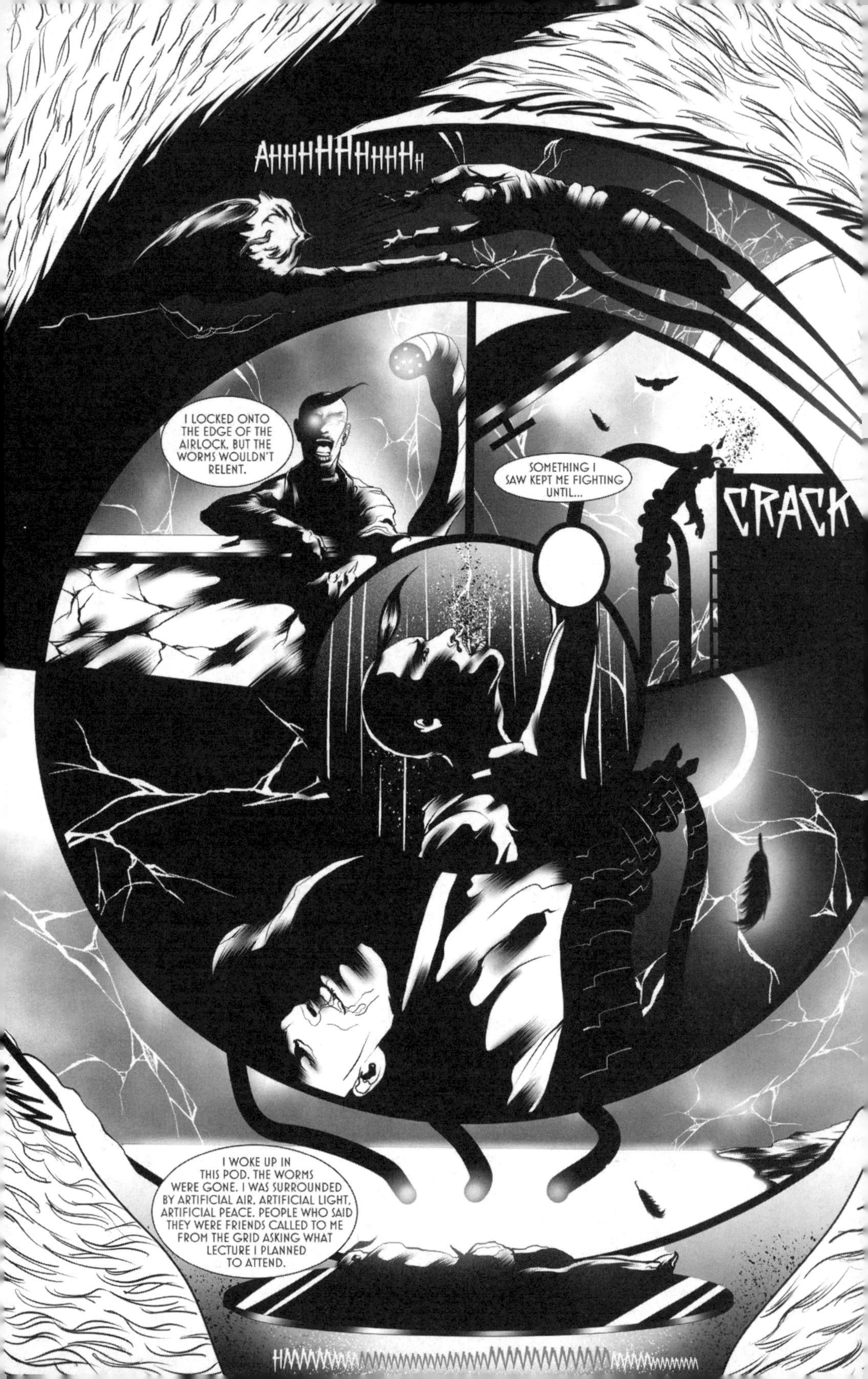
AHHHHAHHHHHH
I LOCKED ONTO THE EDGE OF THE AIRLOCK, BUT THE WORMS WOULDN'T RELENT.
SOMETHING I SAW KEPT ME FIGHTING UNTIL...
CRACK
I WOKE UP IN THIS POD. THE WORMS WERE GONE. I WAS SURROUNDED BY ARTIFICIAL AIR, ARTIFICIAL LIGHT, ARTIFICIAL PEACE. PEOPLE WHO SAID THEY WERE FRIENDS CALLED TO ME FROM THE GRID ASKING WHAT LECTURE I PLANNED TO ATTEND.

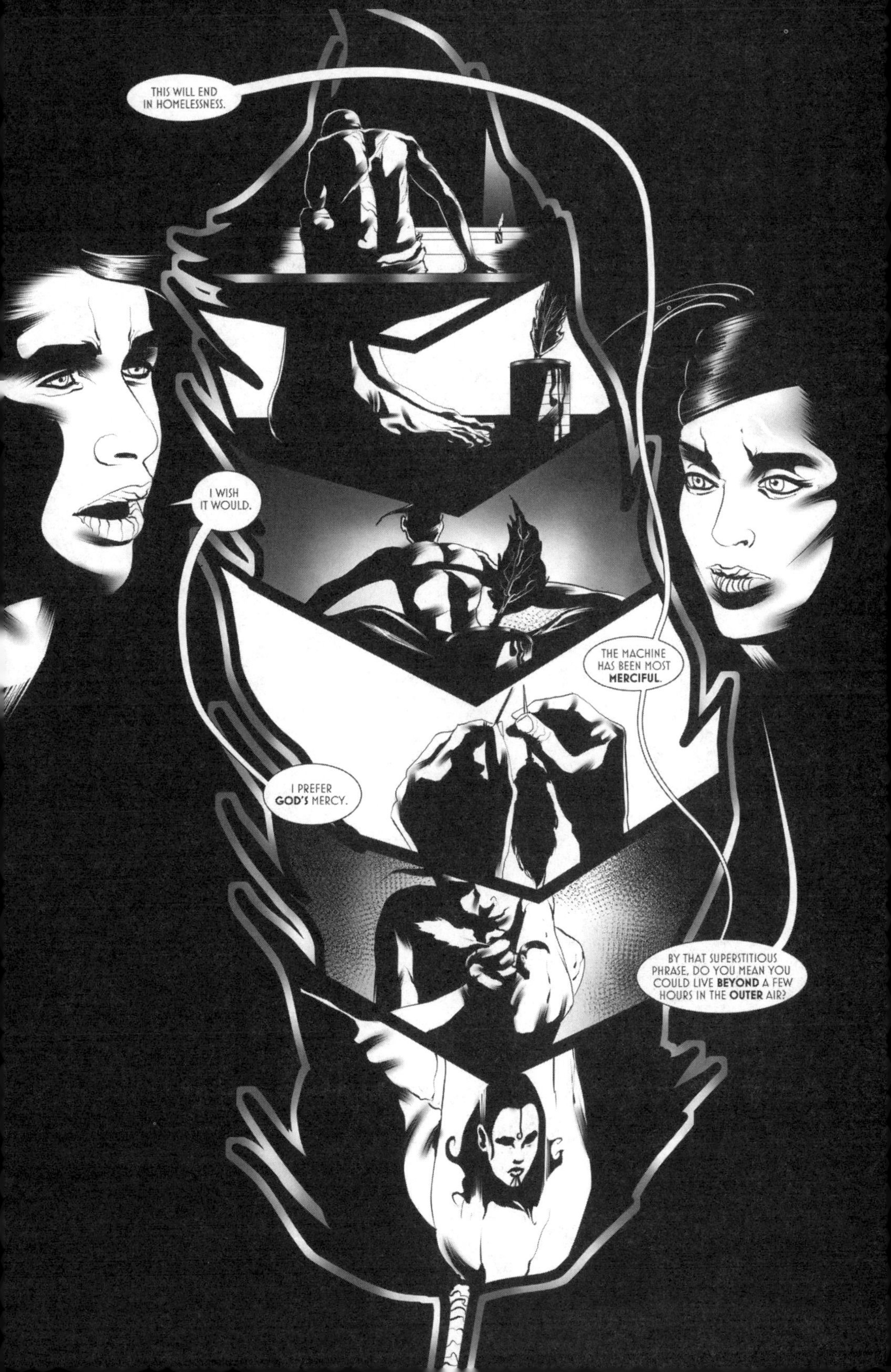
THIS WILL END IN HOMELESSNESS.
I WISH IT WOULD.
THE MACHINE HAS BEEN MOST **MERCIFUL**.
I PREFER **GOD'S** MERCY.
BY THAT SUPERSTITIOUS PHRASE, DO YOU MEAN YOU COULD LIVE **BEYOND** A FEW HOURS IN THE **OUTER** AIR?

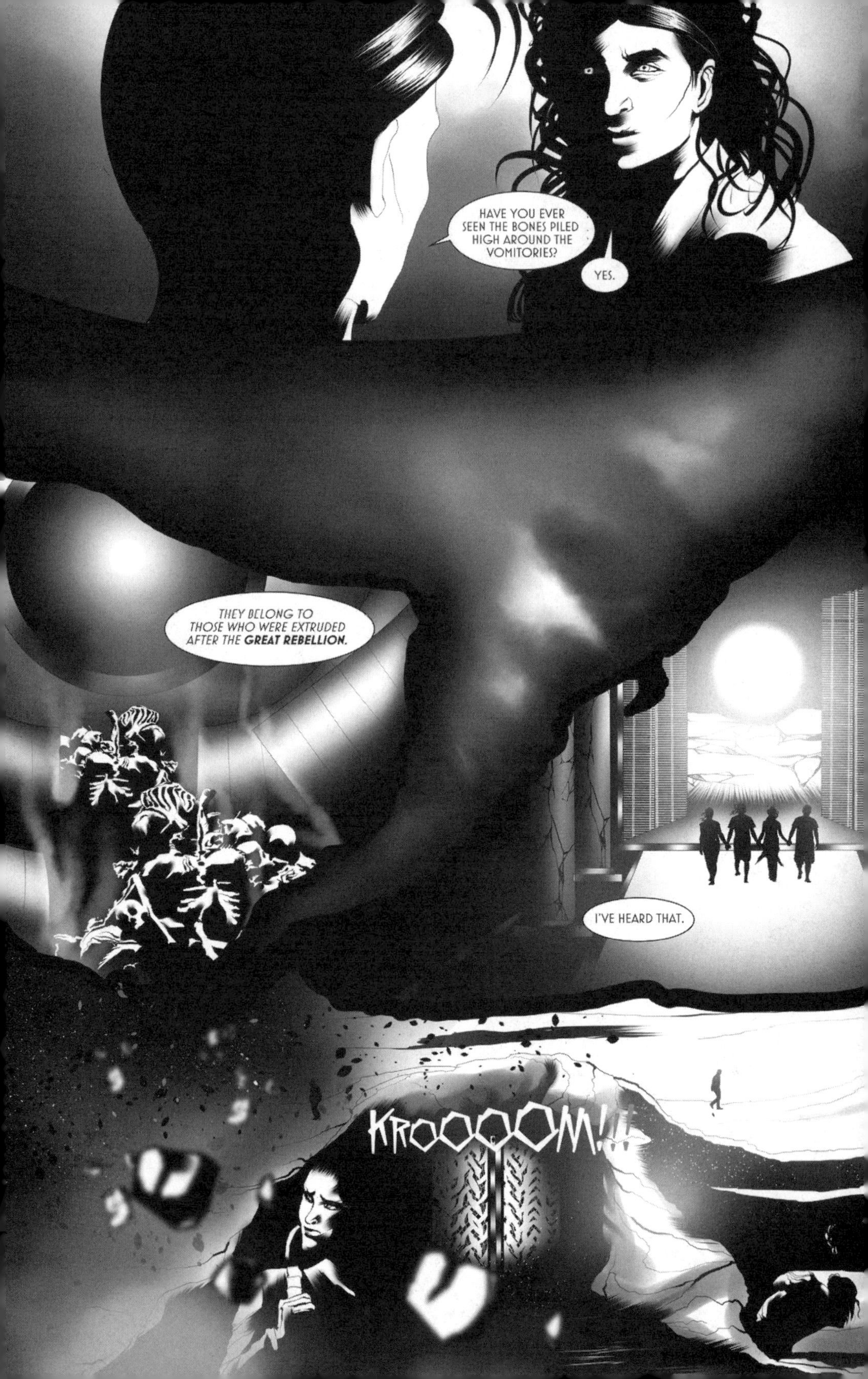
HAVE YOU EVER SEEN THE BONES PILED HIGH AROUND THE VOMITORIES?
YES.
THEY BELONG TO THOSE WHO WERE EXTRUDED AFTER THE **GREAT REBELLION.**
I'VE HEARD THAT.
KROOOOM!!!

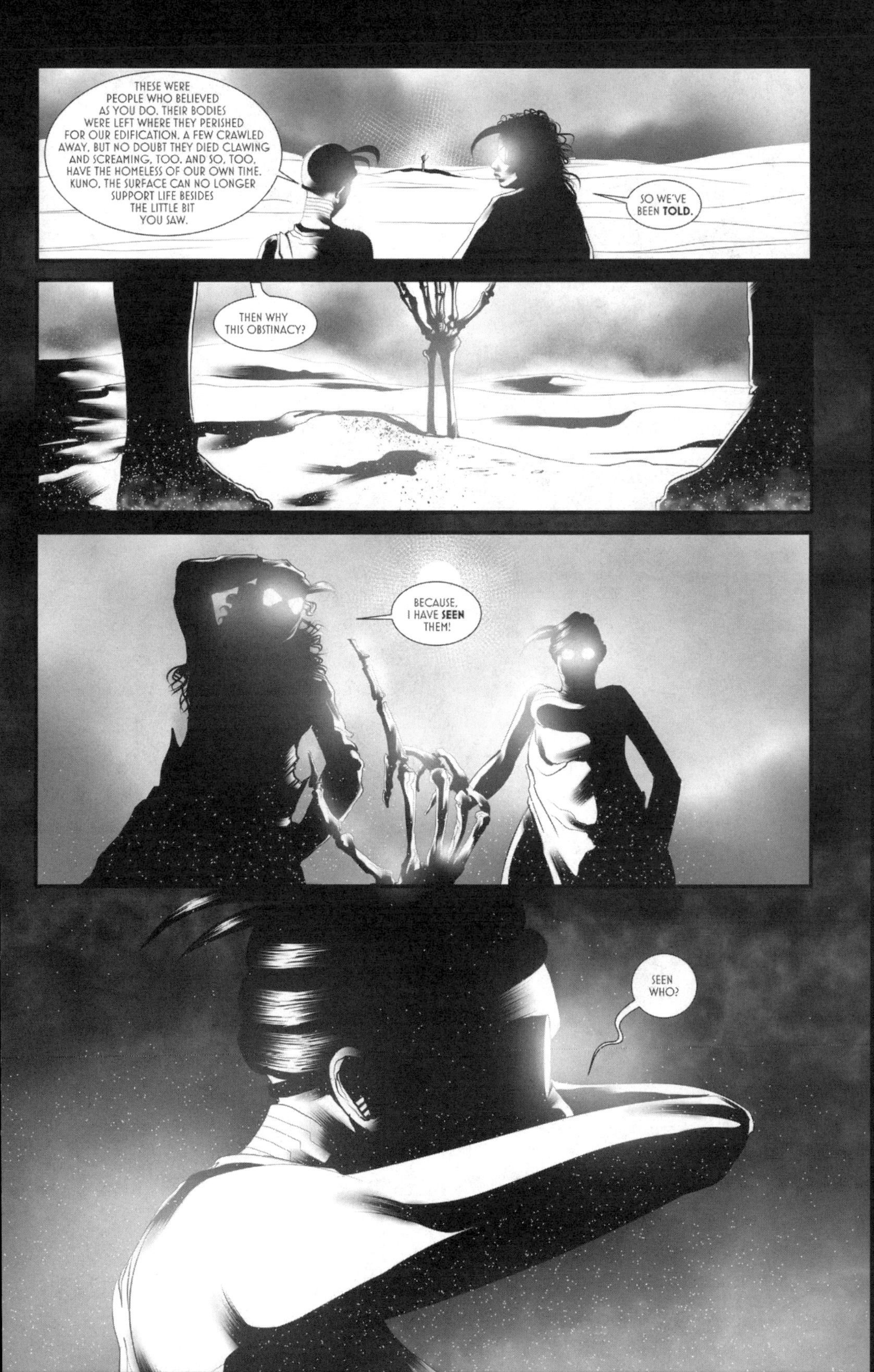
THESE WERE PEOPLE WHO BELIEVED AS YOU DO. THEIR BODIES WERE LEFT WHERE THEY PERISHED FOR OUR EDIFICATION. A FEW CRAWLED AWAY, BUT NO DOUBT THEY DIED CLAWING AND SCREAMING, TOO. AND SO, TOO, HAVE THE HOMELESS OF OUR OWN TIME. KUNO, THE SURFACE CAN NO LONGER SUPPORT LIFE BESIDES THE LITTLE BIT YOU SAW.
SO WE'VE BEEN **TOLD.**
THEN WHY THIS OBSTINACY?
BECAUSE, I HAVE **SEEN** THEM!
SEEN WHO?

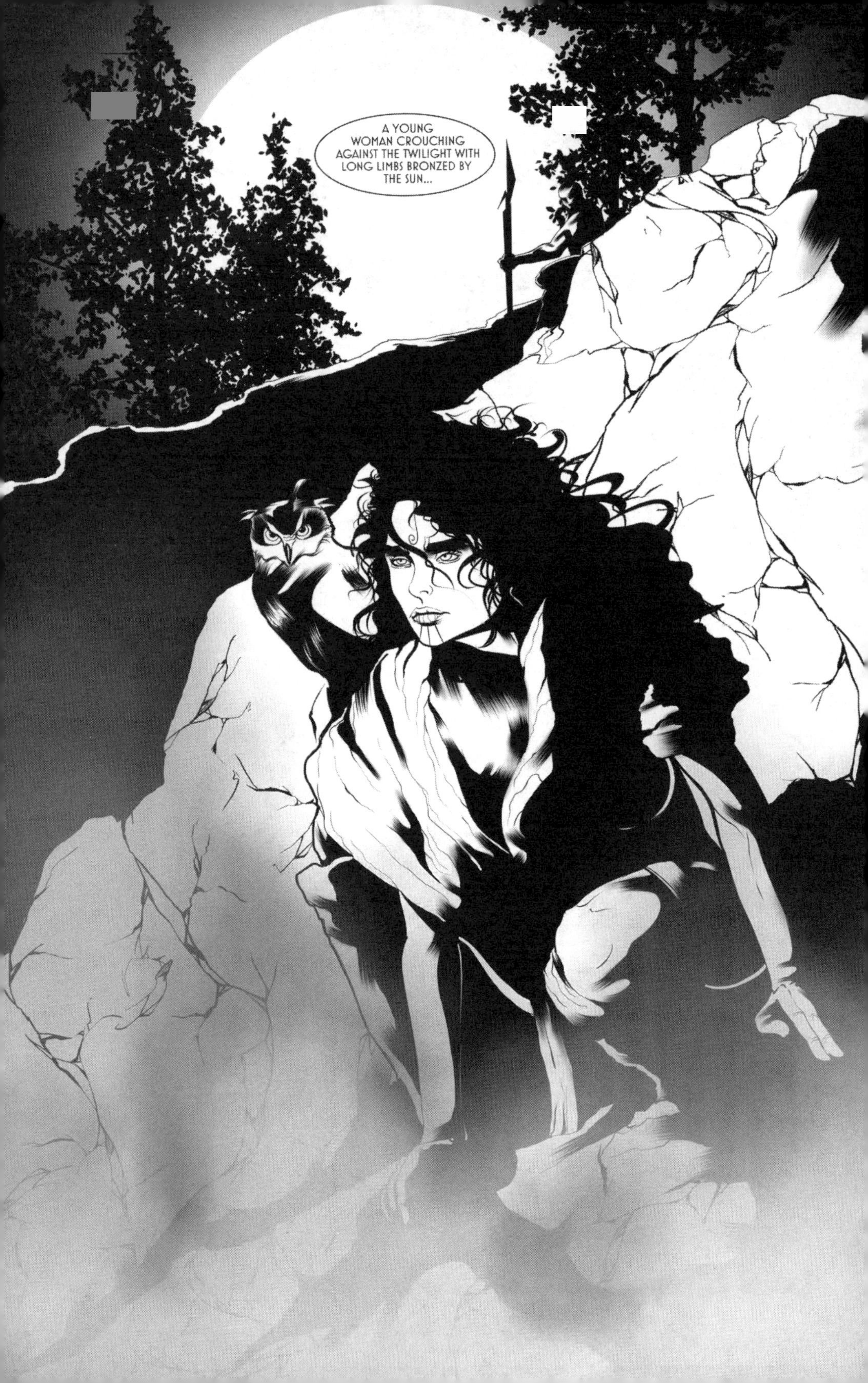
A YOUNG WOMAN CROUCHING AGAINST THE TWILIGHT WITH LONG LIMBS BRONZED BY THE SUN...

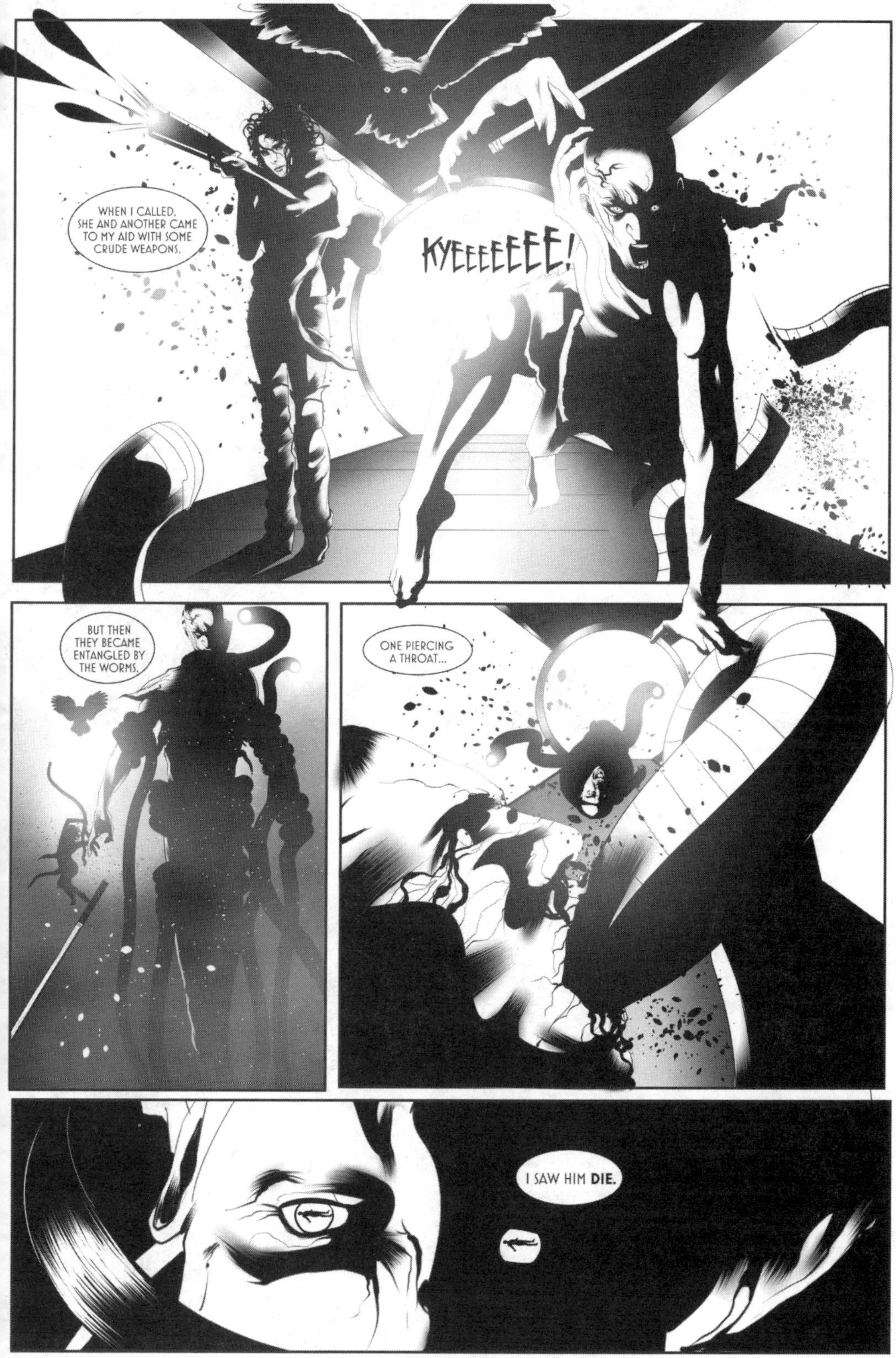

WHEN I CALLED, SHE AND ANOTHER CAME TO MY AID WITH SOME CRUDE WEAPONS.
KYEEEEEEE!
BUT THEN THEY BECAME ENTANGLED BY THE WORMS.
ONE PIERCING A THROAT...
I SAW HIM **DIE.**

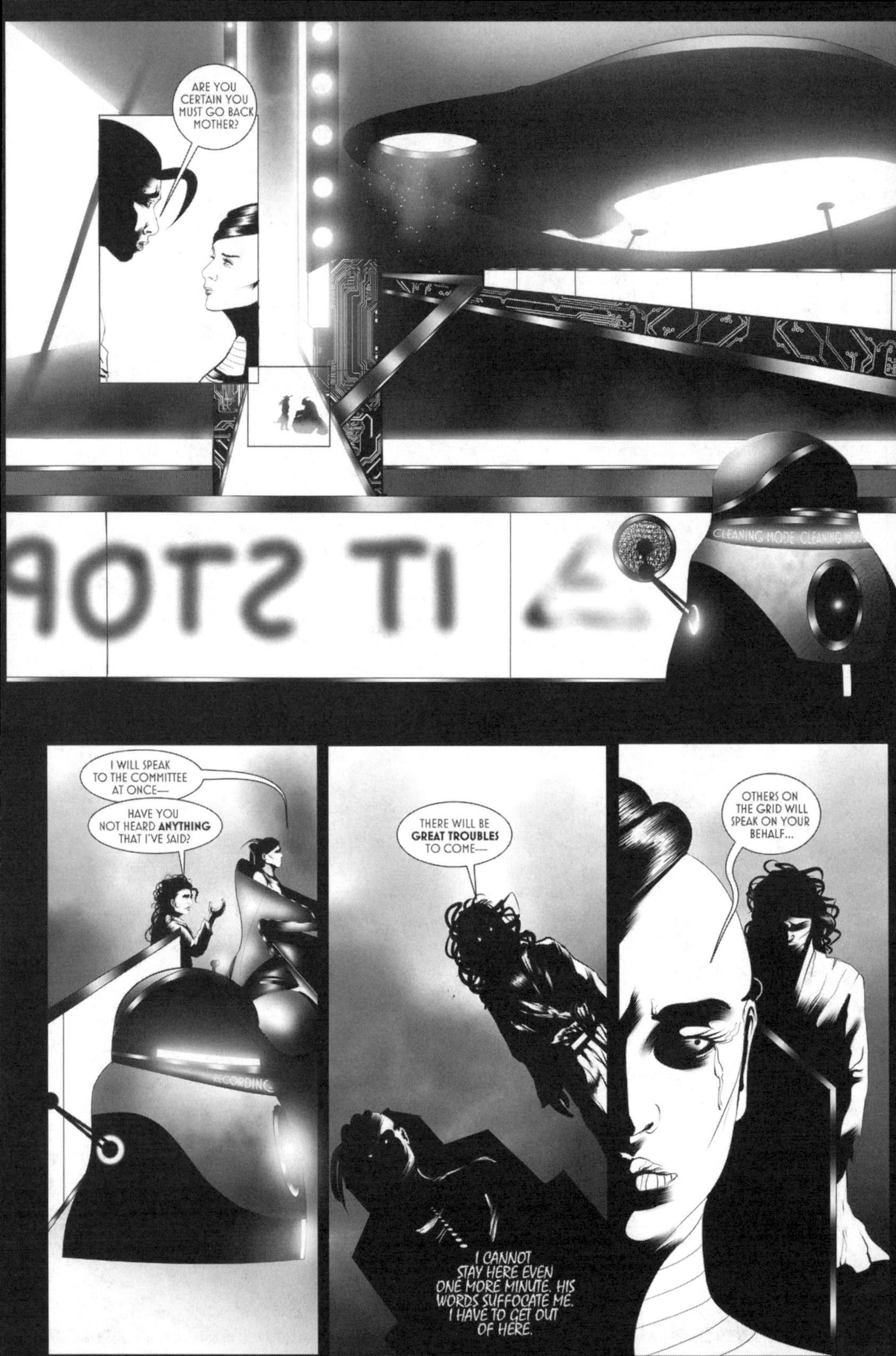

ARE YOU CERTAIN YOU MUST GO BACK MOTHER?
CLEANING MODE CLEANING MODE
I WILL SPEAK TO THE COMMITTEE AT ONCE—
HAVE YOU NOT HEARD **ANYTHING** THAT I'VE SAID?
RECORDING
THERE WILL BE **GREAT TROUBLES** TO COME—
I CANNOT STAY HERE EVEN ONE MORE MINUTE. HIS WORDS SUFFOCATE ME. I HAVE TO GET OUT OF HERE.
OTHERS ON THE GRID WILL SPEAK ON YOUR BEHALF...

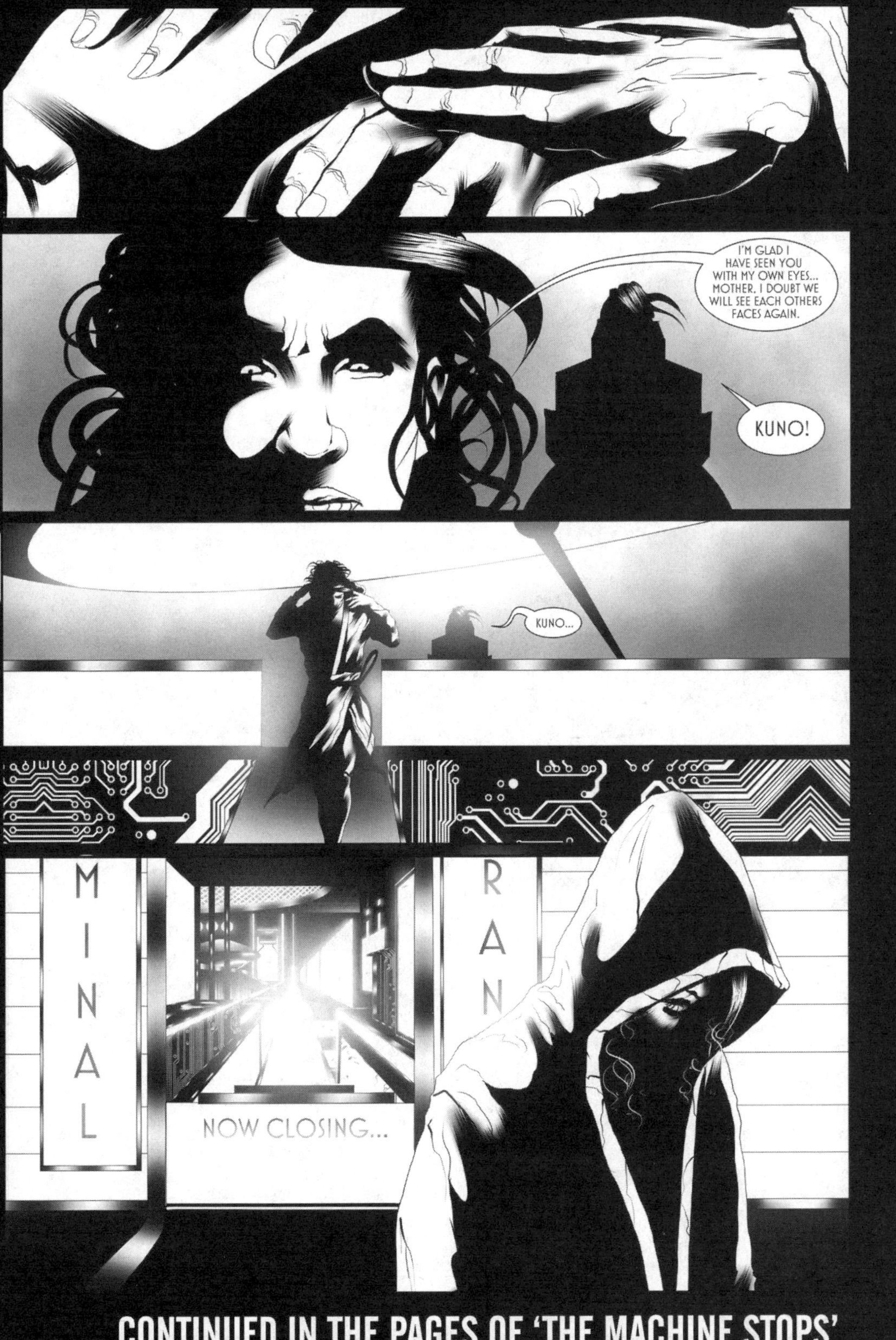
I'M GLAD I HAVE SEEN YOU WITH MY OWN EYES... MOTHER. I DOUBT WE WILL SEE EACH OTHERS FACES AGAIN.
KUNO!
KUNO...
MINAL
RAN
NOW CLOSING...

CONTINUED IN THE PAGES OF 'THE MACHINE STOPS'

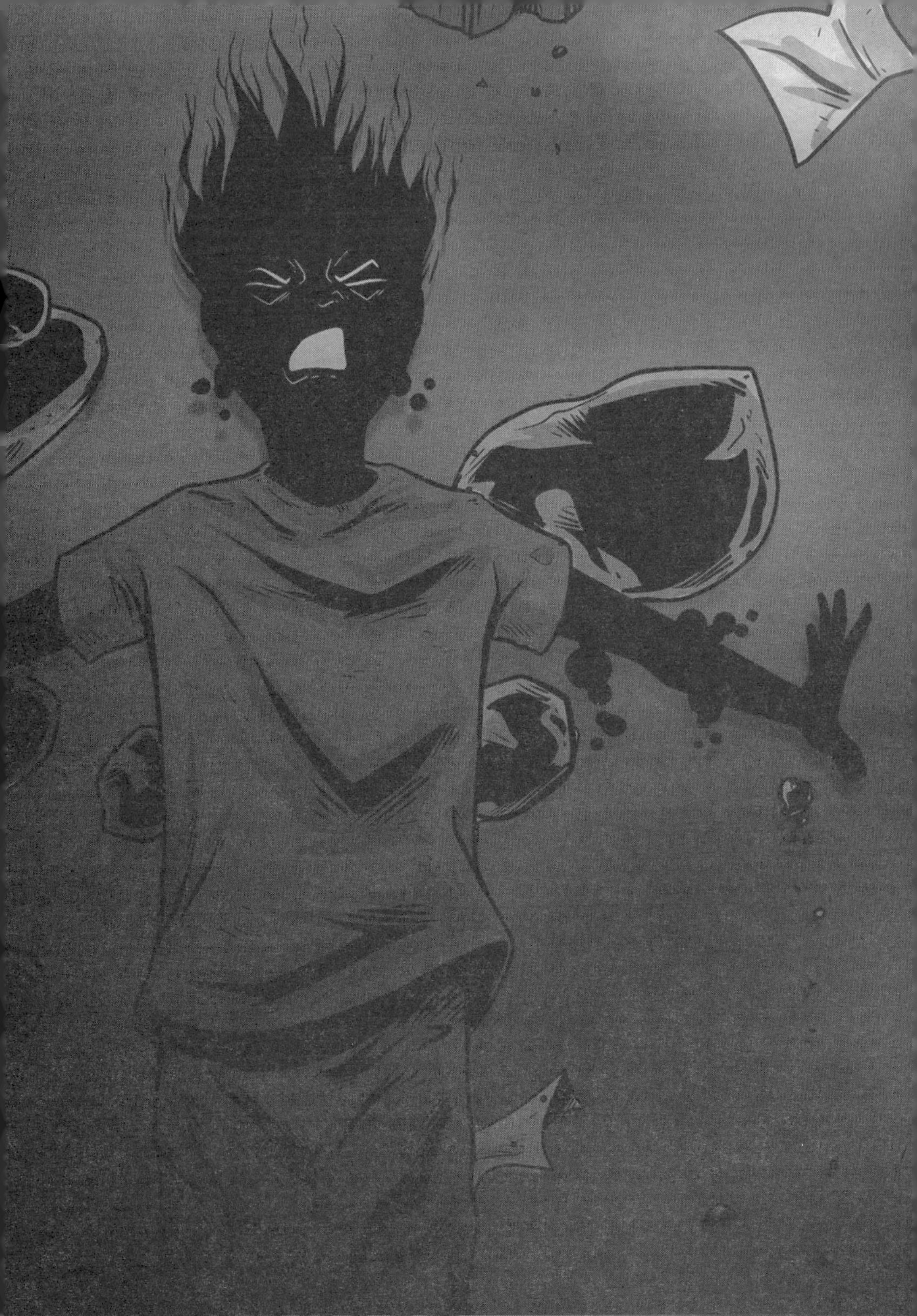

METAPHASE

METAPHASE

OLLIE

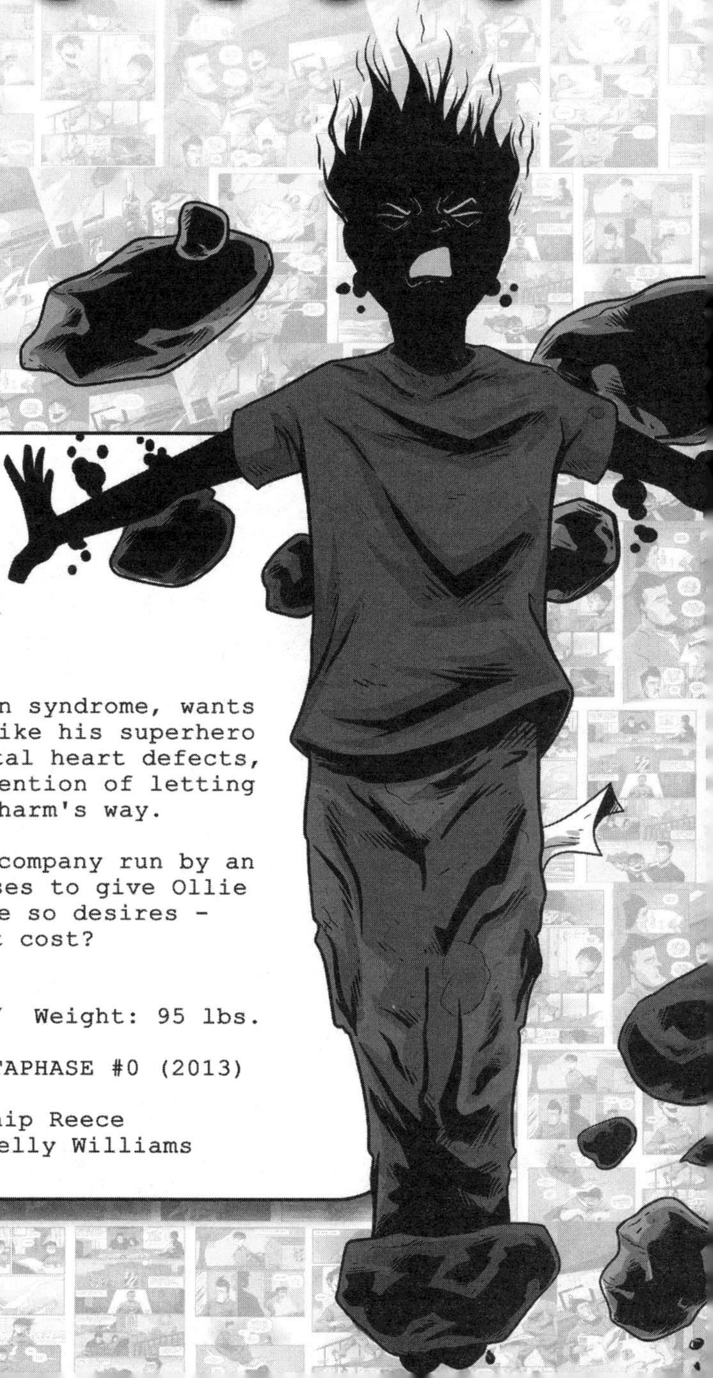

"I have an extra copy of my 21st chromosome... I could be the greatest superhero you've ever made!"

Ollie, a boy with Down syndrome, wants to have powers just like his superhero dad. But with congenital heart defects, his father has no intention of letting his son get in harm's way.

Enter Meta-Makers, a company run by an egomaniac that promises to give Ollie the super powers he so desires - but at what cost?

Age: 16   Height: 5'1"   Weight: 95 lbs.

First Appearance: METAPHASE #0 (2013)

Created by Chip Reece
Illustration by Kelly Williams

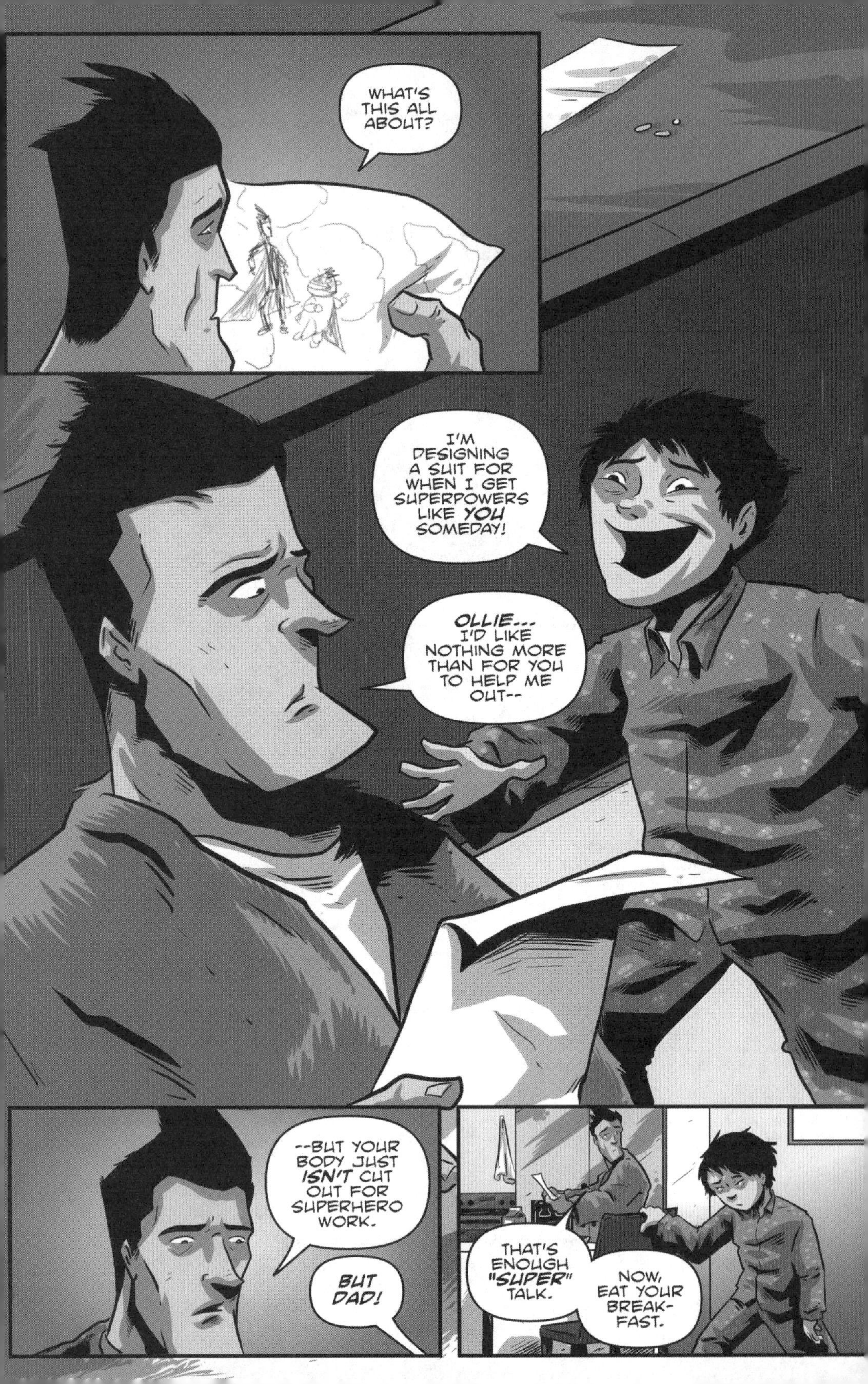
WHAT'S THIS ALL ABOUT?
I'M DESIGNING A SUIT FOR WHEN I GET SUPERPOWERS LIKE YOU SOMEDAY!
OLLIE... I'D LIKE NOTHING MORE THAN FOR YOU TO HELP ME OUT--
--BUT YOUR BODY JUST ISN'T CUT OUT FOR SUPERHERO WORK.
BUT DAD!
THAT'S ENOUGH "SUPER" TALK.
NOW, EAT YOUR BREAK-FAST.

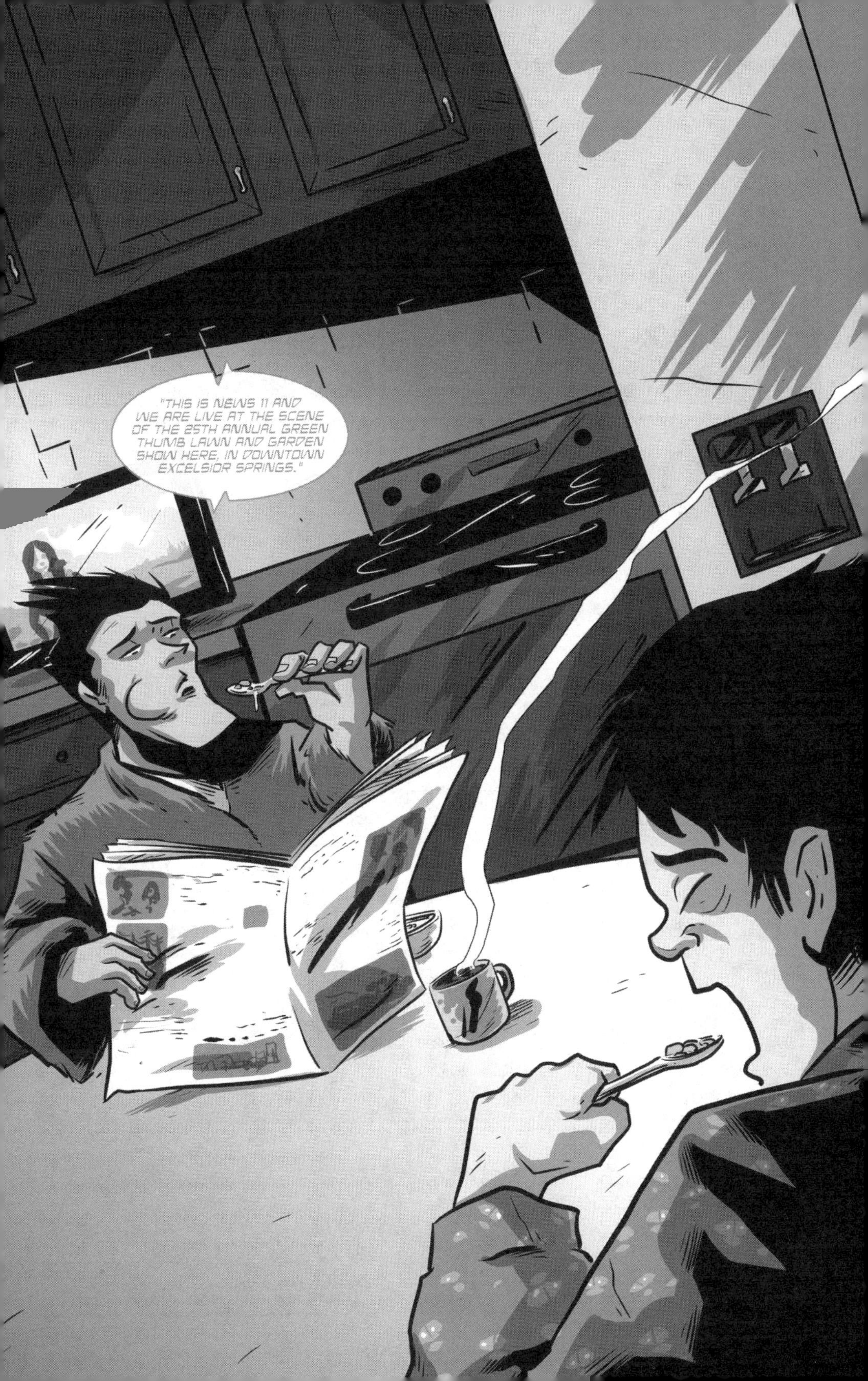
"THIS IS NEWS 11 AND WE ARE LIVE AT THE SCENE OF THE 25TH ANNUAL GREEN THUMB LAWN AND GARDEN SHOW HERE, IN DOWNTOWN EXCELSIOR SPRINGS."

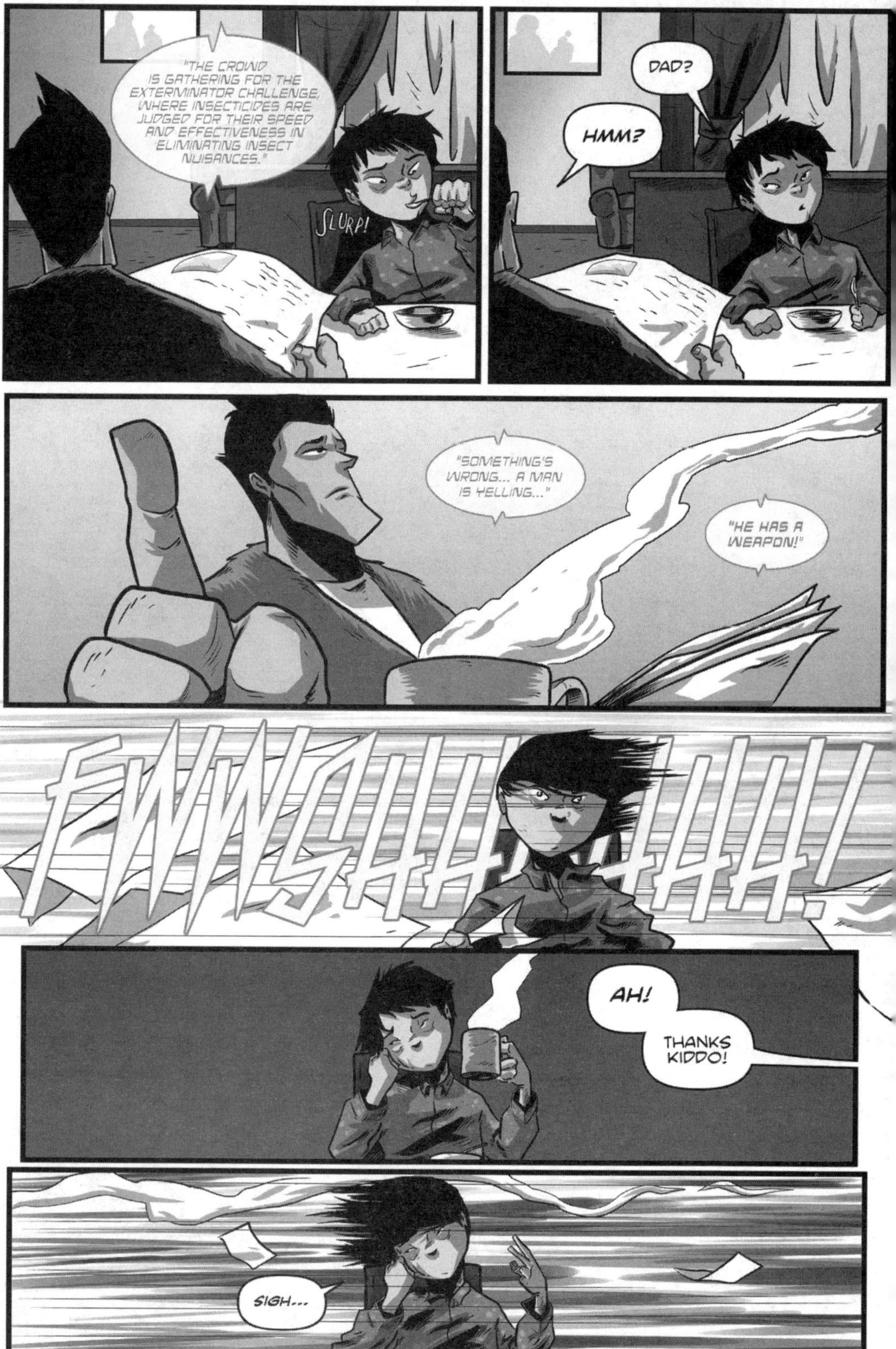
"THE CROWD IS GATHERING FOR THE EXTERMINATOR CHALLENGE, WHERE INSECTICIDES ARE JUDGED FOR THEIR SPEED AND EFFECTIVENESS IN ELIMINATING INSECT NUISANCES."
SLURP!
DAD?
HMM?
"SOMETHING'S WRONG... A MAN IS YELLING..."
"HE HAS A WEAPON!"
AH!
THANKS KIDDO!
SIGH...

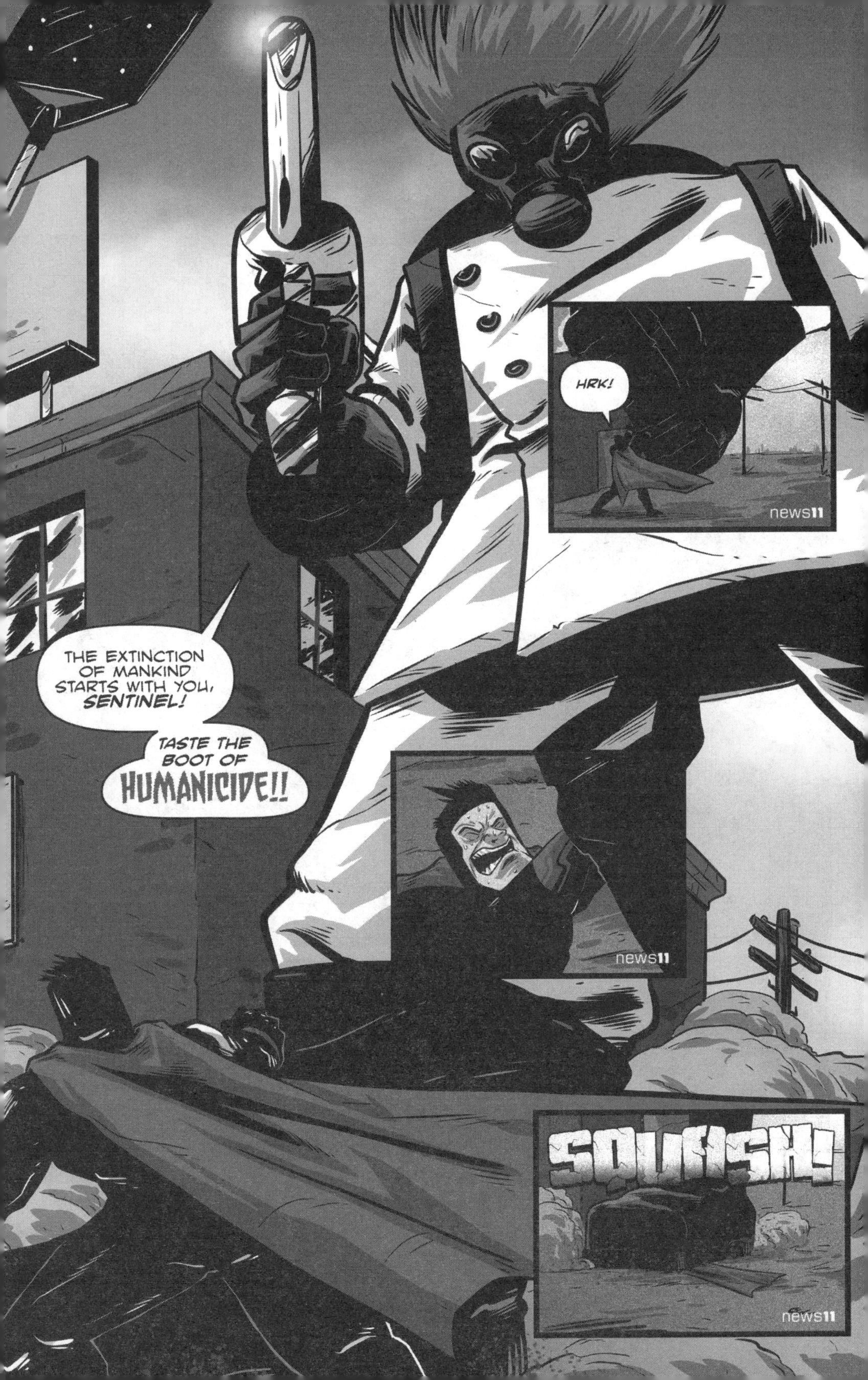
HRK!
news11
THE EXTINCTION OF MANKIND STARTS WITH YOU, SENTINEL!
TASTE THE BOOT OF HUMANICIDE!!
news11
SQUISH!
news11

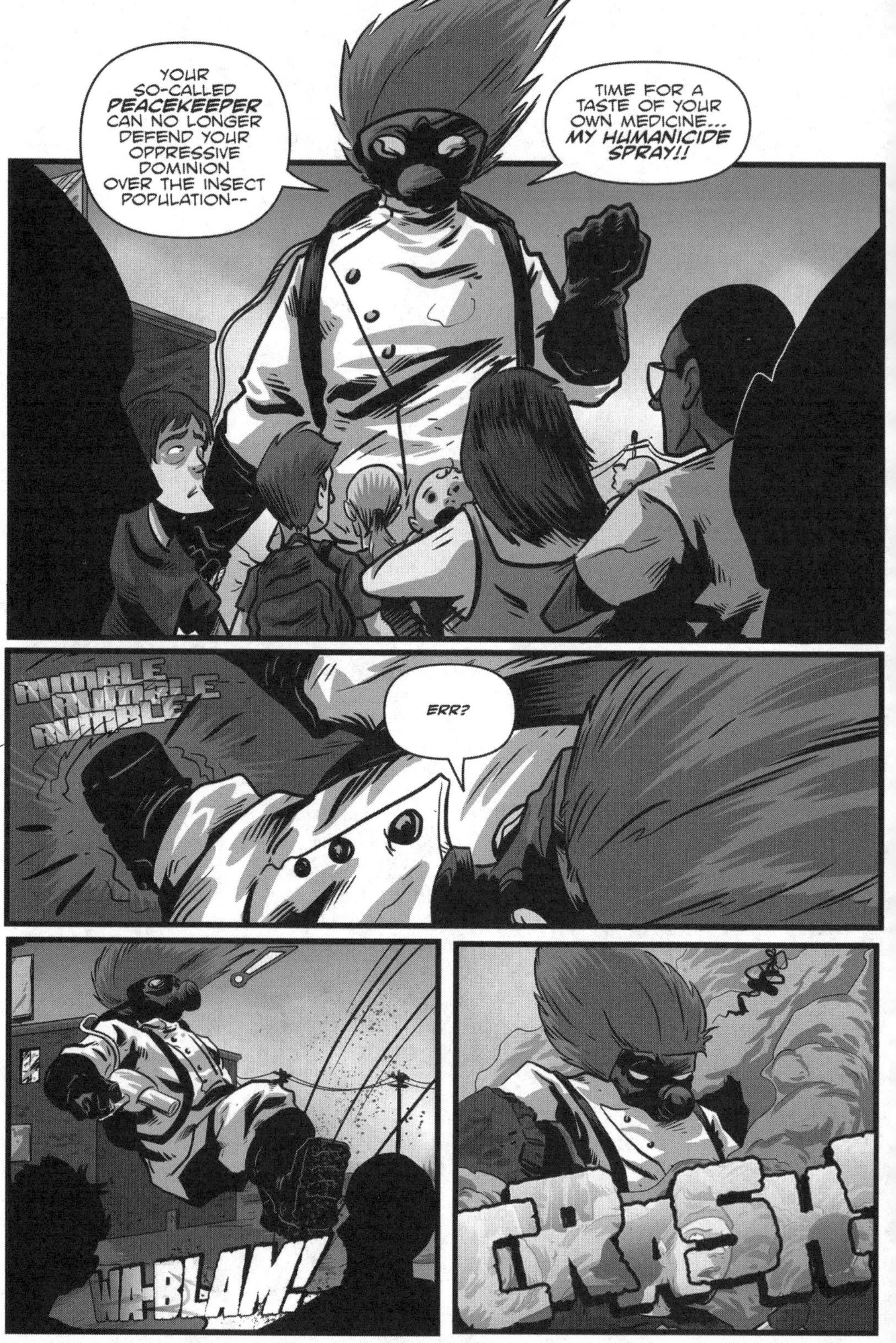
YOUR SO-CALLED PEACEKEEPER CAN NO LONGER DEFEND YOUR OPPRESSIVE DOMINION OVER THE INSECT POPULATION--
TIME FOR A TASTE OF YOUR OWN MEDICINE... MY HUMANICIDE SPRAY!!
RUMBLE RUMBLE RUMBLE
ERR?
!
WA-BLAM!
CRASH!

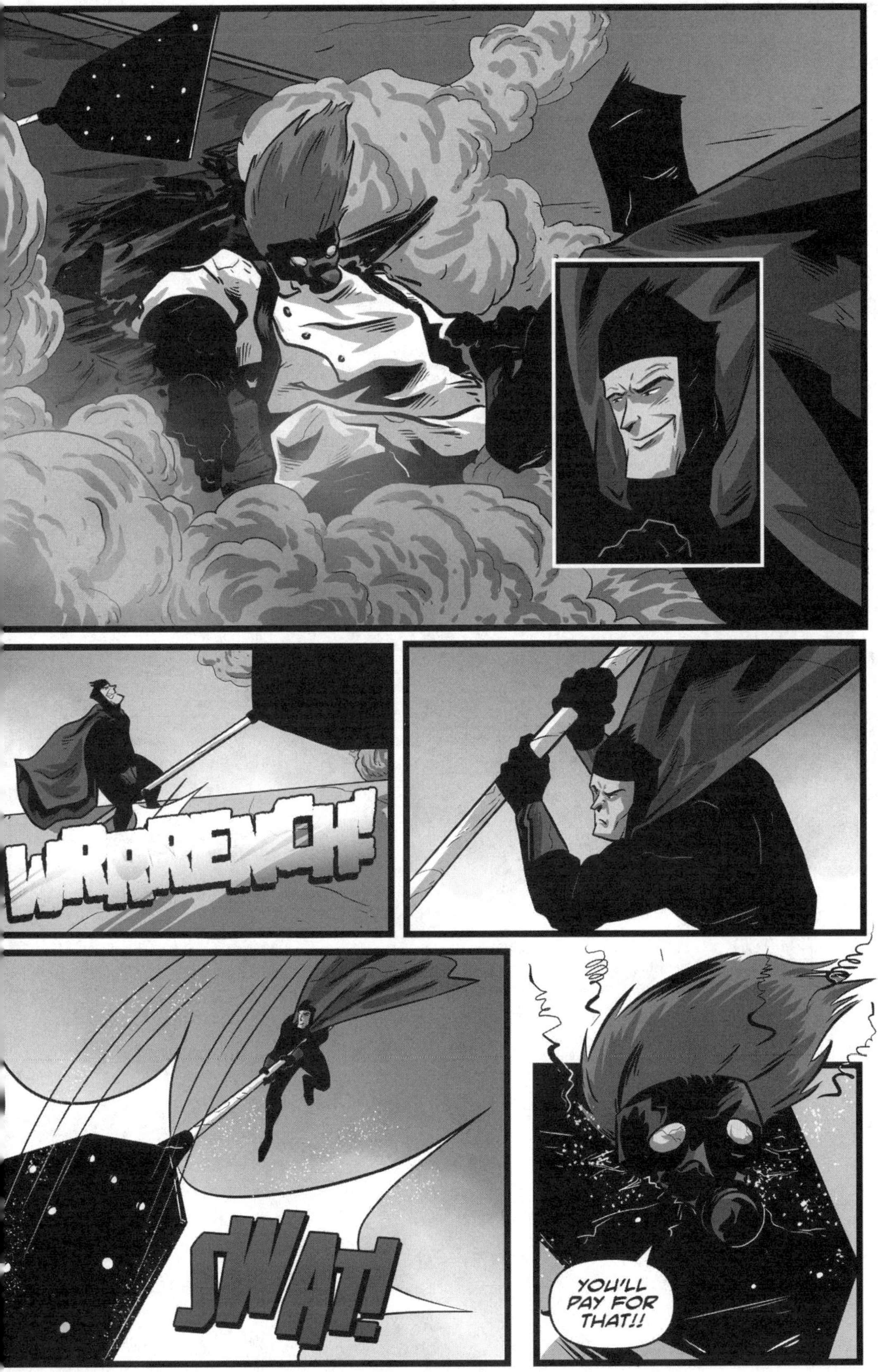
WRRRENCH!
SWAT!
YOU'LL PAY FOR THAT!!

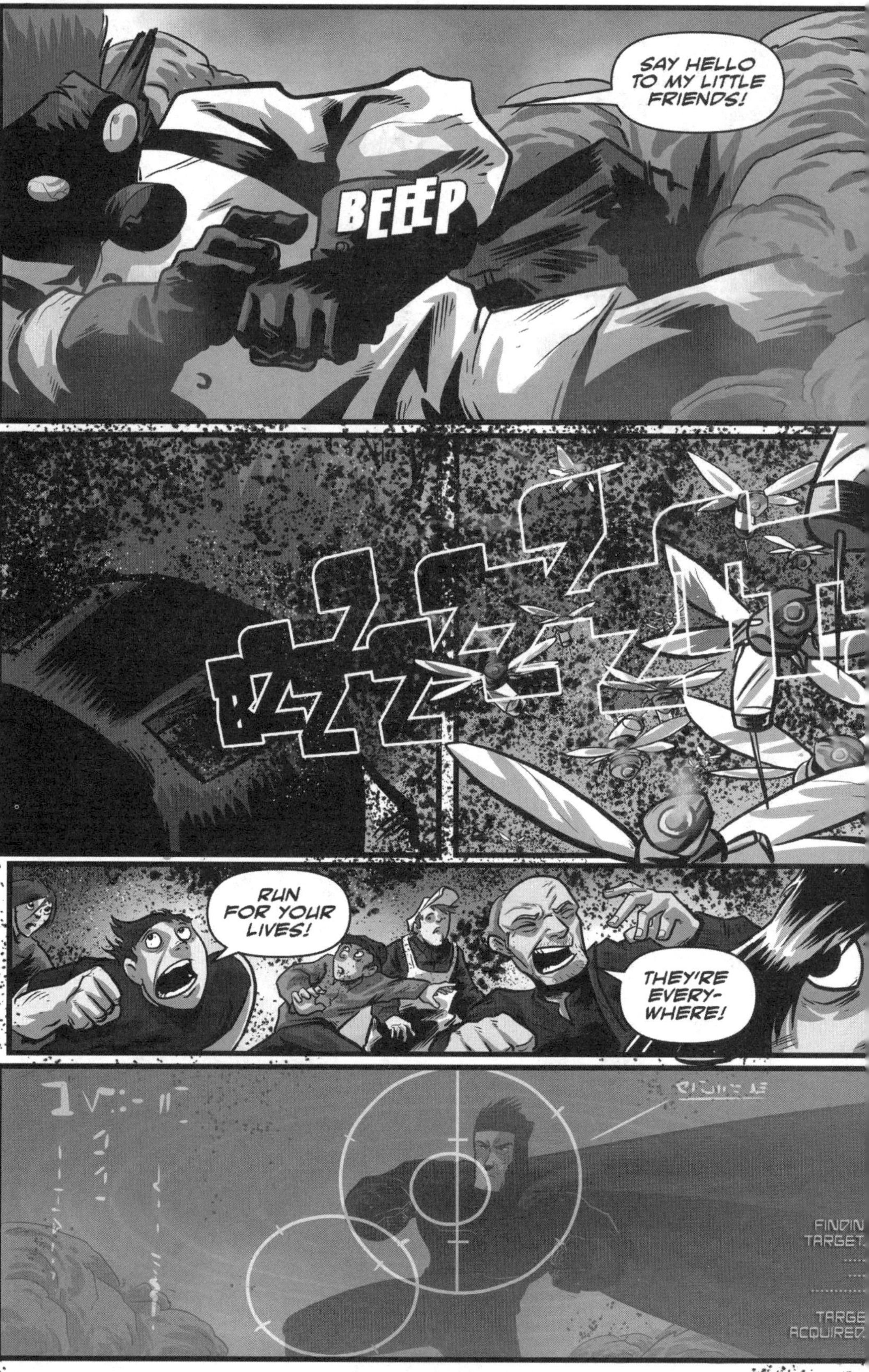
SAY HELLO TO MY LITTLE FRIENDS!
BEEEP
BZZZZ
RUN FOR YOUR LIVES!
THEY'RE EVERY-WHERE!
FINDIN TARGET.
TARGE ACQUIRED.

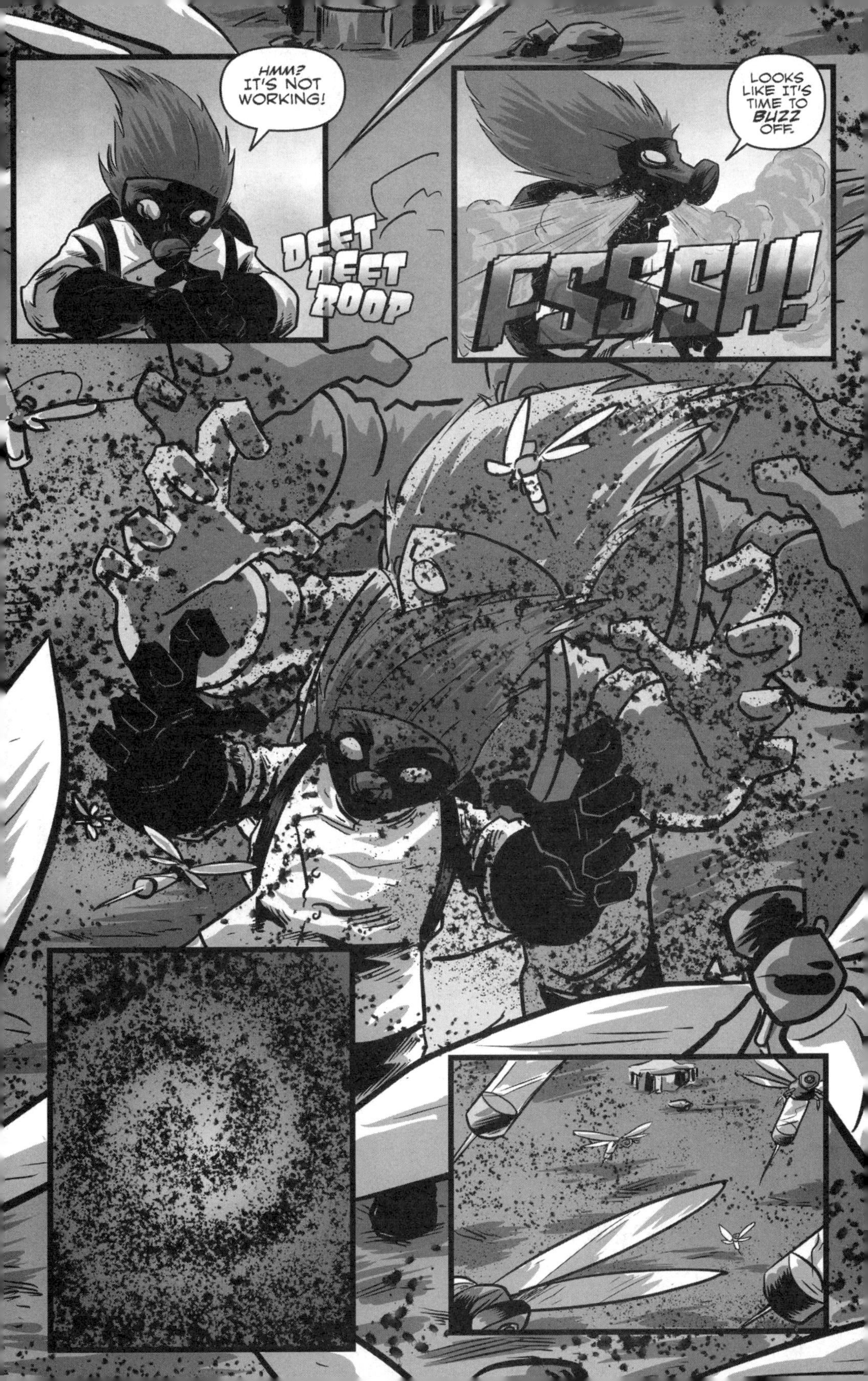
HMM? IT'S NOT WORKING!
DEET DEET BOOP
LOOKS LIKE IT'S TIME TO BUZZ OFF.
PSSSH!

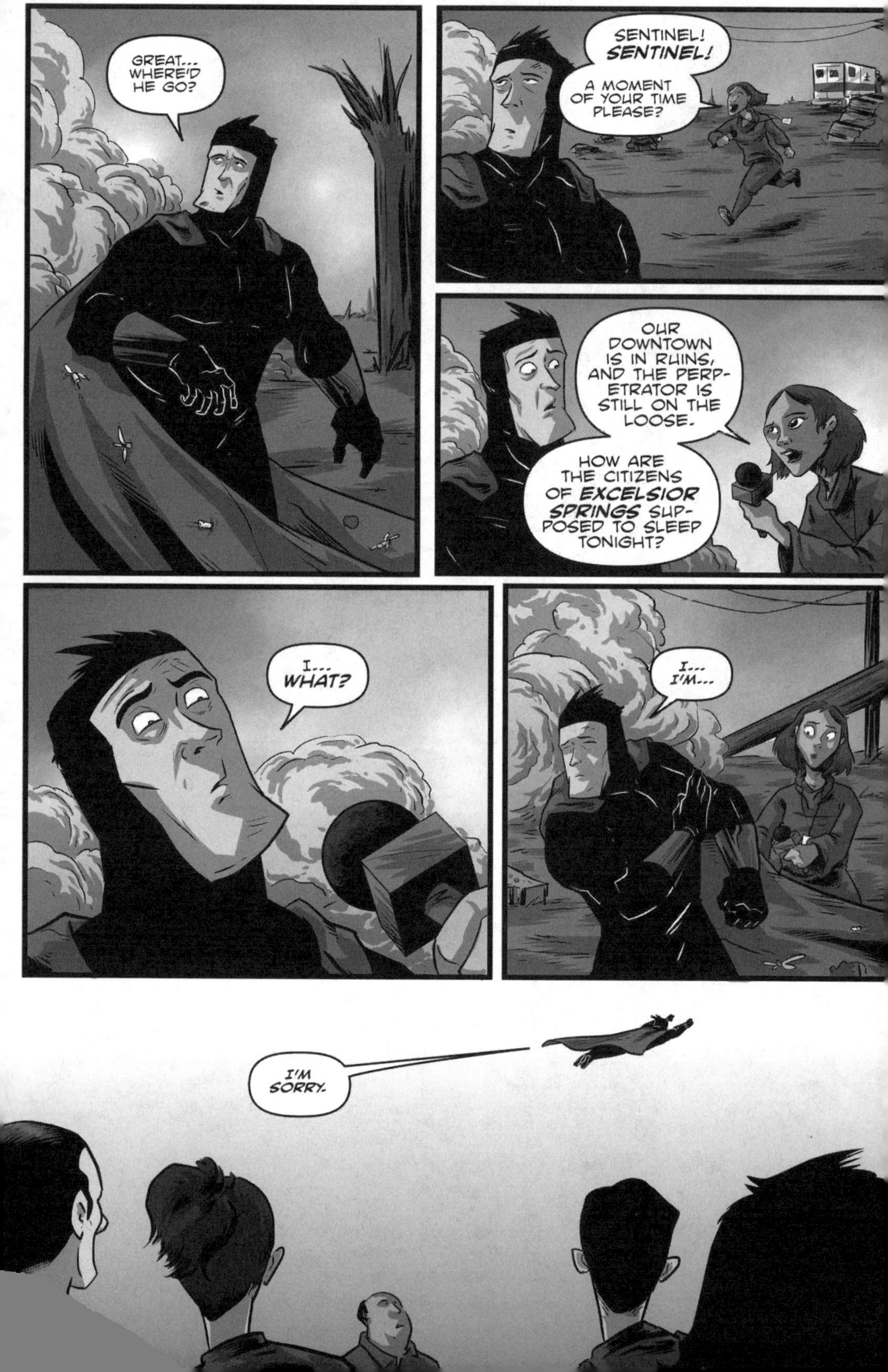
GREAT... WHERE'D HE GO?
SENTINEL! SENTINEL!
A MOMENT OF YOUR TIME PLEASE?
OUR DOWNTOWN IS IN RUINS, AND THE PERPETRATOR IS STILL ON THE LOOSE.
HOW ARE THE CITIZENS OF EXCELSIOR SPRINGS SUPPOSED TO SLEEP TONIGHT?
I... WHAT?
I... I'M...
I'M SORRY.

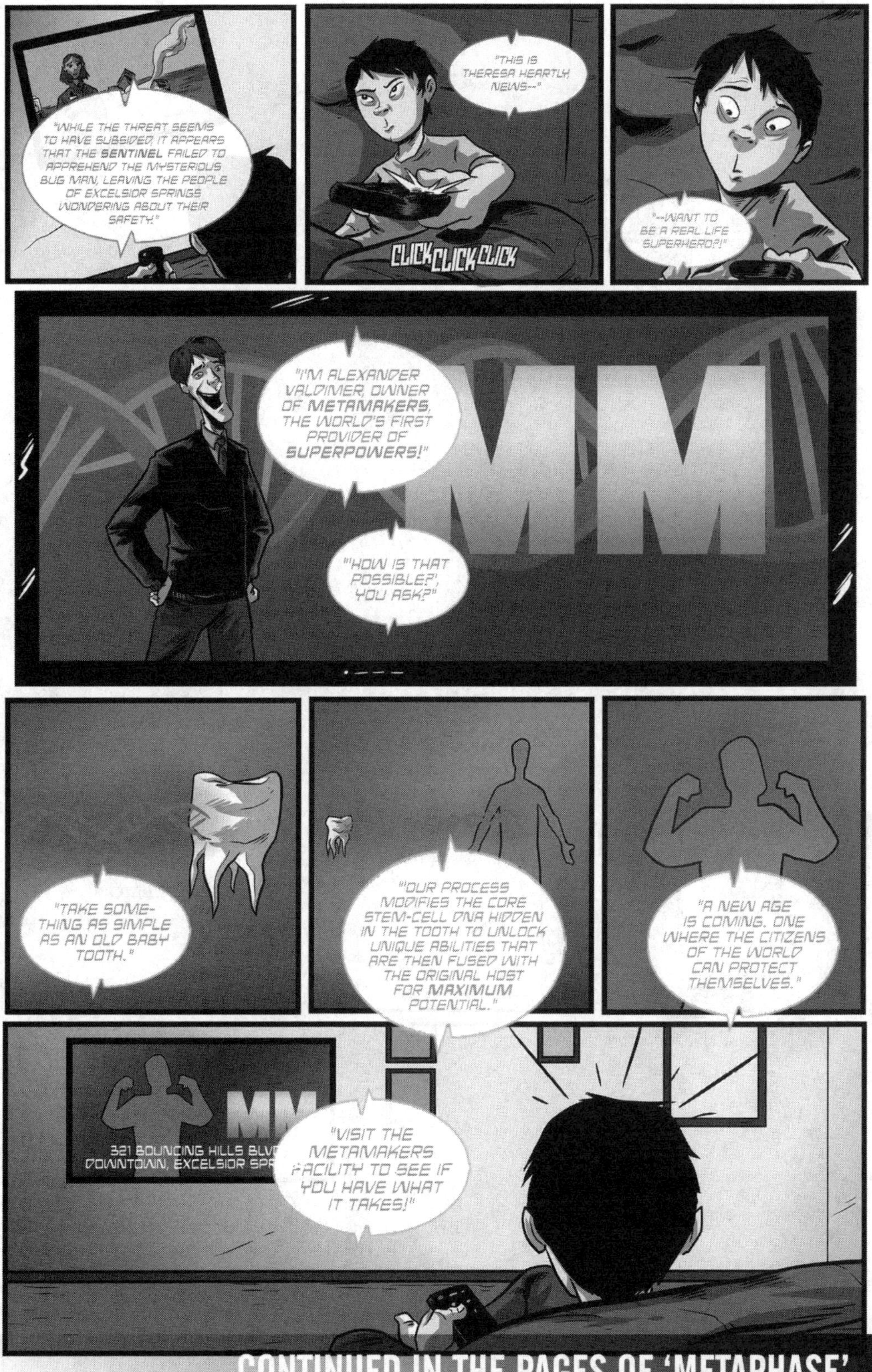
"WHILE THE THREAT SEEMS TO HAVE SUBSIDED, IT APPEARS THAT THE SENTINEL FAILED TO APPREHEND THE MYSTERIOUS BUG MAN, LEAVING THE PEOPLE OF EXCELSIOR SPRINGS WONDERING ABOUT THEIR SAFETY."
"THIS IS THERESA HEARTLY, NEWS--"
CLICK CLICK CLICK
"--WANT TO BE A REAL LIFE SUPERHERO?!"
"I'M ALEXANDER VALDIMER, OWNER OF METAMAKERS, THE WORLD'S FIRST PROVIDER OF SUPERPOWERS!"
MM
"'HOW IS THAT POSSIBLE?', YOU ASK?"
"TAKE SOME-THING AS SIMPLE AS AN OLD BABY TOOTH."
"OUR PROCESS MODIFIES THE CORE STEM-CELL DNA HIDDEN IN THE TOOTH TO UNLOCK UNIQUE ABILITIES THAT ARE THEN FUSED WITH THE ORIGINAL HOST FOR MAXIMUM POTENTIAL."
"A NEW AGE IS COMING. ONE WHERE THE CITIZENS OF THE WORLD CAN PROTECT THEMSELVES."
MM
321 BOUNCING HILLS BLVD
DOWNTOWN, EXCELSIOR SPR
"VISIT THE METAMAKERS FACILITY TO SEE IF YOU HAVE WHAT IT TAKES!"

CONTINUED IN THE PAGES OF 'METAPHASE'

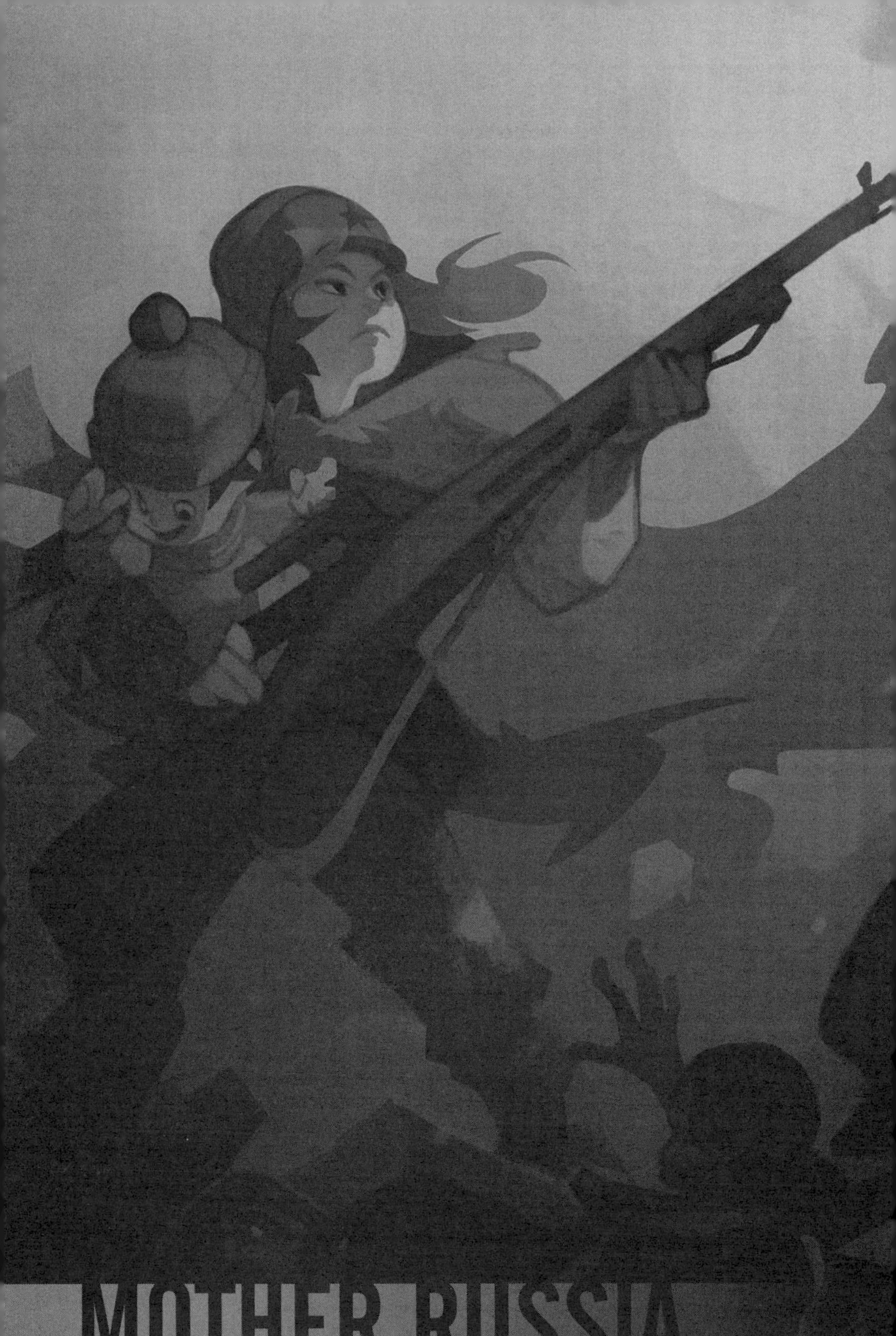

MOTHER RUSSIA

★ MOTH3R ★ RUSSIA

SVETLANA GORSHKOV

*"Anybody worth shooting
is worth shooting twice."*

Svetlana Gorshkov was the feared soviet sniper
"MOTHER RUSSIA" in 1942. She was the scourge of
the Nazi army in Stalingrad but now that the
world went and ended in a zombie apocalypse
she has used her dead eye aim to thin out
the undead population one at a time from the
safety of her well provisioned tower. Trained
as a ballerina her swift feet come in handy
when she leaps from the tower to rescue
a perfectly healthy baby boy.

Age: 22   Height: 5'5"   Weight: None of your business.

First Appearance: FUBAR Vol.1 (2010)

Created by Jeff McComsey
Illustration by Jeff McComsey

CHAPTER TWO:
NO WORSE ENEMY

STORY AND ART BY JEFF MCCOMSEY

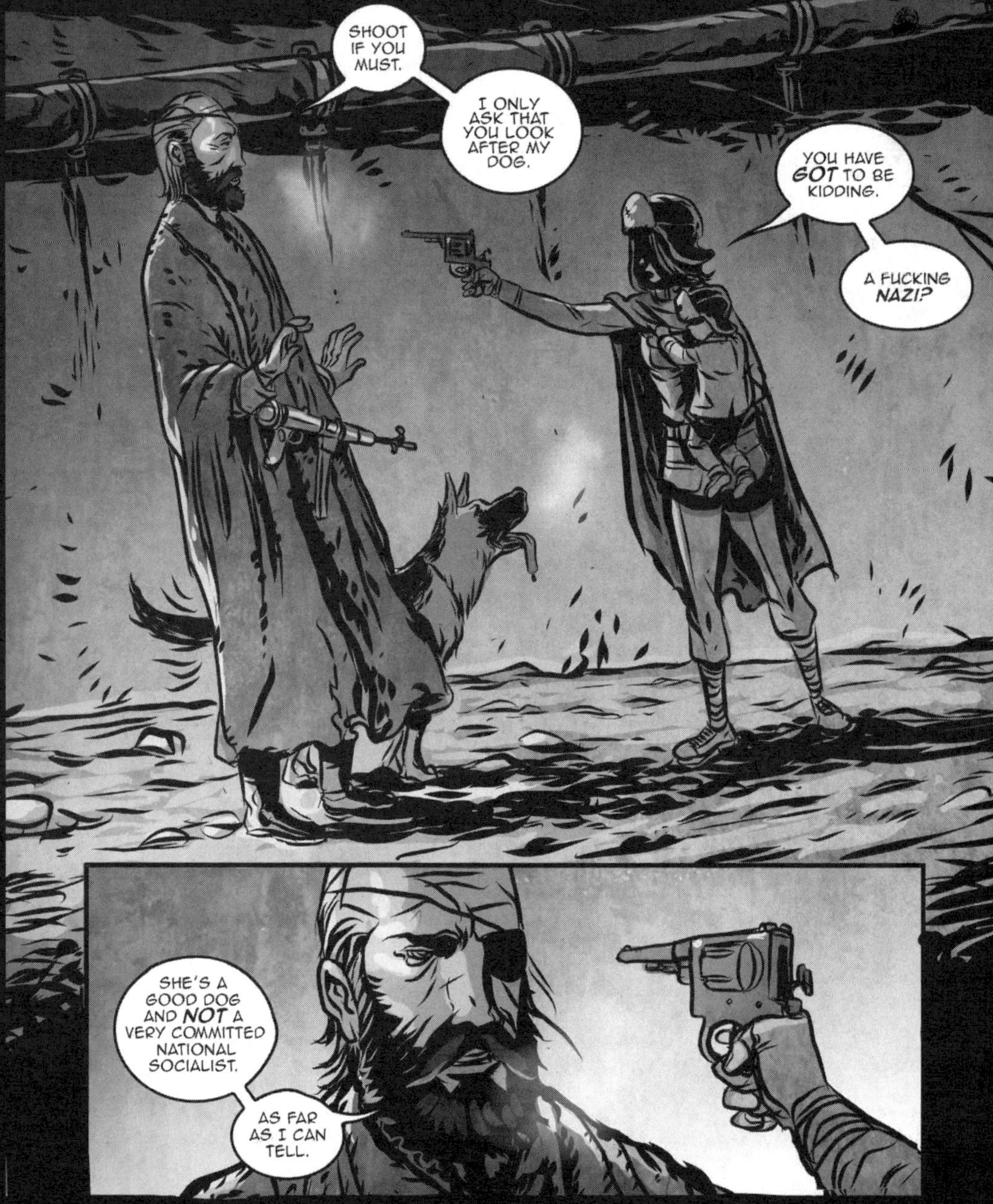
SHOOT IF YOU MUST.
I ONLY ASK THAT YOU LOOK AFTER MY DOG.
YOU HAVE **GOT** TO BE KIDDING.
A FUCKING **NAZI?**
SHE'S A GOOD DOG AND **NOT** A VERY COMMITTED NATIONAL SOCIALIST.
AS FAR AS I CAN TELL.

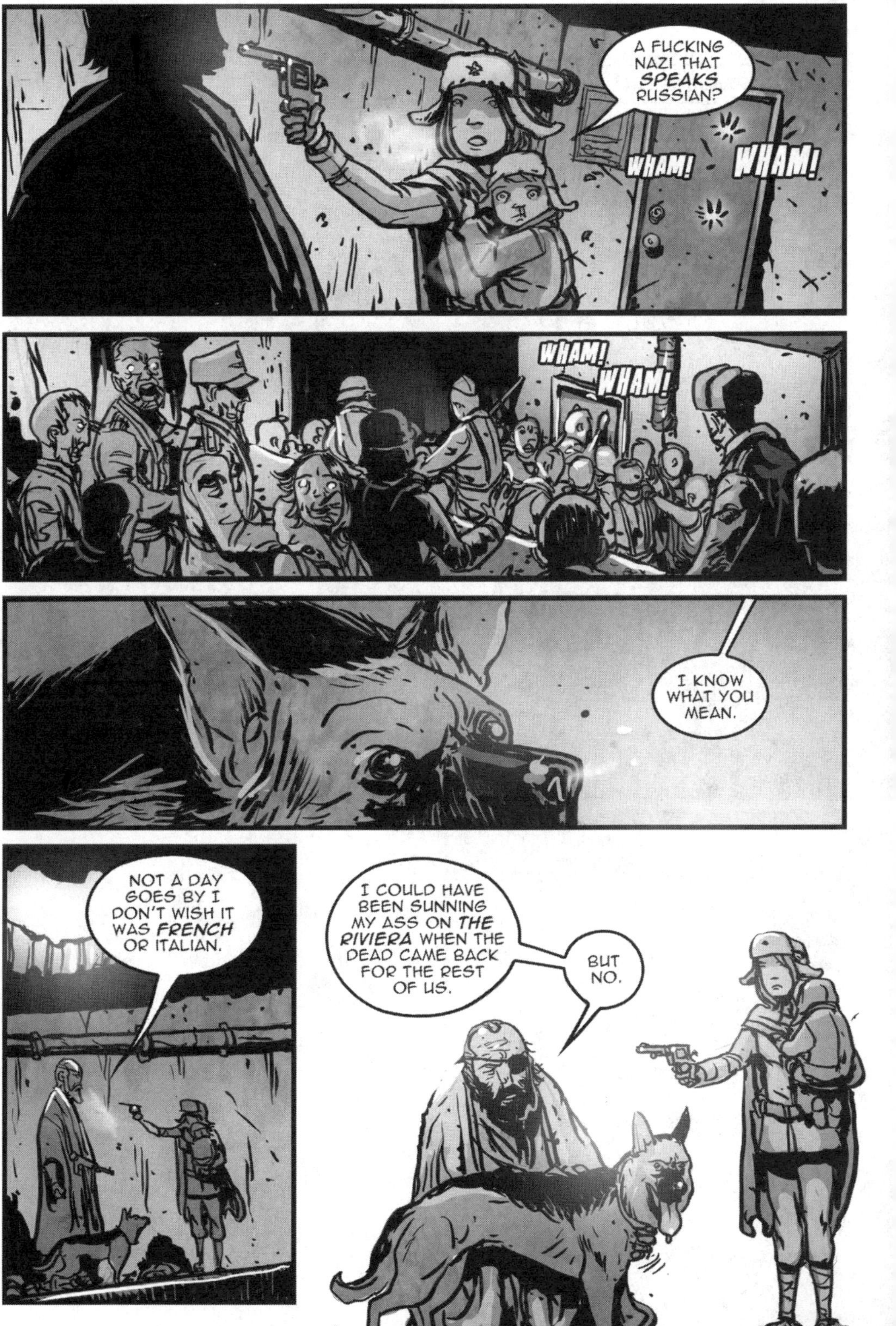
A FUCKING NAZI THAT SPEAKS RUSSIAN?
WHAM!
WHAM!
WHAM!
WHAM!
I KNOW WHAT YOU MEAN.
NOT A DAY GOES BY I DON'T WISH IT WAS FRENCH OR ITALIAN.
I COULD HAVE BEEN SUNNING MY ASS ON THE RIVIERA WHEN THE DEAD CAME BACK FOR THE REST OF US.
BUT NO.

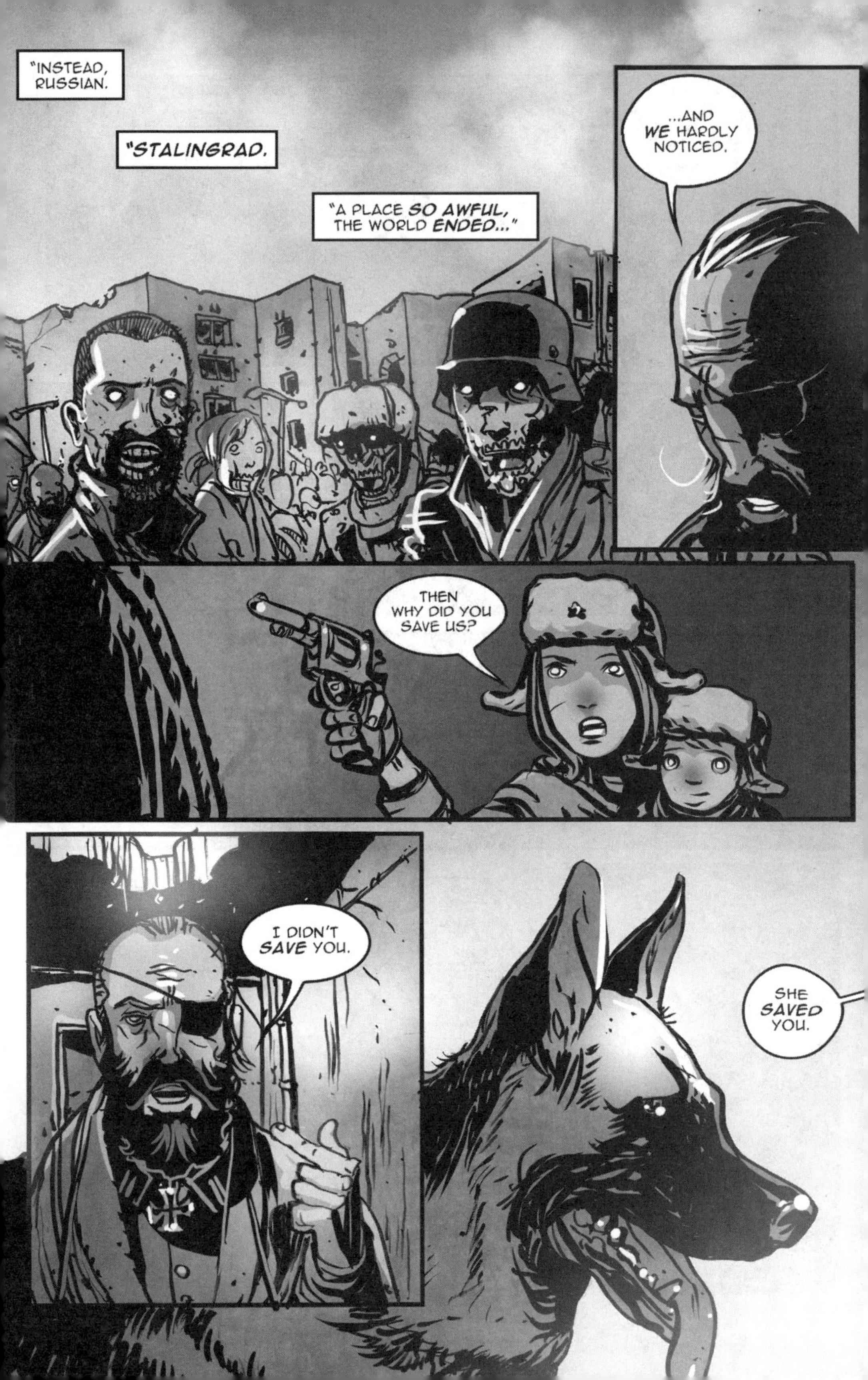
"INSTEAD, RUSSIAN.
"STALINGRAD.
"A PLACE SO AWFUL, THE WORLD ENDED..."
...AND WE HARDLY NOTICED.
THEN WHY DID YOU SAVE US?
I DIDN'T SAVE YOU.
SHE SAVED YOU.

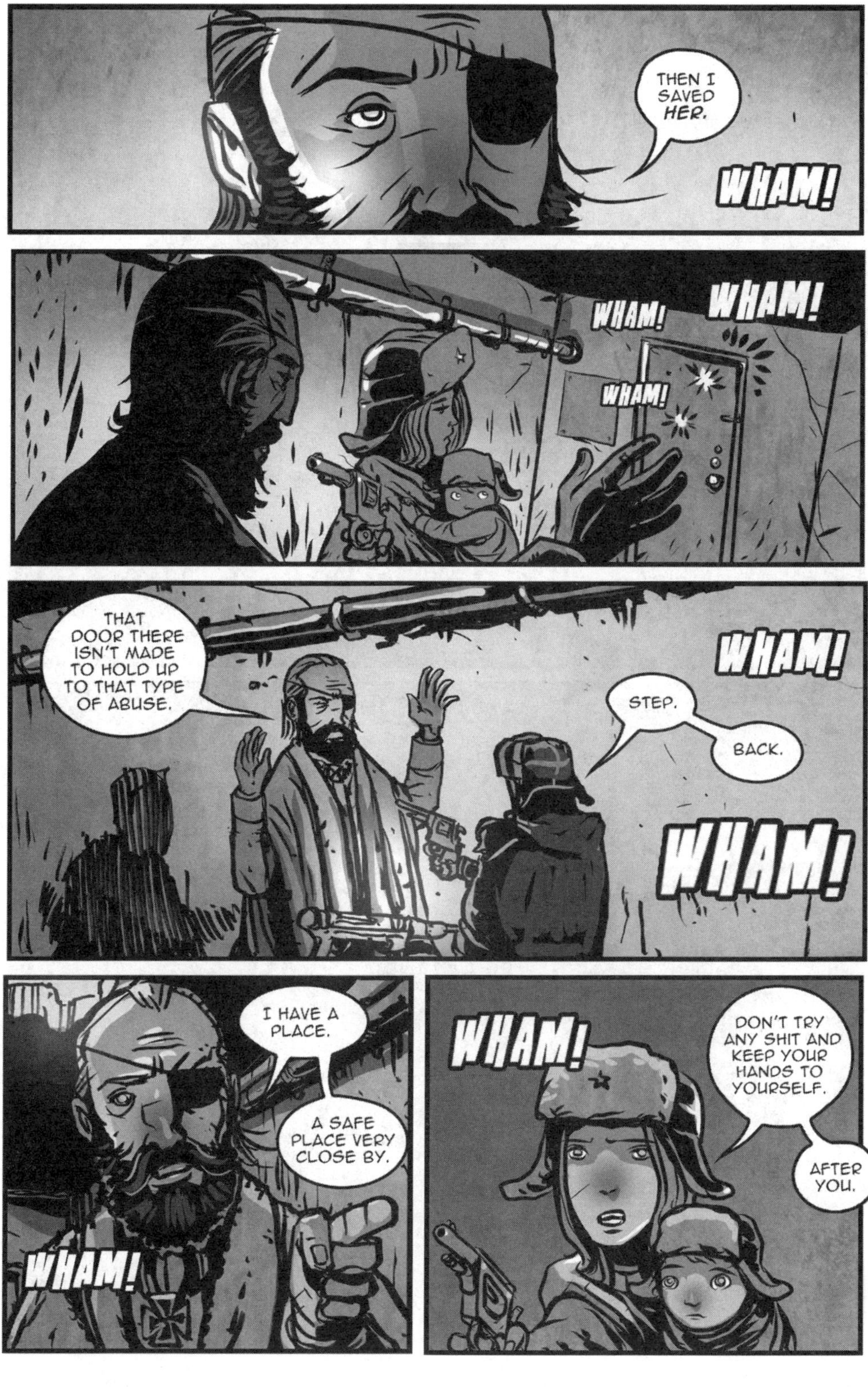
THEN I SAVED HER.
WHAM!
WHAM!
WHAM!
WHAM!
THAT DOOR THERE ISN'T MADE TO HOLD UP TO THAT TYPE OF ABUSE.
WHAM!
STEP.
BACK.
WHAM!
I HAVE A PLACE.
A SAFE PLACE VERY CLOSE BY.
WHAM!
WHAM!
DON'T TRY ANY SHIT AND KEEP YOUR HANDS TO YOURSELF.
AFTER YOU.

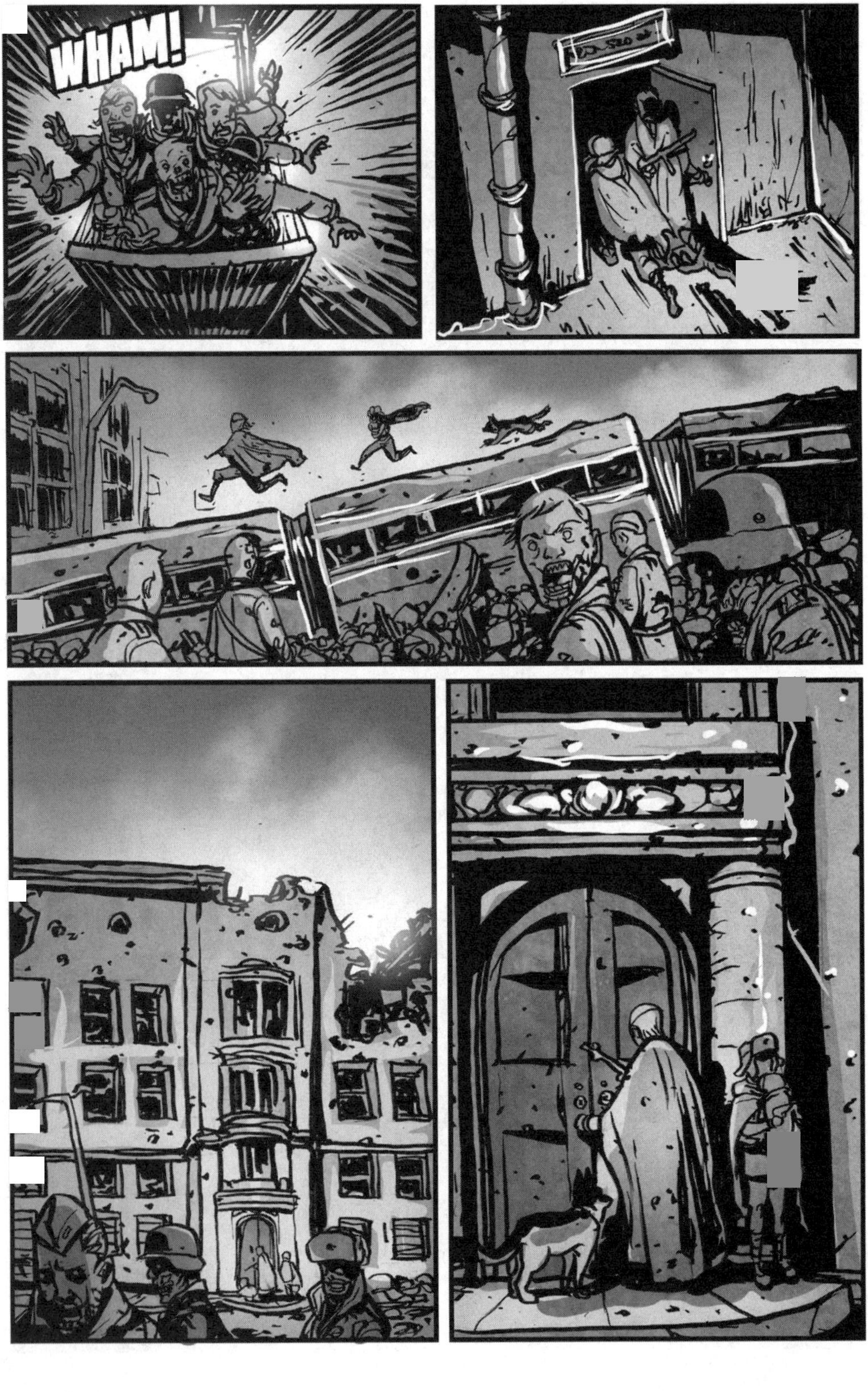
WHAM!

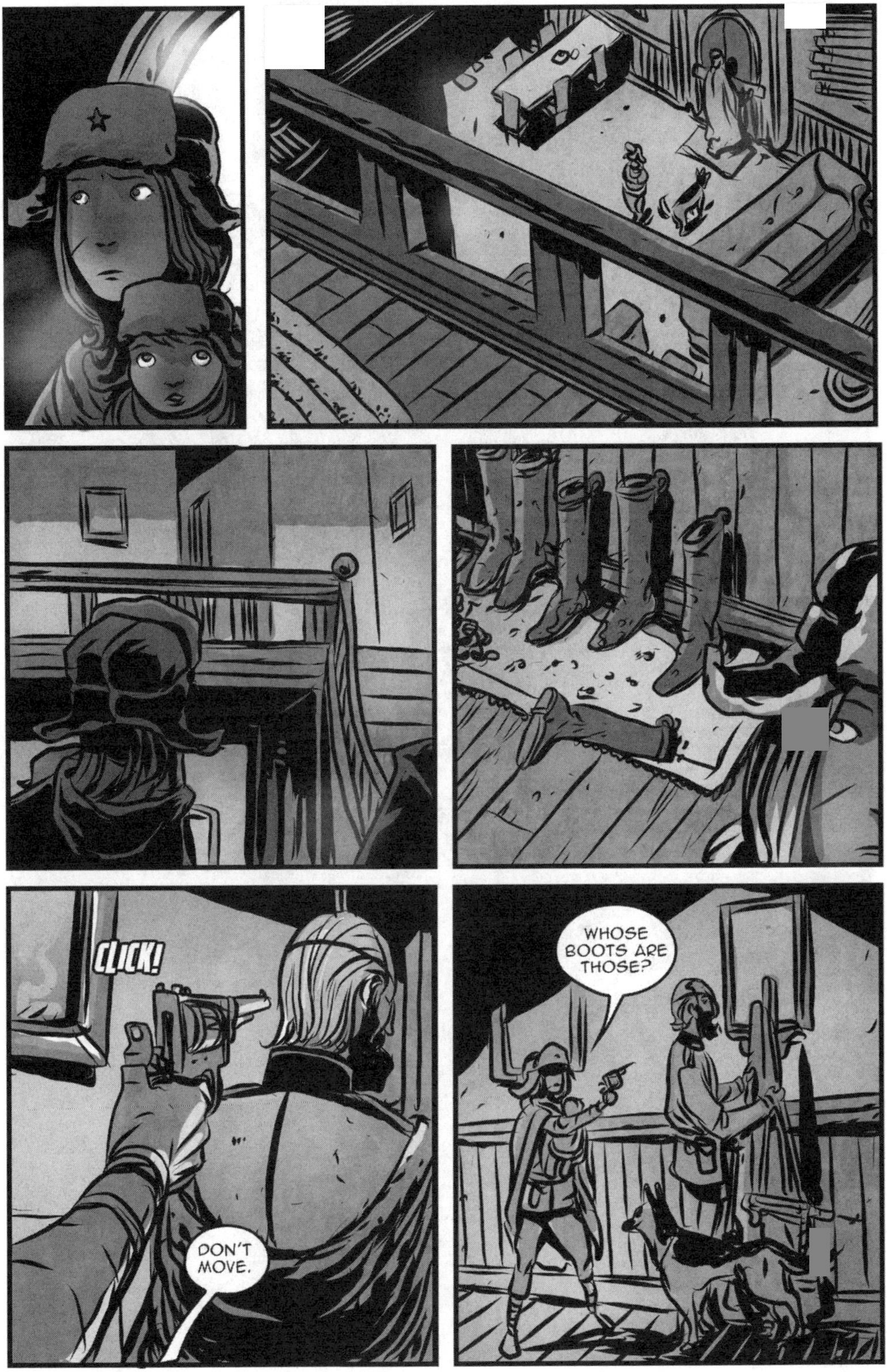
CLICK!
DON'T MOVE.
WHOSE BOOTS ARE THOSE?

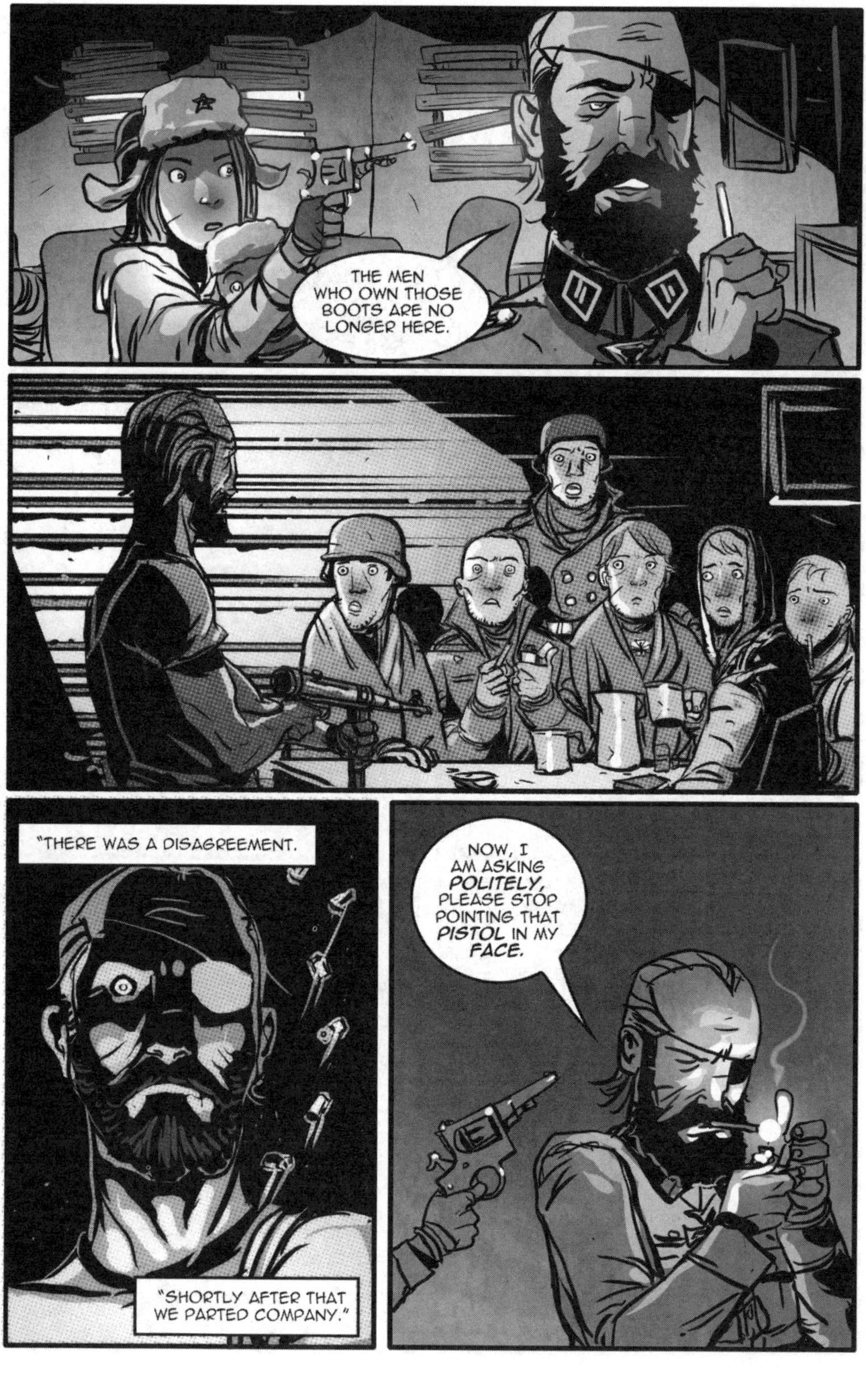
THE MEN WHO OWN THOSE BOOTS ARE NO LONGER HERE.
"THERE WAS A DISAGREEMENT.
"SHORTLY AFTER THAT WE PARTED COMPANY."
NOW, I AM ASKING POLITELY, PLEASE STOP POINTING THAT PISTOL IN MY FACE.

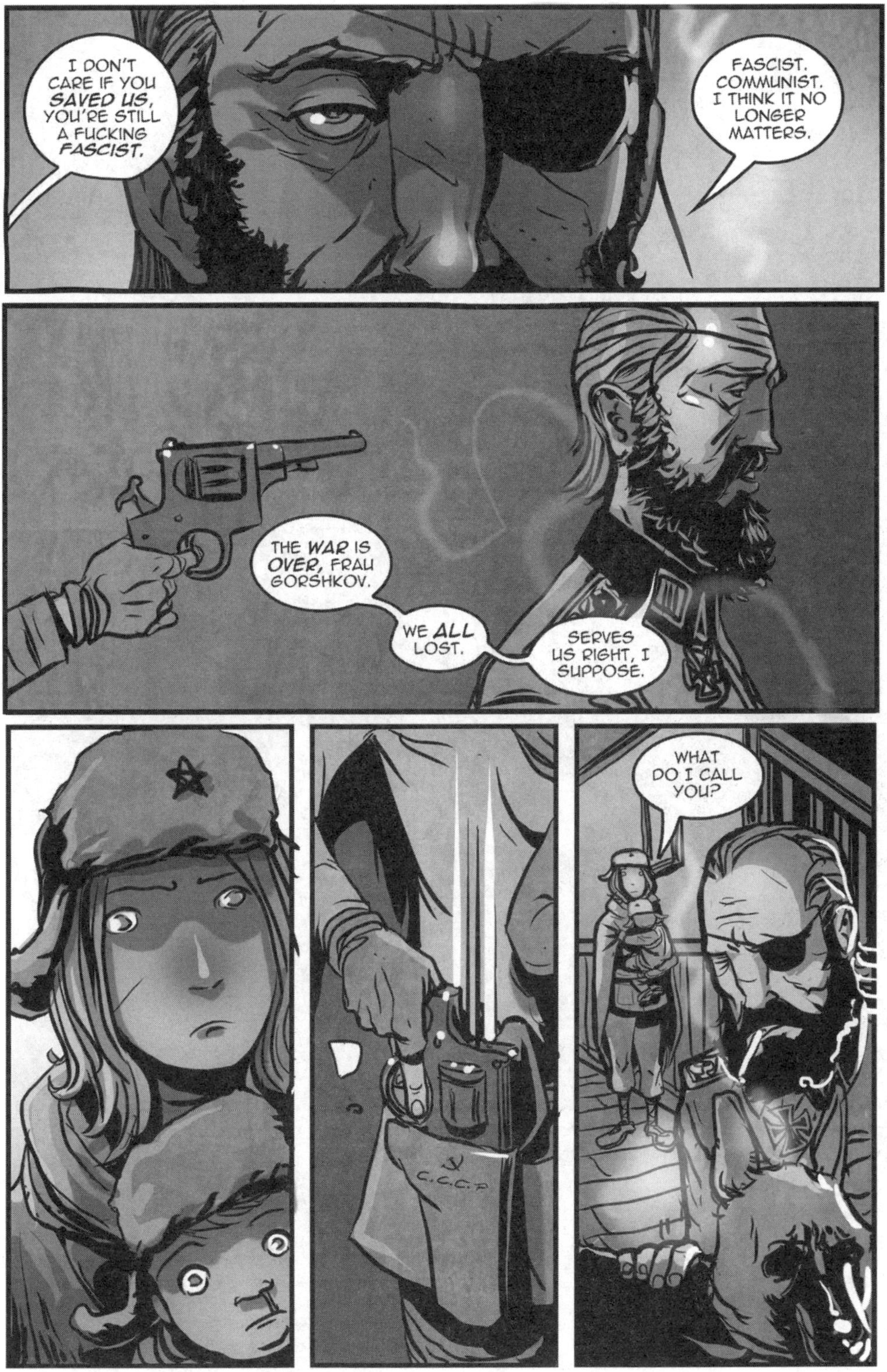
I DON'T CARE IF YOU SAVED US, YOU'RE STILL A FUCKING FASCIST.
FASCIST. COMMUNIST. I THINK IT NO LONGER MATTERS.
THE WAR IS OVER, FRAU GORSHKOV.
WE ALL LOST.
SERVES US RIGHT, I SUPPOSE.
C.C.C.P
WHAT DO I CALL YOU?

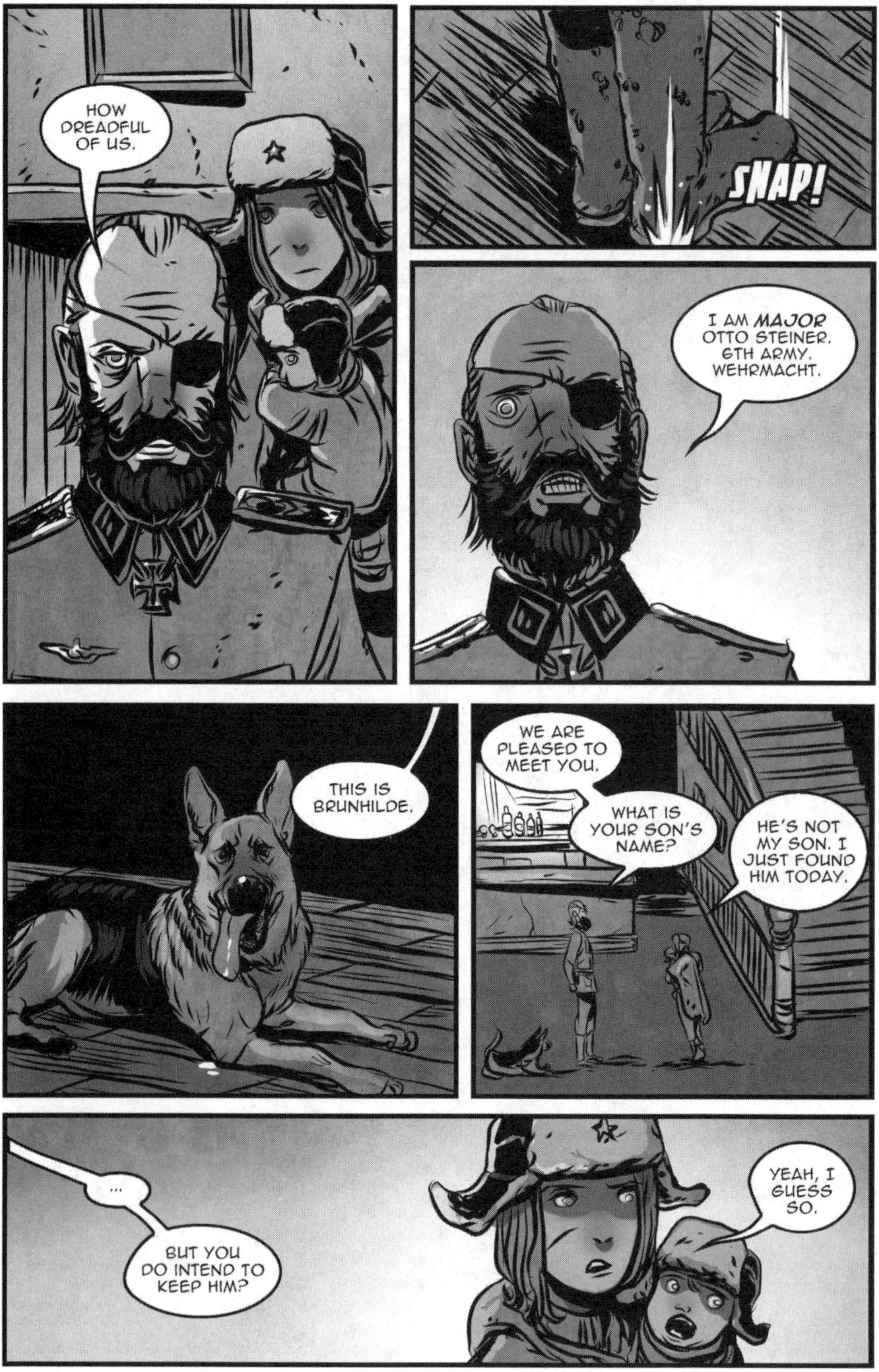
HOW DREADFUL OF US.
SNAP!
I AM MAJOR OTTO STEINER. 6TH ARMY. WEHRMACHT.
THIS IS BRUNHILDE.
WE ARE PLEASED TO MEET YOU.
WHAT IS YOUR SON'S NAME?
HE'S NOT MY SON. I JUST FOUND HIM TODAY.
...
BUT YOU DO INTEND TO KEEP HIM?
YEAH, I GUESS SO.

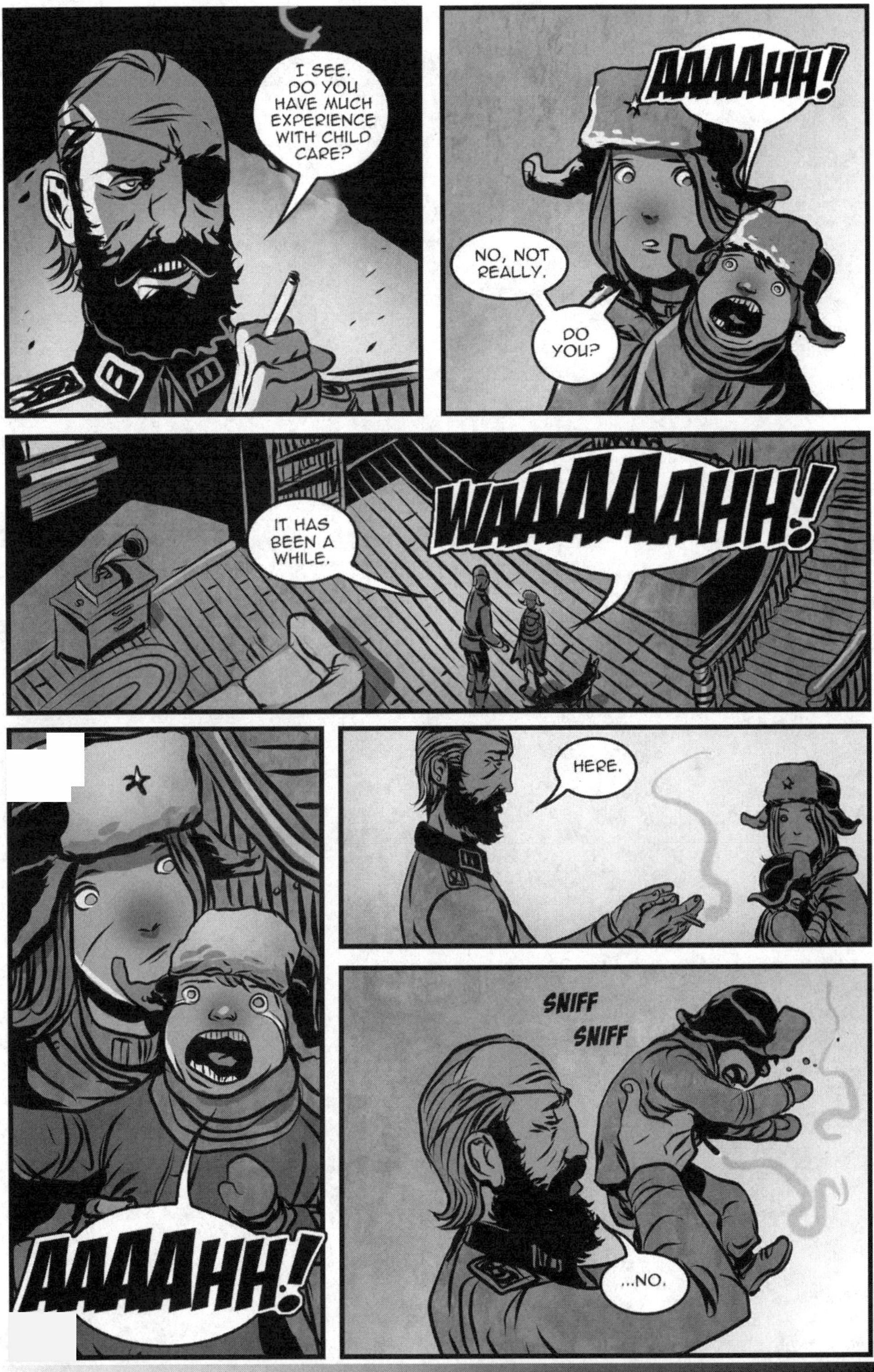
I SEE. DO YOU HAVE MUCH EXPERIENCE WITH CHILD CARE?
AAAAHH!
NO, NOT REALLY.
DO YOU?
IT HAS BEEN A WHILE.
WAAAAAAHH!
AAAAHH!
HERE.
SNIFF
SNIFF
...NO.

CONTINUED IN THE PAGES OF 'MOTHER RUSSIA'

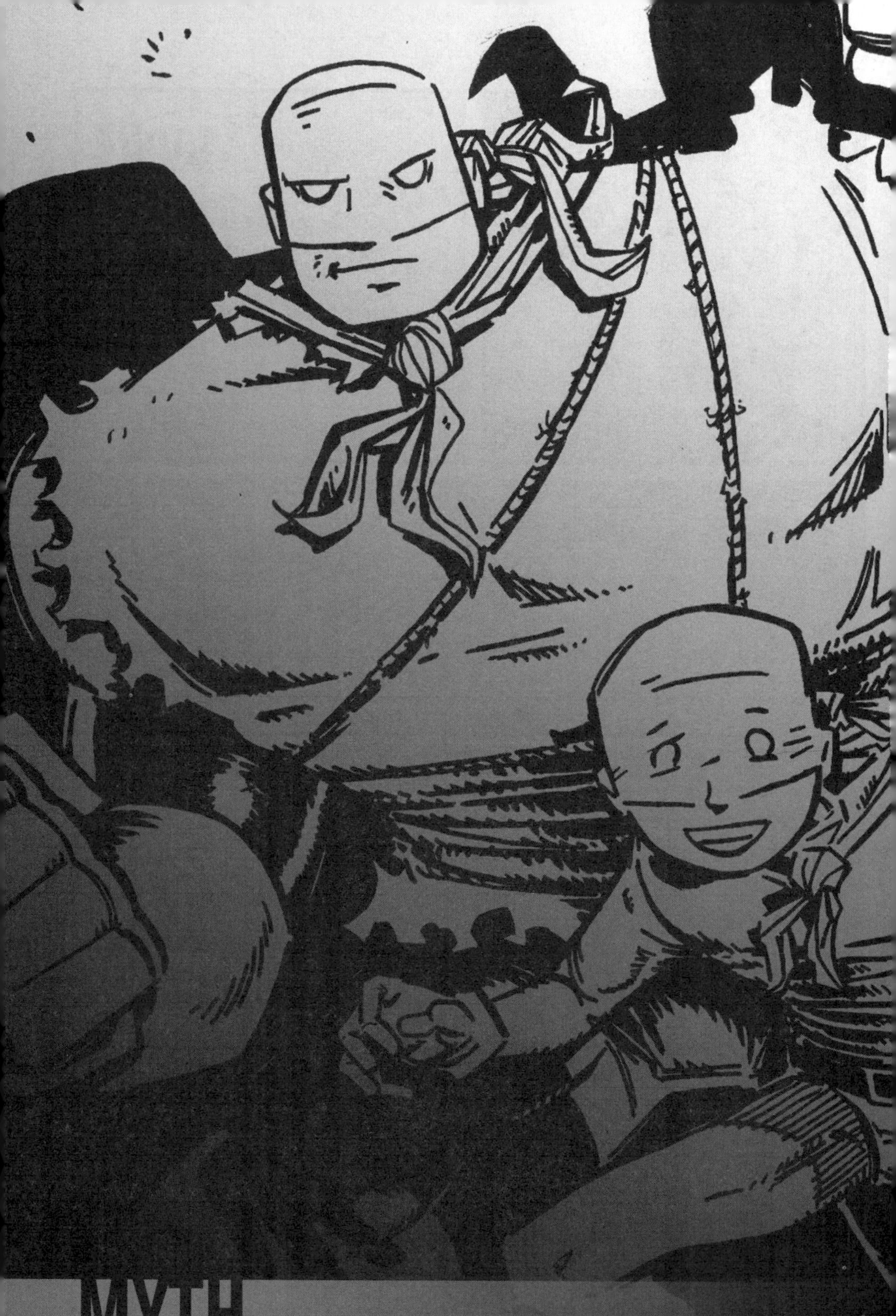

MYTH

MYTH

SAM & GIANT

"That's what's great about superheroes. They aren't afraid to fight the bad guys out there. Kind of like us, right?"

Inspired by the pages of his Golden Age comics, young Sam longs for adventure far from the clutches of the twisted orphanage he calls home. He finds it within the mysterious forest beyond his town, where a fallen kingdom of fantasy awaits. There he befriends a solitary Giant and together they live out the adventures of his favorite heroes as they battle the cruel adults plaguing their small town. But, when an evil far more dangerous than any adult awakens within the ruins of the forest, Sam and his massive sidekick are the only heroes standing in its way.

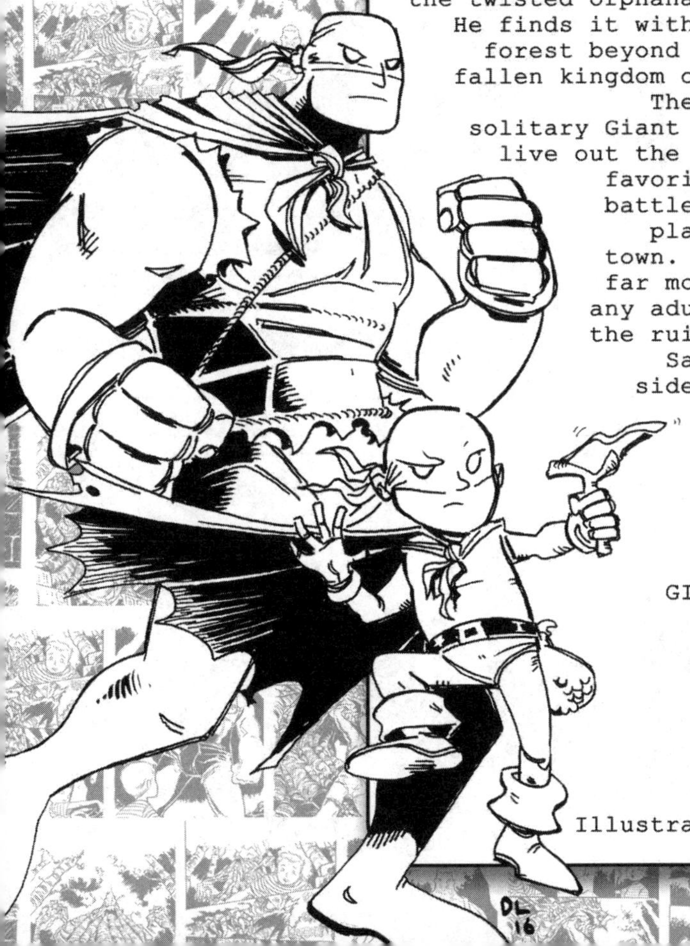

DL
16

SAM Age: 9
Height: 4'9"
Weight: 53 lbs.

GIANT Age: Unknown
Height: 8'4"
Weight: 987 lbs.

First Appearance:
MYTH #1 (2013)

Created by
Mike Loniewski
Illustration by Dan Lauer

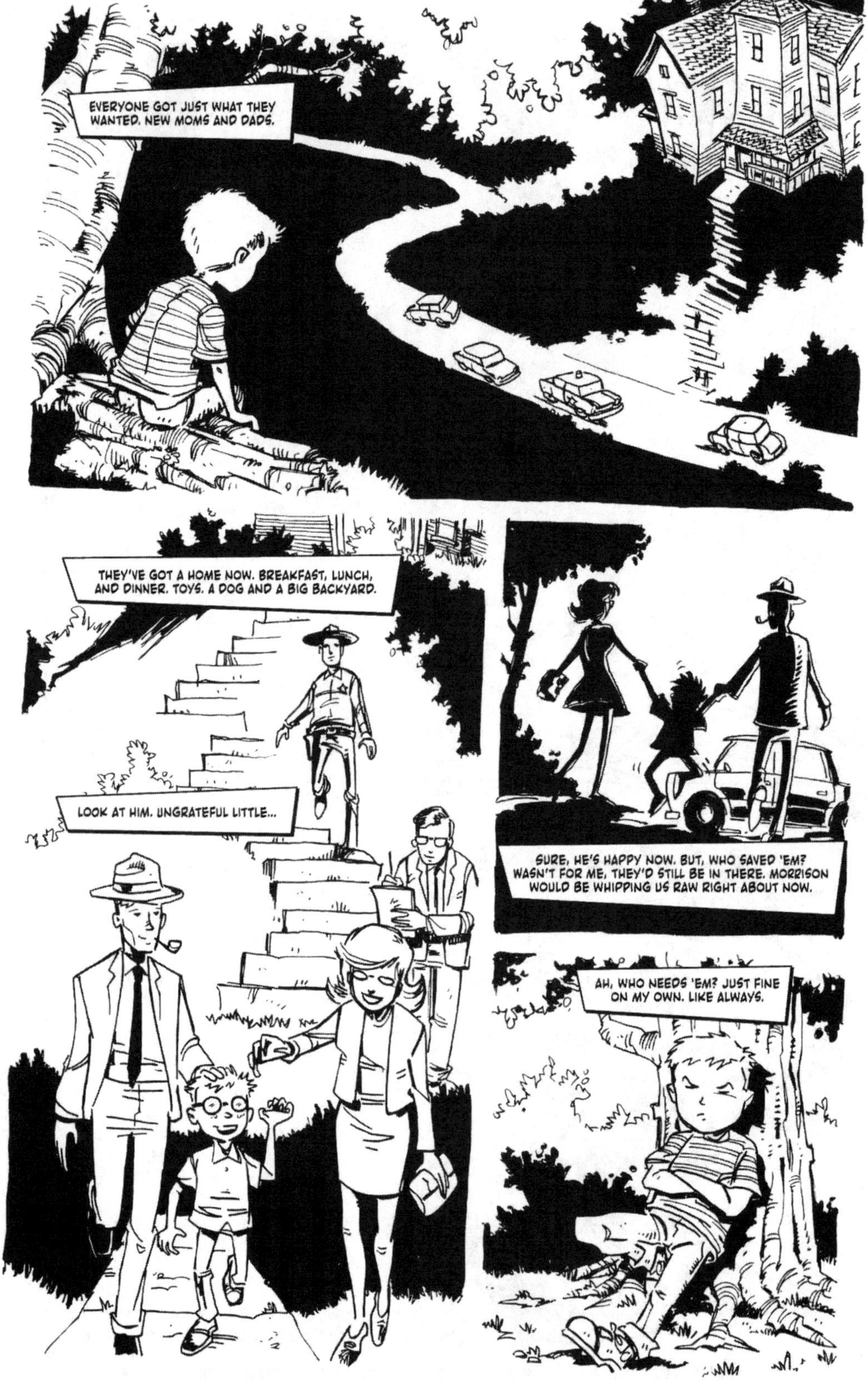
EVERYONE GOT JUST WHAT THEY WANTED. NEW MOMS AND DADS.
THEY'VE GOT A HOME NOW. BREAKFAST, LUNCH, AND DINNER. TOYS. A DOG AND A BIG BACKYARD.
LOOK AT HIM. UNGRATEFUL LITTLE...
SURE, HE'S HAPPY NOW. BUT, WHO SAVED 'EM? WASN'T FOR ME, THEY'D STILL BE IN THERE. MORRISON WOULD BE WHIPPING US RAW RIGHT ABOUT NOW.
AH, WHO NEEDS 'EM? JUST FINE ON MY OWN. LIKE ALWAYS.

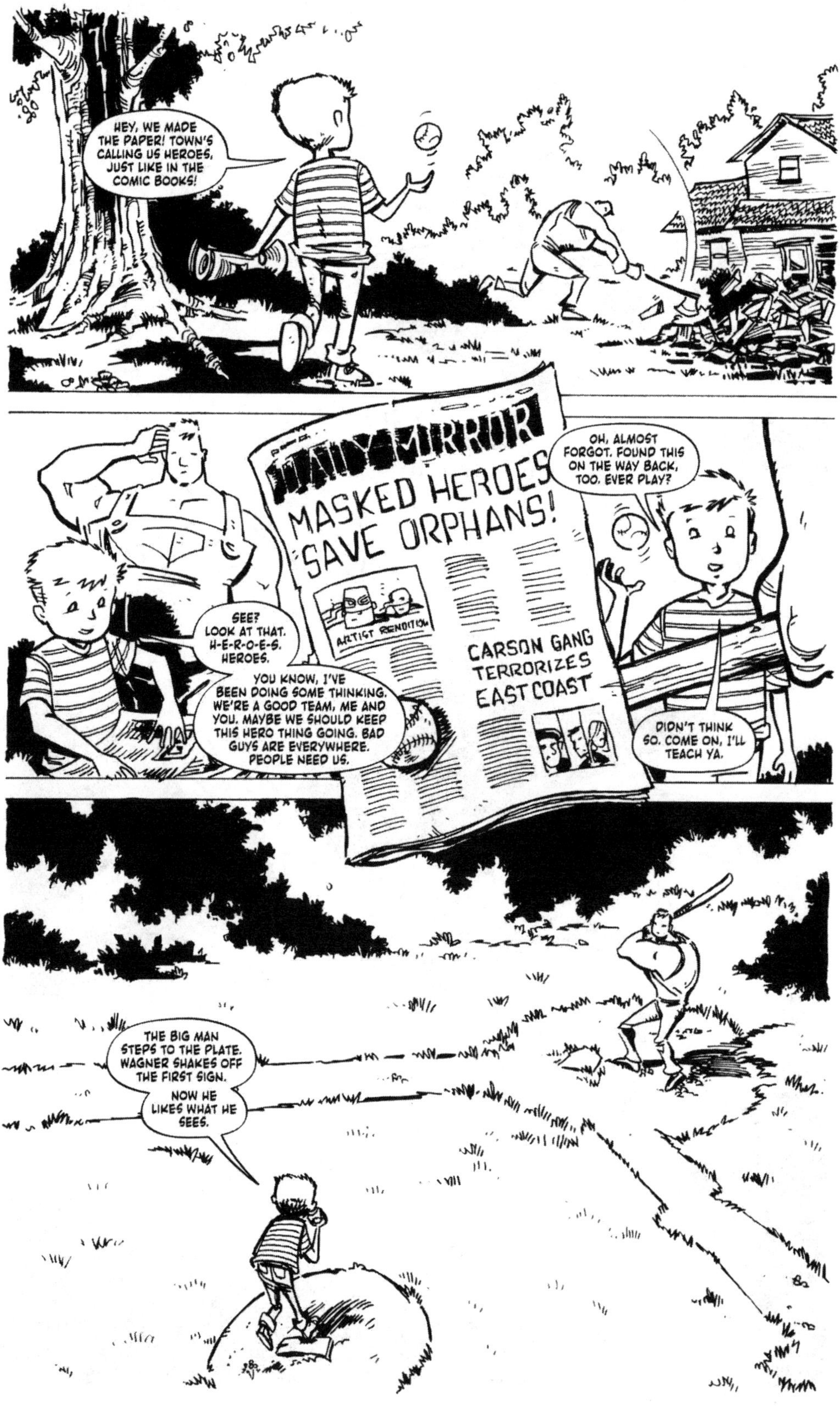

HEY, WE MADE THE PAPER! TOWN'S CALLING US HEROES, JUST LIKE IN THE COMIC BOOKS!
MASKED HEROES SAVE ORPHANS!
ARTIST RENDITION
CARSON GANG TERRORIZES EAST COAST
SEE? LOOK AT THAT. H-E-R-O-E-S. HEROES.
YOU KNOW, I'VE BEEN DOING SOME THINKING. WE'RE A GOOD TEAM, ME AND YOU. MAYBE WE SHOULD KEEP THIS HERO THING GOING. BAD GUYS ARE EVERYWHERE. PEOPLE NEED US.
OH, ALMOST FORGOT. FOUND THIS ON THE WAY BACK, TOO. EVER PLAY?
DIDN'T THINK SO. COME ON, I'LL TEACH YA.
THE BIG MAN STEPS TO THE PLATE. WAGNER SHAKES OFF THE FIRST SIGN.
NOW HE LIKES WHAT HE SEES.

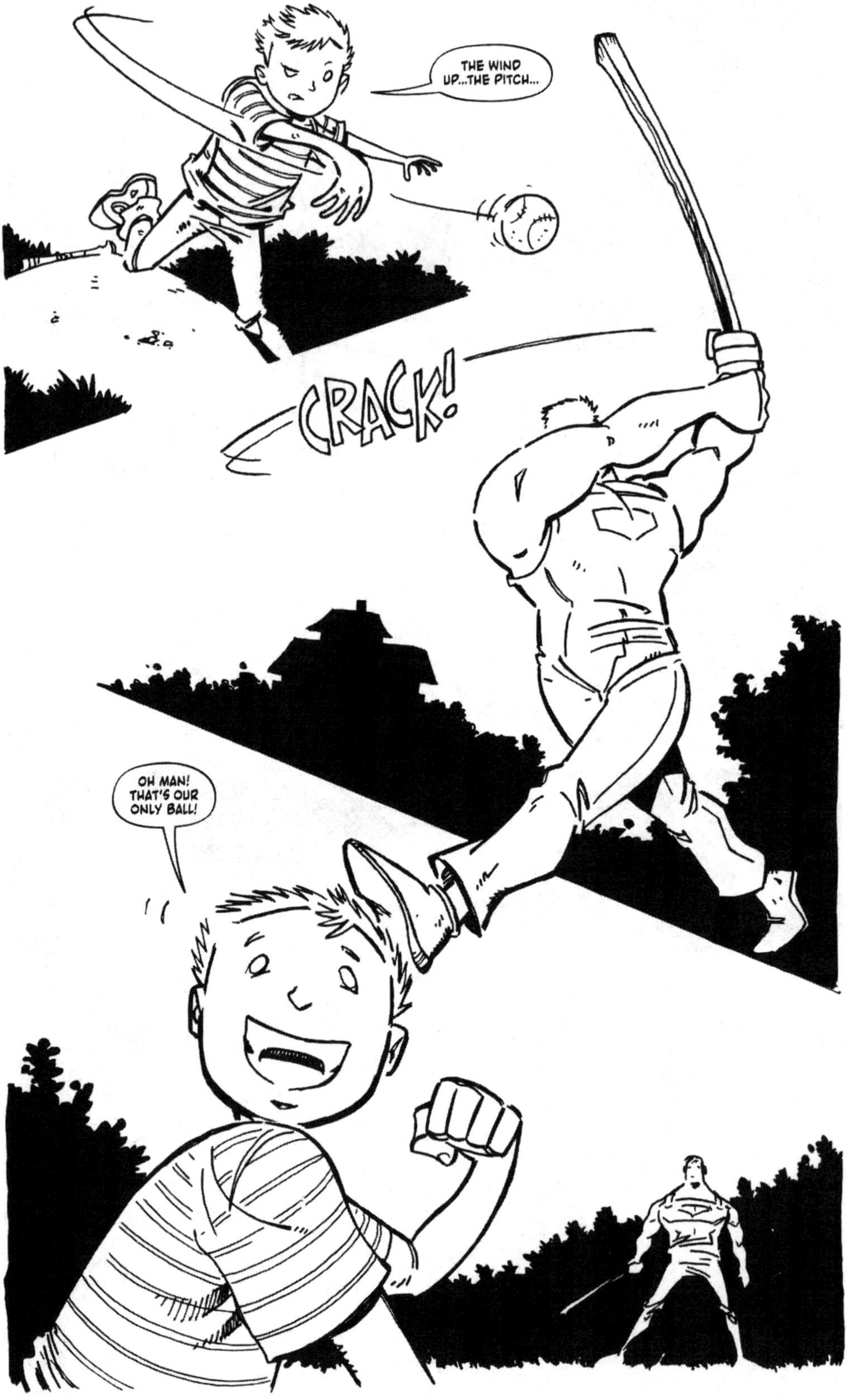
THE WIND UP...THE PITCH...
CRACK!
OH MAN! THAT'S OUR ONLY BALL!

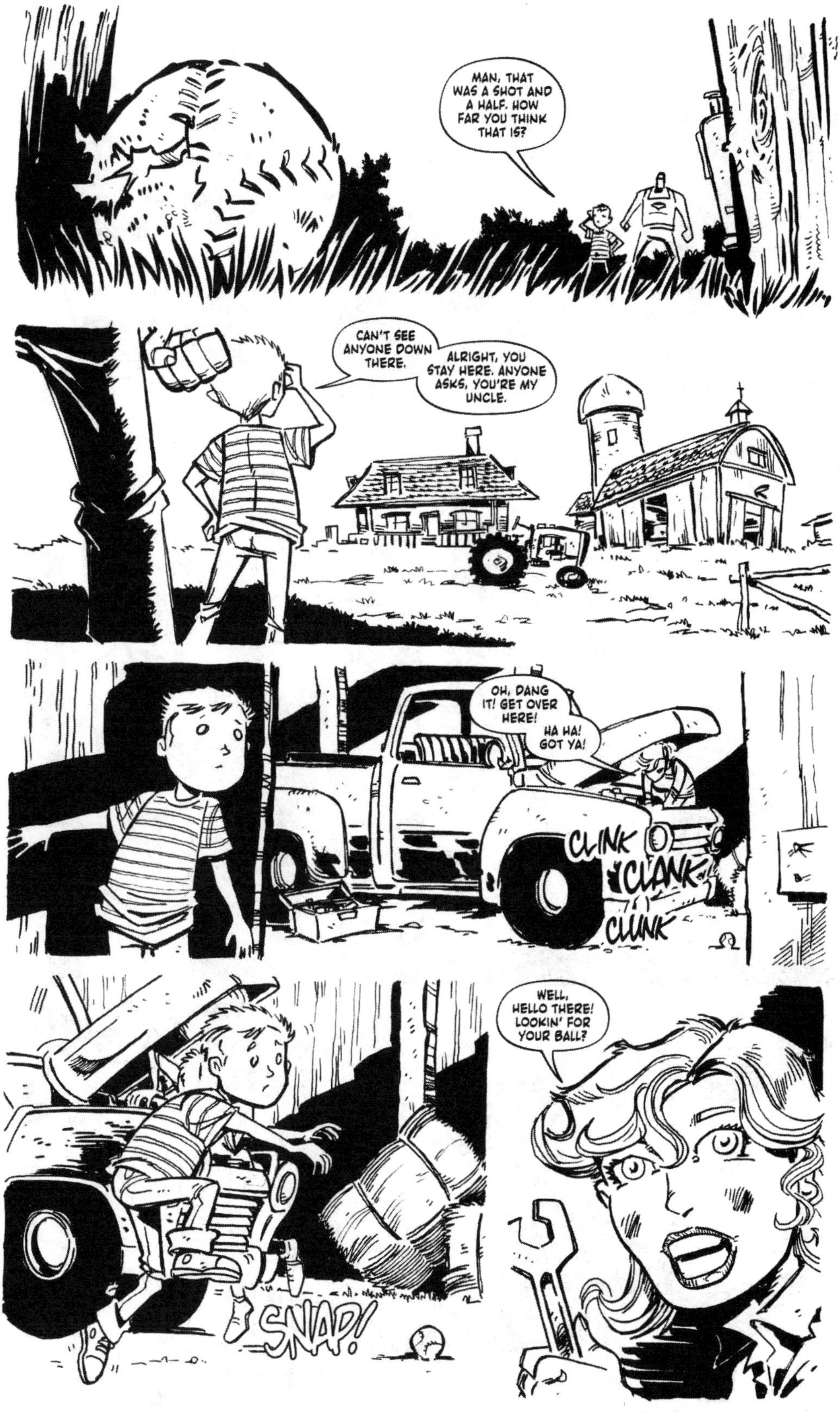
MAN, THAT WAS A SHOT AND A HALF. HOW FAR YOU THINK THAT IS?
CAN'T SEE ANYONE DOWN THERE.
ALRIGHT, YOU STAY HERE. ANYONE ASKS, YOU'RE MY UNCLE.
OH, DANG IT! GET OVER HERE!
HA HA! GOT YA!
CLINK
CLANK
CLUNK
SNAP!
WELL, HELLO THERE! LOOKIN' FOR YOUR BALL?

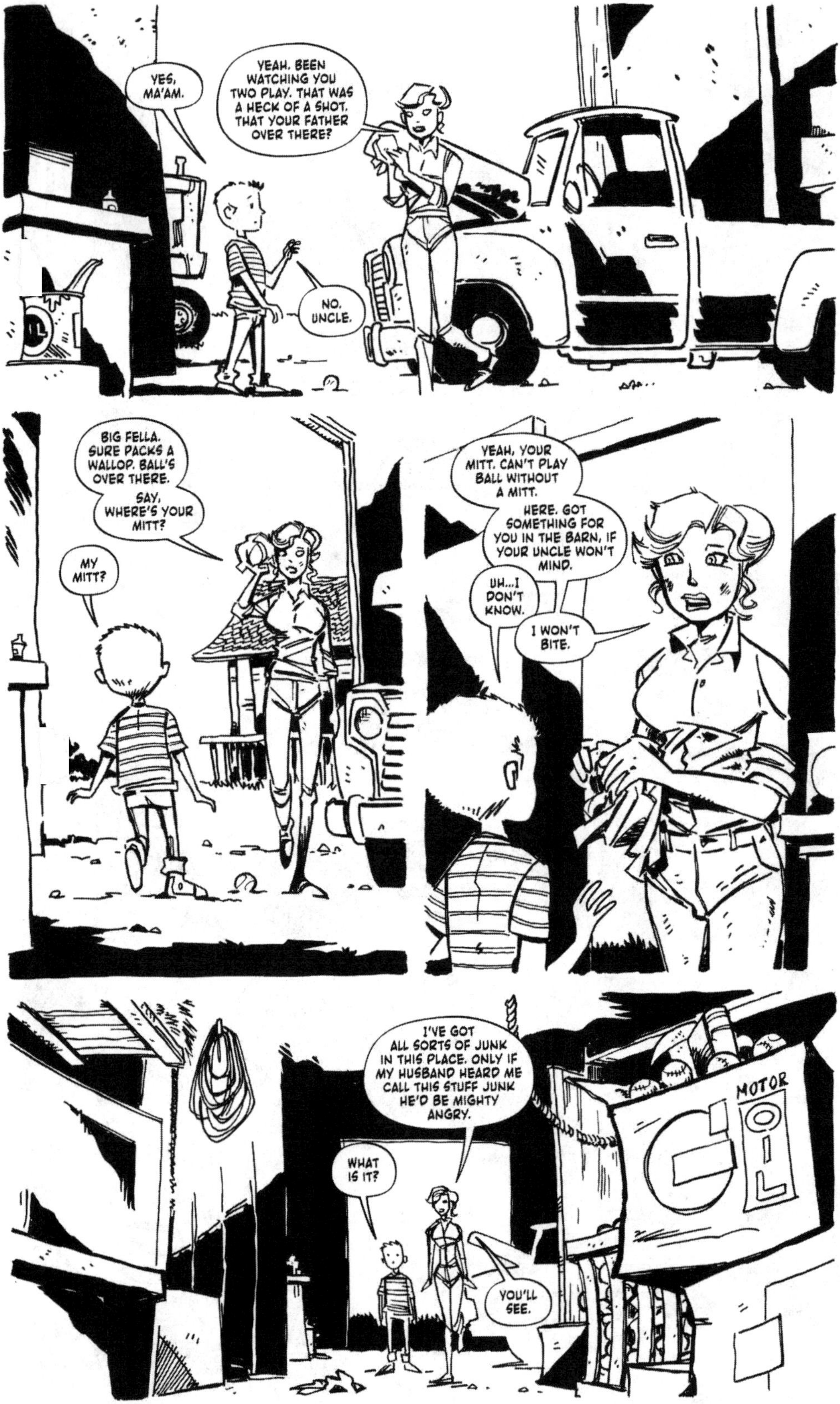
YES, MA'AM.
YEAH. BEEN WATCHING YOU TWO PLAY. THAT WAS A HECK OF A SHOT. THAT YOUR FATHER OVER THERE?
NO. UNCLE.
BIG FELLA. SURE PACKS A WALLOP. BALL'S OVER THERE.
SAY, WHERE'S YOUR MITT?
MY MITT?
YEAH, YOUR MITT. CAN'T PLAY BALL WITHOUT A MITT.
HERE. GOT SOMETHING FOR YOU IN THE BARN, IF YOUR UNCLE WON'T MIND.
UH...I DON'T KNOW.
I WON'T BITE.
I'VE GOT ALL SORTS OF JUNK IN THIS PLACE. ONLY IF MY HUSBAND HEARD ME CALL THIS STUFF JUNK HE'D BE MIGHTY ANGRY.
WHAT IS IT?
YOU'LL SEE.
MOTOR OIL

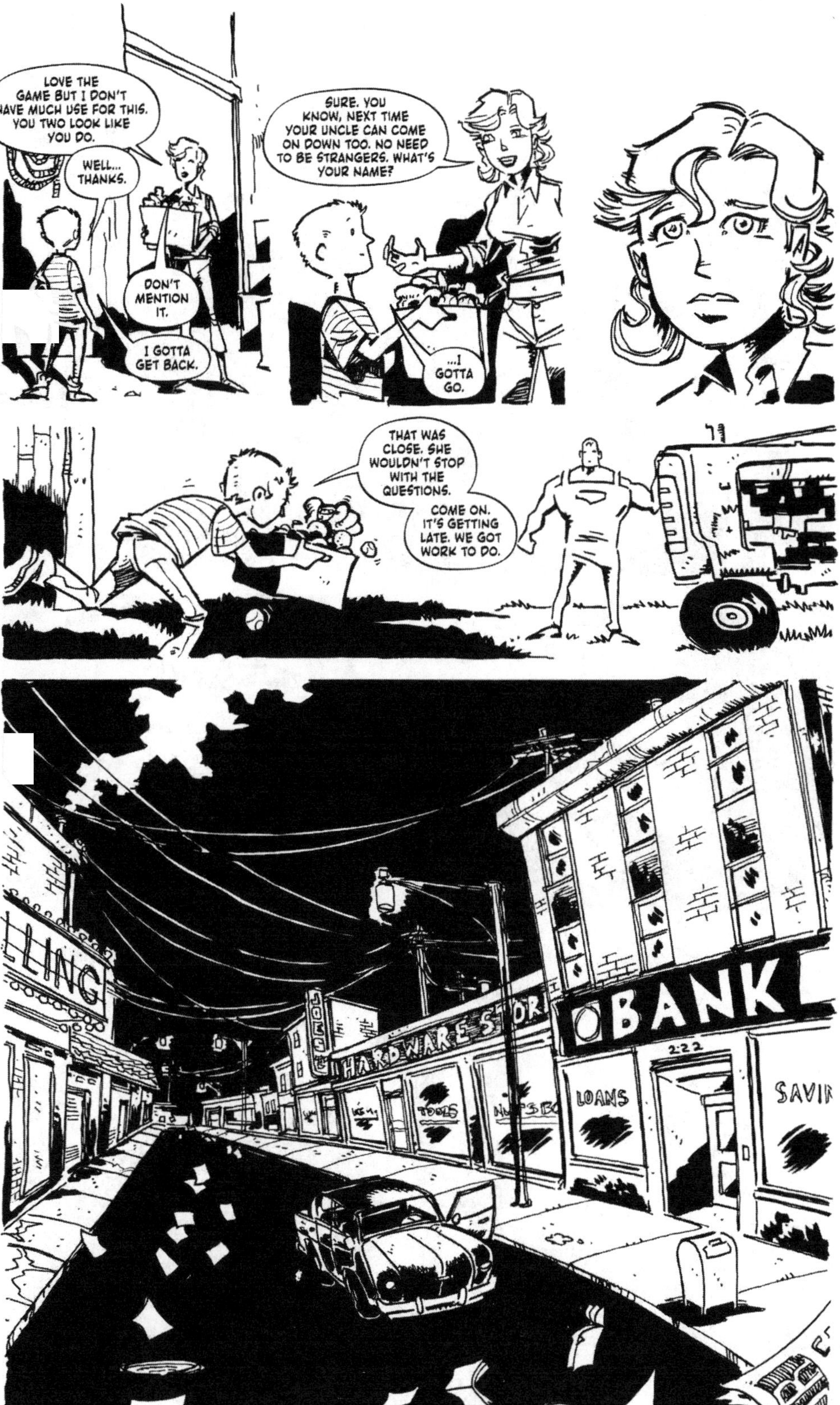
LOVE THE GAME BUT I DON'T HAVE MUCH USE FOR THIS. YOU TWO LOOK LIKE YOU DO.
WELL... THANKS.
DON'T MENTION IT.
I GOTTA GET BACK.
SURE. YOU KNOW, NEXT TIME YOUR UNCLE CAN COME ON DOWN TOO. NO NEED TO BE STRANGERS. WHAT'S YOUR NAME?
...I GOTTA GO.
THAT WAS CLOSE. SHE WOULDN'T STOP WITH THE QUESTIONS.
COME ON. IT'S GETTING LATE. WE GOT WORK TO DO.
BANK
2:22
LOANS
TOOLS

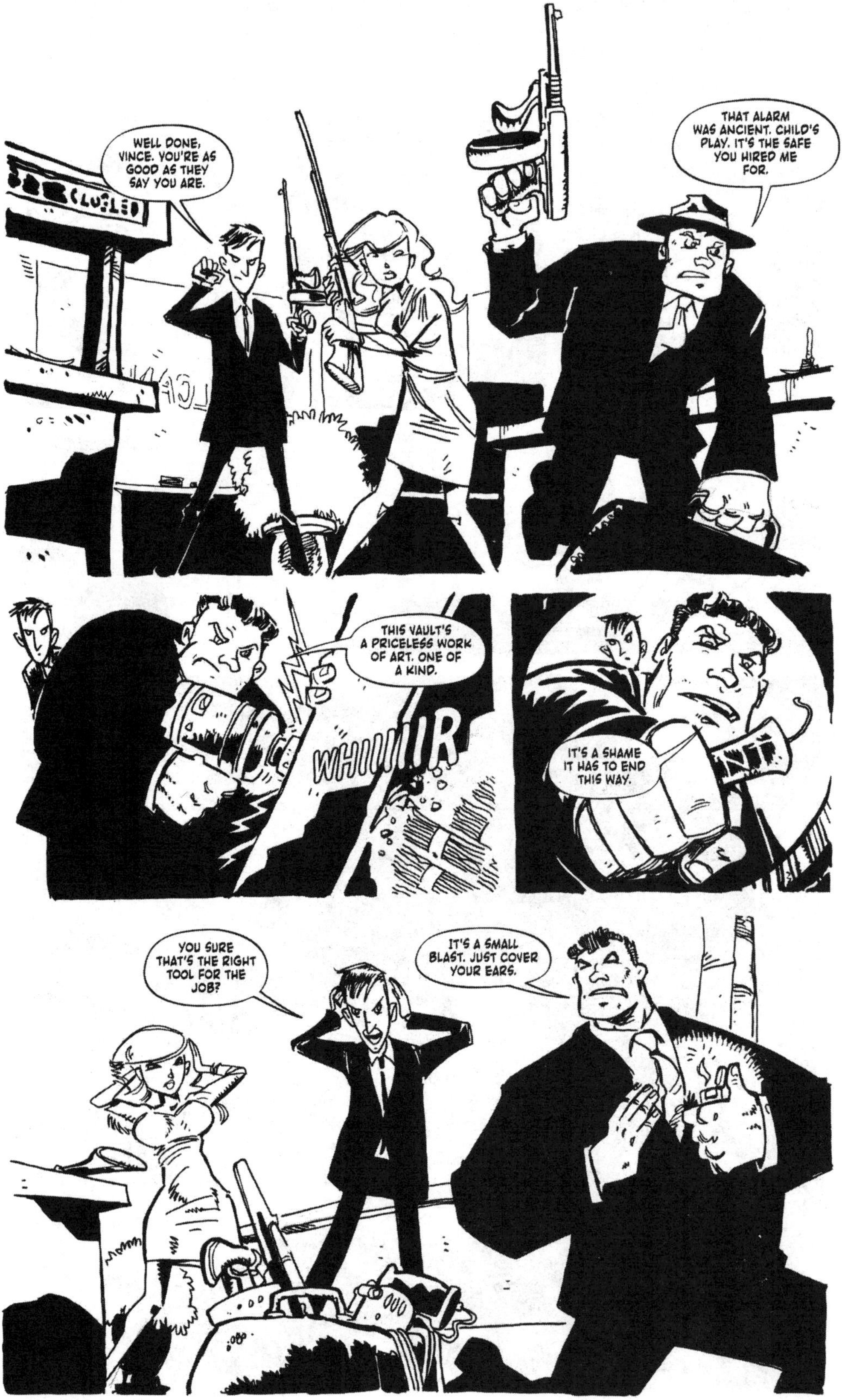
WELL DONE, VINCE. YOU'RE AS GOOD AS THEY SAY YOU ARE.
THAT ALARM WAS ANCIENT. CHILD'S PLAY. IT'S THE SAFE YOU HIRED ME FOR.
THIS VAULT'S A PRICELESS WORK OF ART. ONE OF A KIND.
WHIIIIIR
IT'S A SHAME IT HAS TO END THIS WAY.
YOU SURE THAT'S THE RIGHT TOOL FOR THE JOB?
IT'S A SMALL BLAST. JUST COVER YOUR EARS.

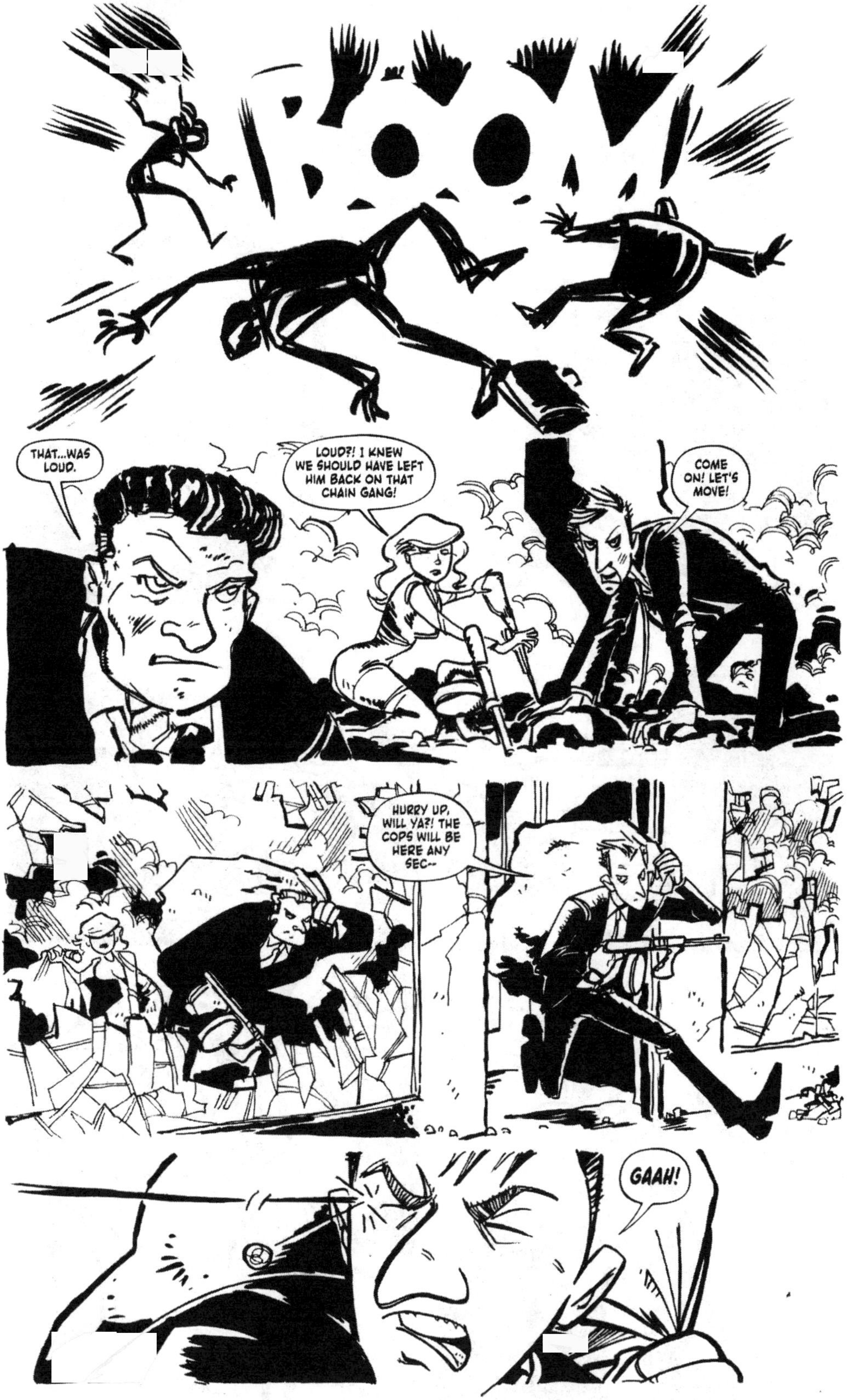
BOOM!
THAT...WAS LOUD.
LOUD?! I KNEW WE SHOULD HAVE LEFT HIM BACK ON THAT CHAIN GANG!
COME ON! LET'S MOVE!
HURRY UP, WILL YA?! THE COPS WILL BE HERE ANY SEC--
GAAH!

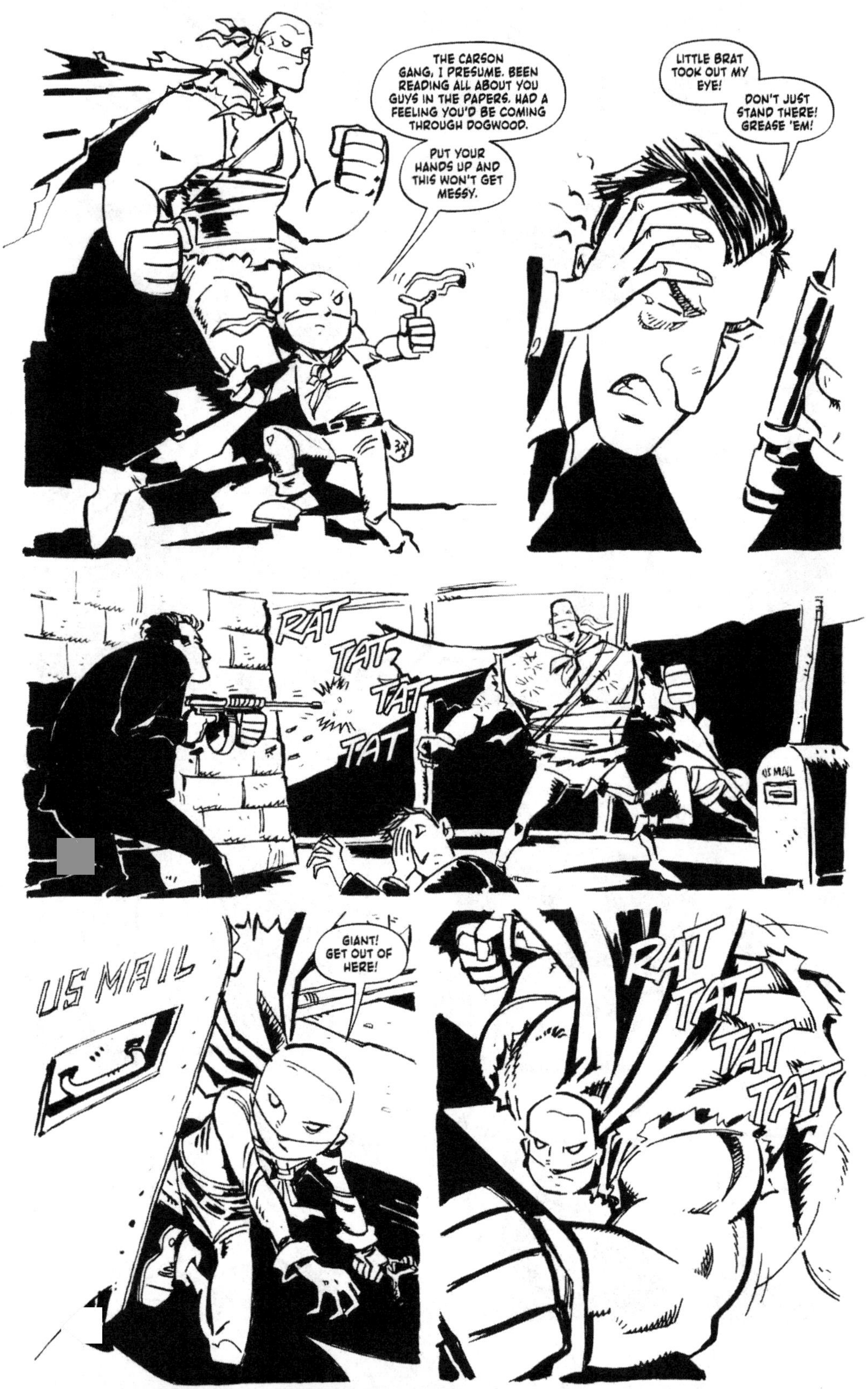
THE CARSON GANG, I PRESUME. BEEN READING ALL ABOUT YOU GUYS IN THE PAPERS. HAD A FEELING YOU'D BE COMING THROUGH DOGWOOD.
PUT YOUR HANDS UP AND THIS WON'T GET MESSY.
LITTLE BRAT TOOK OUT MY EYE!
DON'T JUST STAND THERE! GREASE 'EM!
RAT TAT TAT TAT
US MAIL
US MAIL
GIANT! GET OUT OF HERE!
RAT TAT TAT TAT

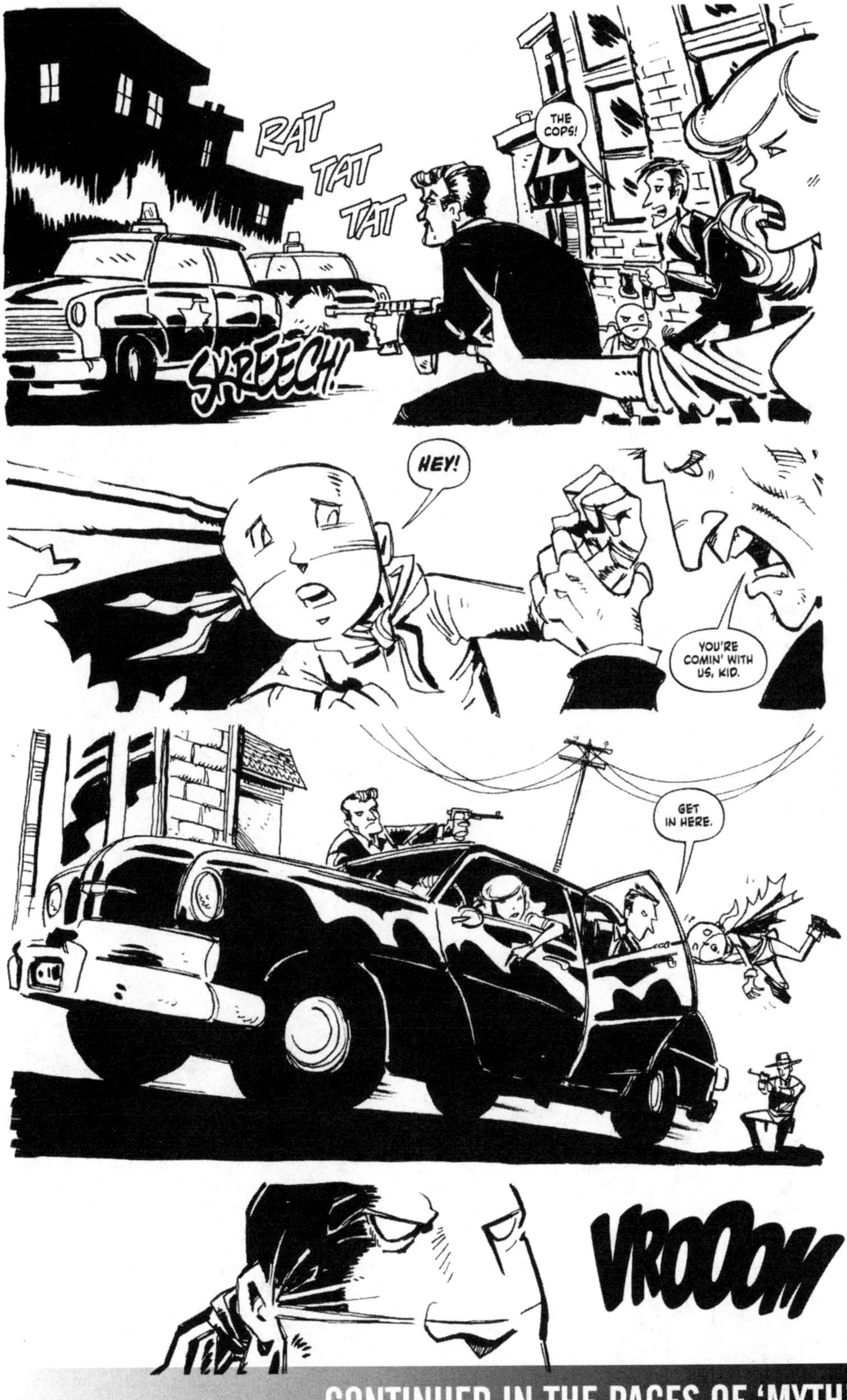
RAT
TAT
TAT
THE COPS!
SKREECH!
HEY!
YOU'RE COMIN' WITH US, KID.
GET IN HERE.
VROOOM

CONTINUED IN THE PAGES OF 'MYTH'

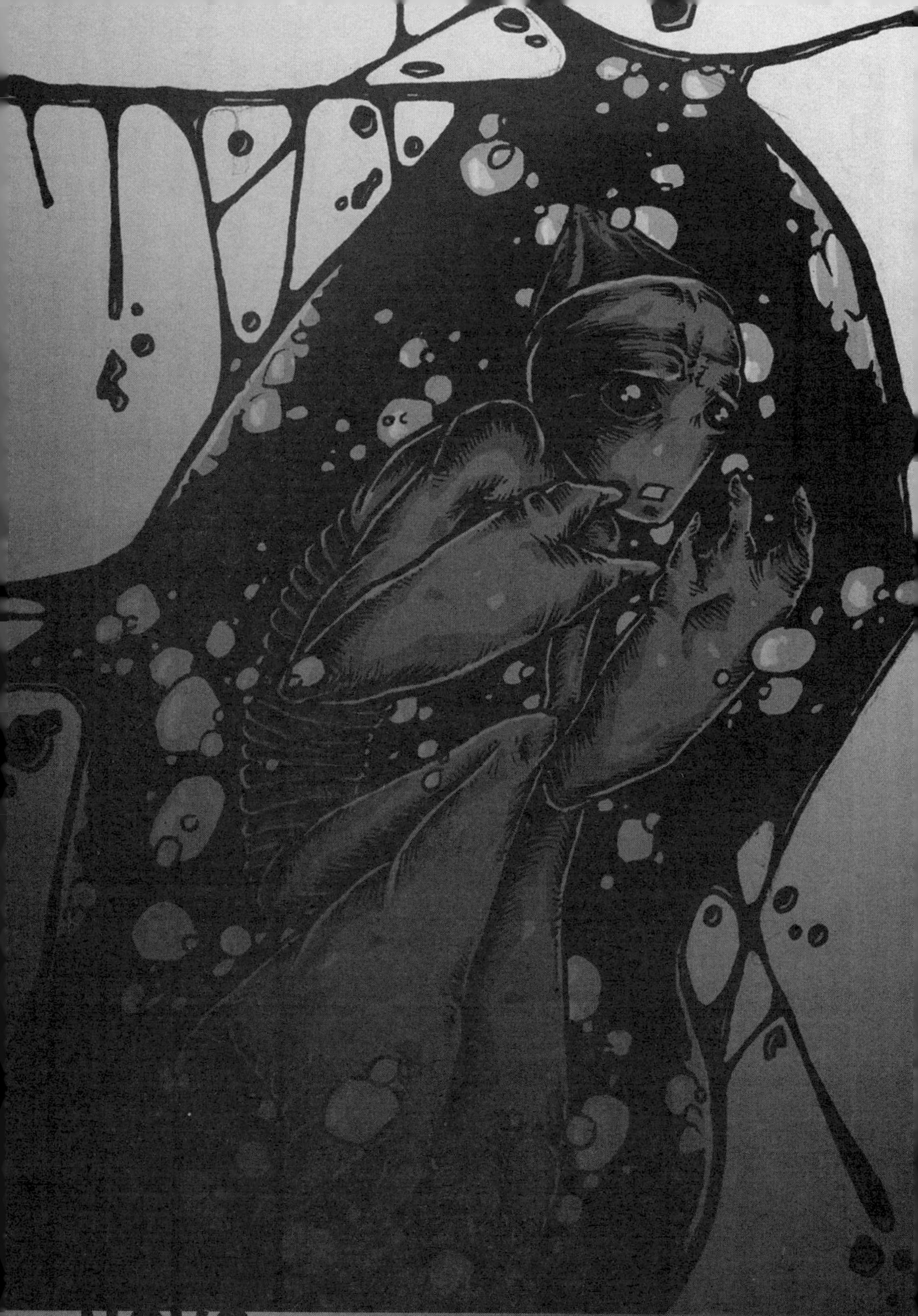

NOVO

NOVO

NOVO

"I hate sleeping… because I know what happens if you don't wake up."

Novo is the offspring of two extinct species, the Aquans and the Terans; who spent their entire existences warring over petty beliefs and ideologies. Now they are all dead and gone and Novo is their last survivor as well as the only member of a new hybrid species. Novo hungers for meaning in his life wandering the deserted planet that was left to him. What he finds on his journey changes him and the lives of countless others throughout the ages.

Age: Adolescent
Height: 5'5"
Weight: 110 lbs.

First Appearance:
BIRTH (2007)

Created by
Michael S. Bracco
Illustration by
Michael S. Bracco

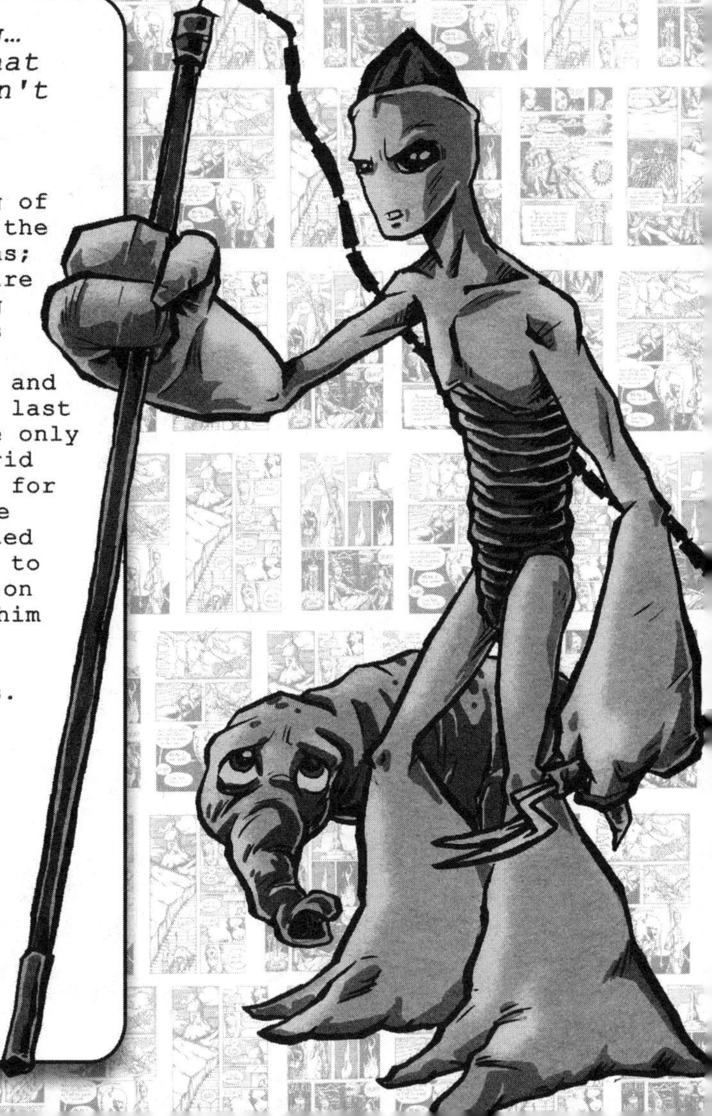

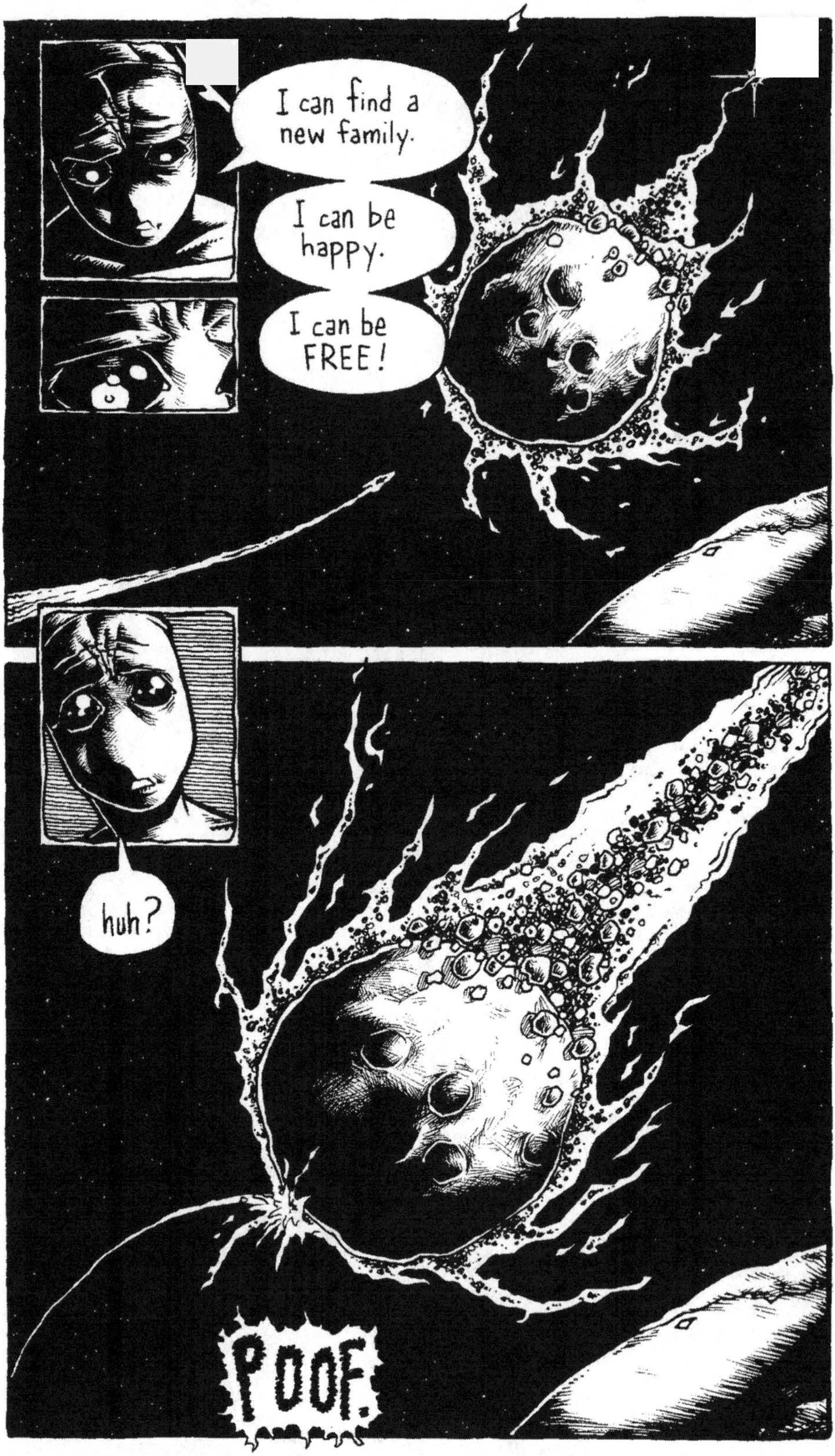
I can find a new family.
I can be happy.
I can be FREE!
huh?
POOF.

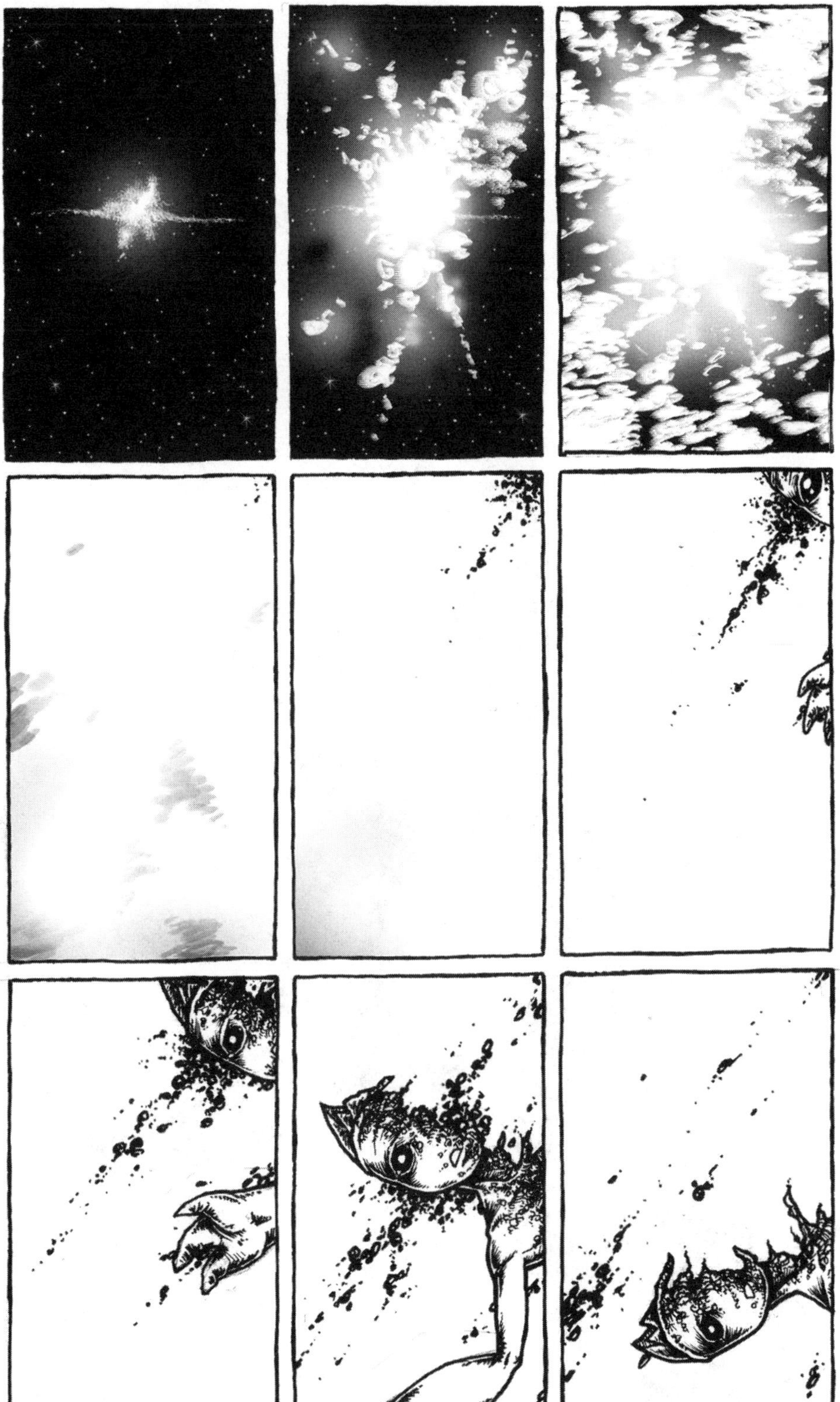

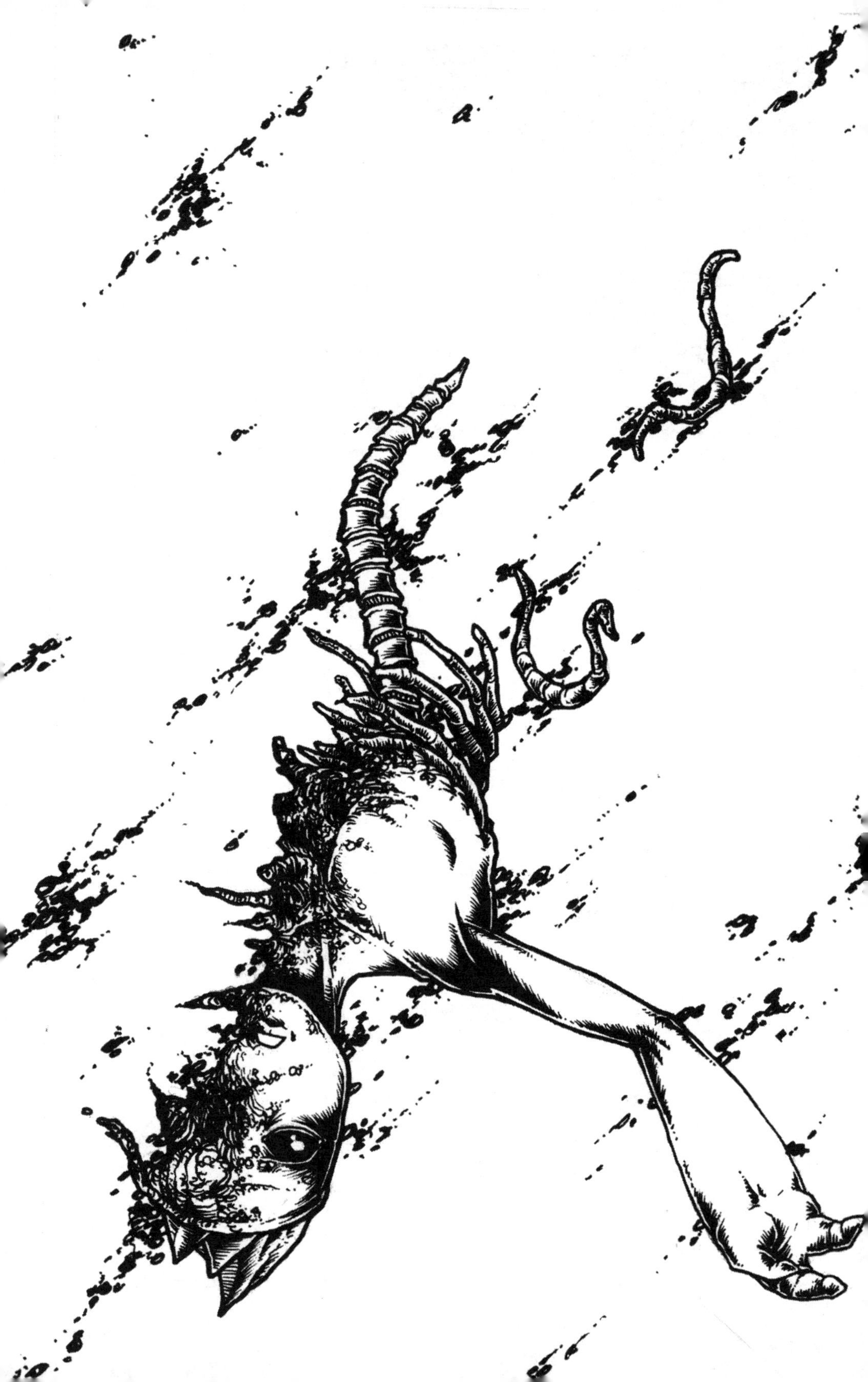

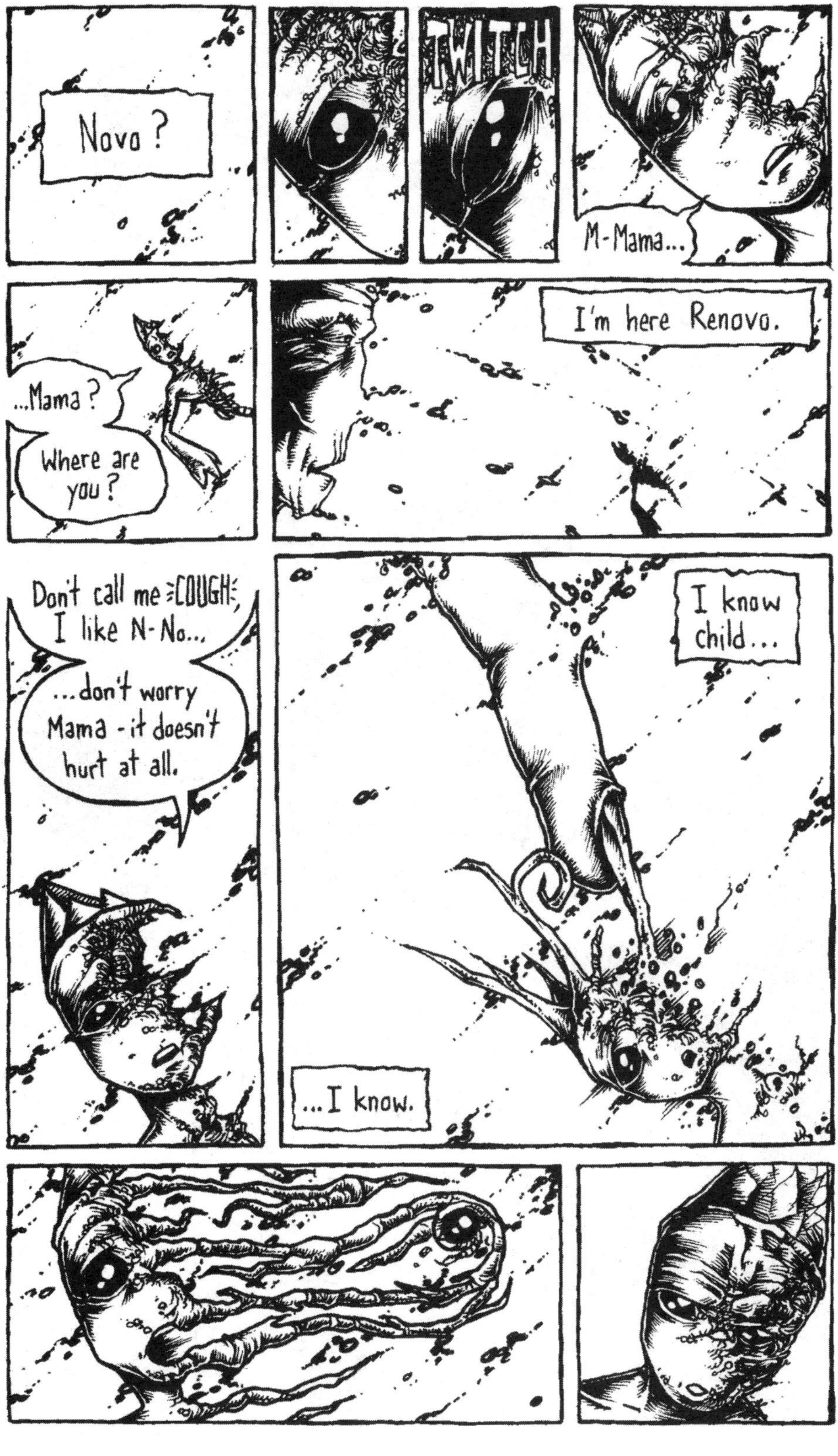

Novo?
TWITCH
M-Mama...
...Mama?
Where are you?
I'm here Renovo.
Don't call me COUGH, I like N-No...
...don't worry Mama - it doesn't hurt at all.
I know child...
...I know.

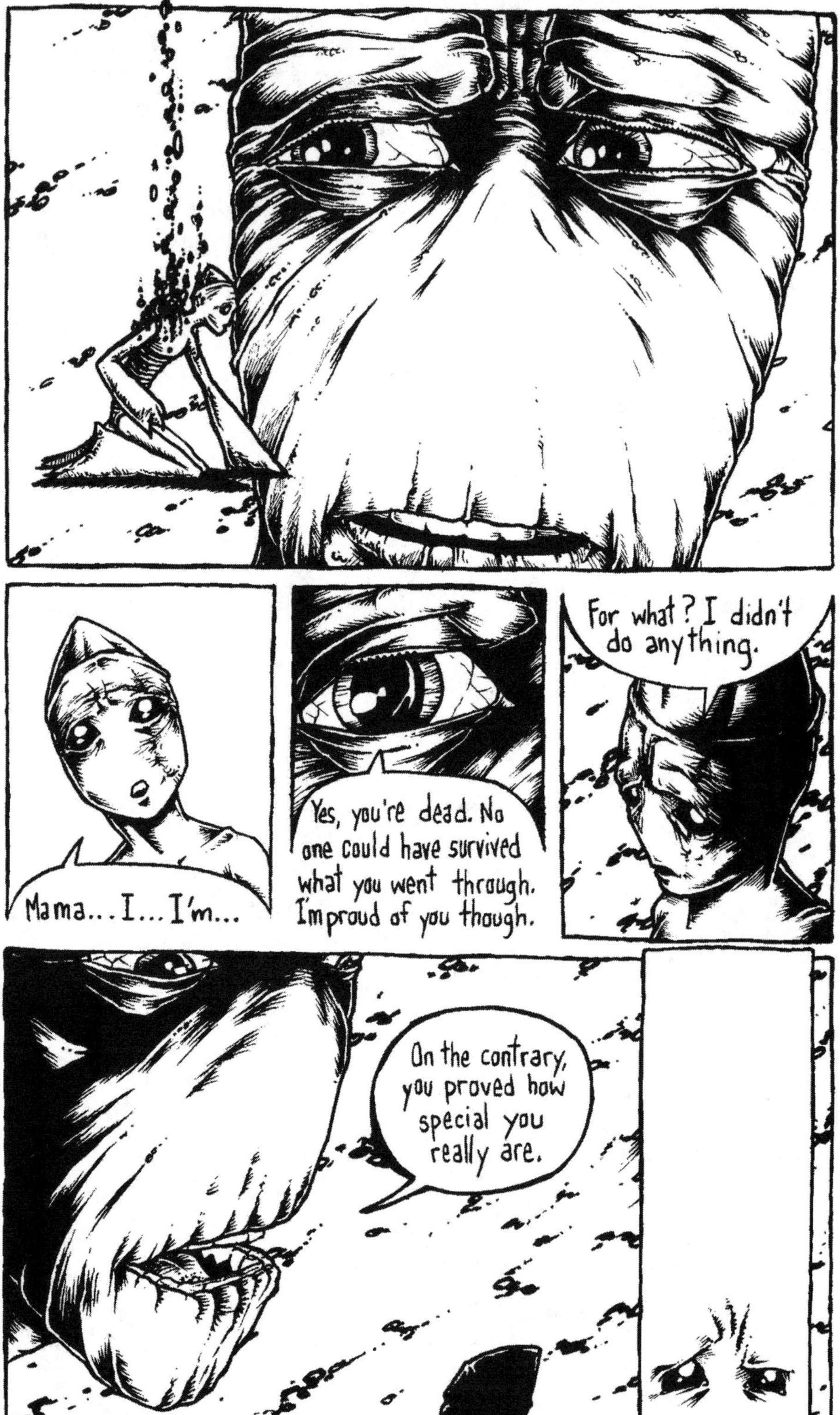
Mama... I... I'm...
Yes, you're dead. No one could have survived what you went through. I'm proud of you though.
For what? I didn't do anything.
On the contrary, you proved how special you really are.

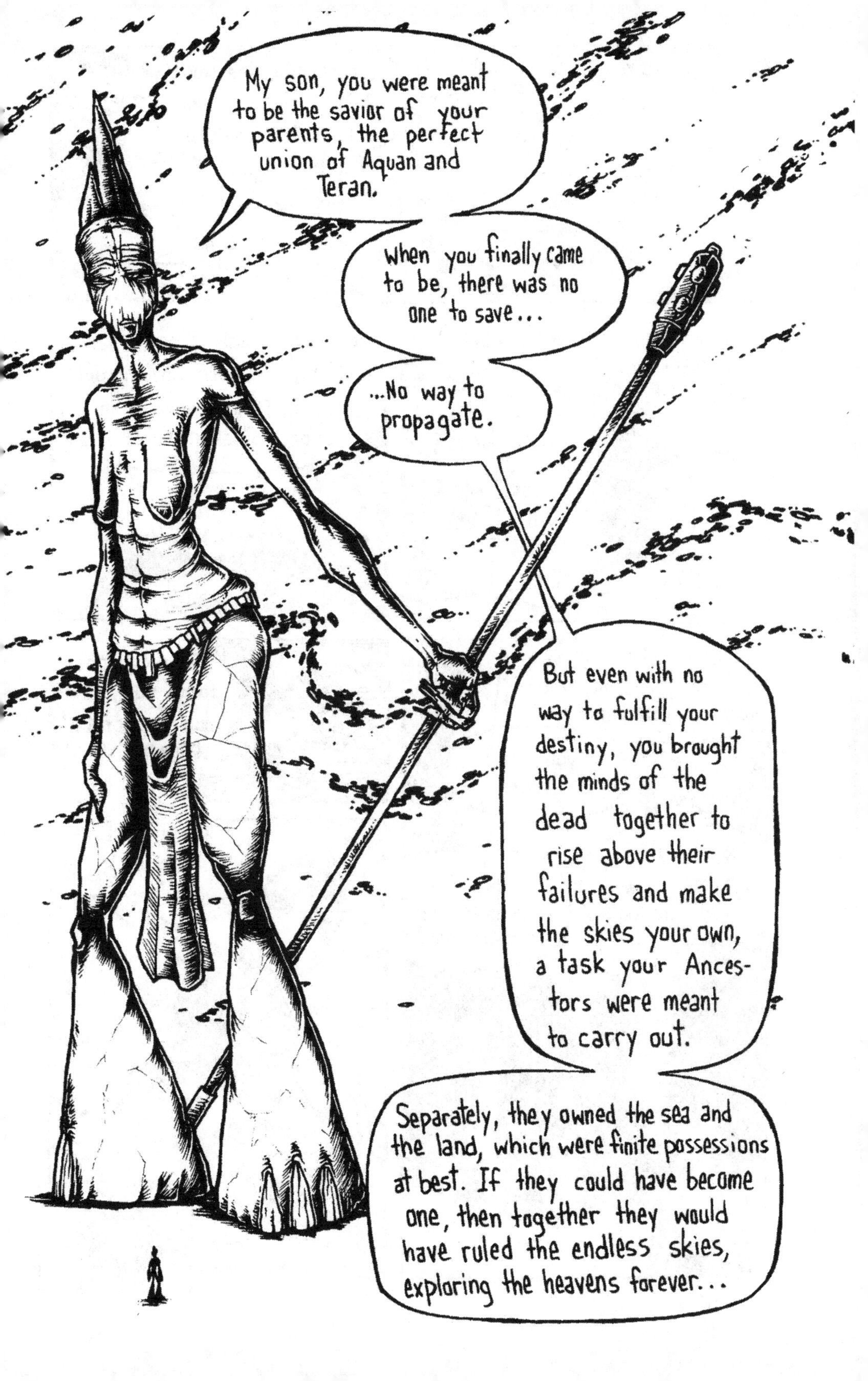
My son, you were meant to be the savior of your parents, the perfect union of Aquan and Teran.
when you finally came to be, there was no one to save...
...No way to propagate.
But even with no way to fulfill your destiny, you brought the minds of the dead together to rise above their failures and make the skies your own, a task your Ancestors were meant to carry out.
Separately, they owned the sea and the land, which were finite possessions at best. If they could have become one, then together they would have ruled the endless skies, exploring the heavens forever...

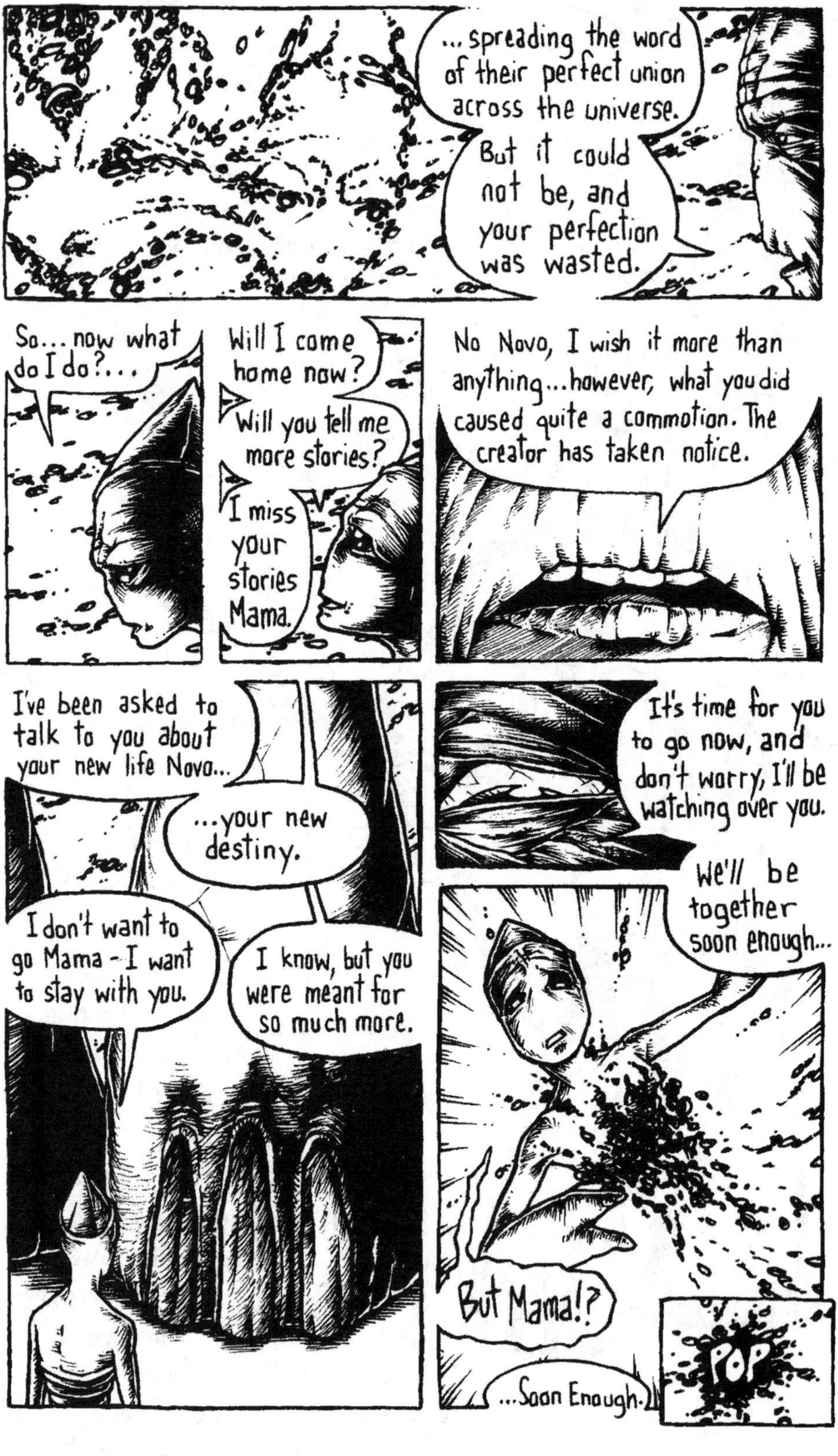
...spreading the word of their perfect union across the universe.
But it could not be, and your perfection was wasted.
So... now what do I do?...
Will I come home now?
Will you tell me more stories?
I miss your stories Mama.
No Novo, I wish it more than anything...however, what you did caused quite a commotion. The creator has taken notice.
I've been asked to talk to you about your new life Novo...
...your new destiny.
I don't want to go Mama - I want to stay with you.
I know, but you were meant for so much more.
It's time for you to go now, and don't worry, I'll be watching over you.
We'll be together soon enough...
But Mama!?
...Soon Enough.
POP

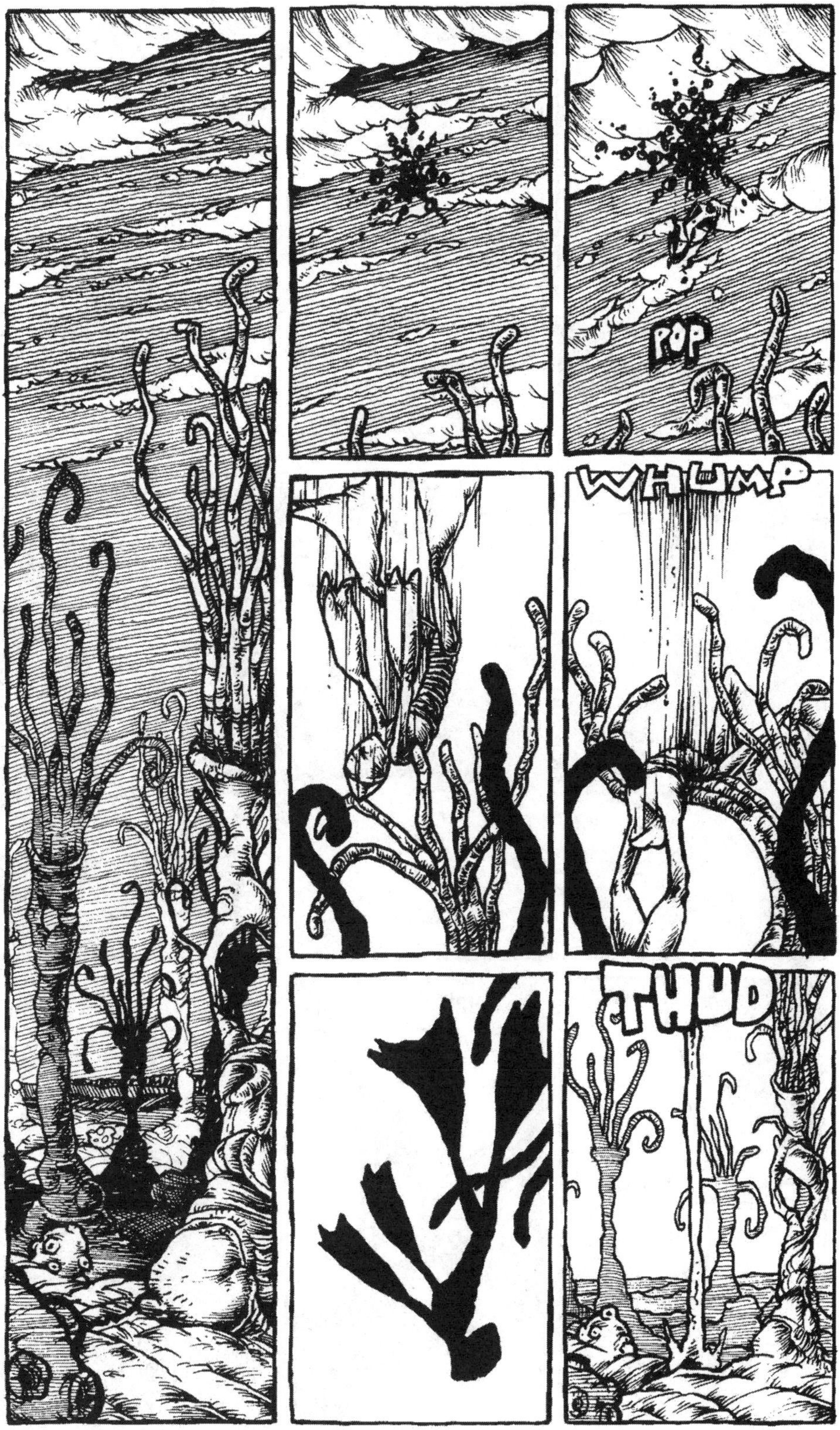
POP
WHUMP
THUD

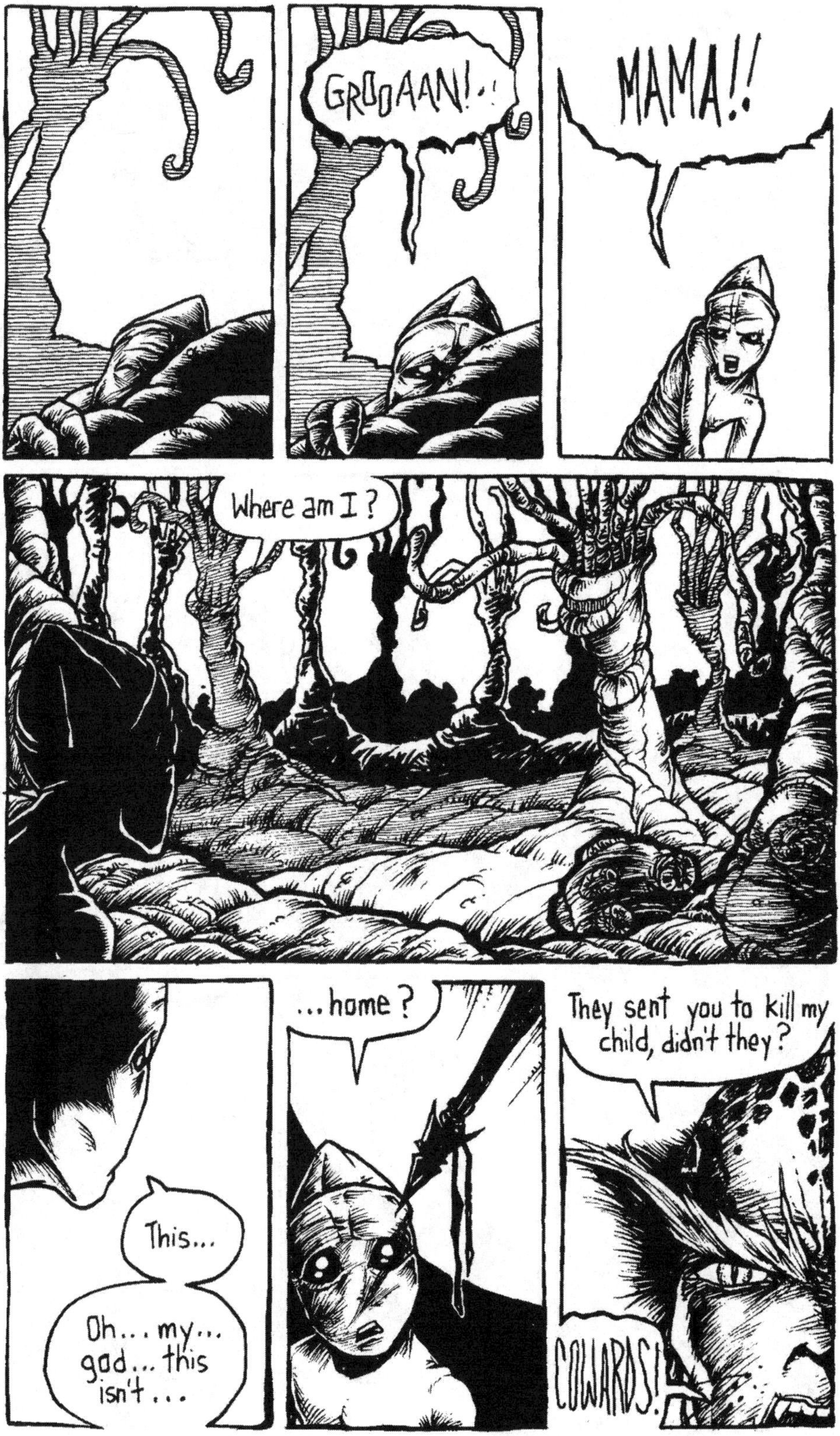
GROOAAN!..!
MAMA!!
Where am I?
This...
Oh... my... god... this isn't...
...home?
They sent you to kill my child, didn't they?
COWARDS!

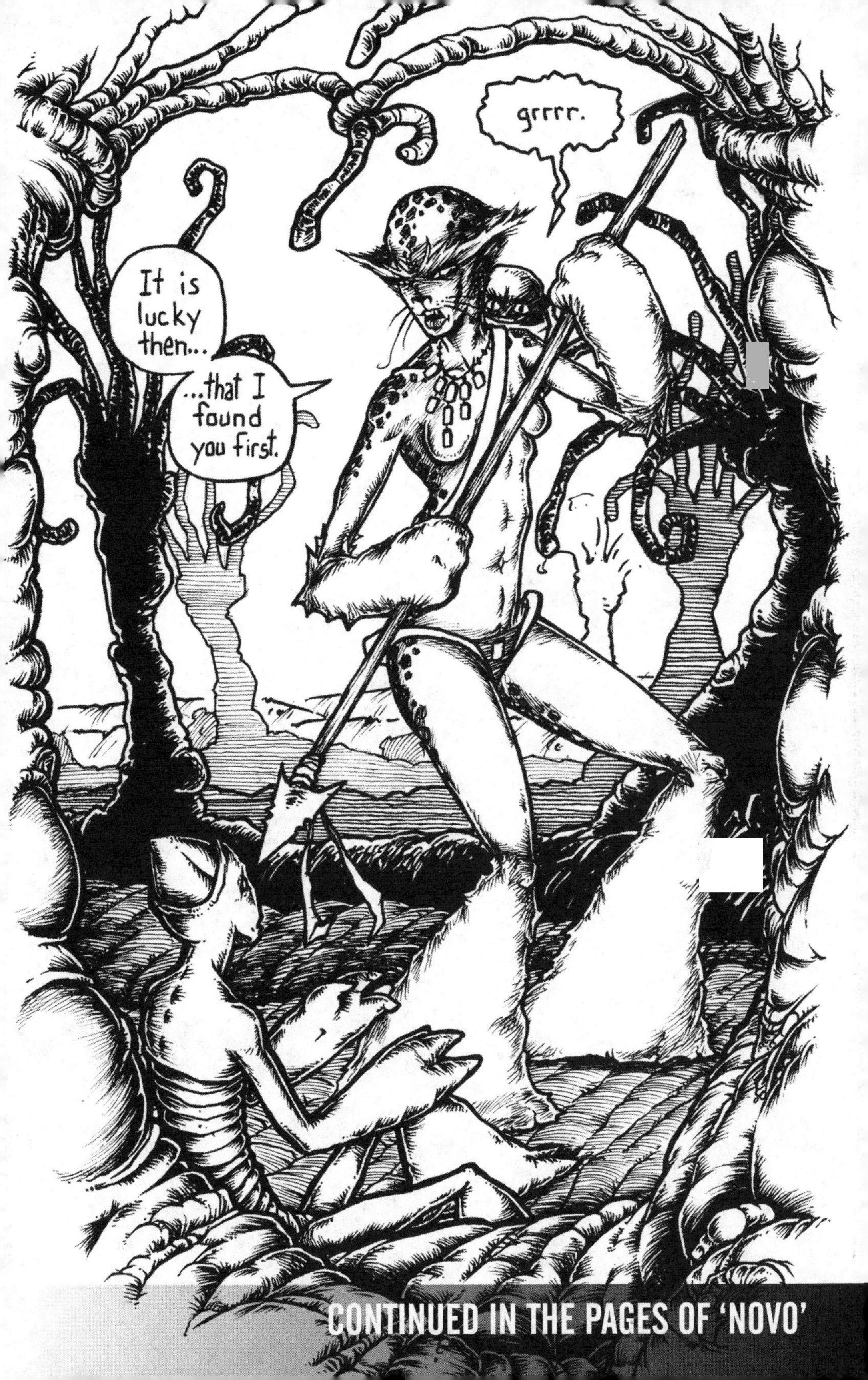
grrrr.
It is lucky then...
...that I found you first.
CONTINUED IN THE PAGES OF 'NOVO'

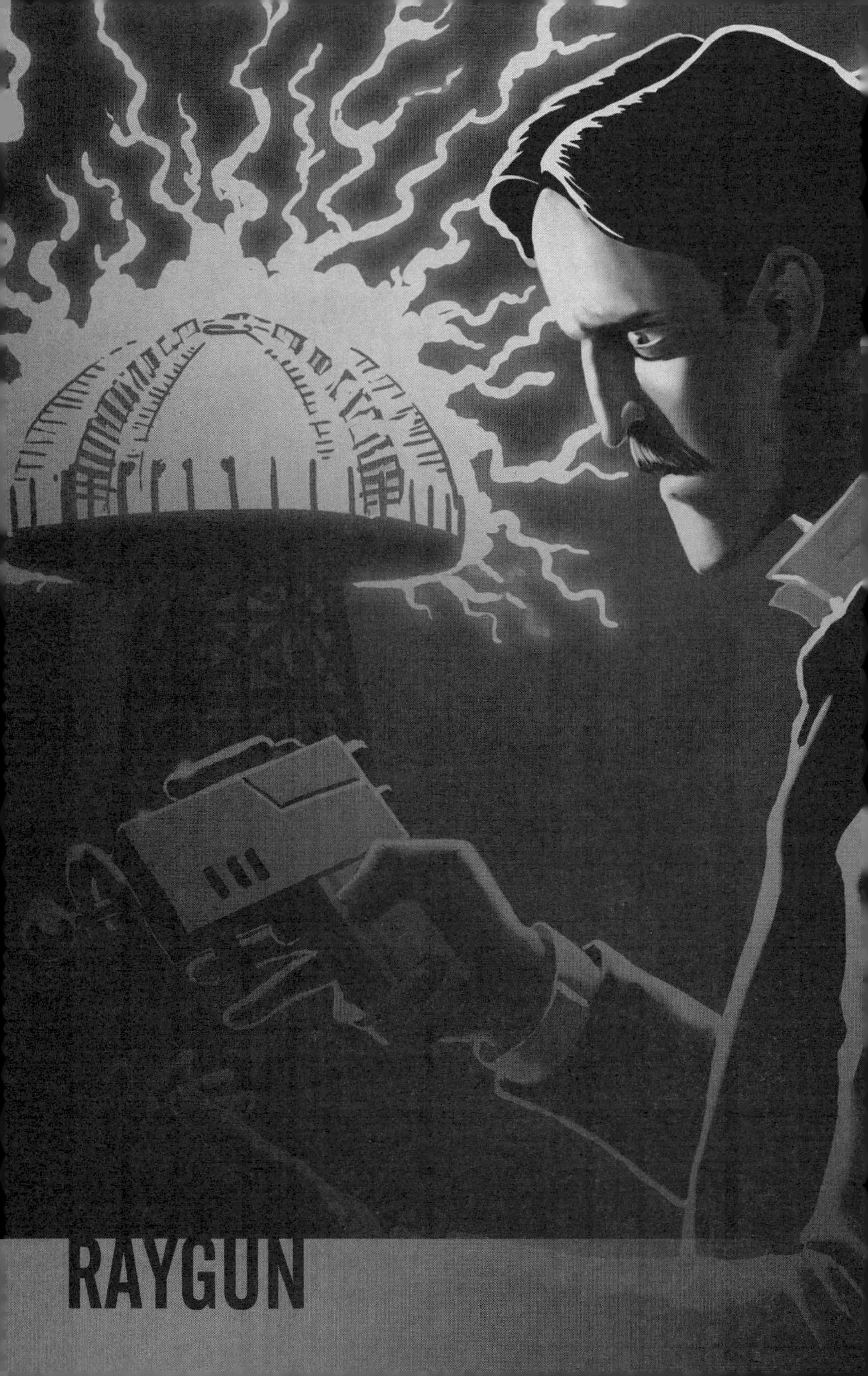

RAYGUN

RAYGUN

MATTHEW BAKER

"...oh crap."

Matthew Baker is a 10 year-old boy who accidentally discovers Nikola Tesla's fabled "Death Ray" and begins a journey of self-discovery that will change the world forever.

Sent to live with his estranged father, David, by his drug addict mother, Karen, life hasn't been easy for Matthew. Soon after dealing with a bully on the first day of school Matthew finds Nikola Tesla's ray gun and is soon pursued by a ruthless government agency, The Strategic Defense Initiative (SDI).

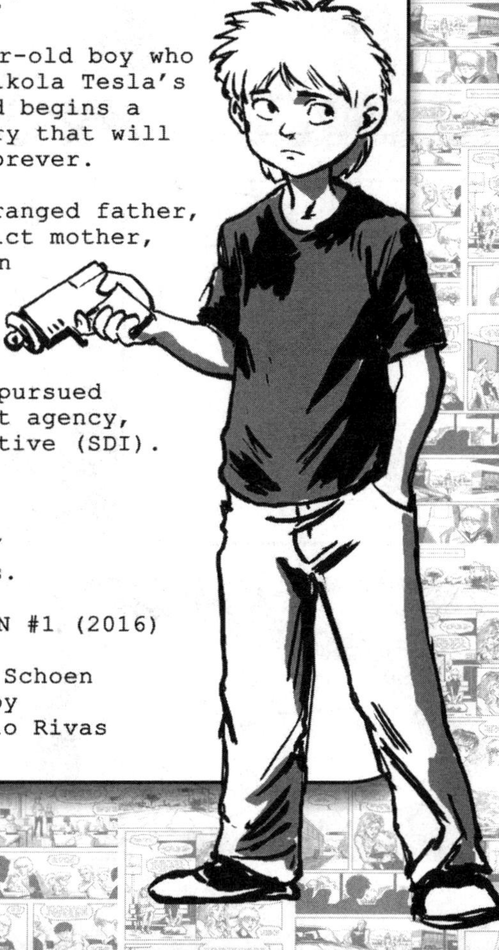

Age: 10
Height: 4'10"
Weight: 72 lbs.

First Appearance: RAYGUN #1 (2016)

Created by Gregory Schoen
Illustration by
Alonso Molina & Paulo Rivas

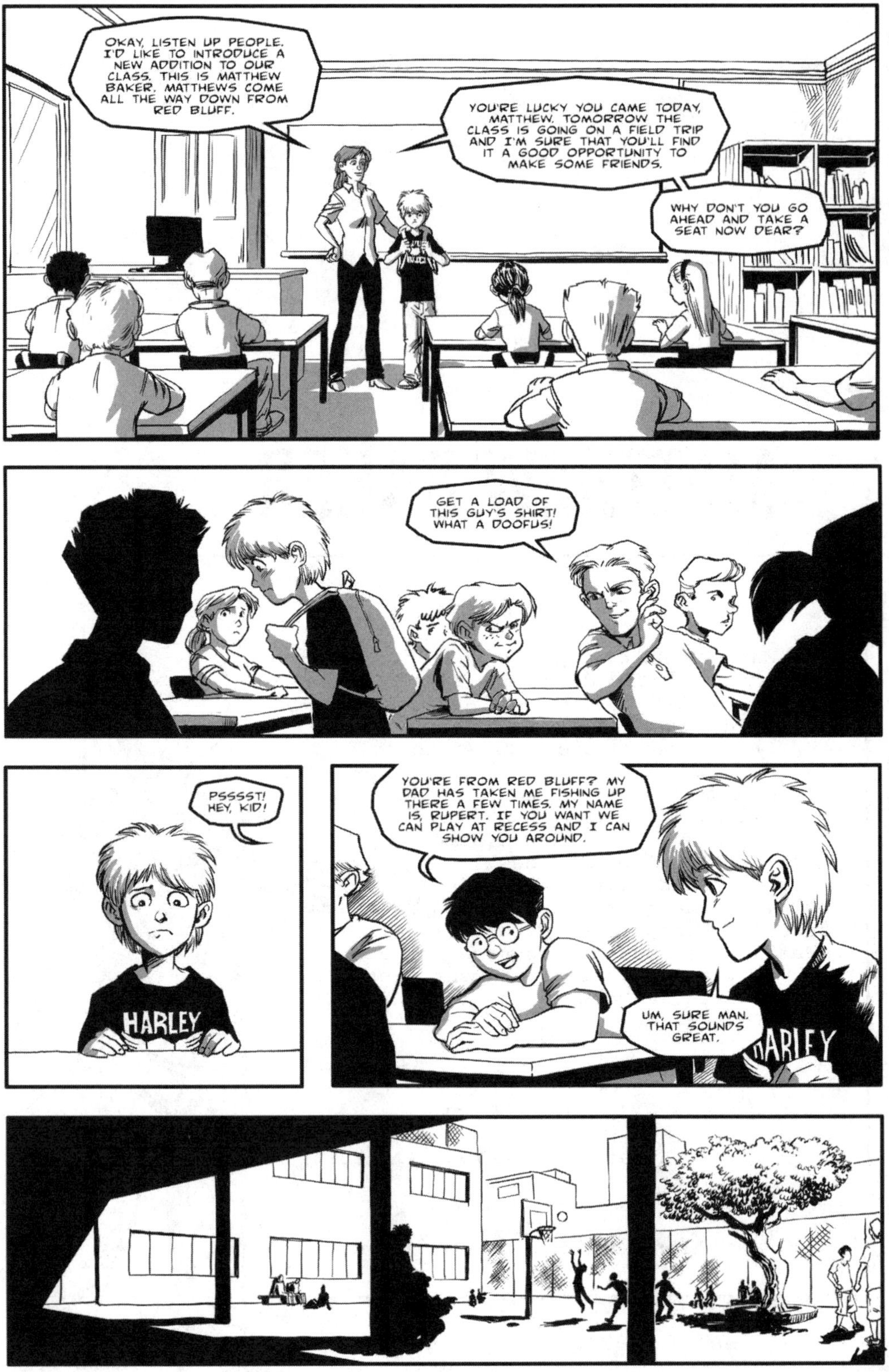
OKAY, LISTEN UP PEOPLE. I'D LIKE TO INTRODUCE A NEW ADDITION TO OUR CLASS. THIS IS MATTHEW BAKER. MATTHEWS COME ALL THE WAY DOWN FROM RED BLUFF.
YOU'RE LUCKY YOU CAME TODAY, MATTHEW. TOMORROW THE CLASS IS GOING ON A FIELD TRIP AND I'M SURE THAT YOU'LL FIND IT A GOOD OPPORTUNITY TO MAKE SOME FRIENDS.
WHY DON'T YOU GO AHEAD AND TAKE A SEAT NOW DEAR?
GET A LOAD OF THIS GUY'S SHIRT! WHAT A DOOFUS!
PSSSST! HEY, KID!
HARLEY
YOU'RE FROM RED BLUFF? MY DAD HAS TAKEN ME FISHING UP THERE A FEW TIMES. MY NAME IS, RUPERT. IF YOU WANT WE CAN PLAY AT RECESS AND I CAN SHOW YOU AROUND.
UM, SURE MAN. THAT SOUNDS GREAT.

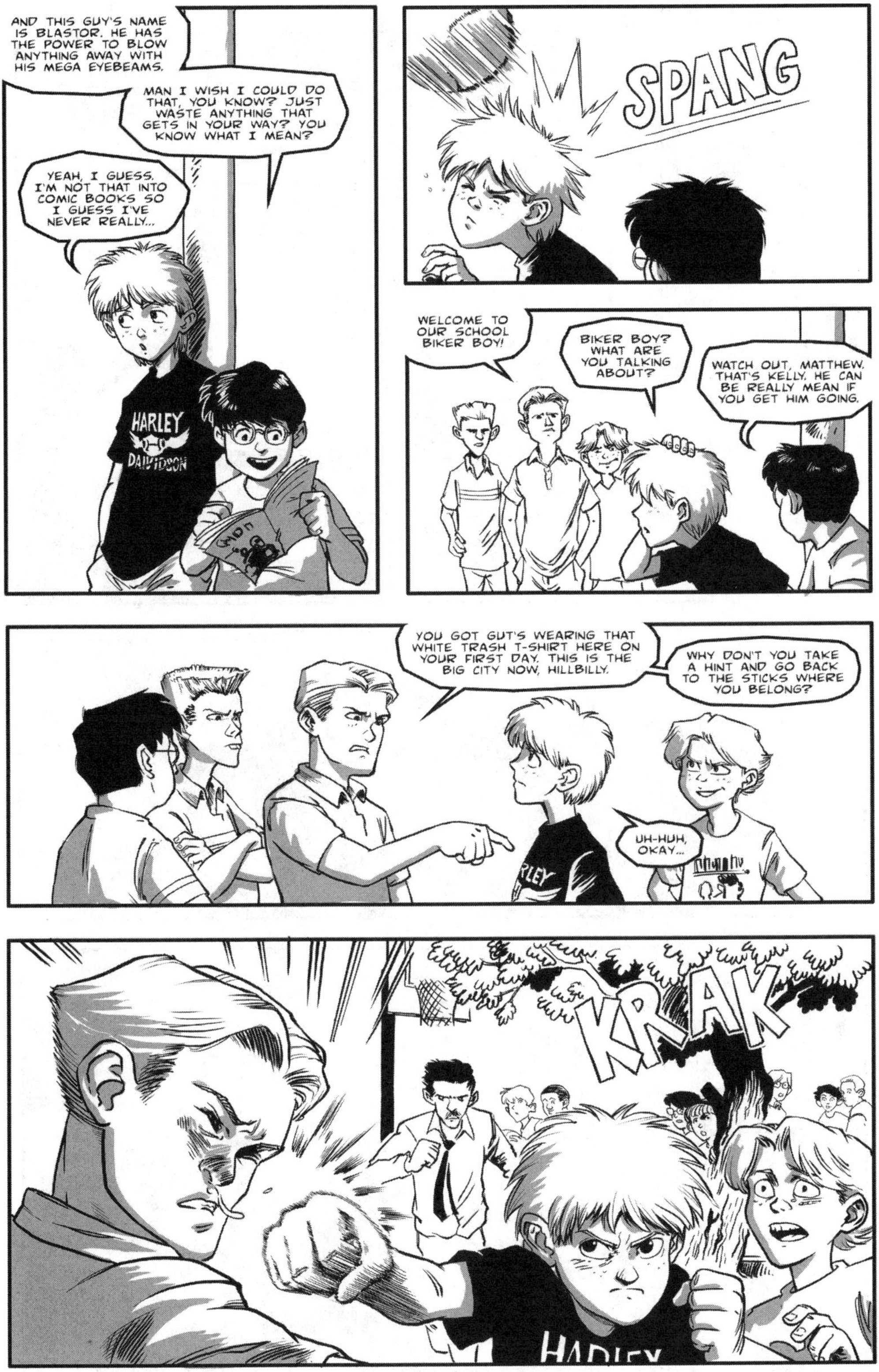
AND THIS GUY'S NAME IS BLASTOR. HE HAS THE POWER TO BLOW ANYTHING AWAY WITH HIS MEGA EYEBEAMS.
MAN I WISH I COULD DO THAT, YOU KNOW? JUST WASTE ANYTHING THAT GETS IN YOUR WAY? YOU KNOW WHAT I MEAN?
YEAH, I GUESS. I'M NOT THAT INTO COMIC BOOKS SO I GUESS I'VE NEVER REALLY...
HARLEY DAVIDSON
SPANG
WELCOME TO OUR SCHOOL BIKER BOY!
BIKER BOY? WHAT ARE YOU TALKING ABOUT?
WATCH OUT, MATTHEW. THAT'S KELLY. HE CAN BE REALLY MEAN IF YOU GET HIM GOING.
YOU GOT GUT'S WEARING THAT WHITE TRASH T-SHIRT HERE ON YOUR FIRST DAY. THIS IS THE BIG CITY NOW, HILLBILLY.
WHY DON'T YOU TAKE A HINT AND GO BACK TO THE STICKS WHERE YOU BELONG?
UH-HUH, OKAY...
KRAK

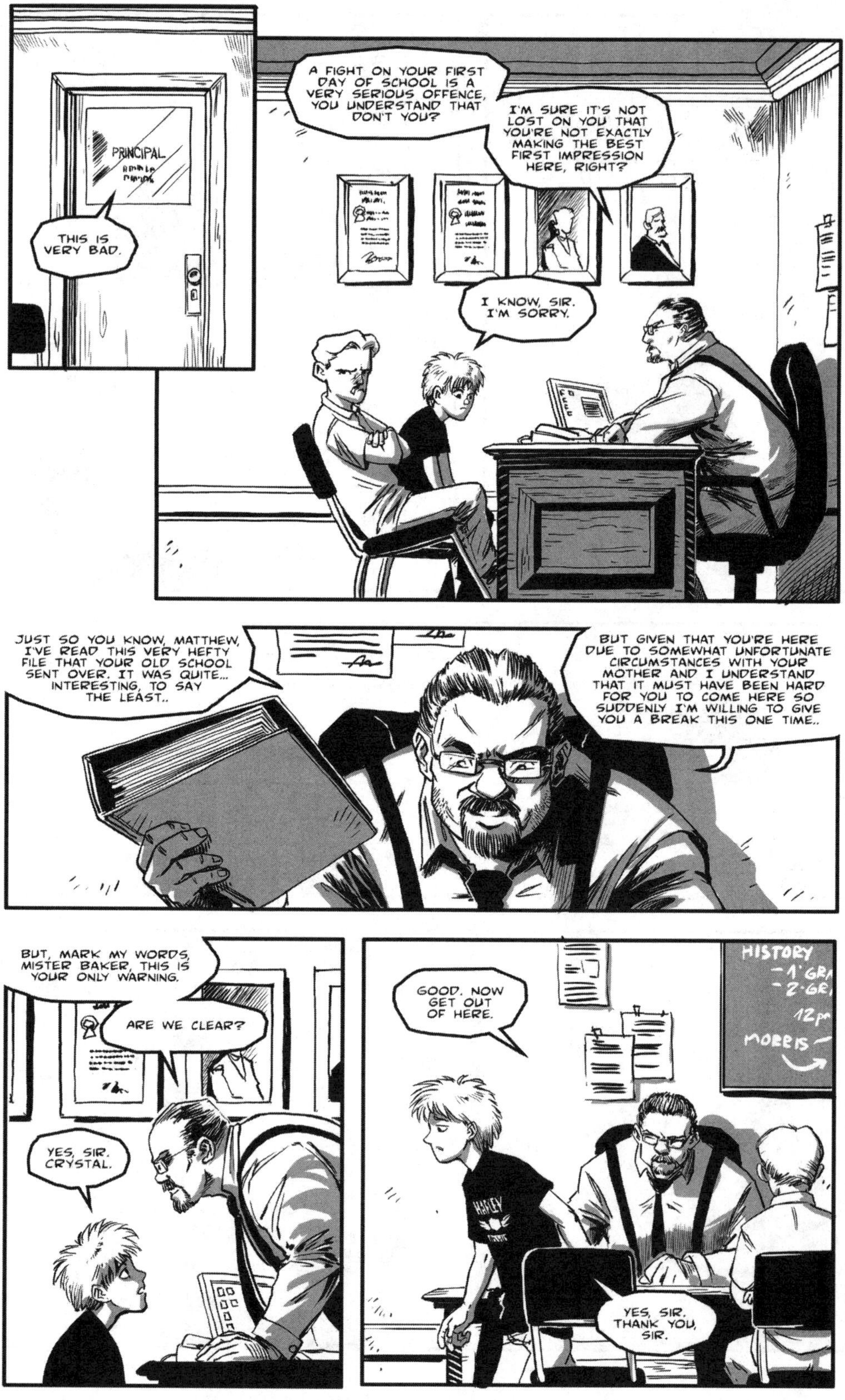
PRINCIPAL
THIS IS VERY BAD.
A FIGHT ON YOUR FIRST DAY OF SCHOOL IS A VERY SERIOUS OFFENCE, YOU UNDERSTAND THAT DON'T YOU?
I'M SURE IT'S NOT LOST ON YOU THAT YOU'RE NOT EXACTLY MAKING THE BEST FIRST IMPRESSION HERE, RIGHT?
I KNOW, SIR. I'M SORRY.
JUST SO YOU KNOW, MATTHEW, I'VE READ THIS VERY HEFTY FILE THAT YOUR OLD SCHOOL SENT OVER. IT WAS QUITE... INTERESTING, TO SAY THE LEAST..
BUT GIVEN THAT YOU'RE HERE DUE TO SOMEWHAT UNFORTUNATE CIRCUMSTANCES WITH YOUR MOTHER AND I UNDERSTAND THAT IT MUST HAVE BEEN HARD FOR YOU TO COME HERE SO SUDDENLY I'M WILLING TO GIVE YOU A BREAK THIS ONE TIME..
BUT, MARK MY WORDS, MISTER BAKER, THIS IS YOUR ONLY WARNING.
ARE WE CLEAR?
YES, SIR. CRYSTAL.
GOOD. NOW GET OUT OF HERE.
HISTORY
YES, SIR. THANK YOU, SIR.

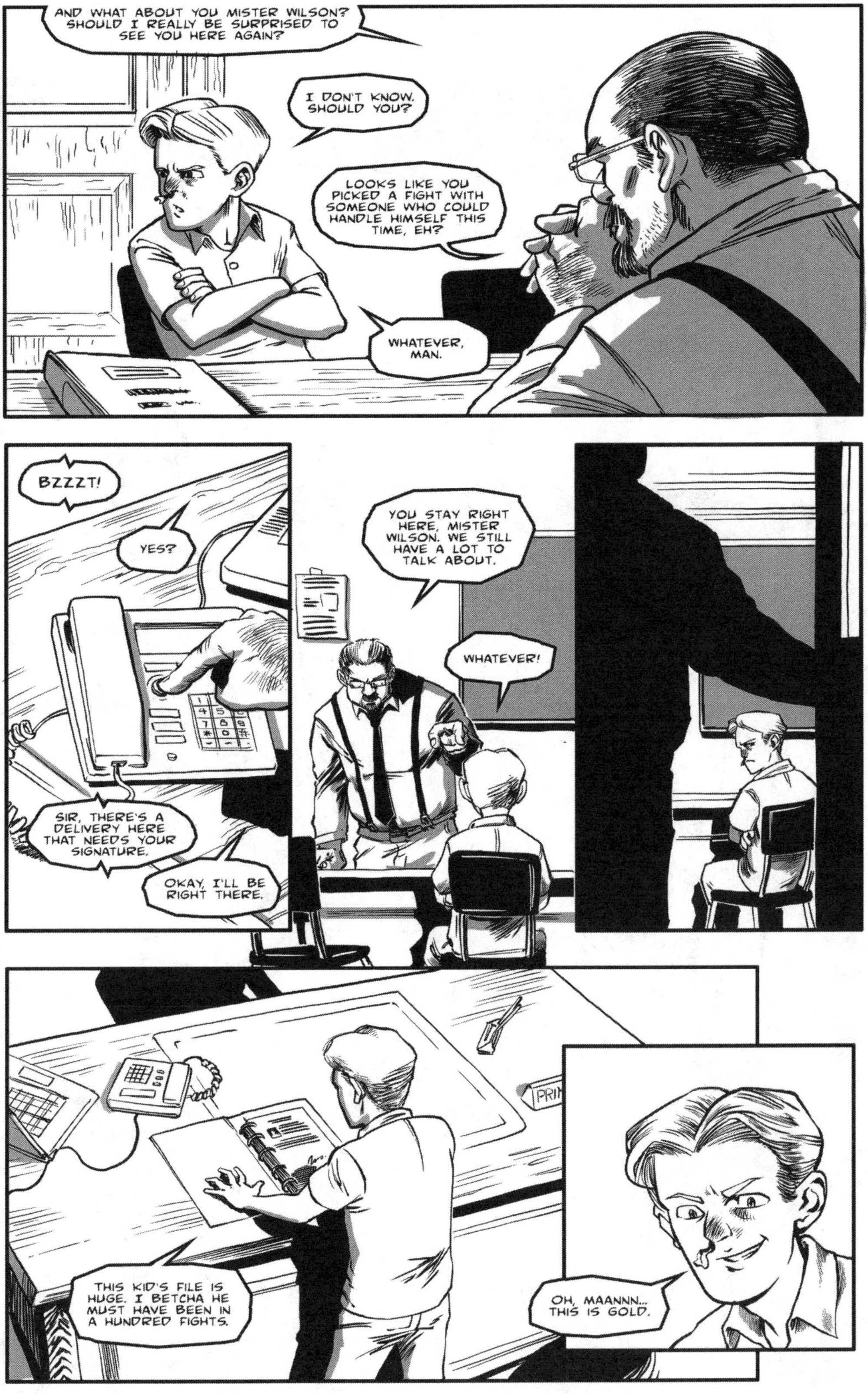
AND WHAT ABOUT YOU MISTER WILSON? SHOULD I REALLY BE SURPRISED TO SEE YOU HERE AGAIN?
I DON'T KNOW. SHOULD YOU?
LOOKS LIKE YOU PICKED A FIGHT WITH SOMEONE WHO COULD HANDLE HIMSELF THIS TIME, EH?
WHATEVER, MAN.
BZZZT!
YES?
SIR, THERE'S A DELIVERY HERE THAT NEEDS YOUR SIGNATURE.
OKAY, I'LL BE RIGHT THERE.
YOU STAY RIGHT HERE, MISTER WILSON. WE STILL HAVE A LOT TO TALK ABOUT.
WHATEVER!
THIS KID'S FILE IS HUGE. I BETCHA HE MUST HAVE BEEN IN A HUNDRED FIGHTS.
OH, MAANNN... THIS IS GOLD.

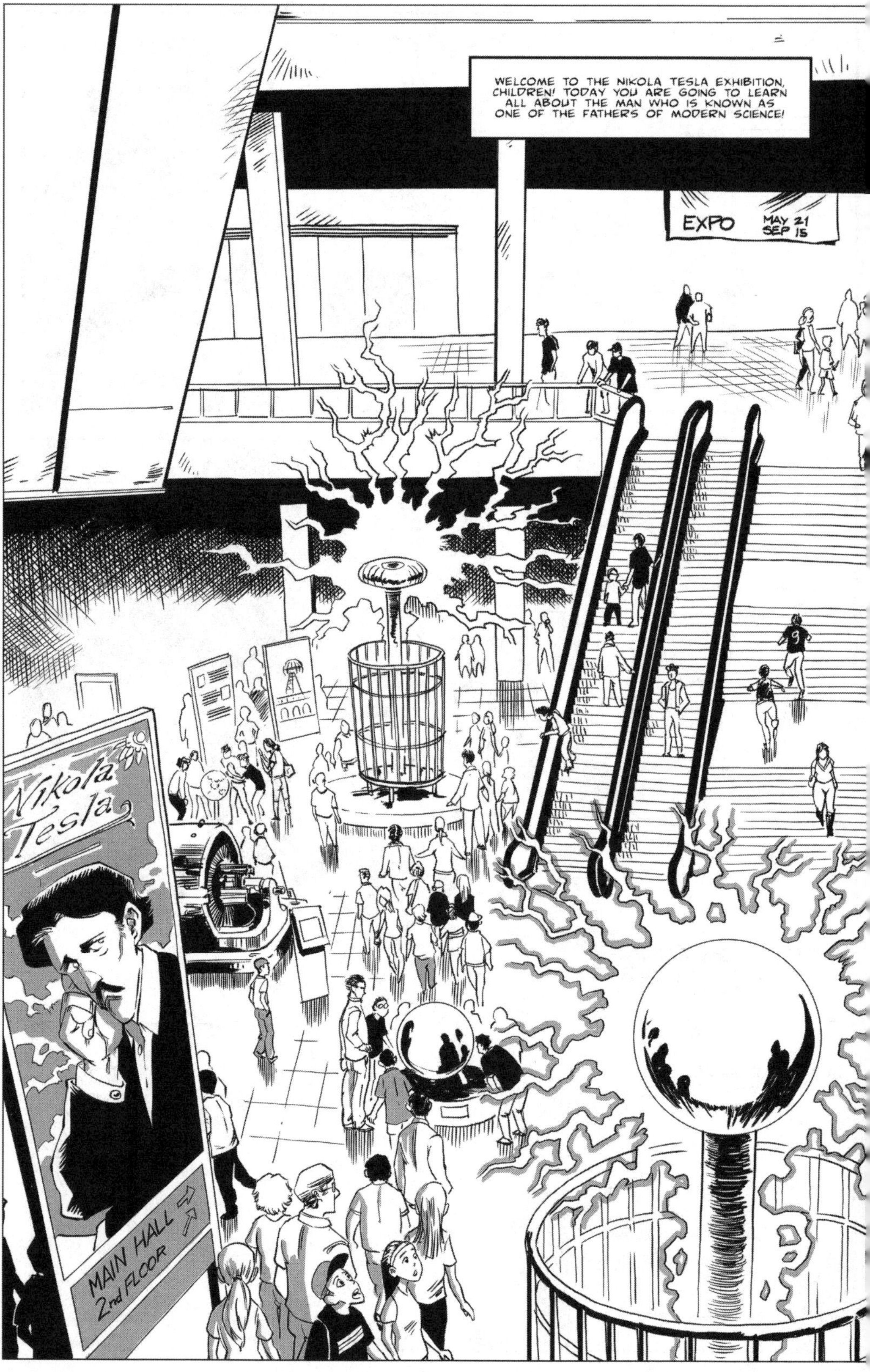
WELCOME TO THE NIKOLA TESLA EXHIBITION, CHILDREN! TODAY YOU ARE GOING TO LEARN ALL ABOUT THE MAN WHO IS KNOWN AS ONE OF THE FATHERS OF MODERN SCIENCE!
EXPO
MAY 21
SEP 15
Nikola Tesla
MAIN HALL
2nd FLOOR

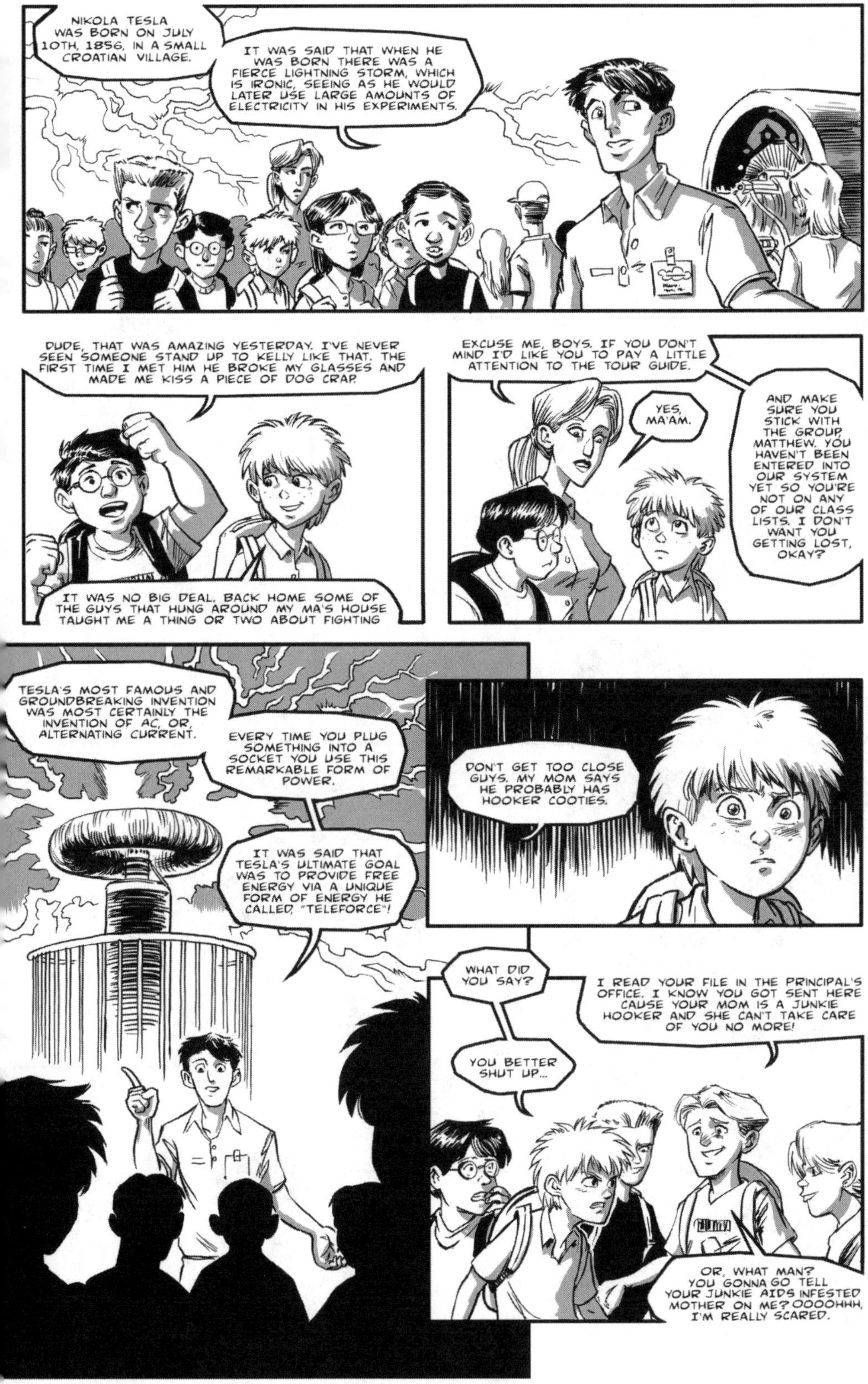
NIKOLA TESLA WAS BORN ON JULY 10TH, 1856, IN A SMALL CROATIAN VILLAGE.
IT WAS SAID THAT WHEN HE WAS BORN THERE WAS A FIERCE LIGHTNING STORM, WHICH IS IRONIC, SEEING AS HE WOULD LATER USE LARGE AMOUNTS OF ELECTRICITY IN HIS EXPERIMENTS.
DUDE, THAT WAS AMAZING YESTERDAY. I'VE NEVER SEEN SOMEONE STAND UP TO KELLY LIKE THAT. THE FIRST TIME I MET HIM HE BROKE MY GLASSES AND MADE ME KISS A PIECE OF DOG CRAP.
IT WAS NO BIG DEAL. BACK HOME SOME OF THE GUYS THAT HUNG AROUND MY MA'S HOUSE TAUGHT ME A THING OR TWO ABOUT FIGHTING
EXCUSE ME, BOYS. IF YOU DON'T MIND I'D LIKE YOU TO PAY A LITTLE ATTENTION TO THE TOUR GUIDE.
YES, MA'AM.
AND MAKE SURE YOU STICK WITH THE GROUP, MATTHEW. YOU HAVEN'T BEEN ENTERED INTO OUR SYSTEM YET SO YOU'RE NOT ON ANY OF OUR CLASS LISTS. I DON'T WANT YOU GETTING LOST, OKAY?
TESLA'S MOST FAMOUS AND GROUNDBREAKING INVENTION WAS MOST CERTAINLY THE INVENTION OF AC, OR, ALTERNATING CURRENT.
EVERY TIME YOU PLUG SOMETHING INTO A SOCKET YOU USE THIS REMARKABLE FORM OF POWER.
IT WAS SAID THAT TESLA'S ULTIMATE GOAL WAS TO PROVIDE FREE ENERGY VIA A UNIQUE FORM OF ENERGY HE CALLED, "TELEFORCE"!
DON'T GET TOO CLOSE GUYS. MY MOM SAYS HE PROBABLY HAS HOOKER COOTIES.
WHAT DID YOU SAY?
I READ YOUR FILE IN THE PRINCIPAL'S OFFICE. I KNOW YOU GOT SENT HERE CAUSE YOUR MOM IS A JUNKIE HOOKER AND SHE CAN'T TAKE CARE OF YOU NO MORE!
YOU BETTER SHUT UP...
OR, WHAT MAN? YOU GONNA GO TELL YOUR JUNKIE AIDS INFESTED MOTHER ON ME? OOOOHHH, I'M REALLY SCARED.

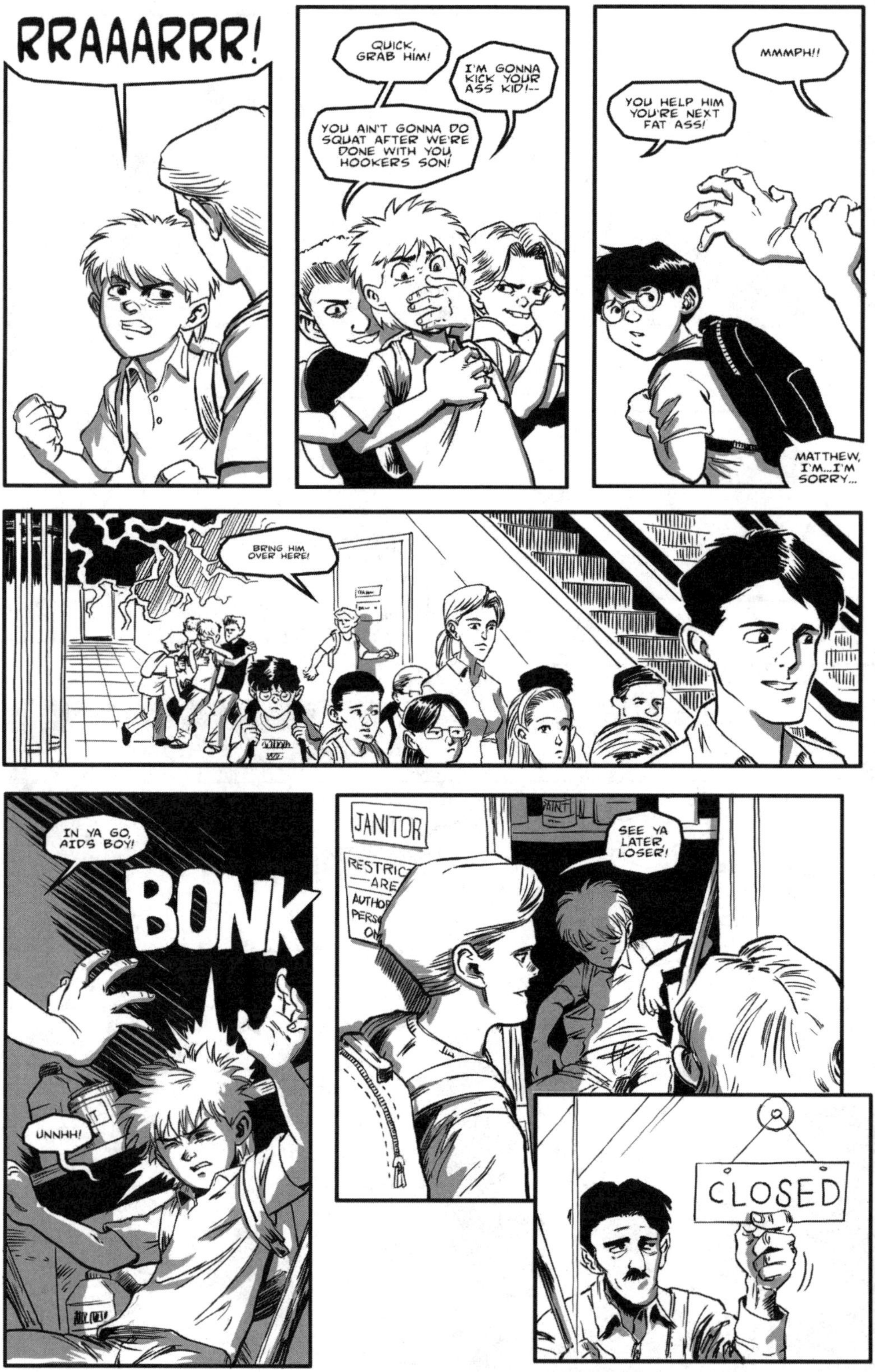
RRAAARRR!
QUICK, GRAB HIM!
YOU AIN'T GONNA DO SQUAT AFTER WE'RE DONE WITH YOU, HOOKERS SON!
I'M GONNA KICK YOUR ASS KID!--
MMMPH!!
YOU HELP HIM YOU'RE NEXT FAT ASS!
MATTHEW, I'M...I'M SORRY...
BRING HIM OVER HERE!
IN YA GO, AIDS BOY!
BONK
UNNHH!
JANITOR
SEE YA LATER, LOSER!
CLOSED

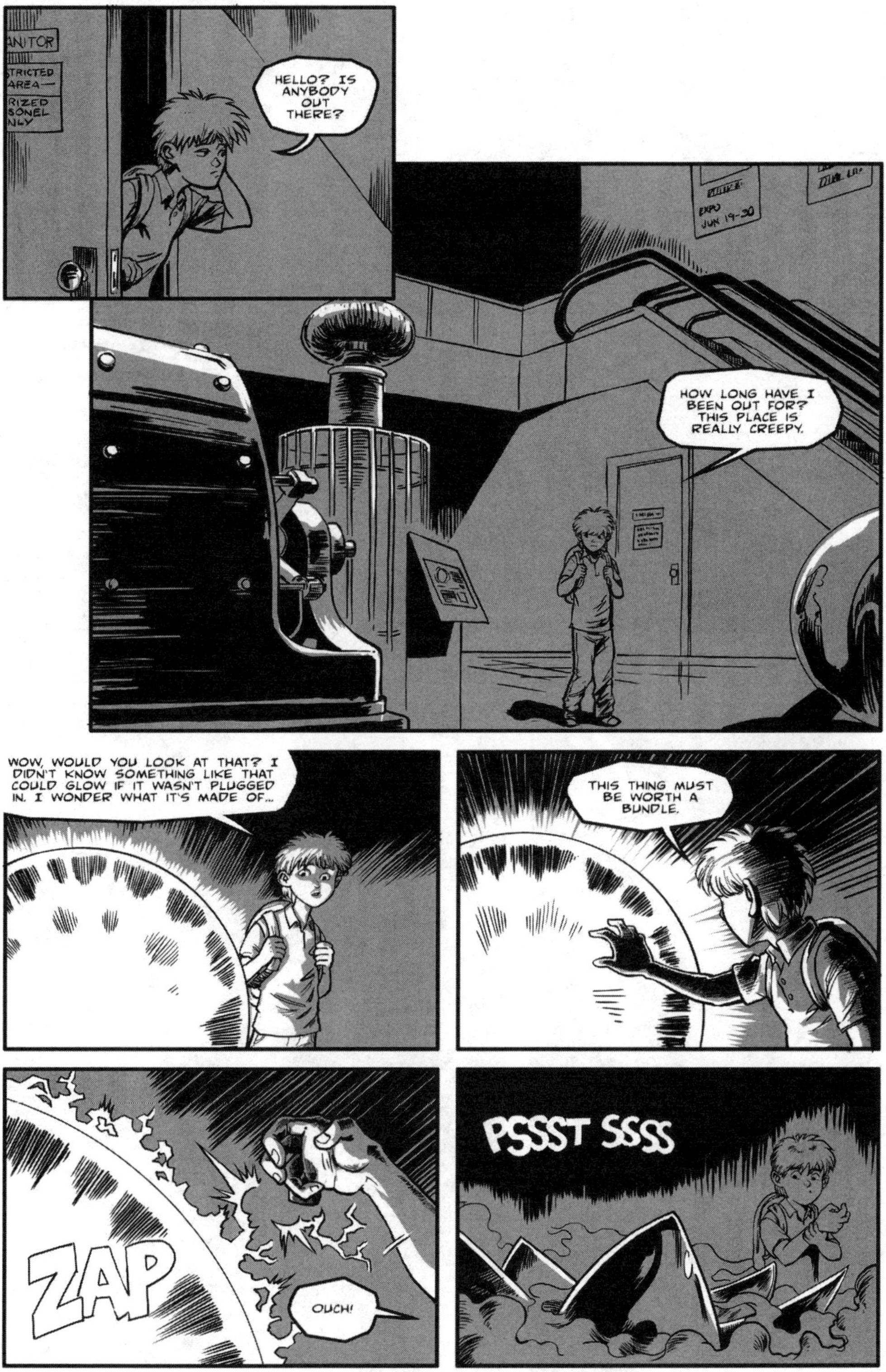
ANITOR
STRICTED AREA—
RIZED SONEL NLY
HELLO? IS ANYBODY OUT THERE?
EXPO JUN 19-30
HOW LONG HAVE I BEEN OUT FOR? THIS PLACE IS REALLY CREEPY.
WOW, WOULD YOU LOOK AT THAT? I DIDN'T KNOW SOMETHING LIKE THAT COULD GLOW IF IT WASN'T PLUGGED IN. I WONDER WHAT IT'S MADE OF...
THIS THING MUST BE WORTH A BUNDLE.
ZAP
OUCH!
PSSST SSSS

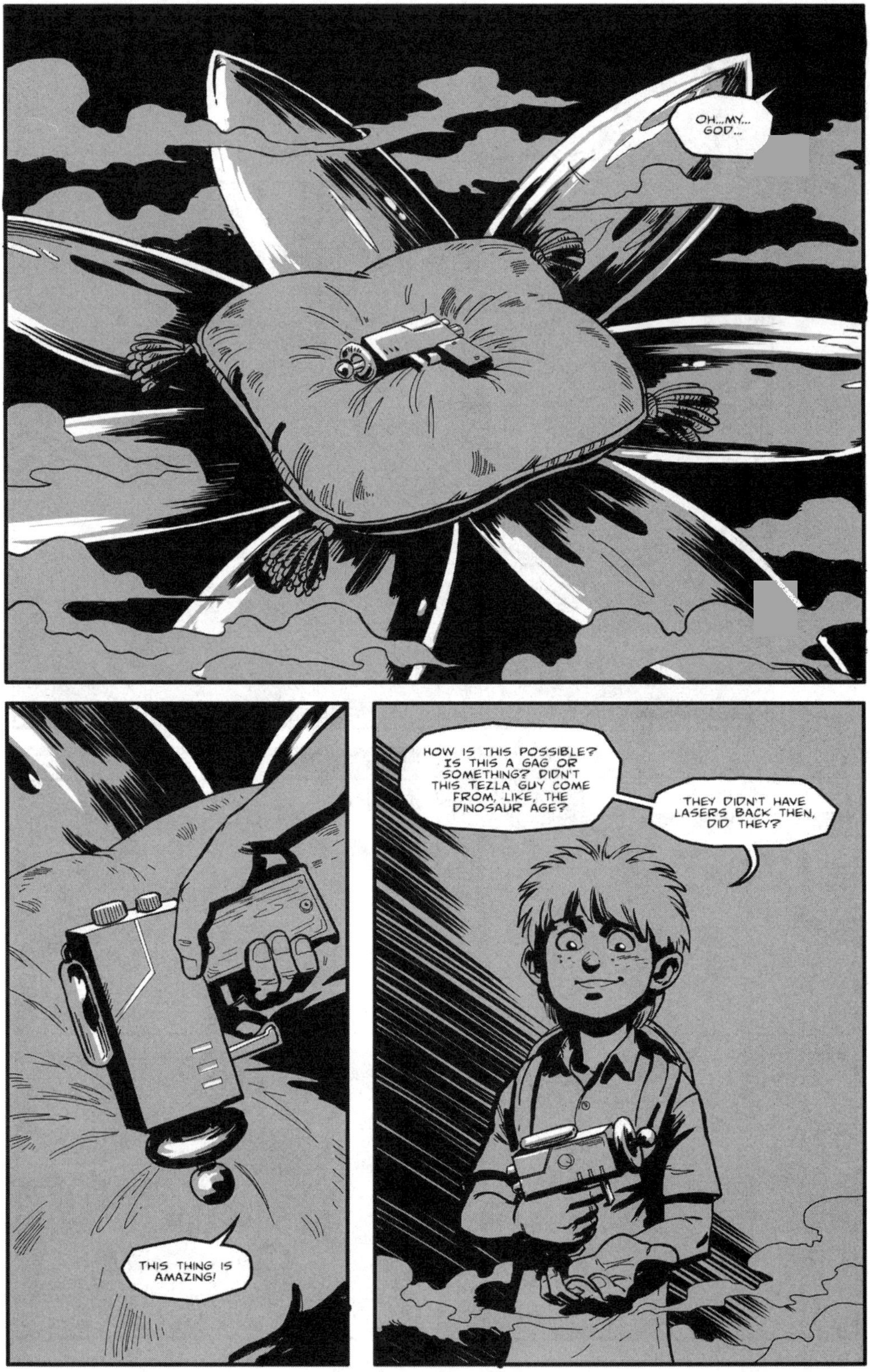
OH...MY... GOD...
THIS THING IS AMAZING!
HOW IS THIS POSSIBLE? IS THIS A GAG OR SOMETHING? DIDN'T THIS TEZLA GUY COME FROM, LIKE, THE DINOSAUR AGE?
THEY DIDN'T HAVE LASERS BACK THEN, DID THEY?

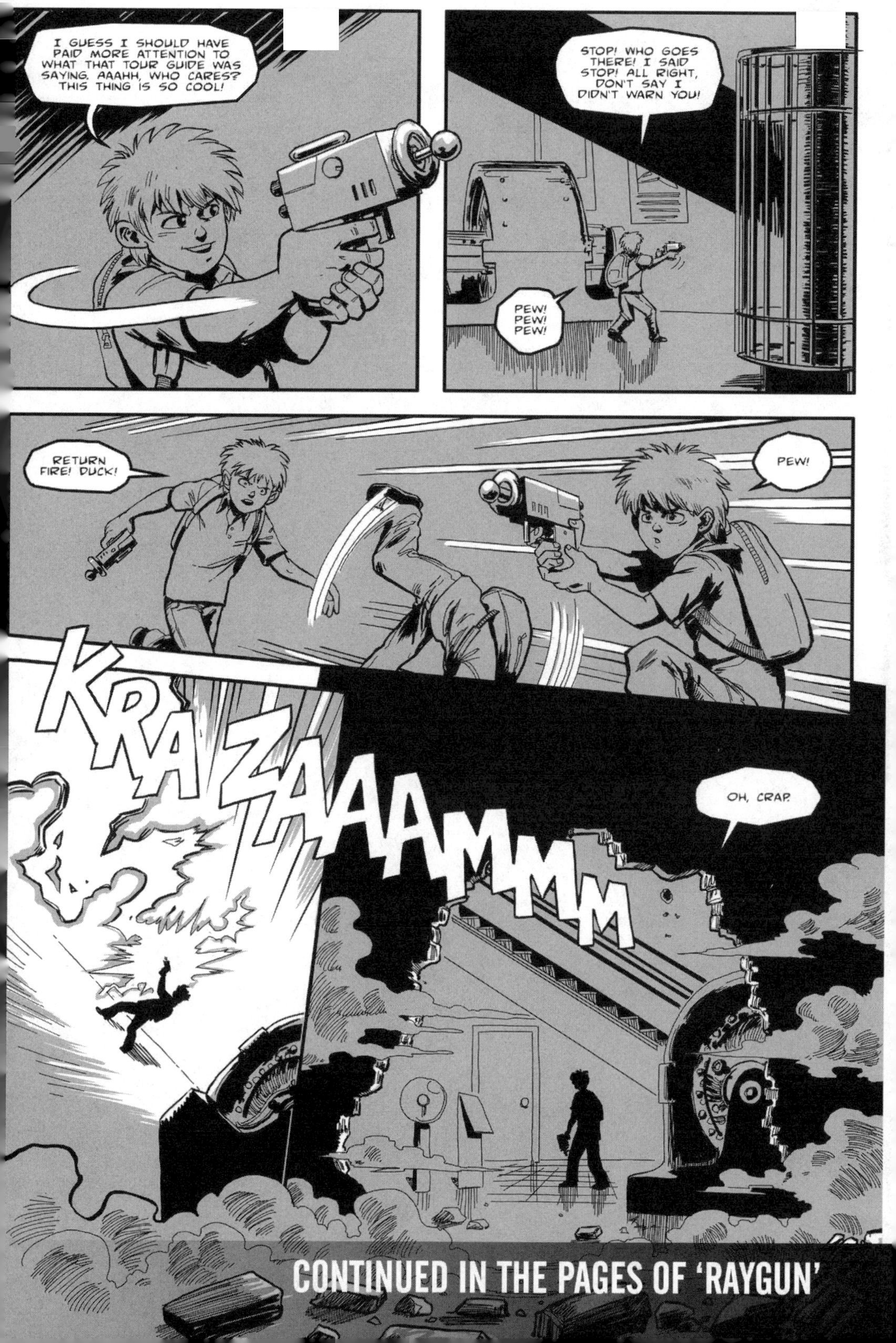
I GUESS I SHOULD HAVE PAID MORE ATTENTION TO WHAT THAT TOUR GUIDE WAS SAYING. AAAHH, WHO CARES? THIS THING IS SO COOL!
STOP! WHO GOES THERE! I SAID STOP! ALL RIGHT, DON'T SAY I DIDN'T WARN YOU!
PEW! PEW! PEW!
RETURN FIRE! DUCK!
PEW!
KRAZAAAMMMM
OH, CRAP.

CONTINUED IN THE PAGES OF 'RAYGUN'

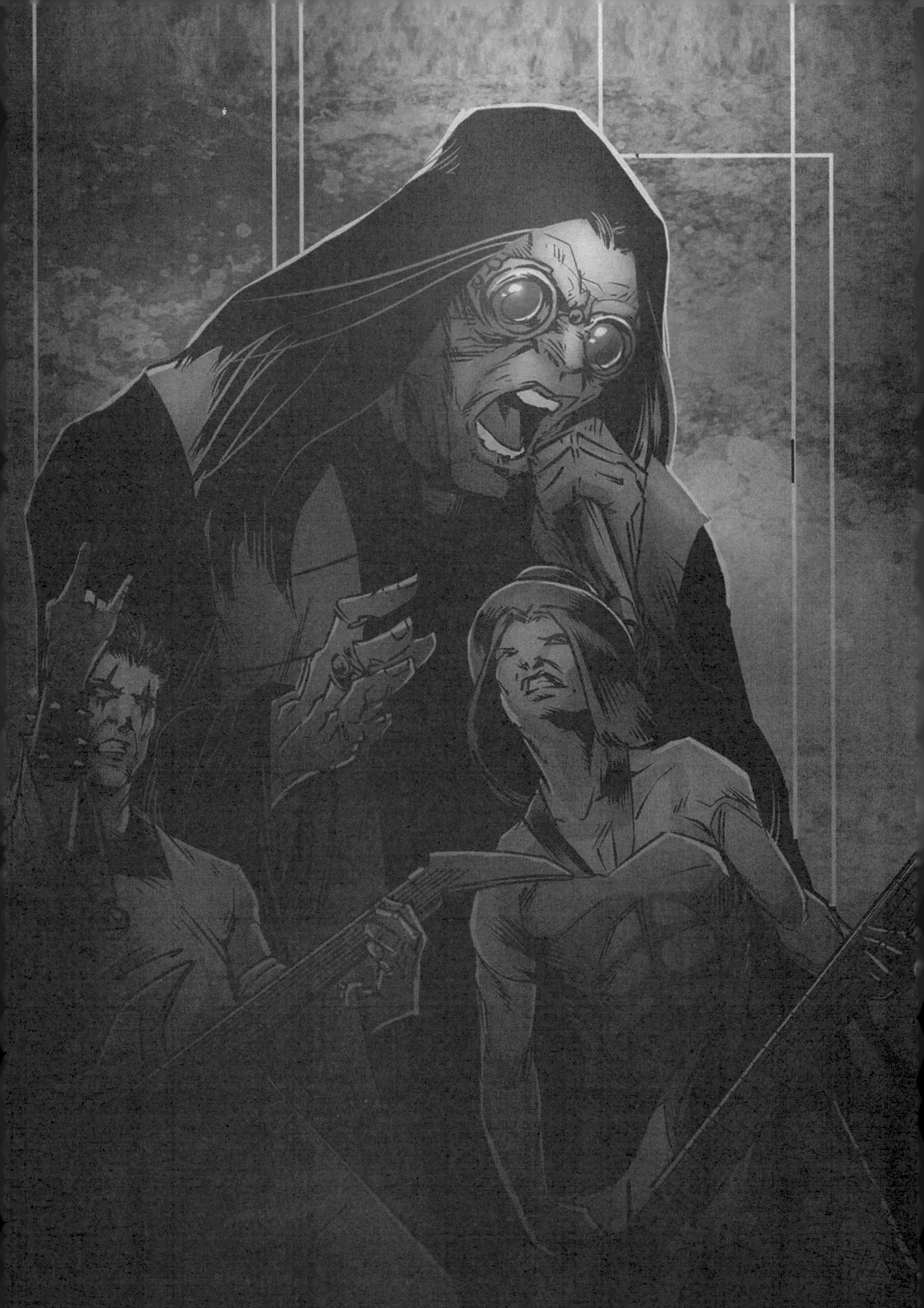

SATANIC HELL

SATANIC HELL

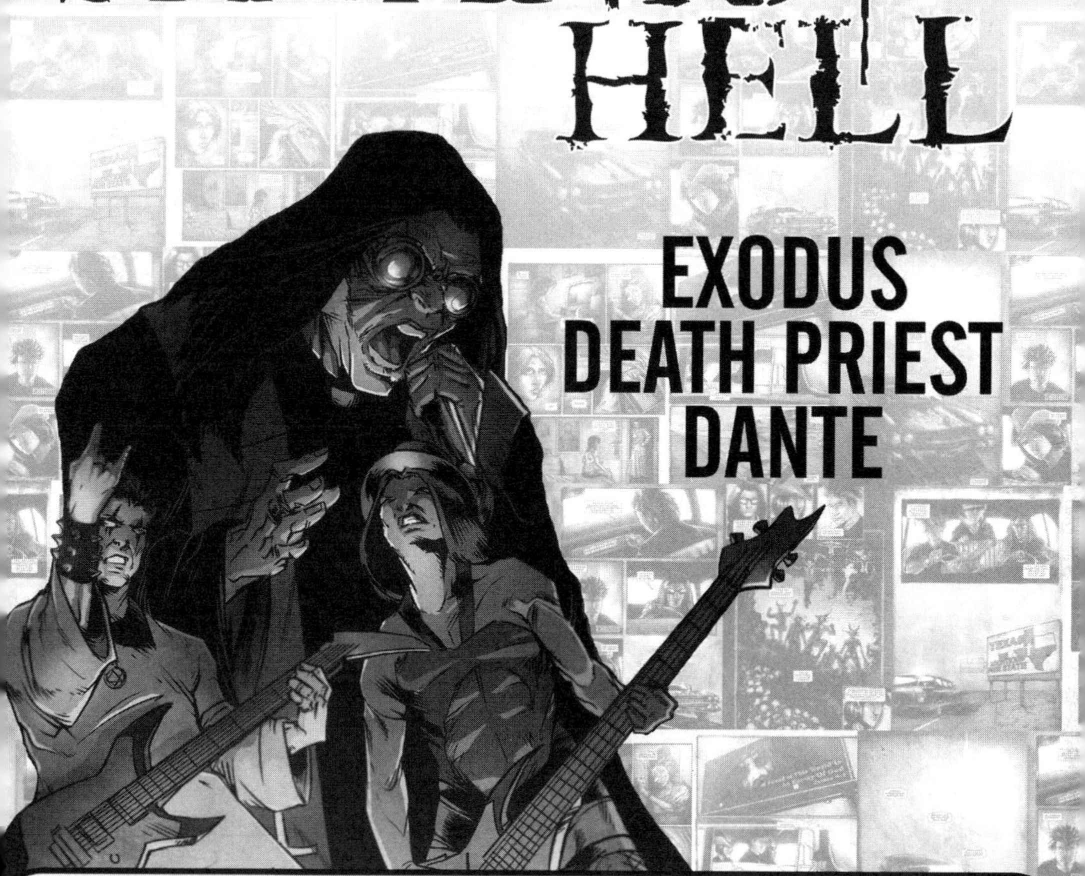

EXODUS
DEATH PRIEST
DANTE

"If we could only get these church guys to sit down and listen to the Butthole Surfers for 72 hours straight, it would change their whole perspective on things."

Exodus and Dante handle guitars in the three-piece metal band Satanic Hell, fronted by lead singer Death Priest. Finding themselves on a make-or-break tour in a Texas ruled by religious fanatics that are bent on their demise, Satanic Hell journey through their own version of Hell on Earth.

EXODUS Age: 26 Height: 5'9" Weight: 174 lbs.
DEATH PRIEST Age: 25 Height: 6'0" Weight: 175 lbs.
DANTE Age: 24 Height: 5'11" Weight: 160 lbs.

First Appearance: SATANIC HELL #1 (2014)

Created by Grigoris Douros
Illustration by Kevin Enhart & Jimmy Kerast

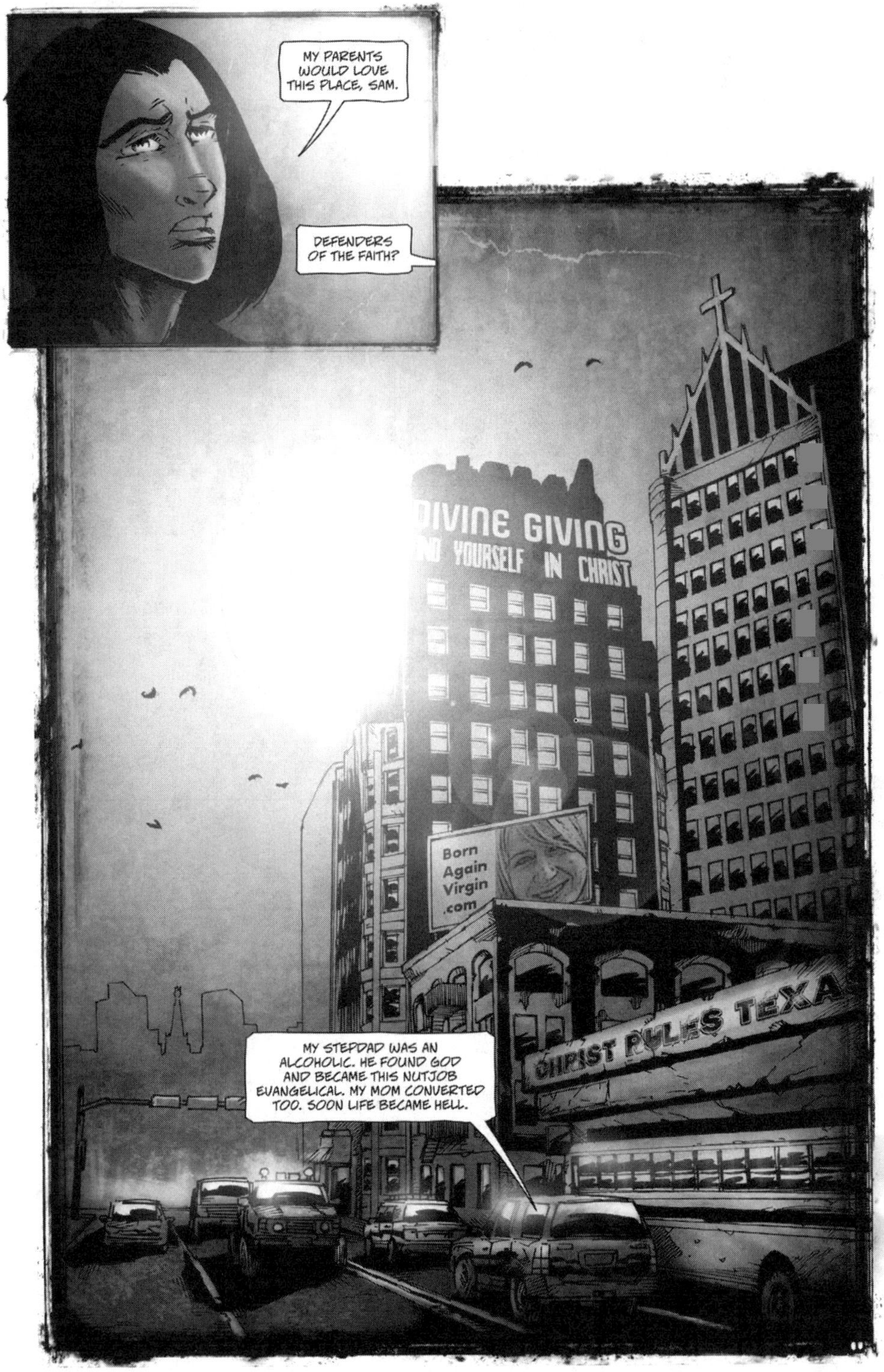
MY PARENTS WOULD LOVE THIS PLACE, SAM.
DEFENDERS OF THE FAITH?
DIVINE GIVING
YOURSELF IN CHRIST
Born Again Virgin .com
CHRIST RULES
MY STEPDAD WAS AN ALCOHOLIC. HE FOUND GOD AND BECAME THIS NUTJOB EVANGELICAL. MY MOM CONVERTED TOO. SOON LIFE BECAME HELL.

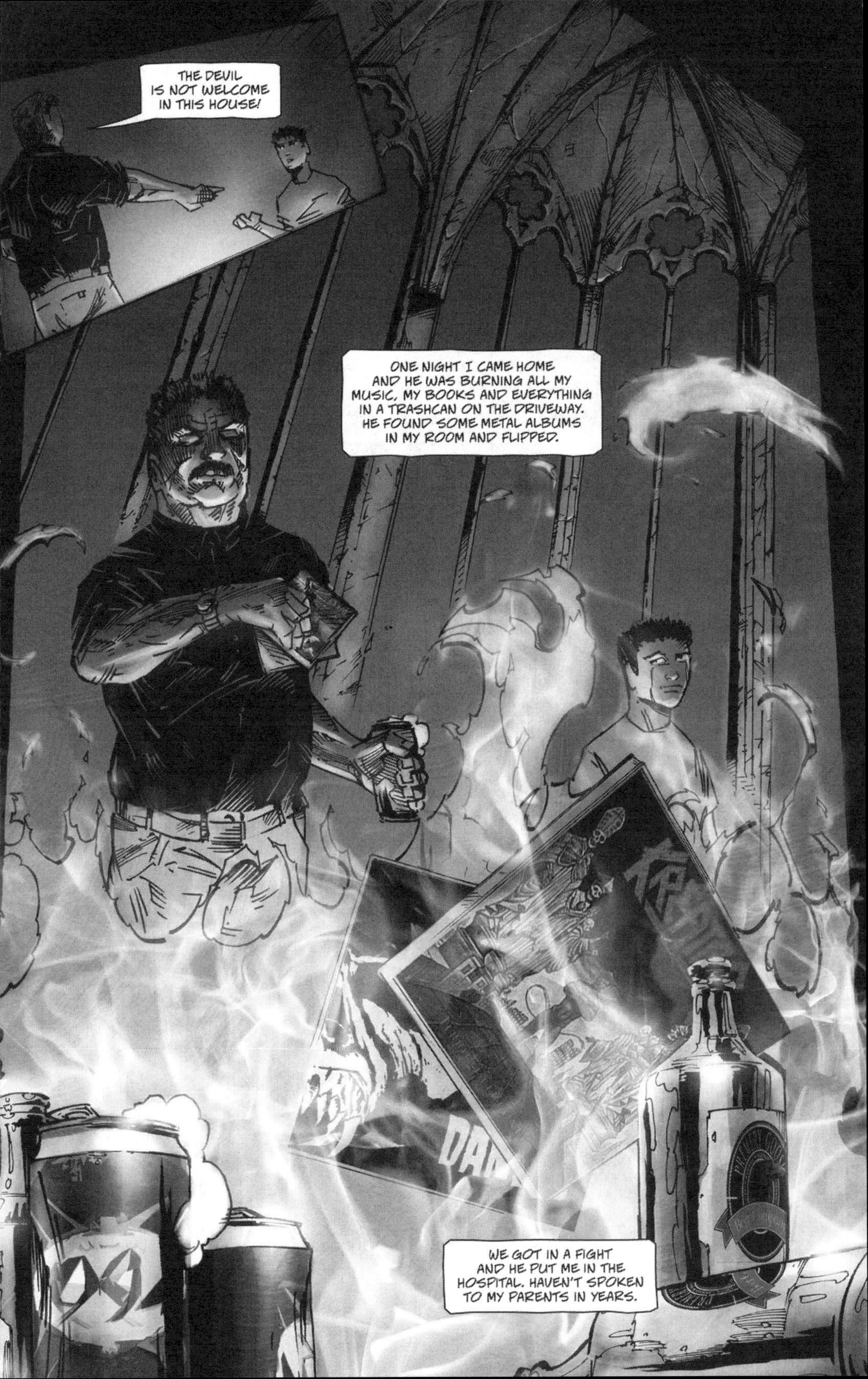
THE DEVIL IS NOT WELCOME IN THIS HOUSE!
ONE NIGHT I CAME HOME AND HE WAS BURNING ALL MY MUSIC, MY BOOKS AND EVERYTHING IN A TRASHCAN ON THE DRIVEWAY. HE FOUND SOME METAL ALBUMS IN MY ROOM AND FLIPPED.
WE GOT IN A FIGHT AND HE PUT ME IN THE HOSPITAL. HAVEN'T SPOKEN TO MY PARENTS IN YEARS.

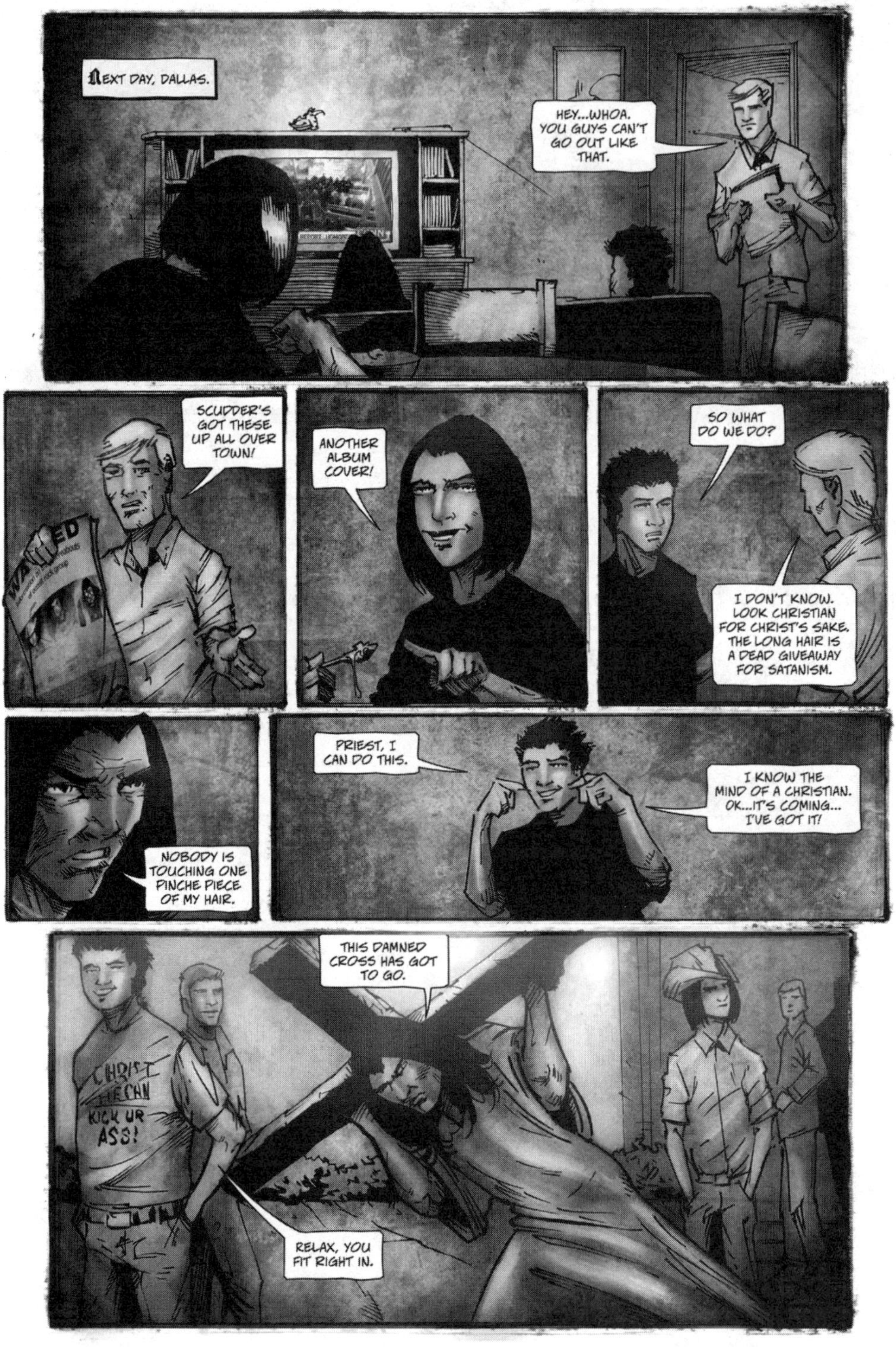
NEXT DAY, DALLAS.
HEY...WHOA. YOU GUYS CAN'T GO OUT LIKE THAT.
SCUDDER'S GOT THESE UP ALL OVER TOWN!
ANOTHER ALBUM COVER!
SO WHAT DO WE DO?
I DON'T KNOW. LOOK CHRISTIAN FOR CHRIST'S SAKE. THE LONG HAIR IS A DEAD GIVEAWAY FOR SATANISM.
NOBODY IS TOUCHING ONE PINCHE PIECE OF MY HAIR.
PRIEST, I CAN DO THIS.
I KNOW THE MIND OF A CHRISTIAN. OK...IT'S COMING... I'VE GOT IT!
THIS DAMNED CROSS HAS GOT TO GO.
KICK UR ASS!
RELAX, YOU FIT RIGHT IN.

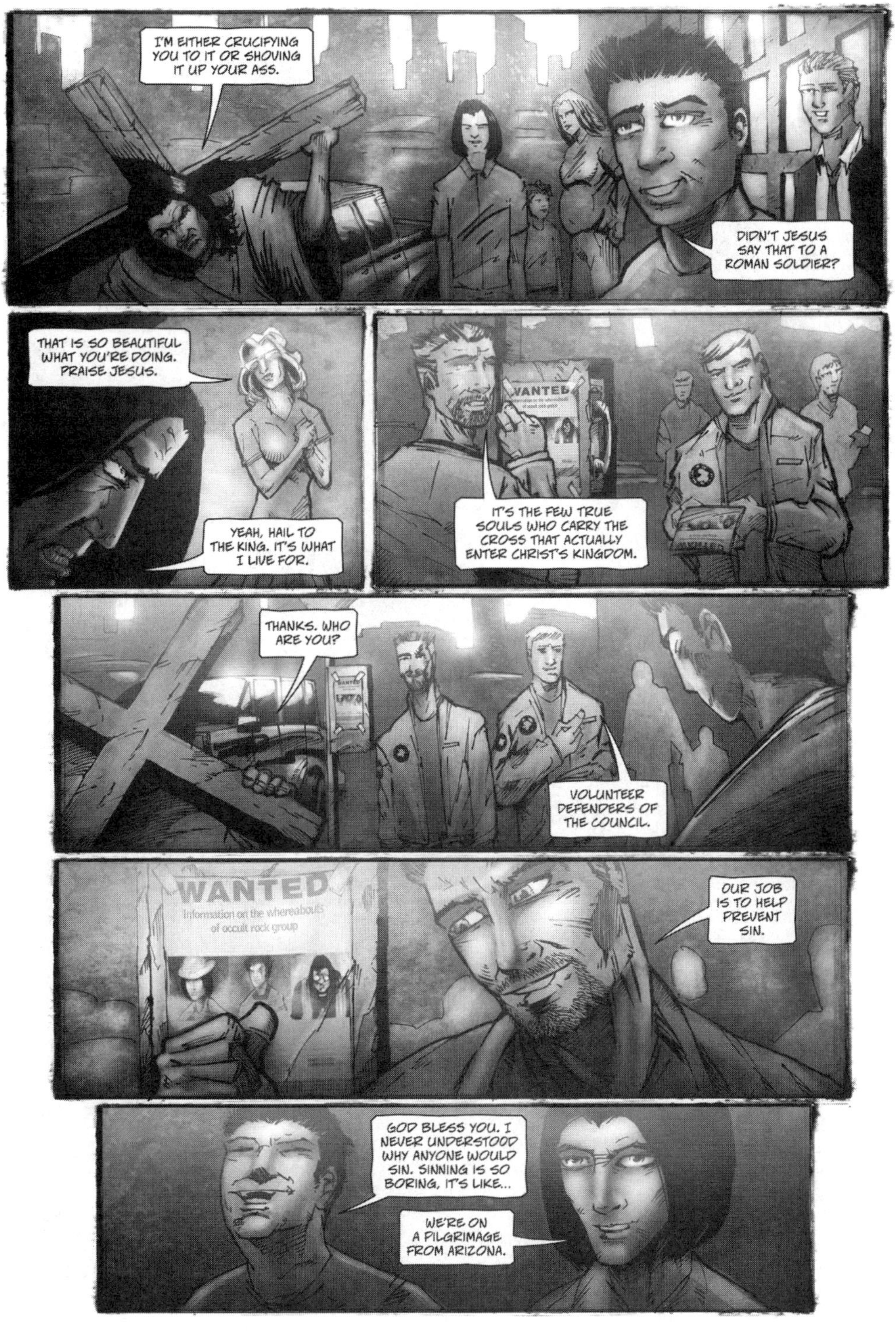

I'M EITHER CRUCIFYING YOU TO IT OR SHOVING IT UP YOUR ASS.
DIDN'T JESUS SAY THAT TO A ROMAN SOLDIER?
THAT IS SO BEAUTIFUL WHAT YOU'RE DOING. PRAISE JESUS.
YEAH, HAIL TO THE KING. IT'S WHAT I LIVE FOR.
WANTED
IT'S THE FEW TRUE SOULS WHO CARRY THE CROSS THAT ACTUALLY ENTER CHRIST'S KINGDOM.
THANKS. WHO ARE YOU?
VOLUNTEER DEFENDERS OF THE COUNCIL.
WANTED
Information on the whereabouts of occult rock group
OUR JOB IS TO HELP PREVENT SIN.
GOD BLESS YOU. I NEVER UNDERSTOOD WHY ANYONE WOULD SIN. SINNING IS SO BORING, IT'S LIKE...
WE'RE ON A PILGRIMAGE FROM ARIZONA.

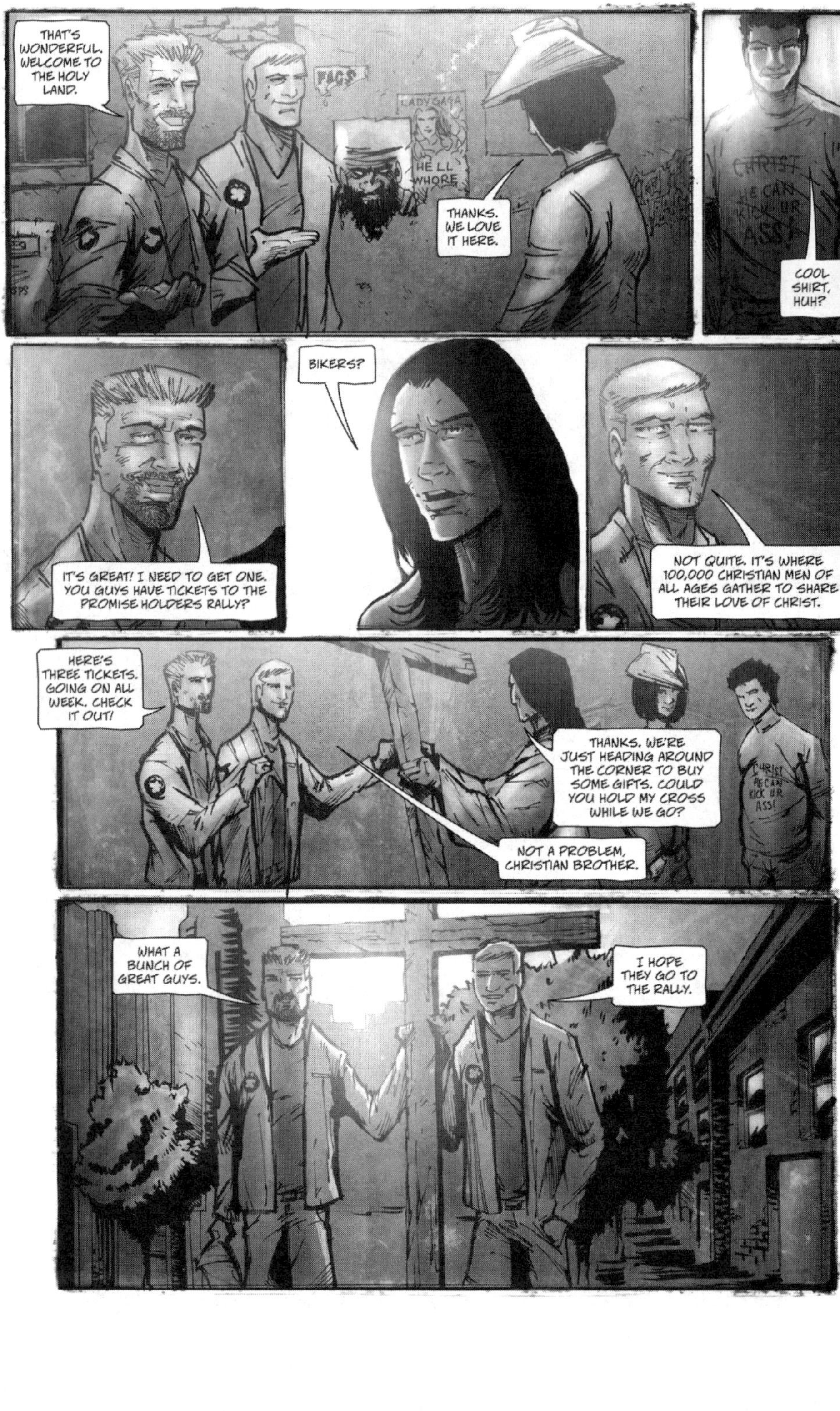
THAT'S WONDERFUL. WELCOME TO THE HOLY LAND.
FAGS
LADY GAGA
HELL WHORE
THANKS. WE LOVE IT HERE.
CHRIST HE CAN KICK UR ASS!
COOL SHIRT, HUH?
IT'S GREAT! I NEED TO GET ONE. YOU GUYS HAVE TICKETS TO THE PROMISE HOLDERS RALLY?
BIKERS?
NOT QUITE. IT'S WHERE 100,000 CHRISTIAN MEN OF ALL AGES GATHER TO SHARE THEIR LOVE OF CHRIST.
HERE'S THREE TICKETS. GOING ON ALL WEEK. CHECK IT OUT!
THANKS. WE'RE JUST HEADING AROUND THE CORNER TO BUY SOME GIFTS. COULD YOU HOLD MY CROSS WHILE WE GO?
NOT A PROBLEM, CHRISTIAN BROTHER.
WHAT A BUNCH OF GREAT GUYS.
I HOPE THEY GO TO THE RALLY.

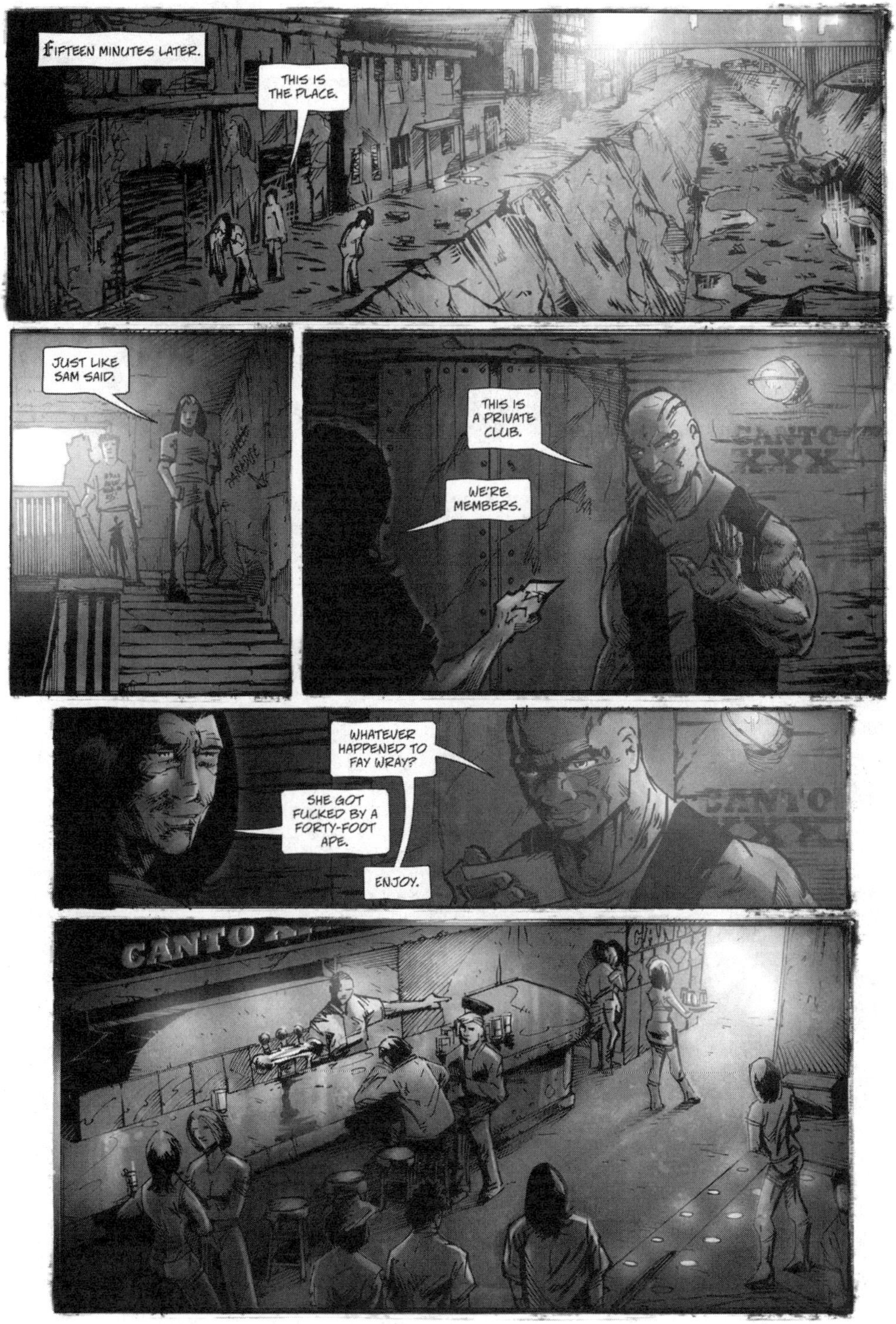
FIFTEEN MINUTES LATER.
THIS IS THE PLACE.
JUST LIKE SAM SAID.
THIS IS A PRIVATE CLUB.
WE'RE MEMBERS.
WHATEVER HAPPENED TO FAY WRAY?
SHE GOT FUCKED BY A FORTY-FOOT APE.
ENJOY.

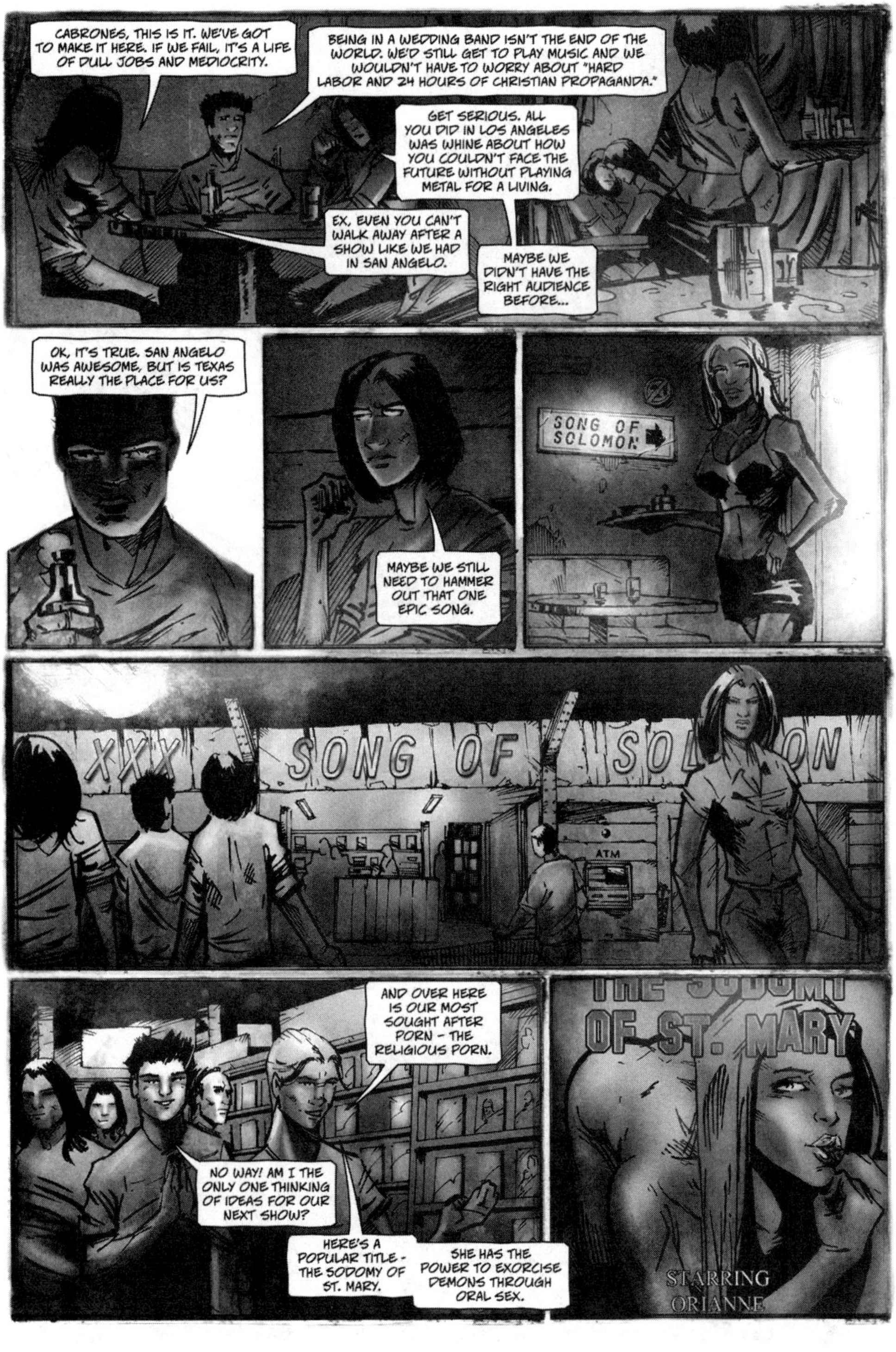
CABRONES, THIS IS IT. WE'VE GOT TO MAKE IT HERE. IF WE FAIL, IT'S A LIFE OF DULL JOBS AND MEDIOCRITY.
BEING IN A WEDDING BAND ISN'T THE END OF THE WORLD. WE'D STILL GET TO PLAY MUSIC AND WE WOULDN'T HAVE TO WORRY ABOUT "HARD LABOR AND 24 HOURS OF CHRISTIAN PROPAGANDA."
GET SERIOUS. ALL YOU DID IN LOS ANGELES WAS WHINE ABOUT HOW YOU COULDN'T FACE THE FUTURE WITHOUT PLAYING METAL FOR A LIVING.
EX, EVEN YOU CAN'T WALK AWAY AFTER A SHOW LIKE WE HAD IN SAN ANGELO.
MAYBE WE DIDN'T HAVE THE RIGHT AUDIENCE BEFORE...
OK, IT'S TRUE. SAN ANGELO WAS AWESOME, BUT IS TEXAS REALLY THE PLACE FOR US?
MAYBE WE STILL NEED TO HAMMER OUT THAT ONE EPIC SONG.
SONG OF SOLOMON
XXX SONG OF SOL ON
ATM
AND OVER HERE IS OUR MOST SOUGHT AFTER PORN - THE RELIGIOUS PORN.
NO WAY! AM I THE ONLY ONE THINKING OF IDEAS FOR OUR NEXT SHOW?
HERE'S A POPULAR TITLE - THE SODOMY OF ST. MARY.
SHE HAS THE POWER TO EXORCISE DEMONS THROUGH ORAL SEX.
OF ST. MARY
STARRING
ORIANNE

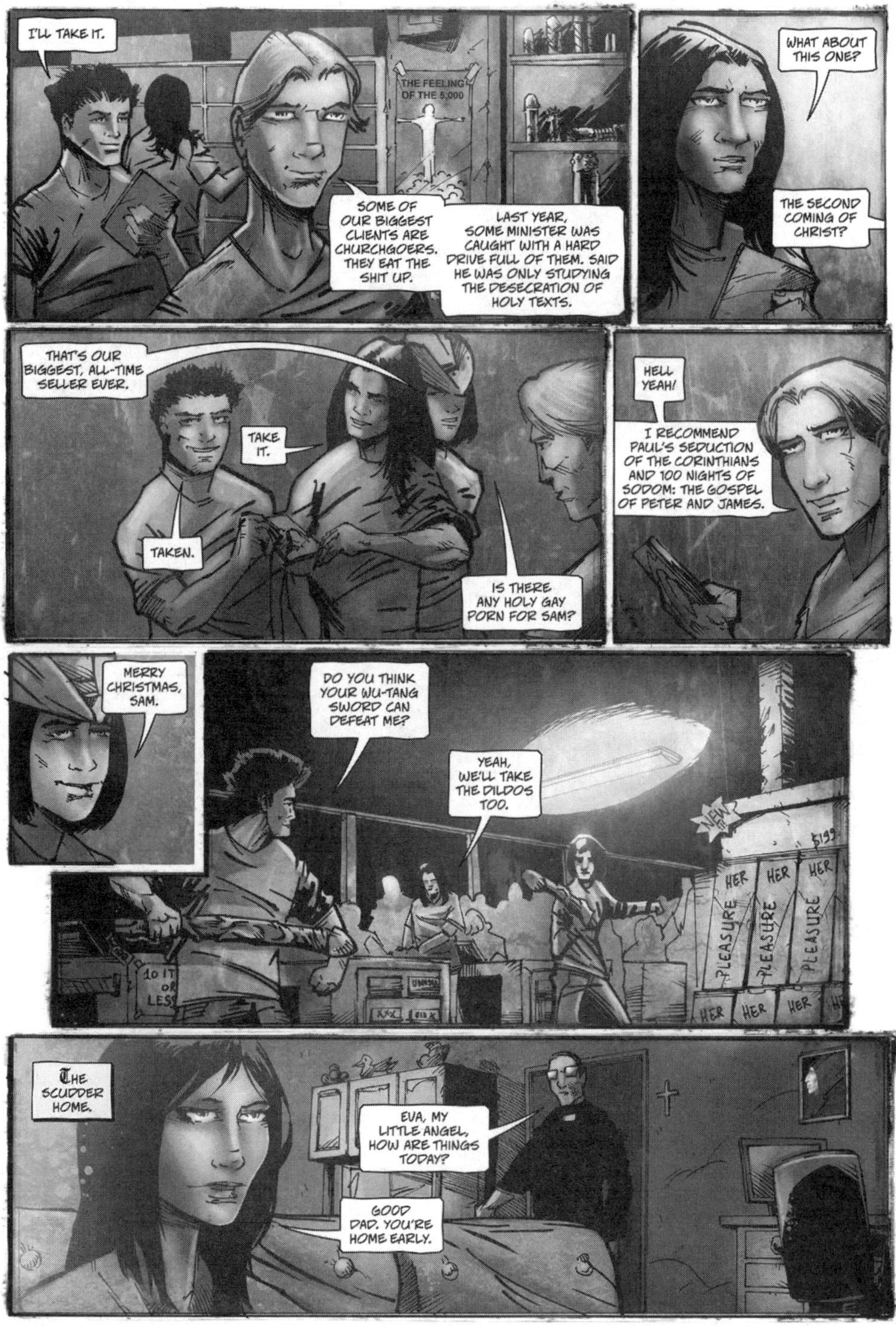
I'LL TAKE IT.
THE FEELING OF THE 5,000
SOME OF OUR BIGGEST CLIENTS ARE CHURCHGOERS. THEY EAT THE SHIT UP.
LAST YEAR, SOME MINISTER WAS CAUGHT WITH A HARD DRIVE FULL OF THEM. SAID HE WAS ONLY STUDYING THE DESECRATION OF HOLY TEXTS.
WHAT ABOUT THIS ONE?
THE SECOND COMING OF CHRIST?
THAT'S OUR BIGGEST, ALL-TIME SELLER EVER.
TAKE IT.
TAKEN.
IS THERE ANY HOLY GAY PORN FOR SAM?
HELL YEAH!
I RECOMMEND PAUL'S SEDUCTION OF THE CORINTHIANS AND 100 NIGHTS OF SODOM: THE GOSPEL OF PETER AND JAMES.
MERRY CHRISTMAS, SAM.
DO YOU THINK YOUR WU-TANG SWORD CAN DEFEAT ME?
YEAH, WE'LL TAKE THE DILDOS TOO.
NEW
HER
PLEASURE
THE SCUDDER HOME.
EVA, MY LITTLE ANGEL, HOW ARE THINGS TODAY?
GOOD DAD. YOU'RE HOME EARLY.

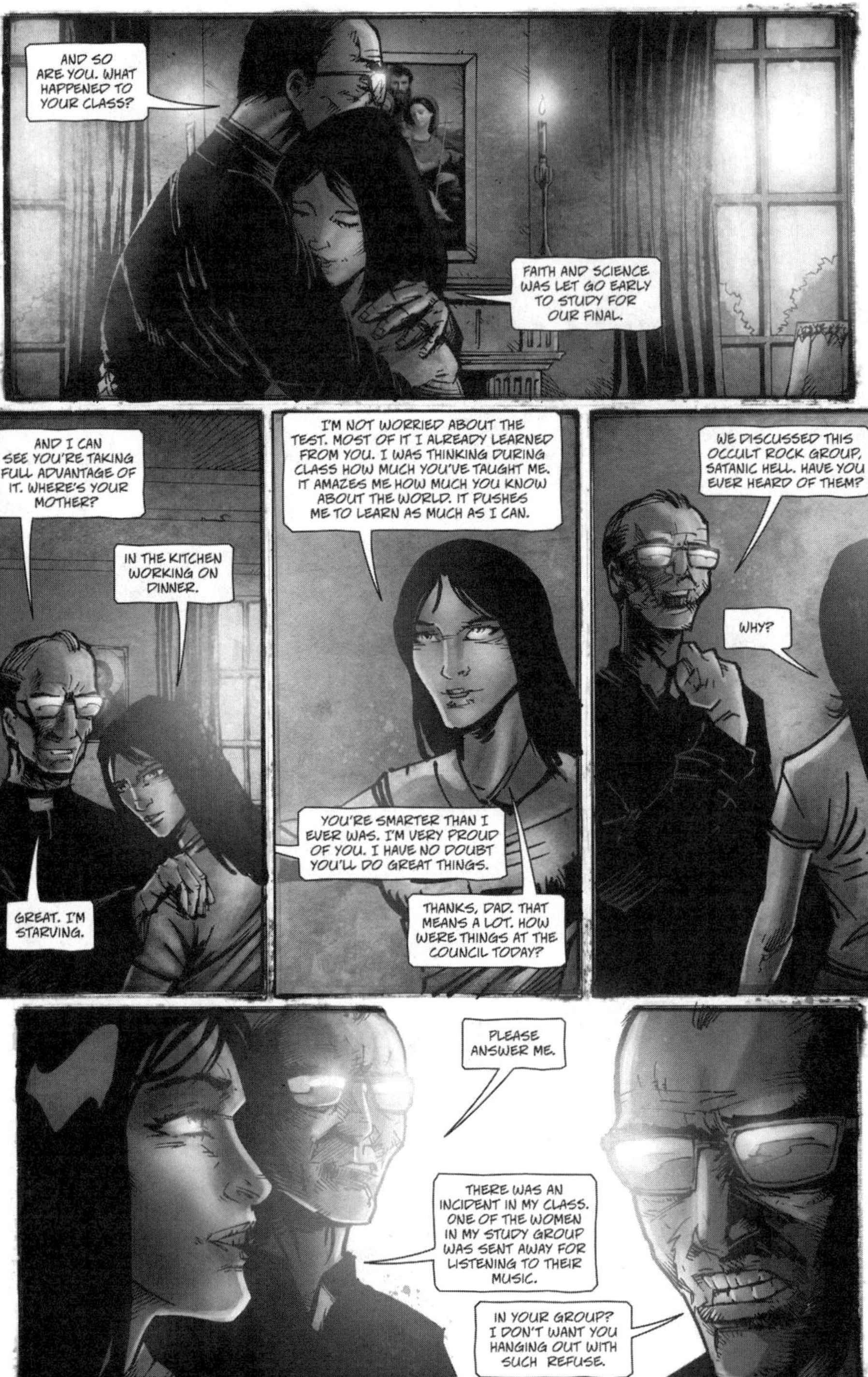
AND SO ARE YOU. WHAT HAPPENED TO YOUR CLASS?
FAITH AND SCIENCE WAS LET GO EARLY TO STUDY FOR OUR FINAL.
AND I CAN SEE YOU'RE TAKING FULL ADVANTAGE OF IT. WHERE'S YOUR MOTHER?
IN THE KITCHEN WORKING ON DINNER.
GREAT. I'M STARVING.
I'M NOT WORRIED ABOUT THE TEST. MOST OF IT I ALREADY LEARNED FROM YOU. I WAS THINKING DURING CLASS HOW MUCH YOU'VE TAUGHT ME. IT AMAZES ME HOW MUCH YOU KNOW ABOUT THE WORLD. IT PUSHES ME TO LEARN AS MUCH AS I CAN.
YOU'RE SMARTER THAN I EVER WAS. I'M VERY PROUD OF YOU. I HAVE NO DOUBT YOU'LL DO GREAT THINGS.
THANKS, DAD. THAT MEANS A LOT. HOW WERE THINGS AT THE COUNCIL TODAY?
WE DISCUSSED THIS OCCULT ROCK GROUP, SATANIC HELL. HAVE YOU EVER HEARD OF THEM?
WHY?
PLEASE ANSWER ME.
THERE WAS AN INCIDENT IN MY CLASS. ONE OF THE WOMEN IN MY STUDY GROUP WAS SENT AWAY FOR LISTENING TO THEIR MUSIC.
IN YOUR GROUP? I DON'T WANT YOU HANGING OUT WITH SUCH REFUSE.

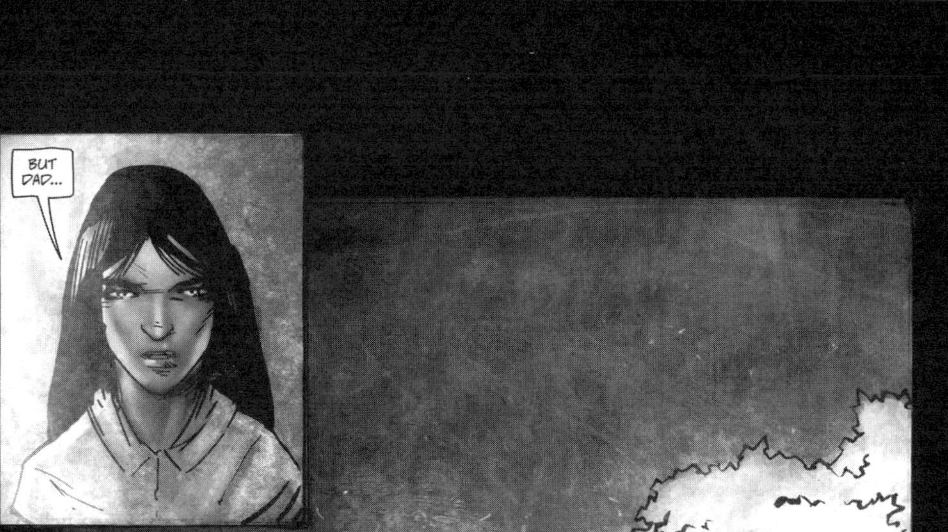
BUT DAD...

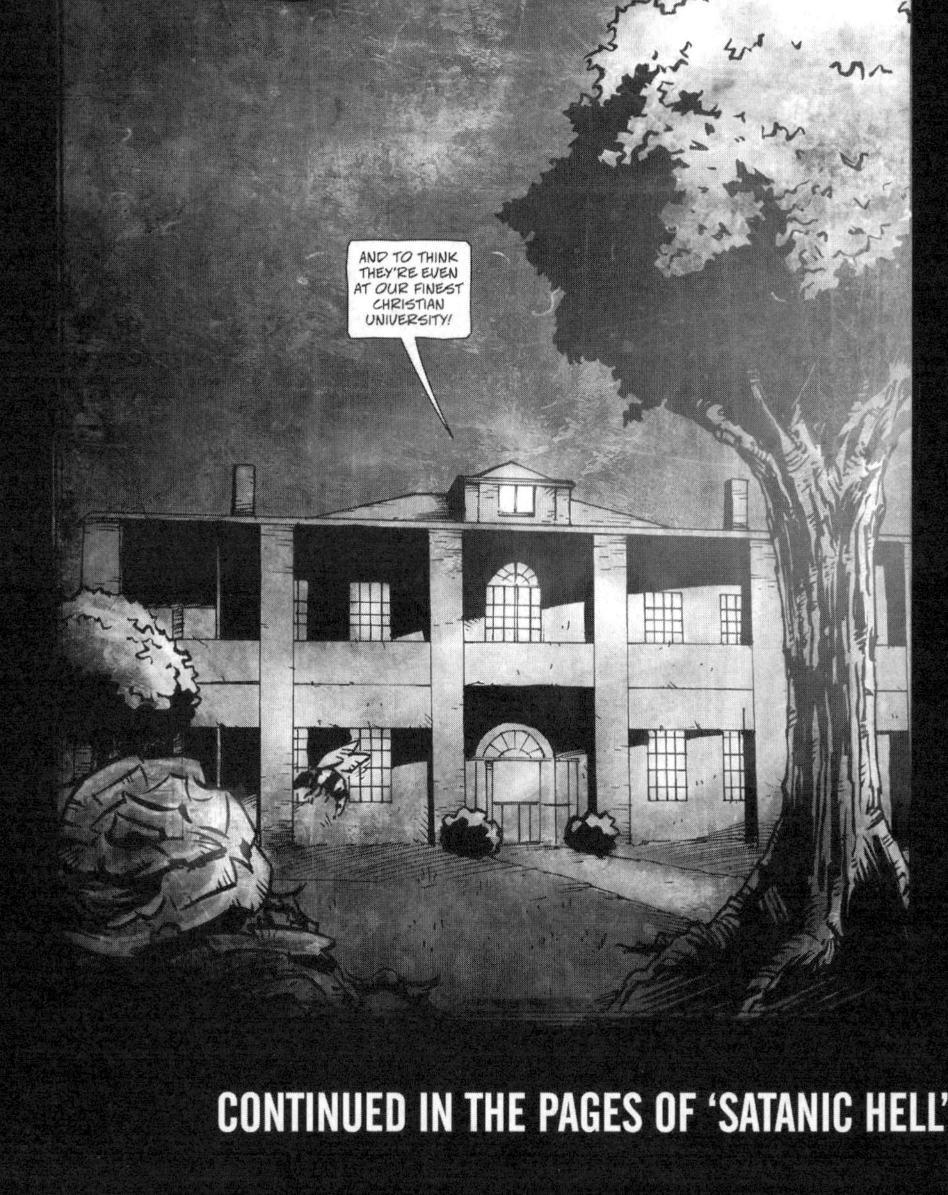
AND TO THINK THEY'RE EVEN AT OUR FINEST CHRISTIAN UNIVERSITY!

CONTINUED IN THE PAGES OF 'SATANIC HELL'

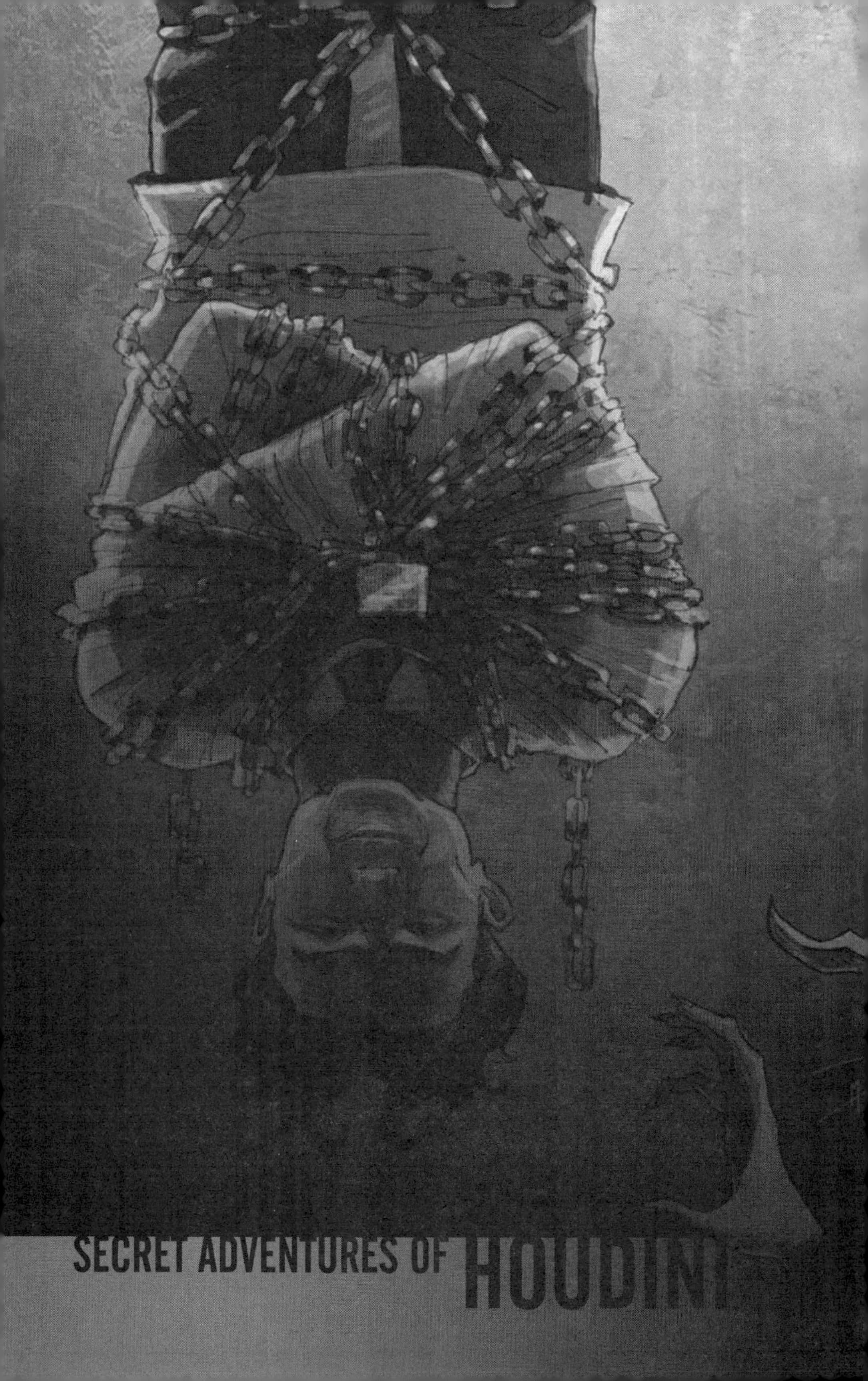
SECRET ADVENTURES OF
HOUDINI

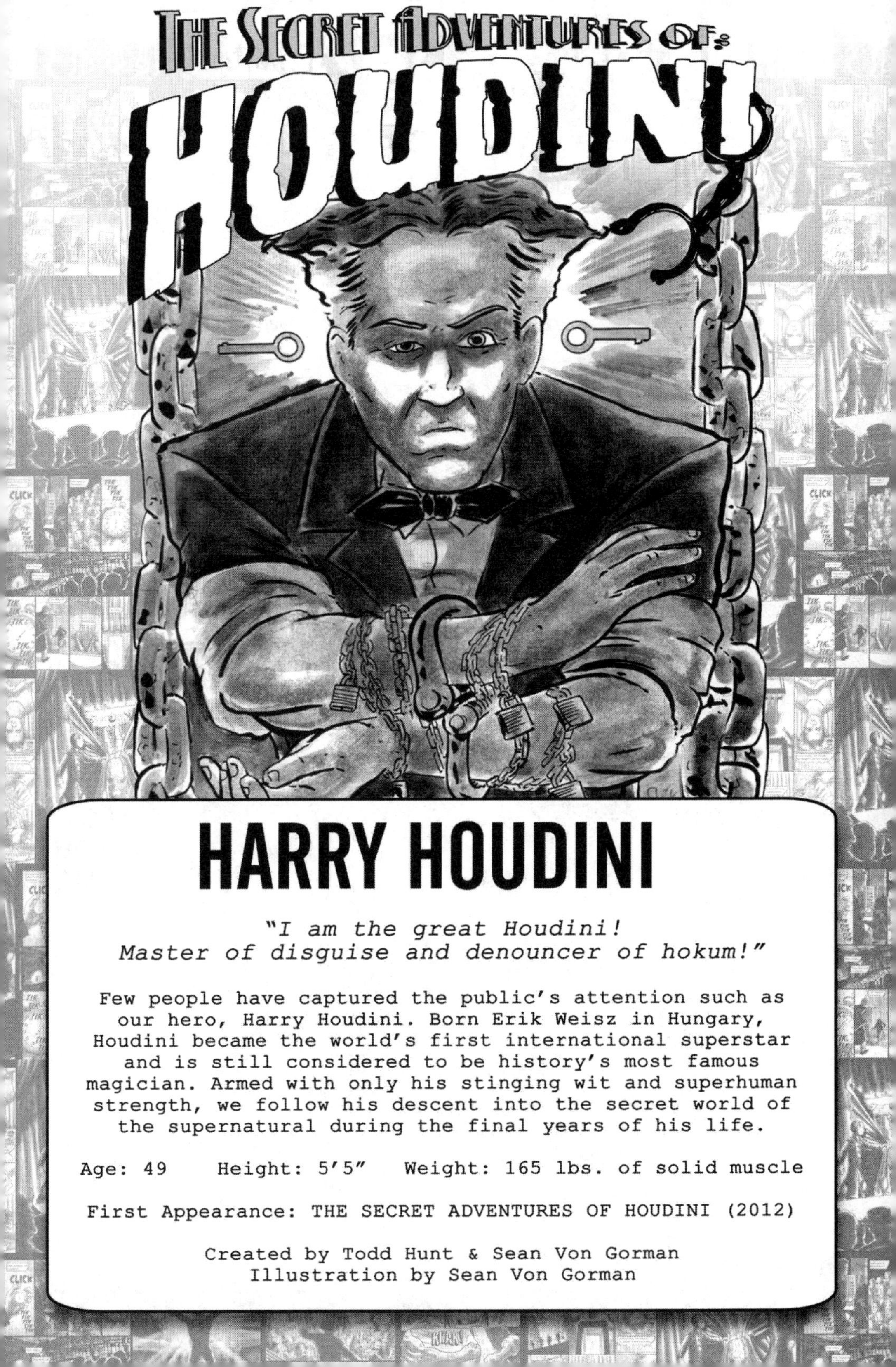
THE SECRET ADVENTURES OF:
HOUDINI

HARRY HOUDINI

*"I am the great Houdini!
Master of disguise and denouncer of hokum!"*

Few people have captured the public's attention such as our hero, Harry Houdini. Born Erik Weisz in Hungary, Houdini became the world's first international superstar and is still considered to be history's most famous magician. Armed with only his stinging wit and superhuman strength, we follow his descent into the secret world of the supernatural during the final years of his life.

Age: 49 Height: 5'5" Weight: 165 lbs. of solid muscle

First Appearance: THE SECRET ADVENTURES OF HOUDINI (2012)

Created by Todd Hunt & Sean Von Gorman
Illustration by Sean Von Gorman

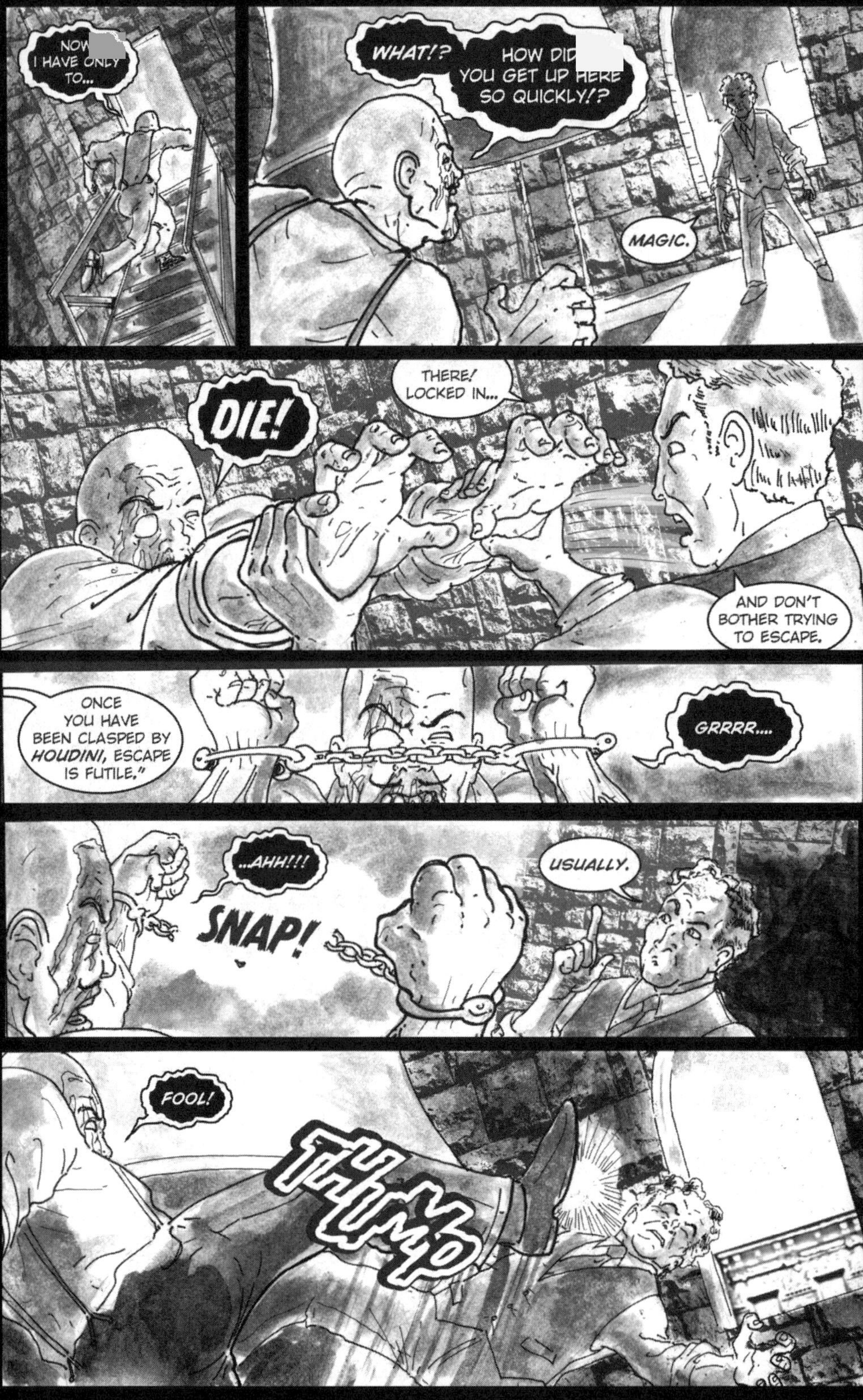
NOW
I HAVE ONLY TO...
WHAT!?
HOW DID
YOU GET UP HERE
SO QUICKLY!?
MAGIC.
DIE!
THERE! LOCKED IN...
AND DON'T BOTHER TRYING TO ESCAPE.
ONCE YOU HAVE BEEN CLASPED BY HOUDINI, ESCAPE IS FUTILE."
GRRRR....
..AHH!!!
SNAP!
USUALLY.
FOOL!
THUMP

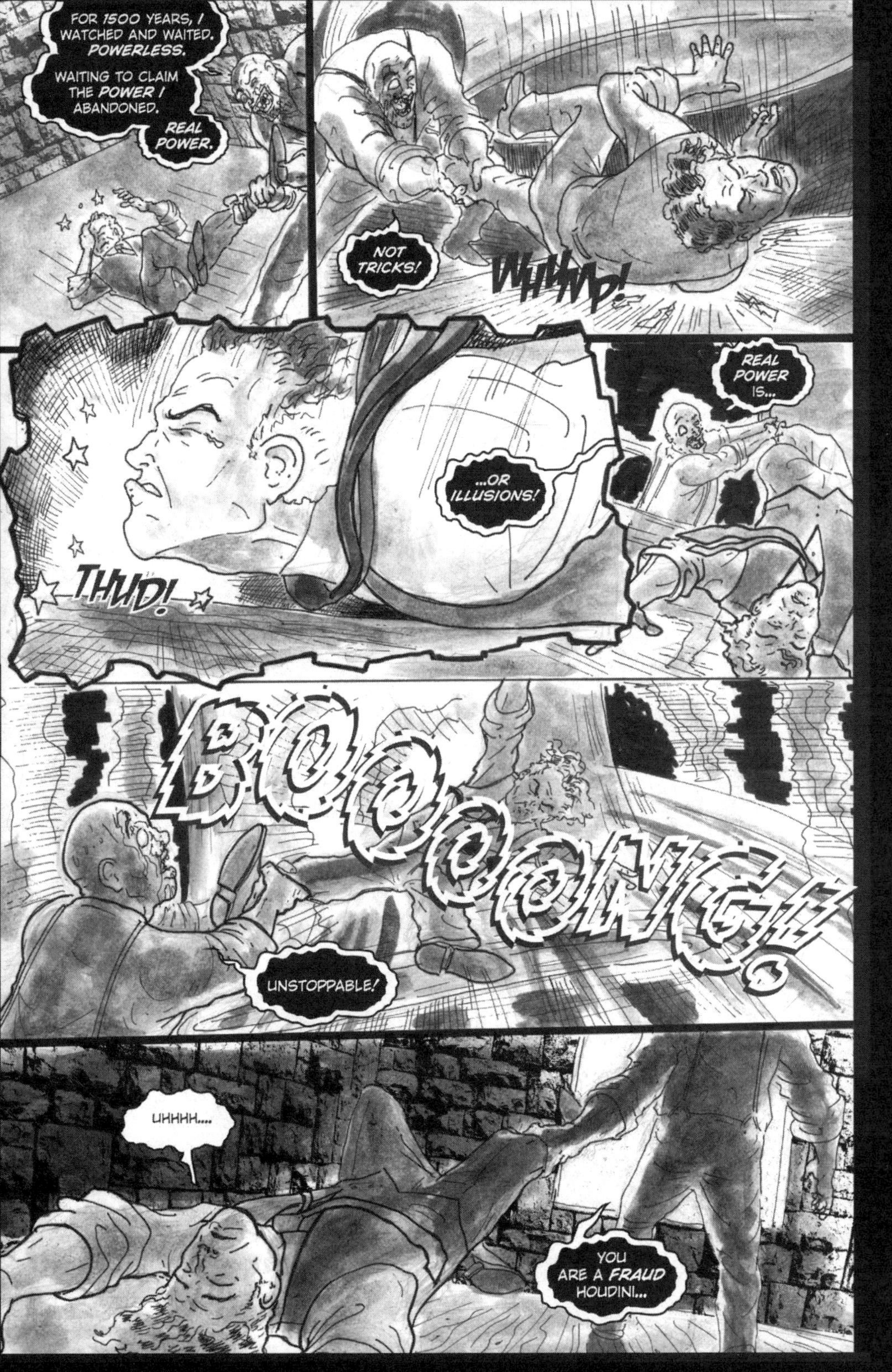
FOR 1500 YEARS, I WATCHED AND WAITED. POWERLESS.
WAITING TO CLAIM THE POWER I ABANDONED.
REAL POWER.
NOT TRICKS!
WHUMP!
...OR ILLUSIONS!
THUD!
REAL POWER IS...
BOOOOING!!
UNSTOPPABLE!
UHHHH....
YOU ARE A FRAUD HOUDINI...

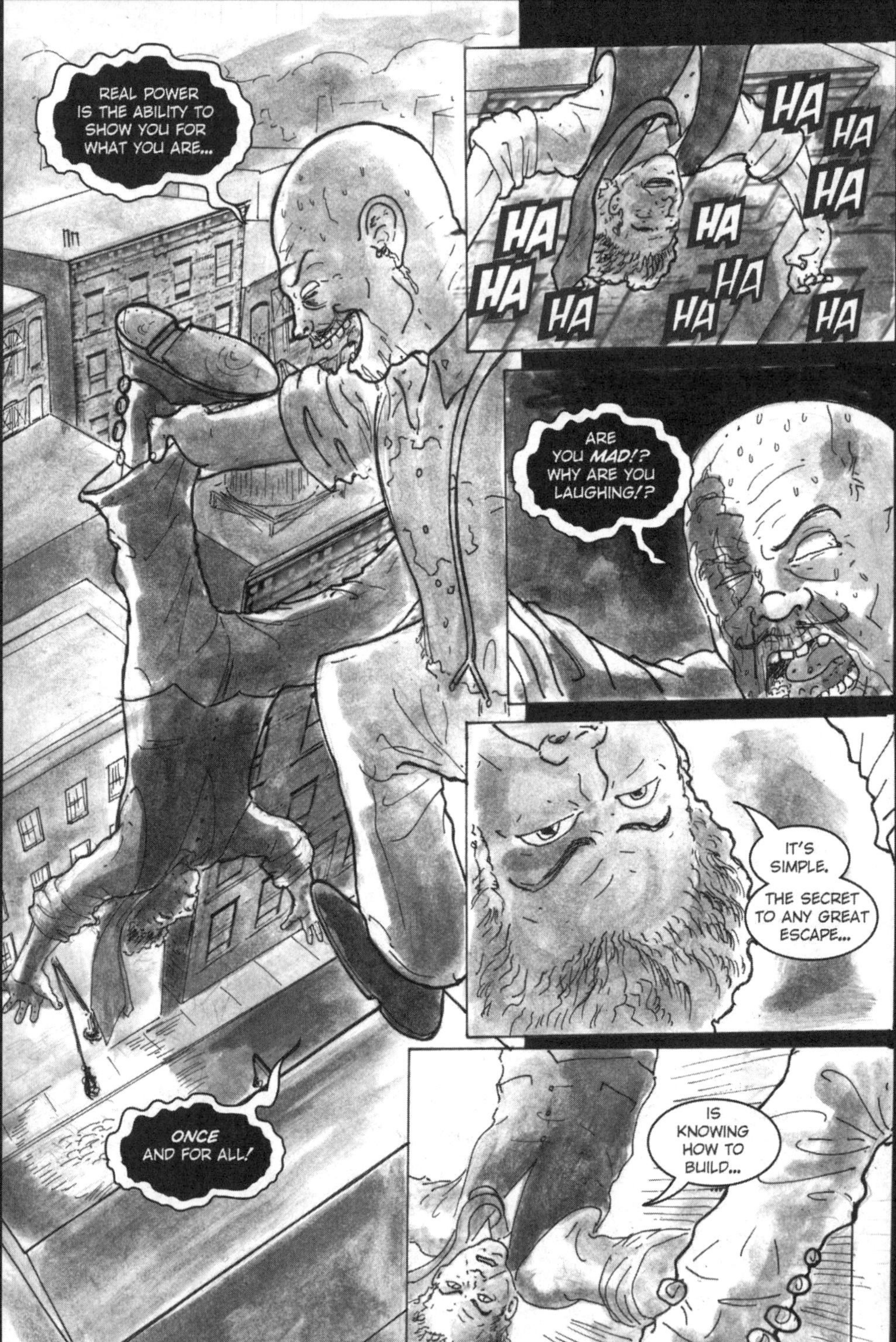
REAL POWER IS THE ABILITY TO SHOW YOU FOR WHAT YOU ARE...
HA HA HA HA HA HA HA HA HA HA HA HA
ARE YOU *MAD!*? WHY ARE YOU LAUGHING!?
IT'S SIMPLE.
THE SECRET TO ANY GREAT ESCAPE...
ONCE AND FOR ALL!
IS KNOWING HOW TO BUILD...

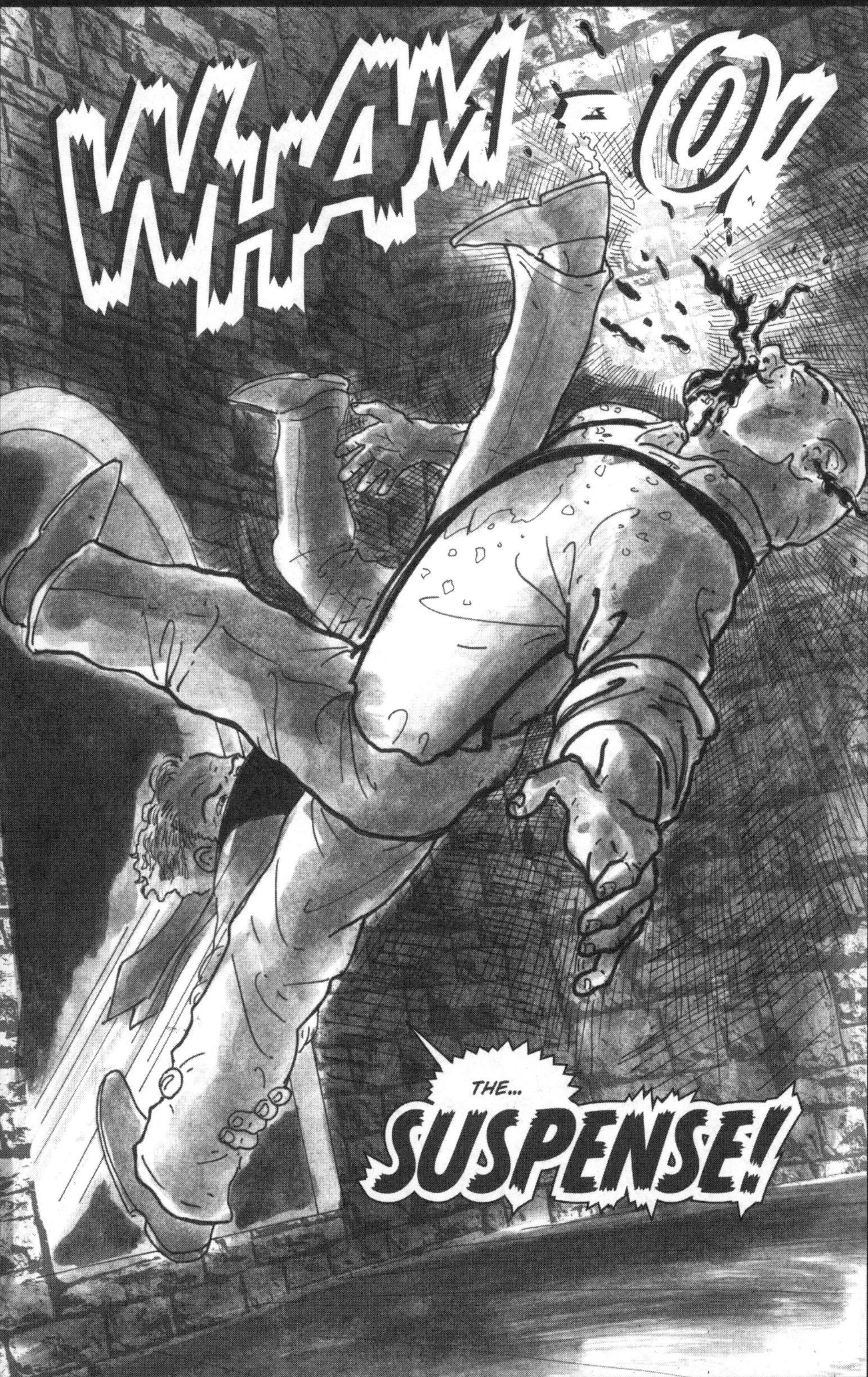
WHAM-O!
THE...
SUSPENSE!

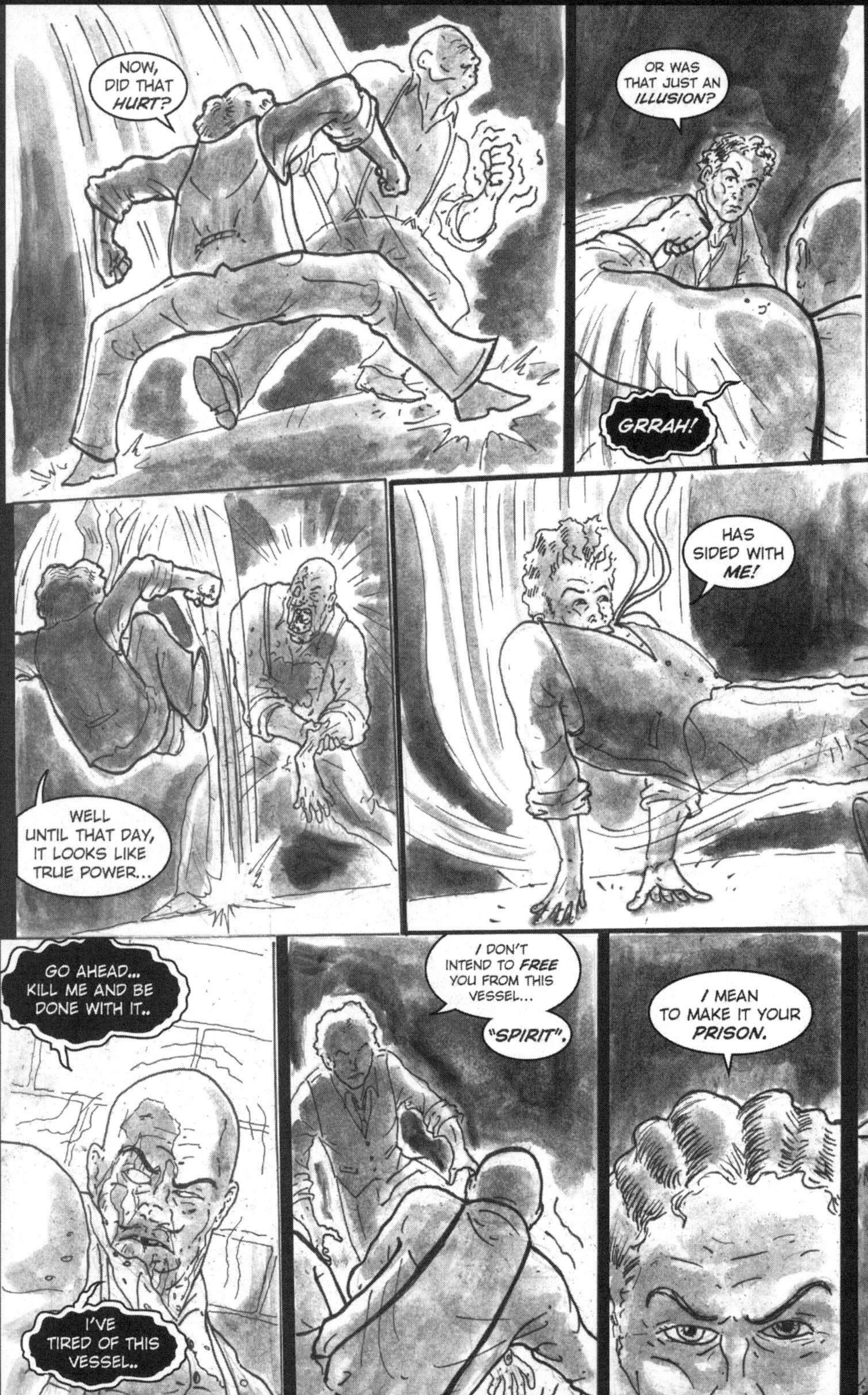

NOW, DID THAT *HURT?*
OR WAS THAT JUST AN *ILLUSION?*
GRRAH!
WELL UNTIL THAT DAY, IT LOOKS LIKE TRUE POWER...
HAS SIDED WITH *ME!*
GO AHEAD... KILL ME AND BE DONE WITH IT..
I'VE TIRED OF THIS VESSEL..
I DON'T INTEND TO *FREE* YOU FROM THIS VESSEL...
"SPIRIT".
I MEAN TO MAKE IT YOUR *PRISON.*

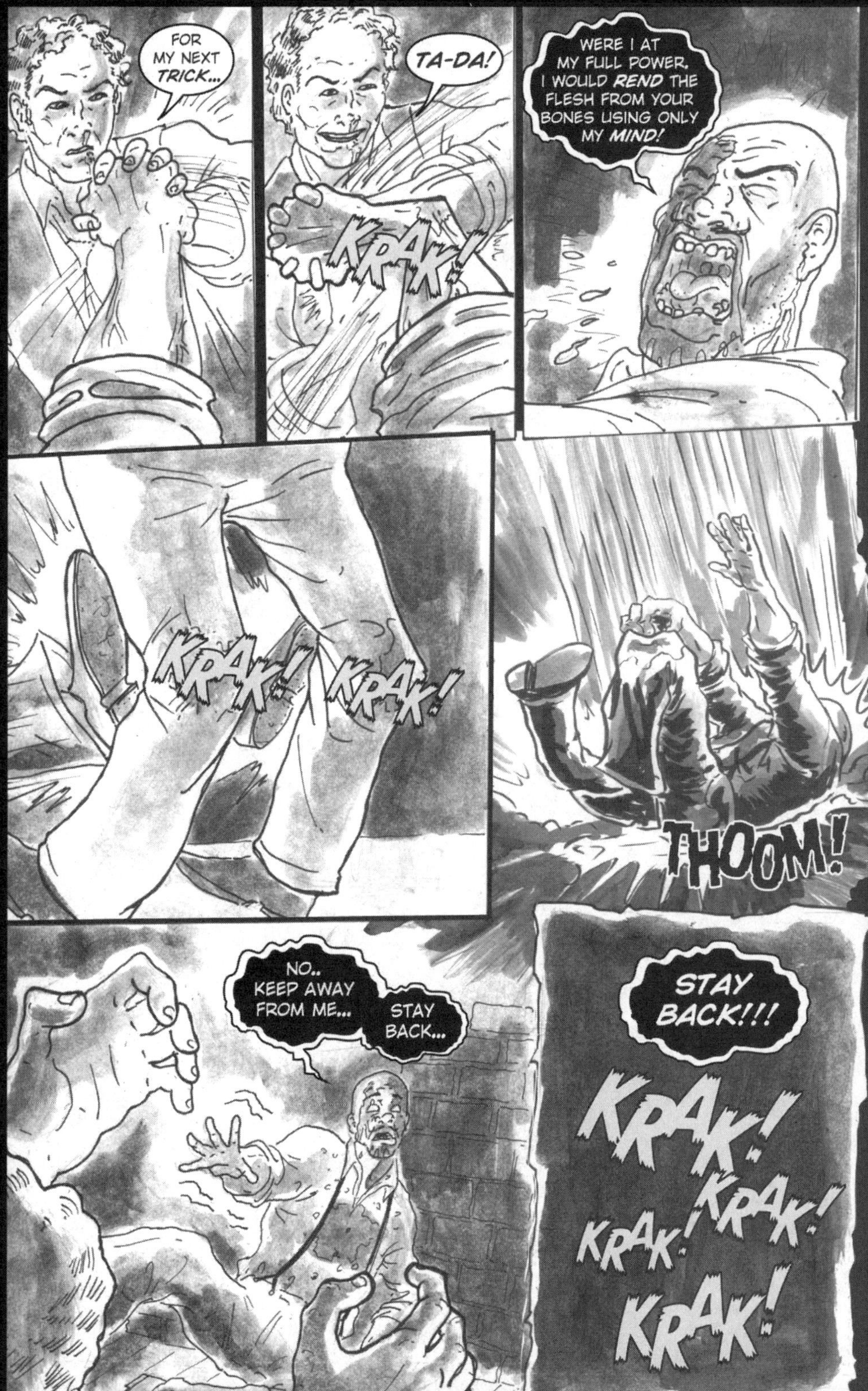
FOR MY NEXT TRICK...
TA-DA!
KRAK!
WERE I AT MY FULL POWER, I WOULD REND THE FLESH FROM YOUR BONES USING ONLY MY MIND!
KRAK! KRAK!
THOOM!
NO.. KEEP AWAY FROM ME...
STAY BACK...
STAY BACK!!!
KRAK!
KRAK!
KRAK!
KRAK!

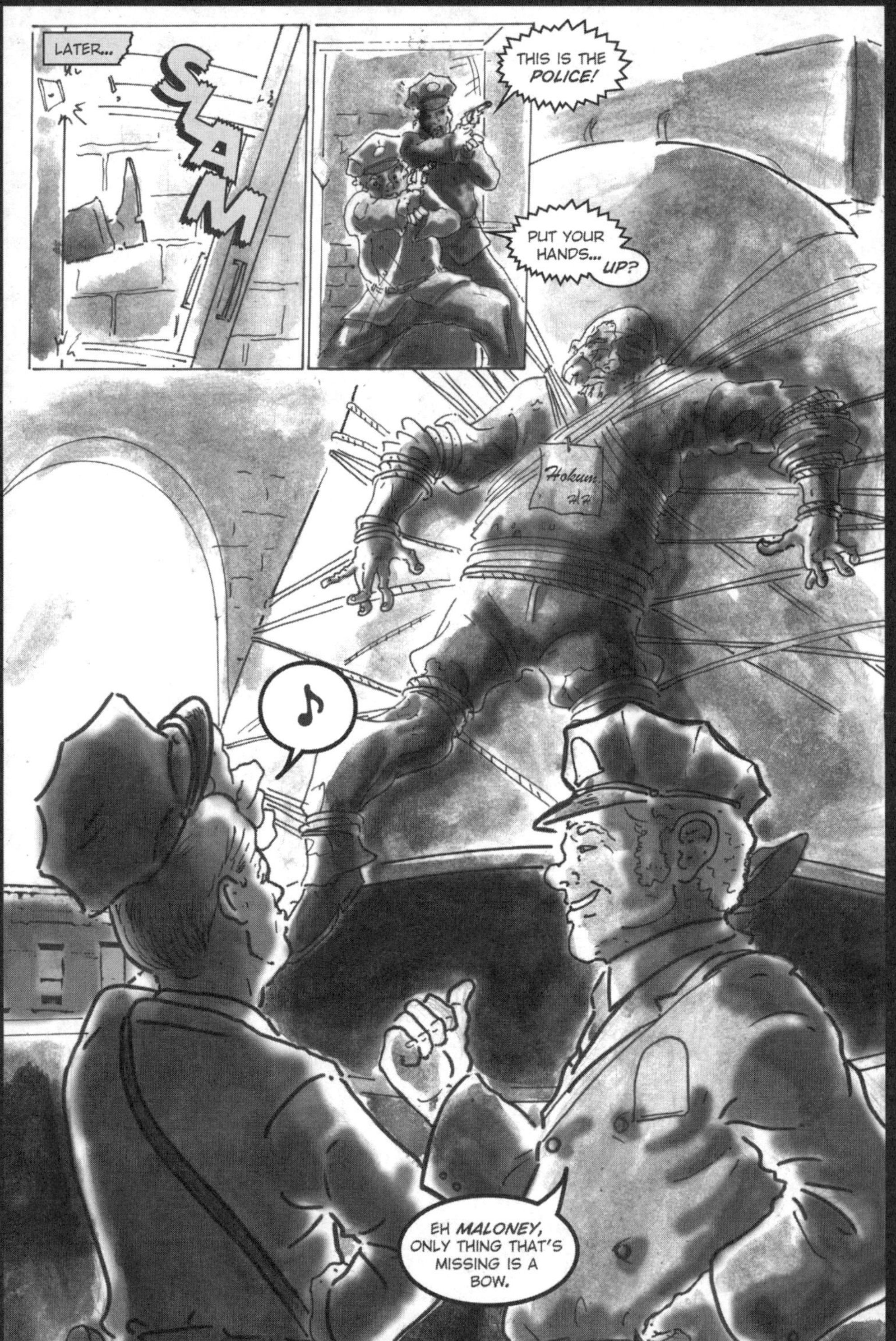
LATER...
SLAM
THIS IS THE POLICE!
PUT YOUR HANDS... UP?
Hokum
♪
EH MALONEY, ONLY THING THAT'S MISSING IS A BOW.

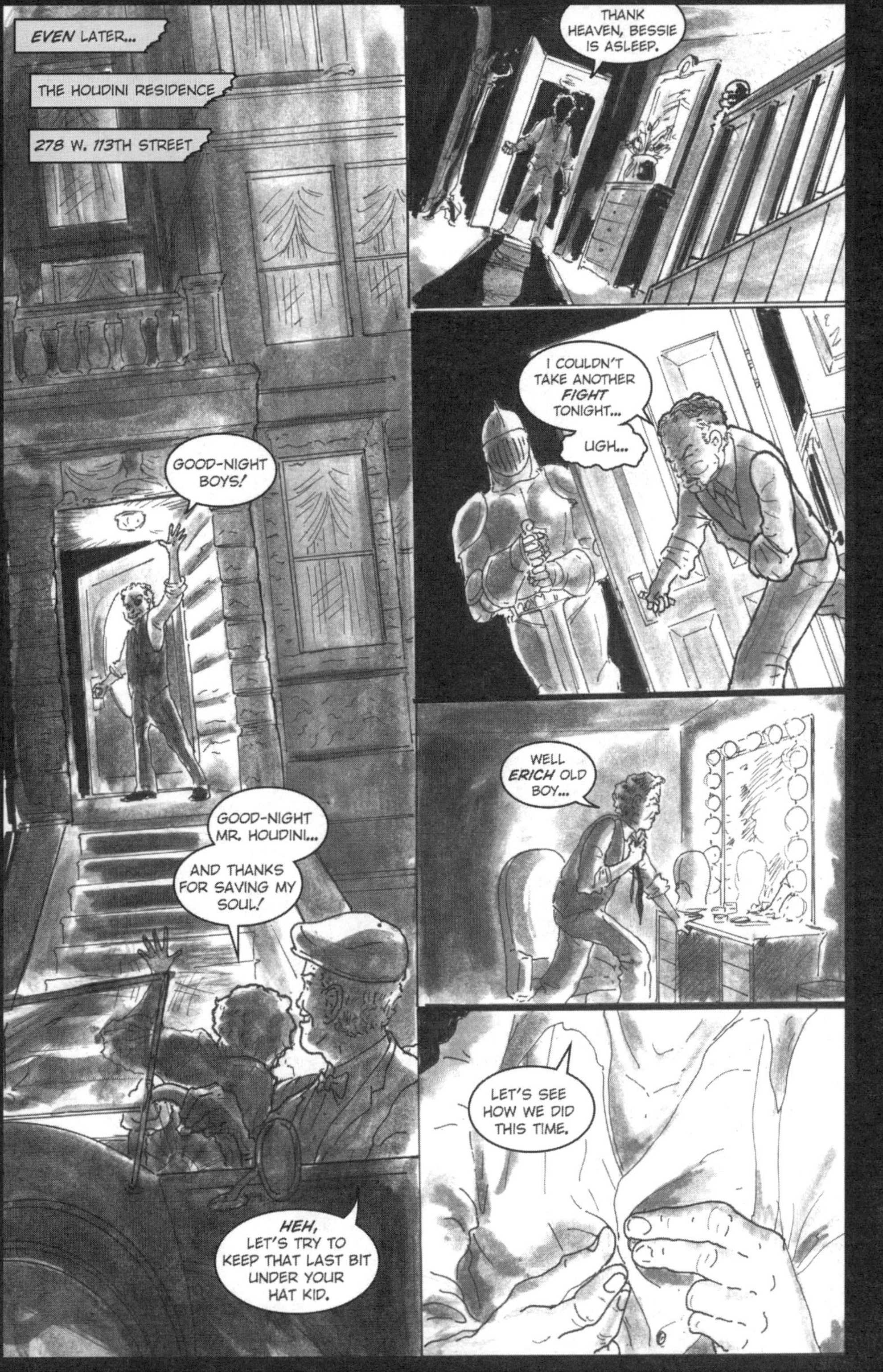
EVEN LATER...
THE HOUDINI RESIDENCE
278 W. 113TH STREET
GOOD-NIGHT BOYS!
GOOD-NIGHT MR. HOUDINI...
AND THANKS FOR SAVING MY SOUL!
HEH, LET'S TRY TO KEEP THAT LAST BIT UNDER YOUR HAT KID.
THANK HEAVEN, BESSIE IS ASLEEP.
I COULDN'T TAKE ANOTHER FIGHT TONIGHT...
UGH...
WELL ERICH OLD BOY...
LET'S SEE HOW WE DID THIS TIME.

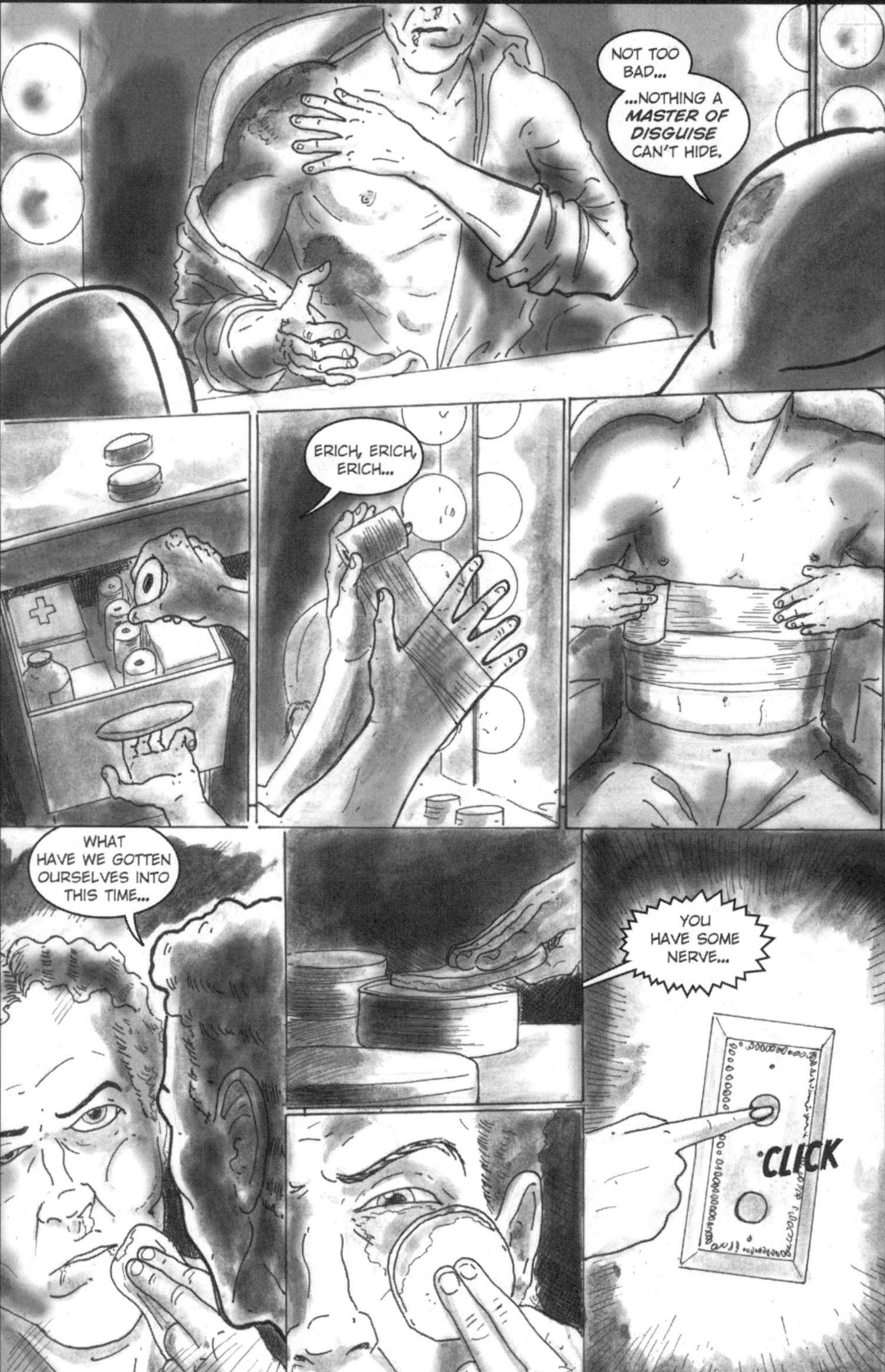
NOT TOO BAD...
...NOTHING A MASTER OF DISGUISE CAN'T HIDE.
ERICH, ERICH, ERICH...
WHAT HAVE WE GOTTEN OURSELVES INTO THIS TIME...
YOU HAVE SOME NERVE...
CLICK

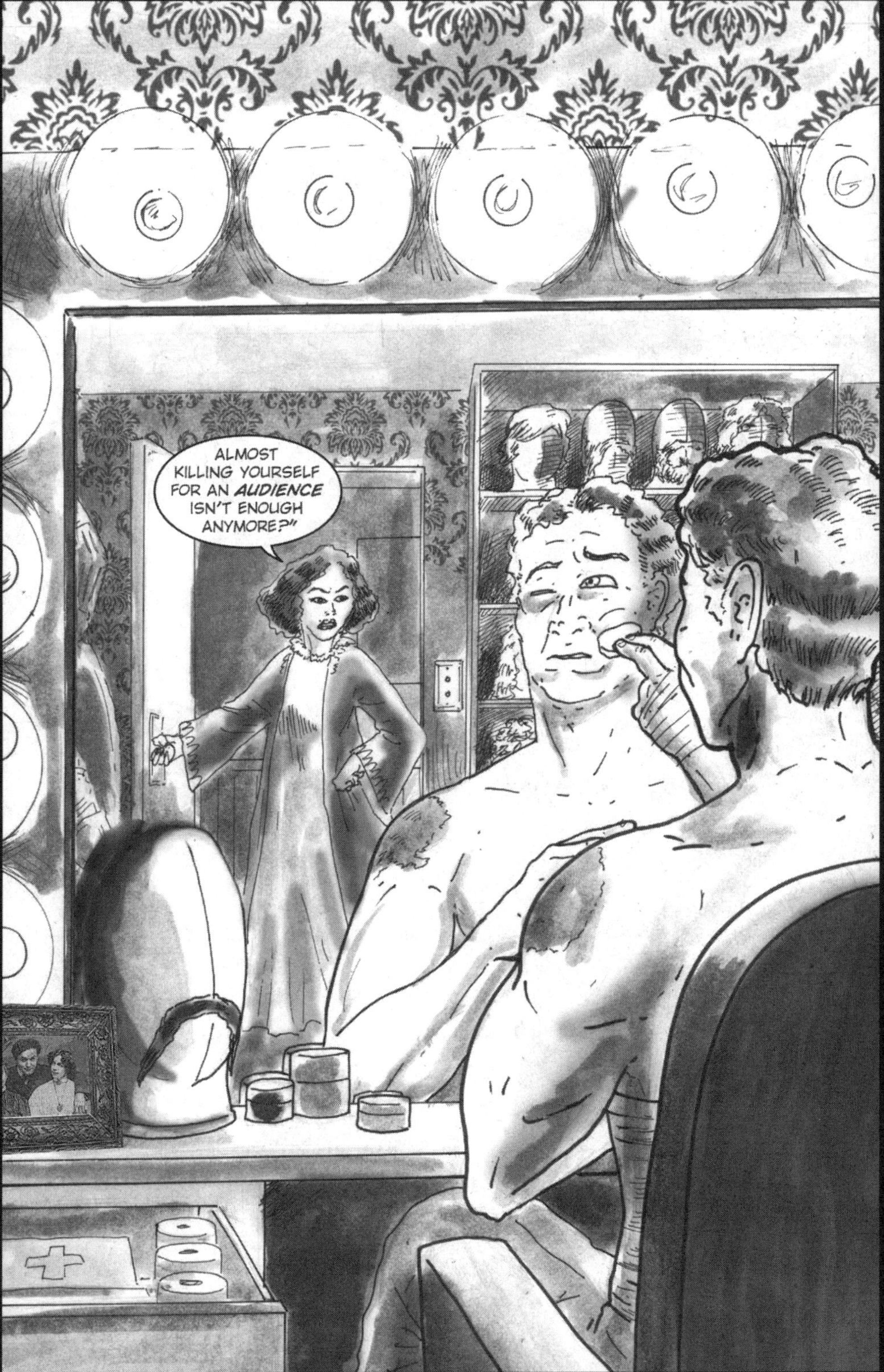
ALMOST KILLING YOURSELF FOR AN AUDIENCE ISN'T ENOUGH ANYMORE?"

CONTINUED IN THE PAGES OF 'SECRET ADVENTURES OF HOUDINI'

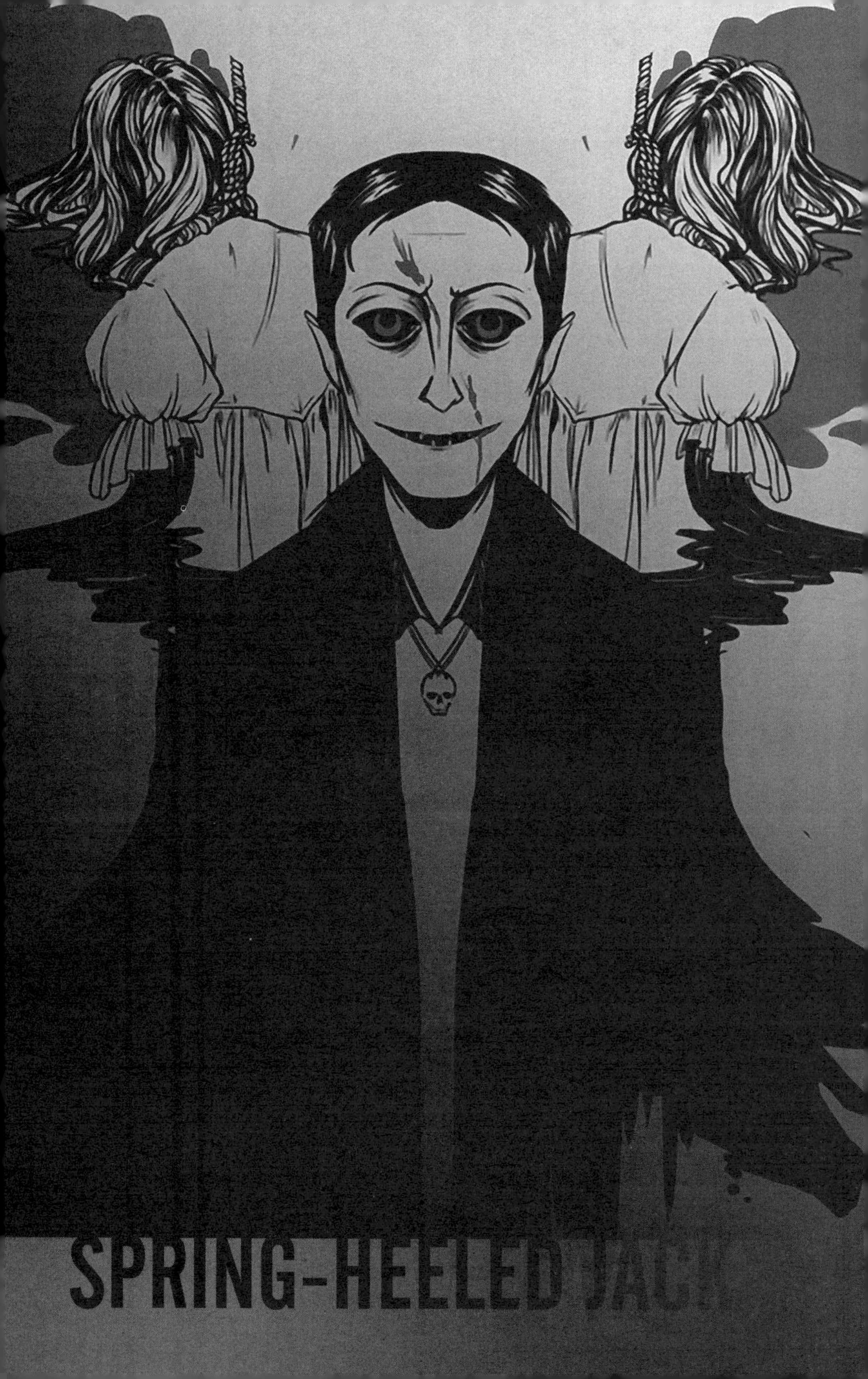
SPRING-HEELED JACK

SPRING-HEELED JACK

SPRING-HEELED JACK

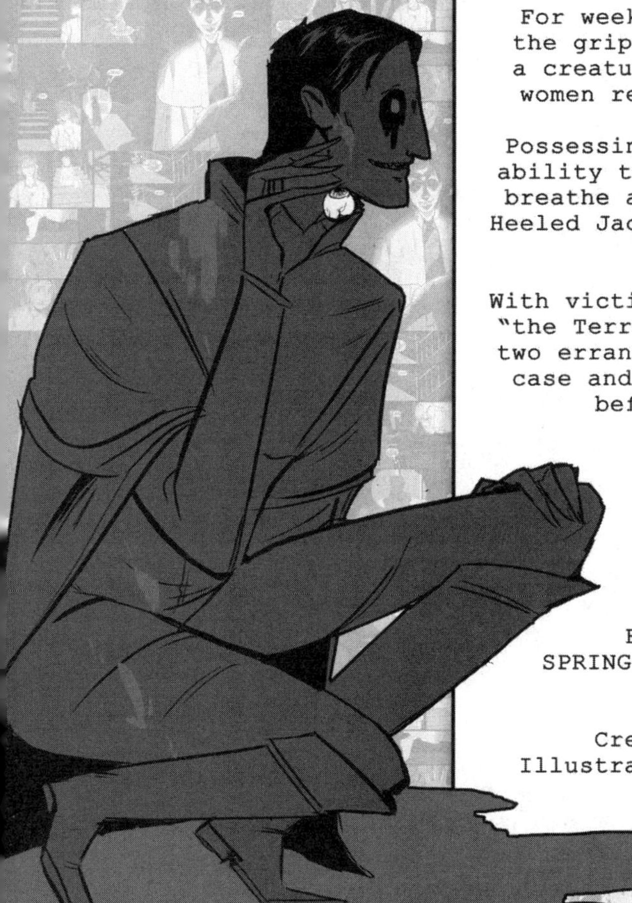

"You've Been Very Naughty..."

For weeks London has been under the grip of a living nightmare - a creature so foul, that men and women refuse to speak his name.

Possessing razor sharp claws, the ability to leap over buildings and breathe a demonic flame, Spring-Heeled Jack has left police baffled and helpless.

With victim after victim falling to "the Terror of London", it's up to two errant Detectives to solve the case and bring peace to the city before it's too late.

Age: Unknown
Height: Unknown
Weight: Unknown

First Appearance:
SPRING-HEELED JACK #1 (2014)

Created by Tony Deans
Illustration by Martha Laverick

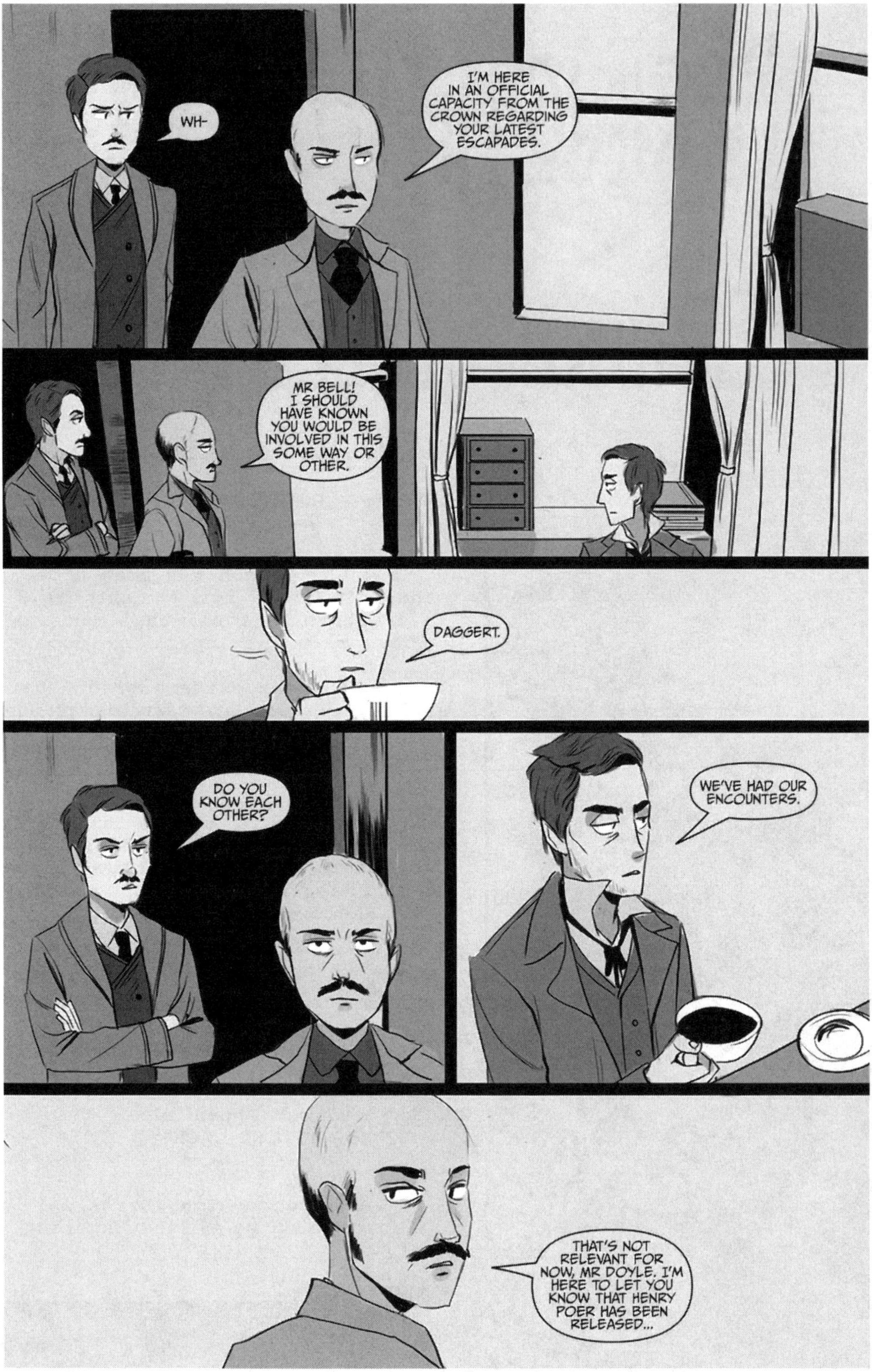
WH-
I'M HERE IN AN OFFICIAL CAPACITY FROM THE CROWN REGARDING YOUR LATEST ESCAPADES.
MR BELL! I SHOULD HAVE KNOWN YOU WOULD BE INVOLVED IN THIS SOME WAY OR OTHER.
DAGGERT.
DO YOU KNOW EACH OTHER?
WE'VE HAD OUR ENCOUNTERS.
THAT'S NOT RELEVANT FOR NOW, MR DOYLE. I'M HERE TO LET YOU KNOW THAT HENRY POER HAS BEEN RELEASED...

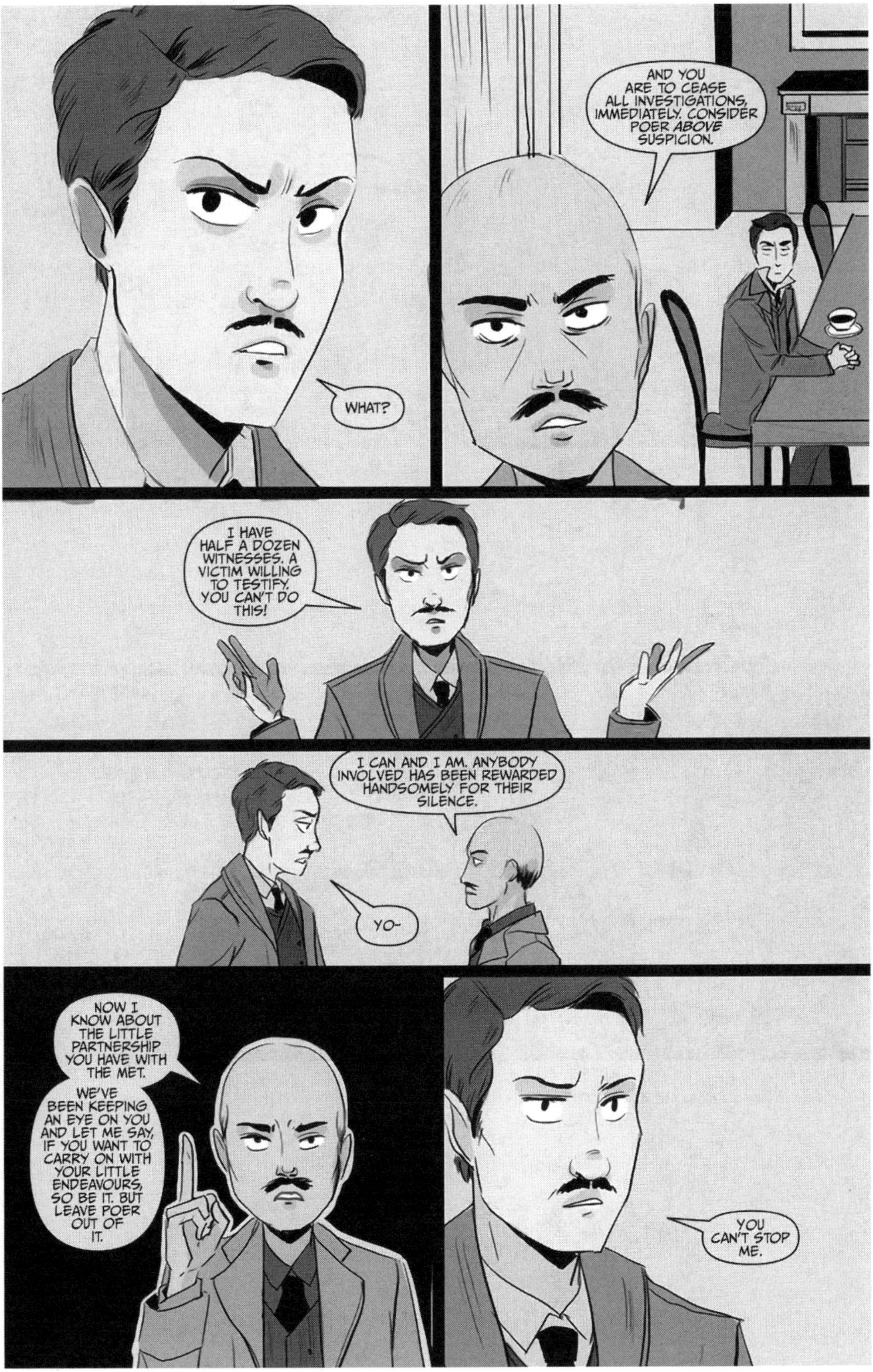
WHAT?
AND YOU ARE TO CEASE ALL INVESTIGATIONS, IMMEDIATELY. CONSIDER POER ABOVE SUSPICION.
I HAVE HALF A DOZEN WITNESSES. A VICTIM WILLING TO TESTIFY. YOU CAN'T DO THIS!
I CAN AND I AM. ANYBODY INVOLVED HAS BEEN REWARDED HANDSOMELY FOR THEIR SILENCE.
YO-
NOW I KNOW ABOUT THE LITTLE PARTNERSHIP YOU HAVE WITH THE MET.
WE'VE BEEN KEEPING AN EYE ON YOU AND LET ME SAY, IF YOU WANT TO CARRY ON WITH YOUR LITTLE ENDEAVOURS, SO BE IT. BUT LEAVE POER OUT OF IT.
YOU CAN'T STOP ME.

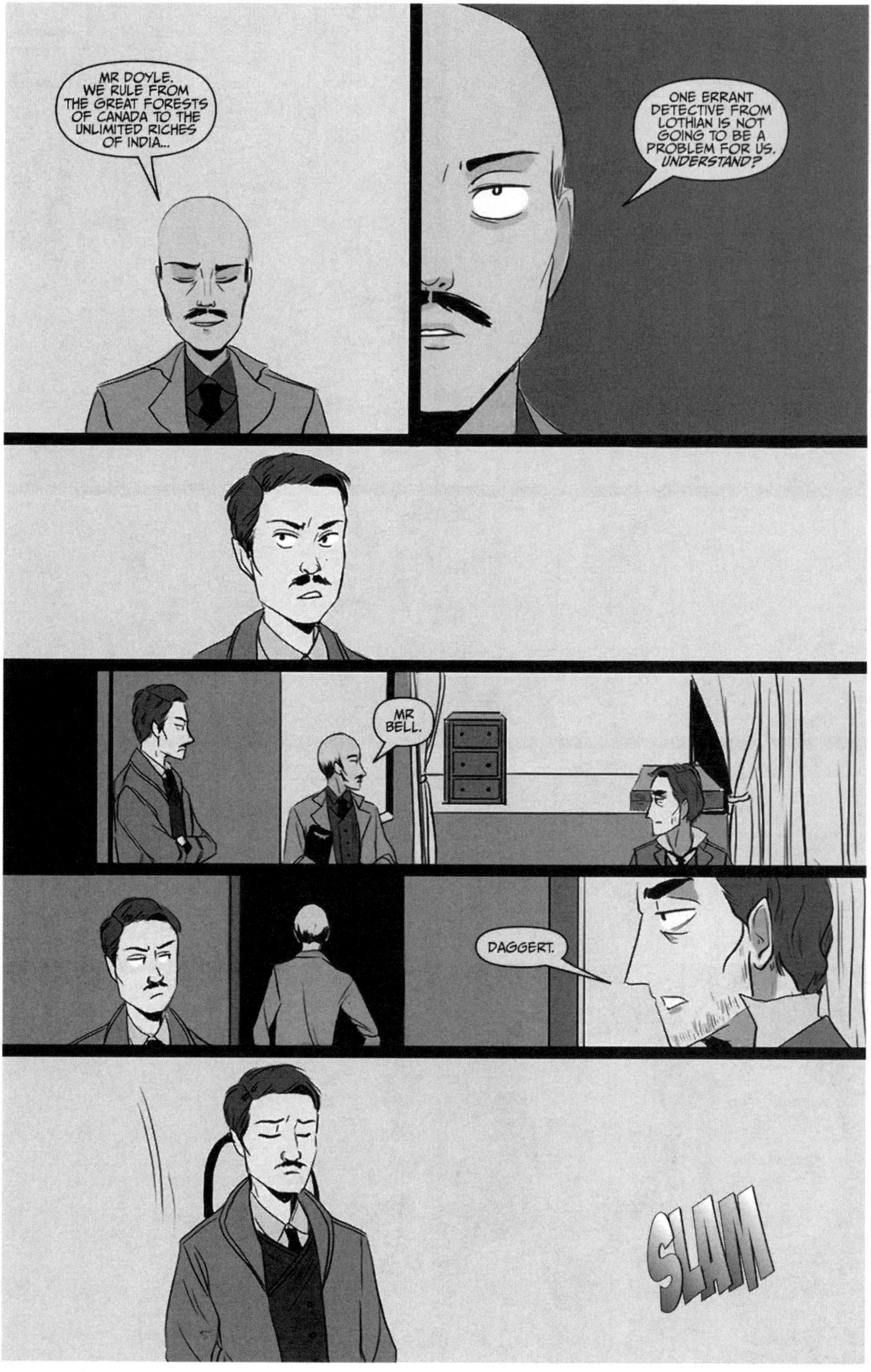
MR DOYLE. WE RULE FROM THE GREAT FORESTS OF CANADA TO THE UNLIMITED RICHES OF INDIA...
ONE ERRANT DETECTIVE FROM LOTHIAN IS NOT GOING TO BE A PROBLEM FOR US. *UNDERSTAND?*
MR BELL.
DAGGERT.
SLAM

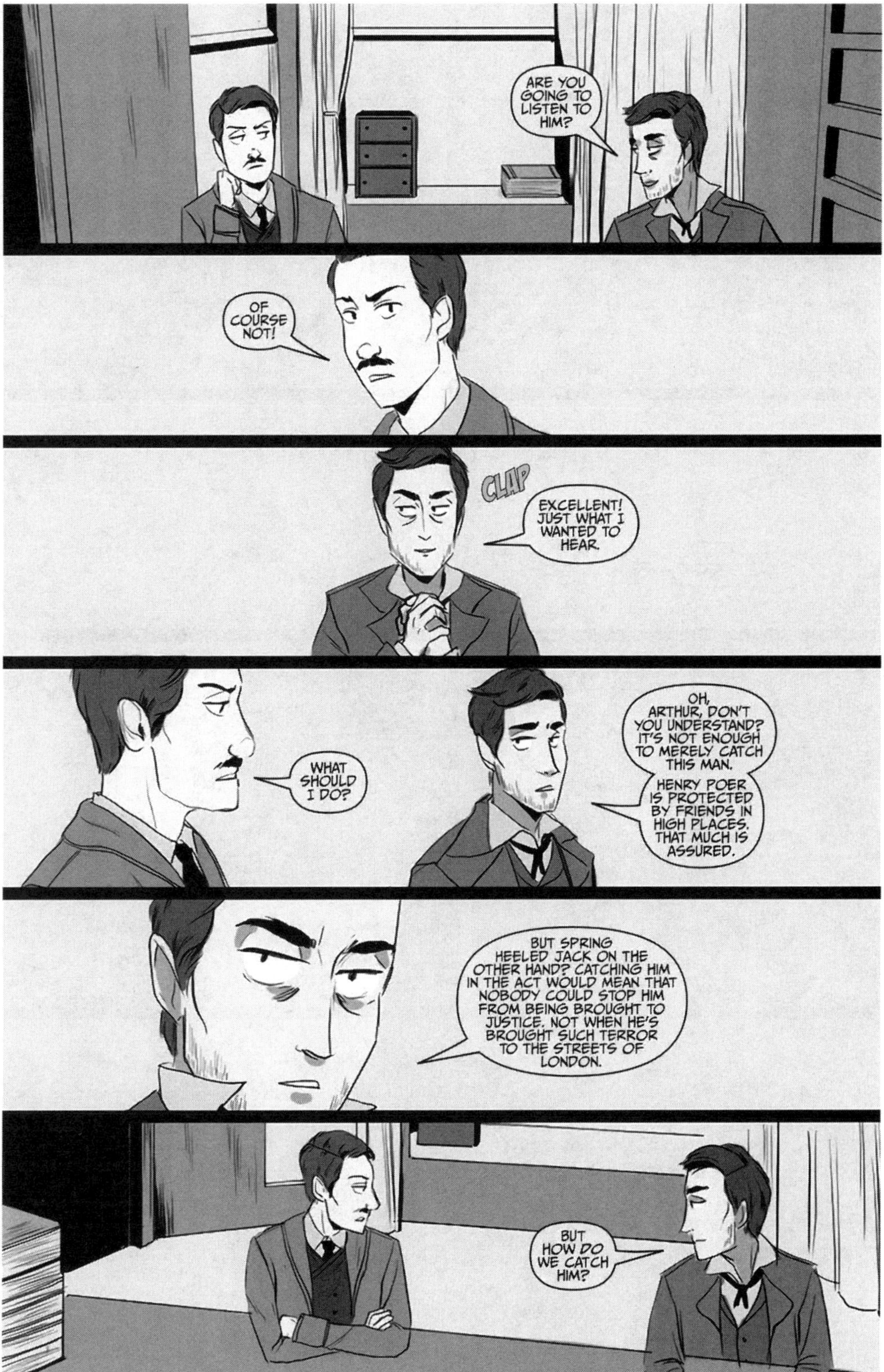
ARE YOU GOING TO LISTEN TO HIM?
OF COURSE NOT!
CLAP
EXCELLENT! JUST WHAT I WANTED TO HEAR.
WHAT SHOULD I DO?
OH, ARTHUR, DON'T YOU UNDERSTAND? IT'S NOT ENOUGH TO MERELY CATCH THIS MAN.
HENRY POER IS PROTECTED BY FRIENDS IN HIGH PLACES. THAT MUCH IS ASSURED.
BUT SPRING HEELED JACK ON THE OTHER HAND? CATCHING HIM IN THE ACT WOULD MEAN THAT NOBODY COULD STOP HIM FROM BEING BROUGHT TO JUSTICE. NOT WHEN HE'S BROUGHT SUCH TERROR TO THE STREETS OF LONDON.
BUT HOW DO WE CATCH HIM?

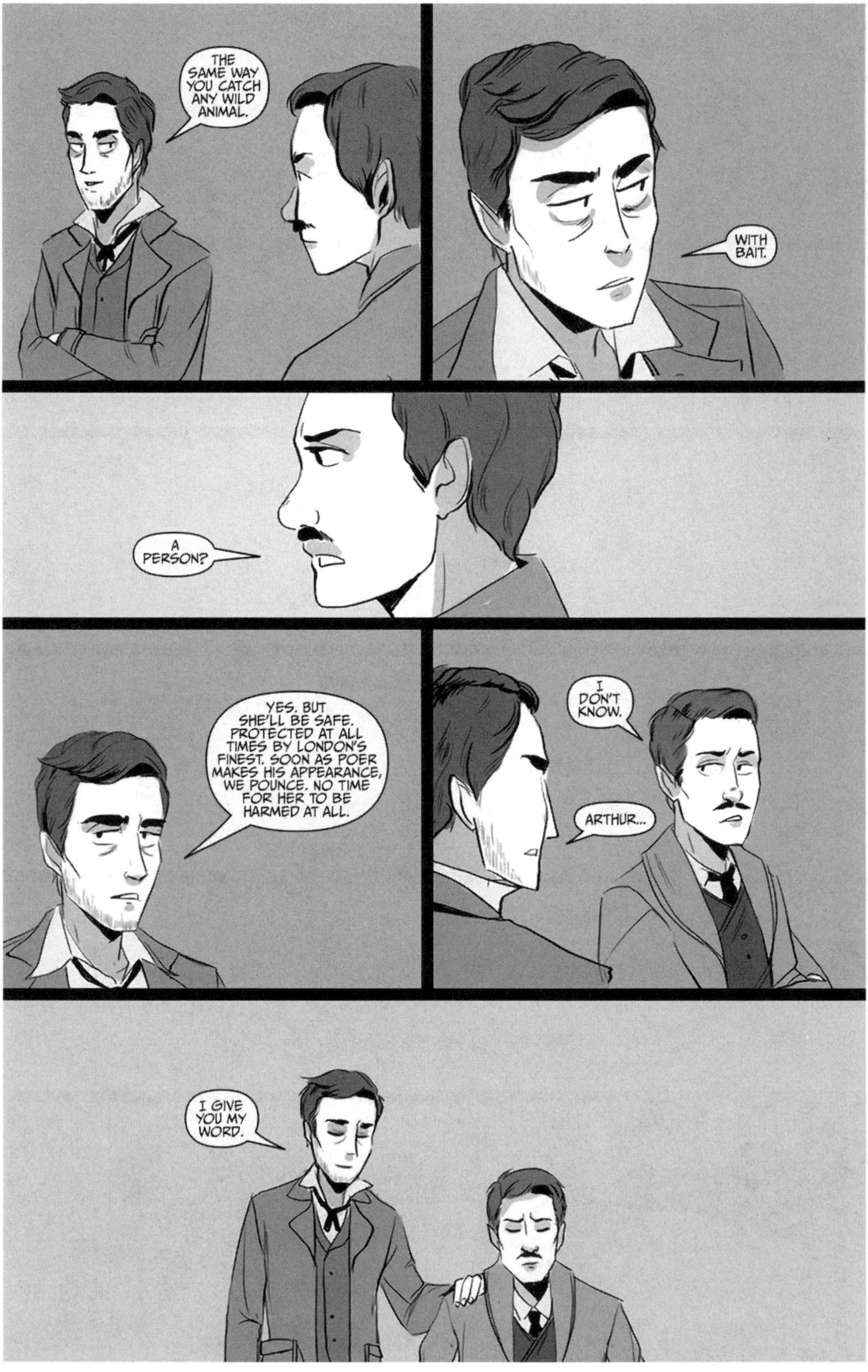
THE SAME WAY YOU CATCH ANY WILD ANIMAL.
WITH BAIT.
A PERSON?
YES. BUT SHE'LL BE SAFE. PROTECTED AT ALL TIMES BY LONDON'S FINEST. SOON AS POER MAKES HIS APPEARANCE, WE POUNCE. NO TIME FOR HER TO BE HARMED AT ALL.
I DON'T KNOW.
ARTHUR...
I GIVE YOU MY WORD.

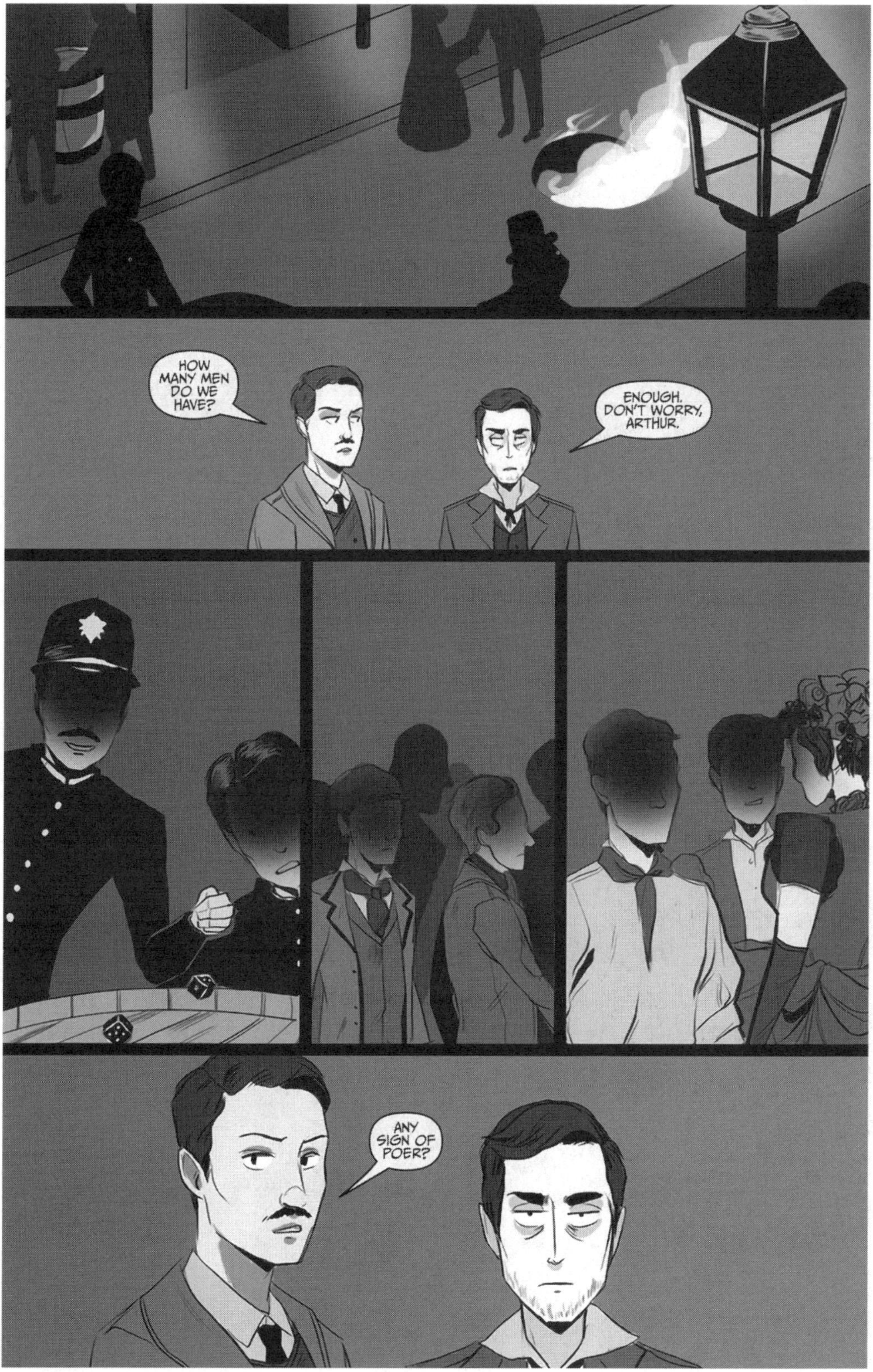
HOW MANY MEN DO WE HAVE?
ENOUGH. DON'T WORRY, ARTHUR.
ANY SIGN OF POER?

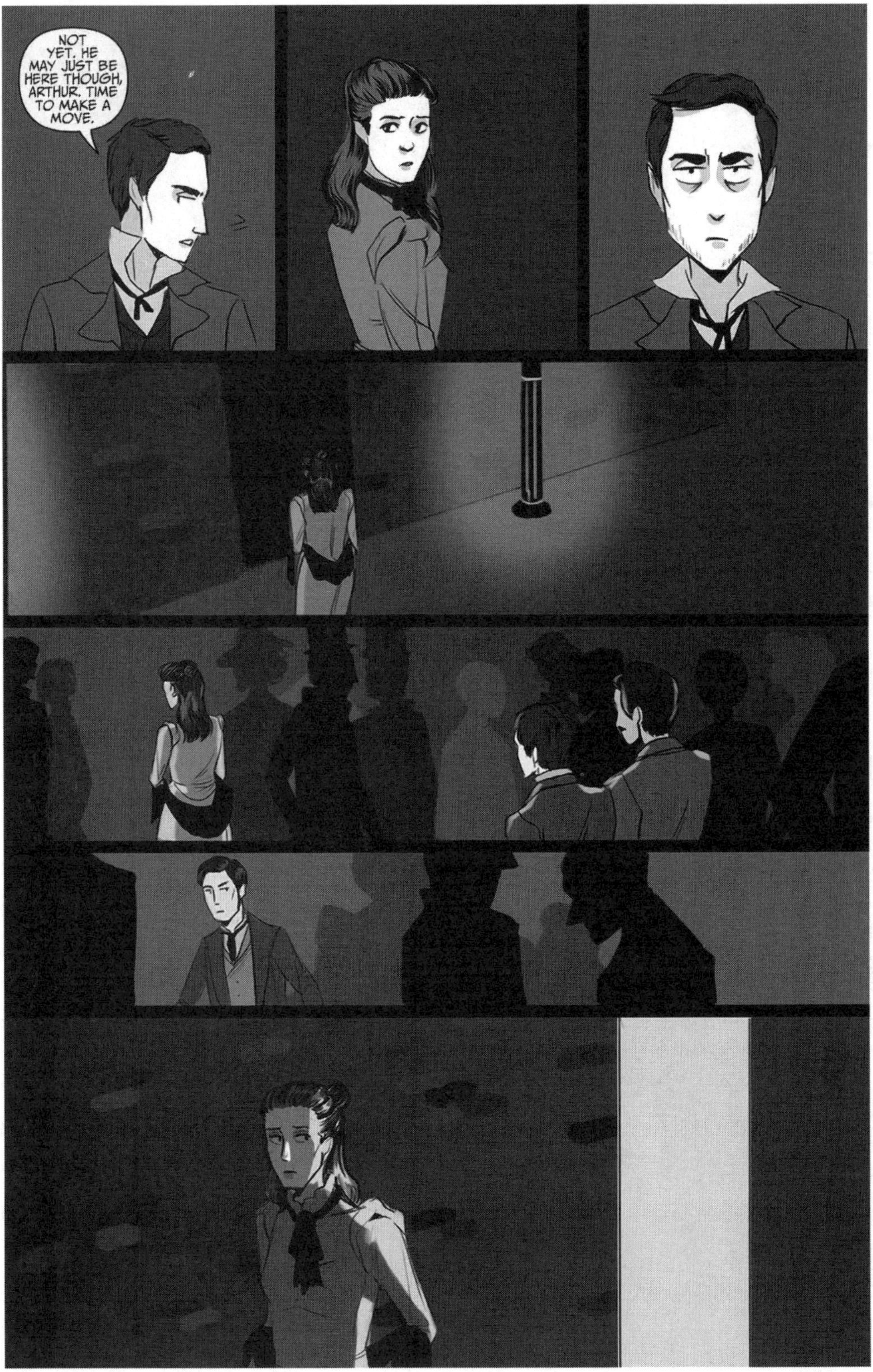
NOT YET. HE MAY JUST BE HERE THOUGH, ARTHUR. TIME TO MAKE A MOVE.

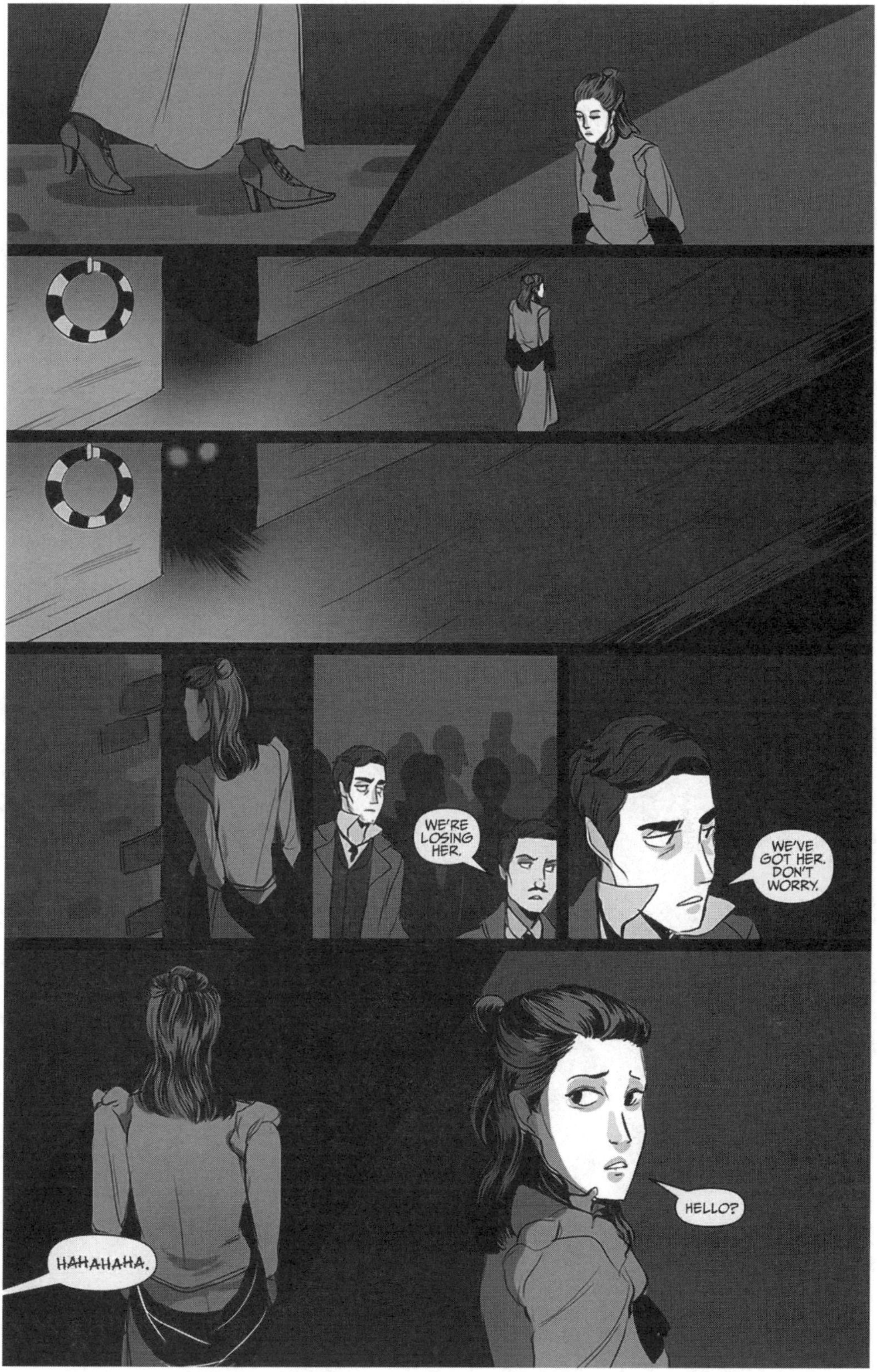
WE'RE LOSING HER.
WE'VE GOT HER. DON'T WORRY.
HELLO?
HAHAHAHA.

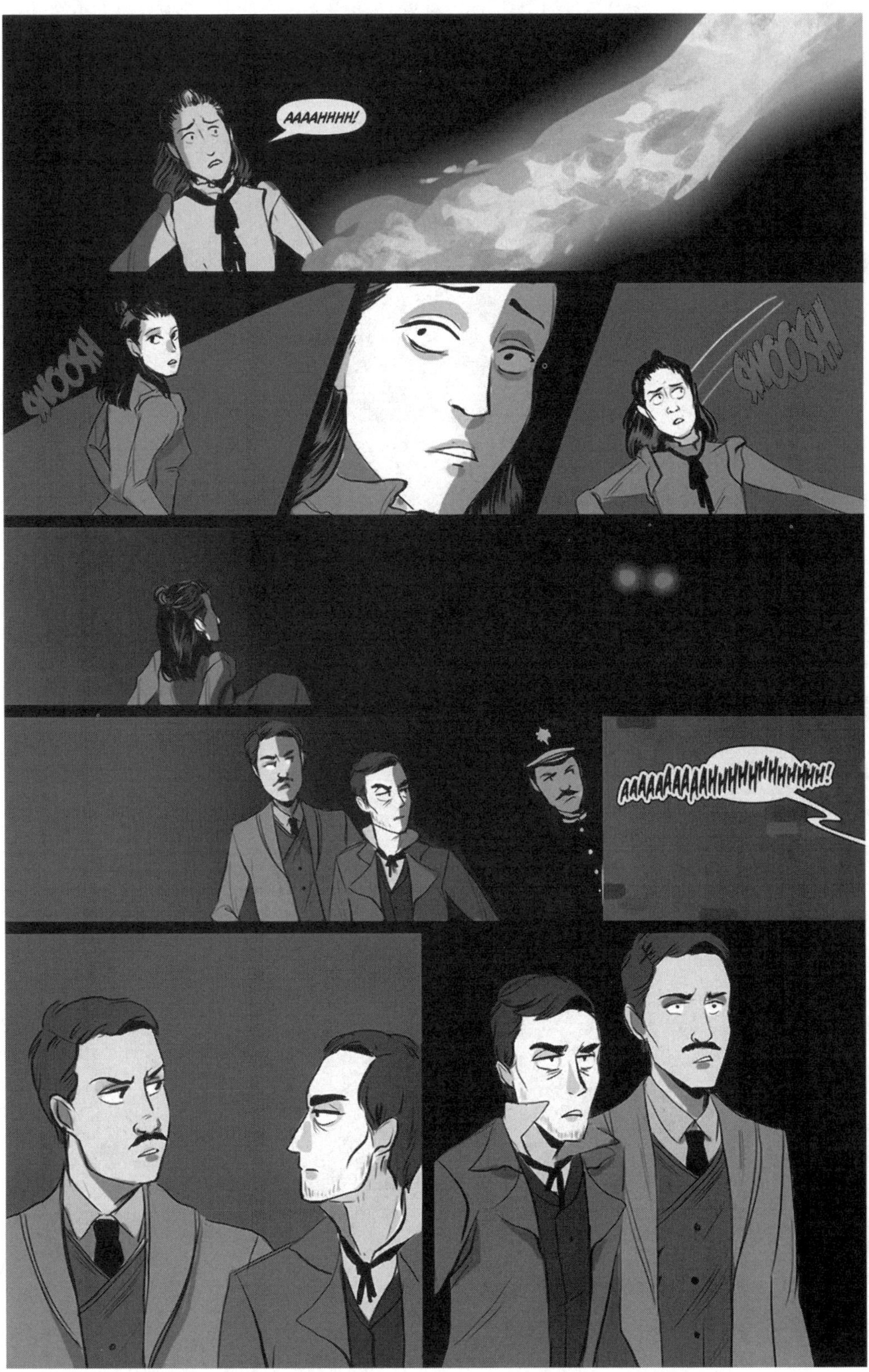
AAAAHHHH!
SWOOSH
SWOOSH!
AAAAAAAAAAHHHHHHHHHHHHH!

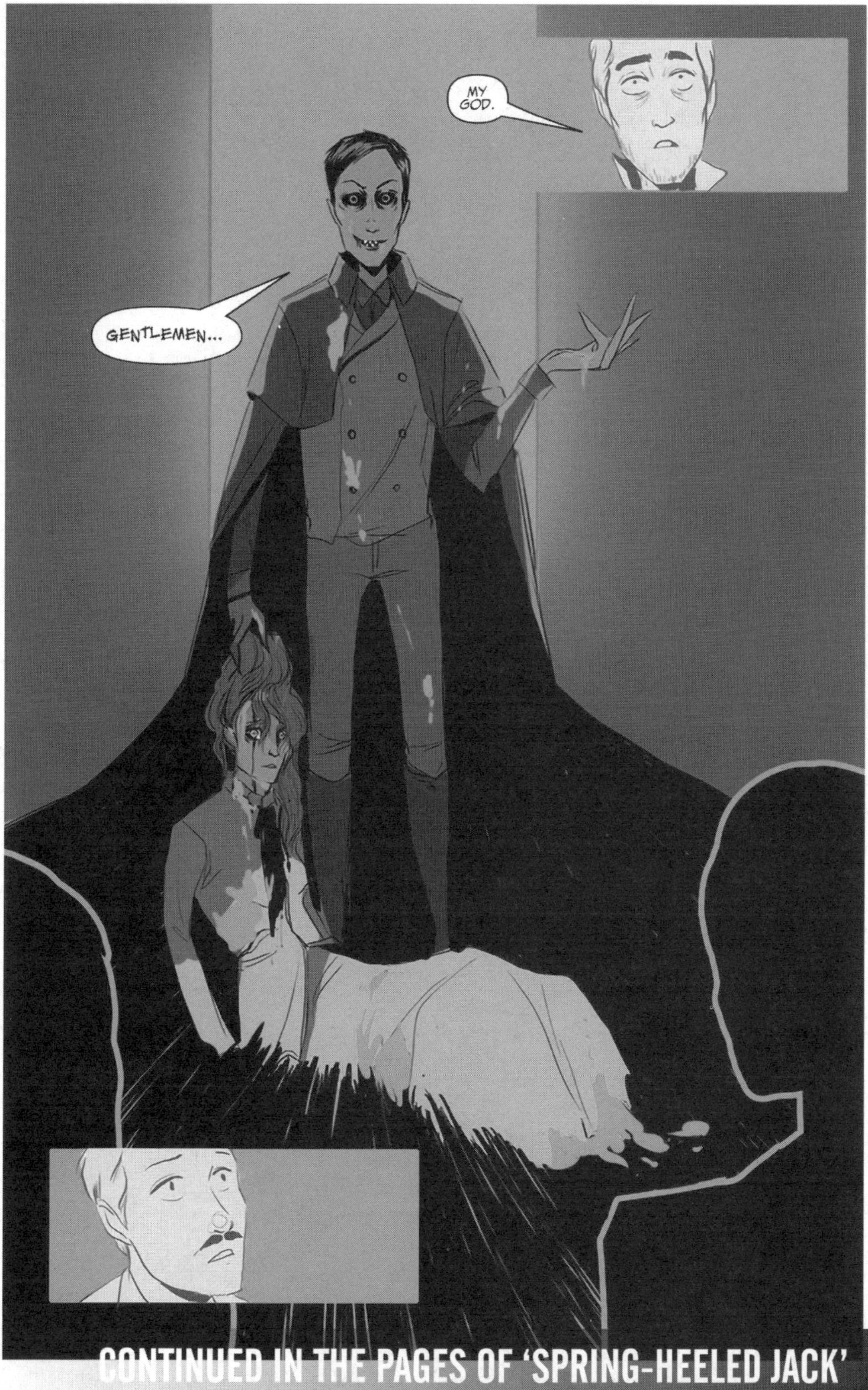
GENTLEMEN...
MY GOD.

CONTINUED IN THE PAGES OF 'SPRING-HEELED JACK'

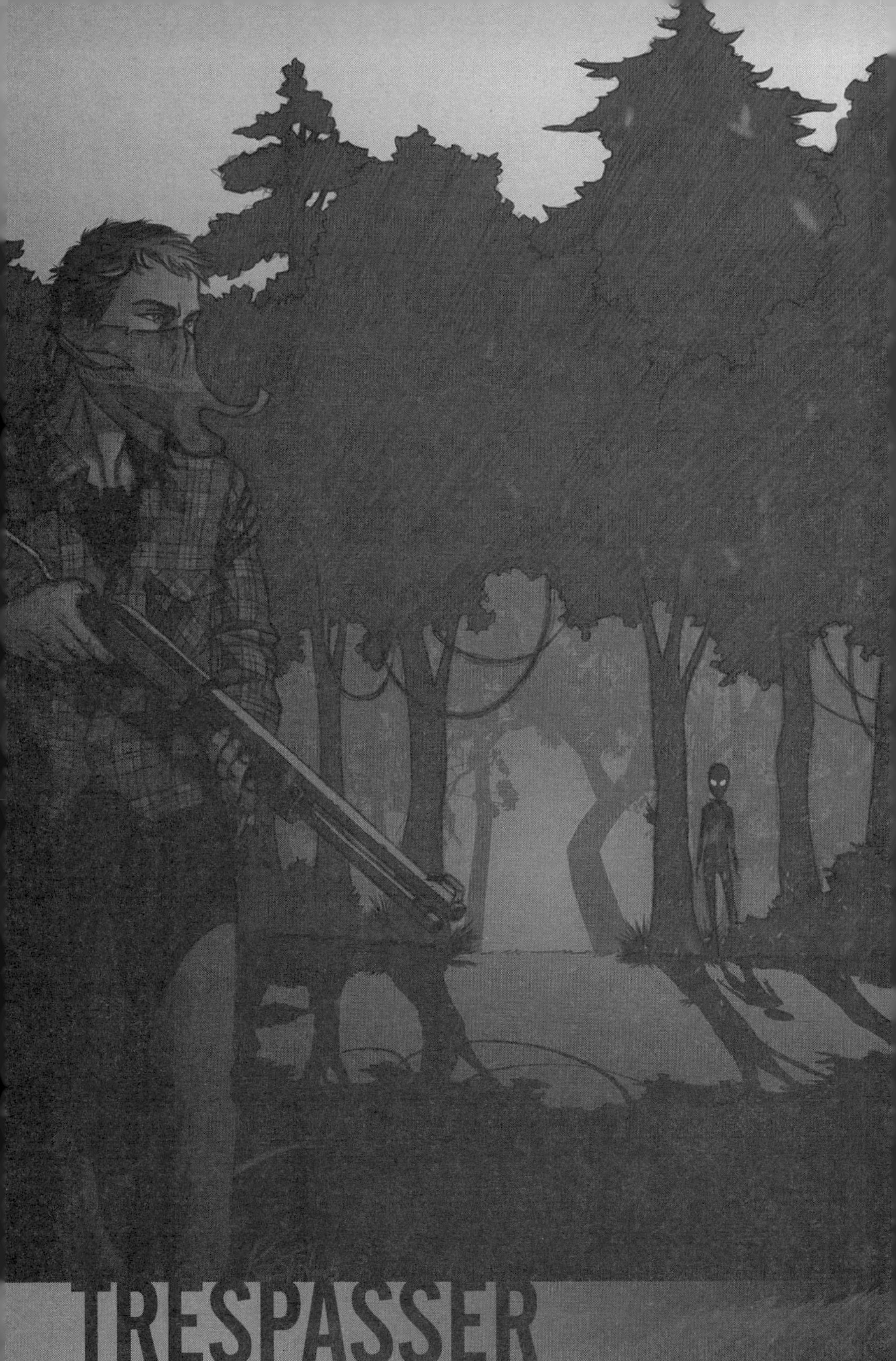

TRESPASSER

TRESPASSER

HECTOR RAMOS

"Things have been a bit desperate the past few years. Makes people dangerous."

A former soldier, Hector retreated from the world after the death of his wife. Returning to his childhood home as the world fell apart around him, Hector insulated himself and his daughter Maria from the worst of it. But solitude comes at a price and when their peaceful existence is threatened by an unwanted visitor, Hector quickly learns how far he will go to protect what's his.

Age: 36
Height: 5'10"
Weight: 185 lbs.

First Appearance:
TRESPASSER #1 (2016)

Created by Justin M. Ryan
Illustration by Kristian Rossi

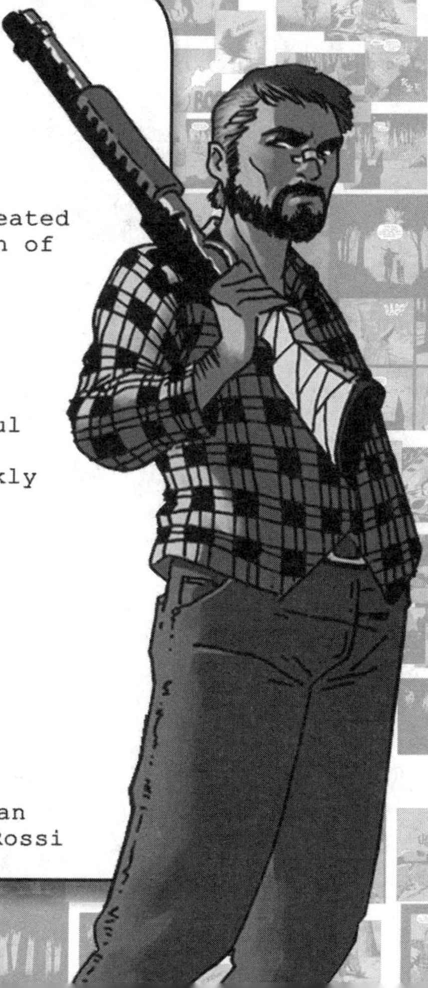

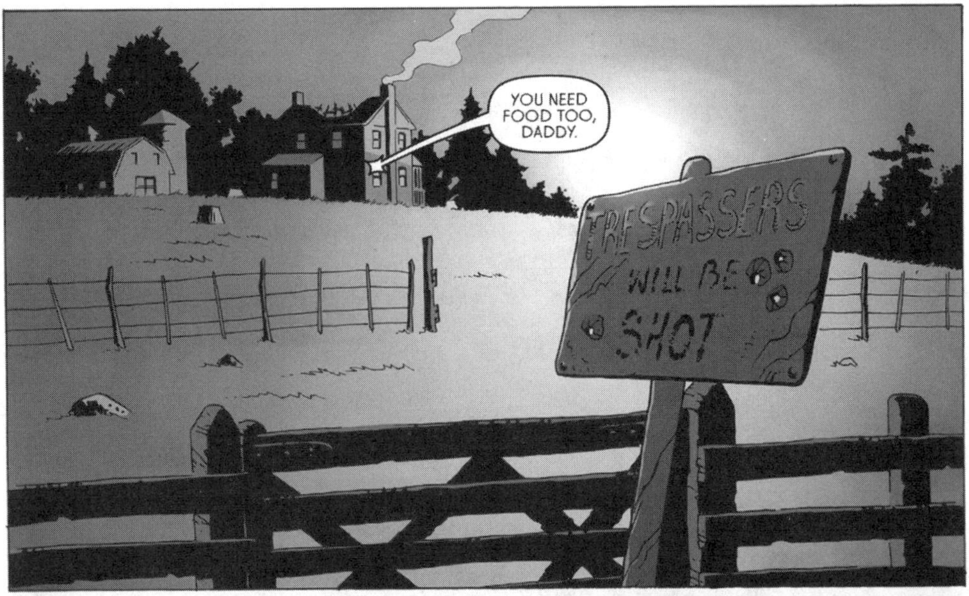
YOU NEED FOOD TOO, DADDY.
TRESPASSERS WILL BE SHOT

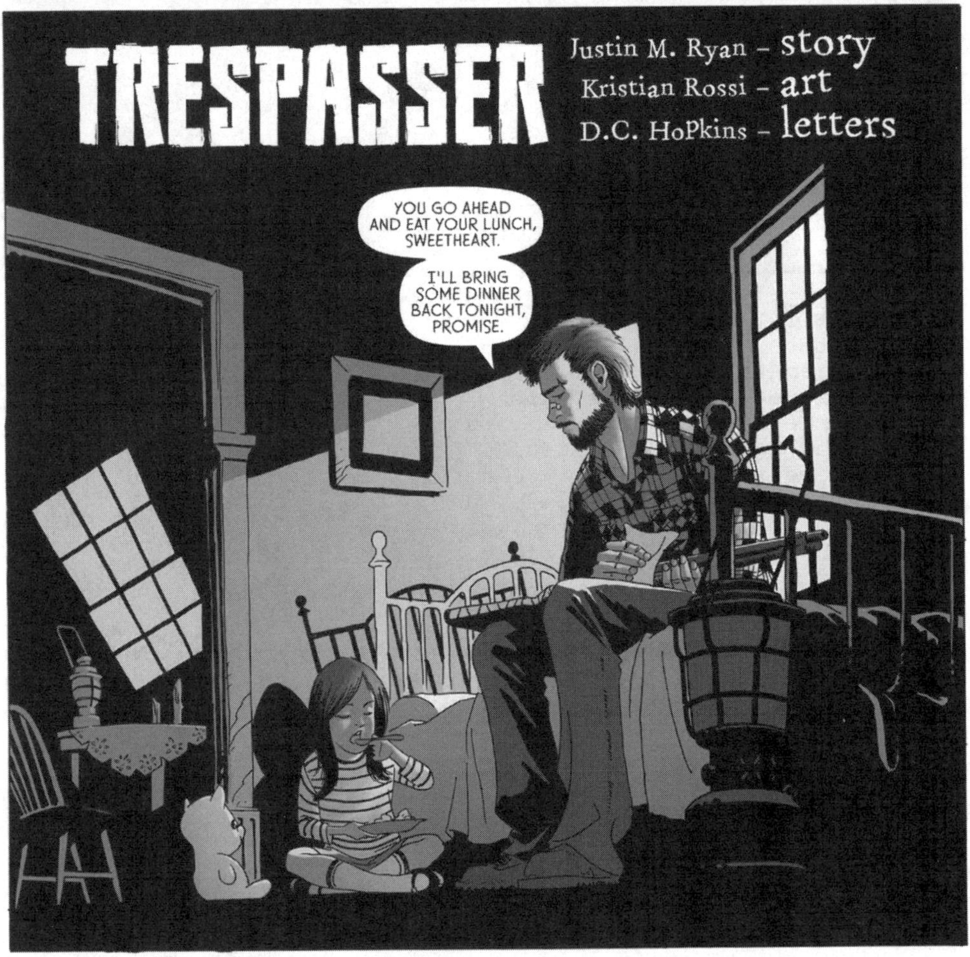
TRESPASSER
Justin M. Ryan – story
Kristian Rossi – art
D.C. HoPkins – letters
YOU GO AHEAD AND EAT YOUR LUNCH, SWEETHEART.
I'LL BRING SOME DINNER BACK TONIGHT, PROMISE.

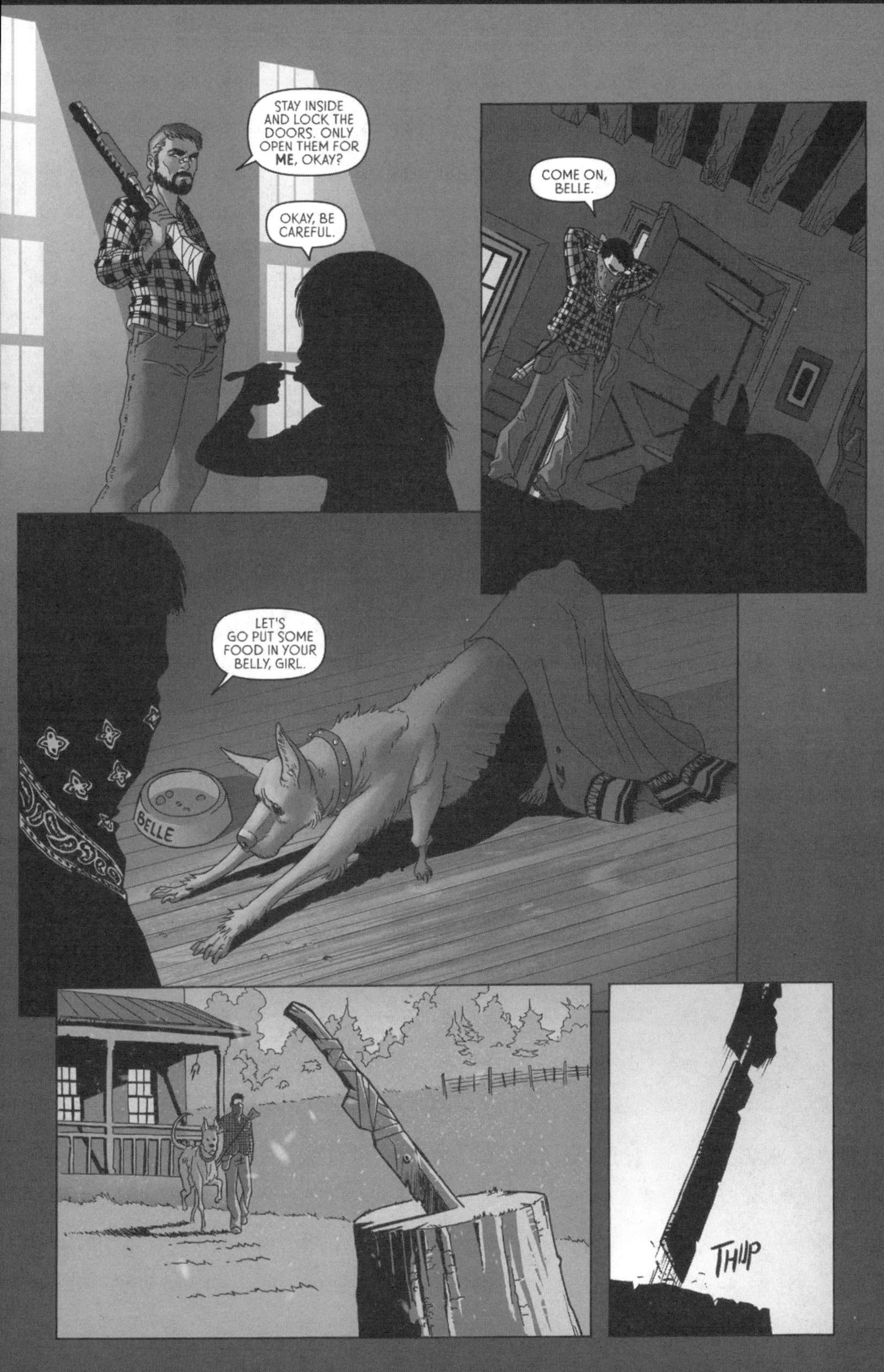
STAY INSIDE AND LOCK THE DOORS. ONLY OPEN THEM FOR **ME**, OKAY?
OKAY, BE CAREFUL.
COME ON, BELLE.
LET'S GO PUT SOME FOOD IN YOUR BELLY, GIRL.
BELLE
THUP

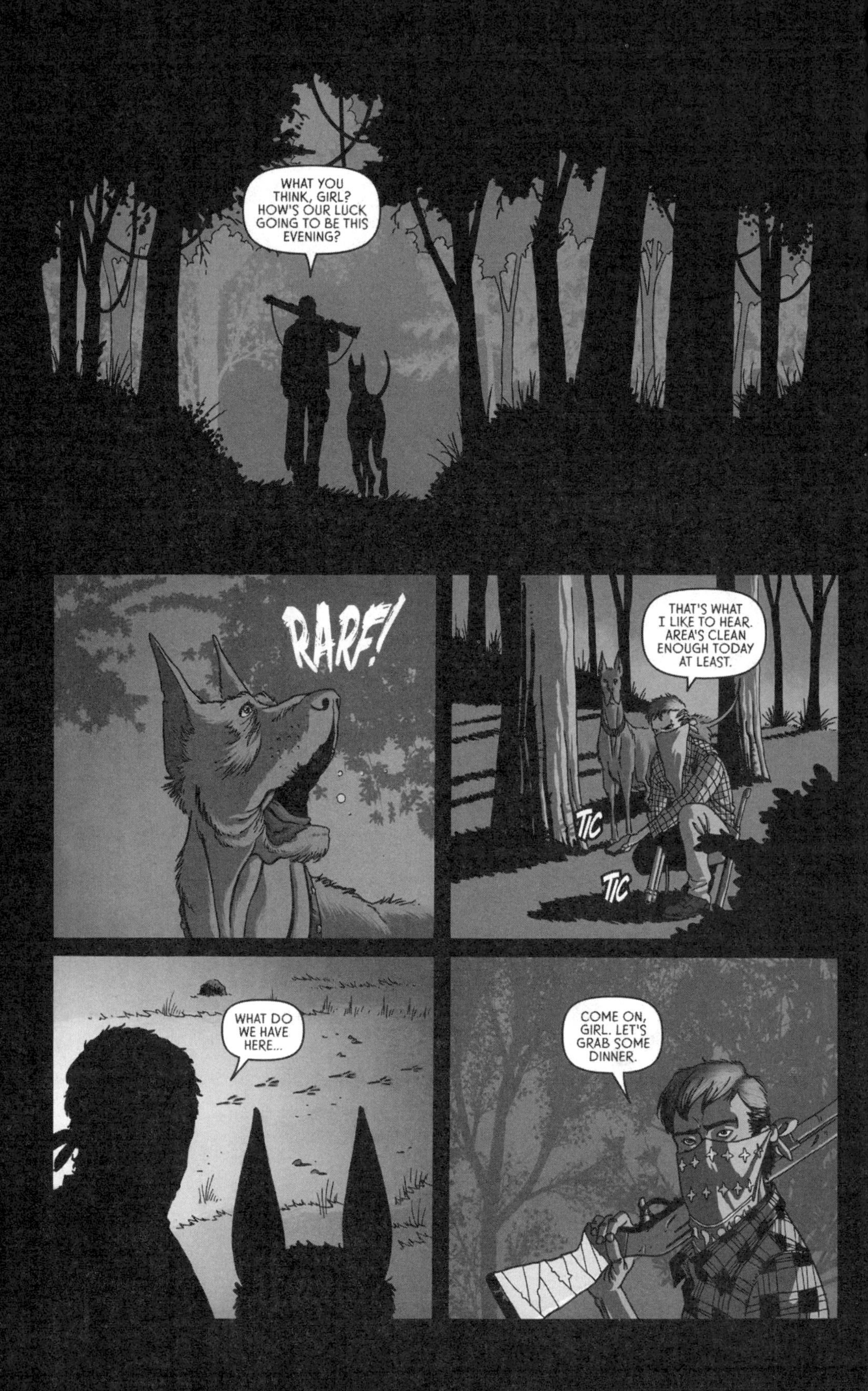
WHAT YOU THINK, GIRL? HOW'S OUR LUCK GOING TO BE THIS EVENING?
RARF!
THAT'S WHAT I LIKE TO HEAR. AREA'S CLEAN ENOUGH TODAY AT LEAST.
TIC
TIC
WHAT DO WE HAVE HERE...
COME ON, GIRL. LET'S GRAB SOME DINNER.

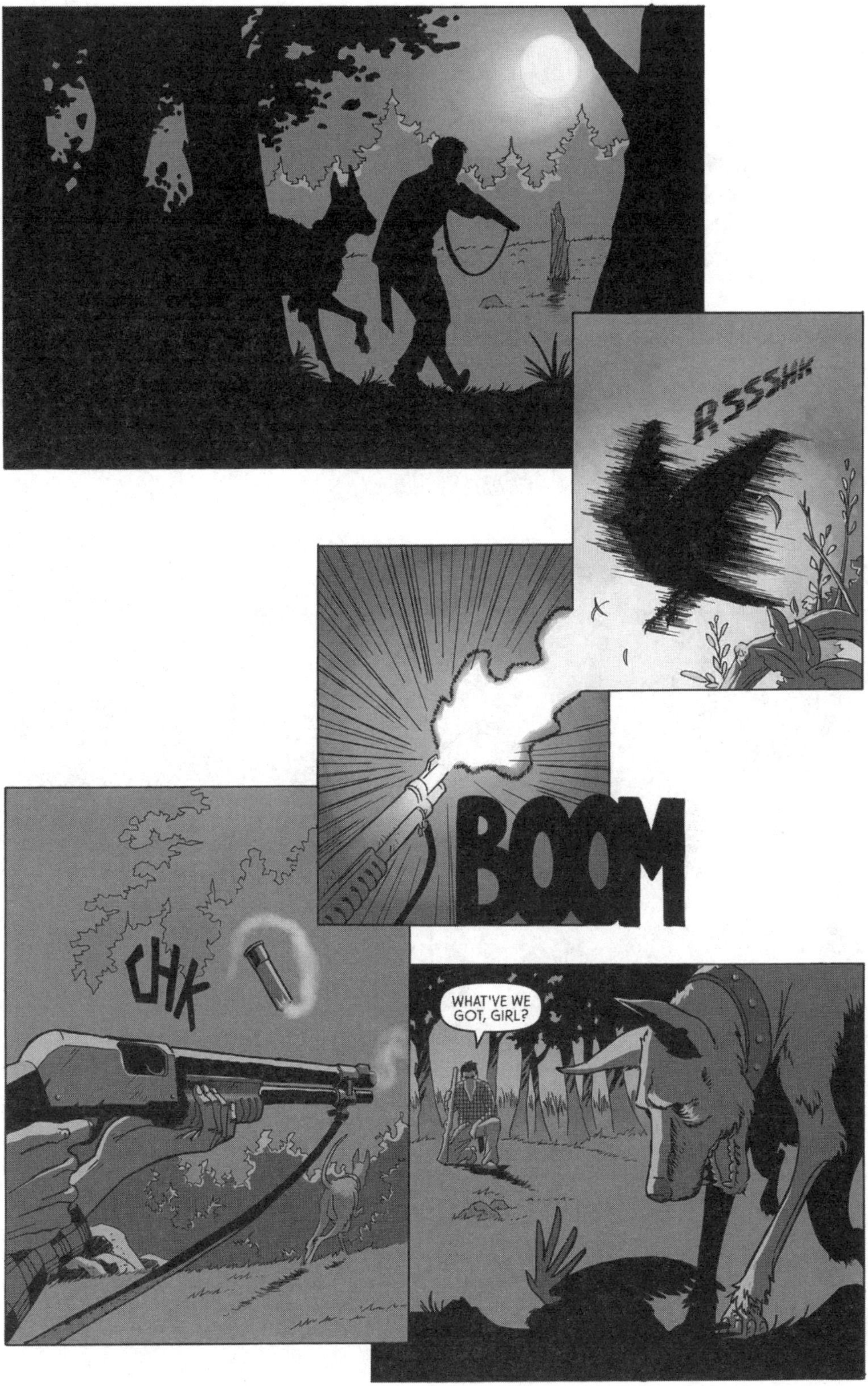
RSSSHK
BOOM
CHK
WHAT'VE WE GOT, GIRL?

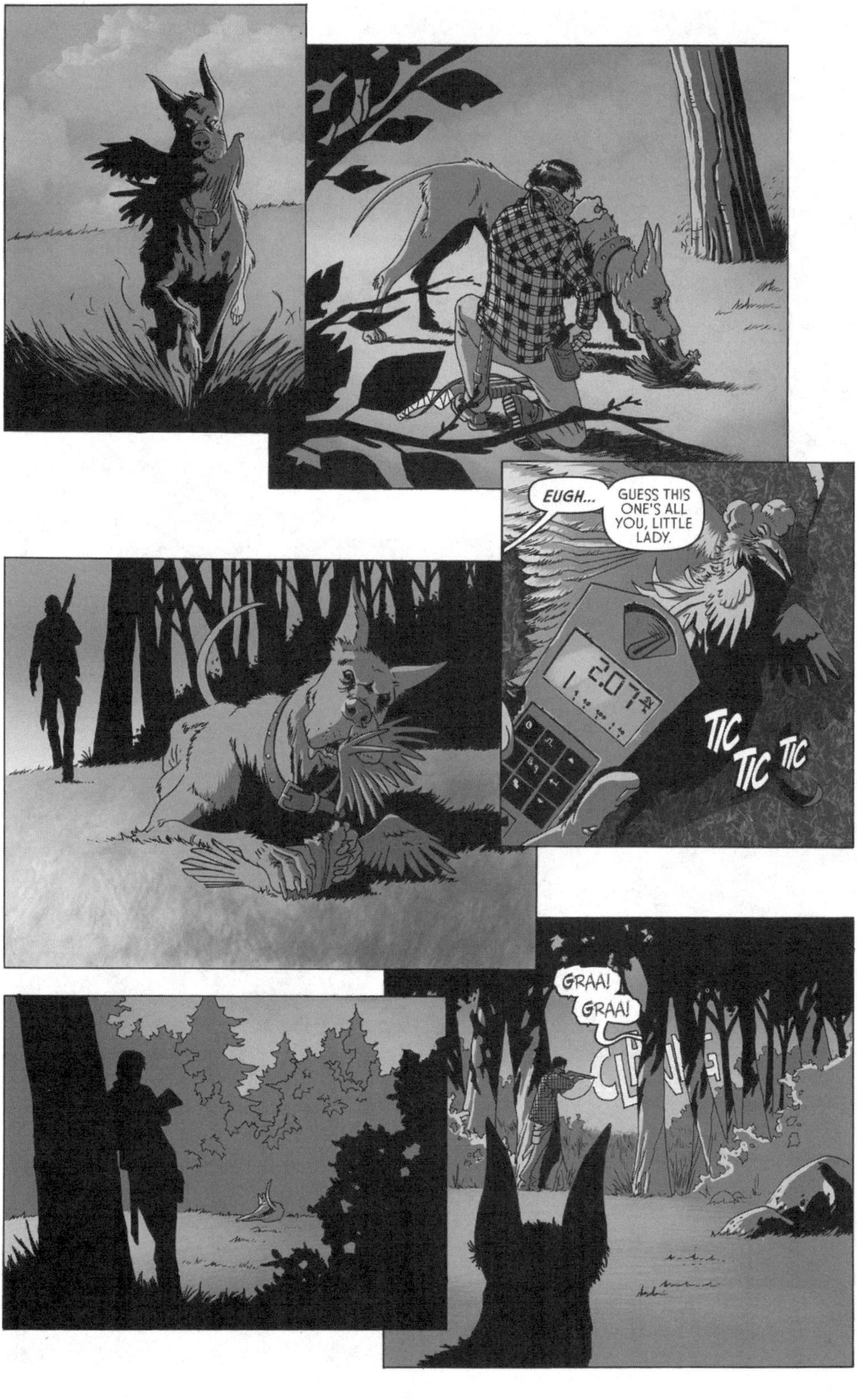
EUGH...
GUESS THIS ONE'S ALL YOU, LITTLE LADY.
TIC TIC TIC
GRAA! GRAA!

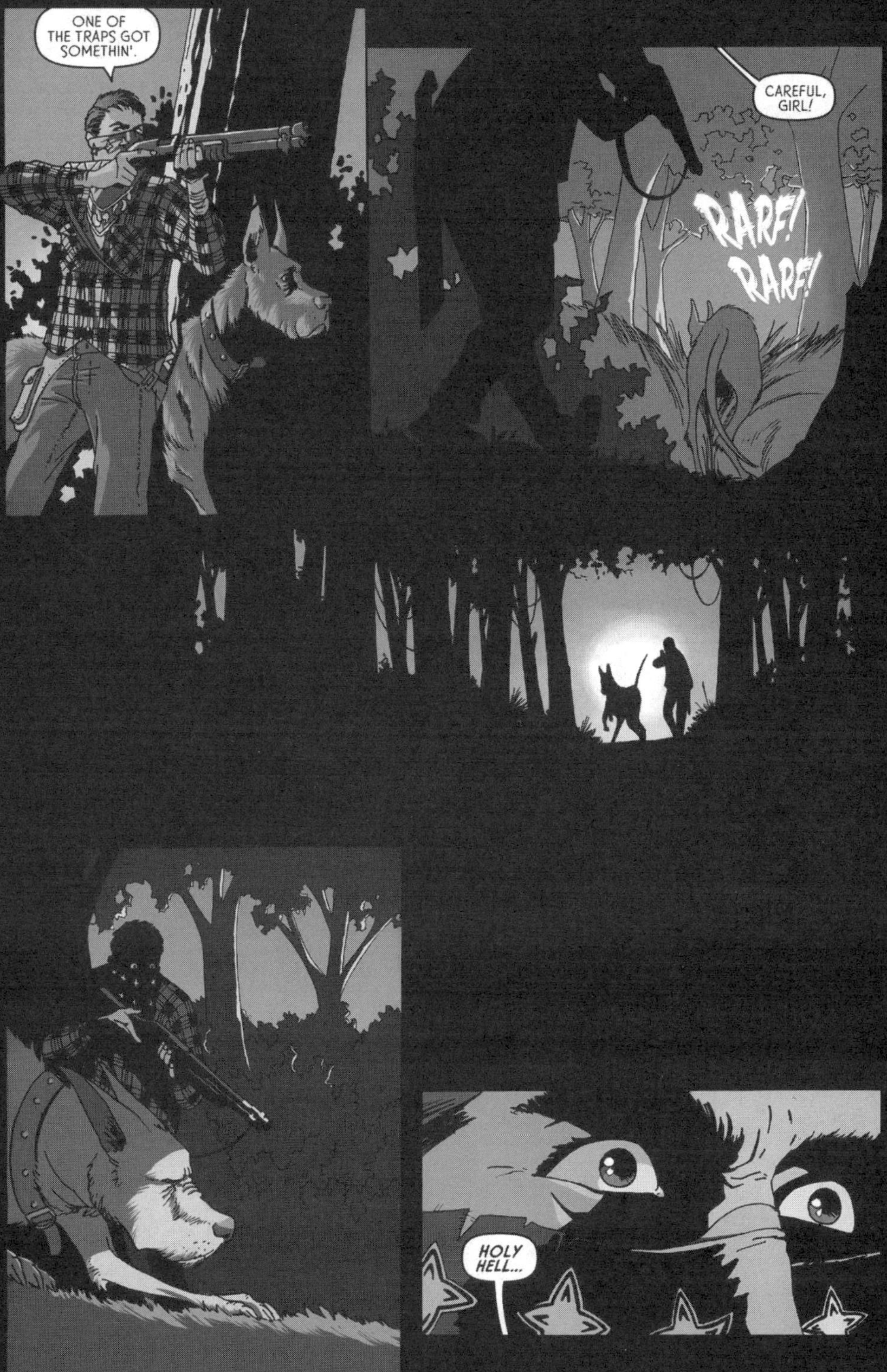
ONE OF THE TRAPS GOT SOMETHIN'.
CAREFUL, GIRL!
RARF! RARF!
HOLY HELL...

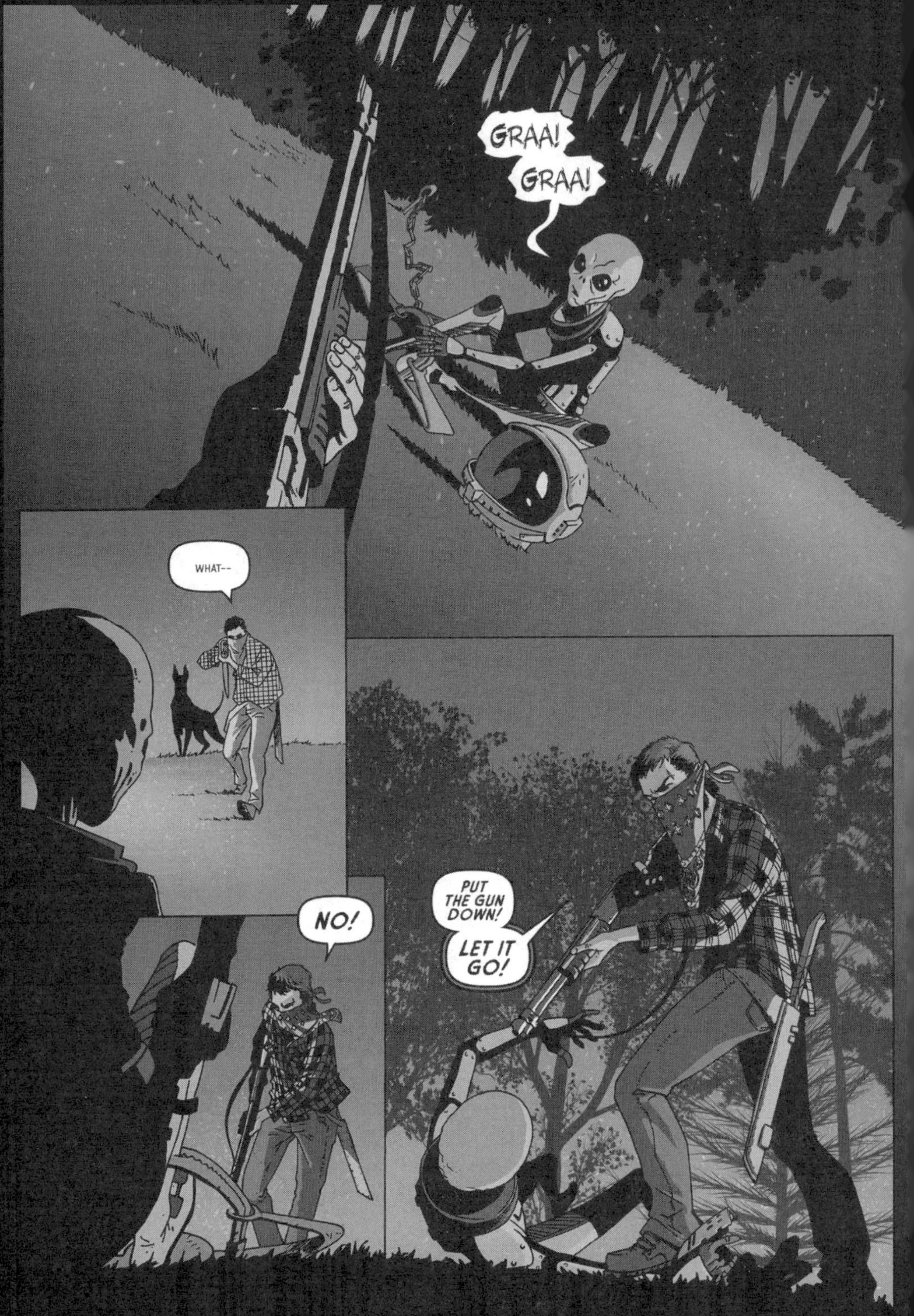
GRAA!
GRAA!
WHAT--
NO!
PUT THE GUN DOWN!
LET IT GO!

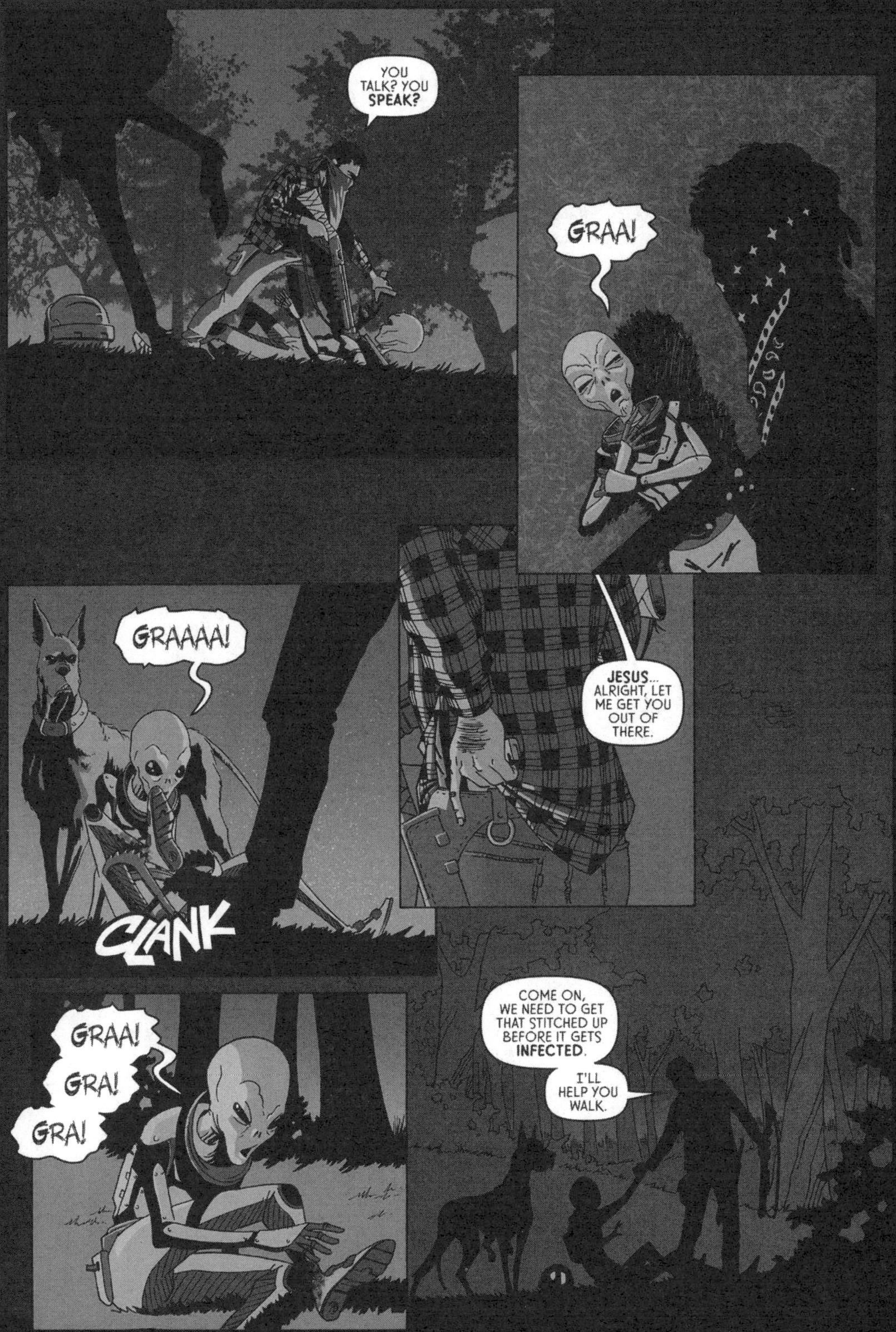

YOU TALK? YOU SPEAK?
GRAA!
GRAAAA!
CLANK
JESUS... ALRIGHT, LET ME GET YOU OUT OF THERE.
GRAA!
GRA!
GRA!
COME ON, WE NEED TO GET THAT STITCHED UP BEFORE IT GETS INFECTED.
I'LL HELP YOU WALK.

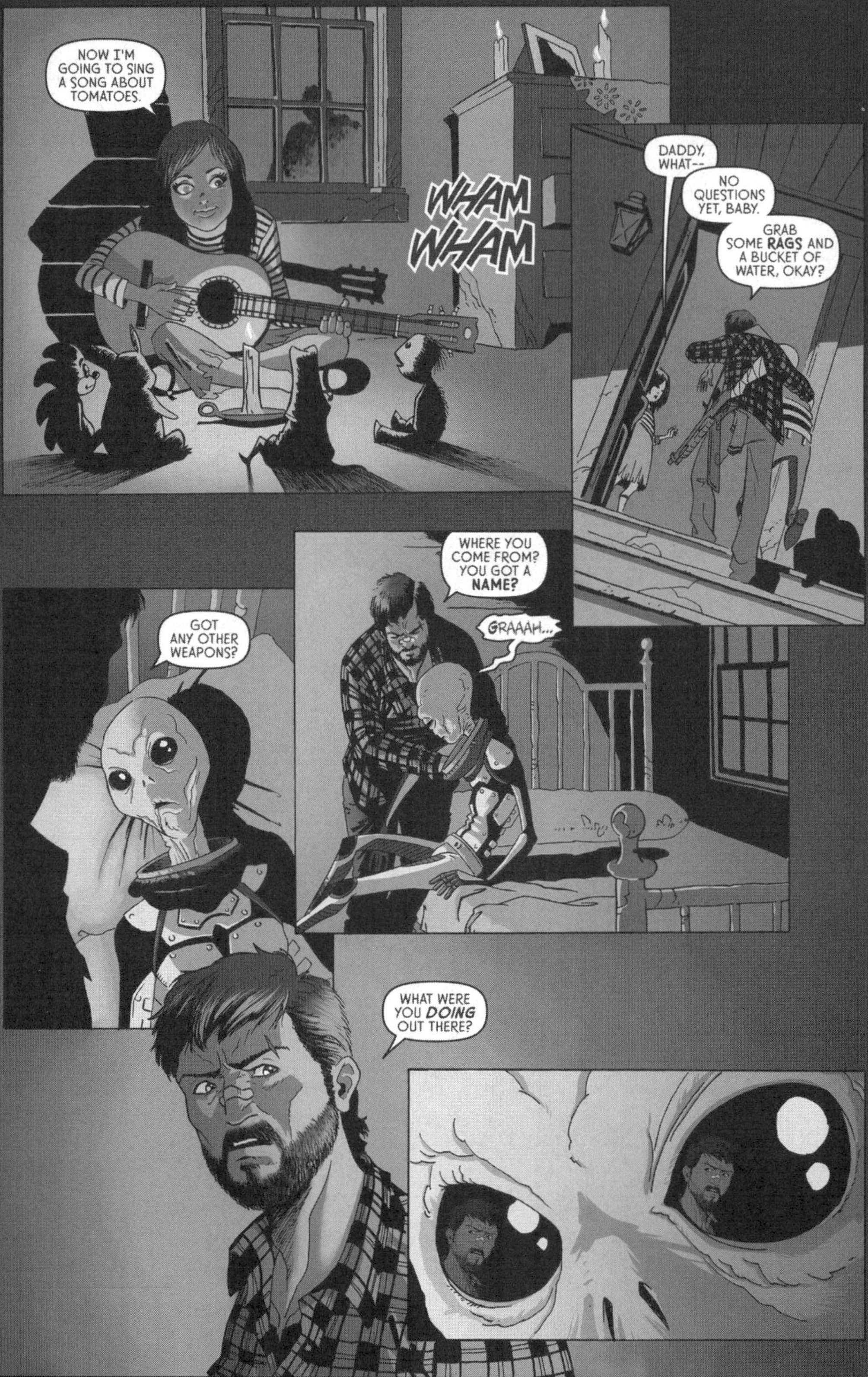
NOW I'M GOING TO SING A SONG ABOUT TOMATOES.
WHAM
WHAM
DADDY, WHAT--
NO QUESTIONS YET, BABY.
GRAB SOME **RAGS** AND A BUCKET OF WATER, OKAY?
WHERE YOU COME FROM? YOU GOT A **NAME?**
GRAAAH...
GOT ANY OTHER WEAPONS?
WHAT WERE YOU ***DOING*** OUT THERE?

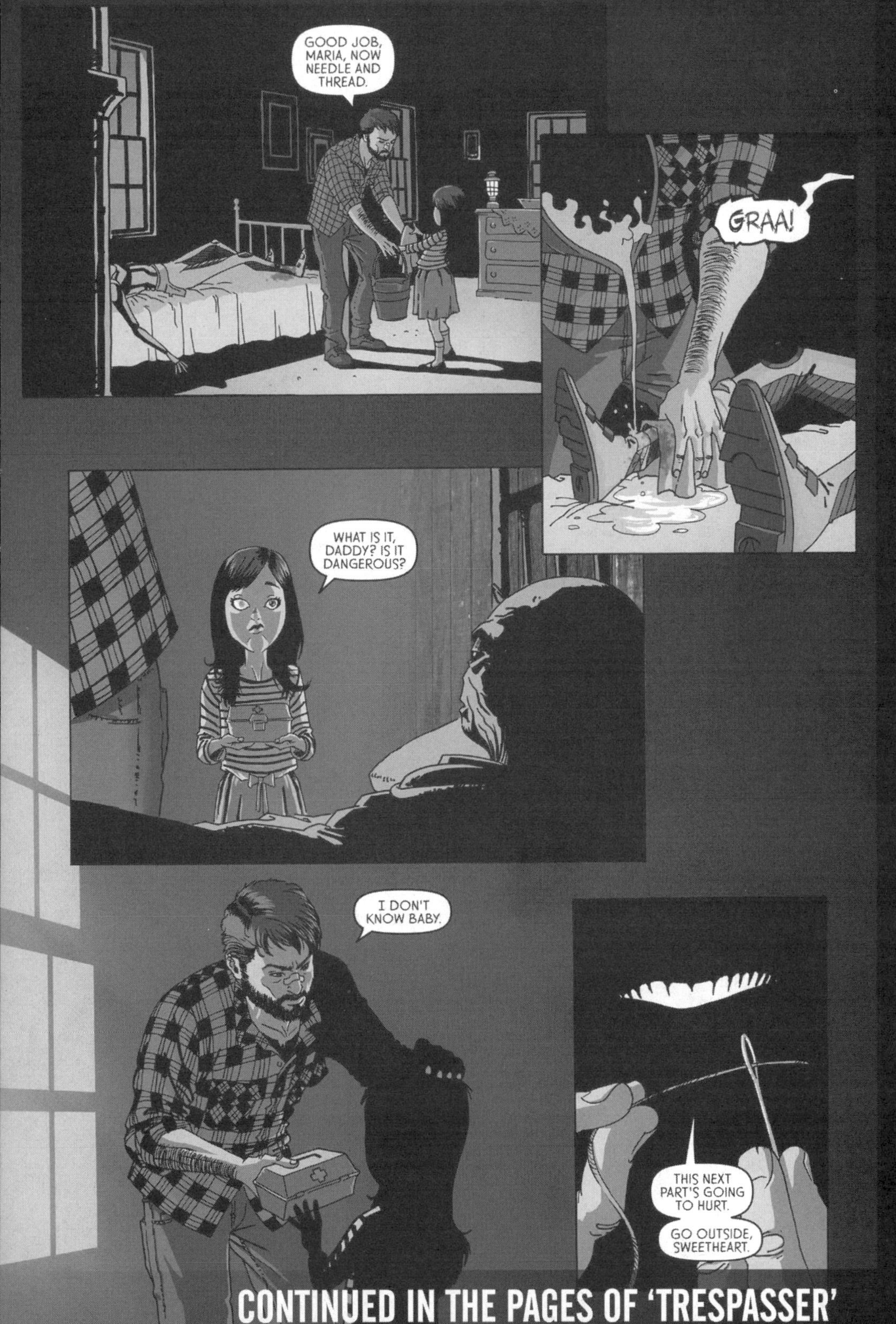
GOOD JOB, MARIA, NOW NEEDLE AND THREAD.
GRAA!
WHAT IS IT, DADDY? IS IT DANGEROUS?
I DON'T KNOW BABY.
THIS NEXT PART'S GOING TO HURT.
GO OUTSIDE, SWEETHEART.

CONTINUED IN THE PAGES OF 'TRESPASSER'

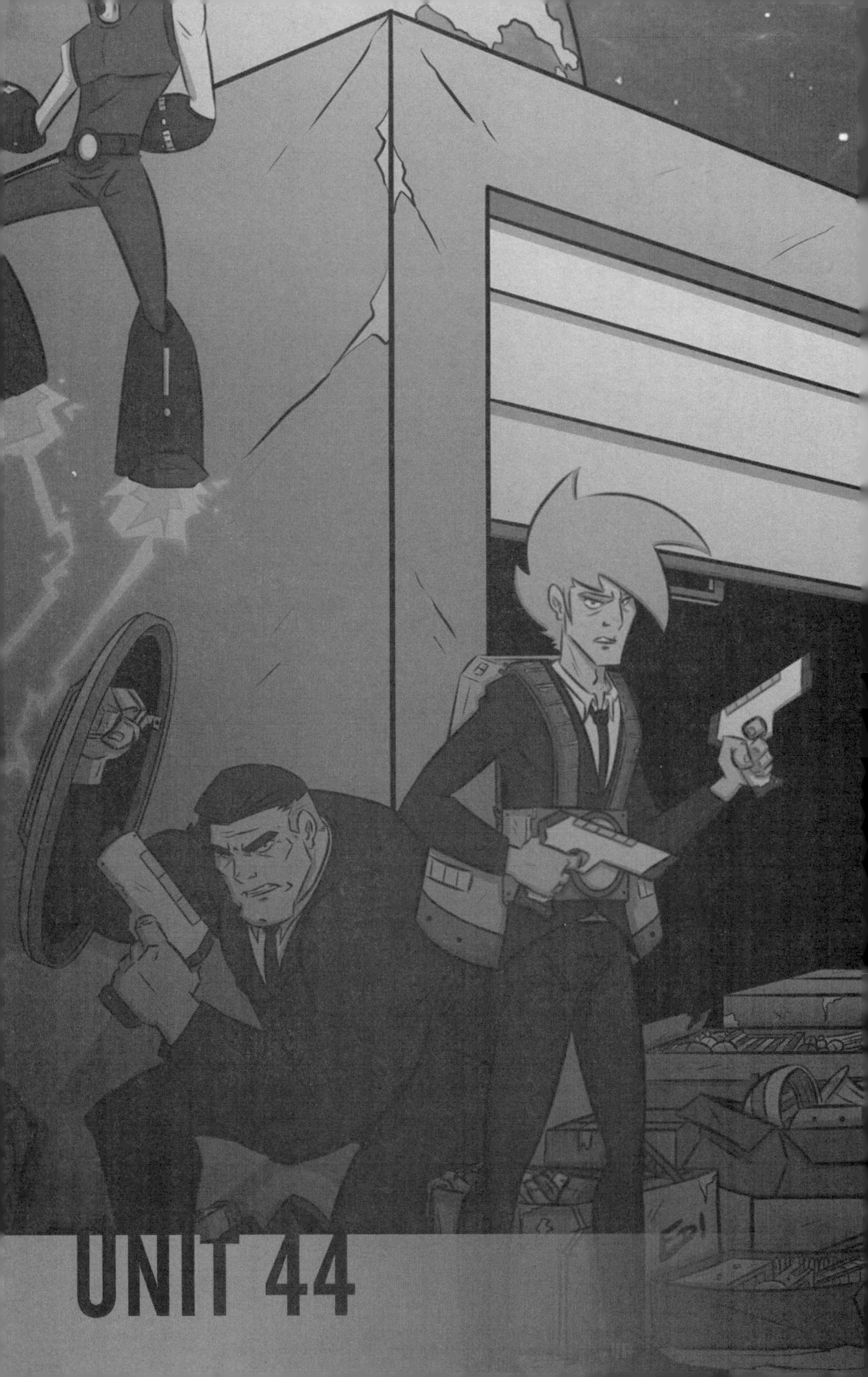
UNIT 44

UNIT 44

GIBSON & HATCH

"In our line of work, it's all about finding the truth. One must demand answers… justice… a hoagie."

Agents Gibson and Hatch, two equally inept employees of the United States Department of Super-Secret Stuff, are sadly the first line of defense in keeping the nation safe from the strange, weird, creepy and out-of-this-world threats it faces on a regular basis. But hey, we're all still here, so how bad a job can they really be doing, right? *…right?*

Agent Gibson
Age: 33
Height: 5'7"
Weight: 115 lbs.
(soaking wet)

Agent Hatch
Age: 47
Height: 6'4"
Weight: 208 lbs.
(completely dry)

First Appearance:
UNIT 44 #1 (2015)

Created by
Wes Locher & Eduardo Jimenez
Illustration by
Eduardo Jimenez

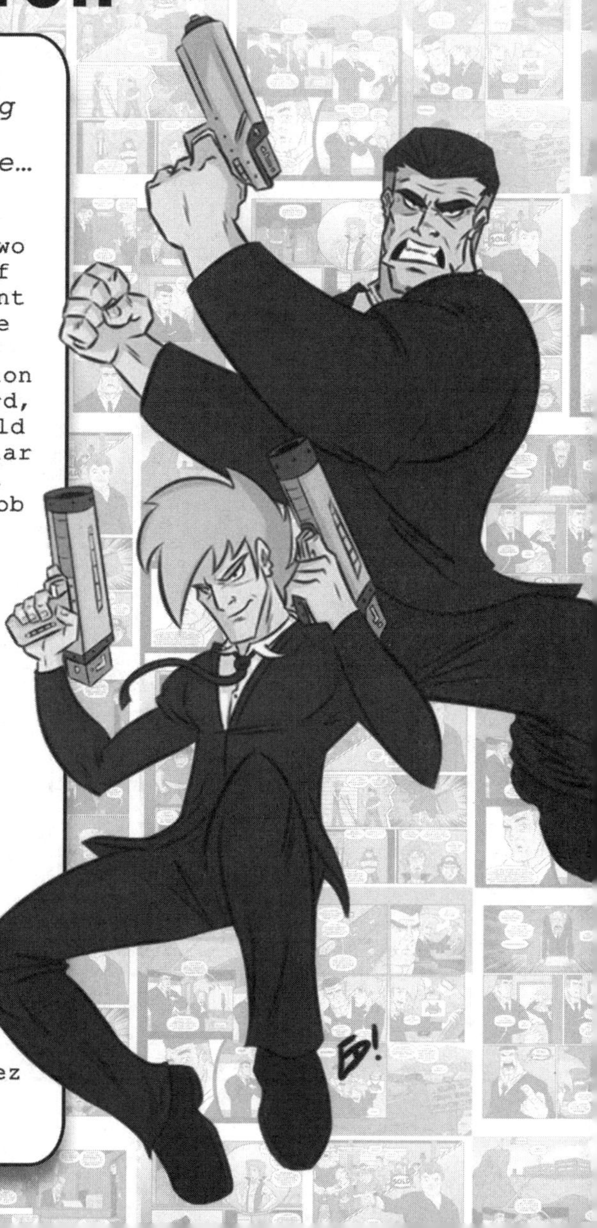
ED!

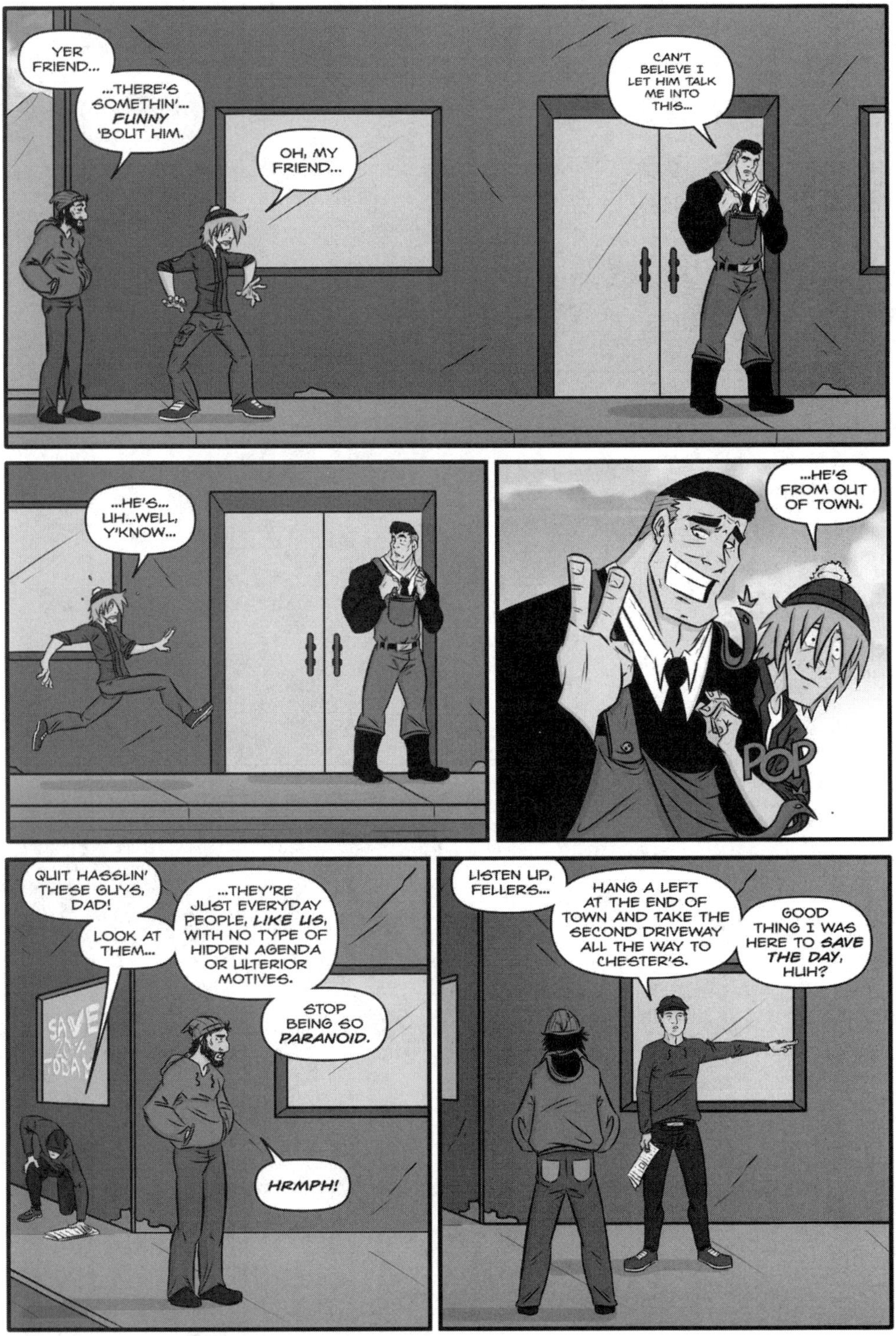

YER FRIEND...
...THERE'S SOMETHIN'... *FUNNY* 'BOUT HIM.
OH, MY FRIEND...
CAN'T BELIEVE I LET HIM TALK ME INTO THIS...
...HE'S... UH...WELL, Y'KNOW...
...HE'S FROM OUT OF TOWN.
POP
QUIT HASSLIN' THESE GUYS, DAD!
LOOK AT THEM...
...THEY'RE JUST EVERYDAY PEOPLE, *LIKE US*, WITH NO TYPE OF HIDDEN AGENDA OR ULTERIOR MOTIVES.
STOP BEING SO *PARANOID*.
HRMPH!
LISTEN UP, FELLERS...
HANG A LEFT AT THE END OF TOWN AND TAKE THE SECOND DRIVEWAY ALL THE WAY TO CHESTER'S.
GOOD THING I WAS HERE TO *SAVE THE DAY*, HUH?

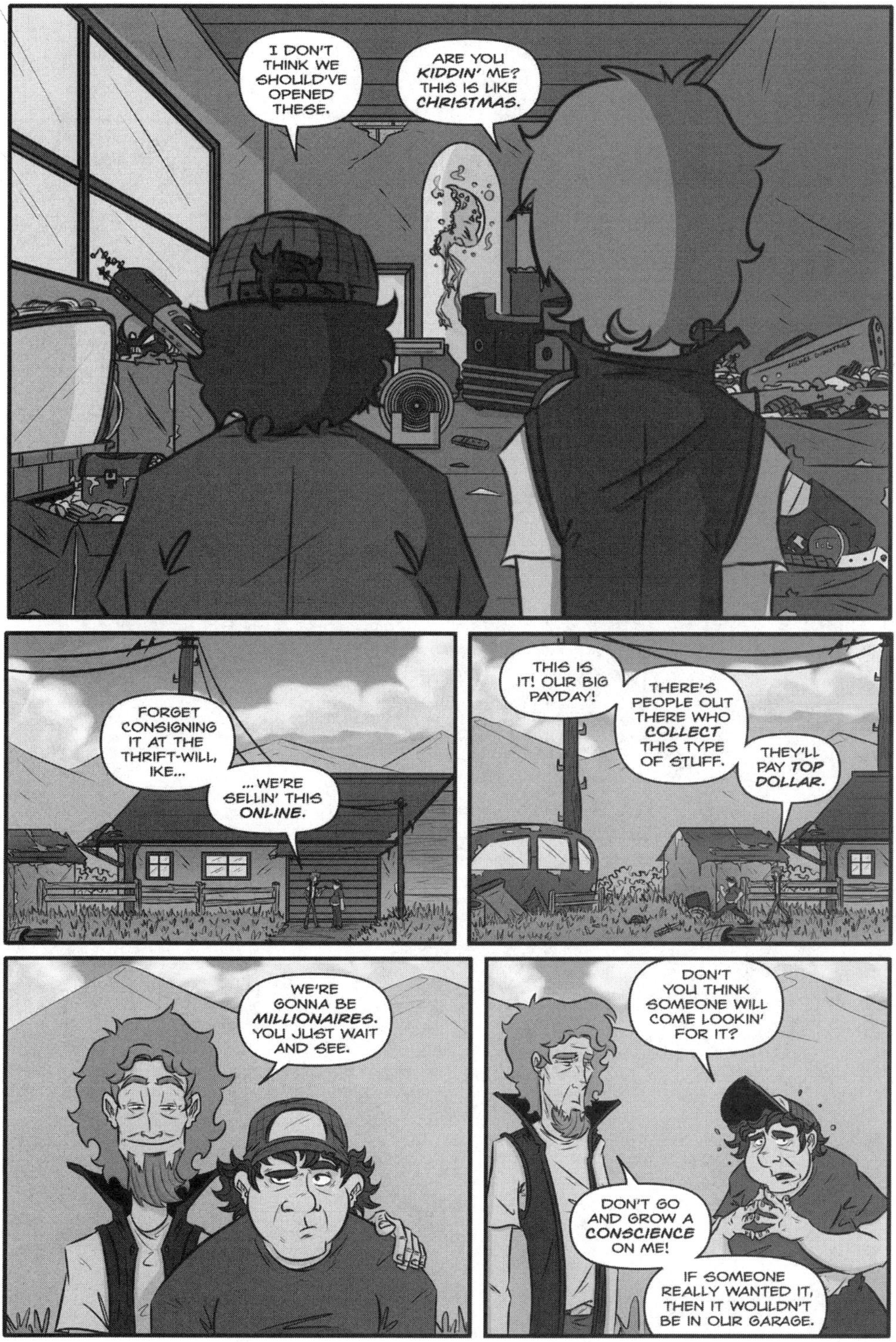
I DON'T THINK WE SHOULD'VE OPENED THESE.
ARE YOU *KIDDIN'* ME? THIS IS LIKE *CHRISTMAS.*
FORGET CONSIGNING IT AT THE THRIFT-WILL, IKE...
...WE'RE SELLIN' THIS *ONLINE.*
THIS IS IT! OUR BIG PAYDAY!
THERE'S PEOPLE OUT THERE WHO *COLLECT* THIS TYPE OF STUFF.
THEY'LL PAY *TOP DOLLAR.*
WE'RE GONNA BE *MILLIONAIRES.* YOU JUST WAIT AND SEE.
DON'T YOU THINK SOMEONE WILL COME LOOKIN' FOR IT?
DON'T GO AND GROW A *CONSCIENCE* ON ME!
IF SOMEONE REALLY WANTED IT, THEN IT WOULDN'T BE IN OUR GARAGE.

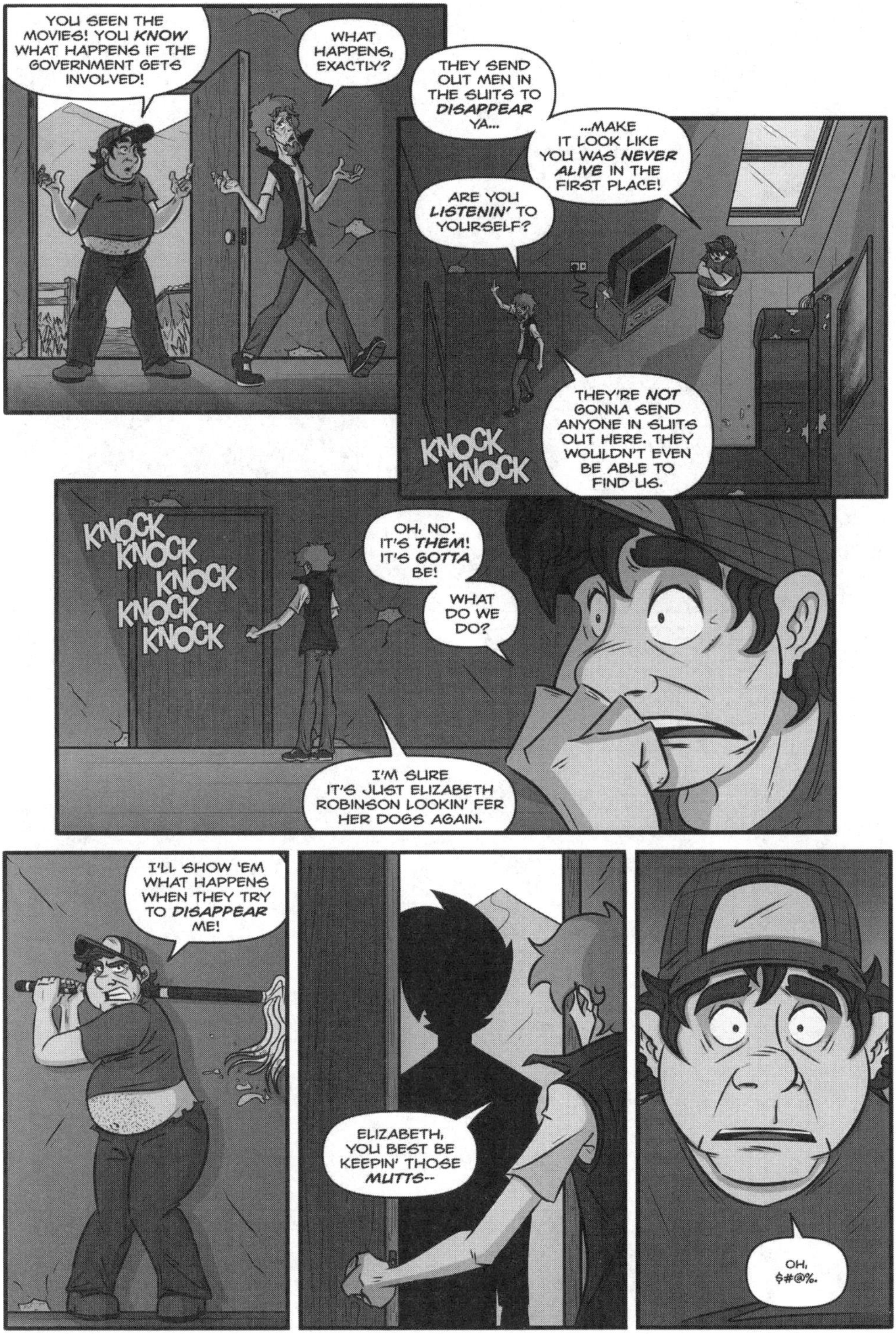
YOU SEEN THE MOVIES! YOU *KNOW* WHAT HAPPENS IF THE GOVERNMENT GETS INVOLVED!
WHAT HAPPENS, EXACTLY?
THEY SEND OUT MEN IN THE SUITS TO *DISAPPEAR* YA...
...MAKE IT LOOK LIKE YOU WAS *NEVER ALIVE* IN THE FIRST PLACE!
ARE YOU *LISTENIN'* TO YOURSELF?
THEY'RE *NOT* GONNA SEND ANYONE IN SUITS OUT HERE. THEY WOULDN'T EVEN BE ABLE TO FIND US.
KNOCK KNOCK
KNOCK KNOCK KNOCK KNOCK KNOCK
OH, NO! IT'S *THEM*! IT'S *GOTTA* BE!
WHAT DO WE DO?
I'M SURE IT'S JUST ELIZABETH ROBINSON LOOKIN' FER HER DOGS AGAIN.
I'LL SHOW 'EM WHAT HAPPENS WHEN THEY TRY TO *DISAPPEAR* ME!
ELIZABETH, YOU BEST BE KEEPIN' THOSE *MUTTS*--
OH, $#@%.

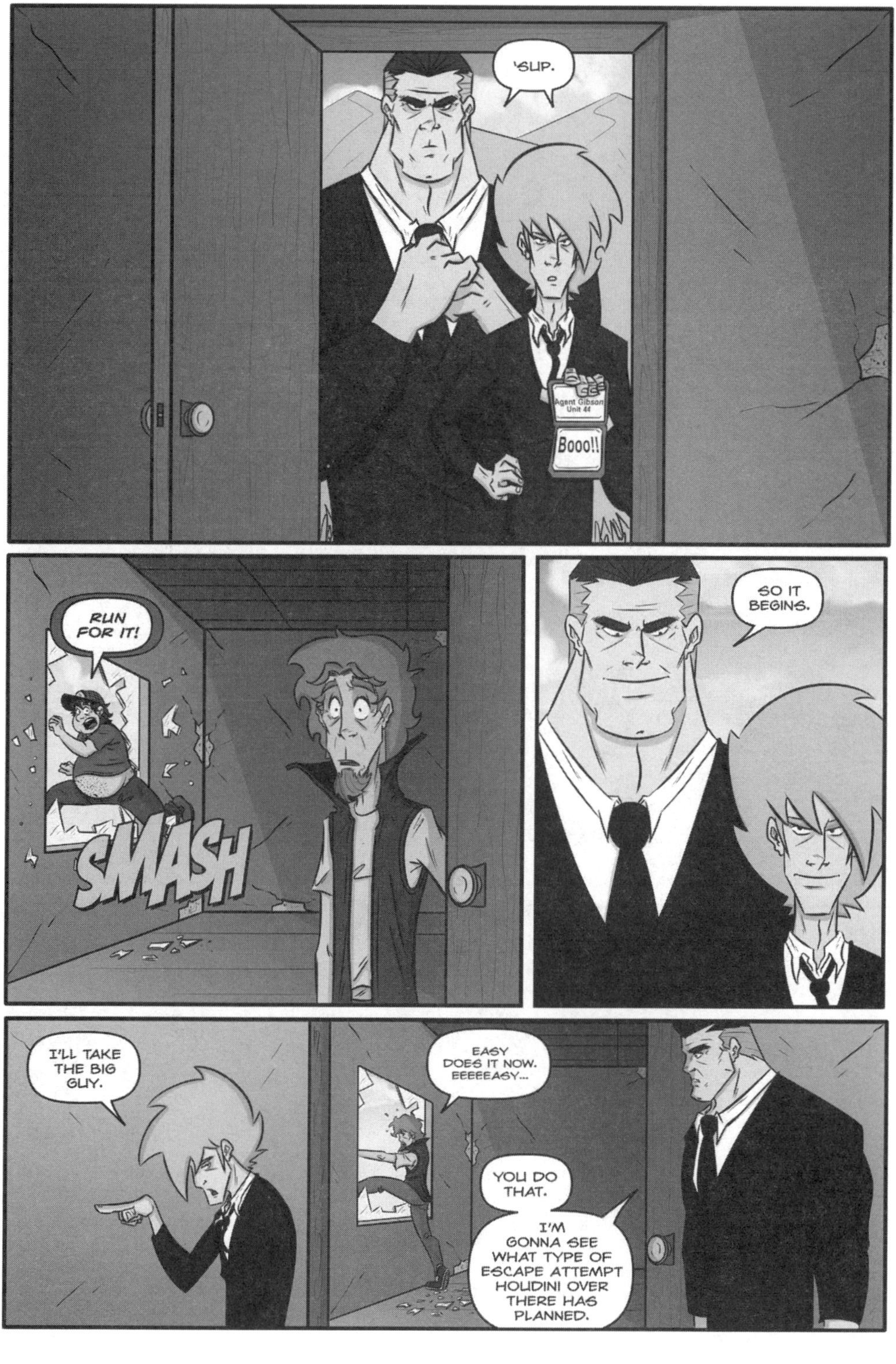
'SUP.
Agent Gibson
Unit 44
Booo!!
RUN FOR IT!
SMASH
SO IT BEGINS.
I'LL TAKE THE BIG GUY.
EASY DOES IT NOW. EEEEEASY...
YOU DO THAT.
I'M GONNA SEE WHAT TYPE OF ESCAPE ATTEMPT HOUDINI OVER THERE HAS PLANNED.

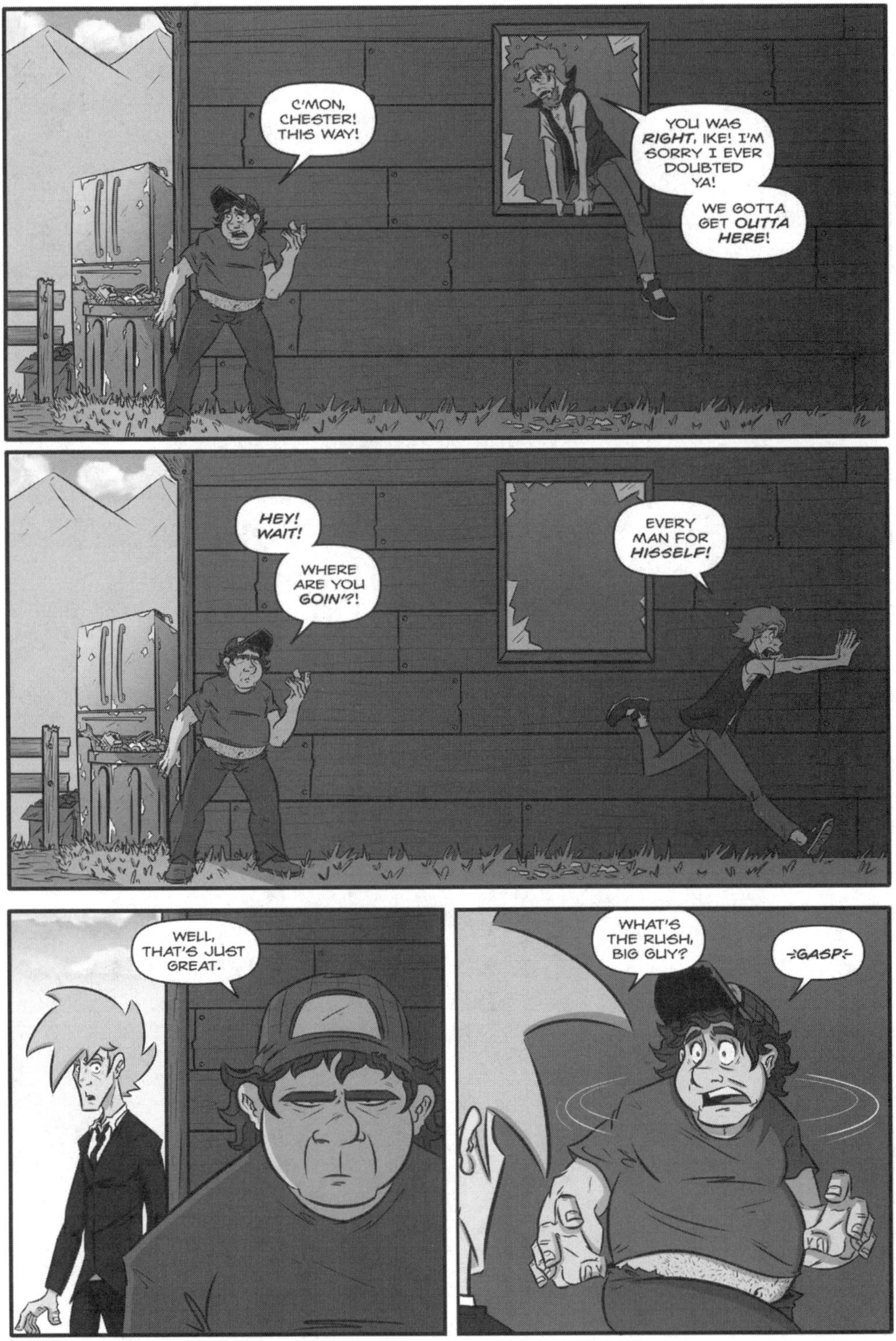
C'MON, CHESTER! THIS WAY!
YOU WAS RIGHT, IKE! I'M SORRY I EVER DOUBTED YA!
WE GOTTA GET OUTTA HERE!
HEY! WAIT!
WHERE ARE YOU GOIN'?!
EVERY MAN FOR HISSELF!
WELL, THAT'S JUST GREAT.
WHAT'S THE RUSH, BIG GUY?
GASP

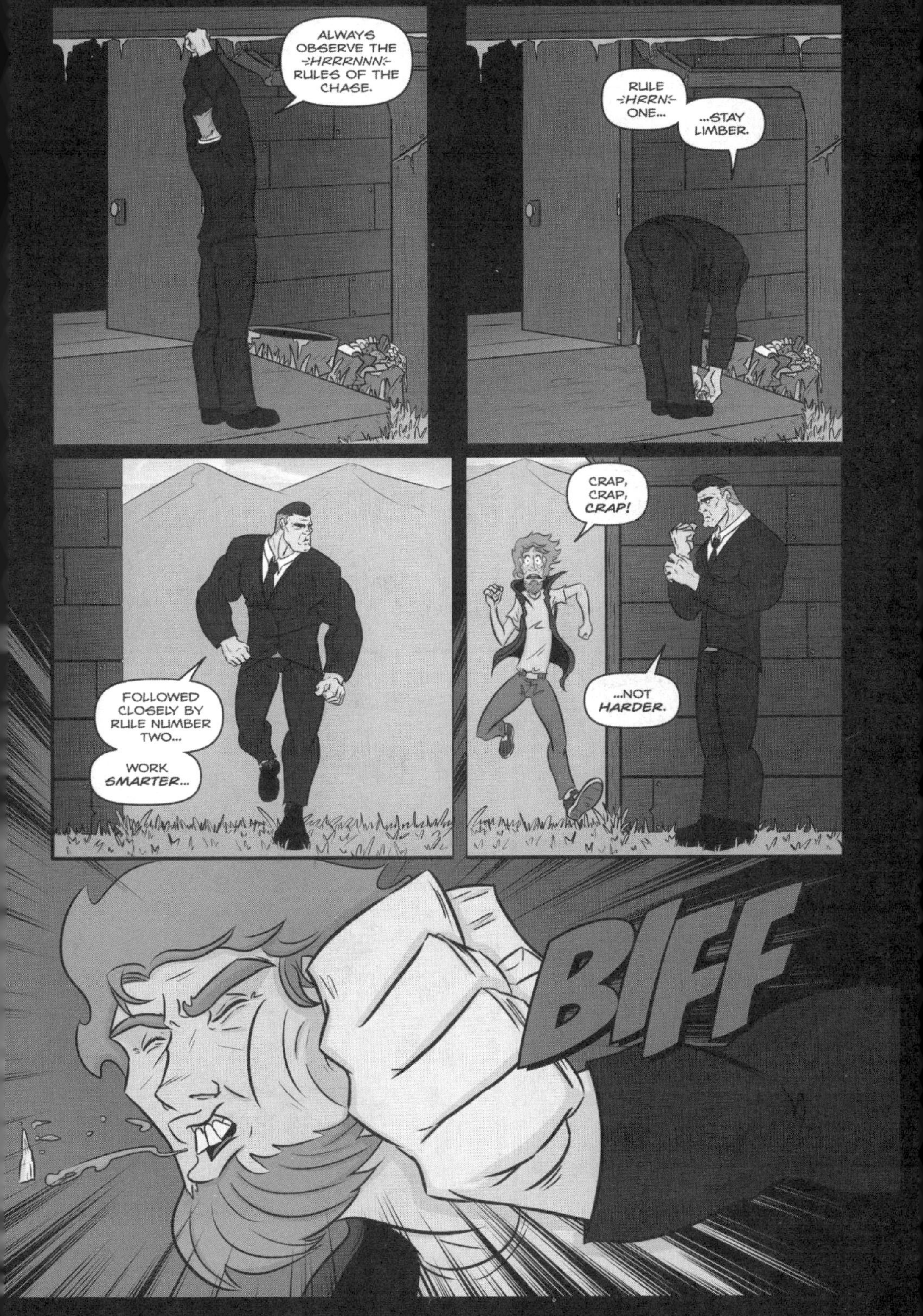
ALWAYS OBSERVE THE -HRRRNNN- RULES OF THE CHASE.
RULE -HRRN- ONE...
...STAY LIMBER.
FOLLOWED CLOSELY BY RULE NUMBER TWO...
WORK SMARTER...
CRAP, CRAP, CRAP!
...NOT HARDER.
BIFF

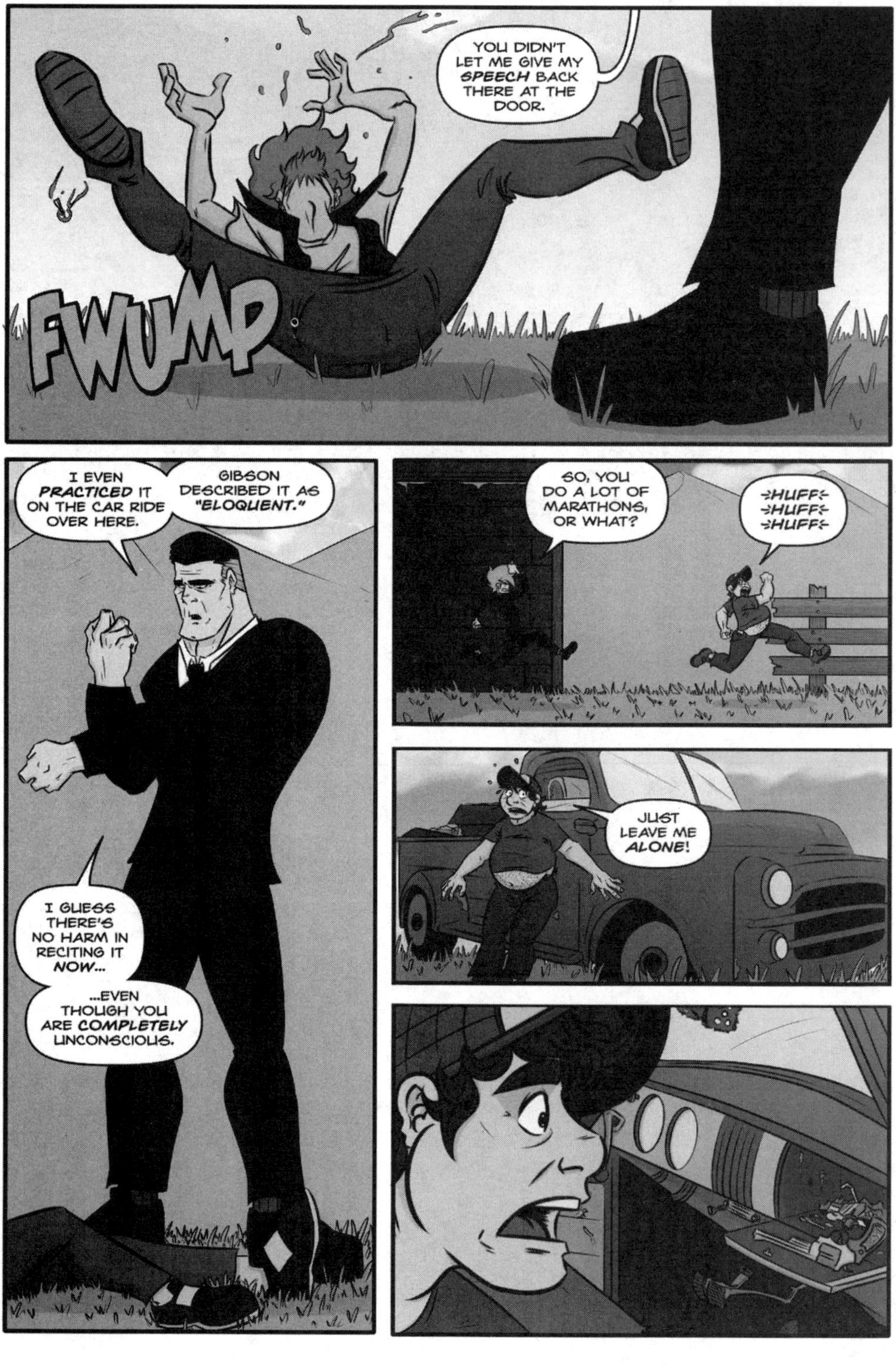
YOU DIDN'T LET ME GIVE MY SPEECH BACK THERE AT THE DOOR.
FWUMP
I EVEN PRACTICED IT ON THE CAR RIDE OVER HERE.
GIBSON DESCRIBED IT AS "ELOQUENT."
I GUESS THERE'S NO HARM IN RECITING IT NOW...
...EVEN THOUGH YOU ARE COMPLETELY UNCONSCIOUS.
SO, YOU DO A LOT OF MARATHONS, OR WHAT?
HUFF HUFF HUFF
JUST LEAVE ME ALONE!

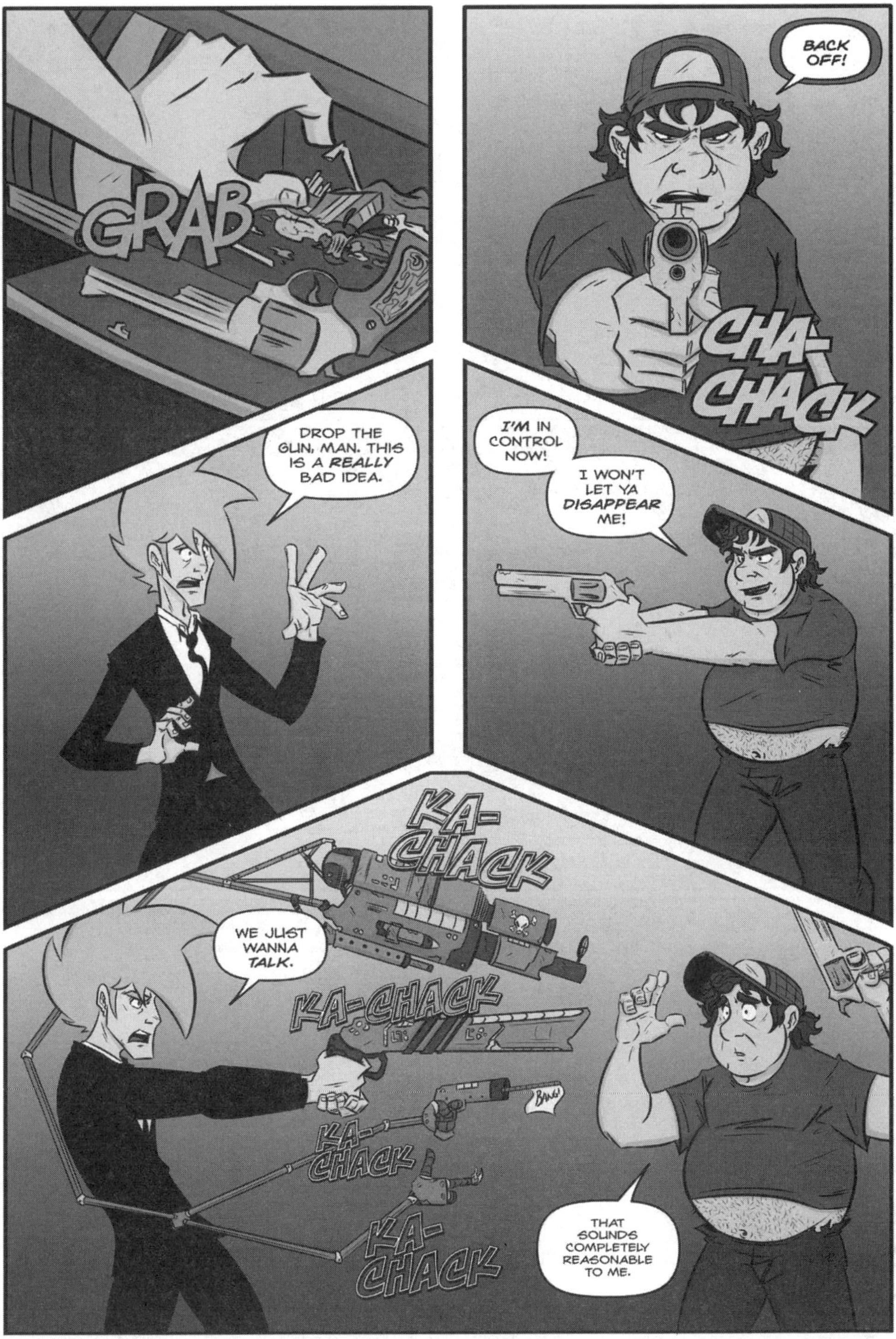
GRAB
BACK OFF!
CHA-CHACK
DROP THE GUN, MAN. THIS IS A *REALLY* BAD IDEA.
I'M IN CONTROL NOW!
I WON'T LET YA *DISAPPEAR* ME!
KA-CHACK
WE JUST WANNA *TALK*.
KA-CHACK
BANG!
KA-CHACK
KA-CHACK
THAT SOUNDS COMPLETELY REASONABLE TO ME.

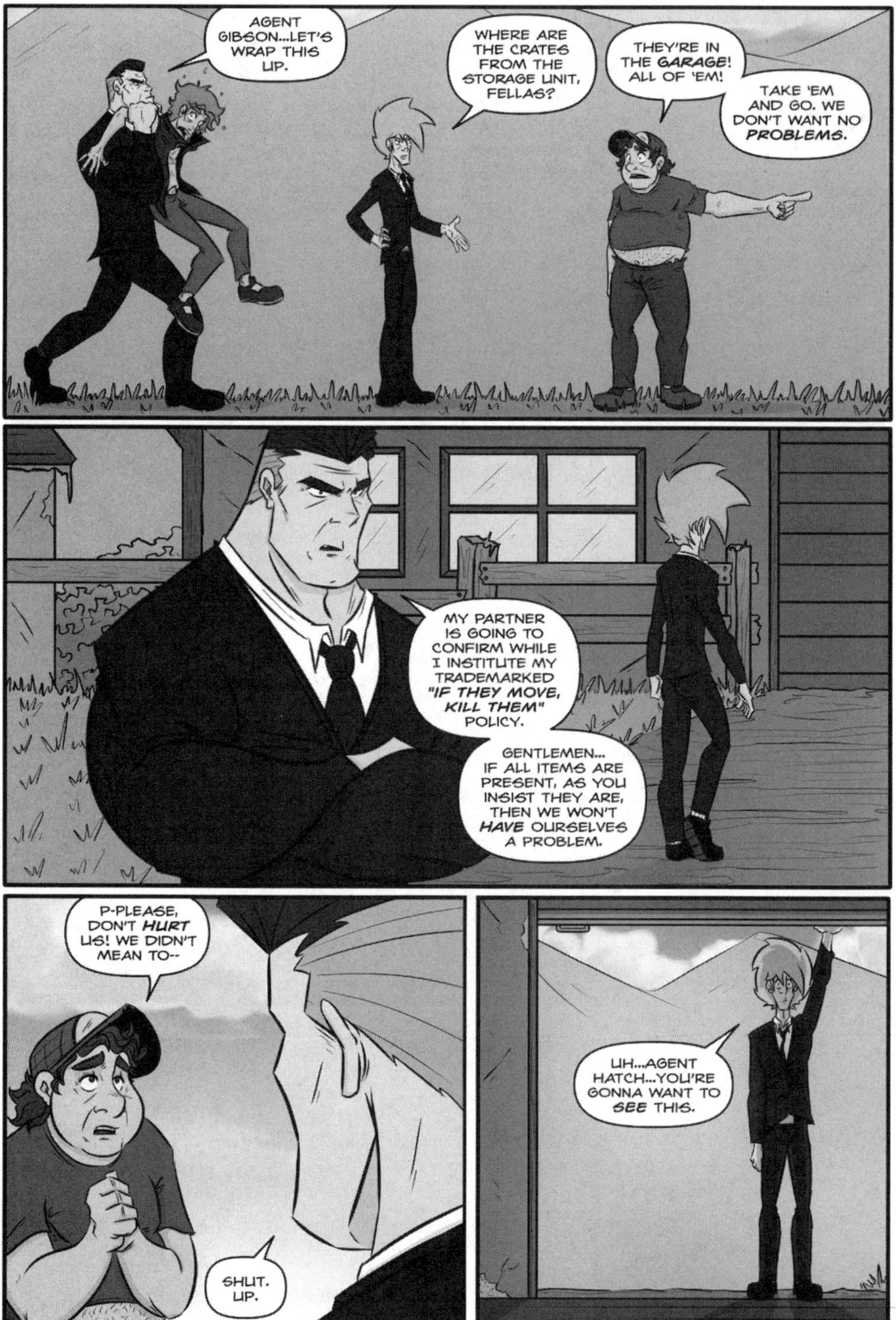
AGENT GIBSON...LET'S WRAP THIS UP.
WHERE ARE THE CRATES FROM THE STORAGE UNIT, FELLAS?
THEY'RE IN THE GARAGE! ALL OF 'EM!
TAKE 'EM AND GO. WE DON'T WANT NO PROBLEMS.
MY PARTNER IS GOING TO CONFIRM WHILE I INSTITUTE MY TRADEMARKED "IF THEY MOVE, KILL THEM" POLICY.
GENTLEMEN... IF ALL ITEMS ARE PRESENT, AS YOU INSIST THEY ARE, THEN WE WON'T HAVE OURSELVES A PROBLEM.
P-PLEASE, DON'T HURT US! WE DIDN'T MEAN TO--
SHUT. UP.
UH...AGENT HATCH...YOU'RE GONNA WANT TO SEE THIS.

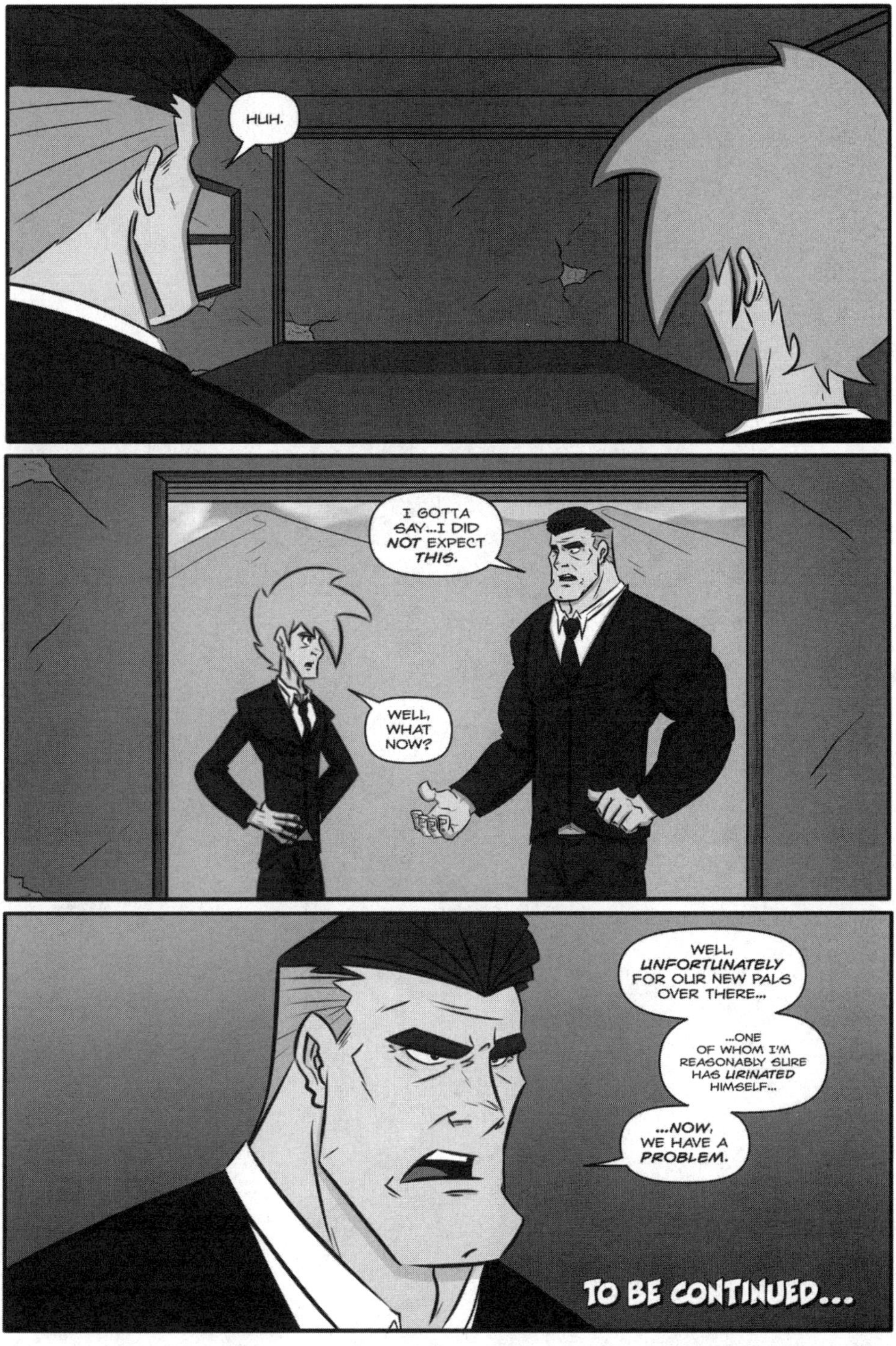
HUH.
I GOTTA SAY...I DID NOT EXPECT THIS.
WELL, WHAT NOW?
WELL, UNFORTUNATELY FOR OUR NEW PALS OVER THERE...
...ONE OF WHOM I'M REASONABLY SURE HAS URINATED HIMSELF...
...NOW, WE HAVE A PROBLEM.
TO BE CONTINUED...

CONTINUED IN THE PAGES OF 'UNIT 44'

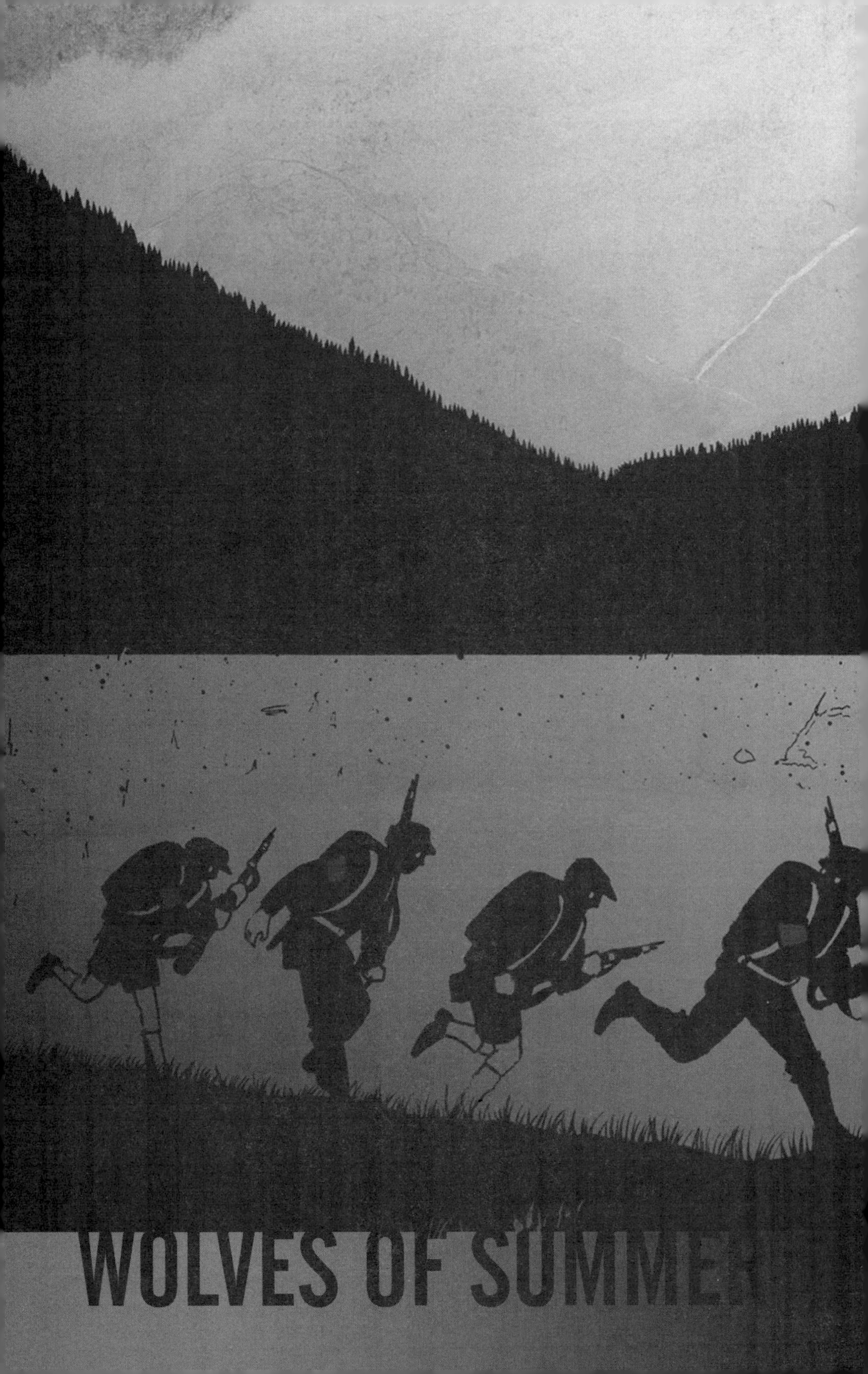
WOLVES OF SUMME

WOLVES OF SUMMER

HANS KRUGER

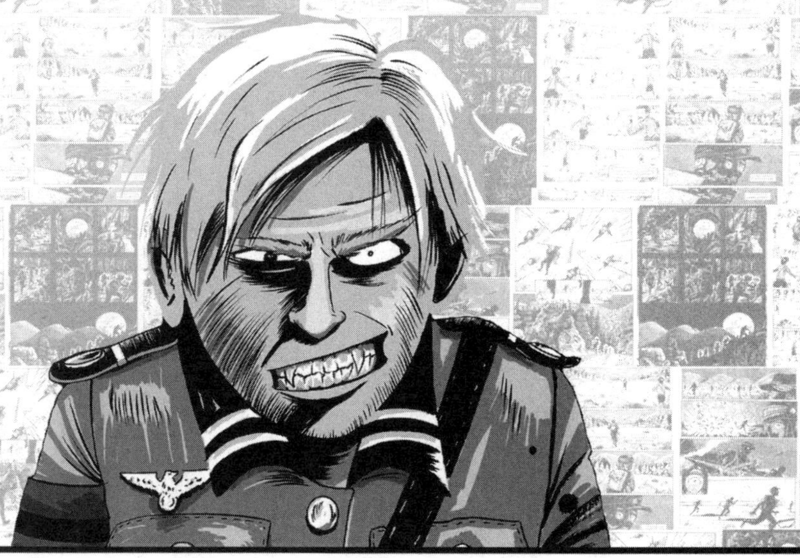

"You may sleep as children, but you must wake as men."

The son of a poor and widowed cobbler, Hans believes he is destined for something more. Seeing Hitler's SS march through his village, he feels inspired by the fear and respect they command. Along with his reluctant younger brother, Rudi, he joins the local faction of Hitler Youth. They are trained to kill at Castle Hulchrath, and hastily thrown into combat. In April of 1945, during the last days of WW2, Hans leads the four surviving members of his Werewolf Squad on a desperate mission of revenge. Believing in the twisted motto of the Hitler Youth, "Live faithfully, fight bravely, and die laughing!", Hans is a frightening example of the evils that mankind is capable of.

Age: 13 Height: 4'9" Weight: 94 lbs.

First Appearance: WOLVES OF SUMMER #1 (2013)

Created by Tony Keaton and Andrew Herbst
Illustration by Andrew Herbst

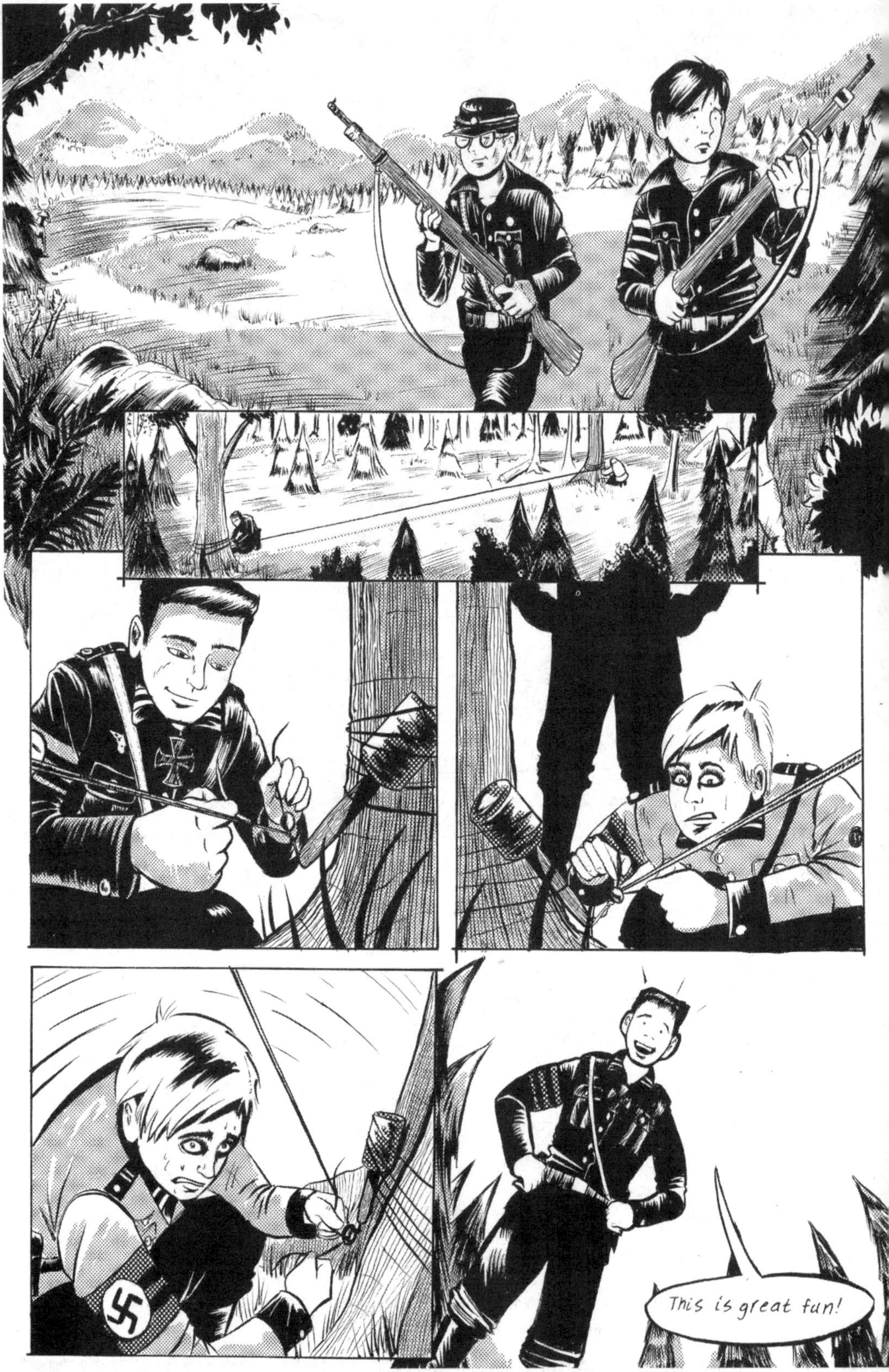
This is great fun!

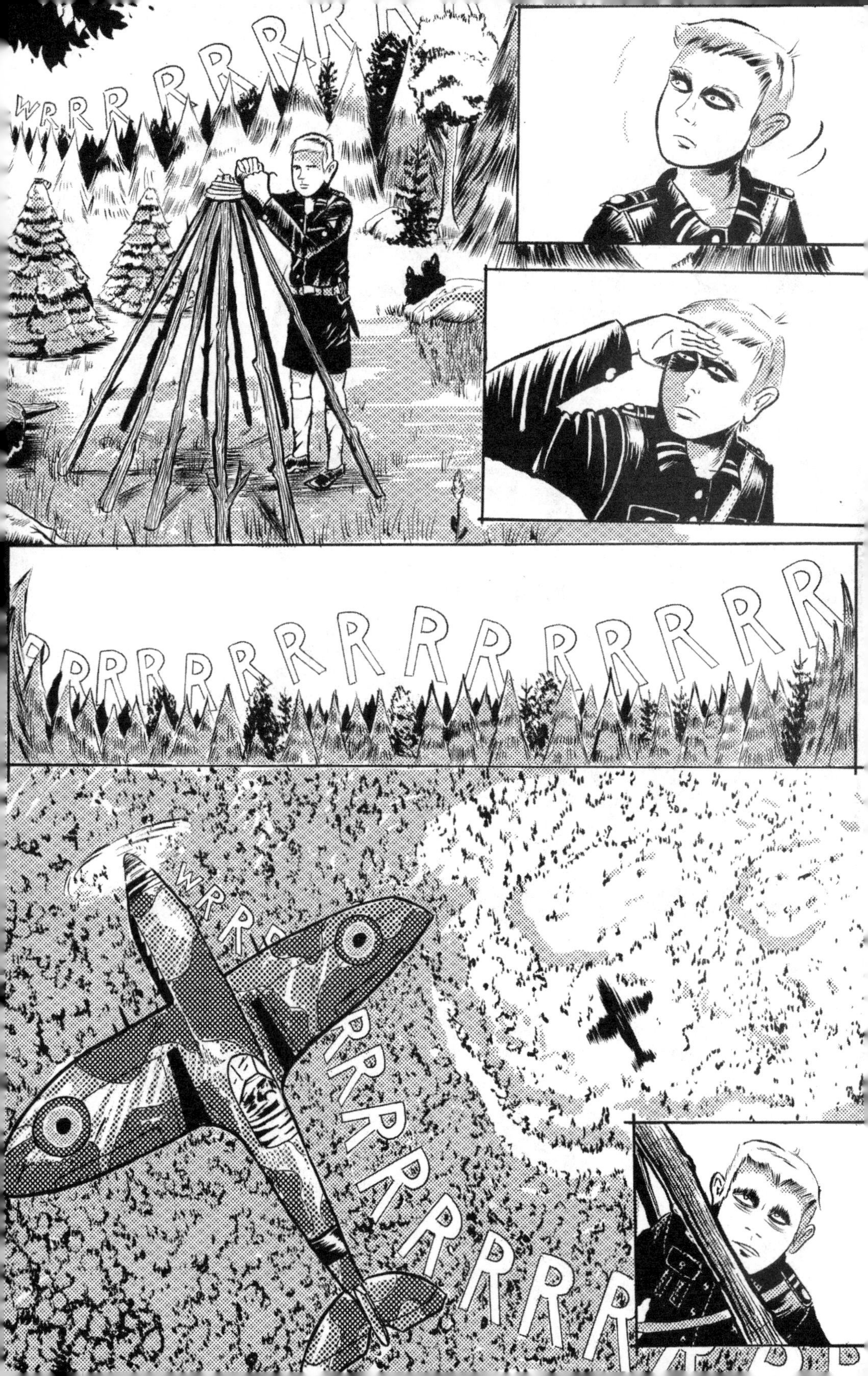
WRRRRRRR
RRRRRRRRRRRRRR
WRRRRRRRRRRRRRRR

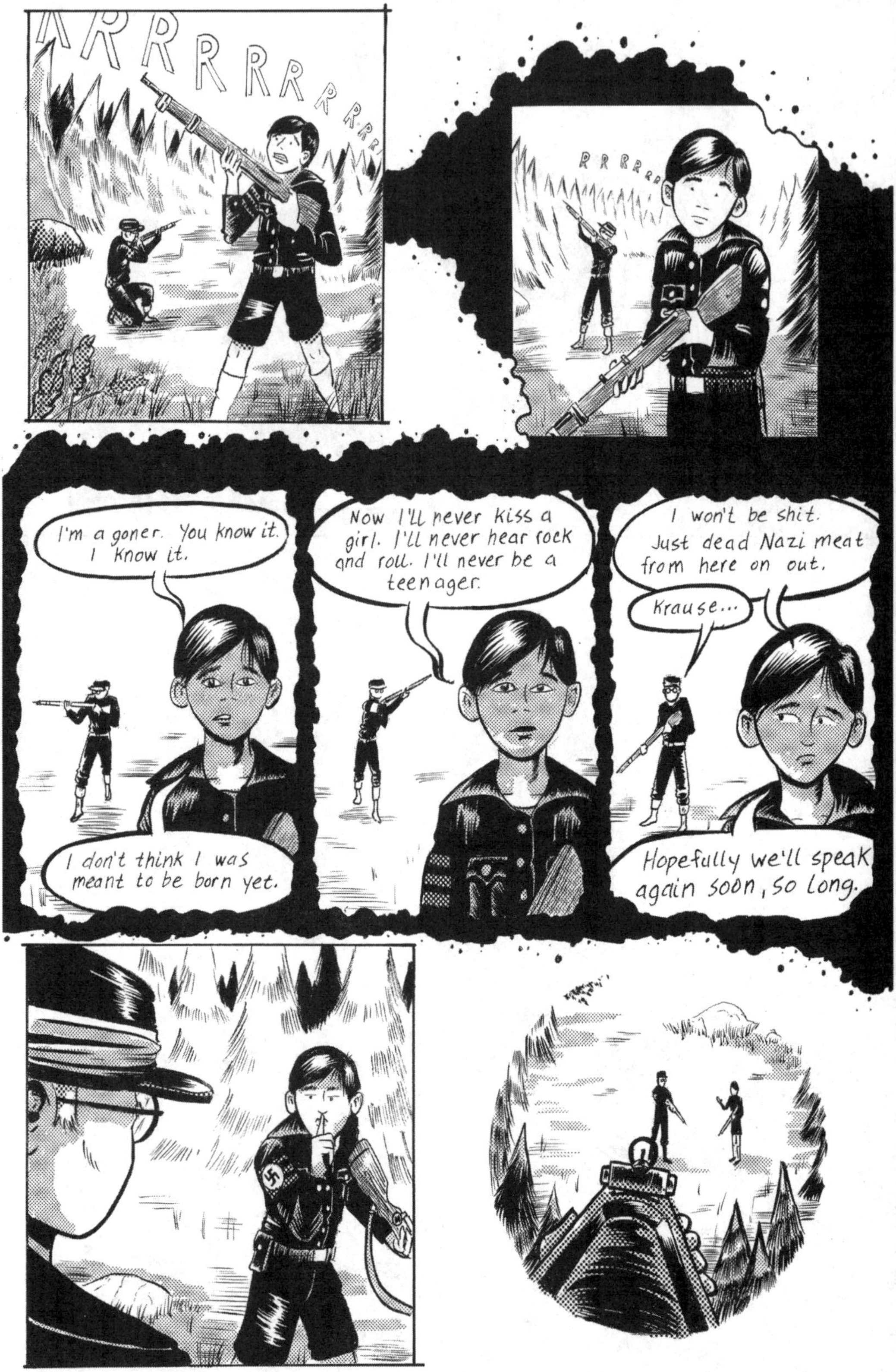
ARRRRRRRRRR
RRRRRR
I'm a goner. You know it. I know it.
I don't think I was meant to be born yet.
Now I'll never kiss a girl. I'll never hear rock and roll. I'll never be a teenager.
I won't be shit. Just dead Nazi meat from here on out.
Krause...
Hopefully we'll speak again soon, so long.

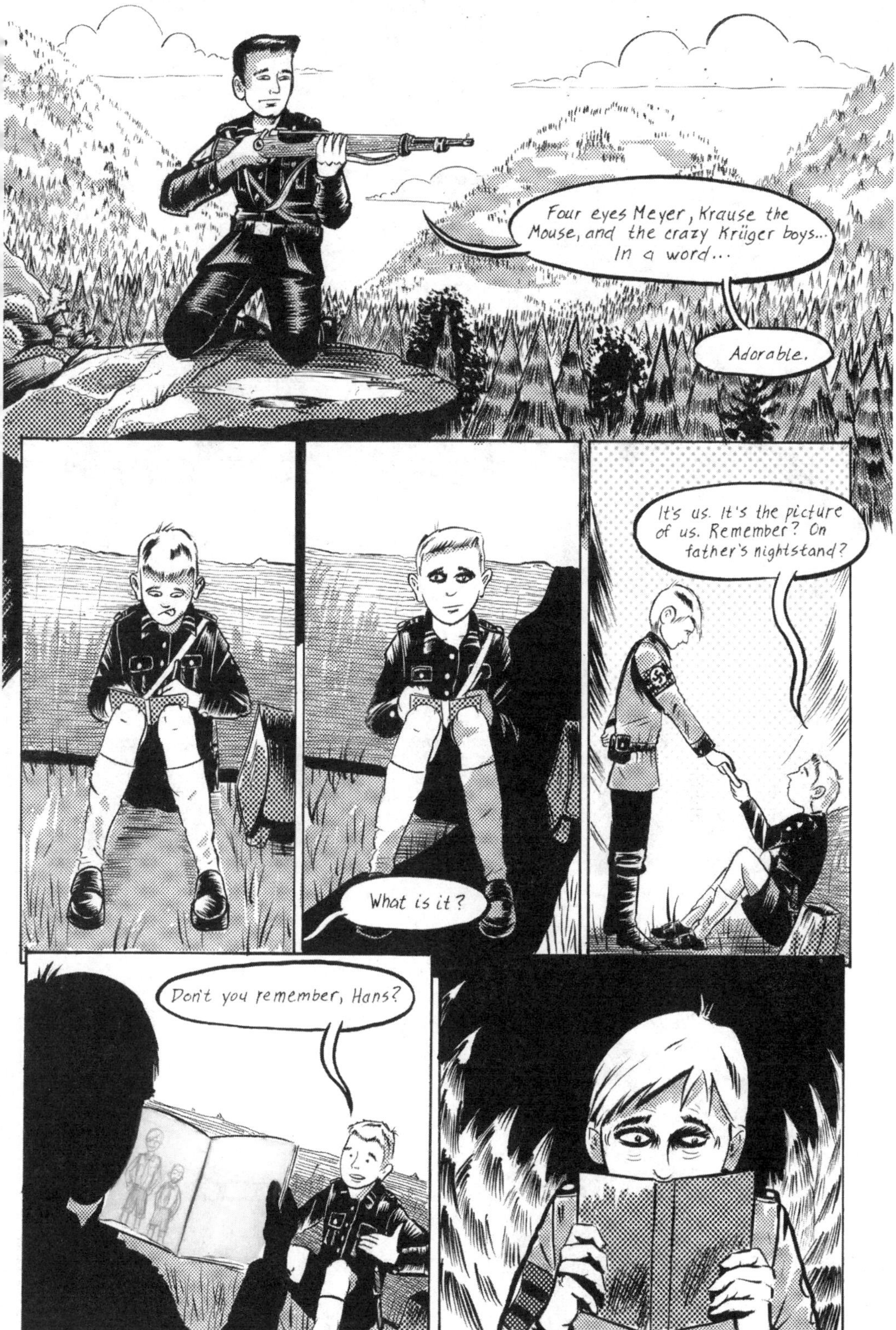

Four eyes Meyer, Krause the Mouse, and the crazy Krüger boys... In a word...
Adorable.
What is it?
It's us. It's the picture of us. Remember? On father's nightstand?
Don't you remember, Hans?

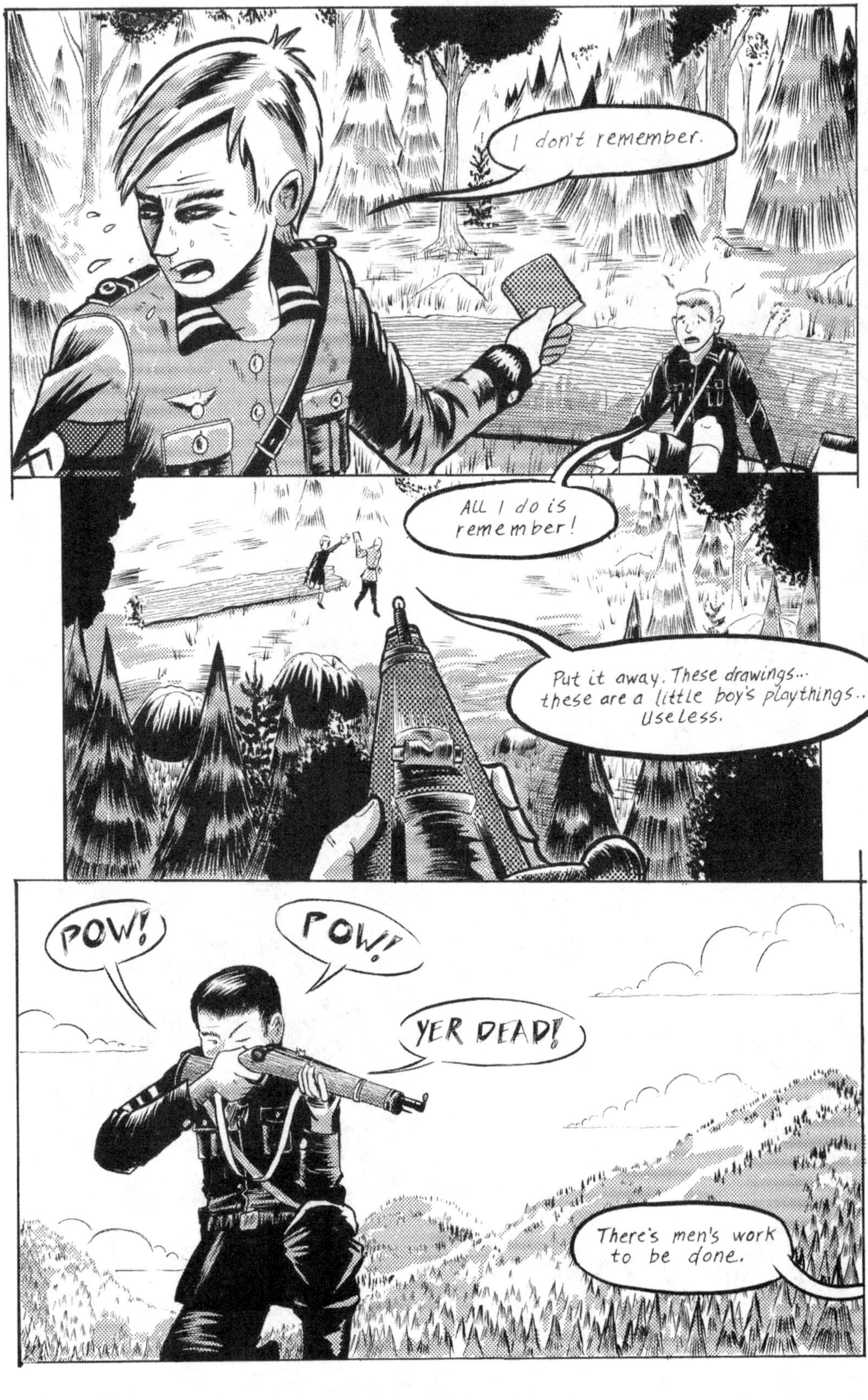
I don't remember.
All I do is remember!
Put it away. These drawings... these are a little boy's playthings... Useless.
POW!
POW!
YER DEAD!
There's men's work to be done.

Dr. Goebbels... you may begin.

THE TERROR RAIDS HAVE DESTROYED OUR CITIES IN THE WEST... OUR STARVING WOMEN AND CHILDREN ALONG THE RHINE RIVER HAVE TAUGHT US HOW TO HATE.

THE BLOOD AND TEARS OF OUR BRUTALLY BEATEN MEN, OUR DESPOILED WIVES AND OUR MURDERED CHILDREN IN THOSE OCCUPIED AREAS CRY OUT FOR REVENGE.

THOSE WHO ARE IN WEREWOLF DECLARE IN THIS PROCLAMATION THEIR FIRM, RESOLUTE DECISION, SEALED WITH THEIR OATH NEVER TO BOW TO THE ENEMY...

EVEN THOUGH WE SUFFER THE MOST TERRIBLE CONDITIONS AND HAVE ONLY LIMITED RESOURCES BUT TO MEET THE FOE WITH RESISTANCE TO DEFY HIM, DESPISING BOURGEOIS COMFORT...

AND SHALL FACE POSSIBLE DEATH WITH PRIDE, AND WE SHALL REVENGE ANY MISDEED WHICH HE COMMITS AGAINST OUR RACE BY KILLING HIM.

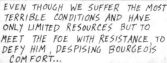

EVERY MEANS IS JUSTIFIED IF IT HELPS TO DAMAGE THE ENEMY, THE WEREWOLF HAS IT'S OWN COURTS OF JUSTICE WHICH DECIDE THE LIFE OR DEATH OF OUR ENEMY AS WELL AS THE TRAITORS AMONG OUR FOLK.

OUR MOVEMENT RISES OUT OF OUR FOLKS DESIRE FOR FREEDOM AND IS BOUND UP WITH HONOR OF THE GERMAN NATION WHOSE GUARDIANS WE CONSIDER OURSELVES TO BE!

HATE IS OUR PRAYER. REVENGE IS OUR BATTLE CRY!!

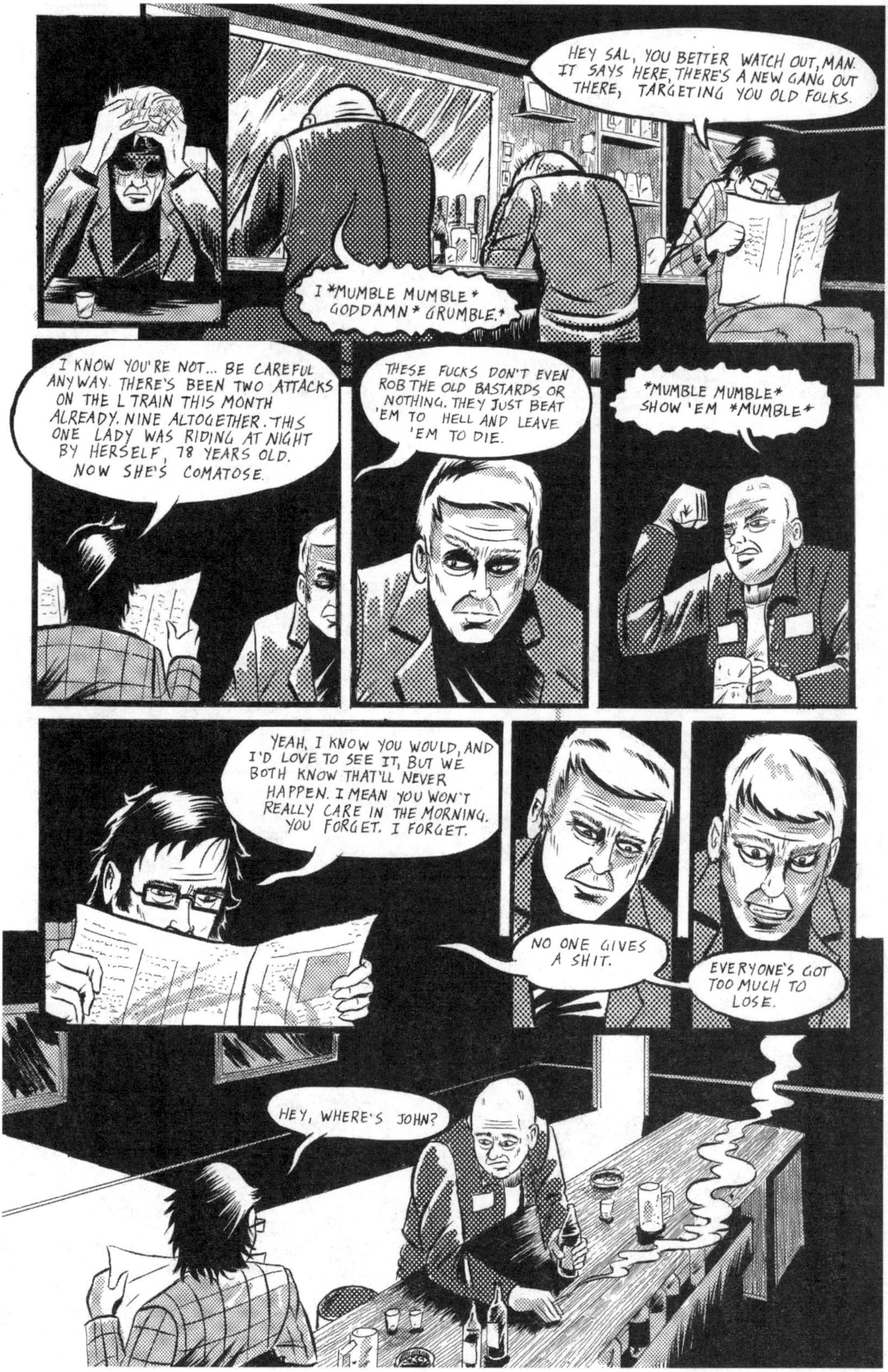
HEY SAL, YOU BETTER WATCH OUT, MAN. IT SAYS HERE, THERE'S A NEW GANG OUT THERE, TARGETING YOU OLD FOLKS.
I *MUMBLE MUMBLE* GODDAMN* GRUMBLE.*
I KNOW YOU'RE NOT... BE CAREFUL ANYWAY. THERE'S BEEN TWO ATTACKS ON THE L TRAIN THIS MONTH ALREADY. NINE ALTOGETHER. THIS ONE LADY WAS RIDING AT NIGHT BY HERSELF, 78 YEARS OLD. NOW SHE'S COMATOSE.
THESE FUCKS DON'T EVEN ROB THE OLD BASTARDS OR NOTHING. THEY JUST BEAT 'EM TO HELL AND LEAVE 'EM TO DIE.
MUMBLE MUMBLE SHOW 'EM *MUMBLE*
YEAH, I KNOW YOU WOULD, AND I'D LOVE TO SEE IT, BUT WE BOTH KNOW THAT'LL NEVER HAPPEN. I MEAN YOU WON'T REALLY CARE IN THE MORNING. YOU FORGET. I FORGET.
NO ONE GIVES A SHIT.
EVERYONE'S GOT TOO MUCH TO LOSE.
HEY, WHERE'S JOHN?

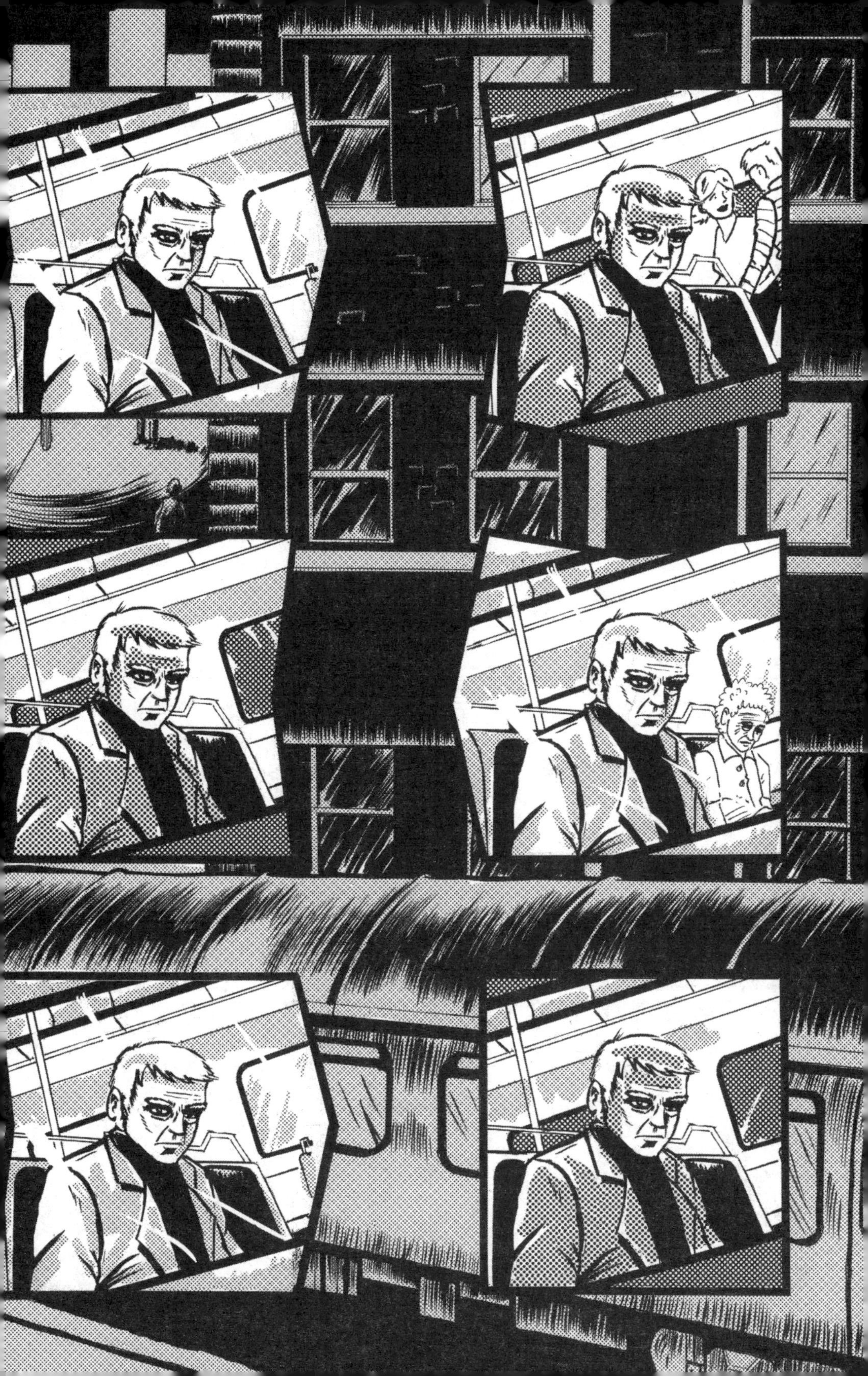

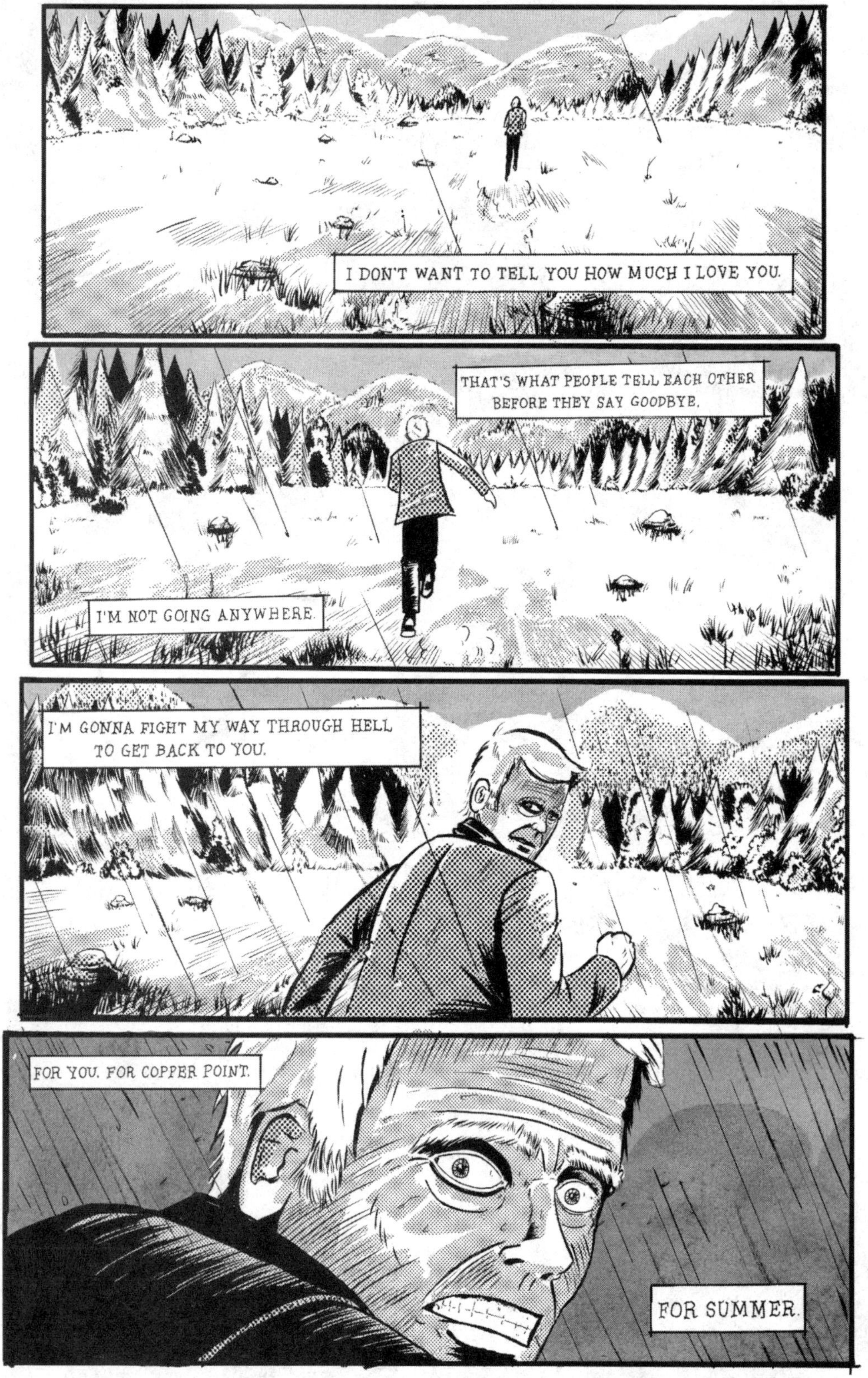
I DON'T WANT TO TELL YOU HOW MUCH I LOVE YOU.
THAT'S WHAT PEOPLE TELL EACH OTHER BEFORE THEY SAY GOODBYE.
I'M NOT GOING ANYWHERE.
I'M GONNA FIGHT MY WAY THROUGH HELL TO GET BACK TO YOU.
FOR YOU. FOR COPPER POINT.
FOR SUMMER.

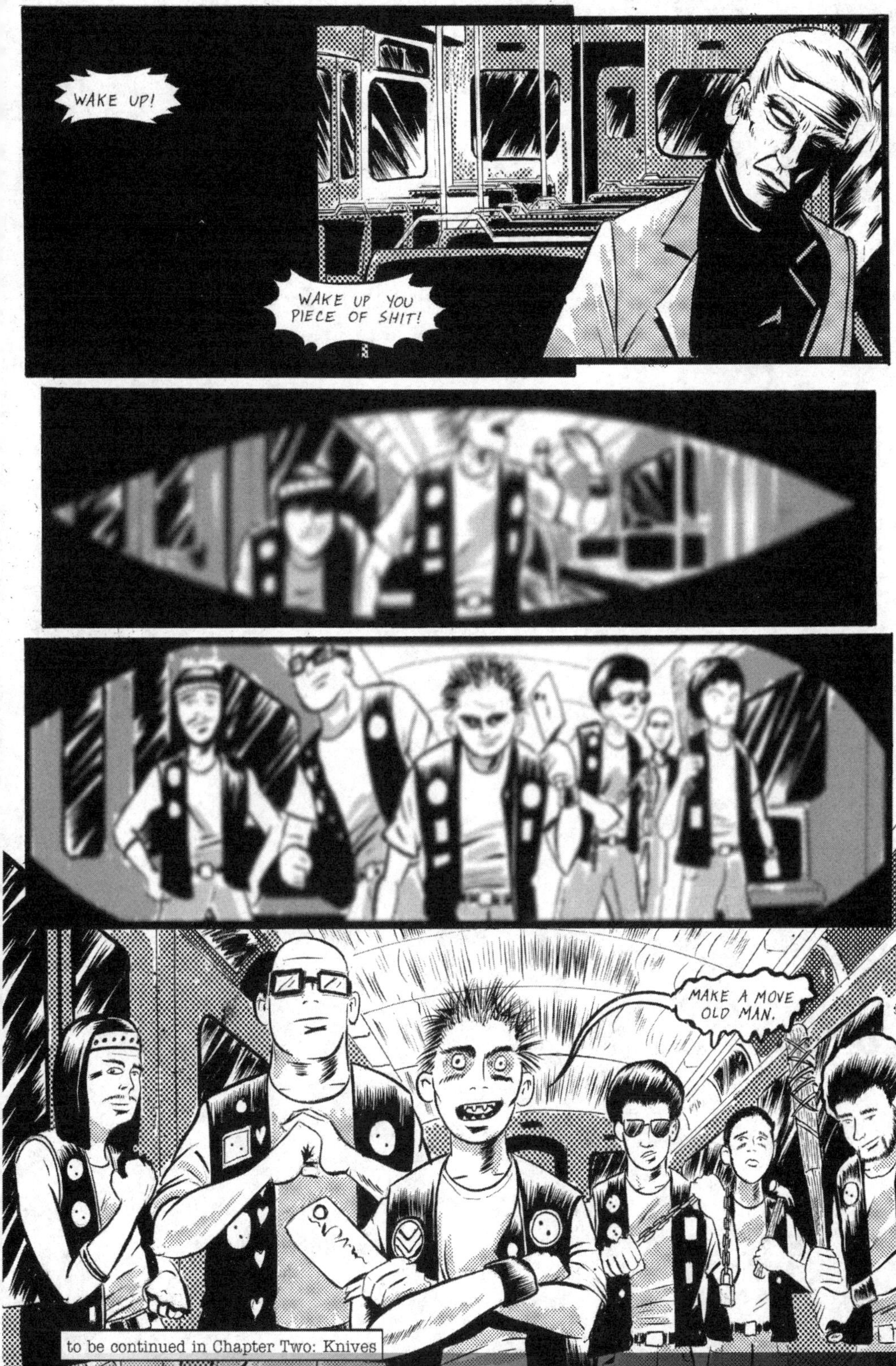
WAKE UP!
WAKE UP YOU PIECE OF SHIT!
MAKE A MOVE OLD MAN.
to be continued in Chapter Two: Knives

CONTINUED IN THE PAGES OF 'WOLVES OF SUMMER'

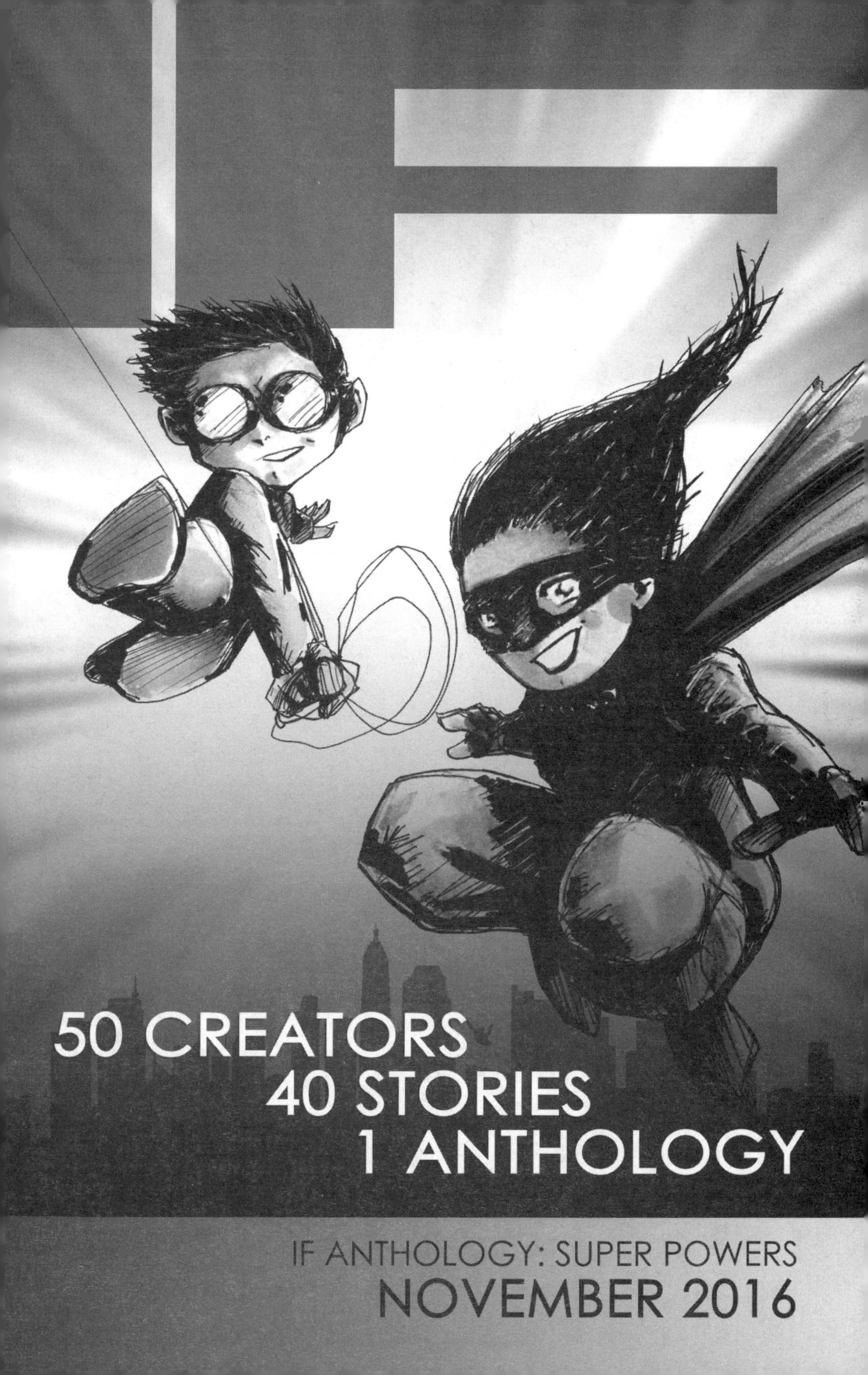
IF
50 CREATORS
40 STORIES
1 ANTHOLOGY
IF ANTHOLOGY: SUPER POWERS
NOVEMBER 2016

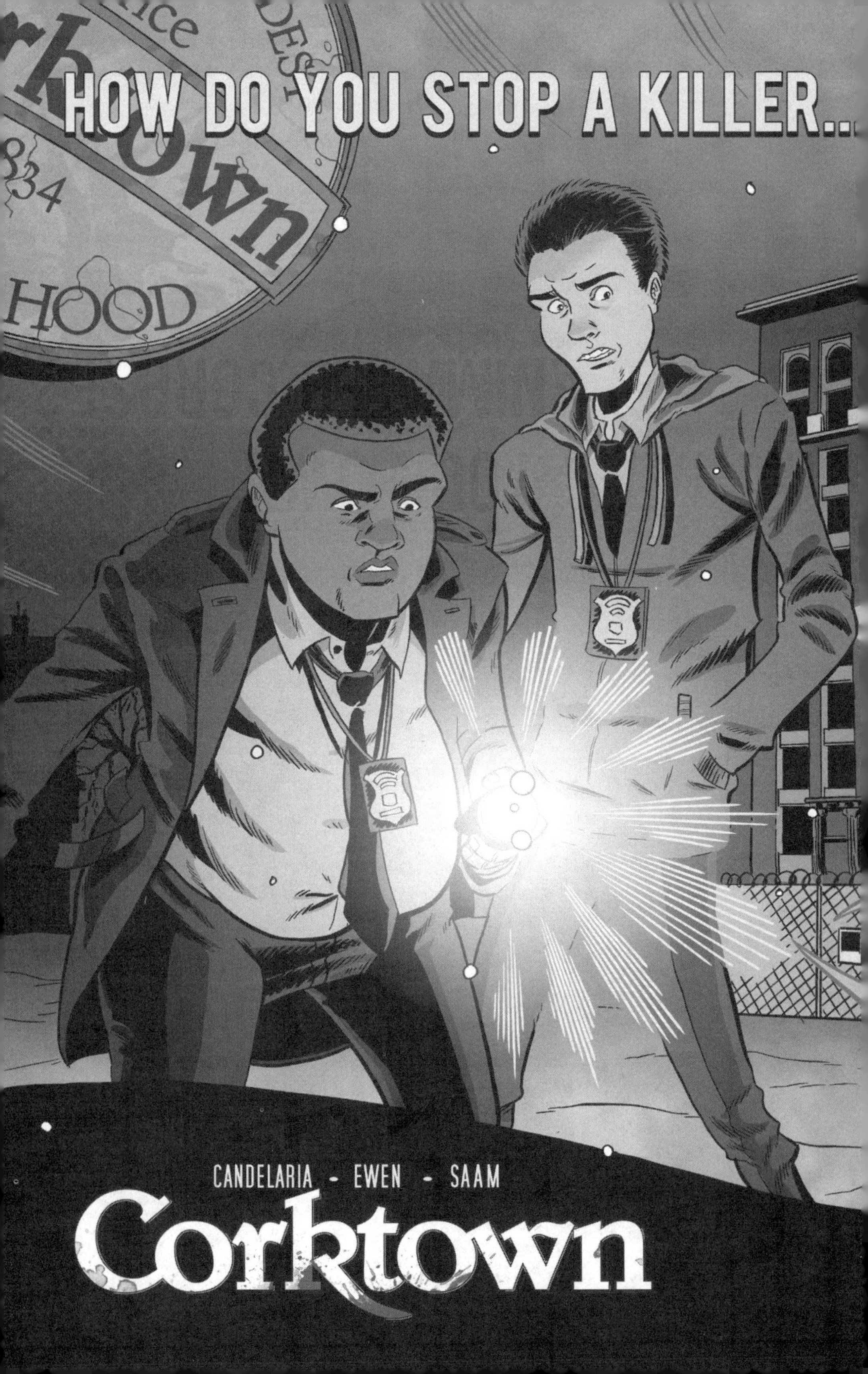
HOW DO YOU STOP A KILLER...
CANDELARIA - EWEN - SAAM
Corktown

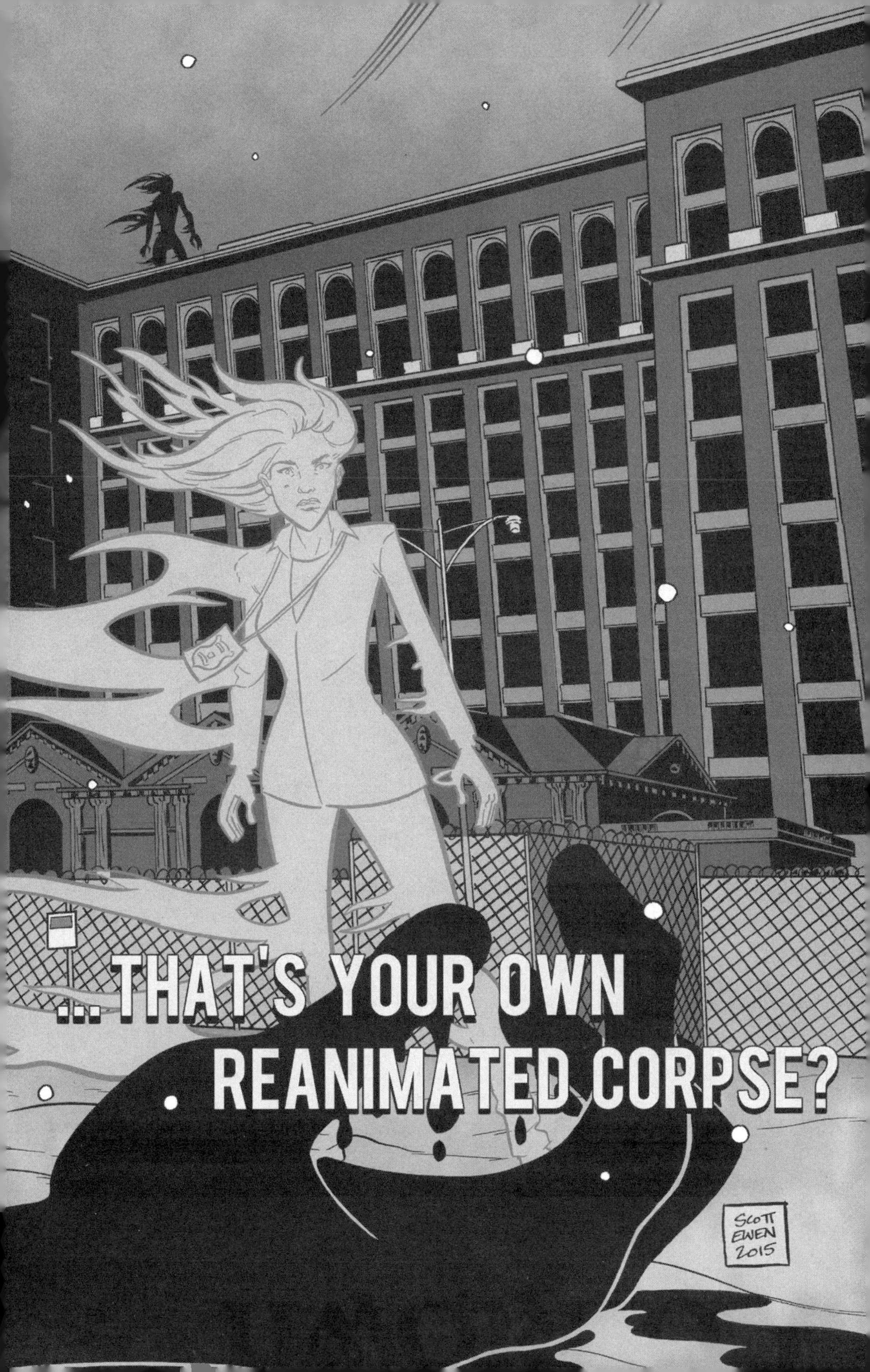
...THAT'S YOUR OWN
REANIMATED CORPSE?
SCOTT EWEN 2015

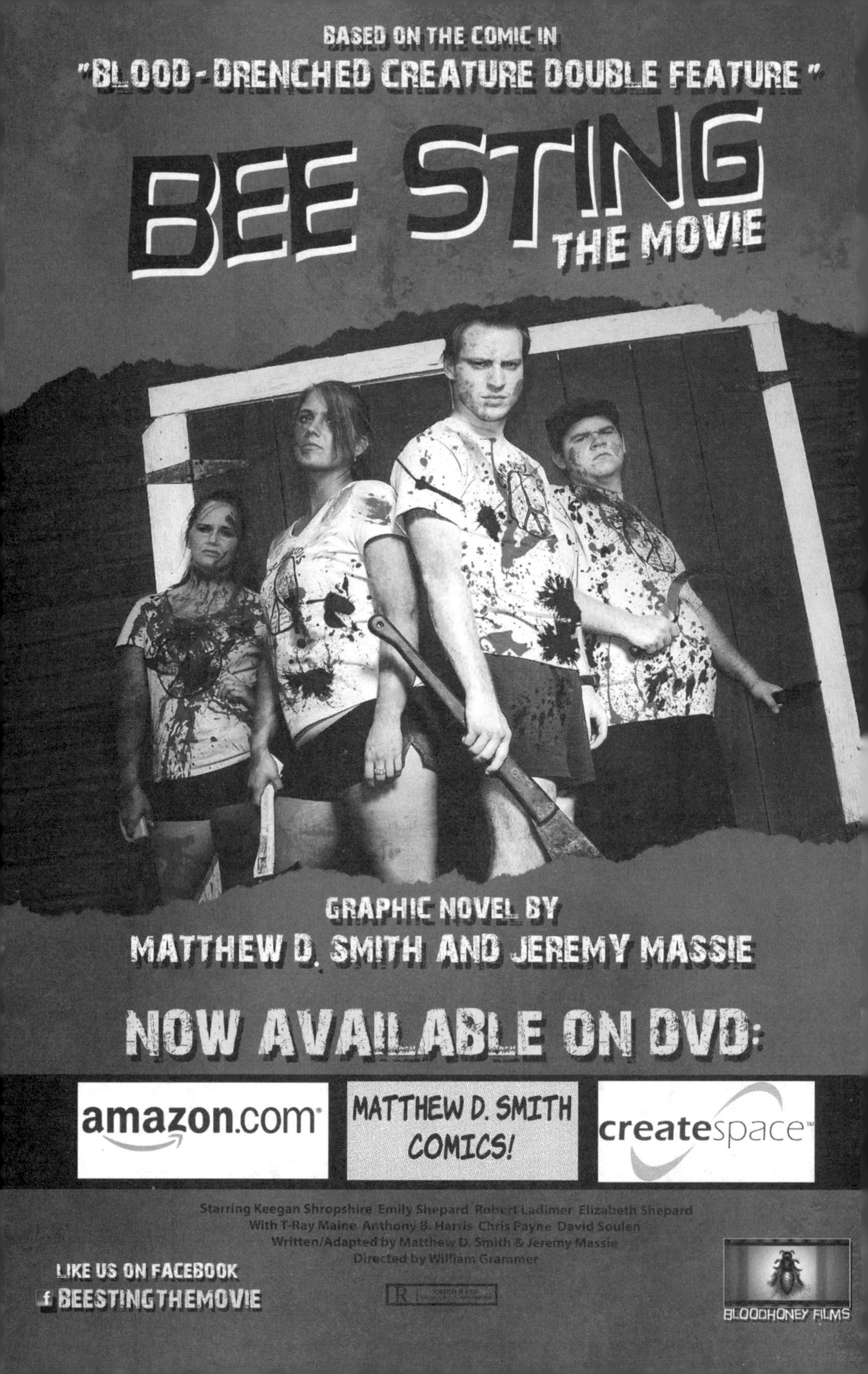
BASED ON THE COMIC IN
"BLOOD-DRENCHED CREATURE DOUBLE FEATURE"
BEE STING
THE MOVIE
GRAPHIC NOVEL BY
MATTHEW D. SMITH AND JEREMY MASSIE
NOW AVAILABLE ON DVD:
amazon.com
MATTHEW D. SMITH COMICS!
createspace
Starring Keegan Shropshire Emily Shepard Robert Ladimer Elizabeth Shepard
With T-Ray Maine Anthony B. Harris Chris Payne David Soulen
Written/Adapted by Matthew D. Smith & Jeremy Massie
Directed by William Grammer
LIKE US ON FACEBOOK
BEESTINGTHEMOVIE
R
BLOODHONEY FILMS

ON DEATH ROW... THE ONLY MONSTER IS MAN

THE CHAIR

BILL OBERST JR.   TIMOTHY MUSKATELL   NOAH HATHAWAY   ZACH GALLIGAN

NAOMI GROSSMAN   EZRA BUZZINGTON   KYLE HESTER   DERRICK DAMIONS

AND RODDY PIPER

BASED ON THE ALTERNA COMICS GRAPHIC NOVEL BY PETER SIMETI & KEVIN CHRISTENSEN
COMING SOON TO FILM   NOT YET RATED   #INWARDENWETRUST

ALTERNA

10 YEARS

c r e a t o r s

SAM AGRO MONSTROSITY; HORROR IN THE WEST; IF ANTHOLOGY - SHAWN ALDRIDGE FUBAR - NEWEL ANDERSON SATANIC HELL - JASON ARTHUR FUBAR GEORGE ATHANASIOU IF ANTHOLOGY - BRANDON BARROWS FUBAR; MONSTROSITY; IF ANTHOLOGY - ZACH BASSETT IF ANTHOLOGY - STEVE BECKER FUBAR DOUG BEEKMAN EMPIRE OF THE WOLF - KURT BELCHER HORROR IN THE WEST; RISERS - CLAIRE BENSON IF ANTHOLOGY - MARK BERTOLINI FUBAR DANILO BEYRUTH FUBAR - ZACH BLOCK GWENDOLYN - MICHAEL S. BRACCO ADAM WRECK; BIRTH; NOVO - DAVID BRAME IF ANTHOLOGY LIEZL BUENAVENTURA THE LAST WEST - JOE CABATIT GWENDOLYN - MARIO CANDELARIA CORKTOWN - DINO CARUSO IF ANTHOLOGY - KOTE CARVAJAL CLUSTERF@#K - KODY CHAMBERLAIN THE LAST WEST - LONNY CHANT FUBAR - KEVIN CHRISTENSEN THE CHAIR - JON CLARK IF ANTHOLOGY - FABIAN COBOS IF ANTHOLOGY - JON A. COLUNGA BLEEN - JASON COPLAND MONSTROSITY; FUBAR; HORROR IN THE WEST - JOSHUA COZINE SPRING-HEELED JACK - BOB CRAM THE BIG BAD BOOK - HELAINE CRAWFORD FUBAR - ZAC CROCKETT ANYONE BUT VIRGINIA - ROB CROONENBORGHS FUBAR - DANIEL CROSIER THE CHAIR MICHAEL CZERNIAWSKI THE BIG BAD BOOK - IAN DAFFERN FREELANCE BLUES - KENTON DANIELS BLOOD FOR STONE - TONY DEANS SPRING-HEELED JACK DEKARA COMPLEX - LOKI DeWITT IF ANTHOLOGY - MARSHALL DILLON EMPIRE OF THE WOLF - MICHAEL J. DiMOTA THE SECRET ADVENTURES OF HOUDINI CHUCK DIXON FUBAR - E.T. DOLLMAN MYTH - JORGE DONIS CANNONS IN THE CLOUDS - GRIGORIS DOUROS SATANIC HELL - CHARLES DOWD LILITH DARK - JOE DUNN FUBAR - ALEX ECKMAN-LAWN IF ANTHOLOGY - JOSH EISERIKE ANYONE BUT VIRGINIA - KEVIN ENHART SATANIC HELL - BRIAN EVINOU MONSTROSITY - SCOTT EWEN CORKTOWN - SALO FARIAS IF ANTHOLOGY - RYAN FERRIER MONSTROSITY - STEVEN FORBES CLUSTERF@#K - JAMES GIAR FUBAR - SERGIO GIARDO THE BIG BAD BOOK - ANNE GRESHAM CANNONS IN THE CLOUDS - MAIA GROSS THE DOLRIDGE SACRAMENT - ERICA J. HEFLIN THE BLACK HAND; IF ANTHOLOGY - ANDREW HERBST WOLVES OF SUMMER - BRET M. HERHOLZ DIARY OF THE BLACK WIDOW; THE SPAGHETTI STRAND MURDER; CONFESSIONS OF A PECULIAR BOY; POLLY & HANDGRAVES; SHERLOCK HOLMES; MURDER, MYSTERY & MAYHEM: THE BRET M. HERHOLZ COLLECTION RICK HERSHEY THE BIG BAD BOOK - DAVID C. HOPKINS TRESPASSER - CHRIS HORAN FUBAR - LANDON HUBER BLEEN - TODD HUNT THE SECRET ADVENTURES OF HOUDINI - MIKE IMBODEN FUBAR - LOU IOVINO THE LAST WEST - MICHAEL ISENBERG FUBAR - NIKOLA JAJIC THE BIG BAD BOOK; HUCK FINN'S ADVENTURES IN UNDERLAND; TOOTH & NAIL - EDUARDO JIMENEZ UNIT 44 - KEVIN JOHNSON FUBAR - KYLE KACZMARCZYK FUBAR; MONSTROSITY - KAY COMPLEX - TONY KEATON WOLVES OF SUMMER - MATT KENDZIOR FUBAR - JIMMY KERAST SATANIC HELL - MICHAEL KOGGE EMPIRE OF THE WOLF CLIFF KUROWSKI THE BIG BAD BOOK - DAN LAUER MYTH; IF ANTHOLOGY - MARIANO LACLAUSTRA IF ANTHOLOGY - MARTHA LAVERICK SPRING-HEELED JACK ROLF LEJDEGARD FUBAR -MICHAEL LENT THE MACHINE STOPS - MIKE LEONE FREELANCE BLUES - WES LOCHER UNIT 44; THE BLACK HAND - MIKE LONIEWSKI MYTH - FARES MAESE THE BLACK HAND - NOVO MALGAPO THE LAST WEST - MICHAEL MALKIN COMPLEX; IF ANTHOLOGY - JEREMY MASSIE ALL MY GHOSTS; THE DEADBEAT; HELLO DO YOU WORK HERE?; BEE STING; FUBAR - GLENN MATCHETT IF ANTHOLOGY - MICHAEL McDERMOTT FUBAR - JEFF McCLELLAND FUBAR; MOTHER RUSSIA; HORROR IN THE WEST - PHIL McCLOREY HORROR IN THE WEST, MONSTROSITY - SHAMUS McGUIGAN FUBAR - JIM McMUNN FUBAR - JEFF McCOMSEY FUBAR; MOTHER RUSSIA; HELLO DO YOU WORK HERE?; AMERICAN TERROR; HORROR IN THE WEST - JASON MEADOWS FUBAR - ROBERT MENEGUS IF ANTHOLOGY - OLIVER MERTZ FUBAR - RICHARD MEYERS FUBAR - ALONSO MOLINA RAYGUN - PEEBO MONDIA IF ANTHOLOGY RONALD MONTGOMERY FUBAR - JONATHAN MOORE FUBAR - DREW MOSS MOTHER RUSSIA - LAURA MULLER MOTHER RUSSIA - JASON NGUYEN FUBAR - KEL NUTALL THE LAST WEST - CHAS! PANGBURN IF ANTHOLOGY - JON PARRISH CLUSTERF@#K - DAN PARSONS EMPIRE OF THE WOLF - GABRIEL PERALTA HUCK FINN'S ADVENTURES IN UNDERLAND; TOOTH & NAIL - PIETRO MOTHER RUSSIA - VLADIMIR POPOV COMPLEX - DAVID RABBITTE EMPIRE OF THE WOLF - CHIP REECE METAPHASE; IF ANTHOLOGY - CASEY REECE IF ANTHOLOGY - JAYMES REED BLOOD FOR STONE - MARC RENE THE MACHINE STOPS - SHANNON RITCHIE BLOOD FOR STONE - RAFER ROBERTS FUBAR - JAMES E. ROCHE IF ANTHOLOGY - KRISTIAN ROSSI TRESPASSER - K. MICHAEL RUSSELL MOTHER RUSSIA JUSTIN M. RYAN TRESPASSER - MIKE SALT IF ANTHOLOGY - ZAKK SAMM CORKTOWN - ANDREW SANFORD GWENDOLYN - ALUISIO CERVELLE SANTOS FUBAR GREGORY SCHOEN RAYGUN - NIC J. SHAW CLUSTERF@#K, IF ANTHOLOGY - JULIE SHELTON FUBAR - TIM SHINN IF ANTHOLOGY - PETER SIMETI THE CHAIR; IF ANTHOLOGY; WILSON PUCK; HELLO DO YOU WORK HERE?; METAPHASE; CANNONS IN THE CLOUDS; HUCK FINN'S ADVENTURES IN UNDERLAND; POLLY & HANDGRAVES; RISERS; SPECTRUM - MATT SMITH MOTHER RUSSIA - MATTHEW D. SMITH BEE STING; THE CURSE OF STRANGLEHOLD; BLOOD-DRENCHED CREATURE DOUBLE FEATURE - GARRETT SNEEN IF ANTHOLOGY - ERIC SPOHN FUBAR - DARRIN STEPHENS FUBAR - MICHAEL SUMISLASKI BLOOD FOR STONE CHRIS SUMMERS EMPIRE OF THE WOLF - KIRSTY SWAM CANNONS IN THE CLOUDS - WILSON TAYLOR THE DOLRIDGE SACRAMENT - DANIEL THOLLIN FUBAR VICKI TIERNEY FREELANCE BLUES - DIEGO TORO CLUSTERF@#K - BEN TRUMAN MONSTROSITY; FUBAR; HORROR IN THE WEST - TIMOTHY TRUMAN FUBAR HANK TUCKER THE ACTUAL ROGER - JORGE VEGA FUBAR - DOMINIC VIVONA FUBAR - SEAN VON GORMAN THE SECRET ADVENTURES OF HOUDINI KRISTOPHER WADDELL MONSTROSITY - WILL WALBER THE CARRIER - JAKE WARRENFELTZ FUBAR- ERIC WEATHERS IF ANTHOLOGY - KELLY WILLIAMS METAPHASE, HELLO DO YOU WORK HERE? - SHAWN WILLIAMS FUBAR - STEVE WILLHITE FUBAR - JENNIE WOOD FUBAR - DANIEL WOOLLEY CANNONS IN THE CLOUDS - MARIO WYTCH FUBAR - CARL YONDER FUBAR - EVAN YOUNG THE LAST WEST; THE CARRIER - TIMOTHY ZAPRALA FUBAR